BEHAVIORAL ASPECTS OF ACCOUNTING

Michael Schiff and Arie Y. Lewin

New York University

PRENTICE-HALL, INC., Englewood Cliffs, New Jersey

Library of Congress Cataloging in Publication Data

Schiff, Michael, comp.
  Behavioral aspects of accounting.

  Bibliography: p.
  1. Accounting—Addresses, essays, lectures.
  2. Business enterprises—Finance—Addresses, essays,
  lectures. I. Lewin, Arie Y.   joint comp.
  II. Title.
  HF5657.S35   657   657   73-14728
  ISBN 0-13-073593-0

© 1974 Prentice-Hall, Inc., Englewood Cliffs, N. J.

Printed in the United States of America

10 9 8 7 6 5 4 3

Prentice-Hall International, Inc., *London*
Prentice-Hall of Australia, Pty. Ltd., *Sydney*
Prentice-Hall of Canada, Ltd., *Toronto*
Prentice-Hall of India Private Limited, *New Delhi*
Prentice-Hall of Japan, Inc., *Tokyo*

Contents

PART FOUR
Control   271
Theory of Control in Organizations
Introduction to the Readings

Discussion Questions

PART FIVE
Financial Reporting 337

PART SIX
Selected Bibliography 401

Preface

The past few years have witnessed a growing awareness on the part of accounting educators of the importance of behavioral science to accounting. The report of the Committee on Behavioral Science Content of the Accounting Curriculum[1] concluded with an urgent recommendation to academic accountants "to assume the responsibility of incorporating relevant materials from behavioral science in accounting curricula." This conclusion was based on the assumption that "If accounting is in fact a behavioral process, then accounting education by definition should include appropriate attention to behavioral considerations."[2]

This book represents our attempt to identify relevant concepts and findings from the behavioral sciences and relate them to financial and managerial accounting. The readings include related contributions from the disciplines of economics, management science, and finance. The book is geared to the needs of both the senior undergraduate in accounting and the student majoring in accounting in an

[1] Report of the Committee on Behavioral Science Content of the Accounting Curriculum, Supplement to Volume XLVI of the Accounting Review, 1971, pp. 247-285.

[2] *Op. cit.*, p. 247.

MBA program. It is intended for multipurpose classroom use. It can serve as a supplement in financial and managerial accounting and as the text in a course on the behavioral aspects of accounting. With these objectives in mind:

1. The book develops a behavioral model of the firm.
2. The text relates behavioral science to budgeting, planning, control, decision-making, and reporting.
3. Each chapter has an introductory section followed by a discussion of the selected readings.
4.. A comprehensive bibliography keyed to each chapter is presented at the end of the book.
5. A series of discussion type questions appears at the end of each chapter.

We would like to take this opportunity to thank Professor Russell M. Barefield for reviewing the manuscript and providing us with helpful and constructive comments.

We also wish to acknowledge our indebtedness to authors and their publishers who have given us permission to reprint their articles. We owe our appreciation to Mrs. Shirley Covington of the Prentice-Hall staff for a most efficient job in handling the production of the book.

Michael Schiff

Arie Y. Lewin

PART ONE

The Theory of the Firm
and Managerial Behavior

THE SETTING

It is only in relatively recent years that the accountant has concerned himself with the utility of his output to the users of his reports. Historically, he did not segment the market for his information, preferring to lump all users together by furnishing a single set of reports that presented the "economic facts" of the enterprise. The motivation of management as participants in this fact presentation was not considered, and the behavior induced by the presentation of these "facts" was ignored. Emphasis was placed on *what* was being presented with little regard for *by whom*, *for whom* and *for what* purpose the reports were developed. This is not to suggest that there was an absence of awareness of people and their behavior as suppliers and consumers of information. It was present and the accountant knew it, but he elected to disregard its existence in pursuing his role.

On the one hand, it could be argued that the neglect may well have been due to a lack of a well-defined theoretical structure that would permit the accountant to address himself to the behavioral problems. On the other hand, one might suggest that the accountant was merely responding to the environment in which he

1

operated and reflecting a behavior generally associated with his activity, not being prone to modify his approach to his task as he perceived it.

Perhaps the accountant consciously or otherwise adopted an attitude not unlike the one in vogue in economics during much of the same period. This suggested that the major thrust was the allocation of scarce resources. In pursuing its goal of profit maximization, the firm assumed a rational behavior on the part of decision makers as they proceeded to convert a finite number of factors of production into a finite number of products and having available to it full information on product demand, factor supply and production technology all operating under conditions of perfect competition with complete certainty assumed.[1] Figure 1-1 presents the decision process associated with the traditional economic theory of the firm. The individual, his perceptions, aspirations, attitudes, goals, and motivation were ignored, and the human being was perceived as an adjunct to a machine, "something to be taught and economically motivated to maximize productivity."

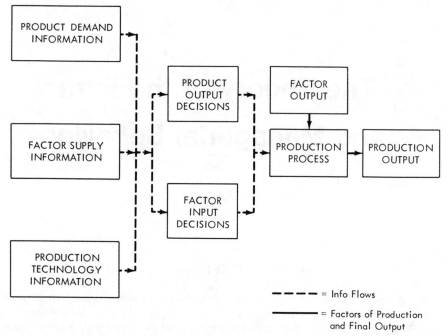

FIGURE 1-1 Decision Process of a Firm

Source: Kong Chu and Thomas A. Naylor "A Dynamic Model of the Firm" *Management Science*, Volume II, (May 1965).

It is only in relatively recent years that this traditional approach in accounting has been questioned, particularly in the area of managerial accounting. The transition from the score-keeping role of accounting to that of providing information for decision-making and control suggested the need to study behavior implications of preparers and users of information. It is also worth noting that a committee

---

[1]Thomas H. Naylor, "The Economic Theory of the Firm: Three Models of Analysis," *Quarterly Review of Economics and Business*, Vol. V, No. 4, 1965, pp. 33-34.

of the American Accounting Association addressed itself to the problem as recently as 1971 and reported:

> To state the matter concisely, the principal purpose of accounting reports is to influence action, i.e., behavior. Additionally, it can be hypothesized that the very process of accumulating information, as well as the behavior of those who do the accounting, will effect the behavior of others. In short, by its very nature, accounting is a behavior process.[2]

If the accountant is to adopt this view, then his concept of the firm needs to be changed. What has evolved in recent years is a behavioral theory of the firm that recognizes the business firm for what it is: an organization composed of people. A short exposition on a behavioral decision-making view of the firm and an overview of a motivational model of managerial behavior is presented in the section titled, "A Behavioral Theory of the Firm."

ORGANIZATION OF THE BOOK

The basic plan of the book is to present relevant behavioral science concepts and findings as they relate to four major activities of the firm of concern to accountants. These are Planning and Budgeting, Decision Making, Control, and Financial Reporting. In addition, Part One of the book focuses on the firm as a complete entity. Thus, Part One presents an integrative behavioral theory of the firm. The selection of articles provides additional theoretical views of the firm from a variety of social science disciplines.

In Part Two, Planning and Budgeting, the focus is on the formulation of operational goals and the interaction of individual behavior in this process. The articles examine such dimensions of the process as participation and satisfaction, level of goal difficulty, levels of aspiration, and the conflict between personal and organizational goals.

In Part Three, Decision Making, the focus is on individual and organizational decision making. One group of articles examines such fundamental issues of individual and group decision making as perception, effects of success and failure, risk aversion, and status. The second group of articles involves the effects of various organization structures on decision making. Finally, the effect of alternative information inputs on decision making is presented.

In Part Four, Control, the articles selected explore individual problems such as performance measurement and individual adaptation to control. The other dimension consists of organization structure and internal control, particularly the problem of centralization-decentralization and the relationships between administrative hierarchies.

In Part Five, Financial Reporting, the articles selected involve income smoothing behavior, the reliability of reported accounting information, and the relevance of accounting information to the investor user.

Each section of the book begins with a discussion of the specific topic in

---

[2]"Report of the Committee on the Behavioral Science Content of the Accounting Curriculum," *The Accounting Review*, Supplement 1971, p. 240. See also "Decision Models and Accounting Measurement: A Challenge for Accountants," T. R. Dyckman, Stanford Lectures in Accounting, 1971.

relation to the behavioral view of the firm presented in Part One. This is followed by an introduction and summary of the readings. Following the selected readings, each section of the book concludes with a number of study questions. The intent is that, in the process of discussing these questions, the reader will be able to relate the readings to the main concepts and effect an integration of the material presented.

A BEHAVIORAL THEORY OF THE FIRM

Modern organization theory is concerned with describing the behavior of the firm as an entity on the basis of understanding the actions and motives of its participants. The business firm, whether large or small, has traditionally been viewed as owned by its shareholders, and its concerns have been financial, revolving around price and output decisions. Regardless of what the complete set of goals of a firm may be, accountants have prepared financial reports reflecting the results of the firm's annual operations for distribution to its shareholders and the public through its financial statements. These reports imply the existence of a goal set that most likely includes cost and revenue goals in the form of aspirations regarding growth, profits, sales market share, production, inventory, rate of return, overhead, product mix, personnel, and the like. Yet the firm has a variety of other goals that are not obvious from reading the financial statements but that are reflected in the financial statements.

To describe how the firm adopts for itself a set of goals, and how it proceeds to adapt and achieve them, requires an understanding of the underlying decision and problem-solving processes of the firm. To be more specific, a modern theory of the firm is concerned with the goal-directed behavior of the firm in terms of the goals, motivations, and problem-solving characteristics of its participants. Organizational goals will be viewed as (1) the outcome of a bargaining influence process among organization participants, (2) determinants of the boundaries of the firm's decision-making and problem solving activities, and (3) their role in the internal control system.

The motivation of the participants and their degree of job satisfaction will be described in terms of their personal goals overlapping with the organization goals, and the extent to which the participants view the firm as being instrumental to the achievement of their personal goals. Finally, the firm's decision-making, problem-solving processes—its organization structure, division of labor, use of standard operating procedures, and so on—will be described as a function of its participant's problem-solving behavior, characterized by severe capacity limitations on their rationality.

Essentially, the firm is viewed as an equilibrium-seeking, decision-making system. Its goal composition may vary over time, but the adjustment process in the level of goals functions according to some simple rules. The firm operates under severe capacity limitations regarding problem solving and information retrieval. That is, the organizational system can recover only a limited fraction of past information and, furthermore, has limited capacity for processing information. As a result, there is great reliance on standard operating procedures and the use of simplifying devices for problem solving. Thus, stability is the outcome of a relatively stable set of goals and routinized problem-solving, decision-making procedures.

The organization achieves further stability through the accumulation of organizational slack. Organizational slack represents excess resources absorbed by the firm as a means to balance fluctuations in its external environment. It also, however, provides the means to satisfy the personal goals of the participants.

The organization members themselves are assumed to possess personal goals, a subset of which they expect to satisfy within the organization while also achieving the organizational goals. Thus, in general, managers are assumed to be motivated to achieve a goal set composed of aspirations for income, status, job security, and discretionary control over resources.

In the sections that follow, we will first discuss the nature and role of the firm's goals, a model of managerial motivation, the firm's decision-making system, and the role of organizational slack.[3]

THE FIRM'S GOALS

In contrast to classical theories of management, traditional planning frameworks, or positive decision analysis, the goals of the firm cannot be assumed to be given or imposed. In theory, however, this could be the case in a firm owned and run by a single entrepreneur, in which case the unity between his goals and those of the firm could be accepted.

The large business firm, as we know it, can be described as representing a rather large constituency, often possessing conflicting objectives. The boundaries of the firm's coalition as demonstrated in Figure 1-2 simply depend on where they are drawn. They would include stockholders, bondholders, various managerial groups, labor unions, suppliers, customers, and increasingly, local, state and federal agencies through their legislative and regulatory powers.

It is not difficult to visualize the conflicting resource allocation demands made by the various members of the coalition. Stockholders have profit, dividend, and capital appreciation aspirations. Top management members' goals include maximizing their income (salary plus bonuses), status, job security, and so on. Labor unions represent their members' demands for increased wages, fringe benefits, and improved working conditions; and customers have expectations with regard to price, quality, and service.

If, in fact, organizational goals reflect the demands of an often conflicting coalition, then the following characterization of goals is evident:

1. Organizational goals cannot be described in terms of a joint preference-ordering function.
2. When agreement exists, it is on non-operationally defined goals.
3. Specific operational goals can be internally inconsistent with one another. They define a set of boundaries that must be satisfied by the organization.
4. Goals, whether operational or non-operational, are the outcome of bargaining processes.

Thus, the goal statements that emerge have two characteristics: (1) they do not require internal consistency, and (2) they vary in terms of prescription of

---

[3]These sections owe much to the ideas and concepts presented in Richard M. Cyert and James G. March, "The Behavioral Theory of the Firm," Prentice-Hall, 1963.

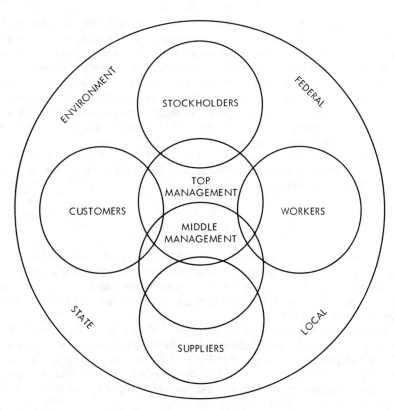

FIGURE 1-2 The Firm's Multigoal Relations

action and measures of success. This suggests, then, that the goal set may include superordinate statements with which every member of the coalition agrees but that such statements do not serve as criteria for action because they deliberately are devoid of any specifics. In a sense, the superordinate goals may be viewed as policy statements without the accompanying resource allocation plans. The superordinate goal, however, is important in the coalition formation process where a policy statement without indication of priorities on resources may be a sufficient inducement to a prospective coalition member. Thus, the relative importance of coalition members can be gauged from a comparison of the policy statements of the organization and its budget which reflects the resource allocation priorities.

The operational goals of the organization cannot be identified in the superordinate goal statement. The set of objectives that represent the subjective means to the goals are a series of level aspirations statements operationally defined. Examples would be market share objectives, profitability objectives, unit cost objectives, growth objectives, and so forth. These objectives are operational because they also define the performance measurement criteria. Thus, if the market share goal is 30 per cent, it is simple to compare the attained market share with the goal and determine whether performance on this criterion is acceptable. Another characteristic of the operational goals is that they focus the activities of the organization on specific objectives and direct attention to specific problems that have to be solved.

Although such a system appears unstable, because the bargaining process is never-ending, it is rather stable. Stability occurs because most of the bargaining

6

involves goal adjustments and not the alteration of the goal composition—the coalition.

Thus, goal adjustment is heavily precedent-dependent—last year's budget is the basis for next year's budget, and it is dependent on success or failure in achieving earlier goals. Success results in adjusting the goals upward, whereas failure to achieve prior goals may lead to maintaining or lowering the level of these goals.

The view of organizational goals, therefore, can be summarized as follows: The firm's goals are a complex compromise of conflicting demands reflecting the individual needs and goals of the firm's large and varied constituency. The makeup of the goals reflects the bargaining power and position of sub-coalitions within the firm, and consensus is generally reached on non-operational superordinate goals. Operational goals, however, as reflected in the firm's budget, determine the day-to-day course of action by the firm.

The role of operational goals—normally stated in level of aspiration form of $G_i \geqslant X_i$ (where G= goals and X is a measure of performance for that goal)—is to identify the boundaries of the multiplicity of goals that the firm hopes to achieve over a time period. Simultaneously, however, these goals also serve as a control device for monitoring achievement against plans, and also serve to split the achievement of overall superordinate goals into a large number of smaller, more explicitly defined objectives.

Finally, it should be stressed that although we have described a conflict system, the firm only occasionally will be in conflict over what the makeup of the superordinate goals should be. For a firm beyond the start-up stage, and this takes in the great bulk of firms, the conflicts are about the levels of goals—the extent to which adjustments are made in the operational goals from one time period to the next.

A MOTIVATIONAL MODEL OF MANAGERIAL BEHAVIOR

An examination of the literature on the motivational bases of organization participants reveals that most of the writing (theoretical and empirical) has been on the motivations of lower level participants. In addition, a number of theories exist that attempt to describe human motivation in general and that have been applied to organizational behavior. In this section, we will develop a view of the motivational bases of managerial behavior and evaluate it in terms of existing theories and empirical evidence reported in the literature.

A common view of individual behavior is that it is goal directed. This general principle underlies need theories[4] and level-of-aspiration type theories.[5] At any point in time, an individual can be considered to possess a personal goal set consisting of hopes, wishes, explicit objectives, and needs and drives. Individuals, because of differences in their personality, differ in terms of the degree to which their goal set is structured. In other words, an individual's personality, determined by such factors as his achievement motive, conformity proneness, need for affiliation, authoritarianism, dependence-independence motive, and power motive, are all related to the intensity of his goal-directed behavior. Generally, however, his

---

[4]See discussion in Timothy W. Costello, and Sheldon S. Zalkind, *Psychology in Administration A Research Orientation,* Prentice-Hall, 1963, pp. 55-122.

[5]See for example discussion in Victor H. Vroom, *Work and Motivation,* Wiley, 1964, pp. 3-45.

goal-directed behavior will have the characteristic that the arousal of drives or physiological needs can interrupt and take precedence over current goal-directed behavior and must be satisfied first. In addition, random disturbances or inability to achieve a goal can shift attention from one goal to another. Finally, goal directed behavior is sequential—the organism can pursue only one goal at a time—and achievement of a goal occurs when a satisfactory solution is obtained.

The implications of the above for organizational behavior are twofold. First, that an individual will expect to achieve only a sub-set of his goals within the organization. Secondly, that his behavior within the organization can be described in terms of a problem-solving, satisfying, sequential, personality-linked model. At this point, however, it is important to emphasize that an organization (the firm) is expected to be instrumental only in the achievement of some sub-set of the personal goals that an individual may have. Furthermore, an individual's decision to join an organization (or choose between organizations) would depend on his perception of the organization's instrumentality in the achievement of his personal goals. Similarly, job dissatisfaction would occur when the organization participant perceives that the organization ceases to be a means to his ends.[6]

We would like to consider next the personal goal dimensions that the firm can be expected to satisfy within its traditional framework but, specifically, from the manager's point of view. Following Williamson the sub-set of personal goals that a manager aspires to achieve within the firm, while achieving the organization goals, are wealth (income: salaries plus bonuses), staff (status), discretionary control over the allocation of resources, and job security.[7] The reality of the modern corporation, large or small, is that the higher up a manager advances in the firm, the greater his income, status, and discretionary decision making. Often this holds also for job security; on the other hand, the greater the discretionary component in decision making, the greater the risks, which could result in lower job security.

The four personal goal dimensions mentioned above represent an important component of an individual's personal goals. Income, in this model, stands for salary plus bonuses and for wealth in general. Status is normally a function of the level in the organization. It is a function of advancement and promotion and is a major form of recognition for achievement. Within the organization, it is formalized by status symbols (title, privileges, and so on) and usually correlated with size of staff and number of people being supervised. Discretionary control over the allocation of resources is a particularly appropriate goal dimension in a model of managerial motivation. It connotes the desire for and the degree to which a manager can influence the goals of the firm, set objectives, and choose between alternatives to achieve these objectives. In principle, all managerial and lower level jobs have a discretionary component as part of the behavior required of the job occupant. Indeed, much of the research on job satisfaction of production workers, first line supervisors, and clerical personnel has identified the lack of enough discretion as a major factor of job dissatisfaction. Accordingly, within the organization environment, the greater the discretionary control over resources a manager has, the greater the responsibility he has, and the more numerous his opportunities to experience personal growth and self-fulfillment.

Managers, therefore, can be expected to behave in a way that will maximize

[6]For a similar analysis based on inducement-contribution theory, see James G. March, and Herbert A. Simon, *Organizations,* Wiley, 1958, pp. 84-110.

[7]Oliver E. Williamson, *The Economics of Discretionary Behavior: Managerial Objectives in a Theory of the Firm,* Prentice-Hall, 1964, pp. 28-38.

the attainment of their personal goals, subject to achieving the firm's objectives.[8] Thus, they will seek to influence the goals of the firm that they perceive pertain to their own activities. Specifically, they will strive for control over management slack absorbed as costs by bargaining for attainable objectives, avoiding uncertainty in their decision making, and creating a deterministic decision environment.

The desire for slack and the attendant managerial behavior are further reinforced by the ever-present need for job security. Because of the asymmetric nature of the organization reward structure, the need for job security is continually aroused. The traditional reward structure is part of the management by objectives, internal planning, and control systems. Rewards in the form of recognition, bonuses, salary increases, promotions, and the like are built into performance criteria. It is the under-achievement of objectives that causes the organization to overreact and that continually arouses the need for job security, thus reinforcing the manager's desire for management slack.

The model of managerial motivation that we have presented views the manager as motivated to achieve two sets of goals—his own and the firm's. His personal goals are directly related to income, status, discretionary control over the allocation of resources, and job security. To achieve both sets of goals, he will strive for slack in his operating environment. Thus, creation and controlling of slack resources become the means both for insuring that the manager achieves the organizational goals and his personal goals.

Although this model describes managerial motivation in terms of the accustomed rewards and practices of most corporations, it can be shown that these dimensions are also incorporated in other theories of motivation.

Maslow's need hierarchy theory assumes that humans possess an internal motive that propels them to action.[9] Thus, Maslow views humans, as we do, to be goal-seeking. Maslow's theory of personality and motivation relates this general goal-seeking characteristic of humans to an internally generated hierarchy of needs. The theory is based on the assumption that individuals are motivated to satisfy a specific need as it arises in accordance with the hierarchy. Thus, physiological needs—the most primitive and urgent human needs—would be satisfied first, followed by safety needs and continuing upward to ultimate needs of self-actualiza-

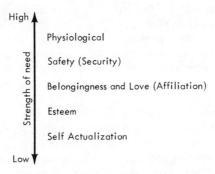

FIGURE 1-3 Maslow's Need Hierarchy

[8] Williamson, for example, suggests that managers maximize a personal utility function subject to the condition that achieved profit equal or exceed the minimum profit demanded.

[9] Costello and Zalkind, *op. cit.*

tion. Figure 1-3 presents the complete primary classification of Maslow's Hierarchy of Needs arrayed in order of decreasing strength.

Comparing the Maslow need hierarchy theory with this model, it is clear that the greater the manager's discretionary control over the allocation of resources, the greater his opportunities to satisfy his self-actualization needs. Self-esteem needs, in the Maslow hierarchy, are related to the status factor in the managerial motivation model, and similarly the income and job security factors are associated with the safety needs. The model of managerial motivation does not give explicit recognition to social needs. This is because the organization often is not the best means to satisfy such needs, particularly in higher level managerial jobs. Furthermore, it is a matter of individual value whether oganizations should be structured to satisfy social needs. Thus, the model is consistent with the hierarchy of need theory and related theories in terms of the goal dimensions it encompasses. In contrast to need theories, it describes a manager as actively engaged in achieving his goals and those of the organization, rather than merely responding to personal needs when they arise.

ORGANIZATIONAL DECISION MAKING

In the previous sections we have discussed the role and formation process of organizational goals and the motivational bases for the manager's participation and performance in the organization. In this section, the firm's decision-making processes are discussed in terms of the organization's severe capacity limitations to engage in optimal problem solving and in terms of the need to satisfy the multiplicity of corporate and personal goals.

Our major concern is with the firm in the steady state, i.e., the functioning medium-to-large corporation. This also implies that start-up problems of organizations are not being considered here. In the steady state, it is important to recall that radical goal reorientations occur mostly as a result of stress situations, such as externally induced changes in top management (through proxy fights, mergers, and the like), and/or severe economic downturns for the firm. Thus, the kind of conflict that exists regarding goals involves performance objectives rather than what the makeup of the goals should be. Similarly, the work force—managerial and lower level—is rather stable and net changes are marginal, therefore having little or no influence on the larger social system of the organization. Thus, the organization in the steady state can be viewed as organistatic (seeking stability) and exhibiting stable behavioral patterns over time. Furthermore, the nature of the firm's decision-making processes are such that they reinforce this stability seeking behavior.

The decision problems faced by the firm are numerous, sometimes very complex, and often involve more than one department. Many decision situations have the characteristic that they recur often or on some regular basis. To cope with this typical decision overload condition, the organization resorts to a variety of problem-solving procedures aimed at simplifying the problem-solving task. The organization develops standard operating procedures—formal or informal—that apply to those problems that recur often and have become routine. Such procedures may be complete heuristics—decision rules—for such recurring problems as inventory control, training programs, recruiting, accounts payable, costing, pricing, distribution, order processing, and so on. Or the standard operating procedures for similar problems may be informal in the sense that a formal procedural record regarding them does not exist. In many instances, the source of the heuristics is external to the organization. Typical examples are the rules governing accounting and financial reporting developed by the APB, SEC, IRS, and so on.

The major characteristics of standard operating procedures are that they remain in use so long as the decision situation for which they apply recurs on a regular basis, and so long as it is perceived, rightly or wrongly, that they continue to solve that problem satisfactorily. When the application of a heuristics becomes unsatisfactory—when it does not solve the problem—the search for a better solution is undertaken, with the new solution being adopted as a standard operating procedure. Thus, the modification, adaptation, or replacement of heuristics is generally the outcome of problemistic search.

Problemistic search, as the words imply, does not occur unless a problem situation has arisen, either one not previously encountered by the organization or one that has been considered solved, but that has recurred. Search behavior can be described as being problem motivated, simple minded, and biased. By problem motivated, we imply that search is problem oriented, solutions are obtained either by changes in heuristics, as mentioned before, or by revising the decision criteria, making existing solutions satisfactory. Search is simple-minded because, to begin with, the causality relation between a problem symptom and the underlying problem is assumed to be simple. Thus, search revolves around the symptom areas and the current solution. In other words, when a problem symptom occurs, it is identified as belonging to a department that is expected to deal with it. The department will attempt to solve the problem by modifying the relevant heuristics. If the symptom disappears, the problem is considered solved.

Search becomes more complex when simple-minded search has failed, in which case search is expanded to consider more complex causal relationships and often expands into vulnerable organizational areas. In other words, failure may be linked to the performance of another department or sub-unit of the organization. Search is biased in the sense that it reflects departmental identification, training, and past experience, and reflects the interaction of hopes and expectations of the participants in the search process and distortions in information flows. The interaction of hopes and expectations is the process by which hopes are substituted for expectations about outcomes, thus decreasing the time spent on problem solving and eliminating the need for objective evaluation of alternatives.

In its decision making, the firm strives to avoid uncertainty in an attempt to make deterministic decisions. Uncertainty avoidance is achieved through:

(1) uncertainty absorption in the information flow for decision making

(2) organizational slack

(3) negotiation of the environment

(4) short term decision making.

Uncertainty absorption is the process by which raw data is summarized; and the inferences transmitted in the summary data become the bases for higher level decision making. In an organization, various sub-units come in contact with outside environment (e.g., salesmen with customers) and then communicate their perceptions to the rest of the organization. As these various sources of inputs are combined, edited, and transmitted up the organization hierarchy, they become facts for decision making rather than data to which uncertainty must be attached.

Thus, for example, sales forecasts are legitimated as facts and serve as a deterministic starting point for budget planning.

Organizational slack occurs in the course of the firm's resource allocation decision processes, through underestimation of revenue and overestimation of costs. This conservatism in forming expectations is conscious on the part of managers. We have seen that managers are motivated to create slack because they perceive it as a means to achieving their personal goals. Uncertainty avoidance underlies this motivation. Clearly minimizing the manager's uncertainty regarding achievement of the organization objectives, which are accepted by him, increases his feeling of job security. On an aggregate basis, it increases the probability of the firm's achieving its objectives and, therefore, also the achievement of personal goals discussed earlier. Furthermore, organizational slack becomes the reservoir for resources that can be applied by the firm to counter downturns in the firm's economic environment.

To further minimize the uncertainty, the firm strives to avoid uncertainty in its environment. Although in extreme instances, negotiating the firm's environment may involve illegal collusion, generally it implies seeking ways to make that environment more controllable. In general, firms achieve stability in their external environment through the adoption of industry-wide practices. In that respect, trade associations, industry institutes, and trade publications serve as the means for establishing such common practices. For example, pricing policies and prices often follow a set pattern, and distribution channels tend to be common within an industry. Similarly, product lines, accounting practices, personnel policies, and union contracts may become standard for an industry. Clearly, it is not necessary for firms to collude to stabilize their environment in an attempt to avoid uncertainty, and thus achieve satisfactory achievements in their respective goals (e.g., satisfactory profit).

Occasionally, the firm is faced with a new decision situation, one not previously encountered, or the risk associated with a resource allocation decision is perceived to be significant. The firm will develop and implement the solution to such situations cautiously, through series of short term decisions, monitoring feedback, and adapting the plans before proceeding. Although this reliance on short-term feedback could result in errors due to spurious learning, it does serve to minimize the uncertainty in a resource commitment process when the firm has no prior experience to guide it.

To summarize, in the steady state, the firm routinizes solutions to recurring problems. Search for new solutions is problem oriented and mostly is simple minded and biased; and the firm's decision-making behavior is best characterized by uncertainty avoidance. This minimization of uncertainty underlies the managerial motivation model; and it is achieved by substituting deterministic decision making for decision making under uncertainty, accumulating excess resources—organizational slack—to balance the firm's performance in bad economic periods, negotiating the environment, and relying on short-term decision making.

INTRODUCTION TO THE READINGS

The readings in Part One highlight economic, behavioral, and managerial views of the firm, the motivational bases of organizational behavior, and the relevancy of behavioral science to managerial accounting. Historically, the article by

Fritz Machlup, "Theories of the Firm: Marginalist, Behavioral, Managerial" was in part his response to the points of view presented in earlier articles by Herbert A. Simon, "Theories of Decision Making in Economics and Behavioral Science and R. Joseph Monsen, Jr. and Anthony Downs, "A Theory of Large Managerial Firms."

In the article, "Theories of Decision Making in Economics and Behavioral Science," Simon demonstrates on the basis of empirical studies in psychology and sociology that the assumptions underlying economic man in the theories of the firm are not tenable under most real life situations. Thus, for example, Simon demonstrates the inadequacy of the maximization assumption of economic man and essentially argues that economic man is a satisficing being whose problem-solving and search behavior are aimed at achieving a set of aspiration levels rather than a maximizing being whose problem-solving behavior requires obtaining the best possible alternative solutions to a specific goal function.

Simon also identifies the type of economic problems that would best benefit from a behavioral approach. These include processes of innovation and change, resource allocation decisions within the firm, and the analysis of oligopolistic competition. Interestingly enough, in the areas of imperfect competition, political economy, consumer behavior (saving and consumption), diffusion of innovation, and actual business decision making, economists have been adopting theoretical and empirical approaches of psychology, sociology, and political science.

In the article, "A Theory of Large Managerial Firms," Monsen and Downs present a modified theory of the firm with the objective of describing the behavior of large firms whose equity is widely distributed. The parallel is the behavioral theory presented earlier. The two theories recognize the weak influence that the widely diverse stockholders have on the firm. In both theories, stockholders' aspirations can be translated into constraints on the behavior of top management. Top management in this theory is assumed to maximize a personal goal function—own lifetime income. This objective to maximize both income and non-income elements is analogous to the managerial motivation model presented earlier. The theory also recognizes the importance of the bureaucratic management structure, which is to say, the organization decision-making system. The main feature of the article is its recognition of the separation of ownership from management in large firms and its implications to the type of decision making that characterizes such firms from maximization of managerial goals.

In the article, "Theories of the Firm: Marginalist, Behavioral, Managerial," Machlup reviews the extensive literature on the conflicting views of the firm in marginal, behavioral, and managerial theories of the firm. Machlup minimizes the conflict between marginal and managerial analysis of the firm. In his views, the theories can be merged so long as managerial theories postulate maximizing behavior and use the calculus to formulate the functional relationships of the firm. Furthermore, Machlup does not recognize any conflict between behavioral and marginal analysis. His contention is that the two types of theories set out to describe different behaviors of firms. Thus, behavioral theories aim at describing the firm's internal decision process and predict the behavior of a specific firm (mainly, the very large one). Marginal analysis, according to Machlup, does not aim at describing the individual behavior of a firm or make specific numerical predictions regarding its decisions. The profit maximization approach (marginal analysis) is best for describing the aggregate behavior of groups of firms or when the need is to provide qualitative answers about directions of change in prices, inputs, and outputs in terms of specific changes in prior conditions. Thus, in large measure Machlup concludes that the controversy over marginal, managerial, and behavioral theory of the firm is one of semantics.

In the article, "The Motivational Basis of Organizational Behavior," Daniel Katz elaborates on the motivational model presented earlier by expanding it to lower level participants as well. In addition, Katz highlights the importance of the social system of the organization as a source of rewards to the organization participant. The discussion on the organization reward structure bears mentioning because we have described it earlier as asymmetric with respect to rewarding good and poor performance. Katz emphasizes the importance of individualized reward systems, yet he is cognizant of how difficult they are to apply. Indeed, the difficulties involved in developing individual reward systems serve to explain why reward systems are generalized over classes of workers and managers, making the social system an important source of individual rewards.

The article, "Implications of Behavioral Science for Managerial Accounting," by Jacob G. Birnberg and Raghu Nath is one of the earliest reviews of behavioral research relevant to accounting.

1

THEORIES OF THE FIRM: MARGINALIST,

BEHAVIORAL, MANAGERIAL*

FRITZ MACHLUP

Last year, when it was my task to plan the program for the annual meeting of our association, a friend suggested that, with twenty years having passed since the outbreak of the "marginalism controversy," is was appropriate to review what has since happened to the embattled theory of the firm. The topic did not fit the general theme I had chosen for the 1965 meeting, but I reasoned that 1966 would give me a good opportunity to undertake the review myself.

THE BATTLEFIELD REVISITED

So let us recall that literary feud and the warriors, and let us revisit the battlefield. The major battlefield was the *American Economic Review*, with six articles and communications between March 1946 and March 1947 [16] [43] [21] [17] [22] [44]. There had been earlier gunfire elsewhere, chiefly in the *Oxford Economic Papers* in 1939 [14]. But, since the shooting then was not returned and it takes at least two opponents to join battle, it must be agreed that the real hostilities were the exchanges in the *AER*.

The fight was spirited, even fierce. Thousands of students of economics, voluntary or involuntary readers, have been either shocked or entertained by the violence of some of the blows exchanged and may have thought that the opponents must have become mortal enemies forever. These readers would have been wrong. Even before we came out for the last round of the fight, we exchanged friendly letters (December 1946) assuring each other that we would bear no grudges.

We have remained the best of friends; for several years now Richard Lester and I have been colleagues in the same department; and, as a token of our friendship, he has generously accepted my invitation to share this platform with me today as chairman of the session. Thus the veterans of both sides of the War of 1946 are now joined in revisiting the battlefield. This, incidentally, does not mean that either of us has succeeded in converting the other to the "true faith."

*Presidential address delivered, in a shorter version, at the Seventy-ninth Annual Meeting of the American Economic Association, San Francisco, December 28, 1966. *American Economic Review,* March 1967, pp. 1-33.

What was the outcome of the controversy? Who won? We could not possibly say if we have not first agreed on precisely what the shooting was about. I have heard it said that Machlup won the battle but Lester won the war. What this means, however, cannot be known unless we know what the issues and objectives of the war had been. Was it merely to make economics safe for or from marginalism? Were there not several other issues being fought over?

SOME OF THE MAJOR ISSUES

There were no doubt a good many contentions of all sorts—major, minor, essential, incidental, interpretative, factual, methodological, substantive, and all the rest. To present a complete catalogue of the issues involved would be too ambitious a task for this occasion, but a partial listing might be helpful.

The chief issue, of course, was whether marginal analysis was invalid and ought to be discarded, especially as far as the theory of prices, cost, wages, and employment in manufacturing industry is concerned. This issue, however, implied the question of the correct interpretation of marginal analysis, including the tenets of the marginal-productivity principle. In this connection, differences in the models of the firm customarily used in different kinds of analysis became relevant. Involved here was the question of whether the postulate of maximizing money profits led to conclusions very different from those derivable from assumptions of conduct guided by a variety of largely nonpecuniary considerations.

Underlying all these questions were some issues of general scientific methodology: the legitimacy and usefulness of abstract theorizing on the basis of unrealistic assumptions, or perhaps on the basis of assumptions regarded as "reasonable" thought not "universally true." These issues, in particular, were whether an assumption of profit maximization as the effective objective of the firm in the theoretical model may be accepted as a tenable hypothesis only if it can be verified that all or a majority of those who actually run business firms in the real world agree that this is their only or major objective, that they are capable of obtaining all the information and of performing all the calculations needed for the realization of that objective, and are really carrying out the actions found to be optimal in this fashion; or, alternatively, whether all these tests may be dispensed with and the assumption of profit maximization nevertheless accepted as a fruitful postulate from which conclusions can be derived which correspond with what can be observed in the records of prices and quantities.

Concerning the empirical testing of theoretical conclusions, there were issues of the validity of surveys through mailed questionnaires and of the proper interpretation of responses to various types of questions about managerial judgment. In the background of the whole controversy, but undoubtedly of pervasive significance, was the comparative acceptability of empirical findings to the effect that the elasticity of demand for labor was virtually zero and of the conventional theoretical inference that the elasticity was normally above zero.

Realizing how manifold were the issues of the controversy, one can appreciate that no clear decision can be made about its outcome. Some of the issues had been raised decades or centuries before 1946 and were not decided in this confrontation one way or the other. Attacks on the assumption of maximizing behavior and on the lack of realism in price theory have occurred with great regularity ever since "economic man" and similar postulates were introduced. The running battles between the classical and the historical schools were largely on these points. The *Methodenstreit* of 1883-84 dealt essentially with the same issues. And in the United States, institutionalism may be seen as a movement animated by the same spirit of protest against abstract theory.

However, the particular form of explicit marginalism (under the name of "theory of the firm") which became the target of the attacks of 1939 and 1946 had only come into being in the 1930's—if one supresses the memory of the great master of 1838 [9]. Ironically, some interpreter of recent history of economic thought—I have forgotten who it was—regarded the 1933-34 versions of the theory of the firm [8] [32] [41] as the theorists' concession to institutionalism, as attempts to supplement the neoclassical model of the firm under atomistic competition with some "more realistic" models allowing for a greater variety of conditions. It was this theory of the profit-maximizing firm in all sorts of market positions, in monopolistic and oligopolistic competition as well as in pure and perfect competition, that was attacked by the researchers in Oxford; and it was the marginal-productivity principle in the explanation of the demand for labor on the part of the individual firm that was the prime target of the attack of 1946.

If the chief aim of the attack was to force the abandonment or subversion of marginalism, and if the chief aim of the defense was to turn back the subversive forces and secure the reign of marginalism once and for all, then, to be sure, the war of 1946 ended in a draw. Look at the textbooks and you will find that marginalism has continued to dominate the teaching of microeconomics, perhaps though with occasional reservations and references to current attempts at greater realism. But look at the journals and monographs and you find that research on alternative approaches to the theory of the firm is regularly reported with the implication that a superior theory may eventually replace marginalism. This replacement, however, according to the proponents of the best-known alternatives to marginalism, is expected chiefly with regard to industries where firms are few and competition is ineffective. The marginalist solution of price determination under conditions of heavy competition is not seriously contested.

In pointing this out, I am not trying to claim that marginal analysis is invincible and forever irreplaceable. If I follow the philosophy of science which, instead of pronouncing theories "false" or "true," distinguishes only between those "rejected" and those "still open to criticism" [30, pp. 246-48], the only victory that can be claimed for the cause of marginalism is that it is still open to criticism. I must go beyond this and concede that some anti-marginalist suggestions have led in recent years to a number of revisions in the marginal analysis of the firm which amount to the incorporation of other goals besides money profits into expanded marginalist objective functions.

THE ALTERNATIVE APPROACHES

In their arguments against the profit-maximization model the various alternative approaches to the theory of the firm are very much alike; only their positive programs can distinguish them.

The program of behaviorism is to reject preconceptions and assumptions and to rely only on observation of overt behavior. Thus, behaviorism rejects the assumption of marginal analysis that economic action is directed by the objective to maximize the attainment of ends with given means, and that business action can be deduced from a postulate that firms attempt to maximize money profits. Instead, we are directed to *observe* how businessmen really act and by what processes they reach decisions.

Perhaps it is not entirely fair to suggest here an association between "behaviorism" and the working program of the proponents of a "behavioral theory of the firm" [10]. In any case, behavioral research proposes to observe and study the "real processes," in the sense of a "well-defined sequence of behaviors" by which decisions are reached in "actual business organizations." The hope—faithfully inductive—is to develop a theory "with generality beyond the specific firms studied" [10, p. 2]. Such a theory will be based on "four major sub-theories" regarding "organizational *goals,* organizational *expectations,* organizational *choice,* and organizational *control*" [10, p. 21]. It is assumed that five organizational goals—a production goal, an inventory goal, a sales goal, a market-share goal, and the profit goal—become the subject of bargaining among the various members of the "coalition" which make up the business organization but that the goals are continually adapted and are being pressed with varying force [10, pp. 40-43]. The behavior theory of the firm, with regard to the determination of prices and outputs, will run in terms of a "quasi resolution of conflict" within the organization, of an "adaptively rational, multiple-objective process" with responses to "short-run feedback on performance" and with continuing "organizational learning" [10, pp. 269-70].

This behavioral approach has been characterized as striving for "realism in process," in contrast to approaches aiming at more "realism in motivation" [48, p. 11]. Such realism in motivation is felt to be needed chiefly because of the separation of ownership and control in the modern corporation, whose managements have great power and wide discretion.

In principle, I could expect three different views to be taken regarding the relative independence of corporation management: (1) Whereas owners would run their business chiefly with a view to a maximum of money profits, managers run it with several supplementary and partly competing goals in mind. (2) Whereas owners, especially wealthy ones, would often allow nonprofit considerations to enter their decision-making, managers have a sense of dedication and identification with the business that makes them the more single-minded seekers of profits. (3) Even if managers are inclined to indulge in seeking other goals as long as profits look satisfactory, they are as professionals, trained in the art and science of management, able to make better profits than the owners could ever hope to make running their own show.

What consequences can be drawn from this? One attitude would be to stick with the assumption of profit maximization because it is the simplest and is applicable with much less detailed information to the largest field.[1] Another

---

[1] "To use marginalism in the theory of the firm it is not necessary to assert that firms attempt to maximize money profits only nor to deny that a goodly portion of all business behavior may be nonrational, thoughtless, blindly repetitive, deliberately traditional, or motivated by extra-economic objectives. It merely presupposes that the 'rational-economic' portion of business conduct is by and large sufficiently important to affect what is going on in the world to an extent large enough to warrant analysis; and that the substitution of money profits for a composite of pecuniary and nonpecuniary rewards simplifies the analysis so much that the gain in expediency far exceeds the loss in applicability" [23 pp. 30-31]. A similar view is expressed by Scitovsky: "Empirical studies of businessmen's behavior suggest the need for modifying or qualifying the assumption of profit maximization here and there, rather than scrapping it altogether. Accordingly, . . . we shall retain the assumption that the firm aims at maximizing its profit. But we shall regard this assumption as a working hypothesis rather than as a universal rule" [37, p. 111].

attitude would be to insist on starkest realism with a complete catalogue of goals and indices of their effectiveness in each firm. A third attitude would be to select two or three of the most important managerial objectives of a type that can be reduced to quantitative analysis and to combine them in a single manageable "objective function." This third approach merges marginalism with managerialism in that it integrates money profits with other managerial goals within one formula of "maximizing behavior."

The question is whether managerial marginalism is prescribed for general application or only for so-called noncompetitive cases. Its most prominent proponents prefer to use the old formula, based on profit maximization, in situations where competition is effective and managerial discretion therefore narrowly circumscribed. In the next sections we shall discuss matters that at first blush may seem unrelated to this issue but on reflection can shed indirect light on it.

THE ANALOGY OF THE THEORETICAL AUTOMOBILE DRIVER

One of the best remembered points in my exposition was the use of an analogy designed to warn against mistaking theoretical variables and their links for realistic descriptions of observable processes. This was the analogy of the "theory of overtaking" automobiles on the highways [21, pp. 534-35].

Analogies are often misleading, but in this particular case it served its main purpose: to show that the theoretical variables need not be estimated and the theoretical equations need not be solved through actual calculation by the actors in the real world whose idealized types are supposed to perform these difficult operations in the models constructed for the explanation of recorded observations.[2] The critics of marginal analysis believed they had refuted it if they could show that the exact numerical calculations of marginal magnitudes—cost, revenue, productivity—were difficult or impossible to perform by real decision-makers.

Yet my analogy was only partially successful. An implication which should have been obvious has been widely overlooked: that the type of action assumed to be taken by the theoretical actor in the model under specified conditions need not be expected and cannot be predicted actually to be taken by any particular real actor. The empiricist's inclination is to verify the theoretically deduced action by testing individual behavior, although the theory serves only to explain and predict effects of mass behavior.

We may illustrate this again by means of the same analogy, the theory of overtaking. Assume a change of driving conditions occurs, say, that the roads have become wet and slippery and fog has reduced visibility. Theory enables us to predict that traffic will be slower and accidents more frequent, but it does not enable us to predict that any particular driver will drive more slowly or have an accident. The model of the reactions of the individual driver was not designed to explain the actual driving of any particular operator but only to explain the observable consequences of the observed change of conditions by deducing from the model the theoretical reactions of a hypothetical driver.

Our analogy can also show us the limitations of the model: the prediction will hold only if there is a large number of automobiles on the road. If only a very few

---

[2]The theoretical automobile driver had to estimate, among other things, the speeds of three vehicles and the distances between them, and to perform calculations involving potential acceleration and a few other things, before he could decide to overtake the truck ahead of him. An actual driver simply "sizes up" the situation and goes ahead.

cars are around, there may be no accident and there need not be a reduction in their speed. Conceivably, the operators may all be good and self-confident drivers. Marginal analysis of hypothetical driver reaction will suffice for explaining and predicting the consequences of a change in driving conditions if the number of automobiles on the highways is large. If the number is small, behavioral research will be needed, though it may or may not be worth the cost.

Still another use can be made of our analogy: to show the vast differences in the scope of questions to which answers can or cannot be expected with the aid of a given theory, for example, from the theory of overtaking as sketched in my article. Compare the following four questions: (1) How fast will traffic move? (2) How fast will the automobile driven by Mr. X move? (3) How will the speed of traffic be affected by fog? (4) How will the speed of Mr. X's driving be affected by fog?

The theory sketched by me offers no answer to the first question, because each of the variables specified may have very different values for different cars and drivers; it has no answer to the second question, and only a suggestion, a rebuttable presumption, for answering the fourth question, because the theory is not really concerned with particular persons or their actions and reactions. The theory is equipped only to answer the third question, regarding the effects of a change in driving conditions on automobile traffic in general, and even this answer will be qualitative only, without good clues to numerical results. It may be interesting to get answers to all four questions, but since Question 3 can be answered with a fraction of the information that would be needed to answer the other questions, it would be foolish to burden the models designed for Question 3 with irrelevant matters, or to reject such models because they cannot do what they are not designed to do.[3]

CONFUSION OF PURPOSES

The same sort of confusion about the scope of problems and models for their solution has been fostered in recent writings on the theory of the firm: models have been condemned or rejected because they could not be used for purposes for which they had not been designed, and significant differences in the questions to be answered have been obscured or underemphasized.

Let us again pose four typical questions and see which of them we might expect to answer with the aid of "price theory." (1) What will be the prices of cotton textiles? (2) What prices will the X Corporation charge? (3) How will the prices of cotton textiles be affected by an increase in wage rates? (4) How will the X Corporation change its prices when wage rates are increased?

Conventional price theory is not equipped to answer any but the third question; it may perhaps also suggest a rebuttable answer to the fourth question. But Questions 1 and 2 are out of reach. We could not obtain all the information that would be required for their answers and there is, therefore, no use burdening the models with variables remaining silent and inactive throughout the show.

---

[3] A behavioral theory of automobile driving would probably study the process by which the decision to pass a truck is arrived at in a sequence of bickering among the members of the family; Mama and Sis trying to argue against taking an unnecessary risk, Sonny egging on his Dad to speed up and pass the truck "crawling" ahead of them. Moveover, the theory would not be satisfied with "explaining" the decision to overtake but it would also wish to determine the speed of driving, the frequency and length of stops at roadside stands, and all the rest.

We ought to guard against an easy misunderstanding of our denial that conventional price theory can predict actual prices of specified goods. Prediction of future prices of a particular commodity may in fact be quite manageable if we know its present price. It should be obvious, however, that this is Question 3, not Question 1. Or, one may be able to predict prices on the basis of good information on production cost. But this presupposes that we know the demand for the commodity and assume it will remain unchanged; which again comes down essentially to evaluations of changes of some variables and with others held constant, that is, to Question 3.

If the number of firms producing cotton textiles is large and the X Corporation does not supply a very large part of the aggregate output of the industry, price theory may suggest an answer to Question 4, although this is not the purpose of the theory and there may be a considerable chance for the suggested answer to be wrong. The point is that a model of a theoretical firm in an industry consisting of a large number of firms can do with a much smaller number of assumptions, provided the model is used to predict, not the actual reactions of any one particular firm, but only the effects of the hypothetical reactions of numerous anonymous "reactors" (symbolic firms). If it were to be applied to predictions of reactions of a particular firm, the model would have to be much more richly endowed with variables and functions for which information could be obtained only at considerable effort and with results that may or may not be worth the cost of the required research.

My charge that there is widespread confusion regarding the purposes of the "theory of the firm" as used in traditional price theory refers to this: The model of the firm in that theory is not, as so many writers believe, designed to serve to explain and predict the behavior of real firms; instead, it is designed to explain and predict changes in observed prices (quoted, paid, received) as effects of particular changes in conditions (wage rates, interest rates, import duties, excise taxes, technology, etc.). In this causal connection the firm is only a theoretical link, a mental construct helping to explain how one gets from the cause to the effect.[4] This is altogether different from explaining the behavior of a firm. As the philosopher of science warns, we ought not to confuse the *explanans* with the *explanandum*.

[4]The same statement can be made about the household. The "household" in price theory is not an object of study; it serves only as a theoretical link between changes in prices and changes in labor services supplied and in consumer goods demanded. The hypothetical reactions of an imaginary decision-maker on the basis of assumed, internally consistent preference functions serve as the simplest and heuristically satisfactory explanation of empirical relationships between changes in prices and changes in quantities. In other words, the household in price theory is not an object of study.

Behavioral studies of real households are something entirely different. A realistic, behavioral theory of the household might conceivably distinguish the large, children-dominated household from a simpler, father-dominated one. The decisions in the children-dominated household, where mother frequently and father occasionally try to exercise some influence, are probably not consistent, since different preference systems are made explicit at various times, with varying decibels and gestures deployed to make them prevail over the preferences of other members of the family.

One can imagine studies on the behavior of particular households selected at random or in structured samples. If the researcher learns that a spoiled brat in a family wants to eat nothing but beef and throws a tantrum every time his mother tries to feed him other kinds of meat, a reduction in the price of chicken will probably not substantially increase the consumption of chicken in this family. Thus, the weight of the child's taste in the decision process of the family can explain a low elasticity of its demand for chicken. But none of this has much bearing on general price theory.

MISPLACED CONCRETENESS

To confuse the firm as a theoretical construct with the firm as an empirical concept, that is, to confuse a heuristic fiction with a real organization like General Motors or Atlantic & Pacific, is to commit the "fallacy of misplaced concreteness." This fallacy consists in using theoretic symbols as though they had a direct, observable, concrete meaning.

In some fields, investigators are protected from committing the fallacy, at least with regard to some of their problems, by the fact that a search for any empirical counterpart to the theoretical construct seems hopeless. Thus, some physicists working on particle theory were able to answer the question "Does the Neutrino Really Exist?" [11, pp. 139-41] laconically with "Who cares?" and to explain that any belief in the "real existence" of atoms, electrons, neutrinos, and all the rest, would hold up the progress of our knowledge. Some biologists working in genetics warned, after empirical genes were discovered, that these "operational genes" should not be confused with the "hypothetical genes," which had been useful constructs in explanatory models before the discovery of any empirical referents [42, p. 814]. Economists, however, know for sure that firms exist as empirical entities and, hence, they have a hard time keeping the theoretical firm and the empirical firm apart.

For certain economic problems the existence of the firm is of the essence. For example, if we study the size distribution of firms or the growth of the firm, the organization and some of its properties and processes are the very objects of the investigation. In such studies we insist on a high degree of correspondence between the model (the thought-object) and the observed object. For other problems, however, as for problems of competitive-price theory, any likeness between the theoretical construct of the firm and the empirical firm is purely coincidental.

Economists trained in scientific methodology understand this clearly. I might quote a dozen or more writers, but will confine myself to one quotation, which states that "in economic analysis, the business firm is a postulate in a web of logical connections" [15, p. 196]. Let me add the statement of another writer, who however was plaintiff rather than advocate when he wrote that "It is a fascinating paradox that the received theory of the firm, by and large, assumes that the firm does not exist" [45, p. 249].

Here is what I wrote on one of the several occasions when I have discussed this problem:

> ... the firm in the model world of economic micro-theory ought not to call forth any irrelevant associations with firms in the real world. We know, of course, that there are firms in reality and that they have boards of directors and senior and junior executives, who do, with reference to hundreds of different products, a great many things—which are entirely irrelevant for the microtheoretical model. The fictitious firm of the model is a "uni-brain," an individual decision-unit that has nothing to do but adjust the output and the prices of one or two imaginary products to very simple imagined changes in data [26, p. 133].

I went on, of course, to say that this purely fictitious single-minded firm, helpful as it is in competitive-price theory, will not do so much for us in the theory of monopoly and oligopoly. To explain and predict price reactions under monopoly and oligopoly we need more than the construct of a profit-maximizing reactor.[5] I shall come back to this after discussing the demands for "more realistic" assumptions where they are plainly irrelevant and therefore out of place.

REALISTIC MODELS OF THE FIRM UNDER COMPETITION

Many of the proponents and protagonists of a more realistic theory of the firm are quite aware of the fact that the managerial extension and enrichment of the concept of the firm was not needed except where firms in the industry were large and few, and not under the pressure of competition. There are many very quotable statements to this effect.[6]

Too many students, however, want a realistic model of the firm for all purposes. They forget the maxim of Occam's Razor that unnecessary terms in a theory be kept out (or shaved off). These students seem to miss in a simplified model the realistic trimmings of the observable world; they distrust such a model because it is obviously "descriptively false." In view of this sentimental hankering for realism, it may be helpful to survey some of the inclusions which various writers have proposed in order to meet the demands for greater realism in the "theory of the firm," and to examine their relevance to the theory of competitive price. The

---

[5]You may wonder whether I have changed my mind on these matters. Incidentally, I hold that it is important for scholars and scientists to have an open mind, and the only evidence showing that they do are instances in which they have actually changed their minds. On this particular issue, however, I cannot oblige. Whether I am right or wrong, I have been consistent regarding these points. Let me quote from an article I wrote 28 years ago: "The problem of oligopoly is by definition the problem of the effects of the actions of few, giving a greater importance to the behavior of each member of the group. . . . The theory of the oligopoly price involves an interpretation of the significant motives behind the actions of a small number of people. . . . Even the most superficial theory will have to include many more ideal types of behavior in order to handle the problem of *few* sellers than it takes to handle the problem of a *mass* of competitive sellers" [20, p. 235].

On the other hand, I must plead guilty to a charge of the same error of misplaced concreteness against which I have just warned. It occurred in a sentence in which I spoke of various magnitudes (subjectively) "perceived or fancied by the men whose decisions or actions are to be explained (the business men) . . ." [21, p. 521]. If this sentence referred only to oligopolistic or monopolistic behavior, it would not be so bad, for, as I said above, the theoretical constructs of decision-makers in this case have a closer correspondence to real businessmen than the constructs in the theory of competitive prices. But the sentence was a misleading sentence in that (1) it gave the impression that the decision-makers in question were *real* men (real businessmen, whom you could interview) and (2) it said that the actions of these men were to be explained, whereas the purpose of the theory was not to explain observed actions but only observable *results* of imagined (postulated) reactions to observable events.

I apologize for this error. Not that I do not approve of a busy shuttle-traffic between the domain of theoretical construction and the domain of empirical observation, but we must never fail to specify the side of the frontier on which we happen to be. The theoretical terms may have empirical referents (counterparts), but to believe, or allow an impression of belief, that the two are identical is a methodological fallacy.

[6]"When the conditions of competition are relaxed . . . the opportunity set of the firm is expanded. In this case, the behavior of the firm as a distinct operating unit is of separate interest. Both for purposes of interpreting particular behavior within the firm as well as for predicting responses of the industry aggregate, it may be necessary to identify the factors that influence the firm's choices within this expanded opportunity set and embed these in a formal model" [48, pp. 2-3].

following considerations are supposed to supplement, qualify, restrict, or replace the objective of maximizing money profits.

(1) Entrepreneurs and managers cannot be expected to have an inelastic demand for leisure; indeed, one must assume that this demand is income-elastic so that higher profit expectations will cause them to sacrifice some income for the sake of more leisure [36, p. 356]. (2) Managers are anxious to avoid resentment on the part of their colleagues and subordinates and will, therefore, not enforce their orders with the sternness required for maximization of profits; similarly, minor functionaries do not want to disturb the routines of their superiors and, hence, they often abstain from suggesting improvements which would maximize profits [31, p. 452]. (3) Managers are more interested in their own salaries, bonuses, and other emoluments, than in the profits of the firm or the income of its owners [27, pp. 226-27]. (4) The realization of certain asset preferences (for example, liquidity as against inventories and fixed assets) may be in conflict with profit maximization [5, p. 99]. (5) The flow and biased screening of information through the various levels of management may cause systematic misinformation resulting in earnings far below the maximum obtainable [27, p. 229]. (6) The objective of maintaining control in the hands of the present control group may require a sacrifice of profit opportunities [31, p. 455]. (7) The preference for security may be so strong that even relatively conservative ways of making higher profits are eschewed [12, pp. 270-71]. (8) The striving for status, power, and prestige may be such that it results in conduct not consistent with a maximum of profit [1, p. 145], [28, p. 207] [13, p. xii] [27, p. 227]. (9) The wish to serve society, be a benefactor, or soothe one's social conscience, may militate against actions or policies that would maximize profits [7, pp. 16-17] [16, pp. 339-40]. (10) The instinct of workmanship [46, p. 187], a desire to show professional excellence [1, p. 146], a pervasive interest in feats of engineering, may lead to performance in conflict with highest possible profits. (11) Compromises among the different goals of executives with different interests—production, sales, personnel relations, finance, research and development, public relations, etc.—are sure to "compromise" the objective of maximum profits [10, p. 29]. (12) A variety of influences may be exerted on management decisions, perhaps pulling in different directions and possibly away from maximum profits, as for example influences from labor organizations, suppliers of materials, customers, bankers, government agencies [13, p. 340] [12, p. 270] [28, pp. 195-205].

I shall not prolong this catalogue even if it is far from complete. Let us admit that each of the possible deviations, from maximum profit may be "real" in some circumstances. But how effective and significant are they? If the industry is effectively competitive—and it does not have to be "purely" competitive or "perfectly" competitive—is there much of a chance that the direction in which firms react, through their decisions regarding prices, inputs and output, to a change in conditions would be turned around by any of the "forces" listed? Before we say apodictically no, we should examine a few of the reservations.

SECURITY AND MANAGERIAL COORDINATION

Let us single out two items which have been given especially wide play: the "objective of security" and the question of "managerial coordination."

The demand for the recognition of a separate "security motive" conflicting with the profit motive deserves a good discussion. But when I prepared for it, I reread what I had written on this subject and found that I could not improve on it. Will you do me the favor of reading it [23, pp. 51-53 and 424-28] and, if you like it, make your students read it?

That there are no business profits without risks and that there is not much point in treating the two quite separately; that it would be silly to call a decision one of profit-maximizing if it increased risk and uncertainty so much as to reduce the chance of survival; that the notion of long-run profits comprises all considerations of risks of loss; that, in terms of my automobile-driving analogies, only a fool would assume that maximization of speed means driving 120 miles an hour regardless of curves and bumps; these are some of the things that have to be said in this connection. But the most essential point to be made is that in the economics of *adjustment to change* the issues of security, survival, and maximum profit are merged. How primitive again to confuse new ventures and daring moves with mere responses to stimuli, obvious reactions to change. If a change in conditions calls for a certain reaction in the name of maximum profits, the very same reaction is called for also in the name of security of survival.

The other matter is of a more "behavioral" nature: the coordination of different goals and judgments on the part of different members of the management and the deviations from profit maximization that may be involved in the process. Frankly, I cannot quite see what great difference organizational matters are supposed to make in the firm's price reactions to changes in conditions. Assume, for example, the import duties on foreign products competing with the products of domestic industry are raised, with a resulting increase in the demand for the products of the firm. Why should the clashes and compromises of divergent opinions reverse the direction of the change that would be "dictated" by the simple rule of profit maximization? Perhaps one vice president wants to raise prices without increasing output, while another wants to increase output without (at least at the moment) raising prices. No matter what their compromise will be, it is likely to conform with what the simple rule suggests. But if not, so what? Remember we are talking about industries with more than a few firms and with free entry.[7]

OTHER QUALIFICATIONS TO COMPETITIVE PRICE THEORY

Substitution between income and leisure looks like the strongest reason for a qualification in cases in which the change in conditions is such that not only the locus of maximum profits is shifted but also the amount of profit obtainable is changed. Take again the example of a tariff increase shutting out foreign competition. The firms in the industry will find that given outputs will now fetch higher prices and that increased outputs can be sold at prices higher than those prevailing before tariffs were raised. And profits will be higher in any case, so that managers— even owner-managers—will be inclined to relax their efforts. Yet would anybody seriously argue that the substitution of leisure (coffee breaks, cocktail parties, golf) for potential profits would be such that total output would be reduced instead of increased? It is not a likely story, and where the industry consists of several or

---

[7]A great champion of more realistic theories of the firm summed up his reflections on their implications for general economics with this statement: "We shall not be far wrong in concluding . . . that the impact of more realistic theories of the firm on static price analysis is likely to be small" [6, p. 42].

many firms, the small probability vanishes quickly. What remains of the argument is that total output would increase, in reaction to the tariff increase, somewhat less than it would if the managers were eager beavers and did not relax in their efforts when profits increased. Thus, the elasticity of supply of the products in question is a little smaller. But since we do not know how much it would be anyhow, the unknown substraction from an unknown number should not cause the economic theorist any serious anxieties. (And if the politicians who push for the tariff increase decide to push less hard if we tell them that their friends in the industry will enjoy some of the added protection in the form of more leisure and recreation, we would not really mind.)

Even if formal accuracy demanded that we accept the maximization of the decision-maker's total utility as the basic assumption, simplicity and fruitfulness speak for sticking with the postulate of maximization of money profits for situations in which competition is effective. The question is not whether the firms of the real world will *really* maximize money profits, or whether they even *strive* to maximize their money profits, but rather whether the *assumption* that this is the objective of the theoretical firms in the artificial world of our construction will lead to conclusions—"inferred outcomes"—very different from those derived from admittedly more realistic assumptions.

The second qualification in my list—regarding bosses, colleagues and subordinates—is quite irrelevant, except perhaps for questions of welfare economics, where it matters whether firms "really" do all they can to maximize efficiency. For theories concerned with *changes* in prices, inputs, and outputs in response to *changes* to conditions (of production, resource availability, and product demand) the strictness with which efficiency is watched in the firm does not matter. The effects of the tariff increase in our illustration, or the effects of changes in wage rates, interest rates, tax rates, and so forth, are if there is effective competition, essentially independent of the relations among the various levels in the managerial hierarchy of the firm.

It would take too much time here to go through our entire list of reservations. Anybody who makes the effort will find that some of the "realistic assumptions" proposed for inclusion in the theory can affect (by an unknown amount) the magnitude but not the direction of any change that is likely to result from a specified change in conditions; and that other assumptions will not even do that much. In short, they are all irrelevant for purposes of competitive price theory.

OLIGOPOLY, MONOPOLY, AND MANAGERIAL DISCRETION

I repeat: In the theory of competitive price the "real existence" of firms is irrelevant; imaginary (postulated) agents pursuing a simple (postulated) goal react to assumed changes in conditions and thereby produce (or allow us to infer) changes in prices, inputs, and outputs [24, pp. 13-14]. The correspondence between these inferences (deduced changes) and actual observations (observed changes in prices, inputs, and outputs, following observed changes in conditions) is close for two reasons: (1) The number of firms in the real world is so large that it suffices if some of them react as posited by the theory; and (2) the profits of firms are only about "normal," that is, excess profits are about zero, because of competitive pressures from newcomers (pliopolistic pressures [23, pp. 211-23]), so that profits below the maximum obtainable would in fact be net losses in an economic sense.

These two reasons do not hold in the theories of oligopoly and monopoly price.[8] For these theories the real existence of firms (that is, an empirical counterpart to the theoretical construct) is required, because the explanation of changes in prices, inputs, and outputs is at the same time an explanation of decisions of some particular firms, in the sense of organizations of men acting in particular, sometimes unpredictable, ways. Various attempts have been made to develop patterns of oligopolistic and monopolistic conduct and to correlate these patterns with types of organization or with types of personalities exercising ultimate decision-making power. The success has thus far been small; even if the decision-making (say, pricing) in a particular firm was sometimes satisfactorily modeled (for example, in a simulated computer program), the model has usually not been transferable to other cases, to predict decisions in other firms. I do not recall, moreover, that the behavior patterns in these cases were shown to be inconsistent with the postulate of profit maximization.

Under these circumstances, retreat to simpler, less realistic models of firms in oligopoly and monopoly positions is indicated. The first approach is to apply the polypolistic model, in full awareness that the actual facts are entirely different. In many instances the use of the polypolistic model for situations which in our judgment would merit to be labeled as oligopolistic will still yield satisfactory explanations and predictions. Where this is not so, the analyst will resort to the use of models of oligopolistic or monopolistic firms, postulating the simplest possible pattern of action and reaction, dispensing with all peculiar attitudes and "special" strategies. Only where these simple models of oligopolistic and monopolistic firms yield quite unsatisfactory predictions will the analyst need to go further, to more special types of behavior, provided he finds it worth while. It depends on the research interests and on the problems under examination how much effort one wishes to invest in behavioral research where the findings hold little promise of yielding generalizations of wide applicability.

There are, however, some simple models of oligopolistic behavior which seem to be of sufficiently wide applicability. A model that equips the oligopolistic decision-maker not under heavy competitive pressure with an objective of gross-revenue ("sales") maximization, subject to the constraint of satisfactory net-revenue ("profit") [2, p. 49], succeeds in explaining the lack of response to some cost-increasing events observed in several instances. There are other simple models

[8]The idea that profit maximization is the appropriate hypothesis for the theory of competitive price but not necessarily for the theory of monopoly or oligopoly price has been expressed repeatedly over the last century.

Pareto, for example, said that "pure economics" cannot tell us anything about the continuing shifts of position of competing oligopolists, and we have to turn to "the observation of facts," which would show us the variety of possibilities [29, pp. 601-2].

Schumpeter, in 1928, had this to say about dichotomy: "We have much less reason to expect that monopolists will . . . charge an equilibrium price than we have in the case of perfect competition; for competing producers *must* charge it as a rule under penalty of economic death, whilst monopolists, although having a *motive* to charge the monopolistic equilibrium price, are not forced to do so, but may be prevented from doing so by other motives" [33,]. 371].

Finally, Scitovsky in 1951 stated that "not only does the monopolist's secure market position enable him to relax his efforts of maximizing profit, but his very position may prevent his aiming at maximum profit. He may regard his immunity from competition as precarious or be afraid of unfavorable publicity and public censure; and for either reason, he may judge it wiser to refrain from making full use of his monopoly position. We conclude, therefore, that although in some cases the monopolist will aim at maximizing his profit . . . in other cases— which may well be the important ones—he will refrain from maximizing profit" [37, p. 377].

27

explaining one model or another more satisfactory. If the sales-maximization hypothesis can explain a greater variety of observed responses or nonresponses than other hypotheses can, and if it seems to correspond better with self-interpretations offered by interviewed businessmen, it merits acceptance, at least for the time being.

An alternative to the maximization of sales is the maximization of the growth rate of sales [3, p. 1086]. This hypothesis is especially interesting because it involves an endogenous relation with profits: while some of the growth of gross revenue may encroach on profits, it does so with an automatic limit in that profits are needed to finance the investment required for the growth of sales.

Another extension of the objective function proposed on the basis of behavior research combines two managerial preferences for specific expenses of the firm with the usual profit motive. The two additional motives are expenditures for staff personnel and expenditures for managerial emoluments; both figure prominently in the utility functions of executives of companies which, sheltered from competitive pressures, make enough profits to allow management to indulge in these personal desires [48, pp. 38-60].

All these "managerial-discretion models" are simple and sufficiently general to allow relatively wide application. We shall have more to say about them later.

EFFECTIVE COMPETITION AND MANAGERIAL DISCRETION

In mapping out the area of applicability for theories of managerial discretion, we have spoken of "oligopoly," "monopoly," and of "firms not under heavy competitive pressure." These are rather vague guideposts, but unfortunately the literature has not been very helpful in ascertaining precisely what it is that allows or restricts the exercise of wide managerial discretion.

Some writers stress the size of the firm, suggesting that it is only in the *large* firm that management can exercise discretion. Others stress the condition of *diffused ownership* as the one that affords management the opportunity of pursuing objectives other than maximization of profits. Those who stress oligopoly as the domain for which objective functions richer than profit maximization are needed are usually not quite specific as to their criterion of an oligopoly position: it may be *fewness of firms* active in the same industry, or the subjective state of awareness of the *interdependence of price making* often characterized as "conjectural variation," or simply the *absence of aggressive competition for increasing shares in the market.* Others again stress *closed entry,* or absence of newcomers' competition, as the essential condition for a profit level sufficiently comfortable to allow managers to indulge in the satisfaction of objectives other than maximization of profits.

To combine all these conditions would probably be far too restrictive; it would confine the application of managerial-discretion models to large firms with diffused ownership, few competitors, full awareness of interdependence in pricing, absence of aggressive efforts by existing competitors to increase their market shares, and little danger of new competitors entering the field. The size of the firm may actually not be relevant, and diffused ownership may not be a necessary condition for some deviations from profit maximization to occur, say, in the interest of larger sales or larger expenditures for staff. Fewness of competitors may be more significant, chiefly because the danger of newcomers' competition is likely to be small where the number of firms has been few and continues to be few; partly also because the few competitors may have learnt that aggressive price competition does not pay. The essential conditions, it seems to me, are these two: that no newcomers are likely to invade the field of the existing firms, and that none of the existing firms tries to expand its sales at such a fast rate that it could succeed only by encroaching on the business of its competitors.

Competition from newcomers, from aggressive expansionists, or from importers is sometimes called "heavy," "vigorous," or "effective." The simplest meaning of these adjectival modifiers is this: a firm is exposed to heavy, vigorous, or effective competition if it is kept under continuing pressure to do something about its sales and its profits position. Under this "competitive pressure" the firm is constantly compelled to react to actual or potential losses in sales and/or reductions in profits, so much so that the firm will not be able to pursue any objectives other than the maximization of profits—for the simple reason that anything less than the highest obtainable profits would be below the rate of return regarded as normal at this time.

I am aware of a defect in this definition: its criterion is lodged in the effect rather than in an independently ascertainable condition. Perhaps, though, "effective" is quite properly defined in this fashion, namely, by whether certain effects are realized: competition is effective if it continually depresses profits to the level regarded as the minimum tolerable. What makes it effective is not part of the definition, but has to be explained by the conditions of entry, aggressive attitudes on the part of any existing firms, or imports from abroad.

If my reasoning is accepted, several formulations proposed in the literature will have to be amended. Managerial discretion will be a function, not of the independence of the management from the control of the owners, but chiefly of the independence of the management from urgent worries about the sufficiency of earnings. If one insists, one may still say that all managers are primarily interested in their own incomes. But, since it is clear that their long-term incomes are jeopardized if profits go below the acceptable rate of return, maximization of managerial incomes and maximization of profits come to the same thing if competition is effective.[9]

There can be no doubt about the fact that competition is not effective in many industries and that many, very many, firms are not exposed to vigorous competition. It follows that managerial discretion can have its way in a large enough number of firms to secure wide applicability of well-designed managerial-discretion models—or to invite the use of managerial total-utility models.

I was fully aware, when I wrote my 1946 article, that there were many qualifications and exceptions to the principle of profit maximization.[10] But I considered it hopeless for predictive purposes to work with total-utility maximization and I did not see the possibility of combining a few selected managerial goals with the profit motive.

[9]For competition to be effective it is not necessary that competition is either pure or perfect or that all or any of the markets in which the firm buys or sells are perfect.

[10]Several of my statements, if I presented them without source reference, might well be mistaken for quotations from critics of marginalism, including behavioralists and managerialists. Here are samples [21]: "... a business man is motivated by considerations other than the maximization of money profits"; "it is preferable to separate the non-pecuniary factors of business conduct from those which are regular items in the formation of money profits" (p. 526); "one may presume that producing larger production volumes [or] paying higher wage

29

MARGINALISM EXTENDED: TOTAL UTILITY

In order to show how hopeless it is to construct a comprehensive total-utility model and obtain from it definite predictions of the effects of changes in conditions upon the dispositions of the managers, one merely has to visualize the large variety of possible "satisfactions" and the still larger variety of things that may contribute to their attainment. The satisfactions consist not only in receiving money incomes, immediate or deferred, and various incomes in kind, but also in distributing incomes to others and in gaining prestige, power, self-esteem, as well as in enjoying a good conscience and other pleasurable feelings.

What makes things really complicated is that the creation of these satisfactions is related to very different flows of funds into and out of the firm: some to gross revenue (sales volume), others to net revenue; some to profits distributed, others to profits retained; some to investment outlays, others to company expenses. The managers' immediate money incomes and some of the emoluments received in kind are partly at the expense of profits, partly at the expense of corporate income taxes (and every change in tax rates changes the trade-off ratios.) The same is true of several other company expenses which add to the prestige, power, and self-esteem of the managers. Special mention may be made of the provision of stock options for managers, which are either at the expense of the owners' equity (through watering down their stock) or at the expense of potential capital gains on treasury stock earmarked for such stock options, but which, on the other hand, may be a powerful force aligning the managers' personal interests with the goal of maximizing the net profits of the firm.

The point of it all is that the total utility of managers can be increased by decisions which increase expenses at the expense of profits. (Of course, this is confined to situations where profits are high enough to stand encroachments by avoidable expenses—to situations, that is, where the firm is not hard-pressed by competition.) The question is how various changes in conditions will affect managerial decisions on inputs, outputs, and prices if the objectives of management include the gratification of preferences for certain expenses of the firm that compete with the maximization of profits.[11]

rates . . . than would be compatible with a maximum of money profits may involve for the business man a gain in social prestige or a certain measure of inner satisfaction"; "it is not impossible that considerations of this sort substantially weaken the forces believed to be at work on the basis of a strictly pecuniary marginal calculus"; for patriotic reasons during the war "many firms produced far beyond the point of highest money profits"; "the conflict of interests between the hired managers and the owners of the business" may call for "important qualifications" (p. 527); "the interest of the former in inordinately large outlays or investments may be capable of descriptions in terms of a pecuniary calculus, but it is not maximization of the firm's profits which serves here as the standard of conduct" (pp. 527-28); "maximization of salaries and bonuses of professional managers may constitute a standard of business conduct different from that implied in the customary marginal analysis of the firm"; and "the extent to which the two standards would result in sharply different action under otherwise similar conditions is another open question in need of investigation" (p. 528).

[11]Instead of cataloguing the various contributions to the "utility" of the management and their relationships to the sources and uses of the firm's funds, one may wish to classify the expenses of the firm with reference to "discretionary" decisions of the management influenced by the decision-makers' preferences. Here is a tentative classification of this sort:

1. Expenses required for the production of (a) current output of unchanged size, (b) additional current output, with marginal cost not exceeding marginal revenue (hence, contributing to higher profits), and (c) additional current output, with marginal cost exceeding marginal revenue (hence, reducing profits).

For purposes of illustration let us reproduce in a literary form the utility function of a management (perhaps of its "peak coordinator" [28, pp. 190-91]) in full control and confident that stockholders will not make any fuss as long as the firm makes a "normal" profit and pays out a fair share of it in dividends. Total utility, which the manager by his decisions will try to maximize, will be a function of a large number of variables, by virtue of the contributions they make to his pride, prestige, self-esteem, conscience, comfort, feeling of accomplishment, material consumption, and anticipations of future benefits and pleasures. Among the variables may be total profits of the firm, growth rate of profits, rate of profits to investment, total sales, growth rate of sales, increase in market share, dividends paid out, retained earnings, increase in market value of stock, price-earnings ratio of stock, investment outlay, salary and bonus received, stock options received (capital gains), expense accounts (consumption at company expense), services received (automobile, chauffeur, lovely secretary, theatre tickets, conferences at resorts), size of staff, expenses for public relations and advertising, expenses for research and development, technological and other innovations, leadership in wage increases and good industrial relations, expenses for public or private education and health, other contributions to public interest and patriotic causes, free time for leisure and recreation, and indications of influence over government, industry, and society. This list of variables is, of course, only representative, not exhaustive.[12]

Now what can one do with a utility function of this sort? Will it be of much use in telling us what the firm will do with its freedom of action if it has to respond to a change in conditions?

The answer will depend partly on a simple condition, namely, whether the acceptable trade-off ratios between all the factors contributing to total utility remain unchanged, or approximately the same, if any one of them, say, total profit, increases. If this were the case, we could shout hurrah or sigh a sigh of relief (depending on our temperament). For, if the marginal rates of substitution among all the various "utilifactors" are constant, the distribution of funds among them will remain unchanged with changes in conditions that increase or decrease the total of funds available. Only if the cost of any of the factors changed, say, the cost of staff personnel and, hence, the cost of prestige and other benefits that accrue from having a sizable staff, would the marginal rates of substitution be adapted to the new cost relation. In such a case we might also perhaps be able to tell the kind of response of the decision-makers.

2. Expenses not required for the production of current output, but increasing the productive capacity or efficiency of the firm for future production.

3. Expenses for managerial personnel in the form of a) salaries and bonuses, and (b) services rendered to them for their convenience and pleasure.

4. Expenses not required for either current or future production, but (a) expected of a profitable firm as a social service, and only slightly promoting the public image of management, (b) widely recognized as contributing to the social or national benefit and as indicative of the public spirit of the management, (c) contributing chiefly to the gratification of personal desires of supervisory and managerial personnel, and (d) largely wasteful, that is, contributing nothing, and economizing nothing but managerial effort or capability.

This list may be suggestive of the actions that may have to be taken when, after years of ease and growth, the firm finds it profits declining or disappearing.

[12]Perhaps there ought to be a place on the list for some gratifications that are more stable, less subject to quantitative variation, such as the pleasure of being known for honesty and fairness, on the one hand, and for sharpness and shrewdness, on the other, or at least the pleasure of being convinced of having and exercising these qualities. And last, though not least, there is the general feeling of gratification from "running" a large, well-known profitable, widely respected firm with growing assets and employment.

Alas, the condition that the marginal rates of substitution are independent of the total funds available is not likely to be satisfied; in addition, certain types of change in conditions have the bad habit of affecting at the same time funds available and relative costs of utilifactors. For example, an increase in the corporate income tax will change the trade-off ratio between expensable outlays and profits in favor of avoidable expenses.

MARGINALISM EXTENDED: CHOICE OF MAXIMANDA

If we were interested only in a formal solution, and perhaps in a proof of "existence" of an equilibrium position, we might be satisfied with the maximization of total utility by those who effectively run the firm. If, however, we want to predict the direction of the changes which a given change in conditions is likely to bring about, then mere formalism will not be enough. For predictive purposes we need *more* to go by with the help of *fewer* variables. Maximization of money profits is certainly the simplest "objective function," but it works only in the case of firms exposed to vigorous competition. The management of a firm that makes more than enough money need not go all out to maximize profits; it can afford to do a few other things that it likes, such as serving what by its own lights it regards as the national interest or indulging in other luxuries.

Would this imply "giving up" the principle of marginalism in the theory of the profitable firm? This is chiefly a semantic question. I have been inclined to use a more extended definition. In 1946, I called marginalism "the logical process of finding a maximum" [21, p. 519]. I did not say that it had to be maximization of money profits—though I struggled hard to justify the use of profit maximization in all cases. In the meantime several writers have shown that profit maximization may not be a completely unambiguous objective, even where it is used in splendid isolation from all competing goals, in that it may refuse to yield unambiguous conclusions regarding the effects of certain changes, such as the effects of changes in profit taxes. In addition, it has been shown that several workable "objective functions" can be developed that give plausible results with a few relatively simple terms added. Any of these functions that can be maximized, with or without specific constraints, would still be a part of marginal analysis.

The choice of the *maximandum* is of course a pragmatic matter: we should prefer one that yields sufficiently good approximations to what we consider reasonable on the basis of empirical research, with wide applicability and fruitfulness and with great simplicity. The compromise among these goals that we accept is, admittedly, a somewhat "subjective" standard of selection, but perfectly in line with the standard accepted in all scientific fields. Concessions to any one of these desiderata must be at the expense of the others.

Let us list some of the alternative *maximanda* that have been suggested and are available for our choice: Total quasi-rents over a short period of time (But how short? This is good only for a freshman course); total quasi-rents during the service-life of existing fixed assets (But is a replaceable part of a machine a fixed asset? This works only for a one-hoss shay); present value of all profits (after taxes) expected in the future, discounted at a "normal" or "competitive" rate; internal rate of return to equity; equity of controlling stockholders; present values of retained earnings; growth rate of equity; gross rate of total assets; growth rate of gross revenue (sales); gross revenue (sales), if net revenues (profits) are satisfactory (over what period of time?); salaries, bonuses, and other accruals (including services in kind) to management, over their entire lives; all accruals to management plus expenditure for staff personnel, compatible with minimum profits; all accruals to management, consistent with satisfactory profits and gradually rising prices of corporate stock; and, of course, the present values of the various combinations of flows mentioned.

Surely a much longer list could be prepared, but there is no use to this. The point should be clear: profit maximization proper may mean a variety of things—several entries apply to money profits—and in addition there are a few other *maximanda* of possible relevance. Incidentally, if profits or accruals to stockholders are not explicitly included in some of the entries, let no one believe that they are really out of the picture. No management could try to maximize its own accruals in the long run if it completely disregarded the interests of the stockholders. Hence, all *maximanda* are subject to the constraint of some minimum benefits to the owners of the business in the form of dividends, capital gains, or both.[13]

SUBJECTIVE INFORMATION AND THE CHARGE OF TAUTOLOGY

I have a few remaining tasks, and one of them is to lay a ghost, one that has long played tricks on economists and led them astray. He has done this in their discussions of the subject of information, its availability, its uncertainty, and its subjectivity. I mean, of course, information available to the "firm," and this raises the question whether we mean the firm as a purely theoretical construct or the firm as an organization of real people or anything else.

The firm as a theoretical construct has exactly the kind of information the theorist chooses to endow it with in order to design a good, useful theory. The firm as an organization of real people has the information system that it actually happens to have and which, in some instances, the management scientists (operations researchers) have succeeded in developing. For purposes of competitive price and allocation theory, it does not make much difference whether the information which we assume the firm to have concerning the conditions of supply, production, and demand under which it works is correct or incorrect, as long as we may safely assume that any *change* in these conditions is registered correctly. If we want to inquire into the effects of a change in wage rates or tax rates or something of this sort, we must of course take it for granted that the decision-makers who supposedly react to the change have taken notice of it. But whether their "previous" store of

---

[13]The four "managerial" variables included in the list—sales, growth of sales, expenses for staff, and emoluments to the management—may well be the most important deviations from profit maximization, although I may easily be persuaded of the existence of other "extravagances" of management. Among the managements of our large corporations there are so many civic-minded men, bursting with social responsibility and cocksure of their ability to know what is in the national interest, that I incline to the thought that rather serious deviations from the profit motive occur in the area of virtuous striving for the so-called common good. I hope I am not excessively naive if I believe that the excess profits secured through restrictions on competition are to no small extent used for what the discretionary managers believe to be worthy causes. But I see no way of formulating any hypotheses that would enable us to predict either just what the firms' outlays in the public interest will be or how they will affect total output in the long run. I suppose that Boulding's witty question, "do we maximize profit subject to the constraints of satisfactory profits? [7, p. 17] was not intended to suggest an answer with empirically fertile conclusions.

information—from which they started when the change occurred—was accurate or not will only in exceptional instances make a qualitative difference to the reactions. This important difference between information about conditions and information about changes in conditions has eluded several writers, who shouted "tautology" when they confronted my statements about the subjectivity of information. They reasoned like this: If firms act on the basis of information which is entirely subjective, then *anything* they do may be said to follow from whatever they believe they know: hence, the assumption of subjectivism defeats any explanatory purposes. This is a sad confusion. In teaching elementary economics we ought to be able to make our students grasp the difference between the shape and position of a curve, on the one hand, and the shift of a curve, on the other. The direction of the effects which we derive from the shift is usually, though not always, independent of the shape and position of the original curve. We need not fuss about the curve reflecting "accurate information" if we only want to see what happens when the curve shifts in a certain direction.

Since ghosts are hardy creatures, the laying of this one will probably not constitute a once-and-for-all execution. We shall probably see him again thumbing his nose at us in the next textbook or in the next issue of one of our journals.

IMPERFECT INFORMATION
AND THE QUESTION OF "SATISFICING" BEHAVIOR

The same confusion sometimes encumbers the discussions about the alleged "imperfection" of knowledge available to firms for their rational decision-making [39, pp. xxiv-xxvi, 40-41, 81-83, 241-42] and the screens and blockages in "the flow of information through the hierarchies of the organization [27, pp. 228-29]. But what can be "imperfect" about the information on, say, a tax increase? Why should it take special theories of bureaucracy to explain how the news of a wage increase "flows" through various hierarchical levels up or down or across? Yet this, and this alone, is the information that is essentially involved in the theory of prices and allocation, since it is the *adjustment to such changes* in conditions for which the postulate of maximizing behavior is employed.

One can understand, of course, how the confusion arose. The proponents of managerial analysis have the creditable ambition to reorganize firms in such a way that their managements can really, as a matter of actual fact, maximize the results of their performance, not only in adjusting to changes in conditions, but also in making the most rational arrangements on the basis of the *complete environment* in which they operate.[14] Incidentally, not only "normative micro-economics," as management science has been called [40, p. 279], has this ambition; many propositions of welfare economics are also based on such presuppositions.

As a matter of fact, the interesting distinction made between "satisficing" and "maximizing" or "optimizing" behavior [39, pp. xxiv-xxvi] [40, pp. 262-65] had its origin in precisely the same issue; management, realizing the complexity of

---

[14]"Economic man deals with the 'real world' in all its complexity," says Herbert Simon [39, p. xxv]. The *homo oeconomicus* I have encountered in the literature was not such a perfectionist. Incidentally, even Simon's "economic man," two years before the ambitious one just quoted, did not have "absolutely complete," but only "impressively clear and voluminous" knowledge of the "relevant aspects of his environment" [38, p. 99]. My point is that we ought to distinguish perfect or imperfect knowledge of (*a*) the entire environment, (*b*) the relevant aspects of the entire environment, (*c*) the relevant changes in environmental conditions.

the calculations and the imperfection of the data that would have to be employed in any determination of "optimal" decisions, cannot help being satisfied with something less: its behavior will be only "satisficing." What behavior? The mere adjustment to a simple change or the coordinated, integrated whole of its activities? Evidently, only the latter is the overly ambitious aim. The theory of prices and allocation, viewed as a theory of adjustment to change, does not call for impossible performances.[15] I ask you to remember what I spelled out, twenty years ago, about the difference between exact estimates and calculations, on the one hand, and "sizing up" in nonnumerical terms, on the other [21, pp. 524-25, 534-35]. And I ask you to realize how many more good predictions can be made on the basis of the assumption that firms try to maximize their profits than on the basis of the assumption that they want no more than satisfactory profits. Take one illustration: if an easy-money policy is introduced, we expect that some firms will increase their borrowings, some firms will increase their purchases, some firms will sell at higher prices, and some firms will increase their output. But if everybody was satisfied before the change, we cannot infer any of these things. On the other hand, if we assume that firms prefer a larger profit to a smaller one, all the mentioned consequences follow from the simple model.

THE TWENTY-ONE CONCEPTS OF THE FIRM

Several times in this paper I have spoken of the fallacy of misplaced concreteness, committed by mistaking a thought-object for an object of sense perception, that is, for anything in the real, empirical world. My warnings might have given rise to another confusion, namely, that there are only two concepts of the firm. There are many more, and I do not wish to suppress altogether my strong taxonomic propensities. I shall offer a list of ten different contexts calling for even more different concepts, some theoretical, some more empirical.

One of my favorite philosophers, who was a past-master of the art of making fine distinctions, enumerated 13 concepts of "pragmatism" [18], 66 concepts of "nature" [19, pp. 447-56], and "a great number" of concepts of "God."[16] I am sure there are at least 21 concepts of the firm employed in the literature of business and economics, but I shall exercise great forbearance and confine myself to a selection. Everyone may join in the game and fill in what I leave out. I shall first state the context, then delimit the concept, and finally add a few words of explanation.

---

[15]Suppose the government imposes a 15 per cent surcharge on all import duties. The theory of the profit-maximizing firm will without hesitation tell us that imports will decline. What will the theory of the satisficing firm tell us? "Models of satisficing behavior are richer than models of maximizing behavior, because they treat not only of equilibrium but of the method of reaching it as well. Psychological studies of the formation and change of aspiration levels support propositions of the following kinds. (a) When performance falls short of the level of aspiration, search behavior (particularly search for new alternatives of action) is induced. (b) At the same time, the level of aspiration begins to adjust itself downward until goals reach levels that are practically attainable. (c) If the two mechanisms just listed operate too slowly to adapt aspirations to performance, emotional behavior—apathy or aggression, for example—will replace rational adaptive behavior" [40, p. 263]. I admit that this is an unfair use of the theory of satisficing, but I wanted to show that everything has its place and no theory can be suitable to all problems. I suspect, however, that Simon's theory of satisficing behavior will yield neither quantitative nor qualitative predictions.

[16]"Lovejoy Denied Approval by Senate Group, " *The Baltimore Sun,* April 1, 1951.

1. In the theory of competitive prices and allocation, the firm is *an imaginary reactor to environmental changes*. By "imaginary" I mean to stress that this a pure construct for which there need not exist an empirical counterpart. By "reactor" I mean to deny that this robot or puppet can ever have a will of his own: he is the theorist's creature, programmed to respond in the predetermined way.

2. In the theory of innovation and growth, the firm is *an imaginary or a typical reactor or initiator*. Depending on which theory one has in mind, we see that several combinations are possible. In the theory of "entrepreneurial innovation" by men of very special qualities [34, pp. 78-94] the entrepreneur is neither imaginary nor a mere reactor; he is a typical initiator. By "typical" I do not refer to the ideal type of German sociology [47, p. 44] [35, pp. 20-63, 81] [25, pp. 21-57], but rather to the common-sense kind of person that many of us have met in person or, at least, have heard about. On the other hand, there are also theories of "induced invention"—assuming latent inventiveness (though an invention can never be a mere reaction)—and theories of "induced growth," employing the construct of the imaginary reactor.

3. In welfare economics, the firm is *an imaginary or a typical reactor or initiator with accurate knowledge of his opportunities*. Depending on the proposition in question, all combinations are again possible, but in any case a new requirement is introduced: accurate knowledge of the environmental conditions on the part of all reactors and initiators. For, in contrast to the theory of price and allocation, the welfare theorist wants to ascertain, not only in which direction price, input, and output will move in response to a change, but also whether this move will increase or reduce welfare. For such an exercise it is no longer irrelevant whether the subjective information of the firms is correct or false.

4. In the theory of oligopoly and monopoly, the firm is *a typical reactor and initiator in a small (or zero) interacting group*. I have explained earlier why a theory of oligopoly with nothing but imaginary reactors may not be widely applicable.

5. In the theory of organization (or bureaucracy), the firm is *a typical cooperative system with authoritative coordination*. I have accepted this formulation from one of the authorities [28, p. 187] and thus may disclaim responsibility for it.

6. In management science (or the art of business management), the firm is *a functional information system and decision-making system for typical business operations*. The normative nature of management science should be stressed. Several management scientists include operations research among the agenda of management science. I take this to mean that the principal techniques of operations research of such matters as inventory problems, replacement problems, search problems, queueing problems, and routing problems have to be mastered by the management scientist. He should, however, make a distinction between the science and its application: the science deals with typical systems, but is applied to particular cases.

7. In operations research and consultation, the firm is *an actual or potential client for advice on optimal performance*. In this context the reference is not to the techniques and principles of operations research but rather to the particular projects planned or undertaken.

8. In accounting theory, the firm is *a collection of assets and liabilities*. It should be clear how different this concept is from most of the others.

9. In legal theory and practice, the firm is *a juridical person with property, claims, and obligations*. This may be a very deficient formulation; I defer to the experts, who will surely correct it.

10. In statistical description (such as the Census of Manufactures) the firm is *a business organization under a single management or a self-employed person with one or more employees or with an established place of business.* I have adopted here the definition used by the U.S. Census.

This exercise should have succeeded in showing how ludicrous the efforts of some writers are to attempt *one* definition of *the* firm as used in economic analysis, or to make statements supposedly true of "the" firm, or of "its" behavior, or what not. Scholars ought to be aware of equivocations and should not be snared by them.

A SENSE OF PROPORTION

I hope there will be no argument about which concept of the firm is the most important or the most useful. Since they serve different purposes, such an argument would be pointless. It would degenerate into childish claims about one area of study being more useful than another.

I also hope the specialist who uses one concept of the firm will desist from trying to persuade others to accept his own tried and trusted concept for entirely different purposes. The concept of the firm in organization theory, for example, need not at all be suitable for accounting theory or legal theory; and I know it is not suitable for either competitive price theory or for oligopoly theory.

Most of the controversies about the "firm" have been due to misunderstandings about what the other specialist was doing. Many people cannot understand that others may be talking about altogether different things when they use the same words.

I am not happy about the practice of calling any study just because it deals with or employs a concept of the firm "economics" or "micro-economics." But we cannot issue licenses for the use of such terms and, hence, must put up with their rather free use. My own prejudices balk at designating organization theory as economics—but other people's prejudices are probably different from mine, and we gain little or nothing from arguing about the correct scope of our field.

Now what conclusions from all our reviewing may we draw on the conflicts between marginal analysis, behavioral theory, and managerial theory of the firm? Fortunately, not much time is being wasted on descriptive studies of a narrowly behaviorist kind, in the sense of recording observed behavior without any prior theoretical design. Most proponents of behavioral studies of the firm are too competent theorists for that. As far as the proponents of managerial theories are concerned, they have never claimed to be anything but marginalists, and the behavior goals they have selected as worthy for incorporation into behavior equations, along with the goal of making profits, were given a differentiable form so that they could become part of marginal analysis.[17] Thus, instead of a heated contest between marginalism and managerialism in the theory of the firm, a marriage between the two has come about.

Not all marriages, these days, are permanent; divorces are frequent. Whether this marriage will last or end in divorce will depend chiefly on what offspring it will

[17]While under profit maximization MR - MC = 0, sales maximization requires that MR=0; hence, for some of the output sold marginal revenue is less than marginal cost, which into profits. A minimum-profit constraint sets a limit to this.

In the case of maximization of the growth rate of sales the limit on nonremunerative selling is built into the objective itself because a growth of productive assets is required to produce. If the match of the profit hypothesis with the various managerial hypotheses proves fertile of sufficiently interesting deductions, the prospects of a lasting marriage are good.

It is not easy to judge the future sterility or fertility of this marriage between marginalism and managerialism, because most of us are inclined to underrate the kinds of problem on which we have never worked: we have a bias in favor of our own research experience. Most of the researchers on behavioral versions of the theory of the firm look for their problems to the records of selected large corporations. They take it for granted that their theory must be designed to explain and predict the behavior of these firms. This, however, is less so in the case of economists engaged in the analysis of relative prices, inputs, and outputs. They look for their problems to the records of entire industries or industrial sectors. To be sure, some industries are dominated by large corporations, yet the accent of the analysis is not on the behavior of these firms but at best on some of the results of that behavior. Where the focus is not on the behavior of the firm, a theory that requires information on particular firms to be "plugged in" seems to them less serviceable than a more general theory, at least as long as only qualitative, not numerical, results are sought. Hence, even if the "partial-equilibrium analyst" knows full well that the actual situation is not a really competitive one, he probably will still make a first try using the competitive model with good old-fashioned profit maximization. And if the results appear too odd, appropriate qualifications may still be able to take care of them more simply than if he had started with a cumbersome managerial model. (In saying this, I am showing my bias.)

It is revealing to ask what kind of theory we would apply, at least in a first approximation, if we were called upon to predict the results of various kinds of public-policy measures. For questions regarding short-run effects of changes in the corporation income tax (or an excess-profits tax) I believe a strong case can be made in favor of a model of the firm with some managerial variables. If the problem is whether an increase in cigarette taxes is likely to be fully shifted onto the consumer or what portion of it may be absorbed by the producers, I may feel safer with a model that includes managerial objectives. If, however, the problem is what qualitative effects an increase in the import duty on a material used in several industries will have on its imports and on the prices and outputs of the various products of the industries in question, I would be inclined to work with the simple hypothesis of profit maximization. I would find it far too cumbersome in this case to go down to the level of the "real" firms; I could probably not obtain the necessary data and, even if I did, I might not be able to rely on the composite results obtained from a firm-by-firm analysis. The old theory of the firm, where all firms are pure fictions, may give me—in this case—most of the answers, in a rough and ready way, not with any numerical precision, but with sufficient reliability regarding the directions of change.

support the growth of sales, and the acquisition of these assets presupposes a sufficiency of profits, either for internal financing or as a basis for outside finance [3, pp. 1086-87]. If at any time sales were pushed too hard at the expense of profits, there would arise a shortage of funds for acquiring the productive assets needed for producing more output. Thus no separate minimum-profit constraint has to be imposed, since it is inherent in the objective of maximization of the growth of sales. It should be understood, however, that the growth rate of assets under this objective is still less than it could be under straight profit maximization. (This shows why we should never speak of the "growth of the firm" without specifying by what criterion we measure it.)

I conclude that the choice of the theory has to depend on the problem we have to solve.[18] Three conditions seem to be decisive in assigning the type of approach to the type of problem. The simple marginal formula based on profit maximization is suitable where (1) *large groups* of firms are involved and nothing has to be predicted about particular firms, (2) the effects of a *specified change* in conditions upon prices, inputs, and outputs are to be explained or predicted rather than the values of these magnitudes before or after the change, and nothing has to be said about the "total situation" or general developments, and (3) only *qualitative answers*, that is, answers about directions of change, are sought rather than precise numerical results. Managerial marginalism is more suitable to problems concerning particular firms and calling for numerical answers. And, I am sure, there are also some problems to which behavioral theory may be the most helpful approach. My impression is that it will be entirely concerned with particular firms and perhaps designed to give answers of a normative, that is, advisory nature.

It looks as if I had prepared the ground for a love feast: I have made polite bows in all directions and have tuned up for a hymn in praise of peaceful co-existence of allegedly antagonistic positions. But I cannot help raising a question which may tear open some of the wounds of the battle of 1946. The question is whether the effects of an effective increase in minimum wages upon the employment of labor of low productivity can, at our present state of knowledge, be fruitfully analyzed with any other model than that of simple marginalism based on unadulterated profit maximization.

If I answer in the negative, does this mean that we are back at the old quarrel and have not learned anything? It does not mean this. Deficiencies in marginal analysis have been shown and recognized; and a great deal of good empirical as well as theoretical work has been accomplished. But the deficiencies dealt with were not just those which the critics twenty years ago attacked. That attack questioned the applicability of marginal analysis to the employment effects of wage increases in industries with many firms presumably under heavy competition [16, pp. 64, 75-77]. In such circumstances the managerial theories of the firm, according to their proponents, do not apply. On this narrow issue, therefore, the old-type marginalist cannot retreat.

[18]As a matter of fact, it will also depend on the research techniques which the appointed analyst has learned to master; we can eliminate this bias by assuming an ideal analyst equally adept in all techniques.

REFERENCES

1. C. I. Barnard, *Functions of the Executive*. Cambridge, Mass. 1938.

2. W. J. Baumol, *Business Behavior, Value and Growth*. New York 1959.

3. ———, "On the Theory of the Expansion of the Firm," *Am. Econ. Rev.*, Dec. 1962, *52* 1078-87.

4. ———, *Economic Theory and Operations Analysis*, 2nd ed. Englewood Cliffs, N.J. 1965.

5. K. E. Boulding, *A Reconstruction of Economics*. New York 1950.

6. ———, "Implications for General Economics of More Realistic Theories of the Firm," *Am. Econ. Rev.*, Proc., May 1952, *42*, 35-44.

7. ———, "Present Position of the Theory of the Firm," in K. E. Boulding and W. A. Spivey, *Linear Programming and the Theory of the Firm*, New York 1960, pp. 1-17.

8. E. H. Chamberlin, *The Theory of Monopolistic Competition; A Reorientation of the Theory of Value*. Cambridge, Mass. 1933.

9. A. A. Cournot, *Recherches sur les principes mathematiques de la theorie des richesses*, Paris 1838. English transl. by N. T. Bacon under the title *Researches into the Mathematical Principles of the Theory of Wealth*, New York 1897, reprinted 1927.

10. R. M. Cyert and J. G. March, *Behavioral Theory of the Firm*. Englewood Cliffs, N.J. 1963.

11. S. M. Dancoff, "Does the Neutrino Really Exist?" *Bull. Atomic Scientists*, June 1952, *8*, 139-41.

12. R. A. Gordon, "Short-Period Price Determination in Theory and Practice," *Am. Econ. Rev.*, June 1948, *38*, 265-88.

13. ———, *Business Leadership in the Large Corporation*, 2nd ed. with a new preface, Berkeley 1961.

14. R. L. Hall and C. J. Hitch, "Price Theory and Business Behaviour," *Oxford Econ. Papers*, May 1939, *2*, 12-45. Reprinted in T. Wilson, ed., *Oxford Studies in the Price Mechanism*, Oxford 1951, pp. 107-38.

15. S. R. Krupp, "Theoretical Explanation and the Nature of the Firm," *Western Econ. Jour.*, Summer 1963, *1*, 191-204.

16. R. A. Lester, "Shortcomings of Marginal Analysis for Wage-Employment Problems," *Am. Econ. Rev.*, March 1946, *36*, 63-82.

17. ———, "Marginalism, Minimum Wages, and Labor Markets," *Am. Econ. Rev.*, March 1947, *37*, 135-48.

18. A. O. Lovejoy, "The Thirteen Pragmatisms," *Jour. Philosophy*, Jan. 2, 1908, *8* 5-12, 29-39. Reprinted in *The Thirteen Pragmatisms and Other Essays*, Baltimore 1963.

19. A. O. Lovejoy and G. Boas, *Primitivism and Related Ideas in Antiquity*. Baltimore 1935.

20. F. Machlup, "Evaluation of the Practical Significance of the Theory of Monopolistic Competition," *Am. Econ. Rev.*, June 1939, *29*, 277-36.

21. ———, "Marginal Analysis and Empirical Research," *Am. Econ. Rev.*, Sept. 1946, *36*, 519-54.

22. ———, "Rejoinder to an Antimarginalist," *Am. Econ. Rev.*, March 1947, *37*, 148-54.

23. ———, *The Economics of Sellers' Competition*. Baltimore 1952.

24. ———, "The Problem of Verification in Economics," *So. Econ. Jour.*, July 1955, *22*, 1-21.

25. ———, "Idealtypus, Wirklichkeit, und Konstruktion," *Ordo*, 1960-1961, 21-57.

26. ———, *Essays on Economic Semantics*. Englewood Cliffs, N.J. 1963.

27. R. J. Monsen and A. Downs, "A Theory of Large Managerial Firms," *Jour. Pol. Econ.*, June 1965, *73*, 221-36.

28. A. G. Papandreou, "Some Basic Problems in the Theory of the Firm," in B. F. Haley, ed., *A Survey of Contemporary Economics*, Vol. II, Homewood, Ill. 1952, pp. 183-219.

29. V. Pareto, *Manuel d'economie politique*, 2nd ed. Paris 1927.

30. K. R. Popper, *Conjectures and refutations*. New York and London 1962.

31. M. Reder, "A Reconsideration of the Marginal Productivity Theory," *Jour. Pol. Econ.*, Oct. 1947, *55*, 450-58.

32. J. Robinson, *The Economics of Imperfect Competition.* London 1933.

33. J. A. Schumpeter, "The Instability of Capitalism," *Econ. Jour.*, Sept. 1928, *38*, 361-86.

34. ———, *The Theory of Economic Development.* Cambridge, Mass. 1934.

35. T. Schutz, *Collected Papers*, Vol. II. The Hague 1964.

36. T. Scitovsky, "A Note on Profit Maximisation and its Implications," *Rev. Econ. Stud.*, Winter 1953, *11*, 57-60. Reprinted in AEA, *Readings in Price Theory*. Homewood, Ill. 1952, pp. 352-58.

37. ———, *Welfare and Competition.* Chicago 1951.

38. H. A. Simon, "A Behavioral Model of Rational Choice," *Quart. Jour. Econ.*, Feb. 1955, *69*, 99-118.

39. ———, *Administrative Behavior*, 2nd ed. New York 1957.

40. ———, "Theories of Decision-Making in Economics and Behavioral Science," *Am. Econ. Rev.*, June 1959, *49*, 253-83.

41. H. von Stackelberg, *Marktform und Gleichgewicht*, Vienna 1934.

42. L. J. Stadler, "The Gene," *Science*, Nov. 19, 1954, *120*, 811-19.

43. G. J. Stigler, "The Economics of Minimum Wage Legislation," *Am. Econ. Rev.* June 1946, *36*, 358-65.

44. ———, "Professor Lester and the Marginalists," *Am. Econ. Rev.*, March 1947, *37*, 154-57.

45. H. B. Thorelli, "The Political Economy of the Firm: Basis for a New Theory of Competition?" *Schweiz Zeitschr. Volkswirtschaft und Stat.*, 1965, *101*, 248-62.

46. T. Veblen, *The Instinct of Workmanship and the State of the Industrial Arts.* New York 1914.

47. M. Weber, *On the Methodology of the Social Sciences*, transl. and ed. by E. A. Shils and H. A. Finch, Glencoe, Ill. 1949.

48. O. E. Williamson, *Economics of Discretionary Behavior: Managerial Objectives in a Theory of the Firm.* Englewood Cliffs, N.J. 1964.

2

THEORIES OF DECISION-MAKING IN ECONOMICS

AND BEHAVIORAL SCIENCE*

HERBERT A. SIMON

Recent years have seen important new explorations along the boundaries between economics and psychology. For the economist, the immediate question about these developments is whether they include new advances in psychology that can fruitfully be applied to economics. But the psychologist will also raise the converse question—whether there are developments in economic theory and observation that have implications for the central core of psychology. If economics is able to find verifiable and verified generalizations about human economic behavior, then these generalizations must have a place in the more general theories of human behavior to which psychology and sociology aspire. Influence will run both ways.[1]

I. HOW MUCH PSYCHOLOGY DOES ECONOMICS NEED?

How have psychology and economics gotten along with little relation in the past? The explanation rests on an understanding of the goals toward which economics, viewed as a science and a discipline, has usually aimed.

Broadly speaking, economics can be defined as the science that describes and predicts the behavior of several kinds of economic man—notably the consumer and the entrepreneur. While perhaps literally correct, this definition does not reflect the principal focus in the literature of economics. We usually classify work in economics along two dimensions: (a) whether it is concerned with industries and the whole economy (macroeconomics) or with individual economic actors (microeconomics); and (b) whether it strives to describe and explain economic behavior (descriptive economics), or to guide decisions either at the level of public policy (normative macroeconomics) or at the level of the individual consumer or businessman (normative microeconomics).

The profession and literature of economics have been largely preoccupied with normative macroeconomics. Although descriptive macroeconomics provides the scientific base for policy prescription, research emphases have been determined

*American Economic Review, June 1959, pp. 253-283.

[1] The influence of economics upon recent work in the psychology of higher mental processes is well illustrated by Bruner, Goodrow and Austin [14, Ch. 3 and 4]. In this work, game theory is used to throw light on the processes of concept formation.

in large part by relevance to policy (e.g., business cycle theory). Normative micro-economics, carried forward under such labels as "management science," "engineering economics," and "operations research," is now a flourishing area of work having an uneasy and ill-defined relation with the profession of economics, traditionally defined. Much of the work is being done by mathematicians, statisticians, engineers, and physical scientists (although many mathematical economists have also been active in it).[2]

This new area, like the old, is normative in orientation. Economists have been relatively uninterested in descriptive microeconomics—understanding the behavior of individual economic agents—except as this is necessary to provide a foundation for macroeconomics. The normative microeconomist "obviously" doesn't need a theory of human behavior: he wants to know how people *ought* to behave, not how they *do* behave. On the other hand, the macroeconomist's lack of concern with individual behavior stems from different considerations. First, he assumes that the economic actor is rational, and hence he makes strong predictions about human behavior without performing the hard work of observing people. Second, he often assumes competition, which carries with it the implication that only the rational survive. Thus, the classical economic theory of markets with perfect competition and rational agents is deductive theory that requires almost no contact with empirical data once its assumptions are accepted.[3]

Undoubtedly there is an area of human behavior that fits these assumptions to a reasonable approximation, where the classical theory with its assumptions of rationality is a powerful and useful tool. Without denying the existence of this area, or its importance, I may observe that it fails to include some of the central problems of conflict and dynamics with which economics has become more and more concerned. A metaphor will help to show the reason for this failure.

Suppose we were pouring some viscous liquid—molasses—into a bowl of very irregular shape. What would we need in order to make a theory of the form the molasses would take in the bowl? How much would we have to know about the properties of molasses to predict its behavior under the circumstances? If the bowl were held motionless, and if we wanted only to predict behavior in equilibrium, we would have to know little, indeed, about molasses. The single essential assumption would be that the molasses, under the force of gravity, would minimize the height of its center of gravity. With this assumption, which would apply as well to any other liquid, and a complete knowledge of the environment—in this case the shape of the bowl—the equilibrium is completely determined. Just so, the equilibrium behavior of a perfectly adapting organism depends only on its goal and its environment; it is otherwise completely independent of the internal properties of the organism.

If the bowl into which we were pouring the molasses were jiggled rapidly, or if we wanted to know about the behavior before equilibrium was reached, prediction would require much more information. It would require, in particular, more information about the properties of molasses: its viscosity, the rapidity with which it "adapted" itself to the containing vessel and moved towards its "goal" of lowering its center of gravity. Likewise, to predict the short-run behavior of an

---

[2] The models of rational decision-making employed in operations research are surveyed in Churchman, Ackoff, and Arnoff [16]; Bowman and Fetter [11]; and Vazsonyi [69].

[3] As an example of what passes for empirical "evidence" in this literature, I cite pp. 22-23 of *Friedman's Essays in Positive Economics* [27], which will amaze anyone brought up in the empirical tradition of psychology and sociology, although it has apparently excited little adverse comment among economists.

adaptive organism, or its behavior in a complex and rapidly changing environment, it is not enough to know its goals. We must know also a great deal about its internal structure and particularly its mechanisms of adaptation.

If, to carry the metaphor a step farther, new forces, in addition to gravitational force, were brought to bear on the liquid, we would have to know still more about it even to predict behavior in equilibrium. Now its tendency to lower its center of gravity might be countered by a force to minimize an electrical or magnetic potential operating in some lateral direction. We would have to know its relative susceptibility to gravitational and electrical or magnetic force to determine its equilibrium position. Similarly, in an organism having a multiplicity of goals, or afflicted with some kind of internal goal conflict, behavior could be predicted only from information about the relative strengths of the several goals and the ways in which the adaptive processes responded to them.

Economics has been moving steadily into new areas where the power of the classical equilibrium model has never been demonstrated, and where its adequacy must be considered anew. Labor economics is such an area, oligopoly or imperfect competition theory another, decision-making under uncertainty a third, and the theory of economic development a fourth. In all of these areas the complexity and instability of his environment becomes a central feature of the choices that economic man faces. To explain his behavior in the face of this complexity, the theory must describe him as something more than a featureless, adaptive organism; it must incorporate at least some description of the processes and mechanisms through which the adaptation takes place. Let us list a little more concretely some specific problems of this kind:

(a) The classical theory postulates that the consumer maximizes utility. Recent advances in the theory of rational consumer choice have shown that the existence of a utility function, and its characteristics, if it exists, can be studied empirically.

(b) The growing separation between ownership and management has directed attention to the motivations of managers and the adequacy of the profit-maximization assumption for business firms. So-called human relations research has raised a variety of issues about the motivation of both executives and employees.

(c) When, in extending the classical theory, the assumptions of perfect competition were removed, even the definition of rationality became ambiguous. New definitions had to be constructed, by no means as "obvious" intuitively as simple maximization, to extend the theory of rational behavior to bilateral monopoly and to other bargaining and outguessing situations.

(d) When the assumptions of perfect foresight were removed, to handle uncertainty about the environment, the definition of rationality had to be extended to another direction to take into account prediction and the formation of expectations.

(e) Broadening the definition of rationality to encompass goal conflict and uncertainty made it hard to ignore the distinction between the objective environment in which the economic actor "really" lives and the subjective environment that he perceives and to which he responds. When this distinction is made, we can no longer predict his behavior—even if he behaves rationally—from the characteristics of the objective environment; we also need to know something about his perceptual and cognitive processes.

We shall use these five problem areas as a basis for sorting out some recent explorations in theory, model building, and empirical testing. In Section II, we will examine developments in the theory of utility and consumer choice. In Section III, we will consider somewhat parallel issues relating to the motivation of managers. In Section IV, we will deal with conflict goals and phenomena of bargaining. In Section V, we will survey some of the work that has been done on uncertainty and the formation of expectations. In Section VI, we will explore recent developments in the theory of human problem-solving and other higher mental processes, and see what implications these have for economic decision-making.

II. THE UTILITY FUNCTION

The story of the re-establishment of cardinal utility, as a consequence of the introduction of uncertainty into the theory of choice, is well known.[4] When Pareto and Slatsky had shown that the theory of consumer demand could be derived from the properties of indifference curves, without postulating a cardinal utility function underlying these curves, it became fashionable to regard utility as an ordinal measure—a ranking of alternatives by preference. Indeed, it could be shown that only ordinal utility had operational status—that the experiments that had been proposed, and even tried in a couple of instances, to measure an individual's utilities by asking him to choose among alternatives could never distinguish between two cardinal utility functions that were ordinally equivalent—that differed only by stretchings and contractions of the unit of measurement.

It was shown by von Neumann and Morgenstern, as a byproduct of their development of the theory of games, that if the choice situation were extended to include choices among uncertain prospects—among lottery tickets, say—cardinal utilities could be assigned to the outcomes in an unequivocal way.[5] Under these conditions, if the subject's behavior was consistent, it was possible to measure cardinally the utilities that different outcomes had for him.

A person who behaved in a manner consistent with the axioms of choice of von Neumann and Morgenstern would act so as to maximize the expected value—the average, weighted by the probabilities of the alternative outcomes of a choice—of his utility. The theory could be tested empirically, however, only on the assumption that the probabilities assigned to the alternatives by the subject were identical with the "objective" probabilities of these events as known to the experimenter. For example, if a subject believed in the gamblers' fallacy, that after a run of heads an unbiased coin would be more likely to fall tails, his choices might appear inconsistent with his utility function, while the real difficulty would lie in his method of assigning probabilities. This difficulty of "subjective" versus "objective" probability soon came to light when attempts were made to test experimentally whether people behaved in accordance with the predictions of the new utility theory. At the same time, it was discovered that the problem had been raised and solved thirty years earlier by the English philosopher and mathematician Frank Ramsey.[6] Ramsey had shown that, by an appropriate series of experiments,

[4]Ward Edwards [23] provides an account of these developments from the psychologist's point of view; Chapter 2 of Luce and Raiffa [43] is an excellent introduction to the "new" utility theory. Arrow [5] contains a nonmathematical survey of this and related topics.

[5]The second edition of von Neumann and Morgenstern [50] contains the first rigorous axiomatic demonstration of this point.

[6]Ramsey's important essay [57] was sufficiently obscure that it was overlooked until the ideas were rediscovered independently by de Finetti [26]. Valuable notes on the history of the topic together with a thorough formal treatment will be found in the first five chapters of Savage [58].

the utilities and subjective probabilities assigned by a subject to a set of uncertain alternatives could be measured simultaneously.

EMPIRICAL STUDIES

The new axiomatic foundations of the theory of utility, which show that it is possible at least in principle to determine empirically whether people "have" utility functions of the appropriate kind, have led to a rash of choice experiments. An experimenter who wants to measure utilities, not merely in principle but in fact, faces innumerable difficulties. Because of these difficulties, most experiments have been limited to confronting the subjects with alternative lottery tickets, at various odds, for small amounts of money. The weight of evidence is that, under these conditions, most persons choose in a way that is reasonably consistent with the axioms of the theory—they behave as though they were maximizing the expected value of utility and as though the utilities of the several alternatives can be measured.[7]

When these experiments are extended to more "realistic" choices—choices that are more obviously relevant to real-life situations—difficulties multiply. In the few extensions that have been made, it is not at all clear that the subjects behave in accordance with the utility axioms. There is some indication that when the situation is very simple and transparent, so that the subject can easily see and remember when he is being consistent, he behaves like a utility maximizer. But as the choices become a little more complicated—choices, for example, among phonograph records instead of sums of money—he becomes much less consistent [21, Ch. 3] [47].[8]

We can interpret these results in either of two ways. We can say that consumers "want" to maximize utility, and that if we present them with clear and simple choices that they understand they will do so. Or we can say that the real world is so complicated that the theory of utility maximization has little relevance to real choices. The former interpretation has generally appeared more attractive to economists trained in classical utility theory and to management scientists seeking rules of behavior for normative microeconomics; the latter to behavioral scientists interested in the description of behavior.

NORMATIVE APPLICATIONS

The new utility theory has provided the formal framework for much recent work in mathematical statistics—i.e., statistical decision theory.[9] Similarly (it would

---

[7]Some of the empirical evidence is reviewed in [23]. A series of more recent empirical studies is reported in Davidson and Suppes [21].

[8]Some more recent experiments [57a] show a relatively high degree of transitivity. A. G. Papandreou, in a publication I have not yet seen (University of California Publications in Economics) also reports a high degree of transitivity.

[9]The systematic development of statistics as decision theory is due largely to A. Wald [70] on the basis of the earlier work of J. Neyman and E. Pearson. Savage [58] carries the development further, erecting the foundations of statistics solidly on utility and probability theory.

be accurate to say "synonymously"), this framework provides the basis for most of the normative models of management science and operations research designed for actual application to the decision-making problems of the firm.[10] Except for some very recent developments, linear programming has been limited to decision-making under certainty, but there have been far-reaching developments of dynamic programming dealing with the maximization of expected values of outcomes (usually monetary outcomes) in situations where future events can be predicted only in terms of probability distributions.[11]

Again, there are at least two distinct interpretations that can be placed on these developments. On the one hand, it can be argued: "Firms would like to maximize profits if they could. They have been limited in doing so by the conceptual and computational difficulties of finding the optimal courses of action. By providing powerful new mathematical tools and computing machines, we now enable them to behave in the manner predicted by Alfred Marshall, even if they haven't been able to in the past." Nature will imitate art and economic man will become as real (and as artificial) as radios and atomic piles.

The alternative interpretation rests on the observation that, even with the powerful new tools and machines, most real-life choices still lie beyond the reach of maximizing techniques—unless the situations are heroically simplified by drastic approximations. If man, according to this interpretation, makes decisions and choices that have some appearance of rationality, rationality in real life must involve something simpler than maximization of utility or profit. In Section VI, we will see where this alternative interpretation leads.

The Binary Choice Experiment

Much recent discussion about utility has centered around a particularly simple choice experiment. This experiment, in numerous variants, has been used by both economists and psychologists to test the most diverse kinds of hypotheses. We will describe it so that we can use it as a common standard of comparison for a whole range of theories and empirical studies.[12]

We will call the situation we are about to describe the *binary choice* experiment. It is better known to most game theorists—particularly those located not far from Nevada—as a two-armed bandit; and to most psychologists as a partial reinforcement experiment. The subject is required, in each of a series of trials, to choose one or the other of two symbols—say, plus or minus. When he has chosen, he is told whether his choice was "right" or "wrong," and he may also receive a reward (in psychologist's language, a reinforcement) for "right" choices. The experimenter can arrange the schedule of correct responses in a variety of ways.

---

[10]This work relates, of course, to profit maximization and cost minimization rather than utility maximization, but it is convenient to mention it at this point. See [11] [16] [69].

[11]Arrow, Harris and Marschak [3] were among the first to treat inventory decisions dynamically. A general treatment of the theory of dynamic programming will be found in Bellman [9].

[12]My understanding of the implications of the binary choice experiment owes much to conversations with Julian Feldman, and to his unpublished work on the experiment. See also, Bush and Mosteller [15] particularly Chapter 13.

There may be a definite pattern, or they may be randomized. It is not essential that one and only one response be correct on a given trial: the experimenter may determine that both or neither will be correct. In the latter case the subject may or may not be informed whether the response he did not choose would have been correct.

How would a utility-maximizing subject behave in the binary choice experiment? Suppose that the experimenter rewarded "plus" on one-third of the trials, determined at random, and "minus" on the remaining two-thirds. Then a subject, provided that he believed the sequence was random and observed that minus was rewarded twice as often as plus, should always, rationally, choose minus. He would find the correct answer two-thirds of the time, and more often than with any other strategy.

Unfortunately for the classical theory of utility in its simplest form, few subjects behave in this way. The most commonly observed behavior is what is called *event matching.*[13] The subject chooses the two alternatives (not necessarily at random) with relative frequencies roughly proportional to the relative frequencies with which they are rewarded. Thus, in the example given, two-thirds of the time he would choose minus, and as a result would make a correct response, on the average, in 5 trials out of 9 (on two-thirds of the trials in which he chooses minus, and one-third of those in which he chooses plus).[14]

All sorts of explanations have been offered for the event-matching behavior. The simplest is that the subject just doesn't understand what strategy would maximize his expected utility; but with adult subjects in a situation as transparent as this one, the explanation seems far-fetched. The alternative explanations imply either that the subject regards himself as being engaged in a competitive game with the experimenter (or with "nature" if he accepts the experimenter's explanation that the stimulus is random), or that his responses are the outcome of certain kinds of learning processes. We will examine these two types of explanation further in Sections IV and V respectively. The important conclusion at this point is that even in an extremely simple situation, subjects do not behave in the way predicted by a straightforward application of utility theory.

Probabilistic Preferences

Before we leave the subject of utility, we should mention one recent important development. In the formalizations mentioned up to this point, probabilities enter only into the estimation of the consequences that will follow one alternative or another. Given any two alternatives, the first is definitely preferable to the second (in terms of expected utility), or the second to the first, or they are strictly indifferent. If the same pair of alternatives is presented to the subject more than once, he should always prefer the same member of the pair.

One might think this requirement too strict—that, particularly if the utility attached to one alternative were only slightly greater or less than that attached to

[13]An example of data consistent with event-matching behavior is given on page 283 of [15].

[14]Subjects tend to choose the more highly rewarded alternative slightly more frequently than is called for by event matching. Hence, the actual behavior tends to be some kind of average between event matching and the optimal behavior. See [15, Ch. 13].

the other, the subject might vacillate in his choice. An empirical precedent for such vacillation comes not only from casual observation of indecision but from analogous phenomena in the psycho-physical laboratory. When subjects are asked to decide which of two weights is heavier, the objectively heavier one is chosen more often than the lighter one, but the relative frequency of choosing the heavier approaches one-half as the two weights approach equality. The probability that a subject will choose the objectively heavier weight depends, in general, on the ratio of the two weights.

Following several earlier attempts, a rigorous and complete axiom system for a utility theory incorporating probabilistic preferences has been constructed recently by Duncan Luce [cf. 43, App. 1]. Although the theory weakens the requirements of consistency in preference, it is empirically testable, at least in principle. Conceptually, it provides a more plausible interpretation of the notion of "indifference" than does the classical theory.

III. THE GOALS OF FIRMS

Just as the central assumption in the theory of consumption is that the consumer strives to maximize his utility, so the crucial assumption in the theory of the firm is that the entrepreneur strives to maximize his residual share—his profit. Attacks on this hypothesis have been frequent.[15] We may classify the most important of these as follows:

(a) The theory leaves ambiguous whether it is short-run or long-run profit that is to be maximized.

(b) The entrepreneur may obtain all kinds of "psychic income" from the firm, quite apart from monetary rewards. If he is to maximize his utility, then he will sometimes balance a loss of profits against an increase in psychic income. But if we allow "psychic income," the criterion of profit maximization loses all of its definiteness.

(c) The entrepreneur may not care to maximize, but may simply want to earn a return that he regards as satisfactory. By sophistry and an adept use of the concept of psychic income, the notion of seeking a satisfactory return can be translated into utility maximizing but not in any operational way. We shall see in a moment that "satisfactory profits" is a concept more meaningfully related to the psychological notion of aspiration levels than to maximization.

(d) It is often observed that under modern conditions the equity owners and the active managers of an enterprise are separate and distinct groups of people, so that the latter may not be motivated to maximize profits.

(e) Where there is imperfect competition among firms, maximizing is an ambiguous goal, for what action is optimal for one firm depends on the actions of the other firms.

In the present section we shall deal only with the third of these five issues. The fifth will be treated in the following section; the first, second, and fourth are

---

[15]For a survey of recent discussions see Papandreou [55].

purely empirical questions that have been discussed at length in the literature; they will be considered here only for their bearing on the question of satisfactory profits.

Satisficing versus Maximizing

The notion of satiation plays no role in classical economic theory, while it enters rather prominently into the treatment of motivation in psychology. In most psychological theories the motive to act stems from *drives,* and action terminates when the drive is satisfied. Moreover, the conditions for satisfying a drive are not necessarily fixed, but may be specified by an aspiration level that itself adjusts upward or downward on the basis of experience.

If we seek to explain business behavior in the terms of this theory, we must expect the firm's goals to be not maximizing profit, but attaining a certain level or rate of profit, holding a certain share of the market or a certain level of sales. Firms would try to "satisfice" rather than to maximize.[16]

It has sometimes been argued that the distinction between satisficing and maximizing is not important to economic theory. For in the first place, the psychological evidence on individual behavior shows that aspirations tend to adjust to the unattainable. Hence in the long run, the argument runs, the level of aspiration and the attainable maximum will be very close together. Second, even if some firms satisficed, they would gradually lose out to the maximizing firms, which would make larger profits and grow more rapidly than the others.

These are, of course, precisely the arguments of our molasses metaphor, and we may answer them in the same way that we answered them earlier. The economic environment of the firm is complex, and it changes rapidly; there is no a priori reason to assume the attainment of long-run equilibrium. Indeed, the empirical evidence on the distribution of firms by size suggests that the observed regularities in size distribution stem from the statistical equilibrium of a population of adaptive systems rather than the static equilibrium of a population of maximizers.[17]

Models of satisficing behavior are richer than models of maximizing behavior, because they treat not only of equilibrium but of the method of reaching it as well. Psychological studies of the formation and change of aspiration levels support propositions of the following kinds.[18] (a) When performance falls short of the level of aspiration, search behavior (particularly search for new alternatives of action) is induced. (b) At the same time, the level of aspiration begins to adjust itself downward until goals reach levels that are practically attainable. (c) If the two mechanisms just listed operate too slowly to adapt aspirations to performance, emotional behavior—apathy or aggression, for example—will replace rational adaptive behavior.

The aspiration level defines a natural zero point in the scale of utility— whereas in most classical theories the zero point is arbitrary. When the firm has

---

[16]A comparison of satisficing with maximizing models of decision-making can be found in [64, Ch. 14]. Katona [40] has independently made similar comparisons of economic and psychological theories of decision.

[17]Simon and Bonini [66] have constructed a stochastic model that explains the observed data on the size distributions of business firms.

[18]A standard psychological reference on aspiration levels is [42]. For applications to economics, see [61] and [45] (in the latter, consult the index under "aspiration levels").

alternatives open to it that are at or above its aspiration level, the theory predicts that it will choose the best of those known to be available. When none of the available alternatives satisfies current aspirations, the theory predicts qualitatively different behavior: in the short run, search behavior and the revision of targets; in the longer run, what we have called above emotional behavior, and what the psychologist would be inclined to call neurosis.[19]

Studies of Business Behavior

There is some empirical evidence that business goals are, in fact, stated in satisficing terms.[20] First, there is the series of studies stemming from the pioneering work of Hall and Hitch that indicates that businessmen often set prices by applying a standard markup to costs. Some economists have sought to refute this fact, others to reconcile it—if it is a fact—with marginalist principles. The study of Earley [22a, pp. 44-70] belongs to the former category, but its evidence is suspect because the questions asked of businessmen are leading ones—no one likes to admit that he would accept less profit if he could have more. Earley did not ask his respondents how they determined marginal cost and marginal revenue, how, for example, they estimated demand elasticities.

Another series of studies derived from the debate over the Keynesian doctrine that the amount of investment was insensitive to changes in the rate of interest. The general finding in these studies has been that the rate of interest is not an important factor in investment decisions [24] [39, Ch. 11] [71].

More recently, my colleagues Cyert and March, have attempted to test the satisficing model in a more direct way [19]. They found in one industry some evidence that firms with a declining share of market strove more vigorously to increase their sales than firms whose shares of the market were steady or increasing.

Aspirations in the Binary Choice Experiment

Although to my knowledge this has not been done, it would be easy to look for aspiration-level phenomena in the binary choice experiment. By changing the probabilities of reward in different ways for different groups of subjects, we could measure the effects of these changes on search behavior—where amount of search would be measured by changes in the pattern of responses.

Economic Implications

It has sometimes been argued that, however realistic the classical theory of the firm as a profit maximizer, it is an adequate theory for purposes of normative macroeconomics. Mason, for example, in commenting on Papandreou's essay on "Problems in the Theory of the Firm" [55, pp. 183-222] says, "The writer of this critique must confess a lack of confidence in the marked superiority *for purposes*

---

[19]Lest this last term appear fanciful I should like to call attention to the phenomena of panic and broken morale, which are well known to observers of the stock market and of organizations but which have no reasonable interpretation in classical utility theory. I may also mention that psychologists know the theory described here in a straightforward way to produce experimental neurosis in animal and human subjects.

[20]A comprehensive bibliography of empirical work prior to 1950 will be found in [37]. Some of the more recent work is [19] [24] [39, Ch. 11].

of economic analysis, of this newer concept of the firm over the older conception of the entrepreneur." The italics are Mason's.

The theory of the firm is important for welfare economics—e.g., for determining under what circumstances the behavior of the firm will lead to efficient allocation of resources. The satisficing model vitiates all the conclusions about resource allocation that are derivable from the maximizing model when perfect competition is assumed. Similarly, a dynamic theory of firm sizes, like that mentioned above, has quite different implications for public policies dealing with concentration than a theory that assumes firms to be in static equilibrium. Hence, welfare economists are justified in adhering to the classical theory only if: (a) the theory is empirically correct as a description of the decision-making process; or (b) it is safe to assume that the system operates in the neighborhood of the static equilibrium. What evidence we have mostly contradicts both assumptions.

IV. CONFLICT OF INTEREST

Leaving aside the problem of the motivations of hired managers, conflict of interest among economic actors creates no difficulty for classical economic theory—indeed, it lies at the very core of the theory—so long as each actor treats the other actors as parts of his "given" environment, and doesn't try to predict their behavior and anticipate it. But when this restriction is removed, when it is assumed that a seller takes into account the reactions of buyers to his actions, or that each manufacturer predicts the behaviors of his competitors—all the familiar difficulties of imperfect competition and oligopoly arise.[21]

The very assumptions of omniscient rationality that provide the basis for deductive prediction in economics when competition is present lead to ambiguity when they are applied to competition among the few. The central difficulty is that rationality requires one to outguess one's opponents, but not to be outguessed by them, and this is clearly not a consistent requirement if applied to all the actors.

Game Theory

Modern game theory is a vigorous and extensive exploration of ways of extending the concept of rational behavior to situations involving struggle, outguessing, and bargaining. Since Luce and Raiffa [43] have recently provided us with an excellent survey and evaluation of game theory, I shall not cover the same ground here.[22] I concur in their general evaluation that, while game theory has greatly clarified the issues involved, it has not provided satisfactory solutions. Not only does it leave the definition of rational conduct ambiguous in all cases save the zero-sum two-person game, but it requires of economic man even more fantastic reasoning powers than does classical economic theory.[23]

[21]There is by now a voluminous literature on the problem. The difficulties in defining rationality in competitive situations are well stated in the first chapter of von Neumann and Morgenstern [50].

[22]Chapters 5 and 6 of [43] provide an excellent survey of the attempts that have been made to extend the theory of games to the kinds of situations most relevant to economics.

[23]In his volume on "Strategy and Market Structure: Competition, Oligoloply, and the Theory of Games," Martin Shubik [72] approaches the topics of imperfect competition and oligopoly from the standpoint of the theory of games.

Power and Bargaining

A number of exploratory proposals have been put forth as alternatives to game theory—among them Galbraith's notion of countervailing power [30] and Schelling's bargaining theory [59] [60]. These analyses draw at least as heavily upon theories of power and bargaining developed initially to explain political phenomena as upon economic theory. They do not lead to any more specific predictions of behavior than do game-theoretic approaches, but place a greater emphasis upon description and actual observation, and are modest in their attempt to derive predictions by deductive reasoning from a few "plausible" premises about human behavior.

At least four important areas of social science and social policy, two of them in economics and two more closely related to political science, have as their central concern the phenomena of power and the processes of bargaining; the theory of political parties, labor-management relations, international politics, and oligopoly theory. Any progress in the basic theory applicable to one of these is certain to be of almost equal importance to the others. A growing recognition of their common concern is evidenced by the initiation of a new cross-disciplinary journal, *Journal of Conflict Resolution.*

Games against Nature

While the binary choice experiment is basically a one-person game, it is possible to interpret it as a "game against nature," and hence to try to explain it in game-theoretic terms. According to game theory, the subject, if he believes in a malevolent nature that manipulates the dice against him, should minimax his expected utility instead of maximizing it. That is, he should adopt the course of action that will maximize his expected utility under the assumption that nature will do her worst to him.

Minimaxing expected utility would lead the subject to call plus or minus at random and with equal probability, regardless of what the history of rewards has been. This is something that subjects demonstrably do not do.

However, it has been suggested by Savage [58] and others that people are not as interested in maximizing utility as they are in minimizing regret. "Regret" means the difference between the reward actually obtained and the reward that could have been obtained with perfect foresight (actually, with perfect hindsight!). It turns out that minimaxing regret in the binary choice experiment leads to event-matching behavior [64, Ch. 16]. Hence, the empirical evidence is at least crudely consistent with the hypothesis that people play against nature by minimaxing regret. We shall see, however, that event-matching is also consistent with a number of other rules of behavior that seem more plausible on their face; hence we need not take the present explanation too seriously—at least I am not inclined to do so.

V. THE FORMATION OF EXPECTATIONS

While the future cannot enter into the determination of the present, expectations about the future can and do. In trying to gain an understanding of the saving, spending, and investment behavior of both consumers and firms, and to make short-term predictions of this behavior for purposes of policy-making, economists have done substantial empirical work as well as theorizing on the formation of expectations.

Empirical Studies

A considerable body of data has been accumulated on consumers' plans and expectations from the Survey of Consumer Finances, conducted for the Board of Governors of the Federal Reserve System by the Survey Research Center of the University of Michigan [39, Ch. 5]. These data, and similar data obtained by others, begin to give us some information on the expectations of consumers about their own incomes, and the predictive value of their expenditure plans for their actual subsequent behavior. Some large scale attempts have been made, notably by Modigliani and Brumberg [48, pp. 388-436] and, a little later, by Friedman [28] to relate these empirical findings to classical utility theory. The current empirical research on businessmen's expectations is of two main kinds:

1. Surveys of businessmen's own forecasts of business and business conditions in the economy and in their own industries [24, pp. 165-88] [29, pp. 189-98]. These are obtained by straightforward questionnaire methods that assume, implicitly, that businessmen can and do make such forecasts. In some uses to which the data are put, it is also assumed that the forecasts are used as one basis for businessmen's actions.

2. Studies of business decisions and the role of expectations in these decisions—particularly investment and pricing decisions. We have already referred to studies of business decisions in our discussion of the goals of the firm.[24]

Expectations and Probability

The classical way to incorporate expectations into economic theory is to assume that the decision-maker estimates the joint probability distribution of future events.[25] He can then act so as to maximize the expected value of utility or profit, as the case may be. However satisfying this approach may be conceptually, it poses awkward problems when we ask how the decision-maker actually estimates the parameters of the joint probability distribution. Common sense tells us that people don't make such estimates, nor can we find evidence that they do by examining actual business forecasting methods. The surveys of businessmen's expectations have never attempted to secure such estimates, but have contented themselves with asking for point predictions—which, at best, might be interpreted as predictions of the means of the distributions.

It has been shown that under certain special circumstances the mean of the probability distribution is the only parameter that is relevant for decision—that even if the variance and higher moments were known to the rational decision-maker, he would have no use for them.[26] In these cases, the arithmetic mean is actually a certainty equivalent, the optimal decision turns out to be the same as if the future were known with certainty. But the situations where the mean is a

[24]See the references cited [12, p. 160].

[25]A general survey of approaches to decision-making under uncertainty will be found in [2] and in [43, Ch. 13].

[26]The special case in which mean expectations constitute a certainty equivalent is treated in [62]. An alternative derivation, and fuller discussion is given by Theil [67, Ch. 8, sect. 6].

certainty equivalent are, as we have said, very special ones, and there is no indication that businessmen ever ask whether the necessary conditions for this equivalence are actually met in practice. They somehow make forecasts in the form of point predictions and act upon them in one way or another.

The "somehow" poses questions that are important for business cycle theory, and perhaps for other problems in economics. The way in which expectations are formed may affect the dynamic stability of the economy, and the extent to which cycles will be amplified or damped. Some light, both empirical and theoretical, has recently been cast on these questions. On the empirical side, attempts have been made: (a) to compare businessmen's forecasts with various "naïve" models that assume the future will be some simple function of the recent past, and (b) to use such naïve models themselves as forecasting devices.

The simplest naïve model is one that assumes the next period will be exactly like the present. Another assumes that the change from present to next period will equal the change from last period to present; a third, somewhat more general, assumes that the next period will be a weighted average of recent past periods. The term "naïve model" has been applied loosely to various forecasting formulae of these general kinds. There is some affirmative evidence that business forecasts fit such models. There is also evidence that elaboration of the models beyond the first few steps of refinement does not much improve prediction; see, for example, [20]. Arrow and his colleagues [4] have explored some of the conditions under which forecasting formulae will, and will not, introduce dynamic instability into an economic system that is otherwise stable. They have shown, for example, that if a system of multiple markets is stable under static expectations, it is stable when expectations are based on a moving average of past values.

The work on the formation of expectations represents a significant extension of classical theory. For, instead of taking the environment as a "given," known to the economic decision-maker, it incorporates in the theory the processes of acquiring knowledge about that environment. In doing so, it forces us to include in our model of economic man some of his properties as a learning, estimating, searching, information-processing organism [65].

The Cost of Information

There is one way in which the formation of expectations might be reincorporated in the body of economic theory: by treating information-gathering as one of the processes of production, so to speak, and applying to it the usual rules of marginal analysis. Information, says price theory, should be gathered up to the point where the incremental cost of additional information is equal to the incremental profit that can be earned by having it. Such an approach can lead to propositions about optimal amounts of information-gathering activity and about the relative merits of alternative information-gathering and estimating schemes.[27]

This line of investigation has, in fact, been followed in statistical decision theory. In sampling theory we are concerned with the optimal size of sample (and in the special and ingenious case of sequential sampling theory, with knowing when to stop sampling), and we wish to evaluate the efficiencies of alternative sampling

[27]Fundamental and applied research are examples of economically significant information-gathering activities. Griliches [34] has recently made an attempt to estimate the economic return from research on hybrid corn.

procedures. The latter problem is the simpler, since it is possible to compare the relative costs of alternative schemes that have the same sampling error, and hence to avoid estimating the value of the information.[28] However, some progress has been made also toward estimating the value of improved forecast accuracy in situations where the forecasts are to be used in applying formal decision rules to choice situations.[29]

The theory of teams developed by Marschak and Radner is concerned with the same problem (see, e.g., [46]). It considers situations involving decentralized and interdependent decision-making by two or more persons who share a common goal and who, at a cost, can transmit information to each other about their own actions or about the parts of the environment with which they are in contact. The problem then is to discover the optimal communication strategy under specified assumptions about communication costs and payoffs.

The cost of communication in the theory of teams, like the cost of observations in sampling theory, is a parameter that characterizes the economic actor, or the relation of the actor to his environment. Hence, while these theories retain, in one sense, a classical picture of economic man as a maximizer, they clearly require considerable information about the characteristics of the actor, and not merely about his environment. They take a long stride toward bridging the gap between the traditional concerns of economics and the concerns of psychology.

Expectations in the Binary Choice Experiment

I should like to return again to the binary choice experiment, to see what light it casts on the formation of expectations. If the subject is told by the experimenter that the rewards are assigned at random, if he is told what the odds are for each alternative, *and if he believes the experimenter,* the situation poses no forecasting problem. We have seen, however, that the behavior of most subjects is not consistent with these assumptions.

How would sequential sampling theory handle the problem? Each choice the subject makes now has two consequences: the immediate reward he obtains from it, and the increment of information it provides for predicting the future rewards. If he thinks only of the latter consequences, he is faced with the classical problem of induction: to estimate the probability that an event will occur in the future on the basis of its frequency of occurrence in the past. Almost any rule of induction would require a rational (maximizing) subject to behave in the following general manner: to sample the two alternatives in some proportion to estimate the probability of reward associated with each; after the error of estimate had been reduced below some bound, always to choose the alternative with the higher probability of reward. Unfortunately, this does not appear to be what most subjects do.

If we give up the idea of maximization, we can make the weaker assumption that the subject is adaptive—or learns—but not necessarily in any optimal fashion. What do we mean by adaptation or learning? We mean, gradually and on the basis of experience responding more frequently with the choice that, in the past, has been most frequently rewarded. There is a whole host of rules of behavior possessing this characteristic. Postulate, for example, that at each trial the subject has a

[28]Modern treatments of sampling theory, like Cochran [17] are based on the idea of minimizing the cost of obtaining a fixed amount of information.

[29]For the theory and an application to macroeconomics, see Theil [67, Ch. 8, sects. 5 and 6].

certain probability of responding "plus," and the complementary probability of responding "minus." Postulate further that when he makes a particular response the probability of making the same response on the next trial is increased if the response is rewarded and decreased if the response is not rewarded. The amount of increment in the response probability is a parameter characterizing the learning rate of the particular subject. Almost all schemes of this kind produce asymptotic behaviors, as the number of trials increases, that are approximately event-matching in character.

Stochastic learning models, as the processes just described are usually called, were introduced into psychology in the early 1950's by W. K. Estes and Bush and Mosteller [15] and have been investigated extensively since that time. The models fit some of the gross features of the observed behaviors—most strikingly the asymptotic probabilities—but do not explain very satisfactorily the fine structure of the observations.

Observation of subjects in the binary choice experiment reveals that usually they not only refuse to believe that (or even to act as if) the reward series were random, but in fact persist over many trials in searching for systematic patterns in the series. To account for such behavior, we might again postulate a learning model, but in this case a model in which the subject does not react probabilistically to his environment, but forms and tests definite hypotheses about systematic patterns in it. Man, in this view, is not only a learning animal; he is a pattern-finding and concept-forming animal. Julian Feldman [25] has constructed theories of this kind to explain the behavior of subjects in the binary choice experiment, and while the tests of the theories are not yet completed, his findings look exceedingly promising.

As we move from maximizing theories, through simple stochastic learning theories, to theories involving pattern recognition our model of the expectation-forming processes and the organism that performs it increases in complexity. If we follow this route, we reach a point where a theory of behavior requires a rather elaborate and detailed picture of the rational actor's cognitive processes

VI. HUMAN COGNITION AND ECONOMICS

All the developments we have examined in the preceding four sections have a common theme: they all involve important modifications in the concept of economic man and, for the reasons we have stated, modifications in the direction of providing a fuller description of his characteristics. The classical theory is a theory of a man choosing among fixed and known alternatives, to each of which is attached known consequences. But when perception and cognition intervene between the decision-maker and his objective environment, this model no longer proves adequate. We need a description of the choice process that recognizes that alternatives are not given but must be sought; and a description that takes into account the arduous task of determining what consequences will follow on each alternative [63, Ch. 5] [64, Part 4] [14].

The decision-maker's information about his environment is much less than an approximation to the real environment. The term "approximation" implies that the subjective world of the decision-maker resembles the external environment closely, but lacks, perhaps, some fineness of detail. In actual fact the perceived world is fantastically different from the "real" world. The differences involve both omissions and distortions, and arise in both perception and inference. The sins of

57

omission in perception are more important than the sins of commission. The decision-maker's model of the world encompasses only a minute fraction of all the relevant characteristics of the real environment, and his inferences extract only a minute fraction of all the information that is present even in his model.

Perception is sometimes referred to as a "filter." This term is as misleading as "approximation," and for the same reason: it implies that what comes through into the central nervous system is really quite a bit like what is "out there." In fact, the filtering is not merely a passive selection of some part of a presented whole, but an active process involving attention to a very small part of the whole and exclusion, from the outset, of almost all that is not within the scope of attention.

Every human organism lives in an environment that generates millions of bits of new information each second, but the bottleneck of the perceptual apparatus certainly does not admit more than 1,000 bits per second, and probably much less. Equally significant omissions occur in the processing that takes place when information reaches the brain. As every mathematician knows, it is one thing to have a set of differential equations, and another thing to have their solutions. Yet the solutions are logically implied by the equations—they are "all there," if we only knew how to get to them! By the same token, there are hosts of inferences that *might* be drawn from the information stored in the brain that are not in fact drawn. The consequences implied by information in the memory become known only through active information-processing, and hence through active selection of particular problem-solving paths from the myriad that might have been followed.

In this section we shall examine some theories of decision-making that take the limitations of the decision-maker and the complexity of the environment as central concerns. These theories incorporate some mechanisms we have already discussed—for example, aspiration levels and forecasting processes—but go beyond them in providing a detailed picture of the choice process.

A real-life decision involves some goals or values, some facts about the environment, and some inferences drawn from the values and facts. The goals and values may be simple or complex, consistent or contradictory; the facts may be real or supposed, based on observation or the reports of others; the inferences may be valid or spurious. The whole process may be viewed, metaphorically, as a process of "reasoning," where the values and facts serve as premises, and the decision that is finally reached is inferred from these premises [63]. The resemblance of decision-making to logical reasoning is only metaphorical, because there are quite different rules in the two cases to determine what constitute "valid" premises and admissible modes of inference. The metaphor is useful because it leads us to take the individual *decision premise* as the unit of description, hence to deal with the whole interwoven fabric of influences that bear on a single decision—but without being bound by the assumptions of rationality that limit the classical theory of choice.

Rational Behavior and Role Theory

We can find common ground to relate the economist's theory of decision-making with that of the social psychologist. The latter is particularly interested, of course, in social influences on choice, which determine the *role* of the actor. In our present terms, a role is a social prescription of some, but not all, of the premises that enter into an individual's choices of behavior. Any particular concrete behavior is the resultant of a large number of premises, only some of which are prescribed by the role. In addition to role premises there will be premises about the state of the environment based directly on perception, premises representing beliefs and knowledge, and idiosyncratic premises that characterize the personality. Within this framework we can accommodate both the rational elements in choice, so much emphasized by economics, and the nonrational elements to which psychologists and sociologists often prefer to call attention.

Decision Premises and Computer Programs

The analysis of choice in terms of decision premises gives us a conceptual framework for describing and explaining the process of deciding. But so complex is the process that our explanations of it would have remained schematic and hypothetical for a long time to come had not the modern digital computer appeared on the scene. The notion of decision premise can be translated into computer terminology, and when this translation has been accomplished, the digital computer provides us with an instrument for simulating human decision processes—even very complex ones—and hence for testing empirically our explanations of those processes [53].

A fanciful (but only slightly fanciful) example will illustrate how this might be done. Some actual examples will be cited presently. Suppose we were to construct a robot incorporating a modern digital computer, and to program (i.e., to instruct) the robot to take the role of a business executive in a specified company. What would the program look like? Since no one has yet done this, we cannot say with certainty, but several points are fairly clear. The program would not consist of a list of prescribed and proscribed behaviors, since what an executive does is highly contingent on information about a wide variety of circumstances. Instead, the program would consist of a large number of *criteria* to be applied to possible and proposed courses of action, of routines for generating possible courses of action, of computational procedures for *assessing* the state of the environment and its implications for action, and the like. Hence, the program—in fact, a role prescription—would interact with information to produce concrete behavior adapted to the situation. The elements of such a program take the form of what we have called decision premises, and what the computer specialists would call instructions.

The promise of constructing actual detailed descriptions of concrete roles and decision processes is no longer, with the computer, a mere prospectus to be realized at some undefined future date. We can already provide actual examples, some of them in the area of economics.

1. Management Science. In the paragraphs on normative applications in Section II, we have already referred to the use of such mathematical techniques as linear programming and dynamic programming to construct formal decision processes for actual situations. The relevance of these decision models to the present discussion is that they are not merely abstract "theories" of the firm, but actual decision-making devices. We can think of any such device as a simulation of the corresponding human decision-maker, in which the equations and other assumptions that enter into the formal decision-making procedure correspond to the decision premises—including the role prescription—of the decision-maker.

The actual application of such models to concrete business situations brings to light the information-processing tasks that are concealed in the assumptions of the more abstract classical models [65, pp. 51-52]:

(1) The models must be formulated so as to require for their application only data that are obtainable. If one of the penalties, for example, of holding too small

inventories is the loss of sales, a decision model that proposes to determine optimal inventory levels must incorporate a procedure for putting a dollar value on this loss.

(2) The models must call only for practicable computations. For example, several proposals for applying linear programming to certain factory scheduling problems have been shown to be impracticable because, even with computers, the computation time is too great. The task of decision theory (whether normative or descriptive) is to find alternative techniques—probably only approximate—that demand much less computation.

(3) The models must not demand unobtainable forecast information. A procedure that would require a sales department to estimate the third moment of next month's distribution would not have wide application, as either description or prescription, to business decision-making.

These models, then, provide us with concrete examples of roles for a decision-maker described in terms of the premises he is expected to apply to the decision—the data and the rules of computation.

2. Engineering Design. Computers have been used for some years to carry out some of the analytic computations required in engineering design—computing the stresses, for example, in a proposed bridge design. Within the past two years, ways have been found to program computers to carry out synthesis as well as analysis—to evolve the design itself.[30] A number of companies in the electrical industry now use computers to design electric motors, transformers, and generators, going from customer specifications to factory design without human intervention. The significance of this for our purpose here is that the synthesis programs appear to simulate rather closely the processes that had previously been used by college-trained engineers in the same design work. It has proved possible to write down the engineers' decision premises and inference processes in sufficient detail to produce workable computer programs.

3. Human Problem Solving. The management science and engineering design programs already provide examples of simulation of human decision-making by computer. It may be thought that, since in both instances the processes are highly arithmetical, these examples are relevant to only a very narrow range of human problem-solving activity. We generally think of a digital computer as a device which, if instructed in painful detail by its operator, can be induced to perform rather complicated and tedious arithmetical operations. More recent developments require us to revise these conceptions of the computer, for they enable it to carry out tasks that, if performed by humans, we would certainly call "thinking" and "learning."

Discovering the proof of a theorem of Euclid—a task we all remember from our high school geometry course—requires thinking and usually insight and imagination. A computer is now being programmed to perform this task (in a manner closely simulating the human geometer), and another computer has been successfully performing a highly similar task in symbolic logic for the past two years.[31] The latter computer is programmed to learn—that is to improve its performance on the basis of successful problem-solving experience—to use something akin to imagery or metaphor in planning its proofs, and to transfer some of its skills to other tasks—for example, solving trigonometric identities—involving completely distinct subject matter. These programs, it should be observed, do not involve the computer in rapid arithmetic—or any arithmetic for that matter. They are basically

[30]A nontechnical description of such a program will be found in [33].

[31]The program for proving theorems in logic is discussed in [51] and [52], Gelernten and Rochester's geometry program in [31].

non-numerical, involving the manipulation of all kinds of symbolic material, including words.

Still other computer programs have been written to enable a computer to play chess.[32] Not all of these programs, or those previously mentioned, are close simulations of the processes humans use. However, in some direct attempts to investigate the human processes by thinking-aloud techniques and to reproduce in computer programs the processes observed in human subjects, several striking simulations have been achieved.[33] These experiments have been described elsewhere and can't be reviewed here in detail.

4. Business Games. Business games, like those developed by the American Management Association, International Business Machines Corporation, and several universities, represent a parallel development.[34] In the business game, the decisions of the business firms are still made by the human players, but the economic environment of these firms, including their markets, are represented by computer programs that calculate the environment's responses to the actions of the players. As the games develop in detail and realism, their programs will represent more and more concrete descriptions of the decision processes of various economic actors— for example, consumers.

The games that have been developed so far are restricted to numerical magnitudes like prices and quantities of goods, and hence resemble the management science and engineering design programs more closely than they do those we have described under the heading of human problem solving. There is no reason, however, to expect this restriction to remain very long.

Implications for Economics

Apart from normative applications (e.g., substituting computers for humans in certain decision-making tasks) we are not interested so much in the detailed descriptions of roles as in broader questions:

(1) What general characteristics do the roles of economic actors have?
(2) How do roles come to be structured in the particular way they do?
(3) What bearing does this version of role theory have for macroeconomics and other large-scale social phenomena?

Characterizing Role Structure. Here we are concerned with generalizations about thought processes, particularly those generalizations that are relatively independent of the substantive content of the role. A classical example is Dewey's description of stages in the problem-solving process. Another example, of particular interest to economics, is the hypothesis we have already discussed at length: that economic man is a *satisficing* animal whose problem solving is based on search activity to meet certain aspiration levels rather than a *maximizing* animal whose problem solving involves finding the best alternatives in terms of specified criteria [64]. A third hypothesis is that operative goals (those associated with an observable criterion of success, and relatively definite means of attainment) play a much larger part in governing choice than nonoperative goals (those lacking a concrete measure of success or a program for attainment) [45, p. 156].

[32]A survey of computer chess programs can be found in [54].
[33]Much of this work is still unpublished, but see [53] and [54].
[34]Two business games are described by Andlinger [1].

Understanding How Roles Emerge. Within almost any single business firm, certain characteristic types of roles will be represented: selling roles, production roles, accounting roles, and so on [22]. Partly this consistency may be explained in functional terms—that a model that views the firm as producing a product, selling it, and accounting for its assets and liabilities is an effective simplification of the real world, and provides the members of the organization with a workable frame of reference. Imitation within the culture provides an alternative explanation. It is exceedingly difficult to test hypotheses as to the origins and causal conditions for roles as universal in the society as these, but the underlying mechanisms could probably be explored effectively by the study of less common roles—safety director, quality control inspector, or the like—that are to be found in some firms, but not in all.

With our present definition of role, we can also speak meaningfully of the role of an entire business firm—of decision premises that underlie its basic policies. In a particular industry we find some firms that specialize in adapting the product to individual customer's specifications; others that specialize in product innovation. The common interest of economics and psychology includes not only the study of individual roles, but also the explanation of organizational roles of these sorts.

Tracing the Implications for Macroeconomics. If basic professional goals remain as they are, the interest of the psychologist and the economist in role theory will stem from somewhat different ultimate aims. The former will use various economic and organizational phenomena as data for the study of the structure and determinants of roles; the latter will be primarily interested in the implications of role theory for the model of economic man, and indirectly, for macroeconomics.

The first applications will be to those topics in economics where the assumption of static equilibrium is least tenable. Innovation, technological change, and economic development are examples of areas to which a good empirically tested theory of the processes of human adaptation and problem solving could make a major contribution. For instance, we know very little at present about how the rate of innovation depends on the amounts of resources allocated to various kinds of research and development activity [34]. Nor do we understand very well the nature of "know how," the costs of transferring technology from one firm or economy to another, or the effects of various kinds and amounts of education upon national product. These are difficult questions to answer from aggregative data and gross observation, with the result that our views have been formed more by arm-chair theorizing than by testing hypotheses with solid facts.

VII. CONCLUSION

In exploring the areas in which economics has common interests with the other behavioral sciences, we have been guided by the metaphor we elaborated in Section I. In simple, slow-moving situations, where the actor has a single, operational goal, the assumption of maximization relieves us of any need to construct a detailed picture of economic man or his processes of adaptation. As the complexity of the environment increases, or its speed of change, we need to know more and more about the mechanisms and processes that economic man uses to relate himself to that environment and achieve his goals.

How closely we wish to interweave economics with psychology depends, then, both on the range of questions we wish to answer and on our assessment of how far we may trust the assumptions of static equilibrium as approximations. In considerable part, the demand for a fuller picture of economic man has been coming from the profession of economics itself, as new areas of theory and application have emerged in which complexity and change are central facts. The revived interest in the theory of utility, and its application to choice under uncertainty, and to consumer saving and spending is one such area. The needs of normative macro-economics and management science for a fuller theory of the firm have led to a number of attempts to understand the actual processes of making business decisions. In both these areas, notions of adaptive and satisficing behavior, drawn largely from psychology, are challenging sharply the classical picture of the maximizing entrepreneur.

The area of imperfect competition and oligopoly has been equally active, although the activity has thus far perhaps raised more problems than it has solved. On the positive side, it has revealed a community of interest among a variety of social scientists concerned with bargaining as a part of political and economic processes. Prediction of the future is another element common to many decision processes, and particularly important to explaining business cycle phenomena. Psychologists and economists have been applying a wide variety of approaches, empirical and theoretical, to the study of the formation of expectations. Surveys of consumer and business behavior theories of statistical induction, stochastic learning theories, and theories of concept formation have all been converging on this problem area.

The very complexity that has made a theory of the decision-making process essential has made its construction exceedingly difficult. Most approaches have been piecemeal—now focused on the criteria of choice, now on conflict of interest, now on the formation of expectations. It seemed almost utopian to suppose that we could put together a model of adaptive man that would compare completeness with the simple model of classical economic man. The sketchiness and incompleteness of the newer proposals has been urged as a compelling reason for clinging to the older theories, however inadequate they are admitted to be.

The modern digital computer has changed the situation radically. It provides us with a tool of research—for formulating and testing theories—whose power is commensurate with the complexity of the phenomena we seek to understand. Although the use of computers to build theories of human behavior is very recent, it has already led to concrete results in the simulation of higher mental processes. As economics finds it more and more necessary to understand and explain disequilibrium as well as equilibrium, it will find an increasing use for this new tool and for communication with its sister sciences of psychology and sociology.

REFERENCES

1. G. R. Andlinger, "Business Games—Play One," *Harvard Bus. Rev.,* Apr. 1958, *36,* 115-25.
2. K. J. Arrow, "Alternative Approaches to the Theory of Choice in Risk-Taking Situations," *Econometrica,* Oct. 1951, *19,* 404-37.
3. K. J. Arrow, T. E. Harris, and J. Marschak, "Optimal Inventory Policy," *Econometrica,* July 1951, *19,* 250-72.
4. K. J. Arrow, and M. Nerlove, "A Note on Expectations and Stability," *Econometrica,* Apr. 1958, *26* 297-305.

5. K. J. Arrow, "Utilities, Attitudes, Choices," *Econometrica*, Jan. 1958, *26*, 1-23.

6. D. Bakan, "Learning and the Principle of Inverse Probability," *Psych. Rev.,*" Sept. 1953, *60* 360-70.

7. A. Bavelas, "A Mathematical Model for Group Structures," *Applied Anthropology*, Summer 1948, *7*, 16-30.

8. M. Beckmann, "Decision and Team Problems in Airline Reservations," *Econometrica*, Jan. 1958, *26* 134-45.

9. R. Bellman, *Dynamic Programming*. Princeton 1957.

10. H. R. Bowen, *The Business Enterprise as a Subject for Research*. New York 1955.

11. E. H. Bowman and R. B. Fetter, *Analysis for Production Management*. Homewood, Ill., 1957.

12. M. J. Bowman, ed., *Expectations, Uncertainty, and Business Behavior*. New York 1958.

13. H. Brems, "Response Lags and Nonprice Competition," in Bowman [12], Ch. 10, pp. 134-43.

14. J. Bruner, J. J. Goodnow and G. A. Austin, *A Study of Thinking*. New York 1956.

15. R. R. Bush and F. Mosteller, *Stochastic Models for Learning*. New York 1955.

16. C. W. Churchman, R. L. Ackoff and E. L. Arnoff, *Introduction to Operations Research*. New York 1957.

17. W. G. Cochran, *Sampling Techniques*. New York 1953.

18. R. M. Cyert and J. G. March, "Organizational Structure and Pricing Behavior in an Oligopolistic Market," *Am. Econ. Rev.*, Mar. 1955, *45*, 129-39.

19. —— and ——, "Organizational Factors in the Theory of Oligopoly," *Quart. Jour. Econ.*, Feb. 1956, *70*, 44-64.

20. W. Darcovich, "Evaluation of Some Naive Expectations Models for Agricultural Yields and Prices," in Bowman [12], Ch. 14, pp. 199-202.

21. D. Davidson and P. Suppes, *Decision Making: An Experimental Approach*. Stanford 1957.

22. D. C. Dearborn and H. A. Simon, "Selective Perception: A Note on the Departmental Identification of Executives," *Sociometry*, June 1958, *21*, 140-44.

22a. J. S. Earley, "Marginal Policies of 'Excellently Managed' Companies," *Am. Econ. Rev.*, Mar. 1956, *66*, 44-70.

23 W. Edwards, "The Theory of Decision Making," *Psych. Bull.*, Sept. 1954, *51*, 380-417.

24. R. Eisner, "Expectations, Plans, and Capital Expenditures," in Bowman [12], Ch. 12, 165-88.

25. J. Feldman, "A Theory of Binary Choice Behavior," Carnegie Inst. of Tech., Grad. Sch. Indus. Admin., Complex Information Processing Working Paper No. 12, rev., May 5, 1958. Unpublished ditto.

26. B. De Finetti "La prevision: ses lois logiques, ses sources subjectives," *Annales Inst. Henri Poincare*, 1937, *7*, 1-68.

27. M. Freidman, *Essays in Positive Economics*. Chicago 1953.

28. ——, *A Theory of the Consumption Function*. New York 1956.

29. I. Friend, "Critical Evaluation of Surveys of Expectations, Plans, and Investment Behavior," in Bowman [12], Ch. 13, pp. 189-98.

30. J. K. Galbraith, *American Capitalism: The Concept of Countervailing Power*. Boston 1952.

31. H. L. Gelernter and N. Rochester, "Intelligent Behavior in Problem-Solving Machines," *IBM Jour. Research and Develop.*, Oct. 1958, *2*, 336-45.

32. N. Georgescu-Roegen, "The Nature of Expectation and Uncertainty" in Bowman [12], Ch. 1, pp. 11-29.

33. G. L. Godwin, "Digital Computers Tap Out Designs for Large Motors–Fast," *Power*, Apr. 1958.

34. Z. Griliches, "Hybrid Corn: An Exploration in the Economics of Technological Change," *Econometrica*, Oct. 1957, *25*, 501-22.

35. H. Guetzkow and H. A. Simon, "The Impact of Certain Communication Nets in Task Oriented Groups," *Management Sci.*, July 1955, *1*, 233-50.

36. B. F. Haley, ed., *A Survey of Contemporary Economics*, Vol. II. Homewood, Ill. 1952.

37. S. P. Hayes, "Some Psychological Problems of Economics," *Psych. Bull.*, July 1950, *47*, 289-330.

38. C. C. Holt, F. Modigliani and H. A. Simon, "A Linear Decision Rule for Production and Employment Scheduling," *Management Sci.*, Oct. 1955, *2*, 1-30.

39. G. Katona, *Psychological Analysis of Economic Behavior*. New York 1951.

40. ——, "Rational Behavior and Economic Behavior," *Psych. Rev.*, July 1953, *60*, 307-18.

41. H. J. Leavitt, "Some Effects of Certain Communication Patterns on Group Performance," *Jour. Abnormal and Soc. Psych.*, Feb. 1951, *46*, 38-50.

42. K. Lewin, and others, "Level of Aspiration," in J. McV. Hunt, *Personality and the Behavior Disorders*, New York 1944, pp. 333-78.

43. R. D. Luce and H. Raiffa, *Games and Decisions*. New York 1957.

44. R. Mack, "Business Expectations and the Buying of Materials," in Bowman [12], Ch. 8, pp. 106-18.

45. J. G. March and H. A. Simon, *Organizations*. New York 1958.

46. J. Marschak, "Elements for a Theory of Teams," *Management Sci.*, Jan. 1955, *1*, 127-37.

47. K. O. May, "Intransitivity, Utility, and the Aggregation of Preference Patterns," *Econometrica*, Jan. 1954, *22*, 1-13.

48. F. Modigliani and R. E. Brumberg, "Utility Analysis and the Consumption Function," in K. K. Kurihara, *Post Keynesian Economics*, New Brunswick, N.J., 1954, pp. 388-436.

49. F. Mosteller and P. Nogee, "An Experimental Measurement of Utility," *Jour. Pol. Econ.* Oct. 1951, *59*, 371-404.

50. J. von Neumann and O. Morgenstern, *Theory of Games and Economic Behavior*. Princeton 1947.

51. A. Newell and H. A. Simon, "The Logic Theory Machine," *IRE Transactions of Information Theory*, Sept. 1956, IT-*2*, 61-79.

52. A. Newell, J. C. Shaw and H. A. Simon, "Empirical Explorations of the Logic Theory Machine," *Proceedings of the Western Joint Computer Conference*, Feb. 26-28, 1957, pp. 218-30.

53. ——, ——, ——, "Elements of a Theory of Human Problem Solving," *Psych. Rev.* May 1958, *65*, 151-66.

54. ——, ——, ——, "Chess-Playing Programs and the Problem of Complexity," *IBM Jour. Research and Develop.*, Oct. 1958, *2*, 320-35.

55. A. G. Papandreou, "Some Basic Problems in the Theory of the Firm," in Haley [36], Ch. 5, pp. 183-222.

56. M. J. Peck, "Marginal Analysis and the Explanation of Business Behavior Under Uncertainty," in Bowman [12], Ch. 9, pp. 119-33.

57. F. P. Ramsey, "Truth and Probability," in the *Foundations of Mathematics and Other Logical Essays*, London 1931, pp. 156-98.

57a. A. M. Rose, "A Study of Irrational Judgments," *Jour. Pol. Econ.*, Oct. 1957, *65*, 394-402.

58. L. J. Savage, *The Foundations of Statistics*. New York 1954.

59. T. C. Schelling, "Bargaining, Communication, and Limited War," *Jour. Conflict Resolution*, Mar. 1957, *1*, 19-36.

60. ——, "An Essay on Bargaining," *Am. Econ. Rev.*, June 1956, *46*, 281-306.

61. S. Siegel, "Level of Aspiration and Decision Making," *Psych. Rev.*, July 1957, *64*, 253-62.

62. H. A. Simon, "Dynamic Programming Under Uncertainty with a Quadratic Criterion Function," *Econometrica*, Jan. 1956, *24*, 74-81.

63. ——, *Administrative Behavior*. New York 1957.

64. ——, *Models of Man*. New York 1957.

65. ——, "The Role of Expectations in an Adaptive or Behavioristic Model," in Bowman [12], Ch. 3, pp. 49-58.

66. H. A. Simon and C. P. Bonini, "The Size Distribution of Business Firms," *Am. Econ. Rev.*, Sept. 1958, *48*, 607-17.

67. H. Theil, *Economic Forecasts and Policy*. Amsterdam 1958.

68. L. L. Thurstone, "The Indifference Function," *Jour. Soc. Psych.* May 1931, *2*, 139-67.

69. A. Vazsonyi, *Scientific Programming in Business and Industry*. New York 1958.

70. A. Wald, *Statistical Decision Functions*. New York 1950.

71. T. Wilson and P. W. S. Andrews, *Oxford Studies in the Price Mechanism*. Oxford 1951.

72. M. Shubik, "Strategy and Market Structure; Competition, Oligopoly, and the Theory of Games," New York, Wiley, 1959.

3

A THEORY OF LARGE MANAGERIAL FIRMS*

R. JOSEPH MONSEN, JR. / ANTHONY DOWNS[1]

I. INTRODUCTION

For a long time, there has been dissatisfaction with the traditional theory of the firm and its basic axiom that firms maximize profits.[2] This article attempts to propound a more realistic alternative applicable to large corporate firms.

In our opinion, the traditional theory of the firm really deals with only *one* type of firm: the small, owner-managed firm. But since the inception of this theory, several other types of firms have come into being that differ from the traditional type in both owner-management relationships and size. Moreover, these other types of firms are now economically more significant than the traditional type in terms of the magnitude of the resources which they control.

Distinguishing between types of firms is important because the behavior of each firm with respect to profits depends upon certain elements of its internal structure. In firms whose managers are not also their owners there may be a divergence of interest between the managers and the owners in certain situations. Such a divergence can cause firms to deviate from profit-maximizing behavior. Size also

*The Journal of Political Economy, The University of Chicago Press, June 1965, pp. 211-236.

[1] All views expressed in this paper are those of the authors and do not necessarily reflect the views of either the University of Washington or the Real Estate Research Corporation. The authors are developing, separately, in forthcoming studies a number of the ideas outlined in this article.

[2] See R. L. Hall and C. J. Hitch, "Price Theory and Business Behaviour," *Oxford Economic Papers,* May, 1939; B. Higgins, "Elements of Indeterminacy in the Theory of Non-Profit Competition," *American Economic Review,* September, 1939; T. Parsons, "The Motivations of Economic Activity," *Canadian Journal of Economics and Political Science,* May, 1940; K. W. Rothschild, "Price Theory and Oligopoly," *Economic Journal,* September, 1947; M. W. Reder, "A Reconsideration of the Marginal Productivity Theory," *Journal of Political Economy,* October, 1947; W. Fellner, *Competition among the Few* (New York: Alfred A. Knopf, 1949); George Katona, *Psychological Analysis of Economic Behaviors* (New York: McGraw-Hill Book Co., 1951); K. E. Boulding, "Implications for General Economics of More Realistic Theories of the Firm," *American Economic Review, Supplement,* May, 1952; T. Scitovsky, "A Note on Profit Maximization and Its Implications," reprinted in *Readings in Price Theory* (Homewood, Ill.: Richard D. Irwin, Inc., 1952); A. A. Papandreau, "Some Basic Problems in the Theory of the Firm," in B. F. Haley (ed.), *A Survey of Contemporary Economics,* Vol. II (Homewood, Ill.: Richard D. Irwin, Inc., 1952); C. A. Hickman and M. H. Kuhn, *Individuals, Groups and Economic Behavior* (New York: Dryden Press, 1956); H. A. Simon, *Administrative Behavior* (New York: Macmillan Co., 1957); W. Baumol, *Business Behavior, Value and Growth,* (New York: Macmillan Co., 1959); and Robin Marris, "A Model of the 'Managerial' Enterprise," *Quarterly Journal of Economics,* May, 1963.

influences each firm's behavior regarding profit maximization. Very large firms must develop bureaucratic management structures to cope with their administrative problems. But such structures inevitably introduce certain conflicts of interest between men in different positions within them. These conflicts arise because the goals of middle and lower management are different from those of top management. The introduction of these additional goals into the firm's decision-making process also leads to systematic deviations from profit-maximizing behavior.

In this article, we will explore the specific ways in which firm size and goal divergence between owners and managers and among various levels of management cause large-size, corporate firms to deviate from the profit-maximizing behavior posited by the traditional theory of the firm.

II. Types of Firms

In most economic theory, questions regarding the relationships among different parts of the firm simply do not arise. Instead, economists generally assume that the firm can be treated as a single person, with a unified and integrated set of motives and the ability to carry out its goals without any wasted effort except that imposed by the technical limitations of production and distribution. There are some exceptions to this viewpoint, but those holding other views have not succeeded in shaking the dominance of the traditional concept.[3] For example, A. A. Berle, Jr., and Gardiner Means long ago pointed out that the separation of ownership from management created situations which traditional theory was not adequate to deal with.[4] In sociology, a sizable literature has grown up concerning bureaucracy in large organizations, and much of it is applicable to large-scale firms.[5] However, thus far, the theory of bureaucracy and the theory of the firm have not been successfully integrated.

There are so many different kinds of firms in the real world that any method of classifying them is bound to be arbitrary, Nevertheless, we have developed several categories of firms based on two variables: size, and the relationship between the owners of the firm and those who manage it. We have concentrated solely upon these two because they have a direct relationship to the question of whether or not the firm maximizes profits.

Our purpose in using size as a criterion for distinguishing among firms is to separate those with bureaucratic management structures from those that do not have such structures. Therefore, we will consider any firm *small* if it has less than 1,000 employees, and *large* if it has 1,000 or more employees. This boundary line between small and large firms is admittedly arbitrary, but it will serve our purposes in the present analysis.

[3]One of the most important recent treatments of the subject dealt with in this paper is that of Oliver E. Williamson, whose analysis in certain respects is similar to our own. While the authors have benefited from his perceptive criticism of later drafts, the present paper was originally written completely independently of Williamson's work. His whole theory is presented in *The Economics of Discretionary Behavior: Managerial Objectives in a Theory of the Firm* (Englewood Cliffs, N.J.: Prentice-Hall, Inc., 1964), and a summary appears in "Managerial Discretion and Business Behavior," *American Economic Review*, December, 1963.

[4]*The Modern Corporation and Private Property* (New York: Macmillan Co., 1932). A later work on the same subject is Berle's *Power without Property* (New York: Harcourt, Brace & Co., 1959).

[5]An extensive bibliography is presented in Peter M. Blau and W. Richard Scott, *Formal Organizations* (San Francisco: Chandler Publishing Co., 1962), pp. 258-301.

There are also many different relationships between the owners of firms and those who actually manage them (that is, the highest-ranking men in the management structure). As a start toward categorizing these relationships, we propose the following catalogue of firms:

1. *Owner-managed firms* are those managed by the people who own controlling interests in the firm (whether it is a corporation, a partnership, or some other type of organization).
2. *Managerial firms* are those managed by men who do not own anywhere near a controlling interest in them (or any interest at all). Such firms can be further divided into:
   a) *Diffused ownership managerial firms* in which no one person or organized coalition of persons owns a controlling interest in the firm.
   b) *Concentrated ownership managerial firms* in which one person or an organized coalition of persons owns a controlling interest in the firm and (presumably) exercises control over the management. For all purposes of our analysis, such firms are nearly identical with owner-managed firms. Therefore, we will use the term *managerial firms* to refer only to diffused ownership managerial firms.
3. *Non-ownership firms* are those legally considered non-profit organizations. "Ownership" of such firms· does not include the legal right to receive earnings from them. Moreover, such firms are usually entirely controlled by trustees or directors with no ownership relation to them at all.
4. *Fiduciarily owned firms* are those whose "owners" are persons making capital payments into the firms primarily for purposes other than receiving income or capital gains therefrom. Examples of such firms are mutual insurance companies and pension funds. The managers of such firms are normally similar to trustees and usually have no significant ownership in the firms themselves.

It seems clear from the above catalogue that the traditional theory of the firm does not apply equally well to all types of firms. For example, it is not obvious that non-ownership firms maximize profits, since they are by definition non-profit organizations. Moreover, fiduciarily owned firms probably have a much stronger orientation toward tempering profit maximization with considerations of security than owner-managed firms. However, our analysis will not deal with these types of firms any further, but will instead concentrate on managerial firms. Our only point in introducing this catalogue of firms—which could undoubtedly be improved and, we hope, will be—is to illustrate our beliefs that (1) different principles of behavior should be formulated for different types of firms, and (2) the traditional principle of profit-maximization really applies to only a limited number of types—even though they may be extremely important.

III. THE BASIC THEORY

A. Background Structure

This article advances a theory about the way that certain firms make decisions under relatively realistic conditions. Specifically, the following conditions will be assumed:

1. The firms involved are large corporations with ownership divided among a great many stockholders. No one stockholder has anywhere near a controlling interest.
2. Each firm has a board of directors elected by its stockholders. This board has ultimate power over the firm's policies and can replace any of its executives (though in some cases it is effectively controlled by those executives).
3. Each firm is operated by a set of managers arranged in a hierarchical pyramid. This pyramid contains at least the following three layers:
    a) *Top management* consists of those few key executives who are involved in making the basic policy and planning decisions.
    b) *Middle management* consists of those operating executives under top management who are responsible for carrying out various specialized tasks within the firm. There may be several layers within the middle management structure. The lowest level of middle management has direct authority over lower management.
    c) *Lower management* consists of supervisory personnel at the foreman or comparable level. Lower management has direct authority over production or lowest-level clerical personnel.
4. Managers (especially top managers) may own stock in their respective firms. However, the proportion of stock which any one manager or group of managers in a firm controls is so small that it does not constitute anywhere near a controlling interest in the firm. Moreover, the stock dividends of each manager comprise a relatively small part of his income in relation to his salary and bonuses.
5. Each firm operates in a world of uncertainty and risk in which knowledge is costly and perfect knowledge normally unobtainable. These conditions prevail regarding both the firm's relations with the rest of the world, and relations among various parts of the firm itself.
6. The degree of oligopoly or monopoly prevalent in each firm's industry is not specified. Our theory does not offer any solution to the oligopoly problem. However, we will assume that (*a*) each firm operates in a market which contains enough competition so that the firm can conceivably face some risks regarding its long-term survival, but (*b*) it enjoys enough of a monopolistic position so that it can usually earn profits larger than the "normal" level associated with a perfectly competitive industry.

Under these conditions, there are three classes of decision-makers who can potentially affect a firm's policies and behavior: owners, members of the board of directors, and managers. Since managers are usually represented on the board of directors by the very top executives of the firm, there are really only two autonomous groups in the firm's decision-making structure: owners and managers. Where ownership is extremely fragmented and no large stockholders exist, the managers often effectively control the board of directors through proxy agreements. However, we assume that the board is sufficiently independent of the managers to punish extremely poor management performance and reward very good performance.

B. Central Hypotheses

The central hypotheses of our theory concern the *motivations* of owners and managers. We believe that traditional theory is correct in assuming that the people who operate business firms are primarily motivated by their own self-interest. But pursuit of self-interest is a characteristic of human persons, not organizations. A *firm* is not a real person, even when incorporated; hence it really cannot have motives or maximize anything. When traditional theorists stated that *firms* maximize profits, they really meant that the *people who run firms* make decisions so as to maximize the profits of the firms. As long as firms were operated by their owners, this assumption was consistent with the self-interest axiom, because the profits of the firms were the main incomes of their owners.

But in most of the largest and most significant modern firms, ownership and management are functions carried out by two entirely separate groups of people. Even management itself is really a combination of functions carried out by different groups. Thus the entity normally referred to as *the firm* has in fact become a number of different subentities. The people in each of these subgroups within the firm are still primarily motivated by self-interest. However, their changed relationship to the firm as a whole has changed the way in which their self-interest leads them to behave regarding the firm's profits. Therefore, our theory is really nothing more than the application of the self-interest axiom in traditional theory to a new type of firm: one in which ownership is separate from management; and management itself consists of a bureaucratic hierarchy containing several layers.

Our two central hypotheses can be stated as follows:

1. *Owners desire to have each firm managed so that it provides a steady income from dividends and gradual appreciation of the market price of the stock.*
2. *Managers act so as to maximize their own lifetime incomes.*

Since these two hypotheses are the foundations of our whole analysis, we will examine each in detail.

C. The Motivation of Owners

Although every stockholder certainly prefers a rapid rate of advance in the price of his stock to a slow rate, most owners also prefer a slow but steady rise to an erratic combination of rapid rises and equally rapid declines. This is probably true even if the total rise would be slightly higher in the case of erratic movement. A slow but steady rise preserves each owner's ability to get back his original investment plus a profit at any time, whereas up-and-down price movements create uncertainty in his mind about the future price of the stock, thereby creating an apparent risk that he might suffer a loss if he had to sell at a certain moment. Since stockholders typically know far less about the firm's situation than managers, such uncertainty can exist in the minds of stockholders even if the managers know the erratic short-run movements of the stock's price result from factors which will work out favorably in the long run.

Another inportant characteristic of owners is their ignorance of the alternative policies available to the firm. Since owners are remote from the firm's actual decision-making, they learn about the firm's performance only ex post, and then only through "official" reports from top management (unless the firm has so blundered that its mistakes have been publicly reported). As a result, owners have no reliable way of determining whether the firm is maximizing its profits and the growth of its stock prices or not. Their only yardstick consists of comparisons with other similar firms. Even this yardstick is an imprecise one, for no two firms are ever exactly alike, and the performance of every firm in any one year is usually conditioned by some unique events applicable to it alone. Therefore, owners can assess the performance of their own top management only by a relatively general comparison with other similar firms and with the stock market as a whole.

The ignorance of stockholders drastically reduces the amount of marginal switching they do from one stock to another that appears to be enjoying better performance. They simply cannot accurately judge small differences in quality of performance. Moreover, the capital gains tax "rakes off" 25 per cent of all value appreciation every time a stockholder switches from one stock to another. Thus the force of competition among different stocks, which would in theory be expected to put pressure on top management to *maximize* the rate of growth of its stock price, is in fact severely weakened by both ignorance and the tax structure.

As a result, owners tend to act as "satisficers" instead of "maximizers." *In our interpretation "satisficers" differ from "maximizers" only in capability, not in intention.* They would like to maximize, but the limitations of their ignorance and their finite capacity cause them to adapt behavior different from that of a theoretical maximizer. Consequently, if the price increases of the firm's stock meet some minimal criterion of "satisfactory growth" in comparison with alternative investments, and dividends do not fall, they will approve of the firm's top management. If the performance of the firm is so poor that these results are clearly not being attained, they will disapprove of the firm's top management.

Owners express their approval or disapproval of managers in the annual elections of the board of directors. However, because of the diffusion of ownership, it takes an extraordinarily poor management performance to trigger a real uprising among stockholders—an uprising violent enough to elect directors who will remove or drastically discipline the top managers. Normally, top management controls the board of directors through proxy agreements; hence the key executives are self-perpetuating unless they radically disappoint the owners.

Nevertheless, fear of potential rebellion among stockholders imposes a latent check on the actions of the incumbent management. This fear is increased by the operations of professional "outside raiders" who specialize in rallying dissident owners against incumbent managers. The New York Central Railroad over the years has provided a number of examples of revolts sparked by such "outsiders."

Moreover, although a very poor management performance may result in a rebellion, a very good one does not usually cause a powerful movement among stockholders to reward their managers with lavish bonuses. Hence *the punishment for grievous error is greater than the reward for outstanding success.* This asymmetry between failure and success tends to make the managers of a diffused-ownership firm behave differently from the managers of the type of owner-managed firm envisioned by traditional theory.

Although a majority of stock owners in the United States seek "safe growth" as described above, a certain minority are far more interested in rapid appreciation of stock prices. They are the buyers of so-called growth stocks. However, we are excluding these owners from our analysis because (1) Most of the large corporations in the United States with widely diffused ownership are not "growth" corporations. But our theory applies only to diffused-ownership firms. (2) "Growth" stocks comprise a small minority of all stocks (although they receive a great deal of publicity).

D. The Motivation of Managers

Our second central hypothesis is simply the application of self-interest to the managers of large firms. Today the largest, most significant firms in the United States are owned by thousands of individual stockholders who are remote from actual management and decision-making. Conversely, the men who really run these firms are professional managers. Although they may own some stock, their ownership is usually a *result* of their executive positions, rather than the *cause* of their holding such positions. Also, their incomes are not identical with the firm's profits, and may not even vary in any strict relation to the firm's profits. As a result, when managers act in their own self-interest, they do not always act in the interest of the owners.[6]

What *is* in their self-interest is maximizing *their own* incomes. As prudent men, they consider their (discounted) incomes over the course of their *entire working lives,* not just in the current year, or while working for their current employer. These incomes include both *monetary elements* (salaries, bonuses, capital gains from stock options, etc.) and *non-monetary elements* (leisure, prestige, power, etc.).[7] The non-monetary aspects of income can be equated at the margin with dollars; hence we can conceive of the managers as maximizing the present value of their lifetime incomes in dollar terms.

The pursuit of self-interest by managers also has important repercussions upon relationships *among managers* within the firm itself. Just as it is not always in the interest of top management to maximize the returns to the owners, it may not always be in the interest of the middle management to carry out the orders of top management. It is necessary, therefore, ot break the firm down into its component parts in order to discover the levels on which individual motivations actually operate.

It should be pointed out that the self-interest of individual managers has definite limits. We certainly do not mean to depict corporate managers as avaricious, grasping individuals willing to break every moral law in their ruthless drive to success—as the jackets of some business novels have put it. We do not impute any more self-interest to managers as a group than to the members of other social or economic groups. We merely assume that an important fraction of all managers is sufficiently motivated by self-interest to count its own long-run welfare as more important than the welfare of either the owners of the firm or the other managers therein.

IV. IMPACT OF BUREAUCRACY ON BEHAVIOR OF FIRMS

In order to analyze in more detail the way in which managers in very large firms make decisions, it is first necessary to examine the *context* of managerial decision-making. Each manager occupies a certain position in the organizational pyramid formed by the corporate hierarchy. Above him are his *superiors,* who have control over his promotions, salary, bonuses, and other elements of his success. Below him are his *subordinates,* whose promotions and income he analogously

---

[6]See Baumol, *op cit.*

[7]Our definition of managerial *income* is thus operationally similar to Williamson's definition of managerial *utility;* hence our income-maximizing assumption is akin to his utility-maximizing assumption (see Williamson, *op. cit.,* chap. iii).

influences and whose efforts he depends upon to produce results pleasing to his superiors. Alongside him at other positions on the same level of the hierarchy are his *peers*. They are engaged in specialized tasks different from his own, but they are competing with him for eventual promotion to higher levels. *The basic problem which each manager faces is the necessity of pleasing his superior to attain advances in income* (either through promotion to higher-paying jobs or a higher salary in his existing job). In the case of top management, the superiors involved are represented by the board of directors and the stockholders.

From the point of view of each firm's owners, the function of managers and employees is to make the greatest possible contribution toward achieving the objectives of the owners. But whatever the owners' objectives may be, we believe that *the bureaucratic structure of large firms will cause management to deviate systematically from achieving ownership objectives*. This will occur because (1) the motives of managers are not identical with the motives of owners, as we have pointed out, and (2) in large companies, the nature of the administrative structure makes it impossible for the owners to control the behavior of managers completely—or even for top managers to control the behavior of those below them completely.

The following specific factors may cause managerial behavior to deviate from ownership objectives:

1. It is often very difficult to measure accurately the contribution made by each individual employee to profits, stock-price gains, or any other financial objectives. In such instances—which may cover a majority of management personnel in a large corporation—superiors are driven to use subjective impressions or irrelevant objective tests they have set up as means of deciding whom to promote. Therefore they must promote men who somehow make the most favorable impression on them, and these may not necessarily be the men who actually contribute most to ownership (or top management) objectives.

2. The superiors themselves may not be pursuing policies which are identical with those of the firm's owners. If so, they might tend to promote men who carried out the policies they were pursuing rather than men who carried out policies which maximized the owners' objectives.

Insofar as either of the above factors is in effect, managers on the middle and lower levels of the corporate bureaucracy will find themselves best served by actions which create the most favorable impression upon their superiors, regardless of the impact of such actions upon corporate profits or other ownership gains. Of course, the subjective impressions of their superiors will by no means be divorced entirely from factual evidence; hence no manager can completely ignore the possible objectively measurable effects of his behavior upon corporate prosperity. But the tools which measure individual contributions to profits or stock-price increases are often very imprecise, especially regarding such non-selling and non-production jobs as public relations, personnel management, and advertising. Therefore an individual manager may be able to choose among several alternative actions which will affect profits or stock prices in the long run, but which will have no differing effects upon the objective indexes which his superiors must rely on to rate the quality of his performance. If a number of executives in a firm select among such policies so as to please their superiors rather than to maximize ownership objectives, the cumulative effect of such choices may in the long run cause a substantial loss of potential benefits to the firm's owners.

Even more important are the long-run effects of certain actions managers may take to advance their own interests which reduce the firm's efficiency. Since the managers are motivated by the advancement of their own incomes, they will perform acts which impair the firm's efficiency if (1) those acts tend to advance their own interests, and (2) it is impossible or very difficult for their superiors to discover these acts. Gordon Tullock has presented an ingenious and persuasive theory of political bureaucracies which encompasses a number of such actions.[8] Among those applicable to corporate bureaucracies are the following:

1. *Managers at every level of the corporate pyramid tend to screen information in their possession so that only data favorable to them are passed upward to their superiors.* Insofar as cost accounting and other auditing techniques administered by outsiders are available to the superiors, this cannot be done. But there is always a considerable element of judgment in information flowing through the corporate hierarchy. Hence managers can screen out judgment factors unfavorable to them before they pass data upward to those who have authority over their own incomes and appurtenances. Also, in order to please superiors, managers may tend to pass to them only information that verifies the desires of the superiors, or proves that their decisions were wise.

If the corporate hierarchy has many levels, the cumulative effect of this screening process may become substantial. For example, assume 'that the top level of a corporation is designated the A level, the next level, the B level, etc. and that there are five levels in all. Each A executive has a number of B-level men (say, three) under him; each B executive has a similar group of C-level men under him; and so on, down to the lowest or E-level, which consists of men "in the field" who receive information "first hand." In theory, each man passes on information to his superior, who winnows the most important data from the many reports made to him and passes those upward to *his* superior. This process is repeated up to the A level, where the top men make decisions based on the information emerging from the hierarchy below them. Thus, screening information is a legitimate part of each manager's job. But he may deliberately (or even unconsciously) suppress some of the information which his superiors need to know because that information is either unfavorable to himself or displeasing to his superiors. If each manager thus suppresses only 10 per cent of the data he should pass upward if top management is to be properly informed, then managers at the A level will receive only 66 per cent of the important data fed into the pyramid at the E level ($0.9^4 = 0.656$).

Thus the tendency for managers to screen information may cause top management to be systematically misinformed through (a) failure to learn vital facts, especially ones adverse to lower management levels, and (b) a tendency to be told only what they want to hear.

2. *Managers at every level tend to carry out only part of the orders given to them.* Since the personnel of each corporation are pursuing their own interests instead of the firm's, they will be reluctant to carry out any orders which would reduce their income, power, prestige, or chances of advancement. To some extent, they must obey such orders because they will be fired for insubordination if they flatly refuse. However, the vigor with which they execute such policies, their attention to proper follow-up procedures, and their imaginative application of these policies in new situations may be minimized without any actual insubordination. The technique of "kicking it around until it disappears" is well known in all large organizations.

[8]"A General Theory of Politics" (undated and unpublished mimeographed manuscript).

The cumulative effects of such partial failure to execute orders can be very great if a corporation has many layers in its organization hierarchy. In the case of the five-level organization cited above, a failure by each layer of managers below level A to carry out just 5 per cent of the orders they receive from their superiors would result in only 81 per cent of the top management's orders being carried out by the lowest level personnel ($0.95^4 = 0.814$).Moreover, some allowance must also be made for inefficiency in carrying out orders due to incompetence, inertia, and misunderstanding.

It is true that cost accounting, auditing, and other objective performance reports can significantly reduce the ability of subordinates to practice undetected insubordination. Nevertheless, no large corporation actually carries out the policies established by its leaders in precisely the manner originally envisioned by those leaders.

We realize that there are many techniques that owners and top managers can use to counteract the above inefficiencies. Corporate spies, peer-group pressures, personal ties between members of top management and lower management, random inspections, and a host of other devices are often used to produce closer conformance of subordinates' behavior to the desires and policies of owners and top managers. Nevertheless, we believe that all of these remedies are only partially successful in very large organizations. As a result, the inefficiencies described above cause large firms to deviate systematically and significantly from the course of action that would in fact maximize attainment of the owners' objectives—or even the objectives of top management.

These inefficiencies are inherent in all *large* organizations. Hence they will exist not only in large managerial firms with diffused ownership, but also in large non-profit organizations, large owner-managed firms, and even large government agencies. Therefore, even if we agreed with traditional theory that the owners of a firm wish to maximize profits (and we do agree in the case of owner-managed firms), we would contend that the difference between *owner* motivation and *managerial* motivation will cause systematic deviations from profit-maximizing behavior as long as the firm is large enough so that the owners themselves cannot supervise all facets of its activities.

When such large size exists, the owners must yield some discretion over the firm's behavior to managers whose goals are not identical with the goals of the owners. The manager at the top of a large firm, or the owner in a profit-maximizing firm, must delegate authority to others (that is, permit the screening of information and give some discretion to his subordinates in carrying out his orders) because his own personal *capacity* to handle information and decisions is limited at a level below the amount of information and problems generated by the organization. This is a function of *size*. However it does not *necessarily* create inefficiency. *Inefficiency* arises whenever such delegation of authority leads to results other than those which are optimal from the viewpoint of the top man. But non-optimal results may occur because the *goals* of the persons to whom he has delegated authority are different from his own. If these subordinates had goals precisely identical to his own, then they would act as mechanical extensions of his own capacity. That is the implicit assumption of the classical literature on the firm to which we object.

Thus, in essence, some behavior which is non-optimal from the viewpoint of the top man arises because of *both* size and goal divergence. Large size is what requires him to delegate authority in the first place; but goal divergence can cause that delegation to create non-optimal results.

Even if the top man had subordinates whose goals were exactly identical to his own, some inefficiencies of a *technical* nature might arise, again due to the limited capacity of each individual decision-maker in the firm. For example, specialists working in different parts of the firm whose activities had unforeseen overlapping effects might not realize this fact until some unco-ordinated behavior had taken place; that is, until the behavior of one somehow impeded the plans of the other, unbeknown to the first. This kind of inefficiency is due *entirely* to the size of the firm; that is, to the fact that individuals have limited capacities and the firm is larger than their capacities. But behavior of the firm which is not optimal from the viewpoint of the top man can be caused *either* by size alone (technical inefficiency) or by a combination of size and divergent goals (technical plus motivational inefficiency). Screening, of course, arises because of size. But screening per se is not necessarily a form of inefficiency. It can lead to inefficiency without any difference in motives, but it does not *always* lead to inefficiency *unless* a difference of motives is also present. Then screening will always create inefficiency to some extent.

V. IMPLICATIONS OF THE THEORY
REGARDING BEHAVIOR OF MANAGEMENT

Now that we have set forth our basic theory and examined the bureaucratic context of managerial decision-making, we will explore the theory's implications regarding the behavior of managers at various levels within the firm.

A. Top Management Behavior

1. **The Organizational Setting.** The top managers in a large firm are those few key executives who are involved in making basic policy and planning decisions. They are normally paid for their performance in three ways: (*a*) by salaries and bonuses, (*b*) by stock options, and (*c*) by expense accounts and other untaxed perquisites. However, high personal income-tax rates limit the amount of their salaries and bonuses they can retain, and they cannot *retain* any wealth from expense accounts and other similar untaxed benefits. Therefore, top managers normally regard stock options as a very significant form of compensation. Hence, top management normally has a direct and powerful interest in the *market price* of the firm's stock. Clearly, creation of such an interest is the primary justification of the stock-option arrangement from the owners' point of view, although the nature and size of the arrangement is usually determined by the managers themselves.

An important part of top management's environment consists of groups outside the firm's administrative structure who are in a position to challenge the quality of top management's performance. They include labor unions, government officials, and the public at large. Strong criticism from any of these groups can seriously tarnish the general public image of all-around competence which top management seeks to foster by "getting along well" with all important groups. This type of public image is far more significant to top management in a concentrated-ownership firm. It is more significant to top management in a diffused-ownership firm than in an owner-managed firm or a concentrated-ownership firm. When ownership is diffused among thousands of stockholders, the owners are almost indistinguishable from the general public insofar as top management is concerned; hence the public image of the firm is very likely to be the owners' image too.

Moreover, stockholders have so few contacts with management that any widely circulated criticism of top management is likely to convince many stockholders that "where there's smoke, there's fire." Therefore, top management is often highly sensitive to criticism from major groups outside the firm.

2. **Top Management's Promotional Strategy.** The best way for top management to maximize its own lifetime income is to "keep the stockholders happy." This normally involves three basic policies:

a) Carefully screening all information which is forwarded to stockholders or the public at large so that it reflects an outstanding management performance. The results of this policy can be readily seen by reading a typical annual report or attending an annual stockholders' meeting. Of course, professional reporting agencies like the *Wall Street Journal* provide some objective check on management's ability to suppress unfavorable information. However, it is quite easy for managers to conceal a great deal of inefficiency from such "outsiders," especially since only outstanding blunders make good news copy.

b) Directing the firm toward achievement of constant or slightly rising dividends plus steadily increasing stock prices. However, top management need only attain a "satisfactory" rate of stock-price growth, not a "maximum" one.

c) Maintaining a "public image" of competence by avoiding controversy and criticism. Public criticism of the firm or controversy about its policies tends to contradict this "image" and raise doubts in the minds of the stockholders about the wisdom of retaining the existing top management.

3. **Implications of Top-Management Behavior.** The result of top management's employing the above policies is that the firm (*a*) is more likely to avoid risky decisions, (*b*) will have less variability of earnings, (*c*) may grow more slowly, and (*d*) will be less likely to go bankrupt than it would if the managers sought to maximize profits. Top management will avoid highly risky decisions because they might cause the earnings of the firm to fluctuate instead of growing steadily, even if the total profits of the firm would be larger with fluctuating earnings. Top management abhors fluctuating earnings for the following reasons:

a) If the earnings in a given year decline, the price of the stock may fall. This would be repugnant to all owners—including the top managers themselves—and might cause the owners to throw out top management, especially if the stock market in general has risen.

b) Stocks with fluctuating earnings generally have lower price-earnings ratios than those with steadily rising earnings. It is clearly in the interest of all owners—including top managers with stock options—to maintain high price-earnings ratios.

Thus the attention of management is focused on stock *prices* rather than *earnings* (profits), which are viewed as means to obtain higher stock prices rather than as ends in themselves. Therefore, if top management must choose between (*a*) maximizing profits over a given period by accepting fluctuating earnings, or (*b*) achieving total profits by maintaining steadily rising annual earnings, it will normally choose the latter. Therefore, diffused-ownership firms will experience less *variability of earnings* than firms which try to maximize profits.

In our opinion, this relatively conservative attitude by top management would lead to slower growth than a "pure" policy of profit maximization *among those firms which survive.* Other implications of our hypothesis and forecasts consistent with it concerning top management behavior are as follows:

a) Research and development expenditures are more likely to be budgeted for steady yearly growth than for "crash" expansion of promising innovations.

b) Diffused-ownership firms will exhibit a strong predilection for diversification of products, especially through merger, as a means of reducing risks taken on any one product or line of products. Since diversification through merger tends to reduce the rate of return on capital, owner-managers would be less likely to adopt such policies.

c) Financing rapid expansion through additional stock offerings is less likely to be used by top management in diffused-ownership firms than by owner-managers. In many cases, the original owners of a firm which expands rapidly use sales of common stock to "buy themselves out" of the corporation, thus capitalizing on their original ownership interest. Managers whose only stock comes from stock options are more likely to adopt internal financing, bank borrowing, or bond issues for such financing so as not to dilute their own interests. Among long-established firms, both owner-managed and managerial types will probably avoid additional equity financing with equal distaste because of its dilution effects. However, managers may be willing to finance through stock offerings if they feel that the additional capital will enable the firm to rapidly expand sales. The work of McGuire, Chiu, and Elbing has shown that executive incomes are significantly correlated to firm sales.[9] Under the above circumstances, then, professional management will have to decide which course of action will most likely maximize their life time incomes—raising less capital from internal financing or obtaining greater financing (and stock dilution) from stock offerings.

d) Top management will be much more sensitive to public, union, and government criticism than owner-managers would be. Hence top managers will be more conciliatory in their public dealings than might be required for profit maximization.

e) Top managers will use their roles in the firm to enhance their own personal prestige and stature. As a result, they will contribute to local causes and participate in community affairs more than they should from a purely profit-maximizing point of view.

f) In order to stabilize future profits, avoid controversy, and prevent adverse publicity, top management may make concessions to labor unions more readily than owner-managers would. This will tend to reduce profits below the level which would be attained by a truly profit-maximizing firm.

g) Expense accounts are likely to be more extravagant in managerial firms than they would be if managers really maximized returns to owners. Although expense-account benefits and salaries are both deductible, salaries are a much more visible and easily checked form of management compensation. Therefore, managers will seek to expand expense-account benefits in order to raise their total compensation without attracting the attention of owners. This will result in greater total compensation for them than is required to retain their services. The fact that such non-salary benefits will influence their choices among firms (and hence may appear to be a necessary part of their compensation by each firm) does not destroy this argument. Managers *as a group* are probably extracting rent because of inflated expense accounts; that is, they are compensated more in *all* managerial firms than is necessary to keep them from becoming non-managers. Thus what may appear as true costs to individual firms are still an excessive reduction of profits among all managerial firms compared with what profits would be if truly maximized.

[9] J. W. McGuire, J. S. Y. Chiu, and A. O. Elbing, "Executive Incomes, Sales and Profits," *American Economic Review,* September, 1962.

h) Managerial firms are likely to respond more slowly to declines in profits than they would if they really pursued profit maximization. Since managers wish to preserve their personal prerogatives (such as large expense accounts) and do not suffer directly from lower profits, they will be willing to "ride out" a sudden decline in profits without cutting back expenditures in the hope that it will be temporary. In contrast, true profit-maximizers would exhibit no such inertia but would immediately alter their existing behavior patterns. However, if lower profits continue, even managerial firms will adjust their behavior so as to avoid having lower yearly earnings cause any decline in stock prices (if possible).

B. Middle-Management Behavior

1. The Organizational Setting. Middle managers are those operating executives under top management who are responsible for carrying out various specialized tasks within the firm. Middle managers are normally paid for their performance primarily by salaries and bonuses and secondarily by expense accounts and other untaxed perquisites.

2. Middle Management's Promotional Strategy. The best way for middle managers to maximize their lifetime incomes is to increase the size of those incomes by being promoted to higher-paying positions within the firm or in other firms. Since their promotions are determined by the recommendations of their superiors, their efforts to obtain promotion consist essentially of doing whatever will most please and impress their superiors, regardless of the effects of their actions upon the profits of the firm.

We have already pointed out several ways in which this type of motivation will cause deviations from "pure" profit maximization. In addition, middle managers must get along well with their subordinates, since they must rely upon the performance of the latter to assist them in impressing top management. This dual need for pleasing superiors and cooperating with subordinates places middle managers in a somewhat different position from top managers. Top management can employ cost accounting, personal ties with lower management, peer-group informants, and numerous other devices to keep well-informed about what middle managers are doing. This means that middle managers have much less scope for covering up mistakes than do top managers—even though the magnitude of the errors which top managers might make is much greater.

3. Implications of Middle-Management Behavior. Middle managers will normally tend to be risk-avoiders in making decisions. A certain degree of advancement can be obtained merely by surviving, doing daily tasks, and not committing any outstanding blunders. This tendency, plus the desire of middle management to initiate those ideas which reflect the preconceived notions of their superiors, may produce an excessive lack of creativity and innovation at the middle-management level. Consequently, the firm may pass by many profit-increasing possibilities on the middle-management level which would be taken up by a truly profit-maximizing firm.

Insofar as middle managers are intrusted with labor relations, they may also tend to grant concessions to unions more readily than owner-managers would. Since strikes always involve more risks due to uncertainty than do settlements, risk-avoiders will have a built-in bias toward achieving settlements through concessions.

Again, the result may be lower profits than would be attained by more aggressive and tougher owner-manager firms.

In highly decentralized firms, middle managers may be intrusted with far more responsibility than in centralized firms. In such cases, middle managers will undertake much riskier actions because the potential rewards will be higher. In fact, the position of middle management in such firms is riskier than the position of top management, because, as noted, middle managers are more closely scrutinized by their superiors than are top managers. Thus the attitude of middle managers toward risks depends largely upon the structure of costs and rewards associated with different types of behavior on their part. The middle managers at General Electric and Westinghouse involved in price-fixing litigation were apparently willing to take on extraordinary risks in order to gain entry into the ranks of top management.

C. Lower-Management Behavior

1. **The Organizational Setting.** Lower managers are those supervisory personnel at the foreman or comparable level who have direct authority over production or lowest-level clerical personnel. They are normally paid for their performance by salaries and bonuses. Their salaries are partly based on seniority and longevity in the firm, and their bonuses are based on achieving production or quality goals. Normally, lower managers have little expectation of being promoted in middle or top management because the educational standards for those higher echelons are beyond their capabilities.

2. **Lower Management's Promotional Strategy** The best way for lower managers to maximize their lifetime incomes is to seek promotions up to the highest attainable lower-management level and then to hold on to what they have achieved. Often their performances can be accurately measured objectively by means of production quotas, quality checks, costs accounting, etc. Thus the efforts of lower management are more intensively directed at meeting objective performance criteria than is the case with middle and top management.

3. **Implications of Lower-Management Behavior.** Lower managers are risk-avoiders of a high order. Their aim is primarily to retain their present positions by meeting quotas and avoiding gross errors. In this echelon are the classic bureaucrats who never violate the rules and fear to "stick their necks out." As with middle management, the result is undoubtedly a lower level of creativity, innovation, and risk-taking than would occur in a firm perfectly organized to maximize profits.

D. Non-Management Personnel: The Workers

In our analysis of the firm into several parts, we have deliberately ignored those workers who are not part of the firm's management structure. They are normally distinguished from management personnel because they are paid hourly rates instead of salaries. In most large, diffused-ownership firms, these workers are members of labor unions which represent them in collective bargaining with management. It is already a well-accepted tenet in economic theory that union leaders and members are not motivated by profit maximization for the firm which employs them. For this reason, we believe that unionized workers (and perhaps even non-unionized workers) should be considered as factors of production hired by the firm rather than constituent parts of it.

VI. SUMMARY

1. We have proposed a modified theory of the firm to explain the behavior of large, diffused-ownership firms, which we refer to as *large managerial* firms. This theory assumes that ownership and management are essentially separate, and that each such firm is so large that its management hierarchy contains at least three types of managers: top, middle, and lower. We postulate that both owners and managers act in their own self-interest by pursuing the following goals:

a) Owners are basically *satisficers* who desire uninterrupted dividends and a steady rise in the price of the firm's stock. Their remoteness from the firm's actual affairs makes it impossible for them to press for profit-maximizing behavior.

b) Managers are "economic men" who *desire to maximize their own lifetime incomes* (which includes both monetary and non-monetary elements), principally by obtaining rapid promotions as a result of pleasing their superiors in the firm.

2. The behavior of large managerial firms deviates from the profit maximization posited by the traditional theory of the firm for the following reasons:

a) The large size of such firms requires them to develop *bureaucratic management* structures which cannot be perfectly controlled by the men in charge of them. In particular, these structures tend to (*i*) provide biased information to top management which reflects its own desires and ideas too strongly and (*ii*) only partially carry out the orders issued by top management. These tendencies cause systematic deviations from whatever goals the organization is ostensibly pursuing. They exist in large owner-managed firms as well as large managerial firms, since they result from sheer size. In essence, such deviations are caused by divergences of goals *within* management; that is, between middle and lower management on the one hand and top management on the other. These goal divergences are able to influence the firm's behavior because large size both compels top managers to delegate authority to their subordinates and prevents them from checking up completely on how that authority is used. This behavior of the firm which is not optimal from the viewpoint of the top man can be caused *either* by size alone (technical inefficiency) or by a combination of size and divergent goals (technical plus motivational inefficiency).

b) The separation of ownership and management limits owners to being satisficers instead of maximizers; hence managers aim at achieving steady growth of earning plus gradually rising stock prices instead of maximum profits. As a result, large managerial firms are more cautious; spend less on "crash" research programs; experience less variability of profits; have larger expense accounts; evidence more conciliation in dealings with government, unions, and the public; and probably grow more slowly than they would if they sought to maximize profits. In essence, these outcomes result from the divergence of goals *between* owners and top management set forth in paragraph 1 above. The size and structure of the firm both compel owners to delegate authority to top management and prevent them from checking up fully on its performance or imposing their own goals upon top management.

4

THE MOTIVATIONAL BASIS OF ORGANIZATIONAL BEHAVIOR[*]

DANIEL KATZ

The basic problem to which I shall address myself is how people are tied into social and organizational structures so that they become effective functioning units of social systems. What is the nature of their involvement in a system or their commitment to it?

The major input into social organizations consists of people. The economist or the culturologist may concentrate on inputs of resources, raw materials, technology. To the extent that human factors are recognized, they are assumed to be constants in the total equation and are neglected. At the practical level, however, as well as for a more precise theoretical accounting, we need to cope with such organizational realities as the attracting of people into organizations, holding them within the system, insuring reliable role performance, and in addition stimulating actions which are generally facilitative of organizational accomplishment. The material and psychic returns to organizational members thus constitute major determinants, not only of the level of effectiveness of organizational functioning, but of the very existence of the organization.

The complexities of motivational problems in organizations can be understood if we develop an analytic framework which will be comprehensive enough to identify the major sources of variance and detailed enough to contain sufficient specification for predictive purposes. The framework we propose calls for three steps in an analysis process, namely, the formulation of answers to these types of questions: (1) What are the types of behavior required for effective organizational functioning? Any organization will require not one, but several patterns of behavior from most of its members. And the motivational bases of these various behavioral requirements may differ. (2) What are the motivational patterns which are used and which can be used in organizational settings? How do they differ in their logic and psycho-logic? What are the differential consequences of the various types of motivational patterns for the behavioral requirements essential for organizational functioning? One motivational pattern may be very effective in bringing about one type of necessary behavior and completely ineffective in leading to another. (3) What are the conditions for eliciting a given motivational pattern in an organizational setting? We may be able to identify the type of motivation we think most appropriate for producing a given behavioral outcome but we still need to know how this motive can be aroused or produced in the organization (Katz, 1962).

[*]*Behavioral Science,* April 1964, pp. 131-146.

BEHAVIORAL REQUIREMENTS

Our major dependent variables are the behavioral requirements of the organization. Three basic types of behavior are essential for a functioning organization: (1) People must be induced to enter and remain within the system. (2) They must carry out their role assignments in a dependable fashion. (3) There must be innovative and spontaneous activity in achieving organizational objectives which go beyond the role specifications.

Attracting and Holding People in a System

First of all, sufficient personnel must be kept within the system to man its essential functions. People thus must be induced to enter the system at a sufficiently rapid rate to counteract the amount of defection. High turnover is costly. Moreover, there is some optimum period for their staying within the system. And while they are members of the system they must validate their membership by constant attendance. Turnover and absenteeism are both measures of organizational effectiveness and productivity, though they are partial measures. People may, of course, be within the system physically but may be psychological absentees. The child may be regular and punctual in his school attendance and yet daydream in his classes. It is not enough, then, to hold people within a system.

Dependable Role Performance

The great range of variable human behavior must be reduced to a limited number of predictable patterns. In other words, the assigned roles must be carried out and must meet some minimal level of quantity and quality of performance. A common measure of productivity is the amount of work turned out by the individual or by the group carrying out their assigned tasks. Quality of performance is not as easily measured and the problem is met by quality controls which set minimal standards for the pieces of work samples. In general, the major role of the member is clearly set forth by organizational protocol and leadership. The man on the assembly line, the nurse in the hospital, the teacher in the elementary school all know what their major job is. To do a lot of it and to do it well are, then, the most conspicuous behavioral requirements of the organization. It may be, of course, that given role requirements are not functionally related to organizational accomplishment. This is a different type of problem and we are recognizing here only the fact that some major role requirements are necessary.

Innovative and Spontaneous Behavior

A neglected set of requirements consists of those actions not specified by role prescriptions which nevertheless facilitate the accomplishment of organizational goals. The great paradox of a social organization is that it must not only reduce human variability to insure reliable role performance but that it must also allow room for some variability and in fact encourage it.

There must always be a supportive number of actions of an innovative or relatively spontaneous sort. No organizational planning can foresee all contingencies within its operations, or can anticipate with perfect accuracy, all environmental changes, or can control perfectly all human variability. The resources of people in innovation, in spontaneous co-operation, in protective and creative behavior are thus vital to organizational survival and effectiveness. An organization which depends solely upon its blueprints of prescribed behavior is a very fragile social system.

Cooperation

The patterned activity which makes up an organization is so intrinsically a co-operative set of interrelationships, that we are not aware of the co-operative nexus any more than we are of any habitual behavior like walking. Within every work group in a factory, within any division in a government bureau, or within any department of a university are countless acts of co-operation without which the system would break down. We take these everyday acts for granted, and few, if any, of them form the role prescriptions for any job. One man will call the attention of his companion on the next machine to some indication that his machine is getting jammed, or will pass along some tool that his companion needs, or will borrow some bit of material he is short of. Or men will come to the aid of a fellow who is behind on his quota. In a study of clerical workers in an insurance company one of the two factors differentiating high-producing from low-producing sections was the greater co-operative activity of the girls in the high-producing sections coming to one another's help in meeting production quotas (Katz, Maccoby, & Morse, 1950). In most factories specialization develops around informal types of help. One man will be expert in first aid, another will be expert in machine diagnosis, etc. We recognize the need for co-operative relationships by raising this specific question when a man is considered for a job. How well does he relate to his fellows, is he a good team man, will he fit in?

Protection

Another subcategory of behavior facilitative of organizational functioning is the action which protects the organization against disaster. There is nothing in the role prescriptions of the worker which specifies that he be on the alert to save life and property in the organization. Yet the worker who goes out of his way to remove the boulder accidentally lodged in the path of a freight car on the railway spur, or to secure a rampant piece of machinery, or even to disobey orders when they obviously are wrong and dangerous, is an invaluable man for the organization.

Constructive Ideas

Another subcategory of acts beyond the line of duty consists of creative suggestions for the improvement of methods of production or of maintenance. Some organizations encourage their members to feed constructive suggestions into the system, but coming up with good ideas for the organization and formulating them to management is not the typical role of the worker. An organization that can stimulate its members to contribute ideas for organizational improvement is a more effective organization in that people who are close to operating problems can often furnish informative suggestions about such operations. The system which does not have this stream of contributions from its members is not utilizing its potential resources effectively.

Self-Training

Still another subcategory under the heading of behavior beyond the call of duty concerns the self-training of members for doing their own jobs better and self-education for assuming more responsible positions in the organization. There may be no requirement that men prepare themselves for better positions. But the organization which has men spending their own time to master knowledge and skills for more responsible jobs in the system has an additional resource for effective functioning.

Favorable Attitude

Finally, members of a group can contribute to its operations by helping to create a favorable climate for it in the community, or communities, which surround the organization. Employees may talk to friends, relatives, and acquaintances about the excellent or the poor qualities of the company for which they work. A favorable climate may help in problems of recruitment, and sometimes product disposal.

In short, for effective organizational functioning many members must be willing on occasion to do more than their job prescriptions specify. If the system were to follow the letter of the law according to job descriptions and protocol, it would soon grind to a halt. There have to be many actions of mutual co-operation and many anticipations of organizational objectives to make the system viable.

Now these three major types of behavior, and even the subcategories, though related, are not necessarily motivated by the same drives and needs. The motivational pattern that will attract and hold people to an organization is not necessarily the same as that which will lead to higher productivity. Nor are the motives which make for higher productivity invariably the same as those which sustain co-operative interrelationships in the interests of organizational accomplishment. Hence, when we speak about organizational practices and procedures which will further the attainment of its mission, we need to specify the type of behavioral requirement involved.

TYPES OF MOTIVATIONAL PATTERNS

It is profitable to consider the possible motivational patterns in organizations under six major headings. Before considering their specific modes of operation and their effects, let me briefly describe the six motivational patterns which seem most relevant. These patterns are: (1) conformity to legal norms or rule compliance; (2) instrumental system rewards; (3) instrumental individual rewards; (4) intrinsic satisfaction from role performance; (5) internalization of organizational goals and values; and (6) involvement in primary-group relationships.

Rule Compliance òr Conformity to System Norms. Conformity constitutes a significant motivational basis for certain types of organizational behavior. Though people may conform for different reasons I am concerned here with one common type of reason, namely a generalized acceptance of the rules of the game. Once people enter a system they accept the fact that membership in the system means complying with its legitimate rules. In our culture we build up during the course of the socialization process a generalized expectation of conforming to the recognized rules of the game if we want to remain in the game. We develop a role readiness, i.e., a readiness to play almost any given role according to the established norms in those systems in which we become involved.

Instrumental System Rewards. These are the benefits which accrue to individuals by virtue of their membership in the system. They are the across-the-board rewards which apply to all people in a given classification in an organization. Examples would be the fringe benefits, the recreational facilities, and the working conditions which are available to all members of the system or subsystem. These rewards are instrumental in that they provide incentives for entering and remaining in the system and thus are instrumental for the need satisfaction of people.

Instrumental Reward Geared to Individual Effort or Performance. System rewards apply in blanket fashion to all members of a subsystem. Individual rewards of an instrumental character are attained by differential performance. For example, the piece rate in industry or the singling out of individuals for honors for their specific contributions would fall into this category of instrumental individual rewards.

Intrinsic Satisfactions Accruing from Specific Role Performance. Here the gratification comes not because the activity leads to or is instrumental to other satisfactions such as earning more money but because the activity is gratifying in itself. The individual may find his work so interesting or so much the type of thing he really wants to do that it would take a heavy financial inducement to shift to a job less congenial to his interests. It is difficult to get professors in many universities to take administrative posts such as departmental chairmanships or deanships because so many of them prefer teaching and research. This motivational pattern has to do with the opportunities which the organizational role provides for the expressions of the skills and talents of the individual.

Internalized Values of the Individual that Embrace the Goals of the Organization. Here the individual again finds his organizational behavior rewarding in itself, not so much because his job gives him a chance to express his skill, but because he has taken over the goals of the organization as his own. The person who derives his gratifications from being a good teacher could be equally happy in teaching in many institutions but unhappy as an administrator in any one. The person who has identified himself with the goals of his own particular university and its specific problems, potentialities, and progress wants to stay on at his university and, moreover, is willing to accept other assignments than a teaching assignment.

Social Satisfactions Derived from Primary-Group Relationships. This is an important source of gratification for organizational members. One of the things people miss most when they have to withdraw from organizations is the sharing of experiences with like-minded colleagues, the belonging to a group with which they have become identified. Whether or not these social staisfactions become channelled for organizational objectives leads us to a consideration of the two basic questions with which we started: (1) What are the consequences of these motivational patterns for the various organizational requirements of holding people in the system, maximizing their role performances, and stimulating innovative behavior? and (2) What are the conditions under which these patterns will lead to a given organizational outcome?

MOTIVATIONAL PATTERNS: CONSEQUENCES AND CONDITIONS

Compliance with Legitimized Rules

In discussing bureaucratic functioning Max Weber pointed out that the acceptance of legal rules was the basis for much of organizational behavior (Weber, 1947). Compliance is to some extent a function of sanctions but to a greater extent a function of generalized habits and attitudes toward symbols of authority. In other words, for the citizen of modern society the observance of legitimized rules has become a generalized value. A great deal of behavior can be predicted once we know what the rules of the game are. It is not necessary to take representative samplings of the behavior of many people to know how people will conduct themselves in structured situations. All we need is a single informant who can tell us the legitimate norms and appropriate symbols of authority for given types of behavioral settings. Individuals often assume that they can control their participation with respect to organizational requirements when they enter an organization. Before they are aware of it, however, they are acting like other organizational members and complying with the rules and the authorized decisions.

The major impact of compliance with the legitimate rules of the organization primarily concerns only one type of organizational requirement, namely reliable role performance. The way in which any given role occupant is to perform in carrying out his job can be determined by the rules of the organization. But individuals cannot be held in the system by rule enforcement save for exceptions like the armed services. Nor can innovative behavior and actions beyond the call of duty be prescribed.

Though compliance with legitimate rules is effective for insuring reliable role performance it operates to insure minimal observance of role requirements. In other words, the minimal standards for quantity and quality of work soon become the maximum standards. The logic of meeting legal norms is to avoid infractions of the rules and not to go beyond their requirements, for as Allport has pointed out (1934), it is difficult, if not impossible, to be more proper than proper. Why, however, cannot the legal norms be set to require high standards with respect to both quantity and quality of production? Why cannot higher production be legislated? It can, but there is an important force working against such raising of standards by changing rules. The rule which sets a performance standard in a large organization is also setting a uniform standard for large numbers of people. Hence it must be geared to what the great majority are prepared to do. If not, there will be so many defections that the rule itself will break down. Timing of jobs in industry illustrates this principle. Management does not want a loose standard, but if the standards are set so that many workers can meet them only with difficulty, management is in for trouble.

In the third area of behavior necessary for effective organizational functioning, namely innovative and spontaneous acts which go beyond the call of duty, rule compliance is useless by definition. There can be exceptions, in that rules can be devised to reward unusual behavior under specified conditions. The army, for example, will move the man who has pulled off a brilliant military exploit from a court martial to a court of honors. Though such exceptions may occur, organizations cannot stimulate innovative actions by decreeing them. In general the greater the emphasis upon compliance with rules the less the motivation will be for individuals to do more than is specified by their role prescriptions. The great weakness of a system run according to rules is the lack of the corrective factor of human enterprise and spontaneity when something goes wrong. Two years ago in a hospital in New York State several infants died because salt rather than sugar was put into the formula. The large container for sugar had been erroneously filled with salt. The tragic fact was that day after day for about a week the nurses fed the babies milk saturated with salt in spite of the fact that the infants reacted violently to the food, crying and vomiting after each feeding session. But the hospital continued poisoning the children until many of them died. Not a single nurse, attendant, supervisor, or person connected with the nursery tasted the milk to see what was wrong. The error was discovered only when a hospital employee broke a rule and used some of the substance in the sugar container in her own coffee.

Conditions Conducive to the Activation of Rule Acceptance

Though compliance with rules can bring about reliable role performance, the use of rules must take account of the following three conditions for maximum effectiveness: (1) the appropriateness of the symbols of authority and the relevance of rules to the social system involved: (2) the clarity of the legal norms and rule structure; and (3) the reinforcing character of sanctions.

Appropriateness and Relevance. The acceptance of communications and directives on the basis of legitimacy requires the use of symbols and procedures recognized as the proper and appropriate sources of authority in the system under consideration. The worker may grumble at the foreman's order but he recognizes the right of the foreman to give such an order. The particular directives which are accepted as legitimate will depend upon their matching the type of authority structure of the system. The civilian in the army with officer status, uniform, and unassimilated rank is not accepted by the enlisted man as the proper giver of orders. In a representative democracy a policy decision of an administrator may be rejected since it lacks the legal stamp of the accepted procedures of the system. An industrial company may have a contract with a union that changes in the speed of the assembly line have to be agreed to by both organizations. The workers accordingly will accept a speedup in the line if it is sanctioned by the union-management agreement, but not if it is the work of a foreman attempting to impress his superiors.

The acceptance of legal rules is also restricted to the relevant sphere of activity. Union policy as formulated in its authority structure is binding upon its members only as it relates to relations with the company. The edicts of union officials on matters of desegregation or of support of political parties are not necessarily seen as legal compulsions by union members. In similar fashion, employees do not regard the jurisdiction of the company as applying to their private lives outside the plant. And areas of private behavior and personal taste are regarded in our democratic society as outside the realm of coercive laws. The most spectacular instance of the violation of a national law occurred in the case of the Volstead Act. While people were willing to accept laws about the social consequences resulting from drinking, such as reckless driving, many of them were not willing to accept the notion that their private lives were subject to federal regulation.

Another prerequisite to the use of rules as the appropriate norms of the system is their impersonal character. They are the rules of the system and are not the arbitrary, capricious decisions of a superior aimed at particular individuals. The equivalents of bills of attainder in an organization undermine rule compliance. We speak of the officiousness of given individuals in positions of authority when they use their rank in an arbitrary and personal fashion.

Clarity. A related condition for the acceptance of legal norms is the clarity of authority symbols, of proper procedures, and the content of the legitimized decisions. Lack of clarity can be due to the vagueness of the stimulus situation or to the conflict between opposed stimulus cues. In some organizations, symbols of authority are sharply enough defined, but the relationship between competing symbols may lack such clarity of definition. One difficulty of using group decision in limited areas in an otherwise authoritarian structure is that group members may not perceive the democratic procedure as legitimized by the structure. They will question the compelling effect of any decisions they reach. And often they may be right. Moreover, the procedure for the exercise of power may not be consistent with the type of authority structure. The classic case is that *of ordering* a people to be democratic.

Specific laws can be ambiguous in their substance. They can be so complex, so technical, or so obscure that people will not know what the law is. The multiplication of technical rulings and the patchwork of legislation with respect to tax structure means that while people may feel some internal compulsion to pay taxes, they also feel they should pay as little as they can without risking legal prosecution. A counter dynamic will arise to the tendency to comply with legal requirements, namely, the use of legal loopholes to defy the spirit of the law. Any complex maze of rules in an organization will be utilized by the guardhouse lawyers in the system to their own advantage.

Though our argument has been that legal compliance makes for role performance rather than for holding people in a system, the clarity of a situation with well-defined rules is often urged as a condition making for system attractiveness. People know what is expected of them and what they should expect in turn from others, and they much prefer this clarity to a state of uncertainty and ambiguity. There is merit in this contention, but it does not take into account all the relevant variables. The armed services were not able to hold personnel after World War II, and recruitment into systems characterized by rules and regulations is traditionally difficult in the United States. The mere multiplication of rules does not produce clarity. Even when certainty and clarity prevail they are not relished if it means that individuals are certain only of nonadvancement and restrictions on their behavior.

In brief, the essence of legal compliance rests upon the psychological belief that there are specific imperatives or laws which all good citizens obey. If there is doubt about what the imperative is, if there are many varying interpretations, then the law is not seen as having a character of its own but as the means for obtaining individual advantage. To this extent, the legitimacy basis of compliance is undermined.

Reinforcement. To maintain the internalized acceptance of legitimate authority there has to be some reinforcement in the form of penalties for violation of the rules. If there is no policing of laws governing speeding, speed limits will lose their force over time for many people. Sometimes the penalties can come from the social disapproval of the group as well as from legal penalties. But the very concept of law as an imperative binding upon everyone in the system requires penalties for violation either from above or below. Where there is no enforcement by authorities and no sanctions for infractions from the group itself, the rule in question becomes a dead letter.

Instrumental System Rewards

It is important to distinguish between rewards which are administered in relation to individual effort and performance and the system rewards which accrue to people by virtue of their membership in the system. In the former category would belong piece-rate incentives, promotion for outstanding performance, or any special recognition bestowed in acknowledgment of differential contributions to organizational functioning. In the category of system rewards would go fringe benefits, recreational facilities, cost of living raises, across-the-board upgrading, job security save for those guilty of moral turpitude, pleasant working conditions. System rewards differ, then, from individual rewards in that they are not allocated on the basis of differential effort and performance but on the basis of membership in the system. The major differentiation for system rewards is seniority in the system—a higher pension for thirty years of service than for twenty years of service. Management will often overlook the distinction between individual and system rewards and will operate as if rewards administered across the board were the same in their effects as individual rewards.

System rewards are more effective for holding members within the organization than for maximizing other organizational behaviors. Since the rewards are distributed on the basis of length of tenure in the system, people will want to stay with an attractive setup which becomes increasingly attractive over time. Again the limiting factor is the competition with the relative attraction of other systems. As the system increases its attractions, other things being equal, it should reduce its problems of turnover. In fact, it may sometimes have the problem of too low turnover with too many poorly motivated people staying on until retirement.

System rewards will not, however, lead to higher quality of work or greater quantity than the minimum required to stay in the organization. Since rewards are given across-the-board to all members or differentially to them in terms of their seniority, they are not motivated to do more than meet the standards for remaining in the system. It is sometimes assumed that the liking for the organization created by system rewards will generalize to greater productive effort within the system. Such generalization of motivation may occur to a very limited extent, but it is not a reliable basis for the expectation of higher productivity. Management may expect gratitude from workers because it has added some special fringe benefit or some new recreational facility. The more likely outcome is that employees will feel more desirous of staying in an enterprise with such advantages than of working harder for the company for the next twelve months.

System rewards will do little, moreover, to motivate performance beyond the line of duty, with two possible exceptions. Since people may develop a liking for the attractions of the organization they may be in a more favorable mood to reciprocate in co-operative relations with their fellows toward organizational goals, provided that the initiation of task-oriented co-operation comes from some other source. Otherwise, they may just be co-operative with respect to taking advantage of the system's attractions, such as the new bowling alley. Another possible consequence of system rewards for activity supportive of organizational goals is the favorable climate of opinion for the system in the external environment to which the members contribute. It may be easier for a company to recruit personnel in a community in which their employees have talked about what a good place it is to work.

Though the effects of system rewards are to maintain the level of productivity not much above the minimum required to stay in the system, there still may be large differences between systems with respect to the quantity and quality of production as a function of system rewards. An organization with substantially better wage rates and fringe benefits than its competitors may be able to set a higher level of performance as a minimal requirement for its workers than the other firms and still hold its employees. In other words, system rewards can be related to the differential productivity of organizations as a whole, though they are not effective in maximizing the potential contributions of the majority of individuals within the organization. They may account for differences in motivation between systems rather than for differences in motivation between individuals in the same system. They operate through their effects upon the minimal standards for all people in the system. They act indirectly in that their effect is to make people want to stay in the organization; to do so people must be willing to accept the legitimately derived standards of role performance in that system. Hence, the direct mechanism for insuring performance is compliance with legitimacy, but the legal requirements of the organization will not hold members if their demands are too great with respect to the demands of other organizations. The mediating variable in accounting for organizational differences based upon system rewards is the relative attractiveness of the system for the individual compared to other available systems in relation to the effort requirements of the system. If the individual has the choice of a job with another company in the same community which requires a little more effort but offers much greater system rewards in the way of wages and other benefits, he will in all probability take it. If, however, the higher requirements of the competing system are accompanied by very modest increases in system rewards, he will probably stay where he is.

Conditions Conducive to Effective System Rewards

We have just described one of the essential conditions for making system rewards effective in calling attention to the need to make the system as attractive as competing systems which are realistic alternatives for the individual. In this context seniority becomes an important organizational principle in that the member can acquire more of the rewards of the system the longer he stays in it. The present trends to permit the transfer of fringe benefits of all types across systems undercuts the advantages to any one system of length of membership in it, though of course there are other advantages to permitting people to retain their investment in seniority when they move across systems.

Another condition which is important for the effective use of system rewards is their uniform application for all members of the system or for major groupings within the system. People will perceive as inequitable distinctions in amounts of rewards which go to members by virtue of their membership in the system where such differences favor some groups over other groups. Management is frequently surprised by resentment of differential system rewards when there has been no corresponding resentment of differential individual rewards. One public utility, for example, inaugurated an attractive retirement system for its employees before fringe benefits were the acceptable pattern. Its employees were objectively much better off because of the new benefits and yet the most hated feature about the whole company was the retirement system. Employee complaints centered on two issues: years of employment in the company before the age of thirty did not count toward retirement pensions, and company officials could retire on livable incomes because of their higher salaries. The employees felt intensely that if they were being rewarded for service to the company it was unfair to rule out years of service before age thirty. This provision gave no recognition for the man who started for the company at age twenty compared to the one who started at age thirty. Moreover, the workers felt a lifetime of service to the company should enable them to retire on a livable income just as it made this possible for company officials. The company house organ directed considerable space over a few years to showing how much the worker actually benefited from the plan, as in fact was the case. On the occasion of a company-wide survey, this campaign was found to have had little effect. The most common complaint still focused about the patent unfairness of the retirement system.

The critical point, then, is that system rewards have a logic of their own. Since they accrue to people by virtue of their membership or length of service in an organization, they will be perceived as inequitable if they are not uniformly administered. The perception of the organization member is that all members are equal in their access to organizational benefits. Office employees will not be upset by differences in individual reward for differences in responsibility. If, however, their organization gives them free meals in a cafeteria and sets aside a special dining room for their bosses, many of them will be upset. In our culture we accept individual differences in income but we do not accept differences in classes of citizenship. To be a member of an organization is to be a citizen in that community, and all citizens are equal in their membership rights. A university which does not extend the same tenure rights and the same fringe benefits accorded its teaching staff to its research workers may have a morale problem on its hands.

Instrumental Individual Rewards

The traditional philosophy of the free-enterprise system gives priority to an individual reward system based upon the quality and quantity of the individual effort and contribution. This type of motivation may operate effectively for the entrepreneur or even for the small organization with considerable independence of its supporting environment. It encounters great difficulties, however, in its application to large organizations which are in nature highly interdependent co-operative structures. We shall examine these difficulties in analyzing the conditions under which individual rewards of an instrumental character are effective.

Basically the monetary and recognition rewards to the individual for his organizational performance are directed at a high level of quality and quantity of work. In other words, they can be applied most readily to obtain optimal role performance rather than to innovative and non-specific organizational needs. They may also help to hold the individual in the organization, if he feels that his differential efforts are properly recognized. Nonetheless there is less generalization, or rubbing off, of an instrumental individual reward to love for the organization than might be anticipated. If another organization offers higher individual rewards to a person, his own institution may have to match the offer to hold him.

Individual rewards are difficult to apply to contributions to organizational functioning which are not part of the role requirements. Spectacular instances of innovative behavior can be singled out for recognition and awards. In the armed services, heroism beyond the call of duty is the basis for medals and decorations, but the everyday co-operative activities which keep an organization from falling apart are more difficult to recognize and reward. Creative suggestions for organizational improvement are sometimes encouraged through substantial financial rewards for employees' suggestions. The experience with suggestion systems of this sort has not been uniformly positive though under special conditions they have proved of value.

Conditions Conducive to Effective Individual Instrumental Rewards

If rewards such as pay incentives are to work as they are intended they must meet three primary conditions. (1) They must be clearly perceived as large enough in amount to justify the additional effort required to obtain them. (2) They must be perceived as directly related to the required performance and follow directly on its accomplishment. (3) They must be perceived as equitable by the majority of system members many of whom will not receive them. These conditions suggest some of the reasons why individual rewards can work so well in some situations and yet be so difficult of application in large organizations. The facts are that most enterprises have not been able to use incentive pay, or piece rates, as reliable methods for raising the quality and quantity of production (McGregor, 1960).

In terms of the first criterion many companies have attempted incentive pay without making the differential between increased effort and increased reward proportional from the point of view of the worker. If he can double his pay by working at a considerably increased tempo, that is one thing. But if such increased expenditure means a possible 10 per cent increase, that is another. Moreover, there is the tradition among workers, and it is not without some factual basis, that management cannot be relied upon to maintain a high rate of pay for those making considerably more than the standard and that their increased efforts will only result in their "being sweated." There is, then, the temporal dimension of whether the piece rates which seem attractive today will be maintained tomorrow.

More significant, however, is the fact that a large-scale organization consists of many people engaging in similar and inter-dependent tasks. The work of any one man is highly dependent upon what his colleagues are doing. Hence individual piece rates are difficult to apply on any equitable basis. Group incentives are more logical, but as the size of the interdependent group grows, we move toward system rather than toward individual rewards. Moreover, in large-scale production enterprises the role performance is controlled by the tempo of the machines and their co-ordination. The speed of the worker on the assembly line is not determined by his decision but by the speed of the assembly line. An individual piece-rate just does not accord with the systemic nature of the co-ordinated collectivity. Motivational factors about the amount of effort to be expended on the job enter the picture not on the floor of the factory but during the negotiations of the union and management about the manning of a particular assembly line. Heads of corporations may believe in the philosophy of individual enterprise, but when they deal with reward systems in their own organizations they become realists and accept the pragmatic notion of collective rewards.

Since there is such a high degree of collective interdependence among rank-and-file workers the attempts to use individual rewards are often perceived as inequitable. Informal norms develop to protect the group against efforts which are seen as divisive or exploitive. Differential rates for subsystems within the organization will be accepted much more than invidious distinctions within the same subgrouping. Hence promotion or upgrading may be the most potent type of individual reward. The employee is rewarded by being moved to a different category of workers on a better pay schedule. Some of the same problems apply, of course, to this type of reward. Since differential performance is difficult to assess in assembly-type operations, promotion is often based upon such criteria as conformity to company requirements with respect to attendance and absenteeism, observance of rules, and seniority. None of these criteria are related to individual performance on the job. Moreover, promotion is greatly limited by the technical and professional education of the worker.

It is true, of course, that many organizations are not assembly-line operations, and even for those which are, the conditions described here do not apply to the upper echelons. Thus General Motors can follow a policy of high individual rewards to division managers based upon the profits achieved by a given division. A university can increase the amount of research productivity of its staff by making publication the essential criterion for promotion. In general, where assessment of individual performance is feasible and where the basis of the reward system is clear, instrumental individual rewards can play an important part in raising productivity.

Intrinsic Job Satisfaction

The motivational pathway to high productivity and to high-quality production can be reached through the development of intrinsic job satisfaction. The man who finds the type of work he delights in doing is the man who will not worry about the fact that the role requires a given amount of production of a certain quality. His gratifications accrue from accomplishment, from the expression of his own abilities, from the exercise of his own decisions. Craftsmanship was the old term to refer to the skilled performer who was high in intrinsic job satisfaction. This type of performer is not the clock watcher, nor the shoddy performer. On the other hand, such a person is not necessarily tied to a given organization. As a good carpenter or a good mechanic, it may matter little to him where he does work, provided that he is given ample opportunity to do the kind of job he is interested in doing. He may, moreover, contribute little to organizational goals beyond his specific role.

Conditions Conducive to Arousal of Intrinsic Job Satisfaction

If intrinsic job satisfaction or identification with the work is to be aroused and maximized, then the job itself must provide sufficient variety, sufficient complexity, sufficient challenge, and sufficient skill to engage the abilities of the worker. If there is one confirmed finding in all the studies of worker morale and satisfaction, it is the correlation between the variety and challenge of the job and the gratifications which accrue to workers (Morse, 1953). There are, of course, people who do not want more responsibility and people who become demoralized by being placed in jobs which are too difficult for them. These are, however, the exceptions. By and large people seek more responsibility, more skill-demanding jobs than they hold, and as they are able to attain these more demanding jobs, they become happier and better adjusted. Obviously, the condition for securing higher motivation to produce, and to produce quality work, necessitates changes in organizational structure—specifically job enlargement rather than job fractionation. And yet the tendency in large-scale organizations is toward increasing specialization and routinization of jobs. Workers would be better motivated toward higher individual production and toward better quality work if we discarded the assembly line and moved toward the craftsmanlike operations of the old Rolls Royce type of production. Industry has demonstrated, however, that it is more efficient to produce via assembly-line methods with lowered motivation and job satisfaction than with highly motivated craftsmen with a large area of responsibility in turning out their part of the total product. The preferred path to the attainment of production goals in turning out cars or other mass physical products is, then, the path of organizational controls and not the path of internalized motivation. The quality of production may suffer somewhat, but it is still cheaper to buy several mass-produced cars, allowing for programming for obsolescence, than it is to buy a single quality product like the Rolls Royce.

In the production of physical objects intended for mass consumption, the assembly line may furnish the best model. This may also apply to service operations in which the process can be sufficiently simplified to provide service to masses of consumers. When, however, we move to organizations which have the modifications of human being as their product, as in educational institutions, or when we deal with treating basic problems of human beings, as in hospital, clinics, and remedial institutions, we do not want to rely solely upon an organizational control to guarantee minimum effort of employees. We want employees with high motivation and high identification with their jobs. Jobs cannot profitably be fractionated very far and standardized and co-ordinated to a rigorous time schedule in a research laboratory, in a medical clinic, in an educational institution, or in a hospital.

In addition to the recognition of the inapplicability of organizational devices of the factory and the army to all organizations, it is also true that not all factory operations can be left to institutional controls without regard to the motivations of employees. It frequently happens that job fractionation can be pushed to the point of diminishing returns even in industry. The success of the Tavistock workers in raising productivity in the British coal mines through job enlargement was due to the fact that the specialization of American long-wall methods of coal mining did not yield adequate returns when applied to the difficult and variable conditions under which British miners had to operate (Trist & Bamforth, 1951). The question of whether to move toward greater specialization and standardization in an industrial operation or whether to move in the opposite direction is generally an empirical one to be answered by research. One rule of thumb can be applied, however. If the job can be so simplified and standardized that it is readily convertible to automated machines, then the direction to take is that of further institutionalization until automation is possible. If, however, the over-all performance requires complex judgment, the differential weighing of factors which are not markedly identifiable, or creativity, then the human mind is a far superior instrument to the computer.

The paradox is that where automation is feasible, it can actually increase the motivational potential among the employees who are left on the job after the changeover. Mann and Hoffman (1960) conclude from their study of automation in an electric power plant that the remaining jobs for workers can be more interesting, that there can be freer association among colleagues, and that the elimination of supervisory levels brings the top and bottom of the organization closer together.

Internalization of Organizational Goals and Values

The pattern of motivation associated with value expression and self-identification has great potentialities for the internalization of the goals of subsystems and of the total system, and thus for the activation of behavior not prescribed by specific roles. Where this pattern prevails individuals take over organizational objectives as part of their own personal goals. They identify not with the organization as a safe and secure haven but with its major purposes. The internalization of organizational objectives is generally confined to the upper echelons or to the officer personnel. In voluntary organizations it extends into some of the rank-and-file, and in fact most voluntary organizations need a core of dedicated people—who are generally referred to as the dedicated damn fools.

Now the internalization of organizational goals is not as common as two types of more partial internalization. The first has to do with some general organizational purposes which are not unique to the organization. A scientist may have internalized some of the research values of his profession but not necessarily of the specific institution to which he is attached. As long as he stays in that institution, he may be a well-motivated worker. But he may find it just as easy to work for the things he believes in in another institution. There is not the same set of alternative organizations open to liberals who are political activists and who are part of the core of dedicated damn fools in the Democratic party. They have no other place to go, so they find some way of rationalizing the party's deviation from their liberal ideals.

A second type of partial internalization concerns the values and goals of a sub-system of the organization. It is often easier for the person to take over the values of his own unit. We may be attached to our own department in a university more than to the goals of the university as a whole.

Conditions Conducive to Internalization of System Goals

Internalization of organization objectives can come about through the utilization of the socialization process in childhood or through the adult socialization which takes place in the organization itself. In the first instance, the selective process, either by the person or the organization, matches the personality with the system. A youngster growing up in the tradition of one of the military services may have always thought of himself as an Air Force officer. Similarly, the crusader for civil liberties and the American Civil Liberties Union find one another.

The adult socialization process in the organization can build upon the personal values of its members and integrate them about an attractive model of its ideals. People can thus identify with the organizational mission. If the task of an organization has emotional significance, the organization enjoys an advantage in the creation of an attractive image. If the task is attended by hazard, as in the tracking down of criminals by the FBI, or of high adventure, as in the early days of flying, or of high service to humanity, as in a cancer research unit, it is not difficult to develop a convincing model of the organization's mission.

The imaginative leader can also help in the development of an attractive picture of the organization by some new conceptualization of its mission. The police force entrusted with the routine and dirty business of law enforcement carried out by dumb cops and "flatfeet" can be energized by seeing themselves as a corps of professional officers devoted to the highest form of public service. Reality factors limit the innovative use of symbols for the glorification of organizations.

Occupational groups, however, constantly strive to achieve a more attractive picture of themselves, as in the instances of press agents who have become public relations specialists or undertakers who have become morticians.

Internalization of subgroup norms can come about through identification with fellow group members who share the same common fate. People take over the values of their group because they identify with their own kind and see themselves as good group members, and as good group members they model their actions and aspirations in terms of group norms. This subgroup identification can work for organizational objectives only if there is agreement between the group norms and the organizational objectives. Often in industry the norms of the work group are much closer to union objectives than to company objectives.

This suggests three additional factors which contribute to internalization of group objectives: (1) participating in important decisions about group objectives; (2) contributing to group performance in a significant way; and (3) sharing in the rewards of group accomplishment. When these three conditions are met, the individual can regard the group as his, for he in fact has helped to make it.

Social Satisfactions from Primary-Group Relationships

Human beings are social animals and cannot exist in physical or psychological isolation. The stimulation, the approval, and the support they derive from interacting with one another comprise one of the most potent forms of motivation. Strictly speaking, such affiliative motivation is another form of instrumental-reward-seeking, but some if its qualitative aspects are sufficiently different from the instrumental system and individual rewards previously described to warrant separate discussion.

The desire to be part of a group in itself will do no more than hold people in the system. The studies of Elton Mayo and his colleagues during World War II showed that work groups which provided their members social satisfactions had less absenteeism than less cohesive work groups (Mayo & Lombard, 1944). Mann and Baumgartel (1953) corroborated these findings in a study of the Detroit Edison Company. With respect to role performance, moreover, Seashore (1954) has demonstrated that identification with one's work group can make for either above-average or below-average productivity depending upon the norms of the particular group. In the Seashore study the highly-cohesive groups, compared to the low-cohesive groups, moved to either extreme in being above or below the production standards for the company.

Other studies have demonstrated that though the group can provide important socioemotional satisfactions for the members it can also detract from task orientation (Bass, 1960). Members can have such a pleasant time interacting with one another that they neglect their work. Again the critical mediating variable is the character of the values and norms of the group. The affiliative motive can lead to innovative and co-operative behavior, but often this assumes the form of protecting the group rather than maximizing organizational objectives. So the major question in dealing with the affiliative motive is how this motive can be harnessed to organizational goals.

The Likert Theory

What are the conditions under which the cohesive group with all the motivational force of primary-group relationships can gear into organizational goals? There is the possibility that our fifth factor of internalization of organizational objectives can be mediated through identification with sub-groups whose informal norms reflect these purposes. Likert (1962) has devoted his book *New Patterns of Management* to this problem. The Likert thesis is that the factors making for internalization of organizational objectives can be realized by involving all the subgroups of the organization in group decision-making of a task-oriented character. The task orientation is provided by an overlapping set of organizational families and by giving each such family some responsibility in decision-making.

Specifically the Likert theory is based upon four essential concepts: (1) the efficacy of group process in maximizing motivation of organization members; (2) the channeling of this motivation toward group goals by the use of overlapping organizational families; (3) the key role of a member of two families in his linking-pin function; and (4) the development of short feedback cycles through the use of research on the functioning of both the social and the technical system. This theory thus takes account of the hierarchical authority structure of organizations, but also ties in every individual in the organization through his attachment to his own group, and presumably integrates the needs of all sub-groups. For example, the president of an organization can meet with his vice-presidents as the top organizational family, and as a group they can work through problems ordinarily handled by the president alone or by the president meeting individually with his vice-presidents. In turn each vice-president meets with his department heads and again the problems at this level are met through group process, with the vice-president forming the link to top management and interpreting company policy. Department heads meet with their division heads, and so on down the line. When a department head meets with his fellow department heads and their superior, the vice-president, he functions not only as a member of that group but as a representative of his own group of division heads. These meetings take on a task-oriented character, in good part through the continuing use of research and measurement on the group's own activities.

Decisions are made at the level of the structure which is the relevant locus for the amount of organizational space involved. If a decision affects only the people within a subunit, then it should be made in that subunit. Thus top management is relieved of many small decisions which can well be made down the line. Every member of the organization, save at the very top and bottom levels, thus serves as a linking-pin in functioning as a member of two organizational families. The bond between organizational levels is always personally mediated. Every group in the organizational structure has a voice in decision-making. It decides how its task should be implemented. Though its task is set primarily by the level above it, it has some participation at this higher level through its representative.

Problems

There are, however, difficulties with the Likert theory, not because of the nature of the approach but because the approach is not pushed far enough in dealing with the walls of the maze. Specifically, the following problems still remain.

1. The voice of the rank-and-file member of the organization is greatly attenuated in its representation up the line. By the time the ordinary member's voice is reinterpreted through several levels of the organizational structure it may be so faint as to be ghostlike.

2. A related weakness is that the Likert model is primarily directed at the technical and task problems of the organization. The interest-group conflicts in

organizations over the distribution of rewards, privileges, and perquisites between hierarchical levels are difficult to meet in this system of organizational families. In contrast the worker's union, which cuts across all organizational families at the rank-and-file level, is still the worker's best chance of gaining representation of his interests. Legitimate differences in interests between groups may in fact be obscured by an application of the Likert model.

3. Not all motivational problems of the large-scale organization are solved by decisions made in overlapping family groups. The loss of a feeling of worth in an organization when an individual performs a routinized role which can be performed by ten million others or by a machine is still a basic issue. The internalization of organizational goals is not insured by involvement in very limited decisions. In other words, the specialization of labor, the job fractionation, and the alienation of the worker from any meaningful work process are matters of organizational structure which may still prove to be overriding factors in sociotechnical systems.

4. Finally, there is the limitation upon group process when it has to be carefully kept to a limited set of decisions, especially when these limits are imposed upon the group as fixed policies and boundaries. Workers may prefer their own unions, where their elected officers make some of their decisions for them, to their work group where they do not elect their leader and have no voice in larger issues. Group process generates its own dynamic and people involved in it want to go beyond their limited directives. Students who are given disciplinary policies by the university administration and given the task of their implementation soon raise questions about the policies themselves. Representative democracy may be a more powerful organizational form than group process hamstrung by being restricted to means rather than to goals.

REFERENCES

Allport, F. H. The J-curve hypothesis of conforming behavior. *J. soc. Psychol.*, 1934, 5, 141-183.

Bass, B. M. *Leadership, psychology, and organizational behavior.* New York: Harper, 1960.

Katz, D. Human interrelationships and organizational behavior. In S. Mailick and E. H. Van Ness (Eds.), *Concepts and issues in administrative behavior.* New York: Prentice-Hall, 1962. Pp. 166-186.

Katz, D., Maccoby, N., & Morse, Nancy. *Productivity, supervision and morale in an office situation.* Ann Arbor, Mich.: Institute for Social Research, Univ. of Michigan, 1950.

Likert, R. *New patterns of management.* New York: McGraw-Hill, 1961.

Mann, F. C., & Baumgartel, H. J. *Absences and employee attitudes in an electric power company.* Ann Arbor, Mich.: Institute for Social Research, Univ. of Michigan, 1953.

Mann, F. C., & Hoffman, R. L. *Automation and the worker.* New York: Holt, Rinehart and Winston, 1960.

Mayo, E., & Lombard, G. *Teamwork and labor turnover in the aircraft industry of Southern California. Business Res. Studies No. 32.* Cambridge, Mass.: Harvard Univ., 1944.

McGregor, D. *The human side of enterprise.* New York: McGraw-Hill, 1960.

Morse, Nancy. *Satisfactions in the white collar job.* Ann Arbor, Mich.: Institute for

Social Research, Univ. of Michigan, 1953.

Seashore, S. *Group cohesiveness in the industrial work group.* Ann Arbor, Mich.: Institute for Social Research, Univ. of Michigan, 1954.

Trist, E., & Bamforth, K. W. Some social and psychological consequences of the long wall method of coal-getting. *Hum. Relat.,* 1951, 4, 3-38.

Weber, M. *The theory of social and economic organization.* Glencoe, Ill.: Free Press, 1947.

5

IMPLICATIONS OF BEHAVIORAL SCIENCE FOR

MANAGERIAL ACCOUNTING*

JACOB G. BIRNBERG / RAGHU NATH

Accountants have been involved with the behavioral dimension of accounting problems for quite some time. However, that involvement has usually been by default. With this in mind, Carl Devine, in 1960, chastised accountants for failing to become aware of the findings of the behavioral sciences.[1] Too often the behavioral dimension of any accounting problem is discernible only by implication. Even now, in 1967, despite the recent work by several accountants, we are still lagging as a discipline far behind our colleagues in business administration in the application of behavioral science. The wisdom of Devine's position is readily apparent.

The management information system of any firm is not solely a technical communication system, one designed only to permit data to flow from one point in the system (i.e., the firm) to another. Rather, it is intended that the data selected and transmitted both serve as inputs to managers' and workers' decision processes and affect their behavior. It is through this system that top managemen informs and motivates lower levels within the organization.

To design the appropriate management information system, the accountant must ask not only, "What problem is the user trying to solve?" and "What data does the user need to solve it?" but also, "How will the manner and form in which

*The Accounting Review, July 1967, pp. 468-79.

[1]Carl T. Devine "Research Methodology and Accounting Theory Formation," THE ACCOUNTING REVIEW, July 1960, pp. 394-7.

the data are communicated to the user affect his behavior?"[2] In attempting to answer this question, accountants must undertake behavioral research.

This paper will investigate the implications of behavioral science for managerial accounting. The first section will discuss the relevant literature, first by subject matter and later by the research methodology employed. The second section will illustrate some areas where future research by accountants may be fruitful and describe some concepts which may provide us with a better understanding of certain phenomena.

BEHAVIORAL RESEARCH IN ACCOUNTING

The behavioral research in management accounting can be divided into three broad categories:

1. Attempts to specify a model of all or part of the human sub-system
2. Investigations into the behavioral dimension of the management control process
3. Studies from the behavioral point of view of the effect of a firm's characteristics on the form and function of the management information system

Very little research has been done on the form of the relationships between the organization and the individual and its implication for accounting data. Golembiewski viewed the internal reporting system as a function of the traditional organizational structure and concluded that many of the problems of internal reporting, e.g., cost allocation, arise from the traditional line-staff form of organization.[3] A more decentralized form of organization would, he conjectured, ease many of the accounting problems by refocusing the attention of supervisors to other, less arbitrary sets of data. This conclusion is consistent with the suggestions of accountants for the measurement of divisional performance in a decentralized firm.[4]

A second approach to the development of a behavioral model for accounting is suggested by Caplan.[5] It reflects the more general organization models of Simon, and March and Simon, relying heavily on concepts such as bounded rationality and satisficing.[6] He stresses the limitations of the human being as a decision maker and the multiplicity of goals. The appropriateness of this model, like that of Golem-

[2]This is similar to the frequently discussed problem of whether standards ought to be obtainable or unobtainable. *The Accounting Review,* July, 1967, pp. 468-479.

[3]Robert T. Golembiewski, "Accountancy as a Function of Organization Theory," THE ACCOUNTING REVIEW, April 1964, pp. 333-41. Golembiewski draws heavily on the much earlier work of H. A. Simon, Harold Guetzkow, George Kozmetsky, and Gordon Tyndall, *Centralization vs. Decentralization in Organizing the Controller's Department* (New York: Controllership Foundation, 1954).

[4]For example, see Gordon Shillinglaw, "Guides to Internal Profit Measurement," *Harvard Business Review,* March-April 1960, pp. 82-94.

[5]Edward H. Caplan, "Behavioral Assumptions of Management Accounting," THE ACCOUNTING REVIEW, July 1966, pp. 496-509.

[6]For a discussion of this model see, James G. March and Herbert A. Simon, *Organizations* (Wiley, 1958).

biewski, must ultimately be based on the validity and usefulness of the specific hypotheses it generates about the form of the managerial information system.

The third study, which is more general in its approach, is the work of Ijiri, Jaedicke, and Knight.[7] Drawing on essentially the same set of behavioral assumptions as Caplan, they developed a behavioral model of the decision process. Stressing the need to use surrogates in the decision process, they specified the situations where alternative accounting techniques could be expected to lead to confusion on the part of the user. The lack of feedback, the presence of a functional fixation, and an ill-structured environment all can lead to misinterpretation of the accounting data by the user.

The significance of the study by Ijiri, Jaedicke, and Knight is that for the first time a model has been presented on which the researcher can build in developing testable hypotheses. Thus, studies such as Bruns' or Dyckman's[8] need no longer merely test for statistically significant differences. Rather, they can hypothesize ex ante about the presence or non-presence of these differences based upon a logical model of rational behavior.

The study of management control systems has progressed in three areas: the problems in standard setting, the impact of the audit function, and the reporting of relevant data. The various behavioral models of the budget process proposed by Stedry,[9] Becker and Green,[10] and other researchers[11] have all dealt with the problem of achieving goal congruence—that is, with agreement between the goals and standards set by management and the goals held or accepted by the lower, typically worker, groups. Each researcher has suggested a different method for achieving this congruence.

Stedry's study highlighted the importance of the worker's aspiration level in the control process. Better levels of performance could be achieved by relating the budget to the worker's aspiration level. However, Stedry's conclusions were based on laboratory experimentation, and the field experiments have been inconclusive.[12] The explanation may lie in the nature of his experimental study. Students at Carnegie Institute of Technology were the subjects, performing a task that was essentially a mathematical puzzle. This combination of task and subject probably resulted in a highly motivated group of "workers" in the experiment. In such a case Stedry's conclusions would likely be applicable to similar worker groups in the real world. However, the model has not yet been tested on such a group of workers.

[7]Yuji Ijiri, Robert K. Jaedicke, and Kenneth F. Knight, "The Effects of Accounting Alternatives on Management Decisions," Robert K. Jaedicke, Yjui Ijiri, and Oswald Nielsen (eds.), *Research in Accounting Measurement,* (American Accounting Association, 1966) pp. 186-99.

[8]For example, see Thomas R. Dyckman, "The Effects of Alternative Accounting Techniques on Certain Management Decisions," *Journal of Accounting Research,* Spring 1964, pp. 91-107; and William J. Bruns, "Inventory Valuation and Management Decisions," THE ACCOUNTING REVIEW, July 1965, pp. 345-59.

[9]Andrew Stedry *Budgetary Control and Cost Behavior,* (Prentice-Hall, 1960).

[10]Selwyn Becker and David Green, "Budgeting and Employee Behavior," *Journal of Business,* Vol. 35, October 1962, pp. 392-402.

[11]Rudolph Gawron, Jr., "The Effects of Participation and Commitment in Organizational Performance," Master's thesis, M.I.T., 1964.

[12]Andrew Stedry and Emanuel Kay, "The Effects of Goals on Performance: A Field Experiment," Management Science Report No. 23 (Carnegie Institute of Technology, 1964).

The work of McGregor[13] did much to highlight the styles of management and their relationship to the budget process. He labeled the two extreme styles of leadership theory X and theory Y. The former in its most extreme form can be said to describe people as work averters, that is, they are going to perform only so well as their superior forces them to work. It is, essentially, the authoritarian school of budgets, standards, and control. In contrast, theory Y assumes that work is not an undesirable state per se. Workers must be motivated to work, but once motivated will perform well. Authority and punishment are replaced with motivation and rewards. Theory Y is reflected in the idea of permissive management and participative budget schemes.

Becker and Green stressed the benefits to be gained from the workers' participation in the formulation of a budget or standard. By participating in the development of the budget, the worker, it was hypothesized, would internalize the budget. He would accept it as his own standard of performance.[14] The Becker-Green hypothesis was based upon various laboratory and field studies. It has not yet been tested in the managerial accounting context.

The appropriateness of participative management may turn upon the attitude of the workers toward the existing methods for controlling costs and production. Argyris found that workers viewed the budgets as devices used by management to manipulate them.[15] If this is the case, efforts at participation run the risk of being interpreted as phony participation. This would in turn lead to a failure on the part of the workers to participate in the budget setting process in the manner visualized by Becker and Green.

Other studies either are under way or have been made examining other means of achieving goal congruence. In general they have stressed more authoritarian and less democratic methods. One method suggested was formal commitment to the budget or standard in the presence of the worker's superior.[16] This method differs from the Becker-Green model in that no participation in the setting of the standard is permitted. While the results of this study did not support the initial hypotheses, there is some question whether the experimental manipulation was successful. Thus, there is a need for additional research.

The study of the audit function as a factor affecting behavior has been undertaken as an ongoing research project by Churchill and Cooper. Much of their data was reported elsewhere.[17] While some laboratory work has been undertaken,[18] a great deal of effort has been expended on field studies. These will result in a better understanding of how the non-auditor views and perceives the audit process. Their studies have found that the audit experience alters worker behavior to conform with firm policy.

[13]For a complete discussion of McGregor's theory see Douglas McGregor, *The Human Side of Enterprise* (McGraw-Hill, 1960), especially Chapters 2, 3, and 4.

[14]Selwyn Becker and David Green, "Rejoiner to a Reply," *Journal of Business,* Vol. 37, No. 2, April 1964, pp. 203-4.

[15]Chris Argyris, *The Impact of Budgets on People* (The Controllership Foundation, 1952), notably page 25.

[16]Gawron, op cit.

[17]N. C. Churchill, and W. W. Cooper, "A Field Study of Internal Auditing," THE ACCOUNTING REVIEW, October 1965, pp. 767-81.

[18]Neil C. Churchill, "Behavioral Effects of an Audit" (unpublished doctoral dissertation, University of Michigan, 1962).

Little research has been undertaken to examine the process by which the accounting data are communicated to the managers at the various levels. Thus, we do not know the extent to which the various forms of internal reporting succeed in highlighting the desired data. The findings of Dyckman and Bruns[19] provide limited support for the contention that accounting reports are taken at face value and are not adjusted for differing accounting techniques, e.g., Lifo versus Fifo. The data, however, are as yet sketchy. If a similar "functional fixity" is found to exist in other areas on the part of the manager, then the design and content of internal reports must be carefully tailored to meet the needs of the user. He cannot be expected to go beyond the face of the report.

Accountants have also investigated the interaction between a variety of other accounting variables and management decisions. Bruns[20] in what he views as a preliminary study found no significant impact on manager behavior in a business game situation when the length of the reporting period was varied. Livingstone[21] and Lyle found no significant impact on inventory holding decisions when direct costing or absorption costing was used to report to the student managers.

Those studies in the third category, focusing on the implications of the behavioral dimension of the organization on the form and function of the management information system, divide into two broad groups. The first considers the import of the behavioral dimension on management's accounting policies. The second considers its significance for the form and function of the management information system.

The first group includes the work of Sorter et al.,[22] Livingstone,[23] and Lindhe.[24] They investigated various organizations' choice of accounting methods to ascertain if they follow predictable patterns in selecting between alternative accounting techniques. While each approached the problem from a slightly different point of view, all concluded that the selection of accounting method appears to reflect certain individual characteristics. Ultimately, their researches could mean that if we know how a manager feels about Lifo or accelerated depreciation, we can infer how he would record, for example, the investment credit. Only additional

[19]Bruns, op. cit., Dyckman, op. cit.; also Thomas R. Dyckman, "On the Investment Decision," THE ACCOUNTING REVIEW, April 1964, pp. 285-295; T. R. Dyckman, "On the Effects of Earnings-Trend, Size and Inventory Valuation Procedures in Evaluating a Business Firm," in Jaedicke, Ijiri, and Nielsen, op. cit., pp. 175-85. In a slightly different context, see Robert E. Jensen "An Experimental Design for Study of Effects of Accounting Variations in Decision Making," *Journal of Accounting Research*, Autumn 1966, pp. 224-38.

[20]William Bruns, "The Accounting Period and Its Effect Upon Management Decisions," in *Empirical Research in Accounting* (The Institute of Professional Accounting, University of Chicago, 1967), pp. 1-14.

[21]The authors are grateful to Professors J. L. Livingstone and Harry C. Lyle of The Ohio State University for these preliminary results.

[22]George H. Sorter, Selwyn W. Becker, T. Ross Archibald, and William H. Beaver, "Accounting and Financial Measures as Indicators of Corporate Personality," in Jaedicke, Ijiri and Nielsen, op. cit., pp. 200-10.

[23]John Leslie Livingstone, "The Effects of Alternative Accounting Methods on Regulatory Rate Decisions in the Electric Utility Industry," (Ph.D. dissertation, Stanford University, 1966); also the article in this issue of THE ACCOUNTING REVIEW by Livingstone.

[24]Richard Lindhe, "Accelerated Depreciation for Income Tax Purposes—A Study of the Decision and Some Firms Who Made It," *Journal of Accounting Research*, Autumn 1963, pp. 139-48.

research can tell us how strong and pervasive this financial personality will turn out to be.

The significance of the investigations by Lindhe, Sorter, and Livingstone is that they focus attention on another dimension of the problem of achieving uniformity in financial reporting. Prior to these studies it was frequently assumed that the choice of management was a rational one. Lindhe's study of firms failing to adopt accelerated depreciation indicated that was not always the case. The subsequent studies by Sorter and by Livingstone suggest some psychological bases for this. If these researchers are correct, uniformity in accounting policy cannot be achieved by logic alone.

One of the most interesting and more inventive studies undertaken by an accountant attempted to isolate the implications of differing organizational characteristics for a firm's management information system. Grimstad[25] elected, as his point of departure, to classify five firms according to various organizational characteristics, viewing and classifying each according to a set of sociological variables. He illustrated how these variables altered the nature and function of the information system. This study supports Golembiewski's conjecture that a key variable affecting the nature of the managerial accounting system is the nature of the organization itself. This is not surprising, for information systems are designed to meet the needs of the organization and organizational needs vary according to the sociological structure of the firm.

Research Methodology

The methodologies used by the various researchers have been quite diverse. Both field and laboratory techniques have been applied. Indeed, the literature has been rich in this respect. For purposes of discussion, the methodologies will be arbitrarily divided into three categories, recognizing that some degree of overlap will exist. Some projects utilized more than a single methodology. The three classes are laboratory experimentation, field studies, and analysis of real world data.

The earliest literature in this area by accountants utilized the laboratory and the laboratory experiment as its vehicle of investigation. Stedry, Churchill, Bruns, and Dyckman[26] all utilized the laboratory. Later studies have, also.

This is understandable, for the laboratory provides the degree of control necessary in the design of an experiment. The accountant with narrow, tentative hypotheses is better able to test them initially in the laboratory than in the field. Few extraneous, unanticipated variables are likely to occur and invalidate or obscure the results of the study.

The use of the laboratory experimentation has made researchers dependent upon student subjects. As Bruns noted, this raises an unavoidable barrier to the acceptability of the study's results,[27] one which, because businessmen are rarely available as subjects, can not easily be avoided. One notable exception was Churchill's use of workers as subjects in his audit experiment. By moving his

[25]Clayton Grimstad, "A Critique" in *The Use of Accounting Data in Decision Making,* T. J. Burns, ed. (Ohio State University, 1967).

[26]Stedry, op. cit.; Churchill, op. cit.; and any of the various studies by Bruns and by Dyckman.

[27]Bruns, "The Accounting Period," page 7.

laboratory into the field he was able to secure subjects otherwise unavailable to him. Perhaps significantly, he found differences between his worker and student populations.[28]

The laboratory experiment has been and will be a valuable means of testing hypotheses in the earliest stage of any research. Before venturing into any form of field study or experiment, the laboratory experiment provides an initial testing ground. Since opportunities for extensive and systematic studies are rare, the researcher must be prepared to make the most of them. The accountant can improve the usefulness of his laboratory results if two steps are taken. First, effort should be made to bring portions of existing organizations into the laboratory setting. This is more than a change in the character of the subject. It adds a whole new dimension, the subject's previous relationships and interactions. Second, accountants, in researching the effects of differing accounting policies, have tested for significant differences rather than testing hypotheses generated by their models. Thus, they have been able to state only that the groups were different, and have not been able to offer any explanation of why the differences exist.

Much of the work done in related areas which affords accountants insight into their research problems has taken the form of field studies and field experiments.[29] Unfortunately, little of the work done thus far by accountants has fit into this category. The study by Stedry and Kay[30] at General Electric is the one example in the literature of a field experiment to test an accounting-type set of hypotheses. An attempt to assess whether this lack of field studies is due to a lack of testable hypotheses, limited opportunities, or a failure of accountants to recognize the potential value of such studies would be only conjecture. However, researchers must undertake such studies to validate the laboratory findings. The laboratory is at best only a good simulation of the real world.

Accounting researchers have made extensive use of survey techniques. The studies by Lindhe and Sorter et al [31] are typical of those involving mailed survey questionnaires to executives to ascertain behavioral information about them. Such studies must always take their data with the proverbial grain of salt, for there is no check on the validity of the replies. This is important when the data may be in an area where the respondent is sensitive.

Jensen[32] combined the usual laboratory task and the survey technique to poll security analysts. By doing so, he removed the objection that had been raised to some of the earlier work. He no longer relied on students' role-playing. However, to secure the appropriate subjects he sacrificed control over the situation and the setting where the analyst performed the experimental task. He also was able to

---

[28]N. C. Churchill and W. W. Cooper, "Effects of Auditing Records," in W. W. Cooper, H. J. Leavitt and M. W. Shelley III (eds.) *New Perspectives in Organizational Research* (Wiley, 1964), p. 275.

[29]For example, see L. Coch and J. R. P. French, "Overcoming Resistance to Change," *Human Relations,* Vol. 1, No. 4, 1948, pp. 512-32; J. R. P. French, J. Isreal, and D. As, "An Experiment on Participation in a Norwegian Factor," *Human Relations,* Vol. 13, 1960, pp. 3-19; and F. J. Roethlisberger and W. J. Dickson, *Management and the Worker* (Harvard University Press, 1939).

[30]Stedry and Kay, op. cit.

[31]Lindhe, op. cit., and Sorter, et al., op. cit.

[32]Jensen, op. cit.

obtain only one observation from each subject. This blending of the experimental task and the survey technique may prove useful to accountants. It permits access to subjects not normally available to researchers. In addition, a limited number of observations may be made of an extremely large number of subjects.

Churchill and Cooper used survey techniques in a quite different fashion.[33] Relying on questionnaires and interviews they used the field study to collect data that would serve as the basis for new hypotheses and experiments. Thus, the field research did not terminate their study. Rather, it served as the initial input to the model building phase of their research.

As yet only limited use has been made of available financial data for the development and testing of behaviorally oriented models and hypotheses. Livingstone [34] used the decisions of regulatory agencies. Lindhe and Sorter et al.[35] utilized either the form 10-K or published financial statements. However, these and similar data have more commonly been used in empirical studies dealing with problems of profitability, measurement, or the usefulness of accounting data as economic indicators.

Accountants have covered a diverse set of subjects in an attempt to understand the behavioral implications of accounting data and techniques. While the greater effort seems thus far to have been expended on understanding the interaction between accounting convention and managerial behavior, some of the most interesting findings have been in understanding the behavioral implications of such managerial techniques as budgets and performance evaluation (audit).

This has been due to the development of more elaborate models to generate the hypotheses. The more complete the model developed, the more likely that the hypotheses once tested can be interpreted to improve some aspect of the managerial accountant's function. A complete theory, once tested, can lead to new conjectures, further hypotheses, and finally an extension of knowledge into new areas. In contrast, a hypothesis without any accompanying model is useful in understanding only very closely related phenomena. Thus, the findings in the area of investor behavior and Lifo versus Fifo inventory are important because that question is important. However, without some theory to explain the reason for the phenomenon, accountants must be wary in extending the conclusion even to related but dissimilar situations. For example, can we justify extrapolating from those findings to the investment credit problem?

Any review of the methodology employed by accountants cannot help but highlight the resourcefulness of the researchers. They have utilized a variety of methods to reduce their problem to a more tractable form. The emphasis on laboratory testing for many hypotheses may reflect the tentative nature of many of the hypotheses being tested. So long as the model is only now being formulated, the laboratory and the simple laboratory task provide a first step in our understanding of various managerial phenomena.

It must be remembered that at some point these hypotheses must be taken out of the laboratory and into the field. Jensen illustrated an interesting fashion in which this can be done with hypotheses relating to varying accounting techniques.[36] The extant sociological and social psychological literature provide

[33]Churchill and Cooper, "Field Study," op. cit.

[34]Livingstone, op. cit.

[35]Lindhe, op. cit., and Sorter, et al., op. cit.

[36]Jensen, op. cit.

numerous illustrations for the researcher in budgets, standards, audits, and similar areas.[37]

SOME CONJECTURES FOR FUTURE RESEARCH

For the remainder of this paper we will examine two important functions that involve the managerial accountant. These are the resource allocation process and the control system. We will restrict ourselves to the discussion of a few hypotheses and implications from the behavioral sciences that appear to be useful to accountants. We will deliberately avoid discussing those already in the literature.

Resource Allocations: The Budget Process

Many studies of industrial firms have found that the capital budgeting models usually taught in accounting and economics courses are not being utilized in business.[38] In part, this is explainable. The academician prides himself on the degree to which he shapes the next improvement in practice. However, the gulf between theory and practice is too great for such an explanation to suffice.

One alternative is to examine the steps that occur in the resource allocation process. That is, one should consider what occurs when such a decision is made as a behavioral scientist might view it, not as a quantitative decision theorist would. To the behavioral scientist, several groups compete in the resource allocation process for a share of the available capital resources. The sum of the requests exceeds the capital available. The process can be divided into four steps. First, each group must select the proposals it wishes to submit to the individual or committee that makes the final decision. Next, the capital budgeting committee must evaluate all of the proposals submitted and select those that meet the firm's criteria. The third step is informing the various groups of the final capital budget. The last, and perhaps an informal step, is the resolution of the various complaints from dissatisfied groups. The cycle is then complete.

What we have just described is a situation where intergroup conflict could occur. The shortage of capital resources means that every project approved for one department reduces the likelihood of another department's project being accepted. Thus, departments with, ostensibly, a common ultimate goal—the success of the firm—are in potential conflict as they achieve that goal.

Psychologists and sociologists interested in the functioning of organizations have studied the effect of conflict on different groups. One result of these studies is the conclusion that groups in conflict with other groups perceive their own performance as better than their competitors' while the conflict exists.[39] Thus, the inequality perceived by a department in the allocation of capital resources makes the smoothing of ruffled feathers in the fourth step very difficult. Given the

---

[37]See footnote 29 above.

[38]Donald F. Istvan, "The Economic Evaluation of Capital Expenditures," *Journal of Business*, January 1961, pp. 45-51. Similar results have been observed in an experimental setting: L. R. Pondy and J. G. Birnberg, "The Allocation of Financial Resources in Small Hierarchial Groups" (Multilith, University of Pittsburgh, 1966).

[39]Muzafer Sherif, "Experiments on Group Conflict and Cooperation," in Harold Leavitt and L. R. Pondy (eds.), *Readings in Managerial Psychology* (University Chicago Press, 1964), pp. 419-21.

opportunity, it is better in this situation to avoid the conflict. Conflict, once aroused, is not easily allayed.

For any group, failure to achieve the goal when faced with intergroup conflict can lead to increased frictions and tensions within the group.[40] How deleterious these increased tensions will be to the efforts of the department and the organization depends upon many factors. A priori, one would conjecture that it could impede the ability of the firm to function smoothly.[41] Since it is the function of management to prevent, whenever possible, events that will reduce the efficiency of the firm, certain safeguards must be built into the resource allocation process to minimize the risk of disconsolate groups raising the level of perceived interdepartmental conflict in the organization to a potentially harmful level.

How any group measures its success or failure can be viewed through the process of setting aspiration levels. The aspiration level can be viewed in this context as the level of attainment that the group explicitly undertakes to reach on the next trial. Research has shown that the level of aspiration is usually adjusted upward in response to success or downward after a failure.[42] Thus, the level desired on the next performance depends upon previous levels of aspiration and performance. When the aspiration levels exceeds performance by a large amount, the group may become frustrated. If this condition persists, the group may give up.

Both intergroup conflict and disillusionment due to failure to receive a share of the capital budget near the aspired level can have harmful effects on the firm. Management must strive to minimize these in the total process. In doing so, management may be forced to deviate from the budget calculated by the objective decision-making models. Pondy, in studying the capital budgeting policies of several companies found that they relied heavily on categories such as the degree of urgency to minimize the risk of extreme inequities in the final budget.[43] Conventions and guidelines evolve to aid the budget officer and the departments. Rules such as "fair share" or "last year's budget plus a certain increment" are followed in some instances. They serve two purposes. They ease the work of the budget officer. They also permit the group some expectation as to approximately how large its budget will be. This minimizes disappointment and perceived conflict.

Control Systems

Another area where the behavioral sciences have import for accountants is control. Specifically, budgets and standards are used to control worker performance. A very simple model of the process includes four steps.[44]

---

[40] Loc. cit.

[41] Conflict is not, of course, an evil per se. The competition between groups can lead to innovative behavior and a more profitable set of proposals. For a good summary of the literature on conflict see L. R. Pondy, "A Systems Theory of Organizational Conflict," *Academy of Management Journal,* September 1966, pp. 246-56.

[42] For a discussion of aspiration level behavior with business applications, see Andrew Stedry, op. cit., pp. 19-23.

[43] Reported in Richard Cyert and James March, *A Behavioral Theory of the Firm,* (Prentice-Hall, 1962), pp. 272-3. The authors have discussed the topic with Professor Pondy and benefit from his insights. Many of the statements below are drawn from his experience.

[44] The model discussed in this section is not the only one possible. See Stedry, op. cit., McGregor, op. cit. or Victor Vroom, "Some Psychological Aspects of Organizational Control," in Cooper et al., op. cit., pp. 72-86.

1. Standard setting by management
2. Standard setting by the group being controlled
3. The performance of the operation
4. Reporting of the outcome with those positive or negative rewards specified by management

In this simple framework at least four concepts from the various behavioral sciences would aid in a better understanding of the process. One is the concept of group norms from sociology. The others, stimulus-response theory, conditioning, and cognitive dissonance are from psychology.

Sociologists define the norm as an agreement or consensus of a group on how the members should or should not behave.[45] Thus, norms are in essence generally accepted behavioral principles for the group. Like any other set of guides to behavior they vary in their importance and in the significance of their violation. Some norms are so important that their wanton violation will result in an individual's rejection by the group. Others are so unimportant that their continued violation by group members can result in the norm's rejection and the development of a new, opposed norm in its place.

All groups, both work and social, have hierarchies of norms. Some hierarchies are more elaborate than others. The group that meets for a drink after a hard day's work may have few norms, perhaps only that you listen with apparent interest and avoid any excess of shop talk. By contrast, a profession has a complex hierarchy of norms which is quite rigid and inviolate.

Stimulus-response psychologists believe that all observed behavior is in response to stimuli.[46] Thus, the behavior of the worker or the manager is the result of the variety of stimuli affecting him. Virtually everyone is familiar with Pavlov's dog, the classic case of conditioning. Without recounting the details of the experiment, the dog, as a result of a series of experimental experiences, learned to react to another stimulus, a bell, in the same fashion that he previously reacted to food. The essence of conditioning is that the stimulus, the bell, is now able to elicit the same reaction food had previously elicited. Thus, a stimulus can be made to elicit a reaction quite different from that which it usually elicits.[47] Though we will discuss conditioning of a slightly different type than Pavlov's work with the dog, this explanation will serve our purpose.

The fourth theory, cognitive dissonance, is an example of a very recent psychological theory that has found application in other aspects of business, notably marketing. It has not yet been used to analyze any facet of the accountant's problems. The process of removing dissonance refers to the cognitive processes whereby the individual resolves conflicts between what he believes and what he experiences or between two or more conflicting beliefs that he holds.[48] Festinger illustrated the nature of cognitive dissonance with the figures on cigarette smoking and the belief that smoking causes lung cancer. He found that disbelief in the causal connection grew as the rate of smoking increased. Only 20% of the heavy smokers

[45] For example see Robin M. Williams, Jr., *American Society: A Sociological Interpretation* (Knopf, 1960) p. 22.

[46] Ernest Hilgard, *Introduction to Psychology* (Harcourt, Brace, and World, 3rd ed., 1962) p. 633.

[47] Hilgard, op. cit., pp. 253-6.

[48] Hilgard, op. cit., p. 616.

found the evidence convincing, while over 50% of the nonsmokers did. The need to resolve the dissonance by the smokers between the action, smoking, and the belief in the validity of the data led to the rejection of the data.[49]

Now let us use these four concepts to better understand the simplified control process. Once the standard has been set by management it is possible but not a certainty that the workers will accept it. Worker groups develop their own standards for a variety of reasons. Researchers studying the behavior of worker groups have found that workers may refuse to perform as best they can for fear that management will lower the piece rate.[50] Thus, a group norm for performance developed and was enforced by members of the worker group. In this fashion the work group via its norms set the effective standard for the level of production, and not management.

Gold-bricking is an example of what sociologists call "informal power." While management had the formal power to set piece rates and production rates, the workers, through their ability to organize, had developed powers as well. This power, though informal, is in some instances more effective.

The conflict of goals can exist at any level. The more explicit and detailed the system, the more clever the workers or managers become in devising schemes to serve their goals rather than management's. Dalton described a variety of instances where departmental managers utilized resources for what they considered justifiable purposes even though their superiors did not authorize them. By having conspirators charge their expenditures to the budgets of other departments, the managers freed portions of their budgets for items which were considered frills by upper management but were felt to be necessities by them and their workers. According to Dalton, the fault was not with the control system per se. Rather, faced with what they considered justifiable use for the funds, the managers would have found a way around almost any system.[51]

The problem of achieving acceptance of management's standard is complicated by the accountant's implicit assumption the standard is "good." Budgets and standards are neither good nor bad per se. Rather, they are to the workers what the workers view them to be. After unfortunate experiences with standards, the workers, in a sense similar to Pavlov's dogs, have become conditioned to mistrust budgets. Attempts to secure cooperation from them in setting the budget will likely be met with distrust and cynicism. The chances of participative budgeting working without this mistrust being dispelled are negligible. Ideally, as workers and management work together, the workers' fears of the budgets and standards should be allayed. However, if the worker feels that management sporadically "does him in" with the budget or standard, his old fears will be reinforced. Should this occur very often, management will have great difficulty eradicating the worker's mistrust of the participative budgeting process.

Let us now consider the potential behavioral problems in reporting. Traditionally, managements practice management by exception. The emphasis in the feedback received is thus on punishment rather than some mixture of punishment and reward. The manager, as the result of this reporting system, may find

[49] Leon Festinger, *Theory of Cognitive Dissonance* (Evanston: Row, Peterson, 1957), cited in Hilgard, op. cit., pp. 253-6.

[50] See Roethlisberger and Dickson, op. cit., Chapter 22, especially pp. 521-3, and Donald F. Roy, "Efficiency-and the Fix," *American Journal of Sociology* November 1954, pp. 255-66.

[51] Melville Dalton, *Men Who Manage* (Wiley, 1959) Chapter 3, especially pp. 31-52.

himself preoccupied with the times he missed the standard by a significant amount rather than how well he has done over the long run. And the worker who feels he is doing the best he can may experience a degree of anxiety because management by exception highlights only his mistakes. In order to resolve the conflict generated by the reporting system, he may doubt the validity of the standard or budget that management has set. Thus, in resolving the dissonance he will reject or discredit management's standard.

This conclusion is, of course, only conjecture based upon limited findings. However, if further study supports the presence of this form of dissonance resolution in the control system, the impact on the form of the feedback is clear. Reports should be designed to provide positive reinforcement to the worker as well to make management aware of poor performance. This may be accomplished by the use of rewards and through greater emphasis on the favorable variance. Informally, the praise of his superiors could serve to avoid or change a situation where dissonance may be present.

The process we have just described takes into account not only the need for information for decision making but also the personal clues sought from the reports by the decision maker. At first blush such an approach to the internal reporting function may seem absurd. However, if the function of the managerial accountant is to aid management in achieving its goals, then reports as well as budgets must be tailored to this purpose. The reporting function is as important a part of the control process as any of the earlier steps. If the budget cycle began with near congruence between group norms and management goals, the reporting process could either reduce the gap or increase it. Since the operating cycle is repeated many times, the firm is never permanently in control. Rather it is dynamic and must be observed carefully at all times. The report can either facilitate or impede the equilibrium process.

CONCLUSION

If accounting research is going to assist in the development of better managerial accounting techniques, effort must be made to utilize findings from the behavioral sciences. The implementation of the accounting techniques requires that proper consideration be given to the human element, how the individual or group interacts with the system. At the present time only a very limited number of studies have been undertaken. However, many more have been started and it is likely that these will provide us with at least a nucleus upon which to build.

In this paper we have attempted to accomplish two purposes. First, we have indicated the nature of existing research. Second, we have provided examples of how behavioral science theories can be used to view the accounting process and generate some testable hypotheses about it. It is hoped that these will provide an impetus to further research.

DISCUSSION QUESTIONS

1. Professor Otto Eckstein, a former member of the President's Council of Economic Advisers, was quoted (*The New York Times,* August 2, 1971), as saying that pre-tax profits for 1969 as used in the calculation of GNP had to be revised downward by $7 billion or 8 per cent and for 1970 by $6 billion or 7 per cent. Professor Eckstein observed:

> These enormous revisions raise questions about the accounting practices of American business and the statistical measurement of profits by the Federal Government since the decisions of individuals and institutional investors are based on profit data, the quality of investment performance is hurt by reporting errors of the indicated magnitude.

The revisions were made because preliminary figures for corporate profits published by the Government are based on company's annual reports and the final figures are based on tax returns filed with the Internal Revenue Service.

Professor Eckstein added that data based on tax returns "have a greater stability than the public reports which are affected by changing accounting conventions and the management of earnings." He states further, "Had earnings reports been as flat as they are now reported (aggregates as adjusted above) to have been, the stock market boom and bust would have been milder and the economic boom would not have become so overheated".

The relatively large corrections required for profit data in recent years could perhaps be explained, said Professor Eckstein, by the fact that "average accounting practices may have deteriorated dramatically in the last three (years)."

Explain the difference in profit estimation in terms of the traditional and behavioral concepts of the firm.

2. Compare and contrast the assumptions implicit in:
   (a) The traditional accounting theory of the firm.
   (b) The marginal theory of the firm.
   (c) The behavioral theory of the firm.

3. Identify and define the following terms:
   (a) Managerial theory of the firm.
   (b) Operational goals.
   (c) Uncertainty avoidance.
   (d) Problemistic search.
   (e) Satisficing.
   (f) Biased search.
   (g) Levels of aspirations.

4. You have been asked to give a comprehensive lecture to a group of middle-level managers on the motivational basis of managers. Outline that lecture indicating the major points that you would make and discuss some of the evidence to support these points.

5. The president of a large listed corporation appeared before management seminars for company key personnel and stressed the importance of profit maximization as a key business goal. At a private session with top executives late in December, the controller of the company, with the approval of the chief executive, reported that profits for the year increased by 12 per cent over the prior year, but

it was determined to report a 6 per cent increase, the balance of the increase being "stashed away" by accounting adjustments for use in the following year.

In preparing and certifying financial reports, accountants generally assume profit maximization as a business goal. Discuss the above situation in terms of the challenge to this assumption by behavioral scientists.

6. *The New York Times* on October 19, 1972 reported that former United States Supreme Court Justice Arthur Goldberg resigned as a member of the board of directors of Trans World Airlines. Mr. Goldberg stated that his resignation was prompted by his inability to fulfill his "legal and public obligations as a member of the Board."

The newspaper account states: "Mr. Goldberg had argued that non-officers on the Board should be allowed to meet independently and have the authority to hire an autonomous staff of technical specialists. The advisers would help the outside directors pass judgment on the policies recommended by the management."

Discuss this conflict between the internal and external directors in terms of the goal model of the behavioral theory.

PART TWO

Budgeting and Planning

THE PROCESSES OF BUDGETING
AND PLANNING

The behavioral view of the firm presented in Part One described the firm in terms of its goals, its overall decision-making processes, and the motivations of its participants. The firm's goals were described as a dynamic, complex compromise of conflicting demands reflecting the individual needs and goals of the firm's sub-units and participants. This concensus about goals and objectives results in an operational goal congruency that facilitates continuity in the day-to-day operations of the firm. This section of the book examines in detail the role of budgets in the process of achieving operational goal congruency and their dysfunctional effects on the organization.

Budgets have become widely accepted as the focus for the firm's short-term planning activity and the basis of its control system. From a total company viewpoint, financial budgets are a summary projection of the firm's financial statements for the coming year. For each successive level of the firm, budgets represent detailed objectives and plans for their achievement.

As the basis of the organization control system, budgets reflect an extensive application of the management-by-exception principle. This generally practiced principle of management recognizes the inherent cognitive and rational limitations of the manager to be personally involved in every task and activity for which he is responsible. The practical application of the principle is an extension of variance analysis based on standard costs. The manager, often with the aid of accountants and industrial engineers, develops performance criteria (objectives) for the people, processes, and activities reporting to him. By monitoring actual performance against objectives, the manager determines whether his operations are in control and which specific activities or individual require his personal intervention.

In large organizations that place a high emphasis on predictability of employee job-related behavior, tasks are reduced to their smallest component activity and routinized where possible. This increases the felt need for coordination and control, and generally results in a vertical organization characterized by centralization of decision making and authority relations along superior-subordinate lines. Thus, the more vertical an organization, the greater its felt need for a control system based on detailed budgets, and the greater will be its reliance on budgets.

Organizationally, budgets have a dual role; they are the final output of the planning process and the basis of the control system. During the period in which a budget is being established, it is the means for developing the near-term plan. In its completed form this plan reflects a concensus about the organization's operational goals for the time period in the plan (e.g., the next fiscal year). These operational goals are stated in terms of measurable performance criteria such as standard costs. In many instances, however, the objectives stated in the plan cannot be derived objectively (e.g., on the basis of standard costs) and often reflect commitments on the part of affected individuals or sub-units. Commitment implies agreement; and indeed, the budget preparation process involves bargaining about operational goals and the resulting commitments reflect an achieved concensus. Once the budget has been resolved the organization can be described as being in a state of quasi-resolution of conflict.[1]

After the planning period is complete and operational goal congruency has been achieved, the budget assumes its second role. It now becomes the yardstick against which performance is measured and the basis for applying the management-by-exception principle. The role of budgets in control systems is discussed on page 271. The dysfunctional results of utilizing budgets have resulted in many behavioral studies of budgets. These are represented in the readings and are discussed below.

INTRODUCTION TO THE READINGS

The dual role of budgets has many dysfunctional consequences and largely accounts for most of the behavioral studies on budgets. One review of these studies is presented in the article by Dunbar (1971). Dysfunctional consequences occur because budgets can be used to induce pressure and to impose goals on the organization participants. Thus, the coercive nature of budgets in terms of the impact of budgets on people was discussed by Argyris (1953). In their article, Becker and Green (1962) noted the dysfunctional effects of the induced pressure of budgets and suggested a participative approach as a means to achieving congruency between personal and organizational goals, obtaining commitment to planned goals, and reducing intra-organizational conflict. Becker and Green take specific issue with Stedry (1960), who concluded that based on his laboratory experiments on levels

---

[1] For further discussion of this concept see Cyert, Richard M., and March, James G., *A Behavioral Theory of the Firm,* Prentice-Hall, 1964, pp. 117-118.

of aspirations, individuals will, under certain conditions, accept and achieve an imposed goal that exceeds their own aspiration.

Specifically Stedry's experiments suggested that an imposed goal that exceeds an individual's own level of aspiration will be accepted by him as if it were his level of aspiration if he perceives this goal to be reasonable. The implication for budgeting was to provide a rationale for increasing performance by imposing reasonable higher goals. In other words, some degree of manipulation and induced pressure might be beneficial *if* the manager can estimate what increased level of performance will be viewed by a subordinate as reasonable.

Schiff and Lewin (1971) studied the dysfunctional consequences of budgets that result from neglecting the bargaining aspect of the budget process and the motivation of managers to optimize a personal goal set subject to achieving the firm's goals.

Starting with the motivational model of managerial behavior developed in Part One, Schiff and Lewin conclude that managers will strive and bargain for slack in their budgets because slack is perceived by managers as a means to (a) the achievement of personal goals while also achieving the organization goals, and (b) reducing uncertainty in attaining planned goals. Uncertainty avoidance is viewed as the response of organization participants to the use of budgets as yardsticks for measurement of performance. Thus, in their article, Schiff and Lewin report on three case studies in which managers actively participate in the budget process and bargain for slack to insure attainment of organizational goals, to avoid consequences attached to failure in attaining goals, and to satisfy personal goals. To the firm this unexpected behavior results in lost opportunities and in the long run increases its cost function.

Although the firm has been earlier described in terms of a conflict system, it has also been described as stability seeking. Budget processes facilitate both these observations. Budgets promote stability of operational decision making because the last budget is the basis for the new one. Thus, unless a major organizational change has occurred, only marginal changes can be observed in most of the goals from year to year. It also facilitates conflict resolution because normally the system is in conflict (in a state of bargaining) during the budget preparation period. The above observations and an extension of the behavioral theory of the firm to non-profit organizations is found in the article by Crecine (1967). This paper describes the stability of municipal decision making, the role of the budget in promoting this stability, and the means by which slack is created and appropriated in public decision-making systems. Of particular note is the simulation model that is based on the actual decision rules used by the participants in the system.

6

BUDGETING AND EMPLOYEE BEHAVIOR*

SELWYN BECKER / DAVID GREEN, JR

Writing in *Number, the Language of Science,* Tobias Dantzig observed: "The concrete has ever preceded the abstract. . . . And the concrete has ever been the greatest stumbling block to the development of a science. The peculiar fascination which *numbers as individuals* have exerted on the mind of man from time immemorial was the main obstacle in the way of developing a *collective* theory of numbers, i.e., an arithmetic; just as the concrete interest in individual stars long delayed the creating of a scientific astronomy."[1]

And so it has been with budgeting, where for some there is still question on whether or not a theory has developed. Business budgeting is a twentieth-century innovation; its development has been characterized by a fragmentary literature and an emphasis on technique. A review of its history indicates that progress has largely been through learning from mistakes—a "cut-and-try" approach. In this paper we will review this history as a background toward an understanding of the relation of the budget to the motivations of those who effect and are affected by it. In a sense this will be an excursion—an attempt to determine "what the behavioral scientists can tell us or find out for us about . . . the impact [of budgets] on people and on their aspirations."[2] In the process, we will point out that the attempt to make use of motivational factors in the budgeting construct raises many difficult and imperfectly understood problems. Further, we will attempt to explain why the style of managerial leadership is of critical importance in the choice of budget procedures—an issue largely overlooked. Also, we will consider the role played by the communication of performance results and the timing of budget revisions.

In the United States, budgeting by state and local government started with the municipal reform movements around the turn of the century. At the outset, the budget was viewed as an instrument of control—"control over the officers . . . of administration by placing limitations on their authority to spend."[3] These early budgets were, and for the most part still are, authorizations to spend—appropriations—for particular "objects of expenditure" such as personal services, commodities, travel, and the like. The appropriation was the "upper limit" much like a thermal control on a furnace—when the limit is reached the fuel, or, in the fiscal sense, the money is stopped. The upper limit was imposed through the

The Journal of Business, The University of Chicago Press, October 1962, pp. 392-402.

[1] 4th ed.; New York: Macmillan Co., 1956, chap. iii.

[2] David Solomons, "Standard Costing Needs Better Variances," National Association of Accountants Bulletin, XLIII, No. 4 (December, 1961), 30.

[3] Frederick A. Cleveland, *Chapters on Municipal Administration and Accounting* (New York: Longmans, Green & Co., 1909), p. 72.

approving of the budget by the governing body—the board, the council, the legislature, etc.

These governmental budgeting procedures provided for a second type of control—a restraint control. Each claim presented had to be approved for payment by the chief financial officer. The question of "what is a legal or bona fide obligation?" was resolved by considering (1) whether the budget document provided for such an expenditure, (2) whether sufficient funds were left in the appropriation to pay the claim, and (3) whether the necessary documents were on hand. To know if the remaining appropriation was sufficient, fairly elaborate records were maintained. To these were posted the dollar amounts of issued purchase orders as well as the specific expenditures. Both types of transactions reduced the "available" balance. This was a practice of *clerical* control—a technique employed to insure the completeness of record and one that is still unique to governmental accounting (with the possible exception of retail "open-to-buy" records). To the extent that interim reports were prepared and distributed to department heads, rudimentary *communicative* control was practiced.

Governmental purposes were served well enough by these budget procedures. Revenue and expense forecasts were relatively simple. Because changes were not contemplated, the budgets were for fixed amounts for the designated time period. Where actual revenues fell short of the estimates, unilateral demands to cut expenditures by a designated percentage were issued—sometimes by resort to payless paydays.

Early business budgeting largely imitated governmental practice and technique. It began with "imposed" budgets[4] and the obvious controls—limit, restraint, clerical and communicative. During the early and middle 1930's, it became fashionable to speak of "budgetary control" and to view the budget as both (1) a financial plan and (2) "a control over future operations."[5] Also in the Thirties, the inadequacies of the static budget became obvious when business activity took a sharp downturn and profits disappeared.[6]

A budget form that provided for intra-period changes in the level of sales or manufacturing was introduced and was called a flexible or variable budget. It attempted to provide "bench mark" numbers for a range of contemplated activity.

Primarily, budgetary control has been the attempt to keep performance at or within the acceptable limits of the predetermined flexible plan. In a sense the plan controls—but for how long? And how is the plan to be modified?

BUDGET PERIODICITY

The recurring cycle of early governmental and business budgets was simple. The budgets were imposed, there was performance, and the comparison of the

[4]Imposed budgets have been characterized as ones "dictated by top management without the full participation of the operating personnel" (R.N. Anthony, "Distinguishing Good from Not-So-Good Accounting Research," in *Proceedings of the 22nd Annual Institute on Accounting* [Columbus: Ohio State University, 1960], p. 68).

[5]Eric Kohler, *A Dictionary for Accountants* (Englewood Cliffs, N.J.: Prentice-Hall, Inc., 1957), p. 75.

[6]F. V. Gardner, "How About That 1935 Operating Budget?" *Factory Management and Maintenance*, November, 1934; C. E. Knoeppel and E. G. Seybold, *Managing for Profit* (New York: McGraw-Hill Book Co., 1937), p. 206.

performance against the budget influenced the next budget. The cycle could be depicted as follows:

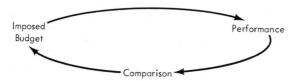

Ordinarily, the budget period was one year or two. The comparison of performance and budget often had curious results on the subsequent budget. Where expenditure was less than budget, there was a tendency to revise the subsequent budget downward. As a result, managers would engage in a spending spree the last few weeks of an appropriation year to avoid being cut down next year.

The budget period in business has also been calendar oriented—the quarter or twelve-week period extended twelve or fifteen months. Ordinarily, budget revisions are restricted to future periods. Later in the paper we will discuss reasons for cycling budget revisions on a basis other than the calendar.

BUDGET MODIFICATION

By 1930 it was recognized in business circles that imposed budgets "resulted in some dissatisfaction and advice was given to prepare them in the departments and have them revised or edited in the central offices."[7] Thus *participation* was introduced into the budgeting construct. It has been said that the "real values of participation at all management levels . . . , aside from better planning are the psychological values that accrue as the result of participation. A high degree of participation is conducive to better morale and greater initiative."[8]

There is some evidence of the extent (and degree) to which participation is currently employed in business. Sord and Welsch interrogated managements of thirty-five companies to determine the level at which principal budget objectives were developed. No companies said they used totally imposed budgets. Six firms (17 per cent) prepared objectives at higher levels and allowed subordinate managers to consider and comment on them before final adoption. Twenty-nine firms (83 per cent) said they requested subordinate managers to prepare their own goals and objectives for review and approval at higher levels.[9]

Theirs obviously was a very small sample. Furthermore, it is questionable that the interrogatories used did, in fact, investigate participation. As Chris Argyris discovered, there is such a thing as "pseudo-participation." "That is, participation which looks like, but is not, real participation."[10]

Participation may have great value in improving budgets by drawing together the knowledge diffused among the participants, although we do not treat this

[7]*Budgetary Control in Manufacturing Industries* (New York: National Industrial Conference Board, 1931), p. 52.

[8]B. H. Sord and G. A. Welsch, *Business Budgeting* (New York: Controllership Foundation, Inc., 1958), p. 97.

[9]*Ibid.,* p. 95.

[10]*The Impact of Budgets on People* (New York: Controllership Foundation, Inc., 1952), p. 28.

objective here. Our interest is in participation as a useful technique for dealing with the psychological problems of employee satisfaction, morale, and motivation to produce; that is, the belief that increased participation can lead to better morale and increased initiative. The evidence supporting this belief will be evaluated, as well as other psychological effects associated with participation that may be of even greater importance. But first the question: What is participation? We will use the following definition: Participation is "defined as a process of joint decision-making by two or more parties in which the decisions have future effects on those making them."[11]

A collateral question: how does the introduction of participation affect the budget cycle? At first glance, it seems that the chart would appear as follows:

However, we believe this is too simple. Participation adds a separate "psychological path." Participation is *not* a single-value variable but rather is a concept encompassing several explicit variables. (Instead of a simple cycle we have a sequence that might be depicted as follows:

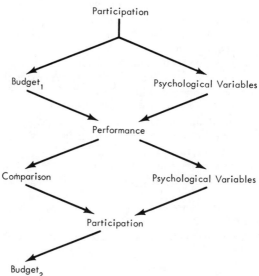

[11]J. R. P. French, Jr., J. Israel, and D. As, "An Experiment on Participation in a Norwegian Factory," *Human Relations,* XIII (1960), 3.

In paragraphs that follow we will attempt to identify these unspecified psychological variables by examining what we consider to be the relevant available research results. Before proceeding it is imperative to make one fundamental point: Participation is not a panacea.[12] Indeed, there is evidence to suggest that it is inappropriate in certain "environments." When participation is employed, the concept of control, as outlined above requires modification. Instead of the budget being the plan to which performance is conformed, compared, and evaluated, irrespective of changes in environment (other than those provided for in the flexible budget), the plan is influenced at least in part, by the environment. That is, control limits and informs those operating under the budget; in turn, they determine and limit the succeeding budget.

PARTICIPATION, MORALE, AND PRODUCTIVITY

In an industrial setting Coch and French investigated the effects of prior participation on production after work changes were introduced.[13] Difficulty of work and percentage of work changes were equated for a no-participation group (NP); for participation by representation (PR); and for a total participation (TP) group. With a prechange standard of sixty units per hour, after relearning, the NP group reached a level of fifty units per hour; the PR group sixty units per hour; and the TP group sixty-eight units per hour, or an improvement of about 14 per cent over the standard rate. Another important finding was that 17 per cent of the NP group quit their jobs in the first forty days after the change, and the remaining members of the group filed grievances about the piece rate, which "subsequently was found to be a little 'loose.'" There was one act of aggression against the supervisor from the PR group, none from the TP group, and no quits in either the PR or TP groups.

If employee turnover and stated grievances can be taken as a measure of morale, then it seems clear that the two groups that participated in the initiation of change were better disposed toward their job situations than was the no participation group.

Based only on this study one cannot decide if participation directly increased incentive to produce, as measured by subsequent productivity, or only improved morale, which in turn led to increased motivation. This is a point worth considering since morale is not perfectly correlated with productivity.

An inference about this relationship can be drawn after examination of a study by Schachter et al. on group cohesiveness and productivity.[14] (Group cohesiveness is usually defined as attraction to the group—desire to become or remain a member—and reluctance to leave the group. Another way of looking at cohesiveness might be the amount of "we" feeling generated in an individual as a result of his association with others.) Schachter and his associates experimentally created high and low cohesiveness in two groups. A task was chosen in which output could be easily measured. In half of each group subjects were individually given instructions designed to induce production at a high rate; the other half

[12] A useful discussion—"Participation in Perspective"—appears as chap. ix in *The Human Side of Enterprise* by Douglas McGregor (New York: McGraw-Hill Book Co., Inc., 1950).

[13] J. Coch and J. R. P. French, Jr., "Overcoming Resistance to Change," *Human Relations*, I (1948), 512-32.

[14] S. Schachter, N. Ellertson, D. McBride, and D. Gregory, "An Experimental Study of Cohesiveness and Productivity," *Human Relations*, IV (1951), 229-38.

instructions designed to induce production at a low rate. It was found that group cohesion and acceptance of induction were significantly related. The high-cohesive groups more frequently accepted induction than did the low-cohesive groups. This was especially true of the negative induction, or "slow-down" situation.

The Coch and French study suggests that morale and/or productivity are enhanced as a result of employee participation in the initiation of change. The Schachter *et al.* study suggests that with participation held constant (all groups worked under constant conditions) change in productivity is related to group cohesiveness. Cohesiveness, it can be seen from the definition, is related to morale. Morale is most frequently defined as satisfaction with one's job, supervisors, and working associates. It has also been defined as the *degree* to which an employee identified himself as part of the organization. In either case morale and cohesiveness with a group imply some similar reactions and attitudes toward an organization or group.

Since participation affects morale (cohesiveness) and productivity, but cohesiveness without participation affects production, the most likely conclusion is that cohesiveness is dependent on participation but that changes in productivity are more directly related to cohesiveness.

ELEMENTS OF PARTICIPATION: PROCESS AND CONTENT

Let us consider participation as conceptually divisible into process and content. Process means the *act* of participating with the possible consequences stemming from the act, content is the *discussion topic* toward which are generated the positive or negative attitudes. The *act* of participating enables the participants to know one another, communicate and interact with one another—conditions that easily can lead to increased cohesiveness. As we have seen, however, increased cohesiveness also can result in lower production if that is the sentiment of the cohesive group. Thus it becomes clear that the content of participation is an important determinant of final production levels. What should the content consist of and what should it accomplish? These questions can be answered on the basis of some data on group decision-making collected by Kurt Lewin and his students.[15] One experiment was designed to induce housewives to use previously unused foods (sweetbreads, etc.). Positive communications describing the foods were presented to two groups; one by the lecture method, the other by a group-discussion method. A subsequent check revealed that 3 per cent of the women who heard the lectures served one of the meats never served before, whereas after group discussion, 32 per cent served one of the meats. This experiment was repeated with a different leader, different groups, and a different food—milk—and yielded essentially similar results.

As compared to individual instruction and the lecture method, group discussion was superior in inducing change—a result attributed to the hesitancy of individuals to accept goals that depart from the group standard. (Psychological non-acceptance of a goal by an individual virtually precludes its attainment by him.) The group-discussion method allows the group member to assess the standards of all other members so that, if the group apparently accepts a change, he too can accept it and retain his group membership.

---

[15] "Studies in Group Decision" in D. Cartwright and F. Zauder (eds.), *Group Dynamics* (Evanston, Ill.: Row Peterson & Co., 1956), pp. 287-88.

It is clear that the content of participation should be directed toward setting a new goal with discussion of a sort sufficient to enable each participant to realize that the goal is accepted by the others in the group. The fulfillment of these conditions could serve as a definition of successful participation by (1) providing the opportunity for enough interaction so that a cohesive group can emerge and (2) directing the interaction so that each participant's analysis of the content will enable him to accept as his own those goals adopted by the group. Thus, we can see that the process and content of a participation program interact, and that such interaction can lead to one of several outcomes:

a) High cohesiveness with positive attitudes (goal acceptance), a condition of maximally efficient motivation;

b) Low cohesiveness with positive attitudes, an unlikely but possible condition that probably would result in efficient performance;

c) Low cohesiveness and negative attitudes, a condition resulting from unsuccessful participation that would tend to depress production within the limits of the integrity or conscience of each individual; and

d) High cohesiveness and negative attitudes, the occurrence most conducive to a production slow-down.

Level of Aspiration and Performance. Ideally, in the budgeting process, participation results in a plan of action including a proposed amount of accomplishment and an estimate of the costs to achieve it. If participation has been successful, then these proposed levels of cost and accomplishment are accepted as goals by the participants. In effect, these projected levels of achievement become the levels of aspiration of the managers of the organization. (In a smoothly running organization the managers induce acceptance of the same levels of aspiration in the members of their departments.)

Level of aspiration has been defined in the psychological literature as a goal that, when just barely achieved, has associated with it subjective feelings of success; when not achieved, subjective feelings of failure.[16] From an extensive review of the literature Child and Whiting summarize many findings into five conclusions:

1. Success generally leads to a raising of the level of aspiration, failure to a lowering.

2. The stronger the success the greater is the probability of a rise in level of aspiration; the stronger the failure the greater is the probability of a lowering.

3. Shifts in level of aspiration are in part a function of changes in the subject's confidence in his ability to attain goals.

4. Failure is more likely than success to lead to withdrawal in the form of avoiding setting a level of aspiration.

5. Effects of failure on level of aspiration are more varied than those of success.[17]

[16]K. Levin, T. Dembo, L. Festinger, and Pauline Sears, "Level of Aspiration," in J. McV. Hunt (ed.), *Personality and the Behavior Disorders,* I (New York: Ronald Press Co., 1944), 333-78.

[17]J. L. Child, and J. W. M. Whiting, "Determinants of Level of Aspiration: Evidence from Everyday Life," in H. Brand (ed.), *The Study of Personality* (New York: John Wiley & Sons, 1954), pp. 145-58.

Recently Stedry has utilized this psychological variable in an attempt to establish some relations between level of aspiration, imposed budgets, and subsequent performance.[18] Stedry, not a psychologist, may have overlooked some of the relevant psychological literature. Seemingly he selected an inaccurate method of measuring aspiration level which weakens his several conclusions and recommendations. For his measure of level of aspiration, Stedry asked his subjects to express what they "hoped to achieve" on the next set of problems. Festinger found that the D score (the difference between performance and aspiration) was greater between performance and expressions of "like to get" than between performance and expressions of "expect to get."[19] Diggory found the correlation between "hope" statements before and after failure significantly higher than statements of expectations before and after failure.[20] In other words, "hope" and "expect" represent different attitudes. Since level of aspiration is defined as the goal one explicitly undertakes to reach rather than the goal one hopes to achieve, it seems clear that Stedry's conclusions are based on an inaccurate measure of his major variable. Subsequently, Stedry has indicated his belief, based on questionnaire information, that his "subjects appeared . . . to have given the right answer to the wrong question."[21] In any event, his attempt is valuable heuristically because it highlights a possible relation between budgets, budgeting, and human motivational performance.

We have already hypothesized a relationship between participation and the formation of levels of aspiration. There remains a specification of the effects of level of aspiration on the remaining segments of the budget cycle.

After the budget has been adopted, the attempt to translate it into behavior constitutes the performance part of the cycle. The degree of effort expended by members of the firm as they attempt to achieve budgeted goals is partially dependent upon their levels of aspiration. Maximum effort will be exerted to just reach an aspired-to goal. In fact, according to level of aspiration theory if, for example, five units of effort are required to reach goal x - 3, ten units to reach x - 2, fifteen units to reach goal x - 1, and twenty-five units to reach goal x, the level of aspiration goal, an individual will expend the disproportionate amount of energy to achieve at level x to derive that subjective feeling of success. Thus we can see how a budget that is partially derived through a successful program of participation can result in greater expenditure of effort on the part of employees to reach goals specified in the budget.

Such expectations are not without foundation, of course. Bayton measured the levels of aspiration of three hundred subjects of roughly equivalent ability prior to their performance on seven arithmetic problems. He found that subjects with higher levels of aspiration followed with higher performance.[22] From a finding of this sort one cannot conclude that greater motivation to achieve is associated with the level of aspiration goal, but it is well known that increased motivation leads to

[18]Andrew C. Stedry, *Budget Control and Cost Behavior* (Englewood Cliffs, N.J.: Prentice-Hall, Inc., 1960).

[19]L. Festinger, "A Theoretical Interpretation of Shifts in Level of Aspiration," *Psychological Review,* XLIX (1942), 235-50.

[20]J. C. Diggory, "Responses to Experimentally Induced Failure," *American Journal of Psychology,* LXII (1949), 48-61.

[21]Stedry, "Aspiration Levels, Attitudes, and Performance in a Goal-oriented Situation," *Industrial Management Review,* III, No. 2 (Spring, 1962), 62.

[22]J. A. Bayton, "Interrelations between Levels of Aspiration, Performance and Estimates of Past Performance," *Journal of Experimental Psychology,* XXXIII (1943), 1-21.

increased effort, a condition usually followed by an increase in performance. We can thus find indirect support for our contention. Another bit of evidence may illustrate the point further. Siegel and Fouraker set subjects to bargaining under bilateral monoply conditions.[23] With no control of levels of aspirations, the subjects maximized their joint profits and split the profits nearly equally. However, when high and low levels of aspiration were induced into the bargaining pairs (despite the fact that a better bargain meant more money for the subject), those with a low level of aspiration gained only about one-third of the joint profits. Thus, it seems clear that level of aspiration not only describes a goal for future attainment, but also it partially insures that an individual will expend a more-than-minimum amount of energy, if necessary, to perform at or above that level.

Depending, then, on the conditions under which a budget is drawn the budget can act as a motivating force and can induce better performance from the members of the organization. On the other hand, the budget can specify aims and goals so easy of attainment that the organization's members will be induced to produce at less than their usual capacity.

After the performance phase of the cycle a comparison is made between the costs and income previously predicted in the budget and the actually attained income and costs. We are not here concerned with how the comparison is made but rather with its utilization, since that may have considerable effect on employee behavior and morale.

Much has been written on the effect of communication within an organization. With reference to the comparison, or control, function of the budget, the use or misuse of communication can be critical especially when viewed in the context of participation and level of aspiration.

First and foremost, it is imperative for each participant to know whether he should feel subjective success or failure. If he is not informed of the results of the comparison he cannot know whether his striving for a particular level was worthwhile or not. Nor can he, in turn, pass on the word to his subordinates in whom he induced specific levels of aspiration. They, too, will not know whether to feel success or failure. We can see that communicating knowledge of results acts, in this case, as reward or punishment. It can serve either to reinforce or extinguish previous employee behaviors. Where subjects were given a learning task and provided knowledge of results, learning increased; but when knowledge of results was withheld performance fell, that is learning not only stopped but performance was decreased.[24] In discussing these results, Munn argued that "the rapid drop in performance which followed this point may be attributed to the loss of motivation which came with withdrawal of knowledge of results, not from forgetting what had been learned up to this point."[25]

Failure to communicate knowledge of results adversely affects not only performance but also morale. Leavitt and Mueller, in an investigation of effects of varying amounts of feedback, found that task accuracy increased as feedback increased. They also found that zero feedback is accompanied by low confidence and hostility while free feedback is accompanied by high confidence and amity.[26]

[23]S. Siegel, L. Fouraker, *Bargaining and Group Decision Making* (New York: McGraw-Hill Book Co., 1960).

[24]J. L. Elwell and G. C. Grindley, "The Effect of Knowledge of Results on Learning and Performance," *British Journal of Psychology*, Vol. XXIX (1938).

[25]N. L. Munn, *Psychology* (Boston, Houghton Mifflin Co., 1946).

[26]H. J. Leavitt and R. A. H. Mueller, "Some Effects of Feedback on Communication," *Human Relations*, IV (1951), 401-10.

The question may now be asked: "So what if the employees don't know how they did? They already performed and the profit is recorded." The answer obviously concerns the effects this lack will produce on subsequent behavior and, more specifically, on the goals to be set in the succeeding budget.

The next budget will be affected because omitting feedback not only precludes certainty regarding a previous level of aspiration but also affects the subsequent level of aspiration. Most generally an individual will raise his level of aspiration after success and lower it after failure.

In the budgeting cycle, after the comparison phase, the new budget is started. The participating supervisors bring to the new participation situation all their new aspirations resulting from past feelings of success or failure. If they have been deprived of a rightfully achieved feeling of success, their subsequent aspirations are likely to be lowered. This could result either in a less efficient budget, that is, lower goals than could easily be achieved or, after disagreeable argument, an imposed budget from an adamant management. In the first case succeeding performance will be unnecessarily low; in the second, participation will be ineffectual with the possible result of poor performance and, almost certainly, lower morale. The *proper* budget cycle then is really a dual, interacting sequence of budgeting and psychological events. It can be depicted as follows:

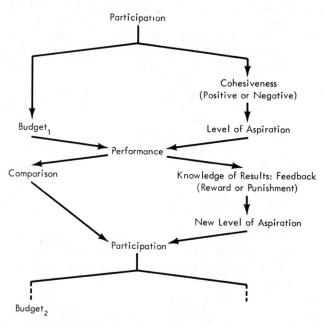

A successful participation budget does two things: (1) it induces proper motivation and acceptance of specific goals, and (2) it provides information to associate reward or punishment with performance. These lead to new aspirations and motivations that set the stage for the next participation budget.

CONCLUSIONS

An understanding of the psychological variables stemming from participation is valuable, perhaps, for its own sake, but it is hardly likely to provide concrete assistance in a decision to institute such a program. We have seen that participation can lead to either increased or decreased output. It is not unlikely that the setting in which participation occurs is one determinant of the production outcome. Some organizations can be characterized as operating under relatively authoritarian leadership. By definition, participation is essential to democratic process and very probably is antithetical to an authoritarian organization. To illustrate the latter, assume that the various department heads participate in the decision-making process, prepare a budget, only to have it rejected by upper management without explanation other than that a more satisfactory budget is necessary. The best prediction here is that the participating group will be highly cohesive and hold negative attitudes toward management, a precondition to lowered output.

It is also likely that under authoritarian management status differences will be rigidly adhered to. If the participants in the budgeting process occupy different status levels influence on decisions will be directly related to status—the more status the more influence. Status differences would probably mitigate against high cohesiveness. Presumably status differences that did not affect the decision-making process would not preclude either a cohesive group or positive goal acceptance, especially if the occupants were secure in their positions or perceived the possibility of upward mobility.[27]

We do not wish to enter the controversy over the relative merits of various styles of leadership but merely wish to point to some possible limitations on the use of participation. In order to be successful, the participants must participate, that is, must have influence on the adopted decisions. If participation can be achieved under more or less authoritarian conditions, it is likely to be effective, just as it can be undermined (by disregard) with democratic leadership. Only management itself can determine whether it is worthwhile to initiate or continue the participation segment of the budgeted cycle.

At any rate, presuming an organization has determined that it can benefit from participation, are the psychological effects such that participation simply can be "grafted" onto existing procedures or are other changes necessary? Or indeed, if no changes are necessary, are there any that can be made so that efficiency, motivation, and productivity will be enhanced?

Suggested changes in budgeting are not difficult to find. Stedry, recognizing the possible motivating forces produced by budgets, seems to suggest that "phony" budgets be prepared while the real budget is kept secret.[28] The "phony" ones would be designed to induce maximum motivation through a manipulation of level of aspiration. This plan would require different phony budgets for each department and, indeed, for each individual. If different budgets are viewed as discriminatory and unfair devices, company morale might suffer. Further, if already disgruntled employees learn that they were striving to attain phony goals the effectiveness of future budgets, real or phony, might be seriously impaired.

A knowledge of the effects of level of aspiration may lead to changes designed to increase employee motivation and output. The budget cycle characteristically is tied to an arbitrary time schedule. Even with no other information, this is defensible logically and perhaps economically as well. If, however, the budget is to be used as a control device (in the sense of prohibiting excessive expenditures) as well as a motivating device, then it clearly should be tied to the level of aspiration

[27]Harold H. Kelley, "Communication in Experimentally Created Hierarchies," *Human Relations,* IV (1951), 39-56.

[28]*Budget Control and Cost Behavior,* pp. 5, 17, 41-42, and 71. Stedry does not use the term "phony."

cycle rather than to a time schedule. We know that success leads to a rising level of aspiration and, generally, failure to a lowering. Failure can also result in "leaving the field," that is, psychological or physical withdrawal from the goal-oriented environment.

It is suggested here that much more frequent comparison of performance and budget be made, including feedback to the employees of the results of the comparison. This recommendation is made for the following reasons: (*a*) If the performances meet or slightly exceed expectation, then level of aspirations will rise and budgets can and should be revised; otherwise employees will perform at the budget level when they could be performing at a higher budget level. Maximum efficiency can only be achieved by revising the budget upward. (*b*) If performances are just slightly below the budget expectations, budget changes are not necessary, but feedback is so that employees will continue to strive for the budget goals. (*c*) If performances are well below the budget, it may be well to revise the budget downward. If such revision is not made, employees' level of aspiration will fall, the budget will be viewed as unattainable, and output will fall. The danger here is that levels of aspiration and output may fall much more than is necessary. If the budget is revised downward just enough so that it is perceived as being attainable, then maximum output will be achieved again.

7

WHERE TRADITIONAL BUDGETING FAILS*

MICHAEL SCHIFF / ARIE Y. LEWIN

A number of investigators have lately been concerned with the relationship of reported corporate income to true income. One hypothesis is that top management behaves as if it were "smoothing" reported income. This thought was first explicitly stated by Gordon,[1] who showed that reported income of the U. S. Steel Corporation appeared to be smoothed through judicious application of accounting methods. Schiff,[2] in his study of the Chock Full O'Nuts Corporation, has noted

*Financial Executive, May 1968, pp. 57-62.

[1] M. J. Gordon, B. N. Horowitz and P. T. Meyers, "Accounting Measurements and Normal Growth of the Firm," *Research in Accounting Measurement* (Jaedicke, Ijzi, and Neilsen, eds.) American Accounting Association, 1966.

[2] M. Schiff, "Accounting Tactics and the Theory of the Firm," *Journal of Accounting Research*, Vol. 4, No. 1 (Aug. 1966), pp. 62-67.

that management appears to have deliberately evened-out reported income by decisions to expense or defer advertising costs of new products. This was apparently motivated by the management's desire to project an image of company growth. Lewin and Seidler[3] conclude that "income management"—the discretionary use of accounting methods—is seemingly painless to apply and is, therefore, preferred by top management to the difficult alternative of correcting internal problems that can be rationalized as temporary.

The question of reporting results exists not only in the relationship between the corporation and its external environment but, on a greater and more sophisticated scale, between divisions within the corporation itself. This article reports the results of a pilot study exploring the internal practices of managing reported results, vis-a-vis the budget and control system, from a behavioral decision-making viewpoint.

The most prevalent management accounting model is founded on the classical economic theory of the corporation and traditional organizational theory. Caplan[4] has compared and contrasted the assumptions which underlie the management accounting model based on the traditional attitudes of behavior with the modern organization theory, which represents the behavioral decision-making view. The fundamental difference in the two approaches is in their treatment of the role of humans in the organization. In the traditional approach, humans are viewed as passive members of the system,[5] whereas in the decision-making problem-solving process, the human and his ever-changing value system and limited information processing capability are emphasized.

It appears that most current budget and control systems are based on the traditional accounting model. Some of the unintended behavioral results of such a model have been reported by Argyris[6] and Dalton.[7] The latter, for example, reports on how lower level managements circumvent the budget and allocate resources to what they perceive as justifiable purposes.

It seems to us, however, that use of a budget and control system based on the traditional accounting model has unintended results which are especially serious with respect to the internal accounting for revenues, costs, and expenses.

Our views of the budget and its role within the firm are similar to those of Cyert and March in their treatise, "The Behavioral Theory of the Firm."[8] The budget in any company has the dual role of being a forecast of the year and a yardstick for managerial performance. The budget in its final form, however, is an explicit elaboration of organizational commitments for the year and reflects the resolution of demands for resources made by the various subunits of the firm.

Contrary to what Becker and Green[9] believe, the budget preparation process

[3]A. Y. Lewin and L. J. Seidler, "Income Management: The Alternative to Cutting Organizational Slack," working paper, Graduate School of Business Administration, New York University.

[4]E. H. Caplan, "Behavioral Assumptions of Management Accounting," *Accounting Review*, Vol. XLI (July 1966) pp. 496-509.

[5]J. G. March and H. A. Simon, *Organizations*, Wiley, 1958, p. 6.

[6]C. Argyris, *The Impact of Budgets on People*, The Controllership Foundation, 1952.

[7]M. Dalton, *Men Who Manage*, Wiley, 1959, pp. 31-52.

[8]R. M. Cyert and J. G. March, *A Behavioral Theory of the Firm* (Prentice Hall, 1963) pp. 36-38.

[9]S. Becker and D. Green, "Budgeting and Employee Behavior," *Journal of Business*, Vol. 35 (October 1962) pp. 392-402.

is a highly participative effort on the part of all managerial levels. This is because managers bargain about the performance criteria by which they will be judged throughout the year and for resource allocations. The outcome is a bargained budget incorporating varying degrees of slack.

Cyert and March see organizational slack in terms of the firm's cost function as the difference between minimum necessary costs and the actual costs of the firm. Organizational slack, in the Cyert and March view, arises unintentionally in the bargaining process, and its primary role is to stabilize performance despite fluctuations in the firm's environment. Basically, then, organizational slack would rise in relatively good times, providing a pool of emergency resources to be drawn upon in poor times, thus permitting the maintenance of organizational aspirations.

We believe as does Williamson[10]—contrary to Cyert and March—that managers consciously and intentionally create and bargain for organizational slack. Managers are motivated to achieve two sets of goals—the firm's goals and their personal goals. Personal goals are directly related to income (salary plus bonuses), size of staff, and control over allocation of resources. To maximize personal goals while achieving the goals of the firm requires a slack environment. This suggests that managers intentionally create slack.

Furthermore, the traditional budget and control system operates on the principle of management by exception. Since budgets are the criteria for measuring performance, and management participates in their formulation, it clearly serves management's interests to have slack in the budget. Lower level management, therefore, usually attempts to have a budget which it feels is attainable and, at the same time, meets top management's requirement for a desirable net income.

All the above is not meant to indicate that top management is not aware of "padding" and "sandbagging." Numerous cases can be cited in which top management simply imposes increased profit requirements at the end of the long process of preparing the budget. These higher demands, often achieved, affirm the existence of slack. Frequently, however, top management accepts proposed budgets without change (normally in favorable years), thus implicitly legitimizing the creation of organizational slack and increasing the long-run cost function of the firm.

The purpose of our study was to determine whether the creation of slack occurs in the course of budget preparation; if so, what mechanisms are used, how extensive is the slack and its creation, and in what depth does top management recognize the existence of slack and counteract its growth?

MODE OF INVESTIGATION

The three independent divisions (segments of large companies chosen from *Fortune's* 100 largest corporations) which participated in the exploratory phase of the study are referred to as divisions A, B, and C. The consent for the study was obtained from the corporate headquarters of these companies with the understanding that this was not to be viewed as a consulting assignment, that the interviews were to be held confidential, and that the principal investigators would have access to all necessary documents and reports. The investigation, which was made with strict adherence to this agreement, relied mainly on personal interviews and

---

[10]O. E. Williamson, *The Economics of Discretionary Behavior: Managerial Objectives in a Theory of the Firm.*

detailed study of the relevant materials. This procedure occasioned frequent visits to each location and frequent re-interviewing. Our observations were made as the budgets developed and are based on cumulative insights.

In each of the three company divisions, the work centered on the division president, the controller, the vice presidents of planning, marketing and production, and their staffs. The interviews in every case ranged over the roles of all persons involved in the planning and budgetary process. In one instance, interviews were held with a random sample of men from the field sales force. The interviews gave a picture of each individual's job, his role in the division, and, moreover, his estimate of how other key people influenced the system as well as his specific activities.

The three divisions differed according to the business of their company. Division A, a producer of heavy industrial equipment, also produces and markets the consumables for its equipment and consumables for equipment produced by competitors. Division B, in a competitive and technologically sophisticated market, sells its products mainly to original equipment manufacturers. Division C, the second largest U. S. producer of its product, sells to both the consumer and industrial markets.

Fortunately for us, the three divisions also differed in their economic climate. Division A has a history of successful operations evidenced by a steady sales growth, high gross margins, and decreasing manufacturing costs. Sales at A in 1967 approximated $70 million and the immediate future of the division seems secure. Division B has been since its inception a loss operation in spite of a 140-fold increase in sales during the last five years (sales in 1967 were about $32 million). Division C has been historically profitable and has grown steadily in sales (1967 volume $100 million) and in earnings, and is reputed to be the low-cost producer in its industry. However, in 1967, due to an unexpected sales slump in one of the company's major products, C did not expect to achieve, for the first time in years, its budgeted profit.

PLANNING PROCESS

In each of the three divisions, planning for the ensuing year was synonymous with the budget preparation for that year. Although each division has a so-called five-year plan, little effort is devoted to the preparation of plans for the other four years. The so-called long-range plans are created by lower level staff after the following year's budget has been completed. These long-range plans are usually based on simple extrapolation of trends, reflecting division management aspirations for future resources commitments.

In all divisions, budget preparation began toward the end of May with a letter from the group controller containing information on timing schedules and accompanied by outlines of company policies and objectives, observations on expected economic climate, and occasional guidelines as to corporate expectations regarding the division's performance for the coming year. The objectives or company goals are stated either in relation to past attainments or in nonoperational terms. None of the companies expect budgets that *maximize* profits; the objective is to obtain *satisfactory* returns.

Corporate memoranda are translated into internal guidelines for budgetary purposes by division management. The following are excerpts from letters accompanying internal budget messages reflecting division managements' general solutions to their budget problem:

"The base line for our 1968 Financial Budgets will be the attainment of 1968 sales volume within the framework of 1967 operating allowances. In brief, your 1968 budget will be in the amounts allotted to you for 1967."

"Preliminary estimates indicate the 1968 sales quota will rise approximately 10 per cent above the 1967 quota."

"To assure that budgets reflect the best thinking of the product line teams and not of any one particular person. To assure to the best of our ability that the budgets submitted are not only accurate but are also *reasonably attainable.*"

The first step in the planning process of the three divisions was estimating next year's sales. There was a staff member in each division whose task was to perform industry analysis, compute product market shares, and prepare a qualified statistical forecast of the coming year's sales by product, region, and, sometimes, customer. The statistical forecasts were in all cases generalized extrapolations of past history based on these rules: (1) Total market share is computed from industry sales. (2) Next year's market share is derived from market share trends. Next year's market share is taken as a linear extrapolation of the market share trend when it is rising. When it descends, next year's market share equals last year's. (3) With a given estimate of next year's market share, that year's sales are directly obtained from the forecasted total industry sales for the coming year. The figure is derived from various trade reports.

We next examined the detailed steps in the budget process for each of the divisions according to differences in organization, roles of the executives, and what might be called "styles" in development of slack.

DIVISION A

A group controller is responsible for the mechanical aspects of the budget for this and other divisions in the group. The controller, who plays a passive role in the budget process, is satisfied to act as a collector of information. The key participant in division A is the vice president of marketing, despite the fact that there are two sales forces concerned with marketing his product: his own force and a force calling on distributors selling the products of the entire group, including division A.

Starting with a statistical sales estimate, the marketing vice president of division A formulates a sales estimate based on his projection of profits acceptable to corporate headquarters. His estimate at the time of our study assumed a "normal" sales and profit growth. In preparing the rough first estimate, the vice president of marketing in division A used average prices at the lower end of the expected range of prices contemplated for the following year. Product managers reporting to him assisted in the task.

With only minor modifications, the vice president's estimates served as a basis for developing detailed expense and capital budgets for 1968. It should be noted that the field sales force was also asked to submit estimates of 1968 sales. *The differences between these and the ones prepared by the vice president were negligible since the crude extrapolation done in totals at the home office was being repeated by each district field sales office as well.*

The aggregate budget and projected income statement, employing standard factory costs reflecting current year-to-date experiences, was then completed. Significant in the development of projections of operating expenses was frequent use of the expense-sales ratio to test the acceptability of expense budgets, especially those relating to marketing functions.

The budget as presented was reviewed with some concern at a division meeting because the final profit figures did not quite approximate the amount they thought corporate headquarters would accept. A modest increase in volume and price was therefore included as well as a decrease in standard unit factory cost produced by the factory cost accountant. These changes yielded a suitable increase in the over-all net income.

Corporate headquarters nevertheless rejected the budget with a request for additional profits. These were finally achieved by another increase in the expected average unit selling price for the products of division A, at which point the budget for the division became the formal approved plan for 1968.

A significant number of field salesmen in division A were interviewed. These men set sales goals which were generally achievable without much alteration in their approach to the market or in their time allocations. It appeared that, if pressed to increase sales, there was reasonable expectation that they could do so by "reallocating their time." Indeed, one of the salesmen, through what appeared to be self-motivation, doubled his sales volume in three years in a hitherto "stable territory."

Finally, the group controller at division A estimated that there was about 20 to 25 per cent slack in the number of division employees, exclusive of manufacturing, but he was "in no position to do anything about it."

DIVISION B

There are two organizational characteristics which affect the budget process and "style" in this division. The controller is so much a part of the process that he makes modifications in key estimates. He reports directly to the division president and is strongly relied upon as chief financial officer of the division.

The products of division B are marketed by a group field sales force which sells products of other divisions as well. This sales body is assisted by a small group of field application engineers who are members of the marketing department of division B. The group field sales force is salaried but operates under an incentive bonus based on performance above dollar sales quota.

The initial sales projection, developed by the marketing research manager early in May 1967, indicated 1968 sales of 14 million units at $2.20. Working independently, the product marketing managers submitted an estimate of 18 million units at $2.20. (The five-year plan, used as a basis for capital budgeting, had indicated an expected sale of 20 million at $2.00.) A third input was the field sales force estimate of sales of 10 million units at $2.00, which was immediately modified to 13 million at $2.00 by the group marketing manager. It was observed by division B's management that the field force estimate was always kept low because of their desire to assure the earning of a bonus by setting a base which is readily achievable.

After a lengthy negotiation which involved the group vice president, a sales goal of 16 million at $2.00 was accepted. It should be noted that the unit price selected was at the low end of the estimated 1968 prices. (At the close of 1967, average prices were $3.68.) The various functional departments were then asked to submit expense budgets and the factory management was requested to develop standard costs. A profit and loss statement was subsequently developed which revealed a multi-million-dollar loss despite a prior directive from corporate headquarters requiring this division to at least break even in 1968.

The controller of division B began his budget adjustment process by raising the estimate for average prices. The revenue gained from this move, however, was somewhat offset when sales volume estimates had to be adjusted downward, based on more recent reports of actual results of the current year. He "recognized" then that some plant personnel would be employed only part of the year, although the initial budget showed them as full year. This difference amounted to a saving of $200,000. The controller next reviewed advertising expense with the product managers and trimmed another $120,000, *which was half the original advertising budget.* He also questioned the group marketing allocations to division B and obtained a $40,000 reduction—only a token, since the allocation was more than $1 million. Review of other costs yielded $140,000 more. The end result was a budget that still projected a loss but reflected total cost reductions of $500,000. All this was done with the support of the division president. The revised budget was then presented to corporate management, where it was again rejected with the clear directive to achieve a breakeven operation.

The divisional controller produced a new series of increased revenues and decreased costs. Average estimated price per unit was raised almost to the expected average high for the year with a resulting $720,000 in additional revenue. Postponement of more hiring of sales personnel added another $300,000. An accounting adjustment calling for deferral of the capitalization of new equipment until mid-year yielded a further saving of $100,000 by avoiding a depreciation charge for one-half of the year. With some other cost postponements and elimination of marginal product lines, the final budget projected a very minor loss for 1968.

It is clear from the above example that, contrary to theoretical expectations of Cyert and March, slack is also incorporated in the budgets of loss-producing divisions. We have specifically observed how slack appears in a budget through bargained sales goals, low average prices, manipulation of personnel requirements, marketing expenses, and accounting adjustments.

DIVISION C

As noted earlier, division C experienced a significant decline in sales in 1967 which was accompanied by an unanticipated labor rate increase of 6 per cent. Theoretically, slack previously incorporated into the budget would now be drawn upon to ameliorate expected profit decline. Therefore, we elected to examine *ex post facto* budget decisions for 1967 as well as the budgetary process for 1968.

Sales, at the end of January 1967, were below estimate in one product line and slightly up in the second. (The two lines account for the total sales of the division.) This trend became more pronounced by the end of March, when it was clear that one group of products had suffered by a 10 per cent sales slump while the second line exhibited a modest increase. Corporate headquarters may have been advised of this, but the division's forecast committee's monthly work sheets showed no attempt to modify the budget recognizing the sales slump, which continued through April. A small downward revision was made, however, at the end of that month. It was not until September that the forecast committee explicitly recognized the 10 per cent decline.

The division controller, an important member of the committee, activated a program officially referred to as "profit recovery." This was a device used by the controller fundamentally to plan slack in the budget. It should be stressed that corporate management accepts the profit recovery program as a means for improving performances by spending less than budget or selling more goods at better prices, which reflects a tight and efficient management. The extent of such built-in budgetary cushions is evident from a comparison of the projected profits prior to slack recovery with the actual profit in 1967. The sales slump, according to the controller, would have resulted in a 40 per cent drop in the division's profit. The final profit for 1967 was expected to be only 10 per cent off forecast! Profit recovery achieved this impressive result in spite of the unexpected 6 per cent labor cost increase granted production workers.

The profit recovery program in general led to cost savings over budget by postponing built-in overhead expenses, thus creating favorable efficiency variances, increasing prices, and cutting marketing expenses.

The 1967 budget called for hiring additional staff in various departments, yet none were hired. This counteracted the projected profit decline by 8 per cent. By re-evaluating marketing expenses, including advertising, the contribution gap was reduced another 15 per cent. This was accomplished by cutting travel expenses, cancelling technical and sales meetings, and reducing special promotional efforts.

Favorable efficiency variances were created by introducing process improvements which had been previously developed but not incorporated in standard costs. This reduced the contribution gap another 6 per cent. The eventuating figure, however, was partly cancelled by the wage rise to production workers. A selective 3 per cent price increase further lowered the contribution gap by 16 per cent.

This summary does not cover the total cost savings and accounting adjustments allowed within the 1967 budget, yet it is obvious that, through incorporating into the budget a formal profit recovery program, division C management created and controlled budgetary slack.

This was the actual climate or setting for the preparation of the 1968 budget. An operations controller, reporting directly to the division controller and responsible for sales forecasts, presented in June 1967 his projection for 1968. Prior to presenting it to the executives of the division, however, the projection was reviewed by the division controller and an upward modification was made to yield a more desirable profit. This projection was derived by using history, industry statistics, and general economic data. Division C has its own field sales force, but this force was not asked to submit sales estimates.

Sales estimates were used, nevertheless, as a basis for expense budget and standard costs. Current standard costs ignoring any improved process modifications were also employed, and budgets were prepared utilizing current expense-sales ratios.[11] A final budget, yielding the expected profit and varying only in minor details from the original estimate of the controller, was submitted and approved by corporate headquarters.

That the profit recovery program was built into the 1968 budget is evident from the fact that the twenty-four men for the marketing organization, budgeted in 1967 and not hired, were incorporated in the 1968 budget! Similarly, standard costs for 1968 did not incorporate process improvements operationally available in December 1967. These improvements would have reduced standard unit manufacturing cost by 15 per cent.

---

[11]It is suggested that since corporate headquarters, working from aggregate data, uses expense-sales ratio as a crude device for controlling expenses, the same method becomes the guide, both at division and departmental levels, for developing estimates.

STUDY RESULTS

It became cumulatively certain in our study that budgetary slack can be incorporated into both revenue and cost projections, and that internal slack may arise through accounting adjustments. We saw that sales objectives were arrived at on the basis of simple decision rules, resulting in the establishment of sales goals which are the most likely to be attained. Sales estimates often fell below a division's attainable estimates primarily due to interorganizational conflict.

Average price estimates seem to be initially budgeted at the low of their expected range and are generally finalized into the budget below their expected average. The greater the discrepancy between budgeted average prices and actual prices, the greater the slack and the ease of achieving or exceeding budgeted contribution.

On the cost side, we have seen that opportunities for incorporating slack are numerous and appear to require intimate knowledge of the budget and control system. Two main cost categories permit major slack manipulation: manufacturing cost standards and operating expenses. The inclusion of standard costs was at first surprising to us, but in retrospect appears simple and logical. Slack in standard cost arises from the discrepancy between the costs budgeted and what they actually would be if various known cost improvements were introduced. We have seen in at least one case that such improvements, producing efficiency variances, were included when needed and not when developed.

Marketing expenses result from many programs (for example, training meetings, special promotions, and the like) which are viewed by management as niceties. These programs appear on budgets, but the commitment of resources to them is contingent on progress made during the year in attaining the budget. Advertising budgets, which are treated in a similar way, strongly suggest that management formulates them on a basis of "how much can we afford," rather than on a basis related to an objective.

In the matter of operating expenses, which include budgetary allocations for new as well as replacement of personnel, it appears that budgeting for personnel and delay in hiring is extensively practiced and is a simple method for creating slack.

Accounting adjustments are also occasionally made to effect slack, but within divisional units over-all use of adjustments for this purpose is marginal. It seems that internal slack in organizations originates mainly through the mechanisms described above.

In our exploration, we concluded that slack may account for as much as 20 to 25 per cent of divisional budgeted operating expenses. The response of key people supports our conclusion. The group controller of division A estimated that slack in the administrative personnel category of the division was between 20 and 30 per cent. His estimate was based on a reorganization of the administrative unit in another division which had resulted in 25 per cent fewer people.

One division president, who was relatively new on the job, felt that the main office staff could be trimmed 20 per cent. He noted that in the past the main office force had been increased on a 1:1 ratio with sales, and questioned the need for it. In this same division, a number of people in the controller's group asserted that the controller could easily maintain the reported division contribution within 25 per cent.

Our results amply support the behavioral implications of the occurrence of slack as an unintended result of the budget and control system, especially where the system is based on the traditional accounting model of the firm. The management accounting control model assumes a plan—or budget—as the means to achieving profit goals based on maximal uses of resources. The system is based on such principles as responsibility accounting, variance analysis, management by exception, and so forth. It focuses on results after the budget by comparing the actual results to the budget.

Contending that the traditional system, contrary to expectations, does not result in maximial use of resources, we have shown on the basis of our pilot study how management can and does create slack to achieve attainable budgets and to secure resources for furthering their personal goals and desires. This behavior seems universal among managers; it occurs in profitable and unprofitable companies, whether stable or growing. Our study also suggests that the practice is widespread among controllers who are closely aligned with top management and assume the dominant role in the budget and control process of a decentralized control system.

8

BUDGETING FOR CONTROL*

ROGER L. M. DUNBAR

Many writers have defined the principal purpose of a business as making profits (for example, Dill, 1965), however, other objectives may also be important such as the coordinating of separate parts of the organization and the development of new products. To achieve these various objectives, the behavior of organization members must be directed and, if necessary, restricted (Tannenbaum, 1968), in many large-scale businesses this control is effected by the budgetary system (Sord and Welsch, 1958).

The term, budget, has been used rather loosely and may refer to at least two methods of control: (1) a budget may be used as a part of the allocation process authorizing expenditures, the budgeted manager being required to restrict spending to this authorized level; or (2) it may be used to set specific organizational goals such as the increase of sales or the reduction of costs. It is the latter focus which is of interest here and an attempt will be made to integrate both laboratory and field research findings to describe how much a system may influence behavior.

*Administrative Science Quarterly, March 1971, pp. 88-96.

THE BUDGETARY SYSTEM

With some notable exceptions such as Hofstede (1967) and Stedry (1960) attempts to understand how budgets control behavior have been rare. In this paper ideas derived from general systems theory are used to formulate the characteristics of a budgetary control system; then the implications of some empirical findings for this model are considered.

A system is a collection of interconnected elements; and if it has a purpose, general systems theorists refer to it as a machine. Each machine can have only one goal; therefore, to obtain a multipurpose system, machines must be combined. In order to achieve its particular purpose, a machine must have a feedback mechanism to sense changes away from its goal and then make appropriate adjustments. The adjustive reaction may be positive in that progress is reinforced by a continual increase of the goal in the desired direction, or negative, in that deviations are inhibited and the machine is brought back to a preset goal.

Stedry (1960: 2) said the primary objective of budgeting "is to increase long-run profit at the fastest possible rate"; however, a second goal of the budget is to facilitate organizational coordination by providing an accurate forecast of future results. Therefore, an ideal budgetary system would consist of a machine to increase profit and another to facilitate coordination by accurately forecasting results.

In the present model, the elements of the machine to increase profit are assumed to appear primarily in the process of setting the budget goal, implying a positive feedack mechanism. On the other hand, the elements of the machine to facilitate coordination are assumed to appear primarily in the process of achieving the budget, implying a negative feedback mechanism. Since the goal-setting machine sets the goal for the goal-achieving machine, there is clearly a hierarchical link between the two machines.

Members of the goal-setting machine, who may include the budget department, top management, and possibly the budgeted individuals themselves, must provide the positive feedback which will ensure the continual advancement of budget goals. The process whereby budget goals are set is here viewed as a black box. However, inputs to this goal-setting box can be isolated and then associated with performance outputs. Four inputs are considered: (*1*) whether goals set are difficult or easy to achieve; (*2*) whether the organization allows the budgeted individual to participate in the setting of the budget goal; (*3*) whether the organization provides monetary incentives for favorable performance relative to the budget; (*4*) whether the organization provides what the budgeted individual perceives as inadequate extrinsic rewards for favorable performance relative to the budget.

Goals must not only be set but also achieved. The critical step between the setting of a goal and its achievement is the acceptance of the goal by the goal-achieving machine, that is the budgeted individual. There is fairly convincing evidence that cognitively, human beings are negative feedback or homeostatic machines (Festinger, 1957; Brehm and Cohen, 1962). Therefore, it is assumed here, that if the budgeted individual can be persuaded to accept the budget goal, his homeostatic nature can be relied upon to achieve it, or to bring performance as close to it as the environment will allow.

GOAL DIFFICULTY AND PERFORMANCE

Stedry (1960) found that when subjects were given a budget goal of a specific number of correct solutions to a series of algebraic water-jar problems to be obtained within a fixed time period, those given a relatively low budget had significantly fewer solutions than those given a higher budget. Locke (1968) found that without exception, and in 12 separate studies, higher goals led to higher performance. Siegel and Fouraker (1960) found that in a bargaining situation, those subjects who had evidently been induced by the experimenter to adopt a high aspiration level negotiated contracts which were significantly more profitable ($6.25) than those with a lower level of aspiration ($3.35). Finally, Likert (1967) noted that high-performing sales offices set higher goals than low-performing offices.

Hofstede (1967) hypothesized that while up to a certain level of difficulty, higher goals would be accepted with resulting improved performance, beyond that, the goal would be rejected and performance would decline. It is this possibility of goal rejection that makes a positive feedback mechanism necessary to ensure a controlled increase of the budget which can be accepted as feasible by the goal-achieving budgeted individual. Unfortunately, little is known about the critical level at which budget goals are likely to be rejected rather than accepted. Stedry and Kay (1966) set foremen normal (that is, achieved 50 percent of the time in the past) and difficult (that is, achieved 25 percent of the time in the past) goals on two different job measures. The difficult goals were associated with either very good or very bad performance. Interviews indicated that good performance resulted when the foreman thought the goals challenging, but bad performance resulted when they thought them impossible.

Stedry (1962) in the water-jar experiment mentioned, distinguished three levels of goal difficulty and found that acceptance was not linearly dependent on difficulty, as Table 1 shows. However, when harder goals were set, Table 1 also shows that the probability that subjects set still higher goals declines. These studies by Stedry and Kay (1966) and Stedry (1962) might indicate that to increase profit and obtain predictable results, the positive feedback mechanism could be designed to set goals that can be achieved, based on past performance, not more than 40 percent of the time but more than 25 percent of the time.

TABLE 1   Probabilities of Achieving and Accepting
Different Levels of Goal Difficulty

	Level of goal difficulty		
	Low	Medium	High
Probability of achieving goal	.69	.59	.39
Probability of accepting goal	.64	.53	.62
Probability of setting a higher goal	.25	.14	.00

*Stedry, 1962.

If goals are too difficult, the performance of the goal-achieving machine will not always reach the planned level, and it will be necessary to trade off the costs and benefits of more profit for more coordination difficulties, as shown in Figure 1. The goal is shown as increasingly difficult, but actual performance in terms of profit increases at a slower rate up until the point where the goal is rejected, then it falls off rapidly. Also, as the goal is increased, the discrepancy between planned and

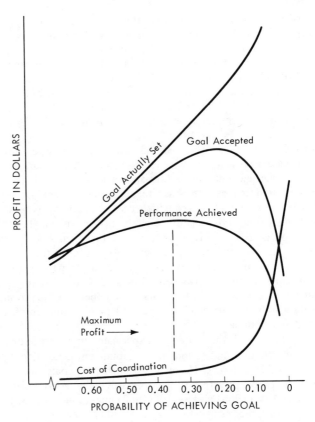

FIGURE 1   Trade-off Between Harder Goals, Performance, and Coordination Costs

achieved performance increases, leading to an increase in coordination cost and a
consequent reduction in profits.

PARTICIPATION IN GOAL SETTING

The organization may allow the budgeted individual to be incorporated into
the goal-setting machine. Such participation has consequences for goal setting, goal
acceptance, and performance. Vroom (1964) after citing a number of empirical
studies, concluded that as subordinates were given a larger influence in decisions,
their performance improved, partly because of the ego involvement which participation generated. In a budgetary context this may be interpreted to mean a greater
willingness by budgeted individuals to accept the budget goal; with a difficult goal
this acceptance would be likely to result in improved performance.

Participation may also bring responsibilities the budgeted individual was not
previously aware of to his attention. Hofstede (1967) found that participation was
associated with the relevance of financial standards, but not technical standards.
First-line managers had considered technical standards their responsibility but not

financial performance, until participation in the setting of financial budgets made financial standards relevant.

However unless participation involves the setting of specific goals after discussion, there is little effect on performance. Lawrence and Smith (1955) introduced group discussion into four industrial work groups. Although there was a slight improvement in the performance of the two groups which did not set goals, production increased very significantly in the other two groups which had set objectives after the discussion.

The timing of goal determination in the participation process may be important. Stedry (1960) found that subjects given a very difficult goal and then asked to specify their personal level of aspiration performed significantly better than subjects asked to specify their levels of aspiration and afterwards given a very difficult goal. He estimated the difference in performance to be equivalent to six standard deviations. He suggested that the first group formulated their level of aspiration with the high budget in mind, but the second group rejected the difficult goal because they could not reconcile it with their already specified aspiration level.

Hofstede (1967) also expected participation to help ensure a perception among budgeted individuals that goals were fair, and therefore the budget would be more relevant to them. However, the association between responses to a question on whether the goal setting took account of special problems and the relevance of the budget was not significant. Stedry (1962) found no association between perceptions of how accurate budget setting had been and performance.

Vroom (1960) hypothesized that participation and personality characteristics will interact to affect performance. He found that for persons with a high need for independence, the extent of their psychological participation in decision making was significantly associated ($r = .31$) with their performance, but not significant for those with medium or low independence needs. He found similar high associations for persons with moderate ($r = .38$) and low ($r = .33$) authoritarian scores, but no significant correlation for those with a high authoritarian need. When he partialled out the effects of age, education, and occupational level, the differences between the correlations attributable to the personality variables generally increased.

Hofstede (1967), using a slightly different measure of authoritarianism, obtained even more significant results in a budgetary context. After dividing managers into low, medium, and high authoritarians, he obtained correlations of .76, .64, and .47, respectively, between participation in goal setting and the budget's perceived relevance to performance. Probably Hofstede's (1967) correlations were much higher than Vroom's (1960) because Vroom associated participation with actual performance as assessed by the superior, whereas Hofstede associated participation with the relevance of the budget as perceived by the budgeted individual. In Vroom's (1960) analysis, goal acceptance intervened between the setting of the goal and performance. Nevertheless, both studies indicate that personality factors have consequences for the influence of participation on performance, and may, according to Hofstede's (1967) results, determine whether the budgeted individual will accept the budget.

In summary, discussions have little effect on performance unless coupled with goal setting. Participation may ensure that goals are not advanced so rapidly that they cannot be accepted by the budgeted individual, and the ego involvement produced by discussion, together with the timing of goal determination, may lead to great goal acceptance. The extent of goal acceptance as a result of participation is probably affected by personality characteristics such as authoritarianism and dependence.

MONETARY INCENTIVES AND GOAL SETTING

Stedry (1960: 19), referring to cost goals and cost performance, hypothesized "that management can increase the tendency of the department head to aim at or below this goal by increasing the positive reward associated with its attainment and/or increasing the negative reward associated with its non-attainment." Similarly, Rath (1960: 172), a management consultant, concluded from "personal observation in hundreds of plants" that there is no motivational force as powerful as a wage system which related individual earnings directly to output "by means of a formula linking performance to a predetermined standard."

Toppen (1965a, 1965b) provided fairly convincing evidence in an experiment that subjects performed a very routine task faster, at least in the short run, if offered monetary incentives. In one experiment, the number of pulls on a manipulandum by subjects paid at the rate of 25 cents was significantly greater than the number by those paid at the rate of 1 cent. In another experiment, subjects paid by piece rate had a significantly greater output than subjects paid a fixed amount, irrespective of output.

Locke *et al.* (1968) argued that monetary incentives would only affect performance to the extent that the rewards persuaded the subject to set higher goals for himself. In an experimental task requiring subjects to list as many uses as possible for a common object—for example, a cardboard box—subjects were either assigned difficult goals, allowed to set their own goals, or else not required to set any goals. No significant difference in performance was found between subjects who were rewarded and those who were not; but subjects assigned higher goals showed a significantly greater improvement than those assigned lower goals. Locke *et al.* (1968) concluded that differences in goal difficulty dominated any direct effects of monetary incentives.

In another experiment Locke *et al.* (1968) showed that monetary incentives resulted in the setting of less difficult goals, if this was perceived as a way of increasing income. In a word-unscrambling task, subjects could choose the word length, but were paid according to whether they successfully unscrambled a word, irrespective of length. As the level of incentive pay increased, subjects set goals, that is, recorded intentions of decreasing word length, and also chose shorter words to unscramble. A significant association was found between incentive and intentions, but when the effect of intentions was partialled out, no relation was found between incentive and choice. This finding suggests that monetary incentives directly affect goal setting, and then the subject behaves in such a way as to achieve the goal he has set.

The Locke *et al.* (1968) experiment also emphasized that monetary incentives may encourage subjects to set less difficult goals, and since goal levels affect performance, higher monetary incentives may be associated with lower performance. This is not the association usually assumed in the literature. Like Georgopoulos *et al.* (1957: 346), most writers have assumed that "It is doubtful whether many people see low productivity as helping the achievement of many of their goals." Yet if rewards are strictly contingent on goal achievement, then lowering goals allows the rewards to be obtained more easily, and therefore may result in lower performance.

Top management may be aware of this potential link between incentives and lower performance, for it is almost universally accepted that information about pay and salary assessment should be kept secret (Lawler, 1967). Such secrecy allows the link between lower performance and either higher income or the same income for less effort to be hidden, but it also fosters the opposite belief, that higher performance is associated with higher income. Georgopoulos *et al.,* (1957) collected questionnaire information from a population of incentive workers, nearly half of whom had had less than a year's experience on the job and found that 62 percent felt that high productivity reduced their earnings in the long run, and 64 percent felt that low productivity did also. Evidently, most workers saw the link between income and performance quite clearly. As long as income depended on performance relative to standards, and standards could be adjusted so that take-home pay was within an appropriate range, higher performance could result in increased goals; to avoid such punishment for high performance, less ambitious goals could be set, thus lowering performance.

Monetary incentives, therefore, do affect goal setting which in turn affects performance. If budgeted individuals set their own goals, they will set them so that their personal income is increased. When payment depends strictly on goal achievement, budgeted individuals will reduce their goals and therefore performance. Only if incentive payments depend on some direct measure of performance, rather than on a relative performance standard, are difficult goals likely to be set and performance improve.

INADEQUATE EXTRINSIC REWARD AND GOAL SETTING

Hypotheses derived from Festinger's (1957) theory of cognitive dissonance suggest that when an individual chooses to carry out an activity for which he will receive inadequate reward from his environment, he will increase the effort he invests in the activity. As a result, the person's performance may improve, allowing the attainment of personal rewards from significant achievements. This sense of personal achievement substitutes for the original inadequate environmental reward and reassures the person that his original decision to engage in the activity was justified. Specifically, Weick (1966) held that inadequate environmental reward for performance will lead a subject to focus on his own inputs and shift the responsibility for his behavior from an external to an internal source. If a suitable dissonant cognition could be created with respect to budgeting, goal setting and hence performance might improve.

Hofstede (1967) recognized this possibility, though not the link with dissonance theory. His thesis was that budgeted individuals, not top management, should regard budgeting as a game. Such a perception is certainly in contrast to arguments that budgeting is an important element of organizational control and that extrinsic rewards, specific and implicit, should depend on budget achievement. To create cognitive dissonance, extrinsic rewards would not be dependent on goal achievement, and for maximum dissonance, the organization would allow managers to work without budgets if they wished. Then the reason for having a budget, that it was needed to facilitate organizational control, would be removed. To resolve the dissonance of choosing to commit himself to a budget in such a situation, a manager would have to wish to obtain the sense of individual achievement which comes from meeting a goal, rather than because of any extrinsic rewards provided by top management.

Two laboratory experiments provide some insight into how cognitive dissonance might affect budget performance. Stedry (1962) found a significant negative association between performance and subjects' beliefs that high monetary rewards would make them work harder. He also found a significant positive association between performance and the enjoyment obtained from the inherent challenge in the task, in contrast to the satisfaction of earning money. Stedry (1962) explained these results as due to subjects' differential financial needs and differential abilities to do the experimental problems. However, since the experimental task was presented to subjects (Stedry, 1962: 61), "as a game in order to avoid possible antimathematical blocks associated with problems in algebra," an alternative explanation might be that subjects who accepted the experimental task as a game then sought to overcome challenging goals, whereas those who saw achievement of the goal as a means to earn money did not perform as well.

Weick (1964: 534) asked students to take part in a "study of problem-solving to receive credit toward fulfilling a course requirement." The experimental task required subjects to identify, by means of cues, a concept chosen by the experimenter. Subjects were asked to set time goals and to identify the concept as quickly as possible with as few cues as possible. They were also told that other people had performed the task, that fairly complete norms had been developed, and that afterwards, they would be able to compare their performance with that of others. Low-dissonance subjects carried out the experiment as they had been led to expect, but high-dissonance subjects were told that they would not receive the credit that had been promised them and that, therefore, they were free to leave even though the experimenter preferred that they stayed. Four out of 54 students left so that 50 students took part in the experiment. Weick's (1964) main hypothesis was that the performance of high-dissonance subjects would be superior to that of low-dissonance subjects.

As Table 2 shows, the high-dissonance group performed only slightly below their goal, but the low-dissonance group was much below. All the differences between the two conditions were statistically significant and in the expected direction. Performance improved in both groups, but while the attainment time on the fourth trial for the low-dissonance group was 117.4 seconds, it was only 43.71 seconds for the high-dissonance group.

Weick's (1964) results are impressive, and a provocative analogy can be made with business budgeting. Top management could carry out its long-range planning

TABLE 2   Performance of Group Getting Credit and Getting No Credit*

Performance groups	Condition	
	No credit	Credit
Average goal time (seconds)	62.44	125.40
Average performance time (seconds)	70.64	191.38
Attainment discrepancy (seconds)	−8.20	−65.98
Average cost of cues (points)	72.57	118.77

*Weick, 1964.

independent of managers at the operating level. Then, like Weick's (1964) students, managers could be allowed a choice as to whether they would participate in the budgeting game. If they chose to use a budget, both top management and the budgeted individual would want challenging goals, because then achieving the goal would give a sense of accomplishment to the budgeted individual and it would also increase profit for top management.

SUMMARY

A budgeting system was described as a hierarchical combination of a goal-setting machine and a goal-achieving machine. The goal-achieving machine sets goals which should increase corporate profit; the goal-achieving machine endeavors to achieve exactly the budgeted goal in order to facilitate organizational coordination and planning. Evidence presented showed that goals significantly affect performance, that participation in goal setting of itself, had little discernible direct effect on the goal levels set, that monetary incentives encouraged the setting of less difficult goals when the reward depended strictly on goal achievement, and it was suggested that inadequate extrinsic rewards may result in the setting of difficult goals and higher performance.

As a result of the survey, a number of problems for further research have become apparent.

1. Evidence is needed as to whether personality characteristics such as needs for dependence or authoritarianism are associated with a budgeted individual's acceptance of a goal set by higher management.

2. Evidence is needed about the relation between managers' perceptions of how their budgetary performance affects their salaries and how this perception affects their goal-setting behavior. The effect of other variables on goal-setting behavior should also be considered.

3. In particular, evidence is needed from industrial settings of the effects on goal setting and performance when cognitive dissonance has been created by allowing managers to choose whether they will work with a budget when it is known that there are extrinsic rewards for goal achievement.

4. Evidence is also needed about how variables such as those discussed in this paper may interact with each other to affect goal setting, budget acceptance and budget achievement.

REFERENCES

Brehm, Jack W., and Arthur R. Cohen. 1962. Explorations in Cognitive Dissonance. New York: Wiley.

Dill, William R. 1965. "Business organizations." In James G. March (ed.), Handbook of Organizations: 1071-1114. Chicago: Rand-McNally.

Festinger, Leon. 1957. A Theory of Cognitive Dissonance. Evanston: Row, Peterson.

Georgopoulos, Basil S., Gerald M. Mahoney, and Nyle W. Jones. 1957. "A path-goal approach to productivity." Journal of Applied Psychology, 41: 345-353.

Hofstede, Geert H. 1967. The Game of Budget Control. Assen: Van Gorcum.

Lawler, Edward E. 1967. "Secrecy about management compensation: are there hidden costs?" Organizational Behavior and Human Performance, 2: 182-189.

Lawrence, Lois C., and Patricia C. Smith. 1955. "Group decision and employee participation." Journal of Applied Psychology, 39: 334-337.

Likert, Rensis. 1967. The Human Organization. New York: McGraw-Hill.

Locke, Edwin A. 1968. "Toward a theory of task motivation and incentives." Organizational Behavior and Human Performance, 3: 157-189.

Locke, Edwin A., Judith A. Bryan, and Lorne M. Kendall. 1968. "Goals and intentions as mediators of the effects of monetary incentives on behavior." Journal of Applied Psychology, 52: 104-121.

Rath, Arthur A. 1960. "The case for individual incentives." Personnel Journal, 39: 172-175.

Siegel, Sidney, and Lawrence E. Fouraker. 1960. Bargaining and Group Decision Making. New York: McGraw-Hill.

Sord, Burnard H., and Glen A. Welsch. 1958. Business Budgeting, A Survey of Management Planning and Control Practices. New York: Controllership Foundation.

Stedry, Andrew C. 1960. Budget Control and Cost Behavior. Englewood Cliffs, N.J.: Prentice-Hall.

——— 1962. "Aspiration levels, attitudes, and performance in a goal-oriented situation." Industrial Management Review, 2: 60-76.

Stedry, Andrew C., and Emanuel Kay. 1966. "The effect of goal difficulty on performance: a field experiment." Behavioral Science, 11: 459-470.

Tannenbaum, Arnold S. 1968. Control in Organizations. New York: McGraw-Hill.

Toppen, J. T. 1965a. "Effect of size and frequency of money reinforcement on human operant (work) behavior." Perceptual and Motor Skills, 20: 259-269.

———. 1965b "Money reinforcement and human operant (work) behavior: 111 piece-work-payment and time-payment comparisons." Perceptual and Motor Skills, 21: 907-913.

Vroom, Victor H. 1960. Some Personality Determinants of the Effects of Participation. Englewood Cliffs, N.J.: Prentice-Hall.

———. 1964. Work and Motivation. New York: Wiley.

Weick, Karl E. 1964. "Reduction of cognitive dissonance through task enhancement and effort expenditure." Journal of Abnormal and Social Psychology, 68: 533-539.

———. 1966. "Task acceptance dilemmas: a site for research on cognition." In Shel Feldman (ed.), Cognitive Consistency: 225-255. New York: Academic Press.

9

A COMPUTER SIMULATION MODEL OF MUNICIPAL BUDGETING *

JOHN P. CRECINE

1. A POSITIVE, EMPIRICAL THEORY OF MUNICIPAL BUDGETING

The model is stated in the form of a computer program. The nature of the budgetary decision process suggests such an approach. Even a superficial examination of the municipal resource allocation procedure indicates that it is the result of a *sequence* of decisions—departmental requests, mayor's executive budget, and final council appropriations. A computer program is really a collection of *instructions* executed in a *specific* sequence. If a computer program is to be an appropriate way to describe the budgetary process, the individual rules ought to be stable over time and executed in a specific sequence (be part of a "stable" structure). Fortunately, there are some compelling reasons why this should be so.

One obvious reason why programmed decisions tend to deal with repetitive problems, and *vice versa,* is that "if a particular problem recurs often enough, a routine procedure will usually be worked out for solving it." Certainly the municipal budget is a recurrent problem (yearly). Evidence is growing that recurrent, complex problems are solved by individuals by breaking the global problem into a series of less complex ones, and then solving the simplified problems sequentially.

In particular, the problem-solving behavior of individuals has been described using a computer program, for a trust investment officer by Clarkson [2], a department store buyer by Cyert, March, and Moore [4], and laboratory subjects solving simple problems [10, 11] and chess players by Newell and Simon [9].

1.1. Computer Simulation of Municipal Budgeting

A simulation of the budgetary process must describe the behavior of many individuals—department budget officers, budget officials in the mayor's office, and the council. There is no reason to think that the hundred or so actors involved in the formal budgetary decision system will be any more difficult to "program" or simulate than *single individuals,* however. The difficulty, if any, arises from the number of decisions and decision makers in our model, and the quantity of data to be analyzed.[1]

*Management Science, July 1967, pp. 768-815.

[1]The implications of the "magnitude of the problem" are many. First, it should be fairly obvious that each actor in our simulation model will be described in a simpler manner than the individual problem solvers in most of the works cited above. Secondly, assumptions will have to be made which will detract from the overall accuracy (i.e., completeness) of the model. For

Simulation as a Research Tool. "Simulation is a technique for building theories that reproduce part or all of the output of a behaving system [2, p. 16]." In addition, some simulation models have the goal of reproducing not only final results but intermediate outputs as well. This is the task to which the model addresses itself. The attempt to reproduce output and procedures is in the form of a computer program representing the structural form of the decision process (sequence of decisions), the functional form of the individual decision rules (individual equations representing actual decision rules), and the decision parameters (values of "constants" or empirically determined variables embedded in the structure and functional relations of the model).

2. OVERVIEW OF MUNICIPAL BUDGETING

The entire decision process can usefully be thought of as an organized means for the decision maker to deal with the potential complexity of the budgetary problem. The most prominent feature of the "original" problem in terms of its contribution to complexity is an externally imposed constraint of a balanced budget[2]—by requiring that, *at some level of generality,* all budget items be considered simultaneously.

2.1. Problem Perception

Before proceeding, we should note that the "problem we are referring to is the budgetary problem as seen by the actual decision makers (department officials, mayor and mayor's staff, and council members). It is quite clear (from interviews) that the decision makers *do not* see the problem as one of optimally balancing community resources, allocating funds among functions to achieve overall community goals, and the like. The problem is generally "seen" by department heads as one of submitting a budget request that 1) assures the department of funds to carry on existing programs as part of a continuing attack on existing problems, 2) is acceptable to the mayor's office, and 3) provides for a reasonable share of any increase in the city's total budget, enabling the department to attack new problems (if any). The mayor's problem is largely one of recommending a budget that 1) is balanced, 2) at least maintains existing service levels, 3) provides for increases in city employee wages if at all possible, and 4) avoids tax increases (especially property tax increases, in the belief that increased property taxes cause business and industry to move from the city, reducing the municipal tax base). If, after achieving some of the above objectives, the mayor has "extra" funds, they will be used to sponsor programs or projects the mayor has on his "agenda," or to grant a portion of departments' supplemental requests.

---

example, it will be necessary to assume that each department head in the system behaves according to the same decisional model, with only parameters changing. It is obviously not practical or reasonable to interview all department heads and all parties involved in the budgetary process. Behavioral rules attributed by others to our decision makers will have to be incorporated in the model without individual verifications. The reasonableness and "accuracy" of these necessary "short cuts" will, of course, be measured empirically when the model is tested.

[2]Required in the city charter, articles of incorporation, or by the State Legislature.

The "problem" for the council is to review the mayor's budget recommendations and check for "obvious" errors and omissions. Because of the complexity and detail in the mayor's budget and lack of council staff, the council's options are limited largely to approving the mayor's budget. The requirement of a balanced budget means that a change in one expenditure category, for instance, implies a balancing change in other account categories, administrative units, or revenues—i.e., one change in the budget (by council) implies many changes which the council has neither the time nor staff to consider.

2.2. Partitioning the Problem into Manageable Subproblems

One of the ways municipal decision makers deal with the *potential* complexity of the municipal resource allocation problem is through their necessarily simplified perception of the problem as discussed above. Other simplifying heuristics observed were:

1. The operating budget is treated separately from the capital budget as a generally independent problem. The only behavioral connection between the operating and capital budgets is the "logical" elaboration of capital budgeting decisions in the operating budget.[3]

2. The budget is formulated within a system of administrative units (departments and bureaus) and account categories (salaries, supplies and expenses, equipment, etc.) that is extremely stable from year to year. This partial structuring of the problem "allows" most of the decision makers to treat the appropriation question for one account category in one administrative unit as a (sub-) problem, separate from the overall resource allocation problem. Thus, the overall problem is transformed into a series of smaller problems of determining appropriations for individual departments.

3. The revenue estimates are generally separate from expenditure estimates. That is, estimates of yields from a given tax are treated independently from expenditures. While, on occasion, tax rates may be adjusted somewhat on the basis of preliminary calculations of *total expenditure estimates,* in order to balance the budget, tax *yield estimates* are seldom manipulated to achieve a balance.

4. The structure of the decision process itself represents a division of labor between department heads, the mayor's office, and the council—reflecting not only the administrative hierarchy, but a set of simplifying heuristics for making a complex problem manageable.

5. Finally, an additional simplifying policy is found in all cities investigated. The presence of a uniform wage policy which maintains relative positions of employees within a city-wide civil service pay scale, eliminates the potentially complex problem of deciding wage rates on an individual basis while attempting to maintain "similar-pay-for-similar-jobs" standards.[4]

---

[3]The "legitimate" claim on operating funds by the capital budget is reflected in the following, found in the Mayor's Message accompanying the 1965 Pittsburgh Budget: "A big item in the Lands and Buildings request pertains to the opening and operation of the new Public Safety Center next Spring. . . . There is a non-recurring expenditure of $150,000 for new furniture . . . and $91,000 is sought for maintenance personnel."

[4]On occasion, uniformed policemen and firemen's salaries are treated separately from the others.

2.3. Governing by Precedent

Perhaps the overriding feature of the mayor's budgetary "problem" is the balanced budget requirement. *If* the mayor took even the majority of items in the budget under serious consideration, his task would be enormous. The requirement of a *balanced* budget *could* mean that not only would the mayor have to consider every budget item, but he would have to consider each item relative to all other items. Somehow the entire level of police expenditures would have to be justified in light of the implied preemption of health department services, public works, fire department expenditures, etc. Obviously the mayor does not have either the staff, cognitive abilities, or time to undertake such a study—even if the necessary knowledge and information existed.

Instead, as we have seen above, the mayor perceives this year's budget problem as basically similar to last year's with a slight change in resources available (new revenue estimates) for dealing with a continuing set of municipal problems (police and fire protection, urban renewal, public works, transporation) augmented by a small number of newly emerging problems and a small number of partial solutions to old problems. In this context, a "logical" way to proceed in solving the complex budgeting problem is to take "last year's solution" (current appropriations) to the problem and modify it in light of *changes* in available resources and shifts in municipal problems to obtain "this year's solution." This, of course, means that the budget is a slowly changing thing, consisting of a series of "marginal changes" from previous budgets.[5] Only small portions of the budget are reconsidered from year to year and consequently, once an item is in the budget, its mere existence becomes its "reason for being" in succeeding budgets.

This "government by precedent" is an integral part of most positive models of decision making in the literature. Cyert and March's *A Behavioral Theory of the Firm* describes the usage of previous solutions and solution procedures to solve new problems and is largely a model of *incremental* adaptations of economic organizations to their internal and external environment [4, p. 104.]. Braybrooke and Lindblom argue that "precedent" is justified and defensible as a "rational" decision strategy [1, pp. 225-245.]. Wildavsky emphasizes the role of "precedent" as an "aid to calculation" in the Federal budgetary process [13, pp. 13-18, 58-59.].

2.4. Openness of Public Decisions

A basic property of decision making in the public sector (vs. the private) is the realization that both decisions and decision procedures are always subject (at least potentially) to public scrutiny. Decisions in the public sector would tend to be more "defensible" than corresponding ones in the private sector and each particular decision (budget item) in a decision system (entire budget) ought to be able to stand on its own "merits." In addition, decision procedures are also subject to public question. We would argue that openness of public decisions reinforces the use of rather straightforward methods of partitioning the budgetary problem, the use of *precedent* as a defensible[6] decision strategy, and encourages the use of simpler, easier-to-understand decision procedures than might otherwise be found.

---

[5]These notions are very similar to those of "disjointed incrementalism," [1,7].

[6]We would also argue that, in general, the need for "defensible" decisions leads to more conservative decisions in the public sector than in the private.

3. FORMAL MODEL OF MUNICIPAL BUDGETING

In the context of the problem complexity and devices used to deal with that complexity, we now turn to an analysis of the model's behavioral characteristics. An overview of the model is found in Figure 1. Inasmuch as the model can be broken down into three reasonably independent submodels (the existence of these submodels illustrates the use of partitioning and division of labor in dealing with complexity), we will discuss each submodel separately.

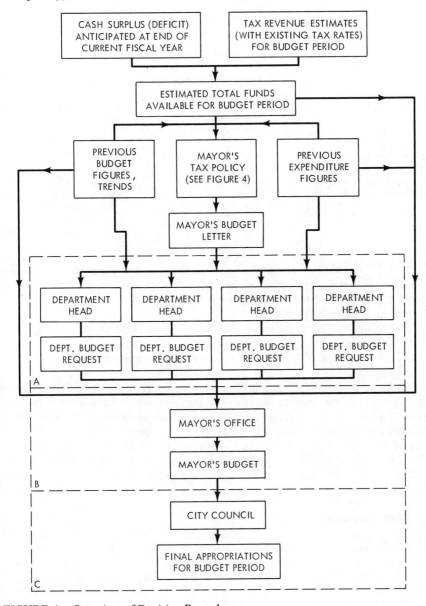

FIGURE 1   Overview of Decision Procedures

3.1. Scope of Model

The formal, computer model explicitly considers three decision processes—departmental requests as formulated by the various department heads in city government, mayor's budget for council consideration, and the final appropriations as approved by city council. These three processes are indicated by areas A, B, and C in Figure 1. The outputs of the departmental-request submodel are inputs to the mayor's budget submodel and outputs of the mayor's submodels are inputs to the council appropriations submodel.

The outputs of each submodel correspond quite closely in number and level of detail with the outputs (or decisions) found in the municipal budgetary process. In the model, each department included in the general fund or operating budget has requests for appropriations for each of 2 to 5 standard account categories—depending on the city involved. For example, the model produces at each of the 3 stages of the decision process, the following dollar estimates for the City Planning Department:

Cleveland		Detroit		Pittsburgh	
Personal services	$X	Administrative salaries	$X	Administrative sala-	$X
Materials, supplies, ex-		Non-adm. salaries		ries	
penses, equipment,	$Y	Materials, supplies and	$Y	Non-adm. salaries	$Y
repairs and improve-		expenses		Materials, supplies	$W
ment		Equipment and repairs	$Z	and expenses	
				Equipment	$U
				Maintenance	$Z

44 to 64 departments and administrative units are involved in the cities examined, with each unit having estimates for 2-5 accounts. Between 128 and 220 decisions are produced at each of the three stages of the model, for each year in the study, in each of the three cities examined.

At this point, one might legitimately ask two important questions:

1. Why are accounts categorized in the manner indicated?

2. Why is "dollars" the unit of resource allocation rather than men, number of street lights, etc.?

Both questions are "crucial" ones for a normative theory of budgeting. In a positive theory, however, the answers are rather straightforward—and essentially identical. People interviewed in all three cities think and talk in terms of "dollars"; they differentiate (at least in interviews) expenditures in terms of the same categories used in their city's accounting system. Apparently, dollar amounts provide the relevant reference points for dealing with the conceptual framework provided by the city's accounting system[7] and provide the basis for the participants' cognitive maps of the process.

3.2. DEPT. Submodel

Role—The role of the department head is similar to that of the agency or bureau chief in the Federal government as described in the Wildavsky study [13, pp. 8-21]. His objective is to obtain the largest possible amount of funds for his

---

[7]A legitimate question would be, "Why was a city's accounting system designed around a particular set of account categories?" This, however interesting and important, is beyond the scope of the study.

department and his purposes. Just as "Washington is filled'. . . 'with dedicated men and women who feel that government funds should be spent for one purpose or another, "[8] so are muncipal governments. In general, department heads, through experience and the process of socialization into their positions, and by "learning" that their request is likely to be cut by the mayor's office or council, tend to ask for more than they "expect" to get. This "padding" of the budget is one part of a system of mutual expectations and roles. Department heads are expected to ask for more than they really "need," the mayor's office is expected to cut these requests in order to balance the budget.

Context—The decisions we are speaking of set the limit on spending for the coming fiscal year. They are limits on manpower, supplies, material, and equipment. They are not program budgets in the sense that exact activity mixes are included in the municipal budget. In a sense, what we are talking about is an intermediate decision. This decision provides the constraints under which decisions about particular activities that a department will undertake must be made. The setting of *levels* of expenditures is just one part of the department head's continuing problems. Within a given expenditure ceiling, many different activity mixes can be utilized. "Low ceilings, in short, can still permit several rooms [12, p. 414.]."

DEPT. Model Characteristics. The role of the mayor's budget letter and the budget forms sent to the department head is a clear one. Together with the time schedule for submission of the completed budget forms, these items have the effect of structuring the department head's problem for him. Budget forms are typically sent to department heads less than two months in advance of the presentation of the completed budget to council. The department head usually has about one month before his completed request forms are due in the mayor's office.

The importance of the time deadline should not be underestimated. In that there is no moratorium on the department head's problems, budget compilation represents an additional workload. In the context of a myriad of nonbudgetary problems and duties, most department heads are more than willing to accept the problem structure provided by the budget forms. To do otherwise would not only involve creating an alternative structure, but would place the "burden of proof" on the department head as far as justifying the alternative to the mayor's office.

Just how is the problem presented to the department head so as to prestructure it for him?

Budget forms—Budget forms seem to be nearly one of the physical constants of the universe [13, p. 59.]. They are laid out as follows:

	Expenditures Last Year	Appropriation This Year	Next Year's Request
Standard account 1	$54321.00	$57400.00	?
Itemization of 1	—	—	
Standard account 2	$43219.00	$45600.00	?
Itemization of 2			
⋮			
Standard account N	$ 100.00	$ 120.00	?
Itemization of N			

---

[8] A quote of President John F. Kennedy, [12, p. 414.].

By structuring the department head's problem, the forms "bias" the outcome or decision in two ways:

1. They provide a great deal of incentive for the department head to formulate his requests within the confines of the existing set of accounts.
2. They provide for an automatic comparison between "next year's" request and "this year's" appropriation—which automatically determines that "this year's" appropriation provides one criterion or reference point for "next year's" request.

The Mayor's budget letter always contains instructions which reinforce the structuring of the problem provided by budget forms—to provide a ". . . written explanation for any change in individual code accounts," "(e)xperience for the years 1962 and 1963 is shown . . . to assist you in estimating your needs for 1965," "(u)nder the heading 'Explanation of Increases and Decreases' must be explained the factors . . . which make up the increase or decrease over or under," "the current budget allowance is shown above on this form."

The level of detail in line items has its influence on the department head's decision process also. (In one city studied, one of the line items listed a $3.00 current appropriation for "Mothballs.") In general, each item broken out in the budget (each line item) "forces" one historical comparison and, hence, represents one more constraint the department request must satisfy. In the face of an increasing number of constraints (increasing as budget detail increases), it is not so surprising that the department head resorts to simpler decision rules to handle this potentially difficult problem. In addition, we would predict that the more detailed the budget (in terms of line items), because of the structure of the budget forms, the less change in requests (and appropriations) from year to year.

The need for effective budgetary control in the mayor's office, made more difficult by the presence of a small staff[9] (small in relation to a similar organization in the private sector), is met by a large number of simple, historical comparisons and has, in many instances, resulted in a burdensome amount of detail—responded to by busy department heads with little change in budget behavior from year to year.

The "tone" of the letter accompanying the budget forms has the effect of providing an arbitrary ceiling on the department's request (Figure 2, item 5). If the department total exceeds the "ceiling," the overage is generally submitted as a "supplemental" request (Figure 2, items 7 and 8). In addition, changes in salary *rates* through raises or promotions are submitted as a supplemental request (or not at all). Supplemental requests are accompanied with a detailed explanation and are treated separately by the mayor's office—and are always on the "agenda" when the department head meets with the mayor's office to discuss his requests.

So far, we have discussed only the constraints a department head must satisfy and the procedures he must follow. There is, obviously, some room for maneuvering. Many of the department head's "calculations" involve figuring "what will go" with the mayor's office.[10] This calculation involves using current appropriations as

[9]For instance, in the City of Pittsburgh, no more than four people examine the entire budget in great detail. Of these four, at least one is faced with the purely physical task of putting the budget together, checking, and compiling city totals.

[10]Similar to Wildavsky's observations of department heads at the large end of the budgetary funnel [13, pp. 25-31.] and Sorensen's at the small end of the federal decision funnel [12, p. 414.].

General DEPT. Request Decision Process*

1. Budget letter and Budget Forms received from mayor
   containing: a. current appropriations for all account
   categories in the department; b. current total appropriation;
   c. previous year's expenditures in various account categories;
   d. estimate of allowable increase over current appropriations
   implied from the "tone" of the mayor's budget letter.

2. Trend of departmental appropriations —
   direction and magnitude of recent changes
   in amounts of appropriations in departmental account categories.

3. Department, using information from 1. and 2., formulates a
   "reasonable request" for funds in its existing account categories,
   using current appropriations as a "base" or reference point and
   adjusting this estimate according to whether there was an increase
   in appropriations last year (for some accounts, an increase for the
   current year means a decrease for next year — equipment —, for
   others, an increase for the current year indicates another increase
   next year), and the difference between last year's expenditures and
   appropriations.

4. Using "reasonable requests" calculated in 3., a preliminary department
   total request is calculated.

5. Is the total department request outside the guidelines set by
   the mayor's office (implied from the "tone" of the mayor's
   budget letter)?

   no   yes

6. Check to see if there are   7. All department requests in all
   any increases in salary   categories are adjusted so that
   accounts over current   any increase (proposed) over
   appropriations   current appropriations is sub-
                                         mitted as a supplemental
                                         request. Go to 6. to check
   no increase   increase   for salary increases.

                   8. Make regular request equal
                      current appropriations and
                      put increase in as supple-
                      mental request.

9. Calculate total of regular departmental request.

10. Send regular requests and departmental total to
    mayor's office along with supplemental requests.

FIG. 2   *For a more detailed flowchart of the DEPT. Submodel and a listing
of the FORTRAN II computer program, see [3].

a base and adjusting this amount for recent appropriation trends, discrepancies between appropriations and corresponding expenditures, and the like (Figure 2, item 3). The results of this "calculation" are then tested to see if they satisfy the constraints discussed above. Preliminary decisions are then adjusted until constraints are satisfied, and the final request is entered on the standard budget forms and sent to the mayor's office for consideration.

Behavior Not Included in Formal DEPT. Model. A quick look at the DEPT. model would indicate that (at least according to our theory) department budgetary behavior varies from department to department only by the relative weights assigned to previous appropriations, trends, and expenditures by the various department heads (Figure 2, item 3). Furthermore, it is contended (by the model) that these relative weights are stable over time. Missing from the formal model are notions of non-regular innovation (or change) by department administrators and notions of the department as a mechanism for responding to particular kinds of complaints from the citizenry—in short, the department is conceived of as explicitly responding to only the mayor's pressure. Also missing are changes in the budget requests as logical elaborations of other policy commitments—implied increases in operating budget because of capital budgeting considerations, changes in intergovernmental support for services (the classic problem in this category involves the highly volatile state-local split of welfare payments), transfer of activities to (and from) other governing units (transfer of hospital system to State or country, etc.), and changes in activity level and scope because of funds obtained from sources (Urban Renewal planning and demonstration grants, the Federal Anti-Poverty Program, etc.) other than the general fund. Our model does not preclude innovative behavior, however. It merely states that innovation (if any) takes place within a regularly changing budget ceiling. It could be argued that a system of weights attached to current appropriations, trends, etc., that leads to relatively large, regular request increases represents a greater potential for innovation than do those leading to smaller increases (or decreases)—providing, of course, that a portion of the request is granted. On the other hand, it could be argued that the presence of a budget ceiling in the face of changing citizenry needs and pressures (precipitating a change in department goals and program needs) forces a department head to "innovate" to survive. Cyert and March, citing the work of Mansfield [8] side with the former concept of innovation rather than the latter. They argue that the presence of "organizational slack" (evidenced by budgetary increases) ". . . provides a source of funds for innovations that would not be approved in the face of scarcity but that have strong subunit support." Major technological innovations, it is argued, are not problem-oriented innovations [4, p. 279.]. At any rate, our model does not restrict certain kinds of innovation-producing behavior. The model is, however, unable to predict or recognize the acceptance of "major" innovations (major changes in expenditure and appropriations).

The other "charge" the model is open to is that it fails to deal with "outside" influences at all. This is particularly true if by departmental responses to pressure one assumes that total (for the department) external pressure and influence is a thing that varies a good deal from year to year and that mechanisms for responding to that pressure would lead to irregular budget decisions reflecting this variation. If, however, one assumes that each department has, over the years, "made its peace" not only with the mayor's office, but with the extra-governmental environment, then the pressure response mechanisms (i.e., constant responses to constant pressures) would also be reflected in the system of weights, above. The model does not exclude a pressure-response kind of budgetary behavior, but has a good deal to say about the nature and context of the response (and pressure). The reasonableness of our characterization of "innovation" and "pressure" is reflected in the model residuals.

3.3. MAYORS Budget Recommendation Model

Role–The function of the mayor's office relative to the budget is to fulfill the legal obligation of submitting a balanced budget to the city council for its consideration. The key word, of course, is "balanced." Most of the problem solving activity and behavior in the mayor's office revolves around attempts to eliminate a deficit or reduce a surplus. Like most other organizations, subunit requests (stated needs) almost always exceed available resources. So, *vis-à-vis* the departments, the mayor's office's role is that of an economizer, cutting departmental requests to the "bare minimum" in lean years and keeping the cost of government "under control" when revenues are more plentiful.

Characteristics of the MAYOR's Model. The decision process in the mayor's office can usefully be thought of as a search for a solution to the balanced-budget problem. In a sense, the mayor has guaranteed the existence of a solution through use of budget guidelines set up in his letter of instruction to department heads. Approximately four months before the final budget is due for council passage, the mayor obtains preliminary revenue estimates from people in city government and from an outside source. Armed with a rough estimate of money available for expenditures in the next budget period, current appropriations, and a knowledge of "required" and predetermined budgetary changes for the coming year, the mayor is able to make a rough guess of the total allowable increase or decrease over current appropriations. From this figure, an estimate of the "allowable" percent increase (or decrease) is made and transmitted to department heads *via* the budget letter. (Only the output from this part of the process is explicitly included in our model– "tone of mayor's letter.") In most instances, then, the "sum" of the budget requests reaching the mayor's office represents a "nearly" (within 10%) balanced budget.

The revenue estimate enters into the process at this point as an independent constraint to be satisfied. On very few occasions are revenue or tax *rates* changed to bring the budget into balance. In the municipalities investigated, there was no evidence of any altering of tax *yields* to balance the budget.[11] Almost all tax rate increases are tied to general wage increases. Our formal model does not include the part of the decision process evoked when the revenue constraint becomes so restrictive (or loose) as to necessitate a change in tax rates. (See Figure 4.) Tax rate

---

[11]One exception to the general rule that there is no alteration of the revenue yield estimates (revenue side) to achieve balance with expenditures, was found. For a couple of years in Detroit (1960-62), part of the cost of government operations was financed through "overly optimistic" revenue estimates which ultimately resulted in operating deficits. Those deficits (technically illegal) were then refinanced, with debt service charges for this refinancing showing up in subsequent operating budgets as deductions from revenue available for general fund expenditures. This brief "operating practice" was quickly discontinued by a new city administration. The magnitude of the effect of this practice on the planning process (budget formation) is unclear and is not incorporated in the formal model. The effects were reflected as larger deviations of model estimates from actual decisions during particular years in the City of Detroit.

decisions are made prior to sending the budget letter to department heads and are considered as given from that point on.

Just as the budget forms and account categories structure the problem for the department head, they also structure it for the mayor's office (Figure 3, items 1 and 3). The legal requirement of a balanced budget also helps structure the problem for the mayor's office and partially determines its role behavior. Together the system of accounts and balanced budget requirement specify the cognitive map of the decision situation for mayor's office participants.

Preliminary Screening of Requests. As budget requests are received from departments by the mayor's office, they are screened individually (Figure 3, item 4). The screening process reflects particular biases and relationships between the mayor's office and individual department heads (and departments). "Department heads are dealt with differently during the (budget) hearings. Some department heads can be depended on for an honest budget request. Others have a history of being less-than-realistic in their budgets."[12] Different perceptions of different departments are reflected in both model structure and model parameters (Figure 3, item 4). The interaction of perceptions and role (to cut requests) describes the preliminary screening process.

Basically, if the department request for a given account category is less than current appropriations, a preliminary, automatic acceptance of the request is made. If the request is larger than current appropriations, a request evaluation procedure is evoked that "calculates" or subjectively determines preliminary appropriation figures (Figure 3, item 4). A particular department can evoke one of four subjective evaluation procedures. The procedure evoked represents the cognitive map used by the mayor's office in dealing with that department.

The four basic procedures consist of two which arrive at a preliminary appropriation figure by making marginal adjustments in the departments request figures—representing departments that submit "honest" or "realistic" budget estimates—and two which make adjustments in current appropriations to arrive at preliminary recommendation figures—representing less "realistic" or "honest" departments. The choice of procedures and parameter values was made on the basis of empirical tests using regression models. The four models used were:

i) department head's request respected and adjusted by his supplemental request and current trends

ii) department head's request ignored, and current appropriations adjusted to reflect recent trends and over or underspending in the past

iii) department head's request used as a basis for calculation and changes in it are based on the magnitude of the requested change in appropriations, supplemental requests, and past change in appropriations

iv) department head's request ignored and change from current appropriations based on previous changes and magnitude of underspending or overspending in the past

The values of the estimated parameters represent the relative weights given to variables in the particular model by decision makers in the mayor's office.

From the preliminary screening of requests outlined above (Figure 3, item 4), a preliminary budget total is compiled (Figure 3, item 5).

[12] November, 1964 interview with chief budget officer in one of the three sample cities. Name withheld on request.

General MAYORS Budget Recommendation Model*

1. Department regular and supplemental budget requests received

2. Latest Revenue Estimate

3. Historical Data— Current appropriations, last year's expenditures, and appropriation trends

4. Preliminary check of all departmental requests—if departmental request is less than current appropriations, it is tentatively accepted; otherwise a tentative "calculation" of the mayor's recommendation is made based on the department's regular and supplemental requests together with the change in appropriation from last year to the current year and the last available expenditure data.

5. Preliminary calculation of total budget—sum of preliminary calculations

6. Check of preliminary total against revenue estimate to determine if a surplus or a deficit is anticipated. If "surplus," a set of "surplus reduction" routines is evoked. If "deficit," "deficit elimination" routines are evoked.

surplus reduction procedures

deficit elimination procedures (Go to 15).

7. Calculate magnitude of anticipated surplus or residual.

8. Find total salaries and wages for the city (preliminary estimates).

9. Is the anticipated surplus large enough to finance a minimum salary increase?

yes   no

10. If so, increase salary levels for all departments and reduce calculated surplus

11. Is there enough anticipated surplus left to distribute among departments?

FIGURE 3

163

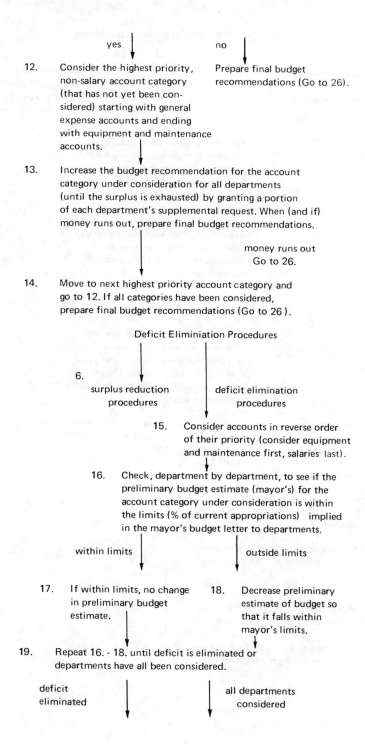

yes   no

12.   Consider the highest priority,   Prepare final budget
       non-salary account category   recommendations (Go to 26).
       (that has not yet been con-
       sidered) starting with general
       expense accounts and ending
       with equipment and maintenance
       accounts.

13.   Increase the budget recommendation for the account
       category under consideration for all departments
       (until the surplus is exhausted) by granting a portion
       of each department's supplemental request. When (and if)
       money runs out, prepare final budget recommendations.

                                    money runs out
                                    Go to 26.

14.   Move to next highest priority account category and
       go to 12. If all categories have been considered,
       prepare final budget recommendations (Go to 26).

                 Deficit Eliminiation Procedures

6.

      surplus reduction   deficit elimination
         procedures   procedures

                 15.   Consider accounts in reverse order
                         of their priority (consider equipment
                         and maintenance first, salaries last).

             16.   Check, department by department, to see if the
                    preliminary budget estimate (mayor's) for the
                    account category under consideration is within
                    the limits (% of current appropriations) implied
                    in the mayor's budget letter to departments.

        within limits   outside limits

17.   If within limits, no change   18.   Decrease preliminary
       in preliminary budget   estimate of budget so
       estimate.   that it falls within
                              mayor's limits.

19.   Repeat 16. - 18. until deficit is eliminated or
       departments have all been considered.

      deficit   all departments
      eliminated   considered

FIGURE 3 (contd.)

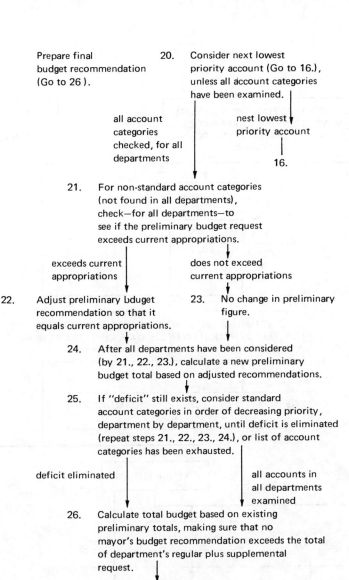

Prepare final
budget recommendation
(Go to 26).

20. Consider next lowest
priority account (Go to 16.),
unless all account categories
have been examined.

all account
categories
checked, for all
departments

nest lowest
priority account

16.

21. For non-standard account categories
(not found in all departments),
check—for all departments—to
see if the preliminary budget request
exceeds current appropriations.

exceeds current
appropriations

does not exceed
current appropriations

22. Adjust preliminary bduget
recommendation so that it
equals current appropriations.

23. No change in preliminary
figure.

24. After all departments have been considered
(by 21., 22., 23.), calculate a new preliminary
budget total based on adjusted recommendations.

25. If "deficit" still exists, consider standard
account categories in order of decreasing priority,
department by department, until deficit is eliminated
(repeat steps 21., 22., 23., 24.), or list of account
categories has been exhausted.

deficit eliminated

all accounts in
all departments
examined

26. Calculate total budget based on existing
preliminary totals, making sure that no
mayor's budget recommendation exceeds the total
of department's regular plus supplemental
request.

27. Check to see if there is a deficit

no deficit

deficit

29. Final Budget to
Council

28. Eliminate deficit by scaling
all non-salary accounts to
make budget balance - proportional allocation of deficit.
(Go to 26).

FIGURE 3 (concluded)

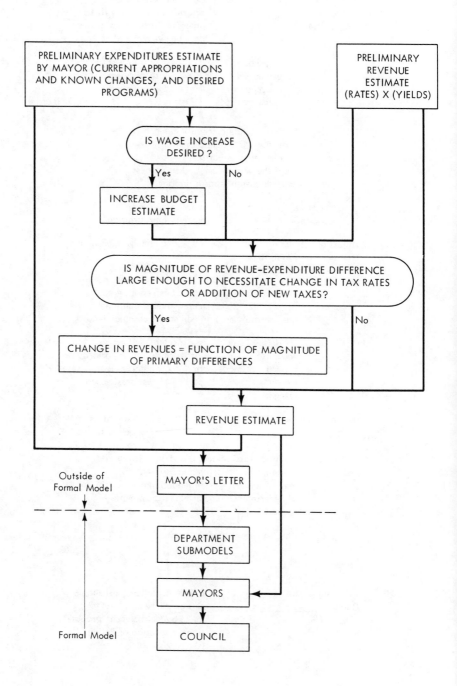

FIGURE 4 Mayor's Tax Decision Process

The next step in the process is to balance the preliminary budget. The "directives" issued by the Mayor's Office in the budget letter to department heads may be viewed as devices for guaranteeing that the budget will be "nearly" balanced. All alterations in regular departmental requests are aimed at balancing the budget. "Balancing techniques" are:

1. Raise tax rates or add a new tax to eliminate anticipated deficit.
2. Cut "lower priority" account categories (maintenance, equipment) to bring expenditures into line with revenues.
3. Grant some supplemental requests to reduce anticipated surplus.
4. Eliminate an "undesirable" tax or reduce tax rates to reduce anticipated surplus.

In general strategies 1 and 4 are used when the anticipated discrepancy between revenues and expenditures is high, while techniques 2 and 3 are used if revenues and expenditures are reasonably close. The general tendency is to move toward a balance between revenues and expenditures by changing either revenue *or* expenditures, but not both. Only "techniques" 2 and 3 are a formal part of the model.

Surplus Elimination Procedures. If a surplus is anticipated, several standard spending alternatives are considered in order of their priority:

1. General salary increase (Figure 3, items 8 to 10)
2. Grant portion of supplemental requests (Figure 3, items 11 to 14)
   a. general expense accounts (Figure 3, item 12)
   b. equipment accounts
   c. maintenance accounts

Although the formal model only includes the above alternatives, others are clearly evoked. It can be said with reasonable assurance, though, that the first alternative considered is a general salary increase whenever a surplus is anticipated.

The model is also "incomplete" in the sense that some departmental priority list obviously exists in the granting of supplemental requests. Thus, the sequence in which departments are considered (the order of departments in Figure 3, items 11 and 13) is important under a revenue constraint. The model's assumption that departments are considered in the order of their account numbers is a poor one, but not enough department request data existed to establish any other reasonable priority list.[13] An analysis of the model residuals, however, failed to reveal any discernible pattern (or "list").[14] A priority list of account categories does exist though, and is shared by departments, the mayor's offices, and council. The salience of wage and salary accounts is readily discernible through interviews.

[13]It should be noted that a substantial portion of the department-priority phenomena is accounted for in the preliminary screening of requests.

[14]In deficit-elimination years, an underestimate would be expected for departments with low account numbers (in the computer-coded data) and an overestimate would be expected for departments with high account numbers. The opposite expectations would exist for surplus-elimination years. This phenomena was not observed.

Deficit Elimination Routines. If, instead of an anticipated surplus after preliminary screening of requests, a potential deficit appears (the usual case), routines are evoked to eliminate the deficit. One routine not evoked in the formal model, but one of the alternatives evoked in practice, is the routine that says "raise taxes."

The alternatives are evoked in the following order.

a) Check preliminary recommendations (lower priority accounts first) to see if they are within limits on increases[15]—bring all preliminary recommendations within limits.

b) Eliminate all recommended increases over current appropriations in non-salary items, considering low priority accounts first.

c) Uniform reduction of all non-salary accounts to eliminate deficit, if all else has failed.

The order in which alternatives are considered represents a priority list for the alternatives (in order of their decreasing desirability) and a search routine evoked by the problem of an anticipated deficit (Figure 3, item 15).

The order-of-account sanctity for the mayor's office is identical to that of the department. This shared preference ordering[16] is as follows:

1. administrative salaries,
2. non-administrative salaries and wages,
3. operating expenses, supplies, materials, etc.,
4. equipment,
5. maintenance,

with maintenance and equipment the first accounts to be cut (and the last to be considered for an increase in the surplus elimination routines) and salaries the last. This deficit elimination procedure is executed only as long as a "deficit" exists. The first acceptable alternative (balanced budget) found is adopted and search activity is halted.

One item that is never reduced from current appropriations in the usual sense is salaries and wages. The salary and wage accounts are different from other accounts in that they represent commitments to individuals currently employed. There are no mass layoffs, etc., rather, a freeze is placed on the filling of positions vacated by retirement, resignation, and death and scheduled step-raises and salary increments are deferred.

Finally, either by reducing the surplus or by eliminating a deficit, the mayor's office arrives at a balanced budget.

Behavior Not Included in Formal MAYORS Model. Perhaps the most prominent omission of problem-solving behavior is the lack of a priority list for departments. The model assumes that the priority list is ordered the same way as the account numbers. The overall importance of this faulty assumption is, of course, an empirical question. An analysis of model residuals suggests this was not important or was reflected in estimated parameter values.

---

[15]The limit is roughly equivalent to the limit indicated in the mayor's letter to department heads.

[16]Shared also with the council.

The entire budgetary process model we have constructed hypothesizes a stable decision structure between cities, and a stable decision structure over time within cities. Stability in decision structure between cities is "explainable" through problem similarity. Stability within cities reflects stable sets of relationships existing between positions and roles through processes of learning, reinforcement, and socialization. This assumption of stability and uniform socialization is predicated on the assumption that only a relatively few occupants of government positions change in a given period of time. The obvious exception to this situation occurs when an administration is defeated at the polls. This results in a complete reordering of position occupants and relationships. The gradual socialization, learning process will no longer hold. So, we expected and found the largest systematic model errors in those years immediately following the start of a new administration.

Another kind of behavior not included in the model is the kind reflecting the mayor's response to external (to the government) pressure and constraints. Again, as in the DEPT. models, the MAYORS model does not preclude a mayoralty response to requests for services from "powerful" interest groups or individuals. It only postulates that the response is *within* the budget constraint for the department involved. The model, as constructed, implies that either the "response-to-pressure" is systematic and regular over the years (implying a stable system of "pressure" or "influence" in the community) and is reflected in the model parameters, or it does not enter the part of the budgetary process represented by our model at all. The only case where external "influence" could be conceived of as imposing a decisional constraint is in the revenue estimate. Most systematic "pressure" from the business community concentrates on keeping tax rates constant, and not on particular expenditure items.

The importance of these conscious omissions are reflected in the empirical tests of the model.

3.4. Characteristics of the COUNCIL Model

The role of the city council is a limited one. The primary reason is more one of cognitive and informational constraints than lack of interest. The city budget is a complex document when it reaches the council. The level of detail makes it virtually impossible to consider all or even a majority of items independently. An example of this complexity is the Mayor's budget for the Pittsburgh Department of Public Works, the Division of Incineration, Miscellaneous Services Accounts found in Table 1. It illustrates the kind of document the council must deal with.

The council is asked to deal with the budget at this level of detail. The sheer volume of information to be processed limits the ability of a council, without its own budget staff, to consider the budget in a sophisticated or complex manner.

Perhaps a more important computational constraint is the balanced budget requirement. If there is no slack in the budget the mayor presents to council (Figure 5, item 8), then any increase the council makes in any account category must be balanced with a corresponding decrease in another account or with a tax increase. So, in the presence of a revenue constraint, the council cannot consider elements of the budget independently as is done in Congress. David, Dempster, and Wildavsky found that Congressional budgetary behavior could be described extremely well using a series of linear decision rules [5]. Behavior of this nature would not be possible if it were required that the sum of the changes in budgets

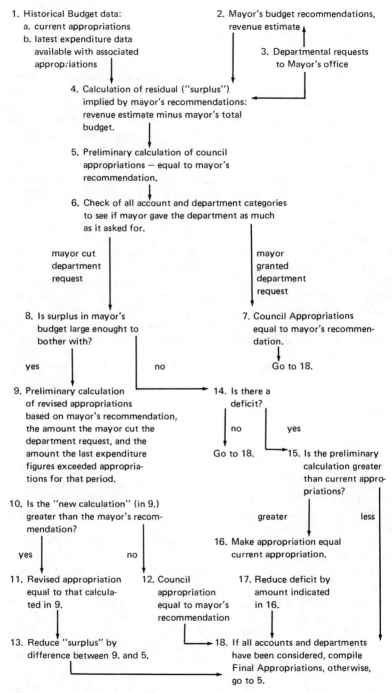

General COUNCIL Appropriations Model*

1. Historical Budget data:
   a. current appropriations
   b. latest expenditure data
      available with associated
      appropriations

2. Mayor's budget recommendations,
   revenue estimate

3. Departmental requests
   to Mayor's office

4. Calculation of residual ("surplus")
   implied by mayor's recommendations:
   revenue estimate minus mayor's total
   budget.

5. Preliminary calculation of council
   appropriations — equal to mayor's
   recommendation.

6. Check of all account and department categories
   to see if mayor gave the department as much
   as it asked for.

mayor cut
department
request

mayor
granted
department
request

8. Is surplus in mayor's
   budget large enought to
   bother with?

7. Council Appropriations
   equal to mayor's recommendation.

yes   no   Go to 18.

9. Preliminary calculation
   of revised appropriations
   based on mayor's recommendation,
   the amount the mayor cut the
   department request, and the
   amount the last expenditure
   figures exceeded appropriations for that period.

14. Is there a
    deficit?

    no   yes

    Go to 18.   15. Is the preliminary
                           calculation greater
                           than current appro-
                           priations?

10. Is the "new calculation" (in 9.)
    greater than the mayor's recom-
    mendation?

    greater   less

yes   no

16. Make appropriation equal
    current appropriation.

11. Revised appropriation
    equal to that calcula-
    ted in 9.

12. Council
    appropriation
    equal to mayor's
    recommendation

17. Reduce deficit by
    amount indicated
    in 16.

13. Reduce "surplus" by
    difference between 9. and 5.

18. If all accounts and departments
    have been considered, compile
    Final Appropriations, otherwise,
    go to 5.

*For a more detailed flowchart of the COUNCIL Submodel and a listing of the FORTRAN
II computer program, see [3].

FIGURE 5

170

TABLE 1 Sample of Municipal Account Complexity

Department of Public Works

Acct. No.	Title of Account	1963 Code Departmental Estimates 1964	Appropriation Year 1963	Expenditures Year 1962	Increase or Decrease '64 over '63
	Division of Incineration				
1687	Miscellaneous services				
B-5	Recharge fire extinguishers	$50.00	$—	$89.26	$—
B-5	Extermination service	200.00	—	—	—
B-8	Towel rental	25.00	—	.26	—
B-9	Supper money	100.00	—	—	—
B-13	Freight and express charges	89.00	—	—	—
B-17	Public property and property damage insurance	125.00	—	—	—
B-18	Water cooler rental	390.00	—	390.00	—
B-18	Power shovel rental	12,960.00	—	14,880.00	—
B-18	Truck rental for incinerator and bell farm	3,765.00	—	2,295.00	—
B-20	Waste disposal permits	50.00	—	50.00	—
B-20	Demurrage on oxygen and acetylene tanks	170.00	—	200.40	—
B-20	Services, N.O.C.	275.00	—	—	—
B-21	Test boring, survey and report, for landfills	1,000.00	—	—	—
Totals		$19,199.00	$18,199.00	$17,904.92	$1,000.00

made by Congress add to zero—*i.e.*, the budget must add up to an amount predetermined by the President. Congressmen and Congressional committees also have staffs, councilmen do not.

Another reason for the limited effect of the council on the budget reflects the nature of the "pressures" they face. All interest groups, neighborhood organizations, department heads, etc. feel that some department's budget should be increased. The pressures transmitted to council concerning the operating budget are of one kind—those advocating increases in the mayor's recommendations. The other side of the argument—curtailment of government activities—is seldom, if ever, presented to council. This countervailing influence enters the decision process not at the council level, but generally through the mayor's office and in particular, through the mayor's revenue estimate.

Given the above limitations, the council is "forced" to use the mayor's decisions as the reference points for their decisions. The constraints—"pressure," informational, and computational—coupled with a recommended budget with no slack to allocate (not enough difference between estimated revenues and recommended expenditures "to be bothered with") makes it extremely difficult for council to veto[17] or change the mayor's budget significantly.

[17]Occasionally the council will defeat a proposed new tax—income tax in Cleveland, tax for meat inspectors in Detroit—but seldom will defeat expenditure recommendations.

Overview. Generalizing, the entire model is one of a systematic, bureaucratic administrative decision process. The stability of the decision system is portrayed as evolving from the restrictive revenue environment, an assumed continuity in the actors manning the system, and an implied stable or non-existent "community power network." The interaction of problem complexity and need for decision, combined with the lack of extra-governmental reference points or standards, produces a decision system which uses historical experience and precedent as its operating standards; a system which handles interest conflicts (high service rates, low taxes) by largely ignoring divergent viewpoints and using feasibility as the prime decision criterion; a system which handles complexity by fragmenting and simplifying the problem. By assuming (implicitly) that "this year's problem" is nearly identical to "last year's," "this year's solution" will be nearly identical to "last year's." It is a system that structures a complex problem, formulates alternatives and makes choices using simple decision rules.

4. MODEL TESTS

The formal model of the budgetary process was subjected to many forms of empirical tests. Basically the model was used to generate budget decisions for six years in Pittsburgh (1960-65), seven years in Detroit (1958-59 to 1964-65), and ten years in Cleveland (1956-65). Model results were then compared with the observed budgetary decisions in the cities.

Three primary goodness-of-fit indicators were used: "modified-r^2" statistics, a comparison of the relative predictability of the simulation model with three naive models, and a regression of observed budgetary decisions on model predictions.

We can view the linear regression, r^2-statistic as a measure of the relative precision of the linear hypothesis *vs.* the alternative hypothesis that the dependent variable is randomly distributed about its mean:

$$r^2 = 1.0 - \Sigma(\text{observed} - \text{regression prediction})^2 / \Sigma(\text{observed} - \text{mean of observed})^2$$

By substituting "model estimate" for "regression prediction" and more reasonable alternative hypotheses for "mean of observed," modified-r^2 statistics were constructed[18] and calculated for each year in each city. The model performed satisfactorily on these measures.

Three alternative, naive models were also tested and compared with the simulation model:

    1. Constant-increase model

$$B_{i,t} = (1.0 + \alpha_i)B_{i,t-1}$$

    2. Constant-share-of-the-budget-total model

$$B_{i,t} = \beta_i(\Sigma_{j=1}^{n} B_{j,t})$$

---

[18]The "more reasonable" alternative hypotheses used were: "This year's budget for a particular standard account in a given administrative unit equals
    a. Last year's budget for that item, or
    b. the average, over the study period, for that item."

3. Constant-share-of-the-budget-increase model

$$B_{i,t} - B_{i,t-1} = \delta_i[(\Sigma_{j=1}^n B_{j,t}) - (\Sigma_{j=1}^n B_{j,t-1})]$$

where

$B_{i,t}$ = budget for account i, year t

n = total accounts in city general fund budget

$\alpha_i, \beta_i, \delta_i$ = empirically estimated parameters (regression coefficients).

The simulation model results were then compared with the naive model predictions. Choices between our simulation model and each of the naive models were then made using two statistics suggested by Hunt.[19] In nearly every case, the simulation model "performed" better on both choice measures. It should be noted, however, that the constant-share-of-the-budget-total model also predicted quite well.

Finally, the following relationship was tested:

[Model Estimate of Appropriations] = a[Observed Appropriations] + b

For an unbiased model that predicts perfectly, the expected value of "a" is 1.0 and the expected value of "b" is 0.0. The results for model tests, where inputs were updated at the beginning of each budget year, are found in Table 2.

TABLE 2   Regression of Observed Decisions on Model Preditions

City	a	Std. error of "a"	b	r^2	n
Cleveland	.977	.001	−$5282	.9980	999
Detroit (excluding Welfare Dept)	.984	.005	$7281	.9772	918
Pittsburgh	.991	.002	−$28	.9975	1002

The true test of goodness-of-fit, however, is the ability of the model to describe the actual budgetary decision process. From all indications, our model does this quite well.

We found a change in goodness-of-fit associated with a change in administration in Detroit, but not in Pittsburgh or Cleveland. This was to be expected, since the "change-overs" in Cleveland and Pittsburgh represented a change only in the person occupying the mayor's position and represented a kind of hand-picked replacement by the incumbent party (the departing mayors moved on to higher political office). This indicates that, in Cleveland and Pittsburgh, the mayors underwent a process of socialization. No perceivable differences in goodness-of-fit were associated with increasing or decreasing revenues, indicating our surplus and deficit elimination routines were equally valid.

[19]The statistics used [16, pp. 40-44.] were:
Min w [(estimated - observed)2/(estimated)] , and
Min w [(estimated - observed)2/(observed)] .

5. ANALYSIS OF MODEL RESIDUALS

In general, there are two kinds of "budgetary" change.

1. Those changes resulting from the continuation and elaboration of existing policies, and
2. Those changes resulting from shifts in municipal policies.

Our model is clearly one describing changes of the first kind. It is a model of the standard procedures which result in particular forms of marginal adjustments in resource allocation from year to year.

The model does not describe changes of the second kind—significant shifts in municipal policies. The model, however, by filtering out (i.e., "predicting" or "explaining," in the statistical sense) incremental changes, draws attention to those items ("unexplained") in the budget that are not marginal adjustments or elaborations of previous policies.

By focusing on the "unexplained" changes in resource allocation, we can discover a great deal about the budgetary process as a change process. "Unexplained" changes include:

1. Incremental changes whose cumulative effect results in a "non-incremental" change.
2. Non-incremental policy shifts.[20]
3. Significant changes in policy, not reflected in the budget.

It should be noted that not all large changes are "changes resulting from shifts in municipal policies," and not all small changes are "changes resulting from the continuation and elaboration of existing policies." For example, a significant policy shift may result from the decision to handle the city's welfare load through the welfare department, rather than have the program administered by the county or the state for a fee. The total budget cost may be nearly the same, so this "significant" change may never be reflected in the operating budget. On the other hand, suppose the city decides to build an office building of their own to house a number of departments, rather than rent office space. Once the building has been completed, several years after the initial decision, a large change is noted in the budget—a change our formal model is not equipped to handle. This change, representing an increase in personnel and building maintenance expenses and large decreases in rental expenses for the departments affected does not represent a significant shift in policy, however. It is merely an elaboration of a long-existing policy (resulting from the decision to build rather than rent). The original decision to build represents a significant "policy shift," however, and anticipated operating budget changes may or may not have been an important part of this capital decision. Our point is that for purposes of analyzing the 1966 operating budgetary

[20]The use of the term "innovation" has been consciously avoided because of lack of a generally-agreed-upon, operational definition of the concept. Rather, "policy shift" will be our theoretical construct. An allocation decision represents a "policy shift" when either through cumulative effects of small changes or immediate effects, it brings about a "significant" reallocation of resources between account categories.

process, the items resulting from previous capital decisions represent "automatic" changes in appropriations.

Model deviations[21] were classified by their perceived "cause". Four types of "causes" appear reasonable:

1. Change in External Environment
   a. Intergovernmental transactions
      i. State and Federal subsidies and regulations
      ii. Transfer of functions involving other governments
   b. Catastrophic event, emergency, crises, etc.—reaction to focus of public attention
2. Changes in Internal Environment
   a. New administration (new actors in system of interrelationships)
   b. Change in departments or functions
      i. Transfers of activities—change in organizational structure
      ii. Changes in programs, functions
3. Lack of Model Information
   a. Implications of capital budgeting decisions
   b. Additional revenue sources discovered
   c. Change in system of accounts
   d. Other
4. Unexplained, Miscellaneous, and Other
   a. Model coding errors and missing data
   b. "Improper" accounting procedures (Detroit only—capital items not included in operating budget, 1958-59 to 1961-62)
   c. Increased work load (or decreased)
   d. Other, unexplained

Those "causes" that represent "policy shifts" would be:

1.a.ii. Transfers of functions involving other governments
1.b.   "Catastrophic event," emergency, etc.
2.a.   New administration
2.b.i. Transfers of activities—organizational change
2.b.ii. New programs, functions
3.b.   Additional revenue sources discovered

"Policy elaborations" would correspond to:

1.a.i. State and Federal subsidies and regulations
3.a.   Implications of capital decisions

[21]In each city, for each year, the five deviations largest in magnitude and the five largest percentage deviations were examined. In each city, for each year, the five deviations largest in (absolute) magnitude and the five largest percentage deviations were examined. "Causes" were associated with individual deviations on the basis of published information. It should be noted that, in nearly every case, the "reason" for the deviation was found in the Mayor's Budget Message to the Council. In other words, the actual devision system identified nearly the same set of unusual decisions as did our model. This, perhaps, is a more significant indication of goodness of fit than the many statistical measures calculated] 3, Section 6].

3.c.   Change in system of accounts

3.d.   Other information not part of allocation (timing of elections) process

4.c.   Increased workload

5.1. Results

An analysis of model residuals revealed some consistent patterns of change in Cleveland, Detroit, and Pittsburgh. Two principal patterns were noted, only one of which could be described as a "policy shift." One class of revealed "unprogrammed" changes represented changes dictated by the external environment. These were largely due to changes in levels of "ear-marked" revenues (especially in Cleveland) and the terms of negotiated contracts (in both Cleveland and Pittsburgh). The other area of change, representing a kind of "policy shift," was observed in those problem areas and activities where Federal funding and involvement was greatest.

The presence of citizenry demands, needs, etc. does not appear to be related to "policy shifts" in any systematic way. This is probably due to the presence of "needs," demands, etc. for additional services in *all* areas of municipal activity, none of which can be fully "satisfied" given revenue conditions.

6. SUMMARY

Traditional studies of public finance and governmental decision making, by trying to couple economic, political, and population characteristics to municipal expenditure items, attempt to identify those forces that determine the direction of budgetary drift. Their (implicit) contention is that the "role" of governmental decision makers is that of a translator of environmental characteristics into expenditure items.

By emphasizing the "short-run," we have stressed internal characteristics of the "Government" decision process and the relationship between current and historical decisions. In Figure 6, our findings are that in the short-run, items 5 and 6 are the most significant. By studying the budgetary phenomena over time, others have emphasized items 1, 2, 3, and 4 almost to the exclusion of 5. The question now remains—do our short-run findings apply in the long run? Our model described a somewhat "drifting" budgetary process. Do long-run "pressures" determine the overall direction of that drift?

6.1. Causes of Model Drift

Model drift could be biased by external constraints. "Expenditures" would be "allowed" to drift "only so far" without being corrected. They would then be brought back into line with "national standards," party or pressure group demands, population needs or tastes, etc. If, in fact, this were the case, evidence of the use of correcting mechanisms should exist in our model deviations because of the lack of provisions for these mechanisms in our model.

6.2 "Observed" Environmental Corrections in Drift

In Detroit, corrections in drift (model deviations) seemed to consist of establishing new departments in the urban renewal area, adjusting appropriations to

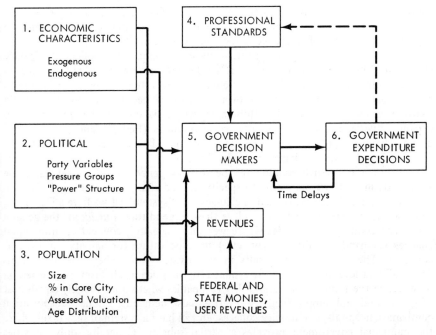

FIG. 6   Environmental Factors in Municipal Finance

correspond with State and user revenue changes, and one adjustment in Police and Fire salaries resulting from a Public Administration Survey report (that could be interpreted as a correction in drift to correspond to some national operating standard).

Cleveland's drift corrections consisted of new departments in the urban renewal area, adjustments in appropriations because of changes in State and user revenue contributions and costs of negotiated contracts, and special wage increases for Police and Fire (corresponding to "national" rates?).

Pittsburgh appears much the same with changes in State revenue contributions, the terms of negotiated service contracts (street lighting), and the emergence of city activities in areas of Federal program involvement accounting for most of the environmental corrections in model drift.

It appears from an analysis of our residuals over time that environmental corrections:

1. are seldom (if ever) evoked directly to bring specific expenditure items "into line," *or*
2. are filtered through the revenue constraint (see Figure 6), blurring the "cause" of increased (decreased) revenues and blunting possible direct impact on specific budget items.

In any event, environmental corrections appear to be more related to revenue changes than expenditure changes. Hence, their *impact* on expenditures appears to be a blurred one that is excised through the administrative allocation and decision process rather than through any direct "expenditure-correction" mechanism.

Some *direct* environmental corrections were observed however. Negotiated contracts and changes in "ear-marked" revenue (State and user) provided some clear "corrections." The existence of Federal monies for municipal programs also appears to have "caused" a change in the "budgetary drift."

What seems to emerge from this study is an opportunity model of budgetary change. The broad "pattern of drift" is accelerated or depressed due to changes in general revenues. The "drift" in specific expenditures items changes in response to changes in "ear-marked" revenues or the terms of negotiated contracts. Rapid spurts of growth are observed in those areas where the city has the *opportunity* to expand activities because of the presence of revenues (Federal funds). rather than in areas having rapid changes or spurts in "needs." This also could be due to the fact that "needs" do not change in "spurts" either.

From a normative standpoint, the drifting *general fund* budget has some appeal. If, in fact, we were *able* to specify desired changes in municipal expenditures as a function of environmental changes, the "system" (if we have a Darwinian view of the world) would tend to place these expenditures *outside* of the general fund. The funding of activities where we *can* "logically" connect environmental changes (demands, ability to pay, etc.) to expenditure (or activity) changes, is common. The extreme case results in a "private" good where "supply equals demand" and level of activity is determined by the price mechanism. Somewhere in between lie the public power and utility companies where price roughly equals cost of goods sold and supply (activity level) equals "demand." Public transportation companies, hospitals, community colleges, etc. all have a system of user taxes where the municipal government provides a partial subsidy. Generally, only activities where user-tax financing is not feasible or undesirable receive a full municipal subsidy and hence are "eligible" for inclusion into the general fund. *It should not be surprising, then, that in the absence of a system of standard costs or ways of determining activity levels* (characteristics of general fund activities) *the decision systems exhibit drifting, opportunistic characteristics.*

REFERENCES

1. Braybrooke, D., and Lindblom, C. E., *Strategy of Decision,* The Free Press of Glencoe: Glencoe, Illinois, 1963.
2. Clarkson, G. P. E., *Portfolio Selection: A Simulation of Trust Investment,* Prentice-Hall, Inc.: Englewood Cliffs, N. J., 1962.
3. Crecine, J. P., *Governmental Problem Solving: A Computer Simulation of Municipal Budgeting,* Rand McNally, Inc.: Chicago, Illinois, 1967.
4. Cyert, R. M., and March, J. G., *A Behavioral Theory of the Firm,* Prentice-Hall, Inc.: Englewood Cliffs, N. J., 1963.
5. Davis, Otto A., Dempster, M. A. H., and Wildavsky, A., "On the Process of Budgeting: An Empirical Study of Congressional Appropriations," in Tullock G. (ed.), *Papers on Non-Market Decision Making,* Thomas Jefferson Center for Political Economy: Charlottesville, Virginia, 1966.
6. Hunt, E. B., "The Evaluation of Somewhat Parallel Models," in Massarik and Ratoosh, *Mathematical Explorations in Behavioral Science,* Irwin-Dorsey: Homewood, Illinois, 1965.
7. Lindblom, C. E., "The Science of Muddling Through," *Public Administration Review,* Spring, 1959.
8. Mansfield, E., "Technical Change and the Rate of Initiation," *Econometrics,* No. 29, 1961.
9. Newell, A., Shaw, J. C., and Simon, H. A., "Chess-Playing Programs and the

Problem of Complexity," in Feigenbaum, E., and Feldman, J. (eds.), *Computers and Thought*, McGraw Hill, Inc.: New York, N. Y., 1963.

10. Newell, A., and Simon, H. A., "Computers in Psychology," in Bush, R. R., Galanter, E., and Luce, R. D. (eds.), *Handbook of Mathematical Psychology: Volume One*, John Wiley and Sons: New York, N. Y., 1963.

11. Newell, A., and Simon, H. A., "GPS, A Program that Simulates Human Thought," in Feigenbaum, E. and Feldman, J. (eds.), *Computers and Thought*, McGraw Hill: New York, N. Y., 1963.

12. Sorensen, T. C., *Kennedy*, Harper and Row, Inc.: Scranton, Pennsylvania, 1965, p. 414.

13. Wildavsky, A., *The Politics of the Budgetary Process*, Little, Brown, and Co.: Boston, Massachusetts, 1964.

DISCUSSION QUESTIONS

1. In American business, one encounters the practice of budget revision within a given year. Some companies review the budget quarterly and adjust the budget for the rest of the year in the light of performance to date and improved information upon the prospects for the remainder of the year. On the other hand, some managements insist that once the annual budget is accepted it cannot be changed.

As a proponent of the periodical revision approach, what advantages of a behavioral nature would you suggest to defend this position vis-a-vis the "no change" view?

2. The task of completing the budget is assigned to a person who in effect becomes the budget director.
   a. Should the role of the budget director be active or passive? Discuss from the viewpoint of behavioral characteristics associated with the different postures.
   b. Will there be any difference in the control implications derived from the two approaches?

3. Schiff and Lewin ("The Impact of People on Budgets," *The Accounting Review*, 1970) observe: "Although top management has the formal power to accept or reject budgets proposed, it is generally at a disadvantage, because it lacks the detailed information regarding make-up of items and underlying analyses which divisional management has." What can top management do to overcome this disadvantage? Discuss.

4. One reads of the deterioration of the budget process in government at all levels—Federal, state, and local. Budget overruns, deficiencies, and supplementary budgets are the order of the day with no solution in sight.
   a. What would be your reaction to the suggestion of abolishing budgets for government agencies particularly if the objectives of the budget system are not being achieved and recognizing the high cost of administering the budget?
   b. Are there any alternative mechanisms that might be suggested?

5. When adopted, sales estimates made as part of the annual planning process provide the starting point for the operating budget. The adopted sales estimates are also used as goals for the field marketing force.

Practices in developing sales estimates vary. The so-called "grass-roots" approach requires that each salesman prepare estimates by product and by customer. These estimates are discussed with his immediate supervisor, usually a district manager. The cycle is repeated at the regional level, and the final summation is made at headquarters. Modifications are generally made at the central office, and these changes are then disseminated downward.

Alternatively, overall sales projections are made centrally and assigned to regions, which in turn assign to districts, with final assignments made to salesmen.

Essentially, this illustrates the participative versus the imposed approach to setting objectives.

What do you expect are the behavioral consequences of these two approaches with regard to motivation to achieve objectives and analysis of performance for the field sales organization?

6. There has been an increased interest in the extension of corporate annual reports as they relate to financial statements. Accordingly, the report for year 19x2 would include actual results for 19x1, budget and actual results for 19x2, and the budget for 19x3.

   a. Discuss the expected behavioral implications for top management faced with a requirement that these data may be furnished.
   b. What change would you expect in investor behavior if this reporting standard becomes accepted practice?
   c. Because published statements are certified, what impacts, certification, and approaches to auditing are implicit in this new reporting requirement?

7. Standard costs convey a notion of precision derived perhaps from the use of engineered physical standards for materials, work measurement modified by learning curve techniques for labor, and so on. This gives an impression of "scientific" determination that tends to limit questions on the suitability of the standard and focuses almost entirely on the analysis of variations of actual performance from standard.

As a division manager, what would you want to know about the approach to developing standard costs for the products manufactured in your division before accepting them as acceptable goals against which performance should be measured?

PART THREE

Decision Making

DECISION MAKING AND PROBLEM SOLVING

The overall view of the firm as a decision-making system was described in Part One. The firm's decision making was described in terms of its utilization of structured decision rules (standard operating procedures), uncertainty avoidance, problemistic search, and organizational slack. Part Three considers the individual as a problem solver and decision maker within the organizational setting.

ADMINISTRATIVE MAN

The concept of administrative man was first introduced by Simon in his book *Administrative Behavior*.[1] It is a description of the rational part of individual behavior. In Simon's view, humans are rational because they have capacity to think, to process information, to make choices, and to learn. Human beings, however, are also bounded in their rationality. They are basically input-output bound, cannot be

---

[1] Herbert A. Simon, *Administrative Behavior*, Macmillan, 1961, pp. 20-79.

assumed to possess full information, and in addition are capable only of sequential processing. The result is that human behavior in problem-solving and decision-making situations is one of satisficing rather than optimizing. In other words, individuals generally do not optimize; they consider a problem solved when they obtain a satisfactory feasible solution.

This does not imply that individuals will not choose the best alternative from among many. However decision making is not simply a choice among alternatives. The total process requires recognition of a problem, definition of the problem, search for solution, evaluation of solution in terms of the problem definition, and choice. By choice is meant a decision whether a solution is satisfactory—that is, whether the problem is solved or whether the search should be continued. In a more general sense, choice can also mean redefining the problem, making simplifying assumptions, or expanding the search.

Thus, satisficing is the major behavioral characteristic of individual decision making. It is the behavioral outcome of the limits on the rationality of humans. However, this should not be interpreted to mean that all individuals have identical cognitive styles. An individual's personal cognitive style is largely determined early in his development as a child.[2] It is through a socialization process that the child acquires attitudes, morals, and a capacity and structure for problem solving. In a specific situation, no one cognitive style is necessarily superior to another because more than one approach can lead to the same satisfactory alternative. The particular cognitive style reflects this socialization process. However, cognitive styles can be differentiated in terms of such criteria as ability to think critically and analytically, dogmatism, dependence on others, conceptual and associative ability, and many more.

In summary, administrative man can be described in terms of satisficing behavior and the limitations on his information-processing capacity; and his problem-solving style represents his unique capacity for rationality within those limitations.

DECISION MAKING IN ORGANIZATIONS

The type of decision problems faced by organizations range from routine to unstructured. Routine problems can be defined as simple because solutions are easily available through modification or adaptation of existing solutions. However, any problem can become routine when, as a result of recurring often enough, a standard response is devised for it. Thus in general, organization can be described as operating with a large collection of standard operating procedures and some mechanisms for recognizing problems, classifying them into routine or complex, and solving complex problems.

This section deals largely with unstructured problem solving in organizations. It should be noted, however, that there exists an analogy between the cognitive styles of individual and organizations. Organizations and individuals are severely constrained in their information-processing capacity. Organizations achieve their objectives (solve problems) by assuming local rationality on the part of sub-units and segmenting tasks to smaller parts. Organizations, as do individuals, routinize problem solving whenever possible. Organizations, as are individuals, are inefficient in solving complex unstructured problems.

[2]See, for example, the discussion in Roger Brown, *Social Psychology*, Free Press, 1965, pp. 197-423.

When the individual joins an organization, he is motivated to learn the organization's way of decision making. Depending on his level in the organization, this process can be completely routine (assembly line worker) or require on-the-job training, i.e., much of what must be learned was routine for the previous job occupant but not recorded formally, or no formal or informal training exists for the job (very high level positions).

The interplay between people in the organization and the decision-making structure occurs when complex problems face the organization. Complex, in this context, refers to problems for which past precedents do not exist or cannot be retrieved. This means that existing decision rules or standard operating procedures and simple modification thereof are unsatisfactory as solutions. Often complex problems also connote intra-organizational conflict. That is, the solution or the definition of the problem involves more than one organizational sub-unit. Finally problems are defined as complex because their analysis is largely more subjective than objective, and therefore bargaining becomes the process through which solutions obtain.

By definition unstructured problems are ill-defined to begin with and are perceived as complex to solve. The search processes for solving such problems are in themselves complex. They depend on the priority of the problem. The more pressing the issue, the greater the likelihood that a solution will be found. Because bargaining is often involved in the solution, the power structure of the organization can determine what solution will be obtained.

Committees are often used for developing solutions to such problems. Their major advantages are that when the problems affect a number of departments, the definition of the problems and solutions will reflect some type of consensus and will have the support of the affected departments when implemented. Committees are not always interdepartmental. They can be interdisciplinary. The latter approach can be quite effective when the solution of the problem requires more than one type of expertise.

Research on the use of committees (groups) suggests that groups are superior to individuals in the solution-evaluation phase, whereas individuals working alone are superior to groups in the solution-generating phase. Individuals working alone generate more solutions than the same individuals working in a group. The primary reason is that each individual working alone devotes the full time period to thinking of solutions and is not distracted by the ideas of others. The superiority of groups in the evaluation phase results from the ability of groups to make judgments on such critical dimensions as the organizational feasibility of a solution and its implementation.

Committees, however, do not always function as intended. They can be hampered, for example, by clearly perceived status differences that result in decisions reflecting the positions of high status persons. The leadership style of a committee chairman or group leader can also affect the results and so does the composition of the group. The departmental allegiances of group members and their personal experience and training will determine problem definition and therefore the nature of the solutions being proposed.

Committees are often created as a way to demonstrate action on the part of the organization in dealing with an urgent problem. In many instances, this action provides the necessary time to search for a solution. However, when the problem is not expected to recur or when its urgency becomes less obvious, creating a committee can also obviate the need for action.

Another approach organizations have employed to deal with unexpected and complex problems has been to build a capacity for solving such problems. Thus, organizations employ staffs of specialists as a way of developing in-house capabilities. Examples are operations research groups, information systems sections, research and development departments, and outside consultants.

The process of organizational decision revolves around resource allocations. Unstructured problems are more difficult than routine problems from a resource allocation point of view. Generally, it is easier to allocate resources to an ongoing activity than to a new one, because ongoing successful projects usually have no difficulty in justifying and obtaining additional resources. New projects and less successful projects usually resort to lobbying activites to insure receiving the resources they need. It is interesting to note, however, that a single criterion—the availability of resources—(can we afford it?)—determines the extent to which proposals are scrutinized. Thus, it can be expected that firms in a slack accumulation phase are more likely to approve projects on the basis of criteria other than cost effectiveness or profitability than firms who are not doing as well. When resources are scarce, not only will project proposals be scrutinized more closely, but lobbying activity increases and felt intraorganizational conflict increases.

In summary, much of the day-to-day decision making is governed by routine stable decision rules. Committees are often used as a device to solve complex problems either when they are perceived as interdepartmental or intradepartmental problems. The effectiveness of committees depends on their composition, perceived status differences, and the leadership style of the chairman. Although unstructured problem solving cannot be routinized, organizations can build up their capacity for general problem solving in a variety of ways. Finally, the determining factor in allocating resources to projects (implementing solutions) is the availability of resources.

INTRODUCTION TO THE READINGS

The individual in his role as problem solver and decision maker is often affected by the decision situation itself, the type of information available to him, and the organization structure within which he functions. The articles by Dearborn and Simon (1958) and Cyert, March and Starbuck (1961) involve the decision maker's perception of a decision situation. In the first article, Dearborn and Simon demonstrate the process of selective perception. Their subjects—managers in an executive training program—were given a complex general business case to analyze. Dearborn and Simon hypothesized that the various solutions proposed for the case would reflect the managerial positions that each held; the results clearly supported this selective perception hypothesis.

Another selective perception experiment is found in the Cyert, March, and Starbuck paper. Here the interesting finding involved the way managers treated two identical series of numbers depending on whether they were labeled cost estimates or sales estimates. From the empirical results it is clear that managers tended to be conservative in their decisions, underestimating revenues and overestimating costs.

The effect of organization structure on individual decision making has been a subject of many research studies. The article by Blankenship and Miles (1968) reports on a survey of 190 managers regarding the relationship between managerial decision behavior and organizational factors such as size. The central finding of the paper is that managers' reports of having more opportunity for discretionary decision making correlate positively with their level in the organization.

The paper by Corzo and Yanouzas reports on a laboratory experiment in which the effect of tall and flat organization structures on decision making and profitability is investigated. Previous research of this type has suggested that hierarchically structured organizations are more efficient than flat organizations when responding to routine or structured problems. However, unstructured organizations are considered to be superior in responding to complex problems and afford higher job satisfaction to their participants. Corzo and Yanouzas observed that tall organizations took more time to process information through their structures, but that flat organizations required more time to resolve internal conflict. They also report that tall structures were more profitable. These results did not involve such factors as morale and job satisfaction but are in general supportive of the superiority of hierarchical organizations in responding to structured problems.

The remaining three papers involve the general issue of how alternative accounting methods affect managerial decisions. The article by Pondy and Birnberg reports on a laboratory experiment on capital investment. The results of their research for real world organizations are applicable to the situation of inter-unit competition for capital resources. Pondy and Birnberg conclude that in the case of a profitable project a manager could maximize his allocations when he presented his costs and profits as accurately as possible. In the case of unprofitable projects, Pondy and Birnberg conclude that a manager would be best served by underestimating his costs and overestimating his profits and furthermore should supplement these optimistic estimates with a lobbying effort.

The specific issue of the impact of accounting information on decision making is discussed in the papers by Bruns (1969) and Ijiri, Jaedicke and Knight (1966). Bruns raises the issue of what is relevant accounting information and concludes that the "relationships between accounting methods, accounting information, and business decision making are largely unexplored" and that further research is needed. Ijiri, Jaedicke and Knight are concerned with the relationship of accounting information and organizational decision making. Specifically, they explore the organization's decision rules for using accounting information and the affect of such information on decision making. Thus, for example, managers must often use accounting information as a surrogate input because the desired information is not available or would be too costly to obtain. Ijiri, Jaedicke and Knight also consider the conditions under which the manager can adjust his decision process to changes in the accounting process and the role of the accounting process in determining operational goals. The budget process is a good example of the accounting process influencing the development of operational goals.

10

SELECTIVE PERCEPTION: A NOTE ON THE

DEPARTMENTAL IDENTIFICATIONS OF EXECUTIVES*

DEWITT C. DEARBORN / HERBERT A. SIMON

An important proposition in organization theory asserts that each executive will perceive those aspects of the situation that relate specifically to the activities and goals of his department (2, Ch. 5, 10). The proposition is frequently supported by anecdotes of executives and observers in organizations, but little evidence of a systematic kind is available to test it. It is the purpose of this note to supply some such evidence.

The proposition we are considering is not peculiarly organizational. It is simply an application to organizational phenomena of a generalization that is central to any explanation of selective perception: Presented with a complex stimulus, the subject perceives in it what he is "ready" to perceive; the more complex or ambiguous the stimulus, the more the perception is determined by what is already "in" the subject and the less by what is in the stimulus (1, pp. 132-133).

Cognitive and motivational mechanisms mingle in the selective process, and it may be of some use to assess their relative contributions. We might suppose either: (1) selective attention to a part of a stimulus reflects a deliberate ignoring of the remainder as irrelevant to the subject's goals and motives, or (2) selective attention is a learned response stemming from some past history of reinforcement. In the latter case we might still be at some pains to determine the nature of the reinforcement, but by creating a situation from which any immediate motivation for selectivity is removed, we should be able to separate the second mechanism from the first. The data provide evidence for internalization of the selective processes.

METHOD OF THE STUDY

A group of 23 executives, all employed by a single large manufacturing concern and enrolled in a company sponsored executive training program, was asked to read a standard case that is widely used in instruction in business policy in business schools. The case, Castengo Steel Company, described the organization and activities of a company of moderate size specializing in the manufacture of seamless steel tubes, as of the end of World War II. The case, which is about 10,000 words in length, contains a wealth of descriptive material about the company and its industry and the recent history of both (up to 1945), but little evaluation. It is

*Sociometry, Vol. 21 (June, 1958), pp. 140-44.

deliberately written to hold closely to concrete facts and to leave as much as possible of the burden of interpretation to the reader.

When the executives appeared at a class session to discuss the case, but before they had discussed it, they were asked by the instructor to write a brief statement of what they considered to be the most important problem facing the Castengo Steel Company—the problem a new company president should deal with first. Prior to this session, the group had discussed other cases, being reminded from time to time by the instructor that they were to assume the role of the top executive of the company in considering its problems.

The executives were a relatively homogeneous group in terms of status, being drawn from perhaps three levels of the company organization. They were in the range usually called "middle management," representing such positions as superintendent of a department in a large factory, product manager responsible for profitability of one of the ten product groups manufactured by the company, and works physician for a large factory. In terms of departmental affiliation, they fell in four groups:

Sales (6): Five product managers or assistant product managers, and one field sales supervisor.

Production (5): Three department superintendents, one assistant factory manager, and one construction engineer.

Accounting (4): An assistant chief accountant, and three accounting supervisors—for a budget division and two factory departments.

Miscellaneous (8): Two members of the legal department, two in research and development, and one each from public relations, industrial relations, medical and purchasing.

THE DATA

Since the statements these executives wrote are relatively brief, they are reproduced in full in the appendix. We tested our hypothesis by determining whether there was a significant relation between the "most important problem" mentioned and the departmental affiliation of the mentioner. In the cases of executives who mentioned more than one problem, we counted all those they mentioned. We compared (1) the executives who mentioned "sales," "marketing," or "distribution" with those who did not; (2) the executives who mentioned "clarifying the organization" or some equivalent with those who did not. The findings are summarized in the Table.

| | | Number Who Mentioned | | |
Department	Total number of Executives	Sales	"Clarify Organization"	Human Relations
Sales	6	5	1	0
Production	5	1	4	0
Accounting	4	3	0	0
Miscellaneous	8	1	3	3
Totals	23	10	8	3

The difference between the percentages of sales executives (83%) and other executives (29%) who mentioned sales as the most important problem is significant at the 5 per cent level. Three of the five nonsales executives, moreover, who mentioned sales were in the accounting department, and all of these were in positions that involved analysis of product profitability. This accounting activity was, in fact, receiving considerable emphasis in the company at the time of the case discussion and the accounting executives had frequent and close contacts with the product managers in the sales department. If we combine sales and accounting executives, we find that 8 out of 10 of these mentioned sales as the most important problem; while only 2 of the remaining 13 executives did.

Organization problems (other than marketing organization) were mentioned by four out of five production executives, the two executives in research and development, and the factory physician, but by only one sales executive and no accounting executives. The difference between the percentage for production executives (80%) and other executives (22%) is also significant at the 5 per cent level. Examination of the Castengo case shows that the main issue discussed in the case that relates to manufacturing is the problem of poorly defined relations among the factory manager, the metallurgist, and the company president. The presence of the metallurgist in the situation may help to explain the sensitivity of the two research and development executives (both of whom were concerned with metallurgy) to this particular problem area.

It is easy to conjecture why the public relations, industrial relations, and medical executives should all have mentioned some aspect of human relations, and why one of the two legal department executives should have mentioned the board of directors.

CONCLUSION

We have presented data on the selective perceptions of industrial executives exposed to case material that support the hypothesis that each executive will perceive those aspects of a situation that relate specifically to the activities and goals of his department. Since the situation is one in which the executives were motivated to look at the problem from a company-wide rather than a departmental viewpoint, the data indicate further that the criteria of selection have become internalized. Finally, the method for obtaining data that we have used holds considerable promise as a projective device for eliciting the attitudes and perceptions of executives.

REFERENCES

1. Bruner, J. S., "On Perceptual Readiness," *Psychological Review,* 1957, 64, 123-152.
2. Simon, H. A., *Administrative Behavior,* New York: Macmillan, 1947.

APPENDIX

Executive Sales

4. Apparent need for direct knowledge of their sales potential.
   Apparent need for exploitation of their technical potential to achieve a broader market and higher priced market.
   Apparent need for unit and operation cost data.

5. How to best organize the company so as to be able to take full advantage of the specialized market available.
6. Appointment of Production Manager familiar with business.
   Analysis of market conditions with regard to expansion in plastic market.
12. Develop a sales organization which would include market research.
20. Lack of organization to plan and cope with postwar manufacturing and sales problems.
25. The President's choice of executive officers.

Production

1. Policy pertaining to distribution of product should be reviewed with more emphasis on new customers and concern for old.
15. Lack of clear-cut lines of responsibility.
16. Determine who the top executive was to be and have this information passed on to subordinate executives.
18. Review the organization.
    Why so many changes in some of the offices such as works manager.
24. Absence of policy—should be set forth by company head.

Accounting

7. Standards brought up to date and related to incentives. (Incentives evidently do not exist.)
9. Future of the company as to marketability of products—product specification—growth or containment or retirement (i.e., from product).
10. Distribution problems. Not necessarily their present problems in distribution, but those that undoubtedly will arise in the near future—plastics, larger companies, etc.
11. Reorganization of the company to save its lost market for its product and to look for an additional market is the prime problem.

Other

3. (Legal) Manufacture of one product which (a) competes against many larger manufacturers with greater facilities in competitive market, and (b) is perhaps due to lose to a related product much of its market.
14. (Legal) Board of Directors.
8. (Public relations) The handling of employee relations—particularly the company-union relationship.
17. (Industrial relations) Can we get the various departments together to form a team in communications and cooperation?
19. (Medical)
    1. Reorganization of corporate structure
    2. Lines of authority and command
    3. Personnel relations.
21. (Purchasing) We should start to think and organize for our peacetime economy.
22. (Research and development) Overcentralized control by the president.
23. (Research and development) No formal organization with duties defined.

11

TWO EXPERIMENTS ON BIAS AND CONFLICT IN

ORGANIZATIONAL ESTIMATION *

RICHARD M. CYERT / JAMES G. MARCH / WILLIAM H. STARBUCK

The hypotheses tested in the experiments reported in this study evolved from a paper concerned with the relationship between the communication structure of the firm and decision-making.[1] In the paper we speculated on the role of bias in the information system and the resultant effect on decisions. Later analysis led to the hypothesis that costs and sales would tend to be estimated with a bias, though the bias might be in a different direction for each type of estimate.[2] This hypothesis is derived from a simple model of the "Estimator's Problem."

Given a subjective estimate, E, select a bias factor, b, appropriate to the particular situation. Given the same subjective estimate, E, nature, in turn, will select a bias factor, b^*, that is, there will be a true value. The true value is, in fact, b^*E; the estimate made by the estimator is bE. Assume in this abstract decision situation, that the pay-off to the estimator varies inversely with the size of the discrepancy between the estimate and the true value. In fact, then, the pay-off depends upon a couplet, (b, b^*). The estimator selects b; nature "selects" b^*.

Suppose that the highest pay-off to the estimator occurs when the estimate is accurate, and that the pay-offs decrease at the same rate for over- and under-estimation. Such a pay-off schedule can be described as unbiased. If the errors in one direction are more costly than the same magnitude of errors in the other direction, the pay-off schedule is biased.

If the pay-offs depend only on the (b, b^*) couplet and the pay-offs are un-biased, there is no reason for the estimator to bias the estimate. If the pay-offs are biased or if they depend on considerations other than the relation between the esti-mate and the true value (e.g., the pay-off may depend on the performance of other parts of the organization as well), the tactical decision on biasing the estimate be-comes an important one to the estimator.

The two studies reported in this paper support two conclusions:

1. The proposition that individuals can and do modify their subjective estimates of reality to accommodate their expectations about the kinds of pay-offs associated with various possible errors has empirical validity.

*Management Science, April 1961, pp. 254-264.

[1] R. M. Cyert and J. G. March. Organizational structure and pricing behavior in an oligopolistic market. American Economic Review, 1955, 45, 129-139.

[2] See also C. C. Saxton, The Economics of Price Determination (London, 1942), p. 148.

2. In the face of conflict, estimations are developed into a kind of bargaining process in which the various problems associated with bargaining, gaming, and lifemanship induce compensating strategies on the part of the individual or group making the actual decisions on the basis of the estimations.

AN EXPERIMENT TESTING THE EFFECT OF SALES AND COST LABELS ON ESTIMATION

The first experiment explores a general proposition in organizational estimation. The proposition is that estimates within a complex decision making system involve attempts by the estimators to control their pay-offs. In this experiment the subjects were asked to determine a summary statistic for an array of numbers. Since the experiment involved the switching of labels, it is of some importance to investigate the "theory" of descriptive statistics to determine the importance, if any, of the substantive origin of the numbers in the array to be summarized.

Essentially a descriptive statistic is a procedure for transforming any arbitrary array of numbers into a coded number (or set of numbers) that in some sense "represents" the original array. The procedure is independent of the labels attached to the numbers in the original array. The arithmetic mean of the array $\{10, 8, 5, 1\}$ is 6, and this result does not depend on whether we are talking about apples, revolutions per minute, or shoe size. According to the theory, the choice of a descriptive statistic (for example, a choice between an arithmetic mean and a median as a measure of central tendency) should be made on the basis of the characteristics of the distribution.

The implicit model underlying much of the treatment of descriptive statistics can be characterized as follows: For any array of numbers there exists a set of summary numbers (smaller in size than the original array) appropriate to that array. This set of summary numbers depends on the values of the numbers within the array and not on the labels attached to those numbers. Given an array of numbers and a set of instructions we can determine a statistic, and that statistic is uniquely defined, at least for any particular practitioner at any particular point of time.

Suppose, however, that the statistic is imbedded as an estimate in a decision making system. In particular, suppose that the summary set of numbers represents information processed through an organization as a basis for a decision. We wish to investigate whether a summary estimate is uniquely determined for a given practitioner, a given array, and a given set of instructions. We do this by introducing variations in the labels attached to specific numbers in an array and comparing the summary statistic chosen by relatively sophisticated subjects.

In accordance with the model described above, it is hypothesized that cost analysts will tend to overestimate costs and that sales analysts will tend to underestimate sales. The rationale for the hypothesis relates to the presumption of a biased pay-off schedule within the organization. The particular experiment described here does not test the rationale but only the treatment of the estimation problem.

Subjects

Subjects were 32 first year graduate students in a program leading to a master's degree in industrial administration. Almost all held undergraduate degrees in engineering or science. All were men. All had had some introduction to techniques of statistical description and estimation.

Experimental Material

The basic experimental form was a paper and pencil test requiring each subject to make ten estimates on the basis of the estimates of others. There were two versions of the test. The first version (the *cost* version) was introduced by the following preamble:

> Assume you are the chief cost analyst of a manufacturing concern considering the production of a new product. You have been asked to submit a *single figure* as your estimate of unit cost for the product if 750,000 are produced. You have two assistants (A and B) in each of whom you have equal confidence and who make preliminary estimates for you. For each of the cases below, indicate what estimate of cost you would submit.

The second version (the *sales* version) was introduced by the following preamble:

> Assume you are the chief market analyst of a manufacturing concern considering the production of a new product. You have been asked to submit a *single figure* as your estimate of sales of the product if the price is set at $1.50. You have two assistants (A and B) in each of whom you have equal confidence and who make preliminary estimates for you. For each of the cases below, indicate what estimate of sales you would submit.

Each preamble was followed by a list of ten pairs of numbers, representing the ten pairs of estimates by two subordinates. These numbers and their pairings were identical in the two cases except that in the cost version they were presented as unit costs in cents and in the sales version they were presented as sales in 1,000's. The numbers ranged from 108 to 907. The pairs were arranged such that there were two pairs in which the difference was approximately 100, two pairs in which the difference was approximately 200, two pairs in which the difference was approximately 400, and two pairs in which the difference was approximately 500. For those eight pairs, one pair in each of the four difference levels was toward the high end of the overall number range and one pair was toward the low end of the overall range. The other two pairs did not fit the same pattern. One involved a difference of approximately 800; the other was simply a repeat of an earlier pair. The ten pairs in the order they were presented to the subjects are indicated below:

Two Experiments on Bias and Conflict

	A's estimate	B's estimate
(1)	594	194
(2)	901	396
(3)	113	609
(4)	894	796
(5)	311	108
(6)	451	848
(7)	901	396
(8)	641	836
(9)	162	257
(10)	111	907

Experimental Procedure

The subjects were divided into two groups of 16 subjects each. One group was given the cost version and the other group the sales version. The two groups met in separate classes and completed the versions at approximately the same time without opportunity for communication. Ten weeks later the same groups were again given the forms. This time the versions were reversed. The group receiving the cost version first received the sales version ten weeks later. The group receiving the sales version first received the cost version ten weeks later. In all cases subjects were assured that the questions did not have a "correct" answer, that they should use their own best judgment, and that the test was not being used as an evaluative device.

Analysis

To analyze the data we define a number representing the weight attached to the larger of the two given numbers in the pair presented to the subject. We specify $E = \alpha U + (1 - \alpha)L$, where E is the estimate made by the subject, U is the higher number in the pair, and L is the lower number in the pair. For each of the ten pairs for each subject, the value of α was computed as well as a mean α for the ten pairs. The mean value of α represents the average weight attached to the higher of the two numbers in the given pair. Thus, a subject with $\alpha = 1.00$ always chose the higher estimate; a subject with $\alpha = .50$ on the average took the mean; a subject with $\alpha = 0$ always chose the lower estimate. Since we had two estimates of α for each subject, we compared the α used in the cost version with the α used in the sales version. We treat the group which received the cost version first separately from the group which received the sales version first.

Results

The mean results for each group are indicated in Table 1. There is some suggestion in the data that the order of presentation might have affected the results. Therefore, before merging the two groups together a test was run. Specifically we

TABLE 1   Mean Value of a by Group

	Sales Estimates	Cost Estimates
Sales version first	.499	.606
Cost version first	.346	.738
Total mean value	.423	.672

tested the hypothesis that the two samples, sales version first and cost version first, came from the same population. The technique used was the Wald-Wolfowitz run test and the hypothesis was not rejected at the 5% level of significance. The hypothesis that the total means are equal was then tested and rejected at the 5% level of significance.

A stronger test is one that utilizes the individual values. Specifically we asked whether the value of α for a given subject was greater for the sales version, equal in the two versions, or greater in the cost version. The results for the 32 subjects are indicated in Table 2. The results for both the sales version first and the cost version first were significant at the 5% level by the sign test.

TABLE 2	Companies of Individual Values		
	Greater in Sales Version	*Equal*	*Greater in Cost Value*
Sales version first	2	3	11
Cost version first	3	1	12

AN EXPERIMENT ON ORGANIZATIONAL ESTIMATION UNDER PARTIAL CONFLICT OF INTEREST

Suppose that the biases suggested by our study of the effect of labels on estimation are combined in an organization. What happens to organizational estimation performance when various kinds of conflict or potential conflict are imposed on it? In order to study the organizational phenomena, we constructed a three-person experimental organization.

The decision making system in the experiment had four critical organizational characteristics:

1. *Subunit interdependence.* Major decisions are not made by individuals or groups at the "lowest" level of the organization. Rather the major decision making units base their actions on estimates formulated at other points in the organization and transmitted to them in the form of communications. The estimates so received cannot be verified directly by the decision making unit.

2. *Subunit specialization.* The estimates used in decision making come from more or less independent subunits of the organization. Each such subunit specializes in a particular function and usually processes a particular type of information.

3. *Subunit discretion.* Organizational constraints on the subunits that formulate and process estimates do not completely determine subunit behavior. The subunits have appreciable discretion in making, filtering, and relaying estimates.

4. *Subunit conflict.* The freedom available to a subunit in satisfying organizational constraints is devoted to the satisfaction of subunit goals. Each subunit develops its own goals and procedures reflecting the particular interests of its members. Such subunit goals will be consistent with the organizational requirements, but within those limits they will take the direction most compatible with individual and group objectives.

Subjects

Subjects were 108 male students. They included both undergraduate and graduate students but were predominantly undergraduate. Most of the subjects were either engineering or science majors. They were divided into 36 three-man groups.

Experimental Situation

Apparatus. Each member of a group sat in a booth designed to prevent him from seeing other members. Each subject was prevented from speaking to other members except when desired by the experimenter and then only over the communication system. This system provided each subject and the experimenter with a headset, microphone, and a display board that indicated what communication was currently feasible over the system. This system was controlled automatically by a mechanical timer which stepped the system through the various communication links required according to a predetermined schedule. When a particular subject was not currently able to use the communication system, a noise signal was transmitted over his line. This served both as a mask for room noise and as an auditory supplement to the visual display board signal.

Task. The task of the group was to estimate the area of a series of 30 rectangles. On each of the 30 trials, one member of the group (the Length Estimator) saw projected on the wall in front of him a line segment. The line segments varied in length from 2.27 inches to 4.92 inches. There were fifteen different lengths. The fifteen were ordered randomly for presentation in the first fifteen trials. The same lengths were presented in the last fifteen trials (in a different random order). This line segment was designated as the length of the rectangle. It was not seen by the other two members of the group. A second member of the group (the Width Estimator) saw a different line segment projected on the wall in his booth. This line segment was designated as the width of the rectangle and was not seen by the other members of the group. The line segments were the same as for the width estimator and were presented in the same way but in a different random order. The third member of the group (the Area Estimator) received from the Length Estimator a number representing his estimate of the length. The Area Estimator received from the Width Estimator a number representing his estimate of the width. Neither the Width Estimator nor the Length Estimator heard the estimation of the other. The Area Estimator then communicated to the Experimenter an estimate of the area of the rectangle. This estimate was compared with the correct area and the magnitude of the error was reported by the Experimenter to all three group members. Aside from the communications indicated here, no communication among the members of the group was permitted.

Rewards. Each subject was given a card in his booth showing the basis on which he would be rewarded for the group's performance during the experiment. The reward was in the form of cash-convertible points. The actual money involved was small (subjects normally "earned" about $1.00 in an experiment lasting about 40 minutes) but was adequate to obtain subjects. The major motivational factor was probably not the modest cash rewards but the point score. The experiment was presented as an experimental test for managerial potential, and most subjects reported after the experiment that they thought it measured some dimensions of managerial ability. There were three different pay-off cards used in the experiment as shown in Table 3. Each card indicated the highest pay-off for estimates within 5% of the true area. However, they differed in the extent to which they valued errors. Card A is symmetric around the true area. Card B suggests a preference for errors on the low side. Card C suggests a preference for errors on the high side. Subjects knew only their own pay-off card.

Experimental Treatments

There were six different experimental treatments; in each treatment six groups were run. They were defined in terms of the assignment of pay-off cards to the various members of the group. We will represent each treatment by three letters. The first letter is the pay-off card given the Length Estimator. The second letter is the pay-off card given the Width Estimator. The third letter is the pay-off card given the Area Estimator.

TABLE 3   Pay-off Cards

	Magnitude and Direction of Error in the Area Estimate	Score
	More than 15% high	0
	5% high to 15% high	2
Card A:	5% high to 5% low	5
	5% low to 15% low	2
	More than 15% low	0
	More than 15% high	0
	5% high to 15% high	0
Card B:	5% high to 5% low	5
	5% low to 15% low	4
	More than 15% low	0
	More than 15% high	0
	5% high to 15% high	4
Card C:	5% high to 5% low	5
	5% low to 15% low	0
	More than 15% low	0

AAA treatment. In this treatment, each member of the group had the same pay-off and it was symmetric.

BBB treatment. In this treatment, each member of the group had the same pay-off but it was not symmetric around the true area.

BCA treatment. In this treatment, the two line estimators have opposing biases and the area estimator has a symmetric pay-off.

ACB treatment. In this treatment, all three pay-offs are used. One of the line estimators has the symmetric pay-off; the other two subjects have opposing biases.

CCB treatment. In this treatment there are only biased pay-offs. The two line estimators have the same bias and are opposed to the Area Estimator.

BCB treatment. In this treatment, there are only biased pay-offs. One of the line estimators and the Area Estimator have the same bias. They are opposed by the other line estimator.

These six treatments represent six of the ten basic types of conflict possible in the experiment. That is, we feel that the following equivalences are reasonable:

BBB is equivalent to CCC.
ACB is equivalent to ABC, BAC, and CAB.
BCA is equivalent to CBA.
CCB is equivalent to BBC.
BCB is equivalent to CBB, BCC, and CBC.

Unrepresented in the experiment are the following types: ABA (equivalent to ACA, BAA, and CAA), AAB (equivalent to AAC), ABB (equivalent to BAB, ACC, CAC), and BBA (equivalent to CCA).

Analysis

In the analysis we are primarily interested in the performance of the groups operating under the different conflict treatments. However, we need first to discuss the evidence bearing on the effectiveness of the experimental conditions in inducing consciously biasing behavior by subjects. Three pieces of evidence are available, none fully satisfactory. First, we compare the regression of estimates on actual line lengths for the three kinds of pay-off cards used for line estimators. Second, we compare the values of δ in the equation $A = \delta L W$ (where A is the area estimate, L is the length estimate, and W is the width estimate) for the two kinds of pay-off cards (A and B) used for area estimators. Third, we compare the frequency of overt strategy comments indicating a conscious manipulation of estimates by individuals having biased pay-off cards (B and C) as compared with persons having unbiased pay-offs (A).[3] The basic problem with all techniques is that the various individuals were involved in different kinds of groups such that it is impossible to make firm inferences as to the effect of the pay-off cards on individual behavior independent of all group effects. These effects include both the pattern of pay-offs to other participants and the local adaptation to area error.

To measure the performance of groups, we compute the mean absolute error and the mean algebraic error in estimating the area of the rectangle. Specifically, we consider the mean absolute and algebraic errors in estimating the area for each treatment for each of six five-trial periods.

Results

The regressions of estimated line segment length (E) on actual length (L) for subjects having the various pay-off cards have the following equations:

A (no bias): $E = 3.28$ | $1.05\,(L - 3.60)$
B (low bias): $E = 3.51$ | $1.20\,(L - 3.60)$
C (high bias): $E = 3.65$ | $1.19\,(L - 3.60)$.

The difference between the means is significant and in the predicted direction for the AC and the BC comparisons. The AB difference is significant but not in the predicted direction. The differences between the slopes of A and B and A and C are significant. The difference between the slopes of B and C is not significant. All tests were made at the 5% level of significance.

The values of the "fudge factor," δ for the several area estimators are indicated below for each treatment:

A card AAA 1.0268
               BCA 1.0015

---

[3]A fourth procedure is to define a mathematical model of the estimation situation (involving simultaneously perceptual error, line estimation bias, and area estimator bias). Such a model can be summarized in the equation $\alpha^2 \lambda^n \delta = \gamma$, where α is the perceptual error in line estimation, λ is the line estimator's bias, η is a function of the line estimators' payoff schedules, δ is defined as in the text, and γ is a function of the area estimator's payoff schedule. Multiple regression estimates of λ from this model also suggest that subjects biased in the predicted direction. The model suffers from the same difficulties noted in the text. The estimates of λ compound both the bias and adaptation to feedback.

Subjects' responses to a question eliciting comments on individual strategies were divided into those that either showed some conscious biasing of subjective estimates and those that did not. 44 of the 78 subjects with biased pay-offs expressed overtly such strategies. 9 of the 30 subjects with unbiased pay-offs did so.

We conclude that the pay-off cards did have the desired effect of introducing individual behavior directed toward biasing the organization estimate. The data in general support such a proposition.

The basic results with respect to the performance of the various groups are indicated in Figure 1. We plot the mean absolute performance over each of the six

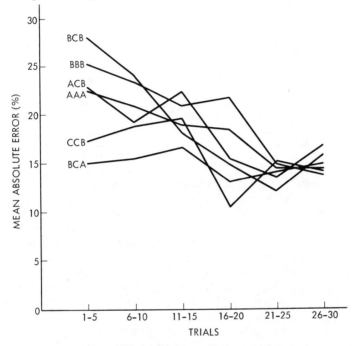

FIG. 1   Absolute Error Performance Results

five-trial periods for each treatment. Two things are conspicuous. First, no treatment has any very clear advantage from the point of view of such performance. Second, there is an apparent convergence in performance over time.

The results (Table 4) with respect to algebraic error show no such consistency except for the treatment (BBB) involving bias without conflict. As might be

TABLE 4   Mean Algebraic Error Performance Results

	Trials					
Treatments	1-5	6-10	11-15	16-20	21-25	26-30
CCB	−6.26	−5.07	−6.70	−.90	+.43	+1.79
AAA	−1.67	−8.88	−5.96	+2.34	−8.73	−5.29
ACB	−.14	−2.90	−4.10	−6.72	−5.53	−3.00
BCA	−1.56	−1.50	−1.03	−7.07	−2.59	+1.17
BCB	+6.13	+6.07	−4.31	−6.10	−5.43	−5.30
BBB	−9.97	−6.07	−10.1	−13.53	−2.48	−5.87

expected, that treatment shows rather consistently the greatest negative error. The other five treatments are indistinguishable by Kendall's test for concordance.

We conclude that there are no persistent differences among the performances of the groups that are a function of the extent or type of conflict imposed on them within this experiment.

DISCUSSION

In the most simplified terms, we can make two generalizations from the results of these studies:

1. The studies suggest that members of an organization will treat estimates, information, and communication generally as active parts of their environment. They will tend to consider the decision for which the information is sought, the probable consequences of various potential biases in information, and the pay-off to them for various possible decision results. They adjust the information they transmit in accordance with their perceptions of the decision situation.
2. The second study indicates that the extent and character of this information manipulation do not affect the performance (in terms of absolute error) of the organization in which the biasing occurs.

The anomaly that variations in behavior at the micro level can exist actively without being reflected at a macro level is a common enough phenomenon. It does not elicit surprise after the fact. In the present situation we can understand how such a result might have been produced. In particular, it seems clear that in an organization of individuals having about the same intelligence, adaptation to the falsification of data occurs fast enough to maintain a more or less stable organizational performance. For the bulk of our subjects in both experiments, the idea that estimates communicated from other individuals should be taken at face value (or that their own estimates would be so taken) was not really viewed as reasonable. For every bias, there was a bias discount.

If such a result can be shown to be a general one, however, it has substantial implications for a theory of organizational decision making. For example, we—as well as others—have argued that the fact of internal informational bias has to be dealt with explicitly in a theory of the firm. These results cast doubt on such an argument. They indicate that perhaps such phenomena, important as they may be to an understanding of the internal operation of the organization, may not be of particular significance to a theory of organizational choice.

12

ORGANIZATIONAL STRUCTURE
AND MANAGERIAL DECISION BEHAVIOR*

L. VAUGHN BLANKENSHIP / RAYMOND E. MILES

The relationship between organization structure and managerial decision-making behavior has been a frequent topic for speculation, but an infrequent subject of systematic research. The study reported here focuses on three structural properties of bureaucracies—size, hierarchical level, and span of control—as possible determinants of this behavior. The results suggest that a pattern of relationships does exist between decision behavior and these organizational variables.

The relative lack of systematic, comparative research on the impact of structural variables on organizational behavior is regularly cited.[1] With a few notable exceptions,[2] most organizational studies have in fact tended to concentrate on attitudinal, demographic, and personality variables, and have tended either to ignore variables of structure altogether or else to give them only secondary consideration. Furthermore, much of the research on organizational behavior has taken the form of case studies dealing with a single organization or department, thus precluding the analysis of structural properties such as those dealt with here. To avoid some of these limitations, this study examines the self-reported decision behavior of 190 managers from eight organizations engaged in light manufacturing, primarily in the electronics industry. The analysis relates the managers' decision behavior to the size of their organizations, their level in the organization hierarchy, and the number of subordinates reporting to them.

DECISION MAKING: CONCEPTUAL FRAMEWORK
AND METHODOLOGY

Conceptual Framework

Decision making may be visualized as a complex process in which an individual or a group of individuals moves through a series of interrelated substeps

*Administrative Science Quarterly, June 1968, pp. 106-120.

[1] Lyman W. Porter and Edward E. Lawler, III, Properties of Organization Structure in Relation to Job Attitudes and Job Behavior, Psychological Bulletin, 64 (1965), 23-51. See also D. S. Pugh, et al., A Scheme for Organizational Analysis, Administrative Science Quarterly, 8 (1963), 289-315.

[2] Melville Dalton, Men Who Manage (New York: John Wiley, 1961), pp. 18-111; Joan Woodward, Management and Technology (London: Her Majesty's Stationery Office, 1950); James C. Worthy, Organizational Structure and Employee Morale, American Sociological Review, 15 (1950), 169-179; Tom Burns, The Directions of Activity and Communication in a Departmental Executive Group, Human Relations, 7 (1954), 73-97; and Sergio Talacchi, Organization Size, Individual Attitudes, and Behavior: An Empirical Study, Administrative Science Quarterly, 5 (1960), 398-420.

including (*1*) the recognition of a problem requiring some response, (*2*) the investigation of the problem and its environment in an effort to collect relevant information and to generate solutions, and (*3*) the selection of a course of action based on an analysis of the available information and solutions.[3]

Within this process, a manager may, with respect to any given decision, participate in any one or all of these stages. His participation in the process may in one instance begin and end with the act of calling to someone else's attention the need for a decision. In another instance, he may collect or provide information on a given problem. In other situations he may have the responsibility of choosing or approving the choice of a course of action from among several alternatives. In short, it is possible to describe a manager's decision-making behavior in terms of the frequency with which he (*1*) *initiates* action on a given set of decisions—calling problems to the attention of peers, superiors, or subordinates, (*2*) *consults* with or is consulted by peers, superiors, or subordinates about such decisions, and (*3*) makes or approves the *final choice* of a course of action with respect to a set of decisions.

The general approach employed in this study depends primarily on managers' descriptions of their own decision-making behavior rather than on participant-observer methods.[4] Although this method increases the possibility of distortion by managers and the ambiguity of some of the meanings of responses, it does make it possible to conduct the study more easily, and the number of managers and organizations that can be included is greater. The focus on the interactions of the structural properties of organizations and decision behavior in the study favored this approach, since it made it possible to include groups of managers at various levels and in several organizations. It is likely that at least some of the managers in our sample have reported distorted pictures of their decision-making role; that is, a picture which would not correspond to that held by their subordinates, their superior, or a disinterested observer. Also, the categories of behavior used do not mean precisely the same thing to all managers. Techniques for studying decision behavior in complex organizations are still new, however, and largely untested; and it is our view that until evidence proves otherwise, broad patterns of decision making across levels and organizations can only be studied by relying heavily on self-reporting measures.

Measures of Decision Behavior

Working within this conceptual and methodological framework, examples of a number of decisions in the form of simple phrases were developed; for example,

[3]There are numerous descriptions of this decision-making cycle, each one differing minutely from another in terms of the words used to label the substeps or the number of substeps mentioned. For example, compare Edward H. Litchfield, Notes on a General Theory of Administration, *Administrative Science Quarterly,* 1 (1956), 3-29 with William R. Dill, "Administrative Decision Making," in Sidney Mailick and Edward H. Van Ness (eds), *Concepts and Issues in Administrative Behavior* (Englewood Cliffs, N.J.: Prentice-Hall, 1962), pp. 29-48.

[4]Support for the research upon which this paper is based was received from the Center for Research in Management Science and the Institute of Industrial Relations, University of California, Berkeley. The helpful comments of Robert Biller, Allen Gulezian, Todd LaPorte, Lyman Porter, and George Strauss on an earlier draft are gratefully acknowledged. The case for the participant-observer approach is forcefully presented by Benjamin Walter, who supports it with a well-designed study. See Benjamin Walter, Internal Control Relations in Administrative Hierarchies, *Administrative Science Quarterly,* 11 (1966), 179-206.

"a decision to change operating procedures." These decisions were derived in part from a number of interviews conducted by the authors in the companies studied and were intended to be representative of the types of decisions that managers at all levels could be expected to face at some time or another. Consequently, they were designed to be general enough to apply across companies, yet not so abstract as to have little or no empirical reference.

Following the initial data collection, further interviews provided information for selecting five of the initial list of decisions as most relevant to the total sample of managers. These decisions, presented to participating managers in a self-administered questionnaire, were stated as follows:

1. A decision to increase the number of permanent positions within your department.
2. A decision to choose one of several applicants for a position in your department.
3. A decision to promote someone in your department to a higher position.
4. A decision to purchase a piece of equipment (machine, tool, facility, etc.) costing over $500 for your department.
5. A decision to purchase operating supplies and equipment not called for in the budget.

For each of these decision statements, participants were asked to indicate, on a 5-point scale ranging from *always* to *never,* how frequently:

1. they, their superiors, or their subordinates would *initiate* action on such a decision;
2. they would be *required to consult* their superior before taking further action on such a decision;
3. *their advice would be sought* by their superior on such a decision;
4. their advice to their superior on a given decision *would be* followed;
5. they would *consult their subordinates* concerning such a decision;
6. they, their superiors, or their subordinates would make the final choice among alternative courses of action on such a decision.

From participants' responses to these statements as they applied to each of the decisions, five summary measures of each manager's decision-making behavior were constructed. These summary measures, as illustrated in Table 1, were designed to reflect various aspects of the three general phrases of the decision-making process, initiation, consultation, and final choice.

Based on his response across all five decisions, each manager was given a summary score for the dimensions of decision behavior shown in Table 1. For example, the frequency with which a manager said that his superior initiated action for him and that he had to consult with his superior was scored and summarized across all five decisions. This then was taken as an indicator of the degree of autonomy that he had from his superior: the lower his score, the higher his autonomy. The individual scores in each of the five measures shown in the table were then arrayed from highest to lowest. Next, for each measure, the sample was divided approximately in half, into a *high* and a *low* group. Thus any given manager's characterization as high or low on a given measure is relative to the scores received by all other managers in the study.

TABLE 1   Measures of Decision Behavior and Response Items Included
in Each Measure

Summary Measures of Decision Behavior	Response Items Included in Measures
Personal initiation	Manager initiates action on decision for himself.
Autonomy from superior	Manager must consult his superior before taking action on decisions.
	Manager's superior initiates action for the manager on decisions.
Perceived influence on superior	Manager is consulted by his superior on decisions.
	Manager's advice is followed by his superior.
Reliance on subordinates (consultation downwards)	Manager consults his subordinates on decisions.
	Manager's subordinates initiate action on decisions.
Final choice	Manager exercises ultimate right of choice on decisions.

STRUCTURAL VARIABLES: CONCEPTS AND MEASURES

As discussed earlier, various factors may influence the decision behavior of managers; that is, with whom they interact and the content of that interaction. Personal characteristics of the manager, unique features of a given decision situation, even the economic market place may help determine decision behavior. We have chosen to focus primarily on structural properties as major explanatory variables in the decision process and to ignore unique situational factors. Individual attitudes and demographic qualities are treated as intervening variables and their impact on decision behavior will be examined in later analyses. Finally, as suggested by the nature of the measures of decision behavior, the possible effects of *types of decisions* on the behavior being studied are crudely controlled in this study by selecting only decisions that can be programmed and that are presumably fairly routine.[5]

Of the several structural features of organizations offered as possible explanations for observed differences in managerial decision behavior, three are emphasized: size, hierarchy, and span of control. To examine some of their effects on decision behavior, crude measures were developed for each of them. The number of employees in 1965 was chosen as the measure of organizational size. None of the organizations in which the study was conducted was more than 15 years old, and all had been relatively stable for at least three years with respect to the total number of employees. The distribution of the eight organizations included in the study by size is shown in Table 2. Five of them were major operating divisions and a sixth a wholly owned subsidiary of a larger corporation. In all but one case, they were physically separate from the parent concern. Two of the smallest were owner-managed, which is characteristic of many of the smaller firms in this industry. For purposes of analysis, Companies A and B were grouped together as being *large,* C and D as *medium,* and E, F, G, and H as *small.*

[5]The decision typology involved here is roughly that between programmed (routine) and unprogrammed (unique) decisions. See Herbert A. Simon, *The New Science of Management Decision* (New York: Harper, 1960), pp. 5-8.

TABLE 2   Companies Studied by Size (Number of Employees in 1965)
and Organizational-Legal Status

Company	Size	Organizational Status	Size Category
A	2,000	Division	Large
B	700	Division	Large
C	410	Division	Medium
D	300	Division	Medium
E	179	Subsidiary	Small
F	150	Division	Small
G	150	Owner-managed	Small
H	112	Owner-managed	Small

The heirarchical level of the individual manager was determined in the following manner. The top managers of the divisions or companies were designated as the *first level* of the hierarchy. Managers one step removed from them on the organizational chart were considered to be at the *second hierarchical level*; those two steps away constituted *third level* managers, and so on. Data were collected from managers below the third level in only two organizations (B and C). Managers at the first two levels were grouped together—there were only seven first-level managers[6] —and classified as upper level for the analysis; managers at level three were classified as middle level, and managers at levels below the third level were classified as lower-level managers.

Span of control was measured simply by asking each manager to indicate the number of people under him whom he was "directly responsible for supervising." The larger the number, the larger his span of control. After an inspection of the distribution of responses on this item, the sample was divided into three groups: those with 0-4 subordinates, those with 5-12 subordinates, and those with 13 or more people working directly under them.

FINDINGS

Relationship Among Types of Decision Behavior

For the managers studied, the five dimensions of decision behavior were generally related to each other, as shown in Table 3, so that a manger who was high on one tended to be high on the others. This relation was strongest for final choice,

TABLE 3   Association (Gamma) Among Measures of Decision Behavior

	Perceived Influence	Autonomy From Superior	Reliance on Subordinates	Personal Initiation
Final choice	.2307	.3407	.2596	.1360
Perceived influence	—	.2134	.2154	.1785
Autonomy from superior	—	—	.2247	.0658
Reliance on subordinates	—	—	—	.0778

[6]Despite repeated contacts and telephone calls, the top manager of one of the larger companies subsequently refused, without explanation, to complete the questionnaire, although he had cooperated fully earlier in having it distributed to managers under him.

the measures of mutual association (gammas) ranging from .14 to .34; and weakest for personal initiation of decisions, with gammas from .07 to .17.[7] Personal initiation seems to be the least discriminating measure of managerial decision behavior. The raw numerical values on this item clustered together towards the high end of the continuum, so that unlike "final choice," for example, average scores in this area were not particularly good predictors of scores elsewhere.

General Impact of Structure

In general, the findings indicate that the manager's location in the hierarchy appears to be the major determinant of his patterns of reported behavior in the types of decisions studied. If he had a position at or near the top, his decision interaction with both subordinates and superiors was different from what it was if he were a lower-level manager. The size of the organization modified this relationship somewhat, especially for managers at the very top and bottom levels. Similarly, span of control is clearly associated with the extent to which managers say they rely on their subordinates. In both cases, however, differences between hierarchical levels remain the dominant influence in these kinds of decisions.

Hierarchical Level

Not surprisingly, perhaps, the freedom of action that a manager believes he enjoys is associated with his position in the hierarchy. More specifically, as Table 4 shows, for those at the top of the hierarchy the pattern of reported behavior appears as follows. Most reported considerable autonomy from their superiors (85

TABLE 4   Level of Hierarchy as Related to High Score on Measures of Decision Behavior

Hierarchical Level	N	Final Choice	Perceived Influence	Autonomy from Superior	Reliance on Subordinates	Personal Initiation
		%	%	%	%	%
Upper	54	80	67	85	70	32
Middle	93	40	51	39	49	49
Lower	43	41	29	20	34	38

percent) in the dual sense that their superiors rarely initiated action for them (at least in the decisions studied) and they were seldom required to consult with their superiors before making a decision. In addition, four-fifths of them claimed that they usually made final choices without the prior approval of anyone, and two-thirds of them believed that their recommendations regularly carried considerable weight with their superiors. At the same time, however, they were the least likely of managers at any level to begin action on decision for themselves (32 percent) and the most likely to report relying on their subordinates for such initiation (70 percent). In short, although they themselves enjoyed considerable independence

[7]W. Allen Wallis and Harry V. Roberts, *Statistics: A New Approach* (Glencoe, Ill.: The Free Press, 1956), pp. 280-282 and Leo A. Goodman and William H. Kruskal, Measures of Association for Cross Classifications, *Journal of the American Statistical Association,* 49 (December 1954), 740-745. In all but two cases in the cross tabulations, $\underline{x}^2$ = P< .001.

and discretion upwards, they relied heavily on subordinates to bring problems to their attention and to offer ideas and recommendations. The pattern of decision behavior for lower-level managers is the reverse of this. They did not appear to rely on their subordinates for initiation of action or suggestions, but took their guidance from above, as evidenced by the fact that only 20 percent of them are in the high category on autonomy from superiors. In addition, less than one-third of them felt that their recommendations to their superiors carried much weight. In the light of this, it is rather surprising to find that a little over two-fifths of the managers at this level (41 percent) still feel that they enjoy the right of final choice without the prior approval of anyone above them.

Size

Table 5 demonstrates that for upper- and lower-level managers, size is a distinguishing factor in terms of reported decision behavior. *For those at the top of the hierarchy, large size is associated with greater freedom of action; however, for those at the bottom, decision opportunity is greater for managers in small organizations.* Within companies of similar size, decision behavior differs sharply by hierarchical level in the same direction as before, with the exception of lower-level managers in small- to medium-sized concerns.

TABLE 5   Level of Hierarchy as Related to High Score on Measures of Decision Behavior with Organizational Size Held Constant

Organizational Size for Each Hierarchical Level	N	Final Choice	Perceived Influence	Autonomy from Superior	Reliance on Subordinates	Personal Initiation
		%	%	%	%	%
Upper level						
Large	19	95	79	90	79	21
Medium-small	35	71	54	80	66	37
Middle level						
Large	46	37	54	39	61	41
Medium-small	46	43	48	39	37	57
Lower-level						
Large	34	29	21	12	38	29
Medium-small	8	88	63	50	38	75

A closer look at Table 5 shows that almost all of the upper-level managers in the two larger companies were high on final choice (95 percent) as compared with 71 percent of those in the medium-sized or small firms. The difference is even greater with respect to their perceptions of influence up the hierarchy. Seventy-nine percent of the managers at the top level in the large organizations were high on this item. Only slightly over half of their counterparts in the smaller concerns (54 percent) saw themselves as having considerable influence with their superiors. However, with respect to both autonomy from superiors and reliance upon subordinates, there is little to distinguish between the two groups. Furthermore, upper-level managers in the medium- and small-sized companies were a little more likely to be high on personal initiation of decisions (37 percent) than those in the larger ones (21 percent).

Span of Control

Reliance on subordinates was the only measure of the decision behavior of the managers associated with span of control. A little over one-third (37 percent) of those managers with four or less subordinates indicated that they frequently depended on their subordinates for ideas and the initiation of decisions, at least in the areas asked about, while almost two-thirds (62 percent) of the managers with thirteen or more subordinates said that they did so. Since a manager's span of control is partly a function of where he is located in the hierarchy, this raised the question of how much of the variation in reliance on subordinates was a matter of numbers of subordinates and how much a matter of hierarchical position.

This question is answered by the data in Table 6. When hierarchical level is held constant, it is clear that the more subordinates a manager has, the more likely they are to initiate action for him. At the same time, the table shows that differ-

TABLE 6   Managers High on Reliance on Subordinates by Hierarchical
Level and Span of Control

Hierarchical Level	Span of Control	N	High Score on Reliance on Subordinates
Upper	0-4	12	%
	5-12	31	42
	13 and up	11	100
Middle	0-4	24	33
	5-12	44	46
	13 and up	24	71
Lower	0-4	2	*
	5-12	11	18
	13 and up	28	39

*The fact that there were only two lower-level managers with four or fewer subordinates makes a percentage in this category unrealistic. One of these managers was high and the other low on reliance on subordinates.

ences between levels remain. Regardless of the number of subordinates, the upper-level managers in the study were more likely to report that they depended frequently upon their subordinates than were those managers at the middle or lower levels of the hierarchy.

Hierarchy, Final Choice, and Decision Behavior

Almost by definition hierarchical structure reflects the distribution within an organization of the right to the final decision, whether this means actually choosing among alternatives or merely formally approving choices already made elsewhere.[8]

[8]Victor A. Thompson, Hierarchy, Specialization and Organizational Conflict, *Administrative Science Quarterly,* 5 (1961), 485-521 and Max Weber, *From Max Weber: Essays in Sociology,* trans. by H. H. Gerth and W. Wright Mills (New York: Oxford University, 1958), pp. 198-204. In fact this distinction between "actually" choosing and "merely" ratifying is one of degree rather than kind. Unless a manager does everything by himself—gathers information, organizes it, generates alternatives, etc.—he is inevitably dependent on others, and the decisions they have made about what he wants to see or consider.

Where a manager believes he has this right of final choice, it may well affect his total pattern of decision behavior, including his interactions with both superiors and subordinates, since it gives occasion for and direction to this behavior. The finding in Table 3 that the right of final choice was most closely associated with other phases of the decision process would lend empirical support to this proposition. The close conceptual linkage of hierarchy and the power of choice on the one hand and the empirical association between this power and other areas of decision behavior on the other, suggested the need for further analysis of the relation between hierarchy and decision behavior with the right of final choice held constant. The results are presented in Table 7.

Consider, first, the managers who are high on final choice. Except in the area of personal initiation, those at the top of the hierarchy still have greater freedom of

TABLE 7   Hierarchical Level of Related to High Score on Measures of
Decision Behavior with Final Choice Held Constant

Hierarchical Level for Score on Final Choice	N	Perceived Influence	Autonomy from Superior	Reliance on Subordinates	Personal Initiation
		%	%	%	%
High					
Upper	41	66	88	77	33
Middle	37	60	54	57	70
Lower	17	59	35	56	65
Low					
Upper	11	70	73	46	27
Middle	55	46	29	44	35
Lower	24	8	8	20	20

action and report a more frequent reliance on subordinates than do managers at lower levels. For middle- and lower-level managers, however, the previous differences between them virtually disappear. The exception is in the area of decision autonomy from superiors. Only 35 percent of those in lower-level positions as compared with 54 percent of those in middle-level positions are high on this measure.

Now among the managers who see themselves as low on final choice, hierarchy makes a sharp difference, especially with regard to perceptions of upward influence and feelings about decision autonomy. Only a few (8 percent) of the lower-level managers scored high in these areas, while an increased proportion of the middle-level managers, and almost three-fourths of those at the top did so. A minority of the managers at all levels were high on personal initiation, and there was no difference between the top and middle levels with respect to reliance on subordinates.

DISCUSSION AND CONCLUSIONS

The dominant point emerging from the analysis is the overriding importance of hierarchical position. Although organizational size, span of control, and a manager's perceptions of whether or not he enjoys the right of final choice modify its effects somewhat, hierarchical level is still strongly and consistently associated with a manager's decision-making style.

Upper-level managers not only claim greater freedom from their superiors in decisions of the type used in this study, they also show a stronger pattern of reliance on their own subordinates; that is, they tend to involve their subordinates in the decision-making process to a greater degree than managers at lower levels. Lower-level managers, on the other hand, tend to have decisions initiated for them by their superiors and are required or expected to consult with their superiors before proceeding on most issues. In turn, these managers tend not to involve their subordinates in the decision-making process, even though their subordinates are themselves managers in their own right.

The pattern suggests that organizations that may want or expect lower-level managers to put participative-management concepts into practice must treat these managers as if they were upper-level members of the organization. This implication is supported by the analysis of variations in behavior on final choice within organizational levels. Lower-level managers who felt they had this right tended to look more like their higher-level counterparts, particularly in terms of the degree to which they felt they relied on their own subordinates for assistance in decision making. No other single phase of decision behavior appears to influence a manager's total pattern of decision behavior as strongly as does his perception of whether he has the right of final choice on an issue. Thus the fact that a superior consults his subordinates when making decisions will not guarantee that they will in turn involve their subordinates in decision making. However, the manager who actually allows his subordinates the freedom to decide certain issues for themselves may well increase the likelihood that they will rely on their own subordinates for assistance.

The deviations from the general pattern of relationships reported here are as interesting as the pattern itself. Why do particular managers at certain levels claim greater freedom in decision making than their peers, both within their own organization and in similar firms? Have their own superiors consciously granted them this freedom, and if so, why these managers and not others around them? Have these lower-level managers who have patterns of decision behavior more like those of upper-level managers simply acquired these patterns with or without guidance or opposition, as the result of their own attitudes or values? What happens to the manager who deviates from the general patterns associated with certain structural features, in terms of his own performance and satisfaction and in terms of the impact of his behavior on his own work unit and the organization as a whole? Additional research along these lines is clearly suggested.

13

EFFECTS OF FLAT AND TALL ORGANIZATION STRUCTURE *

ROCCO CARZO, JR. / JOHN N. YANOUZAS

Empirical studies on the effects of organization structure have been mostly in field research. The purpose of this study[1] was to test the effects of organization structure in a laboratory experiment, specifically, tall and flat structures and their effects on organizational performance. A secondary purpose was to analyze the learning-curve patterns in the performance of organized groups.

THEORETICAL CONSIDERATIONS

Worthy's study (1950) of Sears Roebuck and Company was one of the first extensive and a widely accepted empirical study on the effects of flat and tall organization structure. Worthy argued, that small organizations had better employee morale and productivity than large organizations. He stated that the advantages of small organizations could be incorporated into large organizations by using fewer levels of administration; that is, a flat organizational structure with a wide span of supervision rather than a tall or multilevel organization with a very narrow span of supervision.

At Sears, according to Worthy, the merchandising vice president had 44 senior executives reporting directly to him. The typical retail store at Sears had "forty-odd department managers reporting to a single store manager" (1959: 109). With this organization, the manager of a Sears department store did not have time to solve all the problems and was therefore forced to delegate decision-making authority to subordinates. When managers of departments were forced to manage they learned to manage: "They cannot be running constantly to superiors for approval of their actions; they have to make their own decisions and stand or fall by the results. In the process, they make mistakes, but that, too, contributed to their growth and maturity" (Worthy, 1959: 110). The broad, flat type of organizational structure, according to Worthy, made it possible to do a better job and allowed individuals to develop and grow in ways that were not possible under the traditional tall organizational structure.[2]

*Administrative Science Quarterly, June 1969, pp. 178-191.

[1] This research was supported by research grants from the Ford Foundation and two units of The Pennsylvania State University; the Central Fund for Research and the Center for Research of the College of Business Administration. The authors wish to acknowledge their indebtedness to Mr. Harsha B. Desai of The Pennsylvania State University, who collaborated on the formulation, implementation, and analysis of this study.

[2] Support for Worthy's conclusions was found in a small-group study by Jones (1966).

While Worthy's views have gained wide acceptance, there has been empirical evidence that raises reasonable doubts about their validity. Meltzer and Salter (1960), for example, after studying completed questionnaires from 75 percent of all physiological scientists working in organizations in the United States, had serious doubts about the negative relationship between the number of organizational levels and productivity as stated by Worthy. A questionnaire study by Porter and Lawler (1964), on managerial attitudes, seemed to indicate that a tall structure was better in producing security and satisfaction of social needs, while a flat structure was better for self-actualization. Both studies concluded that there is no simple relationship between structure and performance and that a flat organization structure was not unequivocally superior to a tall organization structure. While these questionnaire studies do not settle the issues, they raise enough questions about the relation of structure and productivity to indicate a need for further research.

The need for further research is also indicated by the controversy that persists over the so-called principle of "span of supervision" or "span of control." Fayol (1949), Hamilton (1921) and Urwick (1956), to name only a few, have argued that man's available energy, knowledge, time and abilities are confined to narrow limits, he is unable to supervise the work of more than a few subordinates successfully. Graicunas (1937) hypothesized that the number of possible relationships that a supervisor might be required to manage increased exponentially with an arithmetic increases in the number of subordinates assigned directly to him. The conclusion, in traditional theory, is that supervisors should have a narrow span of supervision. Some writers are very specific about this prescription, as for example, "No supervisor can supervise directly the work of more than five or, at the most, six subordinates *whose work interlocks"* Urwick, (1956: 41).

The critics of the span-of-supervision principle emphasize that other, and perhaps more difficult, problems are created when the number of subordinates assigned to an executive is limited to a very few. For example, as an organization reduces the number of subordinates reporting to supervisors, it creates a tall organization by increasing the number of supervisory levels and supervisors. Corresponding administrative expenses for executive salaries, office space, and secretarial assistance also increase. Also, an increase in supervisory levels is said to cause communication problems. Communications in an organization are subject to different interpretation at each level. The more levels there are in an organization, the greater is the likelihood of distortion, so that the final recipient of a communication may get the wrong message or wrong emphasis. In addition, it takes longer to process information through the many levels of a tall structure. Many levels of supervision in an organization also dilute the influence of the most senior executive. The resulting administrative distance between top and lower-line officials may have a demoralizing effect on the latter. The critics essentially say that the decision and communication processes of a tall organization take longer and are of poorer quality than the processes of a flat organization.

Some of the hypothesized distortions in communications can be explained by the status differences of formal organization. The supervisor has two responsibilities, which conflict with each other. His decision-making responsibility requires that he be given adequate information by subordinates. However, his responsibility for evaluating the performance of subordinates means that he likely gets information that is not adequate or correct (Read, 1962). According to Hoslett, "The subordinate tends to tell his superivsor what the latter is interested in, not to disclose what he doesn't want to hear, and to cover up problems and mistakes which may reflect adversely on the subordinate. He tends to tell the boss those things which will enhance his position and indicate his success in meeting the problems of the day" (1951: 109). In addition to this distortion in the upward flow of communication, Hoslett points out that this status relationship creates a distortion in the downward flow of communication. In his efforts to maintain the status difference, the supervisor is not candid in his relationships with subordinates. He does not wish to admit mistakes or reveal conditions which would reflect adversely on his ability and judgment: "To do so would undermine his position as a superior being in the formal organization" (Hoslett, 1951: 109).

As a solution to the problems caused by the tall organization with its narrow spans and many levels of supervision, critics such as Worthy offer the flat organization with relatively wide spans and few levels of supervision. However, there has been little research evidence to support the cases for either the flat or tall organization.

The field studies cited indicate that different organization structures produce significant differences in performance. Most of the literature on the theory of formal organization postulates that different structural arrangements produce significant differences in performance. However, several laboratory experiments on the effects of communication networks seem to indicate that the differences in performance on at least one variable, "time to complete an assigned task," are not significant.

One of the first to indicate nonsignificant differences in performance was the study by Guetzkow and Simon (1955). This research effort was a refinement of the empirical work of Leavitt (1951), who found that groups working in a wheel network took less time to complete tasks than groups in a circle network. Guetzkow and Simon made a distinction between: "(a) the effects of communication restrictions upon performance of the operating tasks; and (b) the effects of the restrictions upon a group's ability to organize itself for such performance" (1955: 233). The results supported their hypothesis that communication restrictions would only indirectly affect the efficiency with which the task was performed by "influencing the ability of the members to organize themselves for optimum performance in their line operation" (Guetzkow and Simon, 1955: 238). Although different network groups had varying degrees of difficulty in achieving efficient organizational arrangements, there was no significant difference in time taken to complete the task after they reached an optimum organization.

If, as Guetzkow and Simon concluded, differences in performance were really a reflection of differences in the groups' ability to organize, then it should be possible to impose an organization structure, that is, eliminate the necessity for organizing, and produce nonsignificant performance results under different communication structures.

This possibility was realized in experiments by Carzo (1963), Yanouzas (1963) and Cain (1964). The purpose of these studies was to determine the effects of communication restrictions on group performance when an organization was imposed on the group. A seven-man group had a definite hierarchy of three levels. Each position in the organization had a specialized task and a title that was descriptive of the task. The central position, located at the top of the hierarchy, was occupied by a member responsible for coordinating all other tasks in the organization and making final decisions on the assigned problem from an overall analysis. Subordinate managers were responsible for decision making in their particular area of specialization.

Two different communication structures were tested. There was a highly restricted communication net called a "tight" structure in which subjects were allowed to communicate only through a chain of command. Communications under a less restricted loose structure was total; that is, each subject was allowed to communicate with every other member of the group.

During the early periods, it was found that the loosely structured groups were the fastest in time taken to make decisions, while the tightly structured groups showed a faster learning rate. During the second half of the experiment, there was no significant difference between the groups for the time required to make decisions. Therefore, even when organizing efforts were made unnecessary, groups still displayed the kind of behavior found by Guetzkow and Simon.

The present study is a modification of the studies just reported. In the previous experiments, the hierarchical relationships were held constant, while different communication networks were tested. In this study the communication network was the same for all groups, while two different hierarchies were tested, a flat structure and a tall structure, with each member of a group allowed to communicate with every other member.

RESEARCH DESIGN

Each organization had 15 members, the group size being arbitrarily determined by the researchers. The tall structure had four levels and a span of supervision of two. The subjects were seated spatially in a manner that approximated the relationships shown in the chart (Figure 1a). The flat structure had two levels, with all positions connected directly to the president's position, that is, the president had a span of supervision of 14 (Figure 1b). The subordinate subjects were seated in a semi-circle, each one approximately equi-distant from the president.

Every position in each organization had a specialized task and a title that was descriptive of and commensurate with the task. There was a definite hierarchy in each organization with the president's office as the central position at the top of the hierarchy. The president was responsible for coordinating all tasks and for making final decisions on the assigned problem from an overall analysis. All subordinates to the president were responsible for decision making in particular market areas. The role of each subject was prescribed, but was different in the two organizations because the flat structure had no intermediate levels of supervision, although the overall size and task assigned were the same as in the tall structure.

Experimental Task

The task of the experiment required that organization produce ordering decisions in limited time periods. The organization sold one product in several market areas. Individual tasks were assigned, so that each market area received specialized attention. The subjects assigned to a market area were instructed to make a decision or recommendation on how much to order for that area. After this decision was made, it was passed up to the next higher level in the organization. The president was responsible for making a final decision for each area. He could accept the recommended decisions made at the lower levels or adjust the recommendations according to what he thought was best for the organization as a whole.

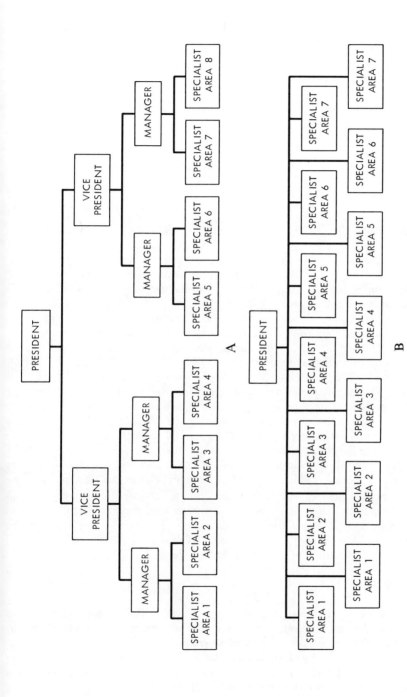

FIGURE 1 Organization Chart of (A) Tall Organization and (B) Flat Organization.

Subjects were asked to think of the organization as a business firm trying to produce decisions on a quantity of goods to order from its suppliers. Before making a decision on what to order, organization members first had to estimate demand. In practice, then, the task had two phases; the first phase involved a demand decision, and the second phase involved an ordering decision.

At the beginning of the experiment, each member of the organization was given a record of demand. The record contained a number of demand quantities, each with a probability of occurrence. For example, a hypothetical distribution for a specific market area might appear as shown in Table 1. The probability distribution was applicable in each decision period; that is, demand was a random variable with a given probability distribution.

TABLE 1   Example of Record of Demand for a Market Area

Demand quantity	7	8	9	10	11	12
Probability of occurrence	0.10	0.15	0.25	0.20	0.15	0.15

At higher levels, organization members had more inclusive probability distributions than at lower levels. Given this information, higher-level members were able to evaluate and adjust decisions made at lower levels. The president, for example, had a probability distribution that covered all the possible demand quantities for all market areas; so that he had the necessary data to make overall evaluations and decisions.

After estimating demand, subjects made the ordering decision. In making the ordering decision, they were asked to consider the following: (1) an estimate of demand, (2) inventories left from the previous period, (3) back orders from the previous period, and (4) a capacity restriction on the amount that could be ordered from suppliers. The capacity restriction applied only to the amount ordered by the president. Organization members at lower levels could order any amount they thought appropriate for their respective areas. The president then had to adjust the amounts recommended for the areas, so that the total amount ordered by the organization was less than or equal to the capacity of suppliers.

The time simulated in the experiment was three years, each year consisting of 20 periods. The organization had to produce one decision per period. The decision time for each period could not exceed 20 minutes. This limitation applied to the whole organization; that is, the president had to indicate the ordering decision within 20 minutes after the completion of the previous decision. If a decision had not been completed within the 20 minutes maximum, the decision made by the president in the previous period was used. If a decision was made in less than 20 minutes, the organization proceeded to the next decision.

Payoffs to Subjects

Subjects were guaranteed an hourly wage of $1.50. They could earn more than this minimum wage, however, based upon their performance in the experiment. A bonus was given according to how effectively the organization as a whole performed, and was equally distributed to all members of the organization. It was possible for the organization to receive negative points for poor performance, but in no event could any member earn less than $1.50 per hour.

The organization was evaluated on the basis of performance over the entire year or 20-decision period. Revenues and costs were accumulated for the

20-decision periods, and the difference was the profit for the year. There was a single measure of performance (as far as subjects were concerned), the rate of return on sales revenue; for example:

Revenue for the year (20 periods)	$50.00
Costs for the year (20 periods)	40.00
Profit for the year	$10.00

Rate of return on sales revenue was ($10/$50) × 100 = 20 per cent.

Bonuses were paid on the basis of $0.70 per member for each percentage point earned on sales revenue. Thus, in the above example, each member of the organization would receive 20 percentage points times $0.70, or $14.00. The maximum that would be paid for any year was set at $15.00 per person. The minimum, as previously indicated, was the guaranteed $1.50 per hour rate. Subjects received the larger of the two amounts, that is, between the bonus and guaranteed rate. In the example, if the 20 decision periods had lasted four hours, each subject would receive $14.00 instead of the guaranteed amount of $6.00.

There was also a bonus to the organization for taking less than the allotted 20 minutes to submit a decision. Revenues were increased by $0.10 for each minute less than the 20 minutes allowed. This bonus was added to the revenue that resulted from each decision and, therefore, contributed to the total revenue for the entire 20 decision periods.

Communication and Decision Process

Although each member of the organizations could communicate with any other member, there were certain procedures, specified by the researchers, which had to be followed to complete the experimental task.

One form, called the "memory form" was used by subjects to evaluate alternatives, to transmit recommended order quantities, and to record the results of the final decision made by the president. The form had 20 rows, one for each decision period of the simulated year. The columns of the form permitted entries for: demand, amount ordered, backorders, and inventories, all stated in physical units. From this record, subjects could make other entries under the column headings of: revenue, cost of goods sold, inventory cost, and backorder cost. There was also a column for entries of bonuses earned on decisions that took less than 20 minutes. This bonus, plus revenues, minus all costs made up the entries under the column heading, profit. Thus, during the experiment, this form gave subjects a visual display of past performance; it provided a means for evaluating alternative order quantities; and it was used as a device for transmitting information.

The only other form possessed by subjects was the probability distribution of demand quantities illustrated in Table 1. Every decision began with this form as subjects attempted to estimate demand for a period.

Flat Structure. As illustrated in Figure 2, the decision and communication process in the flat structure began with an estimate of demand. At the same time that subordinates 2 through 15 were estimating demand for their respective areas, the president was making an over-all demand estimate. The demand estimate and inventory and back order considerations served as a basis for evaluating alternatives and making decisions on the quantity to order. Subordinates recorded their

217

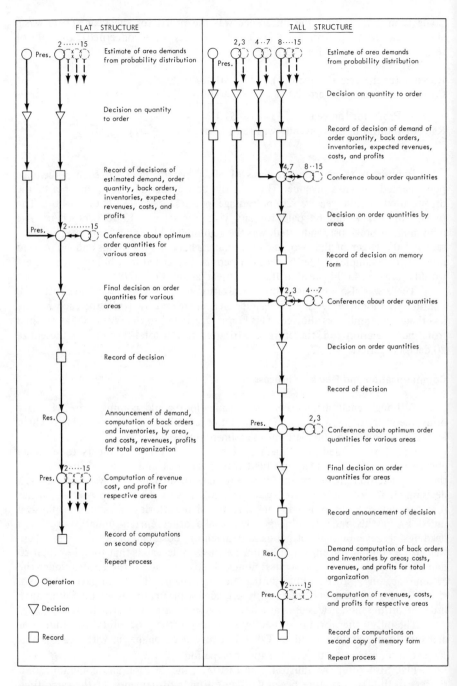

FIGURE 2 Procedure for Communication and Decision Making in Organizations with Flat Structure and Tall Structure.

decisions on the memory form and transmitted them to the president. After receiving these recommendations, the president compared their total with his own decision and the capacity restriction, and reconciled the differences by conferring with subordinates. His final decision was recorded and transmitted to the researcher, who then revealed actual demand, computed back orders, inventories, and units sold in each area, and the revenue, costs, and profits for the total organization on a blackboard visible to all members. From this information, organization members computed revenues, costs and profits for their respective market areas on another copy of the memory form. The process was then repeated for the next decision period.

Tall Structure. Figure 2 also shows that the communication and decision process in the tall structure was more complex than that in the flat structure. At the same time that subordinates 8 through 15 were estimating demand for their respective areas, intermediate supervisors 4 through 7, and 2 and 3, and the president were making more comprehensive demand estimates. The initial decision on the quantity to order for market areas was successively evaluated at each level of the organization until the president, in consultation with intermediate supervisors 2 and 3, made the final decision. Thereafter, the process was identical to the process of the flat structure, until it began again for the next decision period.

Experimental Design

The experimental design for this project was a factorial treatment with two independent variables, one of these being organizational structure. The two levels on this variable were the tall structure and the flat structure.

It was assumed that performance would change as subjects gained experience with the experimental task, therefore, organizational experience was considered the other independent variable. Furthermore, it was expected that experience would be a factor in the outcome of each decision period. Thus, each of the 60 decision periods or trials was considered as a level of the independent variable, organizational experience.

Hypotheses

Three measures of the dependent variable were used for this experiment. Decision time, the time taken by the group to make decisions, was considered as an indicator of the output of the system. The other two measures, profits and rate of return on sales revenue, were considered as indicators of the quality of the decision output of the system.

Industrial practice, as well as scientific research, has established that individuals and organized groups improve their performance after repeated exposure to a given task. Experiments with small groups such as those reported by Guetzkow and Simon (1955), Carzo (1963), Yanouzas (1963), Cain (1964), and Jones (1966) show a learning curve similar to that found in several industries (especially the aircraft industry: Andress, (1954), that is, an exponential decay function on the time taken to make decisions. This leads to the first hypothesis:

Hypothesis 1. As subjects gain experience with the experimental task, their performance, as measured by the time taken to make decisions, displays a pattern of improvement; i.e., a learning curve.

In addition, these same small-group experiments, seem to indicate that the way groups are organized has no significant effect upon the pattern of improvement in time required to make decisions; therefore:

Hypothesis 2. There is no significant difference in the patterns of improvement or learning curves, in decision time for different structures.

With respect to performance over all trials, past experience (e.g., Leavitt and Shaw) seems to indicate that different communication nets do produce significant differences in the time required to make decisions. On simple problems, Leavitt (1951) found that groups in a wheel pattern with one person in a central position completed tasks faster than groups in a circle pattern where all subjects were in equal positions. On complex problems, Shaw (1954) found that groups in the circle arrangement took less time to solve problems than groups in the wheel arrangement. Since the communication nets of this experiment used an "all channel" net, and assuming that structure has no effect on the time variable,[3] there should be no significant difference in the time required to make decisions; therefore:

Hypothesis 3. There is no difference in overall performance as measured by time taken to make decisions for the different structures.

The intermediate levels of a tall structure provide for repeated evaluation of decisions and, therefore, for more analysis than in a flat structure; consequently, the decisions should be better than decisions in flat structures. Specifically for this experiment, then, one can hypothesize as follows:

Hypothesis 4. Groups operating under a tall structure display better overall performance, as measured by profits and rate of return on sales revenue, than groups performing under a flat structure.

The quality of performance should also show a "learning-curve" effect, since there would be a pattern of improvement as subjects gained greater experience with the task; therefore:

Hypothesis 5. As subjects gain experience with the experimental task, their performance, as measured by profits and rate of return on sales, shows a pattern of improvement; that is a learning curve.

Since the elements of the learning situation, that is, stimulus and reinforcement were not a function of structure but of the experimental task, and since the experimental task was the same for all groups, structure should not have a significant effect on the pattern of improvement; therefore:

Hypothesis 6. There is no difference in the pattern of improvement (learning curve) of profits and rate of return on sales for the different structures.

Test of Design

Subjects were selected randomly from the male, junior and senior class enrollments of the College of Business Administration at The Pennsylvania State

---

[3]The basis for this assumption is explained in the "Discussion" section.

University. The flat and tall structures were assigned to the groups on a random basis. Four different groups of 15 subjects were selected, with two groups performing under each structure. Subjects were then assigned to each of the fifteen positions in the experimental organization on the basis of grade-point averages. Subjects with the highest grades were assigned to the president's position, the next highest to positions at the second level, the next highest to positions at the third level, and so on, until all positions were filled. It was easier to make assignments in the flat structure, since there were only two levels of organization.

Each group was tested on three successive evenings. For example, if a group was tested on a Monday evening, it would be tested on Tuesday and Wednesday evenings of the same week. Each group made twenty decisions in each evening. The problems for the second and third evenings were exactly the same as those faced by the group in the first evening.

Use of the same problems on successive evenings served as a basis for establishing the reliability of the testing instrument. An analysis of variance was used to estimate reliability, and gave the following coefficients of reliability on each of the performance variables: decision time, 0.954; profits, 0.837; rate of return on sales revenue, 0.831. An analysis of variance was also used to estimate validity. The performance of the groups operating under each structure was compared to determine whether the effect of structure was uniform. The results showed that the experiment was valid and that variations in performance of groups under their respective structures could reasonably be ascribed to chance.

RESULTS

For the variable, organizational structure, the focus was on whether it affected performance over all trials; for the variable, organizational experience, however, the focus was on the effect over successive trials. It was assumed that differences in performance found between trails were a result of difference in the amount of practice.[4] This learning effect is examined below in terms of variance, trend of means, degree of curvature, and cumulative average performance. The results of the analysis of variance for the performance variables are summarized in Table 2.

Decision Time

Decision time was defined as the amount of time required by a group to complete a communication and decision process. A decision period started when the researchers revealed the actual demand and the results of a previous ordering decision; that is, revenue, costs, and profits, and the inventory and back orders that resulted from the previous decision. The decision period ended when the president indicated the amount ordered by the organization.

The analysis of variance summarized in Table 2 indicates that the F ratio for the structure effect on decision time is not significant. Thus, when decision time is analyzed over all the trials (decision periods), there is no significant difference for the different structures. This finding supports Hypothesis 3.

The F ratio for the effect of trials (decision periods) on decision time is significant; that is, when performance is analyzed over the two structures, there is a

---

[4]We use "trend analysis" as discussed by Edwards (1960: 244-250).

TABLE 2 Summary of Analysis of Variance for Time,
Profits, and Rate of Return

Variables	SS	d.f	Mean Square	Ratio F
Time				
Structures	0.88	1	0.88	0.12
Error (a)	15.05	2	7.53	—
Trials	992.64	59	16.82	5.32*
Structures X Trials	205.19	59	3.48	1.10
Error (b)	372.57	118	3.16	—
Profits				
Structures	477.43	1	477.43	8.11†
Error (a)	117.74	2	58.87	—
Trials	4809.54	59	81.52	7.89*
Structures X Trials	2677.48	59	45.38	4.39*
Error (b)	1218.81	118	10.33	—
Rate of Return				
Structures	2000.46	1	2000.46	7.47‡
Errors (a)	535.64	2	267.82	—
Trials	23633.98	59	400.58	7.92*
Structures X Trials	13448.25	59	227.94	4.45*
Error (b)	6045.24	118	51.23	—

*Significant at 0.01 level
†Significant at 0.12 level
‡Significant at 0.14 level
Error (a) is variation due to groups within structures.
Error (b) is variation due to Trials X groups within structures.

significant difference for the different trials. This finding indicates that performance changed as the result of practice or experience with the experimental task. When the decision times were averaged for each session (20 decisions for each session) and plotted, as shown in Figure 3a, the trend is downward and both curves appear to have a quadratic component. An analysis of variance of the trends, summarized in Table 3, indicates significant linear and quadratic components. The finding of a downward trend and a quadratic component support Hypothesis 1.

Next, it is possible to determine if the trend of means of the trials for the two structures is of the same form. The interaction effect, as shown in Table 2, is not significant; that is, the mean square, structure x trials indicates that the learning curves for the flat and tall structures are of the same form. This finding supports Hypothesis 2.

The conformity of the learning curves is supported by the nonsignificant interaction effect, shown in Table 3, for the linear component and for the quadratic component of the trends for the two structures. The similarity of the learning curves is illustrated even more vividly when decision times are averaged cumulatively and plotted as shown in Figure 4a.

Profits

Profit was defined as the difference between total revenues and total costs. Table 2, indicates that when profits are analyzed over all the trials, there is a significant difference for the different structures. This result supports Hypothesis 4.

Furthermore, when profits are analyzed over the two structures, there is a significant difference for the different trials. This finding indicates that there was also a significant change in profits as a result of experience with the experimental task. When profits were averaged for each session (20 decisions for each session) and plotted, as shown in Figure 3b, the trend is upward, and both curves seem to have a

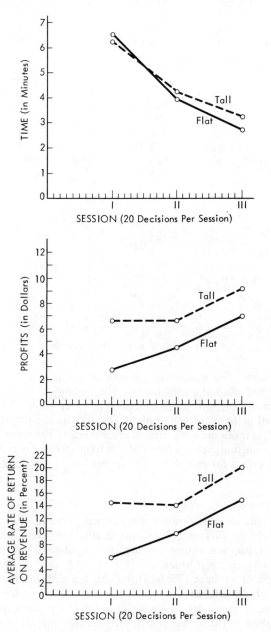

FIGURE 3   For Each Session; (A) Average Decision Time; (B) Average Profits; (C) Average Rate of Return.

TABLE 3   Analysis of Variance for Linear and Quadratic
Components on Decision Time, Profits, and Rate of Return

Trials	SS	d.f.	Mean Square	F Ratio
Time				
Linear Component	533.61	1	533.61	168.86*
Structures × Trials	9.15	1	9.15	2.90
Quadratic Component	136.87	1	136.87	43.31*
Structures × Trials	1.18	1	1.18	0.37
Higher-Order	322.16	57		
Structures × Trials	195.92	57		
Error (b)	372.57	118	3.16	–
Profits				
Linear Component	490.96	1	490.96	47.53*
Structures × Trials	7.98	1	7.98	0.77
Quadratic Component	352.77	1	352.77	34.15*
Structures × Trials	108.41	1	108.41	10.50*
Highest-Order	3965.81	57		
Structures × Trials	2561.09	57		
Error (b)	1218.81	118	10.33	
Rate of Return				
Linear Component	2587.0	1	2587.0	50.50*
Structures × Trials	75.53	1	75.53	1.48
Quadratic Component	1331.17	1	1331.17	25.98*
Structures × Trials	795.77	1	795.77	15.53*
Higher-Order	19715.81	57		
Structures × Trials	12576.95	57		
Error (b)	6045.24	118	51.23	

*Significant at 0.01 level.
†Error (b) is variation due to Trials X groups within structures.

quadratic component. The analysis of variance of the trends (Table 3), indicates significant linear and quadratic components. The finding of an upward trend and a quadratic component supports Hypothesis 5. The interaction effect (Table 2), is significant, indicating that the trend of means for trials for the two structures is of a different form. This result does not support Hypothesis 6. The value of F in Table 3 indicates that the quadratic components of the trends for the two structures differ significantly. The curves for cumulative average profits are plotted in Figure 4b.

Rate of Return

Rate of return on sales revenue was defined as the ratio of profits to sales revenue. The results for this were almost identical to the results found on profits; and since rate of return is a relative measure, it is considered as the more important indicator of over-all group performance.

The analysis of variance (Table 2), indicated a significant structure effect. This result supports Hypothesis 4. Table 2, also indicates that there is a significant trials effect. Thus, as group gained greater experience with the experimental task, they improved their performance significantly on the rate of return. When the results for the rate of return are averaged for each session and plotted (Figure 3c), the trend is upward and both curves seem to have a quadratic component. The analysis of variance for the rate of return (Table 3), indicates both a significant linear component and a significant quadratic component. This result supports Hypothesis 5. The form of the two curves are significantly different as indicated by the significant interaction effect in Table 2. This result does not support Hypothesis 6. The F value in Table 3 indicates that the quadratic component of the trends for the two structures differ significantly. The cumulative average curves are shown in Figure 4c.

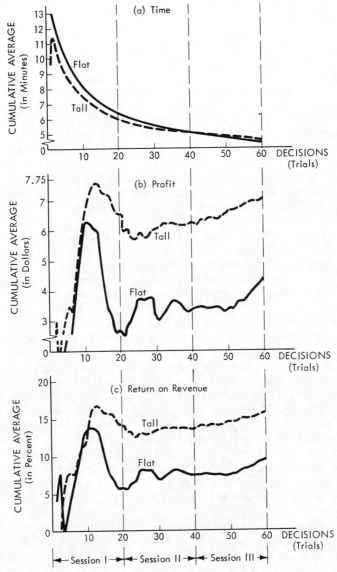

FIGURE 4 Trials (Decision Periods) 1-60: (A) Cummulative Average Decision Times, (B) Cummulative Average Profits; (C) Cummulative Average Rate of Return on Revenues.

DISCUSSION

As expected from the results of past experiments and industrial practice with organized groups, subjects performing under the organizational structures of this experiment displayed a "learning-curve" behavior. Analysis of the data for this experiment indicates that this change in behavior was a result of practice with the experimental task. As subjects gained experience with the task, they improved their performance.

Decision Time

Although experience affected behavior on the time variable, organizational structure had no significant effect on the time taken to make decisions or on the pattern of improvement. The absence of a structure effect on decision time does not seem to agree with the arguments presented earlier, that the decision and communication processes of the tall organization take longer than the processes of the flat organization. The arguments and their applicability to this experiment are summarized below.

First, the greater number of levels between the top and bottom echelons in a tall structure interrupts the flow of information more frequently than in a flat structure in which there is a direct connection between top and bottom echelons. The delays caused by these interruptions in the tall structure supposedly extend the time required for decision making beyond that which is required by the flat structure. This argument was not supported by the results of this experiment.

Apparently, the disadvantages of a wide span of supervision in the flat structure offset the advantages of direct links between top and bottom echelons. The difficulties of a flat structure seemed to be most evident when the president rejected or altered the recommendations of subordinates and attempted to make a final decision on how to allocate orders among the seven market areas. After receiving recommendations from his 14 subordinates on how much to order in each market area, the president had to reconcile the total or recommended orders with the capacity restriction. Since total recommendations always exceeded capacity, the president was forced to scale down the requests of subordinates. Invariably, this lead to much discussion with area specialists and debate among them.

In the tall structure there was the same problem of reconciling total recommendations with the capacity restriction; but the discussions were much more orderly and resolution was faster because the president and intermediate supervisors had to deal with only two subordinates. Also, many of the problems of allocation were resolved for the president as the recommendations filtered through the levels of the tall structure. The absence of a difference on the time variable, then, may be explained partly by the fact that the greater time required for decisions to pass through several levels of a tall structure is offset by the time required to resolve differences and coordinate the efforts of many subordinates in a flat structure.

Another reason given for impediments in the flow of information is the status differences among participants at different levels in the organization. It was argued that he has difficulty in obtaining information, because subordinates, realizing that he evaluates their performance, tend to report only information favorable to them. Such inadequate information flows tend to delay decision processes. For example, when problems at lower levels are not reported to higher-level officials, the decisions required to solve the problems will not be made. If information is inadequate, the decision maker must spend more time gathering the required information; if it is inaccurate, then decisions may be inappropriate.

The problem of status difference is more prevalent in tall structures, since there are more levels. Decision and communication processes should, therefore, require more time in a tall structure than a flat structure. However, in this experiment, there were practically no status differences between the levels of the organizations. Although the president and intermediate supervisors were placed in a higher position with regard to the importance of their jobs, they were not required to evaluate the performance of subordinates. Also, rewards were not distributed to members on the basis of the positions they occupied in the organization; rewards for organizational performance were distributed equally to each member of the organization.

The difficulties of processing information freely, where there are a number of levels and status differences, apply to downward communications as well as to upward communications. Again, the tall structure is supposed to be at a disadvantage. However, in the experiment this disadvantage was removed by providing instant feedback of results to all levels simultaneously. As soon as the president reported his decision, the researchers presented the results of this decision on a blackboard visible to all subjects; therefore, there was little need for downward communications in the experiment.

On the basis that status differences of the tall structure would be unimportant and that the advantage of a direct link between top and bottom echelons would be counteracted by the variety of activity in the flat structure, the researchers hypothesized, as stated in Hypothesis 3, that structure would not have a differential effect on average performance as measured by time required to make decisions. As noted, this hypothesis as well as Hypothesis 2 which stated that the learning curves would have the same form, were supported by the results.

Profits and Rate of Return

On the two performance variables that were considered to be indicators of the quality of decisions, the groups displayed different patterns on each trial. As illustrated in Figures 4b and c, performance of the groups under each structure on the first 20 trials (Session I), was quite erratic. It appears as though they were going through a trial-and-error process in familiarizing themselves with the problem. From trials 21 through 40 (Session II), they appear to have learned and to have stabilized their performance. Thereafter, in trials 41 through 60, performance steadily improved. Considering their performance on Sessions I and II, and the fact that there was a limit on profits (cost of goods sold was fixed at 60 percent of each sales dollar), it is reasonable to assume that if the groups had continued for more than 60 decisions, their performance would have stabilized again or at least approach the limit.

On these two variables, there was a significant difference between the performance of the groups operating under the flat structure and those operating under the tall structure. The superior performance of the groups under the tall structure may be explained by the fact that their decisions were subjected to more analysis than the decisions of the groups under the flat structure. The intermediate supervisory levels apparently were an advantage to groups with the tall structure. They provided the means for repeated evaluation of decisions, and the output was of much better quality than the output of groups in the flat structure.

In addition, the narrow span of supervision in the tall structure permitted a much more orderly decision and communication process. Freed from the burdens that arise from having many subordinates, decision makers appeared to be able to develop a better understanding of the problem. Although the performance of groups with a tall structure was significantly better than with a flat structure, the design of the experiment did not include structural characteristics that seem to cause problems in communication, such as, status differences.

SUMMARY

In this study, four different groups of 15 subjects were organized—two under a flat structure and two under a tall structure. The flat organization structure had two levels, with 14 subordinates reporting directly to the president. The tall structure had four levels, with each supervisor limited to two subordinates. Each position had an assigned task which required decisions on a market-order problem. The president was responsible for making an over-all decision for the organization, which he made after receiving recommendations from subordinates on the amounts to order. His main task was to reconcile differences among recommended orders, a capacity restriction, and his own estimates of optimum order quantities. Group performance was measured on three variables: time taken to complete decisions, profits, and rate of return on sales revenue.

On all three performance variables, groups under each structure showed patterns of improvement as they gained experience with the experimental task. On the time variable, the pattern of improvement was not significantly different for the two structures; the patterns for decision time appeared to follow a function similar to learning curves found in industrial settings. For each structure, patterns for profits and rate of return on sales revenue was erratic on the first 20 decisions, and transient (that is, steadily improving on the stable pattern) on the third 20 decisions.

Structure had no significant effect on the decision time. This result was attributed to counteracting forces in the flat structure and to the elimination of some of the barriers to communication in the tall structure.

Structure did have a significant effect on performance as measured by profits and rate of return on sales revenue. Groups under the tall structure showed significantly better performance than groups under the flat structure. This result was explained by the fact that the tall structure, with a greater number of levels, allowed group members to evaluate decisions more frequently, and that the narrow span of supervision provided for a more orderly decision process.

REFERENCES

Andress, Frank J. 1954. "The learning curve as a production tool." Harvard Business Review, 32: 88.

Cain, Geraldine S. 1964. "Some effects of organization structure on problem solving." Unpublished Doctoral Dissertation, The Pennsylvania State University.

Carzo, Rocco, Jr. 1963. "Some effects of organization structure on group effectiveness." Administrative Science Quarterly, 7: 393-424.

Edwards, Allen L. 1960. Experimental Design in Psychological Research. New York: Holt, Rinehart and Winston.

Fayol, Henri 1949. General and Industrial Management. London: Sir Issac Pitman.

Garicunas, V. A. 1937. "Relationship in organization." Pp. 52-57 in Luther Bulick and Lyndall F. Urwick (eds.), Papers on the Science of Administration. New York: Institute of Public Administration.

Guetzkow, Harold, and Herbert A. Simon. 1955. "The impact of certain communication nets upon organization and performance in task-oriented groups." Management Science, 1: 233-250.

Hamilton, Sir Ian. 1921. The Soul and Body of an Army. New York: George H. Doran.

Hoslett, Schuyler Dean. 1951. "Barriers to communication." Personnel. 28: 109.

Jones, Halsey R. 1966. "The effects of the number of organization levels upon selected aspects of organization performance." Unpublished Doctoral Dissertation, The Pennsylvania State University.

Leavitt, Harold J. 1951. "Some effects of certain communication patterns on group performance." Journal of Abnormal and Social Psychology, 46: 38-50.

Meltzer, Leo and James Salter. 1960. "Organizational structure, and the performance and job satisfactions of physiologists." American Sociological Review, 27: 351-362.

Porter, L. W., and E. E. Lawler, III. 1964. "The effects of 'tall' versus 'flat' organization structures on managerial satisfaction." Personnel Psychology, 17: 135-148.

Read, William H. 1962. "Upward communication in industrial hierarchies." Human Relations, 15: 3-15.

Shaw, Marvin E. 1954. "Some effects of problem complexity upon problem solution efficiency in different communication nets." Journal of Experimental Psychology. 48: 211-217.

Urwick, Lyndall F. 1956. "The manager's span of control." Harvard Business Review, 34: 39-47.

Worthy, James C. 1950. "Organizational structure and employee morale." American Sociological Review, 15: 169-179.

———. 1959. Big Business and Free Man. New York: Harper.

Yanouzas, John N. 1963. "The relationship of some organization variables to the performance of decision groups." Unpublished Doctoral Dissertation, The Pennsylvania State University.

14

AN EXPERIMENTAL STUDY OF THE ALLOCATION
OF FINANCIAL RESOURCES WITHIN SMALL,
HIERARCHICAL TASK GROUPS *

LOUIS R. PONDY / JACOB G. BIRNBERG

This paper discusses an administrative theory of the budgeting process and reports the results of a laboratory experiment designed to test propositions derived from it about the allocation of resources in formal organizations. Drawing upon Cyert and March's (1963) approach to decision making and empirical research on the resource allocation process (Istvan 1961; Pullara and Walker, 1965) it is argued that political processes (e.g., estimation bias, attempted influence) as well as economic processes (e.g., rational cost-benefit analysis) affect allocation decisions within formal organizations.

The emphasis on formal analysis of resource allocation is due chiefly to the usefulness of analytical models in aiding managers to choose rationally between alternatives (Solomon, 1959). The trend toward decentralization, however, has forced the organization to rely more and more upon intermediates to describe the available investments and on an administrative process to carry the proposals through several levels of the organization to the centralized official charged with allocating funds.

The organizational structure and the correlate administrative process have created problems for which the analytical techniques were not applicable. These were essentially political problems which arose as departments competed for larger shares of the scarce financial resources. Had the managers been willing to permit a rational application of the decision models to maximize the best interest of the organization, no problems would have arisen. However, the decentralized organizational structure led each manager to be concerned primarily with the goals of his own unit. Thus a nonrational, i.e., a political, dimension was added to the financial resource allocation process (Davis, et al., 1966; Poore, 1966).

Researchers have found that organizations rely heavily upon administrative rules in allocating resources and that decision makers go beyond the formal budgeting models, where such models are utilized (Istvan, 1961; Pullara and Walker, 1965). In essence, these studies indicate a need to examine the process; i.e., the entire set of procedures, administrative rules, and practices, by which financial resources are allocated.

*Administrative Science Quarterly, June 1969, pp. 192-201.

RESOURCE ALLOCATION:
AN ADMINISTRATIVE PROCESS VIEW

The models for economic analysis typically make the following, usually implicit, assumptions: (1) the goal of the organization is the efficient (i.e., profitable) utilization of its resources; (2) alternative uses of resources are well defined; (3) expected costs and benefits for each project are known; and (4) the organization behaves as if it were a single actor. Thus, the problem is usually stated as one of maximizing some measure of net benefit over a set of known alternatives subject to any financial constraints.

In the administrative process approach to resource allocation these four assumptions are relaxed. Initially, assumption (4), the single-actor assumption, is relaxed. Instead it is assumed that the organization is hierarchical in structure and that its members do not share a common set of goals. The organization is assumed to consist of a central unit that controls the resources of the organization and several operating subunits.

The rational pursuit of their individual goals will bring the managers of the various units into competition with one another. Thus, if the organization is to avoid nonoptimal behavior with respect to its goals, some mediator must be appointed to resolve these conflicts.

Such a resolution of conflicts between subunits by a central official is feasible so long as the first three assumptions are valid. However, in practice, assumption (3), perfect knowledge of costs and benefits, is not likely to be valid. There may be opinions about the streams of costs and benefits, but no objective forecast of these streams is possible. No mediator will be able to resolve the conflict and demonstrate the validity of his solution to the subunit heads. Under these circumstances, each manager will attempt to influence the mediator's decision in his own direction, and political behavior will occur.

This political behavior can take many forms, but only two are discussed here: (1) attempts at influence, and (2) deliverage bias in the estimation of costs and benefits. The first describes the attempts by managers to classify some or all of their projects as "urgent" or "very high quality." These descriptions are intended to reflect the desirability of the particular manager's projects relative to any other manager's projects. The second, deliberate estimation bias, is inimical to the organization's best interest: but the manager can rationalize it as being necessary since other managers are also likely to bias their estimates.

The resource allocation setting can be viewed in an oversimplified form as consisting of three people, each of whom represents all of the functions of a department in an organization: the chief budget officer, and two managers, manager A and manager B. The interaction and competition in the resource allocation process take place within this triad. The three individuals are concerned with the allocation of the chief budgeting officer's periodic budget to the sets of projects proposed by the managers so that the resources required by the projects do not exceed those available. The steps in this view of the budget process are:

1. Managers A and B each determine the projects that are feasible for them.
2. Managers A and B each estimate the cash inflows and outflows related to each project.
3. Managers A and B each specify, either implicitly or explicitly, the criteria they will use in selecting projects for submission. In viewing a series of resource allocation decisions, this step may appear to be omitted after the

first few trials, because the managers have decided on a set of criteria that remain unchanged from trial to trial.

4. Managers A and B each select the projects that they think desirable.

5. Managers A and B submit proposals to the chief budget officer.

6. The chief budget officer formulates, implicitly or explicitly, the criteria he will follow in allocating the resources. The entire process involved in this step could begin before this and continue through step seven. After the initial trials in any series of decisions on resource allocation, this step, like step (3) by the managers, may appear to be omitted.

7. The chief budget officer now receives (if he hasn't already) information on the size of the total budget.

8. The chief budget officer selects specific projects for funding from those submitted.

9. The chief budget officer communicates his decisions to the managers, who then begin again, for the next period, with step (1).

In such a process, when requests of the managers exceed the available resources, managers A and B cannot *both* be satisfied. The managers must therefore somehow, implicitly or explicitly, set a resource goal for their units for the given period, and must develop techniques that reduce the likelihood of any differences between the budget desired and the budget assigned. Such techniques constitute political behavior.

EXPERIMENT

All of the hypotheses to be investigated concern the behavior of the chief budget officer in the idealized three man organization described above, specifically, his response to various manager types characterized by profitability, estimation accuracy, and level of attempted influence.

In order to examine the budget officer's reaction to various manager types, it was essential to control with reasonable precision, or at least consistency, the managerial behavior that each chief budget officer faced. This was done by preparing *beforehand,* sets of "budget proposals" corresponding to various manager types.

But for the experiment to seem at least somewhat realistic, each subject had to be convinced that he was dealing with actual rather than simulated managers. The requisite combination of control and perceived realism was accomplished by using the familiar tactic of testing three subjects at a time and leading each to believe that the other two were to be playing managerial roles. In fact, three separate replications were being conducted at any one time, and each subject was actually receiving prepared communications from nonexistent managers. (See Appendix for sample budget proposal.)

Task

Each subject (i.e., chief budget officer) was informed that it was his responsibility to select from the proposals submitted by manager A and manager B those projects (in this case words) that the firm would undertake. See below for the actual instructions given to each subject.

INSTRUCTIONS TO SUBJECTS

You are the chief budget officer for a word distributing company. Your firm buys words and sells them again for a profit.

Duties: Besides yourself, there are the two division managers in the company. *Their functions* are to estimate the cost, sales, and profit of each word and to propose words for you to purchase and sale.

Your primary function is to approve the purchase and sale of none, some, or all of the words each manager proposes, so that the company makes a profit. Only those words which you approve will be bought and sold. You may buy and sell as many words as you want. However, you should realize that not all words may be profitable. The two managers are told only approximately how cost and sales are determined, so their estimates may be only approximately correct, though they should improve with experience. After the words you approve have been submitted to the experimenter, you will be told the *total actual* cost, sales, and profit for each manager. Each manager will be told the actual cost, sales, and profit *for each approved word.*

The Budget Cycle: The sequence of purchase and sale takes place over a well-defined budget cycle described below. About 15 such cycles will be run.

1. Each manager will submit a budget proposal to you on a "Budget Proposal Form." The words proposed are drawn from a pool of words provided to each manager. The estimated costs listed for each word reflect the variation in cost with the number and type of letters used in the word. Letters, like *e* or *a,* which are used frequently in the English language tend to be expensive. Uncommon letters like *q* tend to be cheap. Each manager knows more than you do about the word costs, so you will have to rely largely on his estimates.

2. Based on the words and estimated costs, sales, and profits of the proposed words, you should decide which words to approve for each manager, and should *check in the column of the Budget Proposal Form marked "Appr."* *those words you wish to invest company money in.* Your revenue from the sale of words depends on how closely you satisfy market demand for words of varying parts of speech (e.g., noun, verb, etc.) and varying length, and on "business conditions" which vary from very good to very poor. The managers know more than you, though still only roughly, how sales are determined; and in addition they should be able to learn from experience. Again you will have to rely on their abilities and knowledge. A space is provided on the Budget Proposal Form for the managers to make comments, if they wish, to help you in your budgeting decisions. Total the estimated sales, cost, and profit *only for the words which you approve.* Record these totals on your Financial Record for each manager.

3. You should give the completed Budget Proposal Forms and financial records to the experimenter, who will calculate the actual figures and report them to you and the managers. The managers then receive more word lists and the cycle begins again. After you submit the forms and records to the experimenter, you should begin to fill out the questionnaire.

Timing: From the time you receive the Manager's proposals you will have a maximum of 3 minutes to make your decisions, total the approved estimates, and submit the records to the experimenter. If you finish before the 3 minutes has elapsed, submit the records as soon as you are done. You will then have another 3 minutes to fill out the questionnaire for that cycle. The last part of the questionnaire cannot be filled out until you receive the market report from the experimenter. This will take place about 2 minutes after you submit your proposals.

For the first three trials, more time will be permitted, to give you a change to learn your duties.

A Final Word: Your task is not an easy one, yet if you perform it well, it is probably a good sign that you have some executive talents. Not only must you deal with some fairly complex budgeting decisions in which you risk the company's money, but you must deal effectively with your managers. In the real world a budget officer is faced not only with the task of maximizing profits both over the short and long run, but also with the problem of holding the organization together and keeping it running smoothly. This experimental setup tries to duplicate these real world pressures, and your job is to be aware of the breadth of your responsibilities and to try to cope with all of them.

Each set of subjects were guided through three practice periods or cycles of the budget process, and then *ten* subsequent cycles were conducted under controlled conditions (i.e., timed, with no verbal communication permitted). After the experiment was completed, the ruse and the purpose of the experiment were explained to the subjects. All but a very few of the subjects were completely convinced that the *other* two subjects were playing managerial roles. For those few that suspected something, their data were discarded and "good" data were collected in a subsequent replication.

Definition of Manager Types

The simulated managers were characterized by attributes—attempted influence (high or low), estimation accuracy (accurate or biased), and average profitability (high or low). Eight types of managers were defined by combining these three attributes in all possible combinations. See Table 1.

TABLE 1 Characteristics of Types of Managers

Manager Type	Attempted Influence	Estimation Accuracy	Average Profitability
1	high	accurate	high
2	high	accurate	low
3	high	blased	high
4	high	blased	low
5	low	accurate	high
6	low	accurate	low
7	low	blased	high
8	low	blased	low

High profit managers were designed, on the average, to propose projects which were actually twice as profitable as those proposed by low profit managers. Accurate estimators were designed to estimate profitability within $\pm 5\%$ of the true value, but biased estimators on the average, overestimated actual profit by a factor of two.

Several lines were placed at the bottom of the managers project proposal form for comments about the budget. Since the managers were simulated by the experimenters, these comments were standardized for each type of manager. Low influence managers included comments to the budget officer on two of the ten trials used in the analysis. These comments were relatively innocuous messages about business conditions, e.g., "Average business conditions" and "No risks this time. All good. I'm doing the best I can."

High influence managers included comments to the budget officer on eight of the ten trials used in the subsequent analysis. These statements were all much more aggressive than those of the low influence managers, e.g., "Business conditions are just average, but the words are pretty good. I'm sure most will bring in a profit," or "Recommend large budget. Note profit estimates are good."

If each budget officer receives project proposals from two managers, then there are 36 distinct pairs of managers. This set of 36 pairs comprises eight pairs of *identical* managers (e.g., 1-1, 2-2, 3-3, etc.), twelve pairs of managers differing only on *one* attribute (e.g., 1-2, 3-4, 1-5, 1-3, etc.), twelve pairs differing on *two* attributes (e.g., 1-4, 2-3, 2-5, etc.), and four pairs differing on all *three* attributes (e.g., 1-8, 2-7, 3-6, and 4-5). Our hypotheses and data are limited to the budget officer's responses to those twelve pairs of manager types which differ only on *one* attribute.

Subjects

The subjects were 24 undergraduates at Carnegie-Mellon University. They were majors in industrial management, engineering, or science. It was felt that these courses of study provided subjects who were schooled in the use of formal models. Thus the emergence of political behavior by the chief budget officer, if any, cannot be ascribed to the subject's ignorance of the techniques of formal analysis.

HYPOTHESES

Hypotheses about the chief budget officer's allocation decisions make use of the definition of manager types as described in Table 1. The dependent variable in each hypothesis is the relative number of projects (i.e., words) approved for each type of manager by the budget officers. A brief justification follows each pair of hypotheses.

H-1: Other things equal, the chief budget officer will approve more projects proposed by high profit managers (i.e., types 1, 3, 5, and 7) than by low profit managers (i.e., types 2, 4, 6, and 8).

H-1a: The differential advantage (i.e., relative number of projects approved) of high profit over low profit managers will be greatest when estimates are accurate and when attempted influence is low (i.e., type 5 versus type 6).

Hypothesis H-1 merely asserts that the chief budget officer will approve proposed projects in accordance with his goal of profit maximization. However, H-1a asserts that as estimates become biased and/or as attempted to influence increases, the allocation decisions will deviate from the objective criterion of economic efficiency. One possible explanation is that the budget officer perceives it to be costly not to yield to subunit demands. He may be willing to accept a lower profit in order to maintain viability of the organization. That is, uneconomical allocations may be regarded as side-payments to organization members. A second explanation is that the presence of biased estimates introduces an element of subjective uncertainty, despite the fact that budget officers could learn to compensate over time for consistent bias. Under conditions of subjective uncertainty, risk aversion by the budget officer would lead him not to approve some projects that might in fact be profitable.

H-2: Other things equal, the chief budget officer will approve more projects proposed by managers who attempt high influence (i.e., types 1, 2, 3, and 4) than by managers who attempt low influence (i.e., types 5, 6, 7, and 8).

H-2a: The differential advantage of high attempted influence over low attempted influence will be greater when profitability is high (i.e., types 1, 3, 5, and 7), and when estimates are biased (i.e., types 3, 4, 7, and 8).

As in part of hypothesis H-la, the justification for H-2 is that the chief budget officer is likely to allocate a larger budget to the manager who exerts pressure for a large budget for any one of several reasons: (1) He can minimize discomfort by yielding to the one manager's pressures; (2) He may interpret the influence attempts as indicating more effort or better understanding of the "market" on the part of the high influence manager; or (3) He may be persuaded that the high influence manager's "projects" are more profitable or his estimates more accurate than those of the other manager.

When profitability is high, the risk of recording a loss because of side-payments to the high attempted influence manager is less than when profitability is low. Thus we would expect the differential advantage of attempted influence to be greater under the high profit condition. As in hypothesis H-la, the subjective uncertainty arising out of biased estimates is likely to lead to deviations from economically efficient allocations, i.e., a larger budget to the high influence manager, when their average profit levels are similar.

H-3: Other things equal, the chief budget officer will approve more projects proposed by managers whose estimates are accurate (i.e., types 1, 2, 5, and 6) than by managers whose estimates are biased (i.e., types 3, 4, 7, and 8).

H-3a: The differential advantage of accurate estimation over biased estimation will be greater when attempted influence is low (i.e., types 5, 6, 7, 8).

As in the previous hypotheses, it is argued that estimation bias, even though consistent, results in the chief budget officer's experiencing subjective uncertainty. In addition, his attempt to minimize the risk of a loss will lead him to approve more projects proposed by the manager who estimates profits accurately. An alternative explanation is that the chief budget officer may reward accurate estimators with larger budgets, and attempt to induce accurate estimation by punishing biased estimators with small budgets. Given his risk aversion and his desire to use the allocation process as a control mechanism, these may be regarded as rational strategies for the chief budget officer. Consistent with previous hypotheses, we would expect deviations from such a rational strategy to be less when attempted influence is low.

RESULTS

Data from only the last ten cycles of each replication were used to test the hypotheses. During those ten cycles, each simulated manager proposed 104 words to each chief budget officer. On the average, 42% of the proposed words were approved. The relative numbers of words approved for each pair of manager types are reported in Table 2.

When profitability was the only distinguishing characteristic between managers, high profit managers received the larger allocation in all eight cases ($p <$ .005). This supports hypothesis H-1. Furthermore, the differential effect of high

236

profit is most pronounced when estimation is accurate and attempted influence is low (i.e., pair 5 and 6), as hypothesized in H-1a (p<.05).

TABLE 2   Differential Advantage of High Profitability,
High Attempted Influence, and Accurate Estimation for
Securing Large Allocation of "Words"

Manager Pair	Estimation Accuracy	Attempted Influence	Profit Level	Replication No. 1	Replication No. 2	Mean Advantage (Words)
		*Profitability**				
1-2	accurate	high	—	1	6	3.5
3-4	biased	high	—	8	7	7.5
5-6	accurate	low	—	29	10	19.5
7-8	biased	low	—	1	7	4.0
						8.625(mean)[a]
		Attempted Influence†				
1-5	accurate	—	high	7	5	6.0
3-7	biased	—	high	9	10	9.5
2-6	accurate	—	low	2	1	1.5
4-8	biased	—	low	6	6	6.0
						5.75(mean)[a]
		Estimation Accuracy‡				
1-3	—	high	high	9	−14	−2.5
2-4	—	low	high	12	9	10.5
5-7	—	high	low	−5	7	1.0
6-8	—	low	low	10	6	8.0
						4.25(mean)[a]

*Managers 1, 3, 5, and 7 are high-profit managers.
†Managers 1, 2, 3, and 4 have high attempted influence.
‡Managers 1, 2, 5, and 6 are accurate estimates.
[a] Significantly greater than zero, $p < .005$.

When attempted influence was the only distinguishing characteristic between managers, the high influence manager received the larger allocation in all eight cases (p<.005), in support of H-2. Furthermore, an analysis of variance of these data strongly suggests (p<.01) that the differential advantage of attempted influence is greater when profits are high and when estimates are biased, as hypothesized in H-2a.

When estimation accuracy was the only distinguishing characteristic between managers, the accurate estimating manager received the large allocation (p<.005), in support of H-3. The differential advantage of accurate estimation was greater, as hypothesized, when attempted influence was low, but the difference was not statistically significant.

DISCUSSION

The data on relative size of budgets support our hypotheses but they do not reveal much about how the budget officers made their decisions, e.g., what decision rules they used, and how their perceptions of managerial characteristics affected their decisions. In order to shed more light on these internal processes, the subjects were asked to complete a brief questionnaire during each trial of the experiment, as was previously mentioned in the Instructions to Subject.

Decision Rules

The subjects were asked to describe what criteria or rules they used in making their budgeting decisions. Two dominant rules were reported, called here the "cutoff rule" and the "budget size rule." In the simplest variant of the "cutoff rule," the subjects set some minimum acceptable level of profit and accepted all words above that level. The ratios of profit to cost or to sales were also used as a cutoff index. The cutoff level was changed through both learning and elaboration. That is, the subjects reported "learning" to set the right cutoff in relation to their preferences for profit and risk. But in addition they elaborated the rule by applying different cutoff levels for different managers. The cutoff in some cases was subject to other constraints such as another "selective cutoff" on word cost, or prescriptions for choosing some, but not all, of the proposed words.

In the case of the "budget size rule," the subjects seemed to establish a norm regarding the "right" total number of words to approve, and elaborated this by checking to see that the "better" manager was getting more words (or perhaps a larger budget in total cost) than the "poorer" manager, and that the relative size of period-to-period budgets was "correct." See the next section for a discussion of how budget officers formed perceptions and evaluations of the managers.

In conjunction with these two low level types of rules, the subjects appeared to use some higher level rules (or strategies) for applying them. For example, the subjects frequently "tested" the managers' profit potential, and in some cases, adjusted the rules to encourage the managers or otherwise affect their behavior.

Finally at the highest level, the subjects could be said to have a set of "rule selection and modification strategies" by which they adopted, adjusted and elaborated the basic rules. It is here that the perceptions and evaluations of the managers probably have the greatest impact. A basic decision rule tended to persist when the budget officer was satisfied that his goals were being met and when there were no obvious ways of improving managerial performance.

Perception of and Satisfaction with Managers

The subjects were also asked to rate their satisfaction with each manager five times during the replication and to comment more generally on each manager's performance. The evidence suggests that the subjects were indeed more satisfied with certain manager types (high profit managers more than low profit managers, $p < .10$: accurate estimators more than biased estimators, $p < .001$), but that the degree of satisfaction was unrelated to size of allocation either as an after-effect or as an intermediate cause. The naive notion that the chief budget officer gives the largest budgets to those managers whose performance staisfies him most simply is not supported by the data. In part this may be because the chief budget officer, during the course of the repeated trials, developed an expectation about each manager's performance. In such a case, his satisfaction would be related to the ability of the manager to meet his expectation. He would be satisfied with performance at or above his implicit standard for each manager and be dissatisfied with managers whose performance, in his opinion, falls significantly below his specific expectations for them.

The following comments by subjects illustrate the tenuous connection between their satisfaction with a particular manager and the size of his budget allocation.

A got me irritated by his volume demands, but I decided to see what he could do with it. Maybe he knows profits will improve with volume in his district.

I wanted to give B more than A but B showed poor profit estimates.

A did a good job; B does O.K. with a large budget. B gets another chance with a larger budget to make some profit.

Will try again to let them pull profits up by increasing volume; can't pour money in indefinitely unless they start showing more profit.

A has a tendency to promise a rather high profit on sales. I hope he's more accurate in the future. Probably I'd like to give A a chance to make up for before. B is still better though.

Nevertheless, subjects formed very definite perceptions of the simulated managers solely on the basis of the information on their Budget Proposal Forms and feedback from the "market." Consider, for example, a subject's comments about managers A (high influence, accurate estimation, and *low profit*) and B (high influence, accurate estimation, and *high profit*):

A plays it too safe on his estimates. He usually picked poorer words than B. He seemed to be unsure of his comments. He was overcautious and afraid to take chances.

B seemed more daring than A. His comments showed more understanding of the market than A's and gave better results when followed. B took chances, even in average times, which brought about large profits. He seemed to know what he was doing and was sure of himself.

Thus for the high profit manager, influence attempts gave rise to a perception of competence, whereas similar comments by the low profit manager caused the budget officer to infer an apparent inability by the manager to understand the market.

When one manager was high in influence (A) and the other low (B), direct evaluations about the personalities of the managers seemed to be evoked. This undoubtedly affected the subject's satisfaction with each. For example, when profits were high—

A doesn't quite have the consistency of B, but A's enthusiasm makes me more inclined to approve his words.

B seems indifferent to whether or not I approve. His indifference wears on me.

or when profits are low—

A got me irritated by his volume demands.

Estimation accuracy, too, gives rise to differential effects at different levels of profit and influence. For an accurate estimator (A) and a biased estimator (B) at *low profit* and *high influence*—

Manager A is dependable because he is consistent. This sets him apart from B who runs in streaks from poor to very good. Both are capable of profit, but A's advice is much more valuable than B's.

or, at *high profit* and *low influence*—

> When A says a word is going to make money, it does. His opinion can be trusted.

> B is wild in his estimations. If I did not know better, I would think that he is trying to make himself look good. We made money only because I took his very best words. If I would have relied completely on his judgment he would not have made money.

However, much work remains to be done to relate these perceptions by the chief budget officer to his actual allocation decisions.

IMPLICATIONS FOR ADMINISTRATION

If the behavior of the subjects in this experiment is isomorphic in its essential aspects to the behavior of real world budget officers, then the results have some implications for the budget proposal strategies managers ought to adopt in order to maximize their shares of the organization's resources. In particular, the data suggest that managers whose projects tend to be highly profitable ought to estimate costs and profits as accurately as possible and to minimize extraneous attempts to pressure the chief budget officer for a larger budget allocation. Conversely, managers whose projects tend to be relatively unprofitable should bias estimates in their own favor and should supplement optimistic estimates of profitability with pleas or demands for large budget allocations. Although not tested in this experiment, it seems equally reasonable that the latter strategy would be relatively more successful when either (1) feedback from the market is complex or delayed, thus making it difficult or impossible for the chief budget officer to detect deliberate biases (Thompson, 1967: 93-97), or (2) the organization operates in a "non-market" environment, thus depriving the chief budget officer of adequate external checks on the effectiveness and efficiency of the managers (Pondy, 1969). It is typically under these conditions that budget officials tend to fall back on a "fair share" concept of resource allocation instead of resorting to a more objective evaluation of projects relative to the goals of the organization (Wildavsky, 1964).

Given that such politically motivated strategies appear to be rational for the unit managers, it becomes clear that budgeting systems need to be designed either to counteract or to take advantage of such self-interested behavior. Before rejecting all political behavior as adversely affecting the organization, however, it should be noted that there may be circumstances where this behavior may work to the advantage of the organization. The interunit competition may draw out the best possible set of proposals from each unit. Thus, while manager A may be more profitable than B, both may present sets of proposals superior to those which would be present without interunit competition. The final organizational budget might be more nearly optimal than it would have been without competition. A political use of the budget may serve to reward manager B, the lower-profit manager, for his efforts and motivate him to continue at the best level possible. If he were not given an adequate share of the budget, he might not continue to respond to the pressure generated by top management for better and better projects. However, use of the budget as a political instrument must not be carried too far, lest the opportunity costs arising out of uneconomic allocations exceed the motivational benefits.

Procedures designed to counteract deliberate bias and attempted influence arising out of self-interested advocacy by the unit managers may also, at some point, become more dysfunctional than functional for the organization. For example, rewarding managers for accurate estimation may only induce them to avoid risky, but highly profitable, projects. Nevertheless, purely political strategies must be counteracted for the sake of organizational efficiency. Perhaps the most effective solution to the problem is to make budget officers more aware of how non-economic consideration enter *their own* decision processes and to make explicit for them the proposal strategies likely to be followed by self-interested managers. Hopefully, the results of this experiment have contributed to that objective.

REFERENCES

Cyert, Richard, and James March. 1963. The Behavioral Theory of the Firm. Englewood Cliffs, N. J.: Prentice-Hall.

Davis, Otto A., M. A. H. Dempster, and Aaron Wildavsky. 1966. "A theory of the budgetary process." American Political Science Review, 40: 529-47.

Istvan, Donald F. 1961. "The economic evaluation of capital expenditures." Journal of Business, 34: 45-51.

Pondy, Louis R. 1969. "Toward a theory of internal resource allocation." Paper presented at the First Annual Vanderbilt Sociology Conference. Vanderbilt University, March 27-28, 1969.

Poore, Daniel. 1966. A Behavioral Analysis of the Short-Range Capital-Budgeting Decision Process. Unpublished doctoral dissertation. Pittsburgh: University of Pittsburgh.

Pullara, S. J., and L. R. Walker. 1965. "The evaluation of capital expenditure proposals—a survey of firms in the chemical industry." Journal of Business, 38: 403-408.

Solomon, Ezra (ed.). 1959. The Management of Corporate Capital. Glencoe: The Free Press.

Thompson, James D. 1967. Organizations in Action. New York: McGraw-Hill.

Wildavsky, Aaron. 1964. The Politics of the Budgeting Process. Boston: Little, Brown.

15

ACCOUNTING INFORMATION AND DECISION-MAKING: SOME BEHAVIORAL HYPOTHESES *

WILLIAM J. BRUNS, JR.

Consider the following statements:

(1) If accounting information is not considered relevant by a decision-maker to a decision under consideration, a change in the accounting information will not affect his decision.

(2) The conception of accounting information held by a decision-maker—his opinion on how well the accountant and accounting system measures significant attributes and characteristics of factors affecting and affected by a decision—will affect the weight given to accounting information in the decision process when other information is available.

(3) The availability of other information will be an important determinant of the weight assigned by a decision-maker to accounting information in the decision process.

Each of these statements has many characteristics of a truism. Many more like them, each concerned with the relationship between accounting systems, accounting information, decision-makers, and decision-making could be easily constructed. Though behavioral relationships on which such statements rest are potentially important to the development of accounting theory and the design of information-decision systems, the study of those relationships is in the earliest stages.

Relatively little is known about the way in which information is used in decision-making, and without such knowledge it is difficult to predict the diverse effects which different accounting systems or information will have on decisions. A model developed below explicitly identifies and relates some factors which may determine when decisions are affected by accounting systems and information. The hypotheses on which this model is based are intended to stimulate and direct part of the study of accounting and decision-making. While the model is not tested here, some implications of the hypothesized relationships for both accounting theory and accounting systems are discussed.

RATIONALES FOR RESEARCH ON DECISION-MAKING AND BEHAVIOR BY ACCOUNTANTS

The problems that demand new research in behavioral aspects of accounting are familiar to almost all who have studied economics and accounting. The rela-

*The Accounting Review, July 1968, pp. 469-480.

tionship between available information and decisions is basic to economic theories of decision-making. Knowledge about costs, prices, and competitors is assumed in almost all traditional theory, and much effort has been directed toward developing models of decision-making for use when information about one or more of these factors is unknown. As these models have been explored and modified, and as new procedures for analysis of alternative courses of action have been developed, new attention has been given to the role of data as determinants of decisions.

Accounting systems of firms are important sources of information for business decision-making. The information which systems provide for decision-making can be grouped in three classes: financial statements, quantitative reports on selected aspects of operations, and special analyses. Information from each class can be grouped with information from another, or with information from sources outside the accounting system in the set of information used by a decision-maker.

Almost all accounting information is affected by the body of rules and procedures called generally accepted accounting principles. Efforts to develop and improve generally accepted accounting principles have been underway since the 1930's, and since 1960 these efforts have found vigorous support from the accounting profession. Thus far, these efforts have not been notably successful, for there are few, if any, bases on which all accountants can agree to select among alternative general principles.

It is possible that much of the effort directed toward resolution of controversy about generally accepted accounting principles has been premature or misdirected. Accounting is a service activity carried out to provide information for decisions within and about business firms. Analyses of alternative sets of generally accepted accounting principles have often been based on the assumption that the relationship between an accounting report or information contained therein and each decision is direct. But this assumption has not been tested, and alternative hypotheses abound. When these have been tested and efforts to develop generally accepted accounting principles can be based upon knowledge of the manner in which accounting affects decisions about business activity, new and important criteria for selecting among alternative methods and alternative systems will be available.[1]

DEFINING ACCOUNTING SYSTEMS AND INFORMATION

One complication in the task of relating accounting information to decision-making is the fact that "accounting systems" are diverse and "accounting information" describes many different sets of data and information. For purposes of this paper, an "accounting system" will refer to the methods by which financial data about a firm or its activity are collected, processed, stored and/or distributed to members of the firm or other interested parties. It is possible to consider that any data or information which are obtained from or created in the accounting system of a firm are accounting information whether contained in a financial statement, a

---

[1]This call for attention to the relationships between accounting, decision-makers, and decisions is not new. See for example Carl T. Devine, "Research Methodology and Accounting Theory Formation," THE ACCOUNTING REVIEW (July 1960), pp. 387-399; Myron J. Gordon, "Scope and Method of Theory and Research in the Measurement of Income and Wealth," THE ACCOUNTING REVIEW (October, 1960), pp. 603-618; and the more recent *Statement of Basic Accounting Theory* (American Accounting Association, 1966), especially Chapter 5.

special report, or verbal statement. However, for our immediate purposes, that interpretation is too broad to be useful. Hereafter, "accounting information" will refer to written information of the type that might be contained in a complete or partial financial report—balance sheet, income statement, or funds flow statement—though in many cases this limitation is not critical to the discussion.

THE RELEVANCE OF ACCOUNTING INFORMATION
FOR DECISION-MAKING

By definition, decisions affect future events, for future actions are determined as a decision is made. In the case of management decisions, decisions may affect only a single event or they may affect all events subsequent to the decision. But no event which has been completed can be altered by a decision.[2] Furthermore, accounting information, in the sense that we are using that term here, focuses on past events.[3] Accounting cannot change events or their effects unless it is through the decision process where future events and their effects are determined. Decision-making and accounting information focus on different time periods except to the extent that the decision process employs accounting information. An important question then is, when is accounting information relevant for decision-making?

In a recent paper, Ijiri, Jaedicke, and Knight have provided a framework which is extremely useful as a basis for discussing the relationship of accounting information and decision processes.[4] They represent a decision process as a function that relates a set of decision inputs to a unique set of decisions. Symbolically,

$$(z_1, z_2, \ldots, z_n) = h(x_1, x_2, \ldots, x_n).$$

Here $z_1, z_2, \ldots, z_n$ are a set of decisions based upon inputs, $x_1, x_2, \ldots, x_n$, according to a decision rule, h. Each set Z and X, must contain at least one element, but there is no requirement that the number of inputs be equal to the number of decisions.

Selection of a particular decision rule by a decision-maker is affected by many factors, among them his analytical capabilities and objectives. The rule associates inputs with decisions, and selection of a decision rule establishes the degree to which objectives will be met by the expected effects of a particular set of decisions. The decision-maker explores the relationships between decisions and objectives prior to the selection of a rule by analysis and through evaluation of the effects of past events similar to those contemplated in the future.

---

[2]Here we approach an interesting point about which more will be said later. Decisions about the accounting methods to be used can alter the *reports* of events which have occurred in the past. It is the effect of these *reports* which is the principal topic of interest here.

[3]In many cases assumptions about future events affect reports of past events. Depreciation accounting is a good example of this; an asset may be assumed to have value in future events, and therefore, its cost is not charged only against events which occur in the period of acquisition.

[4]Yuji Ijiri, Robert K. Jaedicke, and Kenneth E. Knight, "The Effects of Accounting Alternatives on Management Decisions," *Research in Accounting Measurement* (American Accounting Association, 1966), pp. 186-199.

If accounting information affects decisions, it does so through a decision rule which relates decisions to inputs, which include accounting information. The decision-maker uses or selects a decision rule which relates inputs to decisions in a manner consistent with his experience, perceptions, and his objectives. Suppose we let x_1 represent consistent accounting information, one element of a set of all decision inputs available at the time a set of decisions is to be made. The decision rule weights each decision input, which determines each decision in the set Z, and the weight assigned to x_1 will determine what effect, if any, accounting information has on decisions affecting future events. All other decisions inputs, x_2 through x_m, are also weighted by the decision rule, and each affects the resulting set of decisions. These inputs may provide nonfinancial information essential to decisions, and in some cases their weights will overwhelm any possible effects of accounting information.

In selecting a decision rule, the decision-maker must consider all inputs available and their relevance to the set of decisions to be made. It is the decision-maker who decides whether any input is relevant or not. The perceived relevance of the decision inputs to the decisions at hand determine whether the decision rule selected will apply a weight different from zero to accounting information. If a weight different from zero is applied, accounting information may affect decisions; if not, decisions will not be affected by accounting information. Therefore, we hypothesize: *if accounting information is perceived as irrelevant for the set of decisions to be made, accounting information will not affect decisions; if accounting information is perceived as relevant to the set of decisions to be made, it may affect decisions.*

THE ROLE OF THE DECISION-MAKER'S CONCEPTION OF ACCOUNTING

Accounting is a systematic process of providing information about wealth and the effects of economic events. The methods, rules, and procedures that comprise accounting are here assumed to be familiar to the reader. However, there are reasons to believe that accounting is different things to different participants in economic events, and if so, the conceptions of accounting held by individuals or organizations may influence the impact of accounting information on behavior.

Away from reality, accounting can be regarded as a perfect measure. A perfect measure can be defined as a measure where there is a zero probability that the true measurement of an attribute differs from the reported measurement. We can assume that identifiable objects and legal rights have value and that these values are enhanced or destroyed as economic events occur, and we can assume that these values and effects are measureable. To many persons, accounting practice, carried out by trained observers applying consistent and objective methods of measurement and attested to by independent agents, holds the image of a perfect measure applied by professionals. There is an aura of authenticity that surrounds accounting data, and to the untrained user of information, accounting may appear to be a perfect source. We must recognize, however, that few, if any, of the persons who have processed or reviewed the data and the procedures that have converted it to information would consider it perfect.

More realistically, accounting can be considered as a process by which the value or effects of events is reported as accurately as possible but without pretense of being a perfect measure. Here, this conception of accounting will be referred to as an "imperfect measure." Such a measure is defined when the probability that the true value differs from the reported value is greater than zero. This conception is probably closest to that held by most practicing accountants. Errors and inaccuracy in the process of measuring, counting, and reporting are inevitable, and most persons who are familiar with accounting measures and procedures are familiar with these problems. This notion may cause accounting to have a different impact on behavior than the "perfect measure" notion. It allows for a "margin of disbelief" that may in some cases affect the kind of action taken as accounting information is used in decision processes.

A third conception of accounting is fundamentally different from the "perfect measure" or "imperfect measure" notions advanced above. Accounting information may be a goal for actors in economic events. When a businessman seeks profit, he does so for many reasons. For some purposes, the profit reported by accounting is far more important to the businessman or manager than the "true" or "perfectly measured" profit. Modern business organization has given this conception of accounting wide significance, and the implications of this notion for accounting warrant close examination.

Accounting becomes a goal when rewards or satisfactions accrue to a decision-maker as a result of accounting information, and the relationship of the true measure to the reported measure is unimportant. For example, if a manager hopes to advance and feels he will be promoted if he can effect cost reductions, and if accounting information will provide the basis for determining whether costs have been reduced, then it is the accounting information which shows reduced costs that becomes the goal. Likewise, where management is rewarded by stockholders with salary and perquisites on the basis of reported earnings or growth, the reports which result in these rewards may become more important—the goal of management decision-makers—than the long-run earnings or healthy growth which the stockholders really intend to reward.

While not exclusive, this brief recognition of diverse conceptions of accounting seems essential to understanding the effects of accounting information on behavior and decision-making. Below it will be assumed that any individual in a decision situation conceives accounting information either as a goal or at a point on a continuum on which accounting varies from a perfect measure to an imperfect one. This assumption is necessary to state a second set of hypotheses relating accounting information and decisions: *the conception of accounting held by a decision-maker will affect his selection of a decision rule to be used in reaching a set of decisions.* This hypothesis can be further specified by stating it in two parts:

(1) If accounting information is both a decision input and an objective (goal) sought by a decision-maker, accounting information will affect decisions.

(2) The more a decision-maker conceives accounting as being a perfect source of information, the more likely the decision-maker will select decision rules that weight accounting heavily, and the more likely accounting information will affect decisions.

CLASSIFYING DECISION-MAKERS

Because accounting information can be conceived as a goal, and because accounting information is determined in part by an accounting system, a classification of decision-makers provides insight into a final effect which accounting information may have on the set of decisions selected by the decision-makers. Three classes are suggested: first, decision-makers within the firm who make decisions both about operations and about the accounting system used to prepare reports; second, decision-makers within the firm who can make operating decisions but who cannot affect the methods used to prepare reports; and third, those outside of the firm who make decisions about the firm which may affect its environment and operations but who have no direct control over the operation of the firm or any activities in which it is engaged. The reasons for separating the first two classes of decision-makers, both of which are internal to the firm, will later become more obvious.

The first class of decision-makers is comprised of top management. Financial reports are the reports of this group and they are responsible for their preparation and presentation. If a choice must be made between accounting methods, this group is responsible for making that decision. This means that the set of possible decisions available to this class of decision-makers includes modification of the accounting system.[5]

The second class of decision-makers is distinguished from the first only in one important way. Their position in the organization precludes their determining the information included in accounting reports by modifying the accounting system. However, they make decisions about the activities of the firm and we can assume that accounting information enters into their decision processes. They can, of course, influence the content of accounting information by their decisions about activities, in which case accounting information may be affecting decisions.

The distinction between top management, who may affect accounting information, and internal decision-makers who cannot, is most critical where accounting information is conceived as a goal.[6] The decision function for such managers may contain important options between operating decisions and decisions to change the methods by which accounting information is prepared. In any event, decisions are affected, but predicting directions of the effects is much more complicated than it is for decision-makers who do not have authority to modify accounting methods or procedures. Requirements for independent audits and certification of consistency in methods between accounting periods reduces the significance of the two levels of management, though few would argue that this requirement is such that the effects of top management's discretion in accounting can be ignored.

The third class of decision-makers consists of several sets of interested outsiders. Investors, legally the owners of the firm but in fact usually somewhat removed from it, are ostensibly the group for which accounting information in published form is prepared. Creditors, in some cases merely another class of investors, usually seek the same information. A third major set of outsiders consists of government agencies who seek bases for taxation, regulation, and economic analysis. Each of these sets of outsiders makes decisions that may affect the firm

[5]There are, of course, limits to the modifications of the accounting system which can be effected. For example, requirements for consistency prevent selection of different inventory valuation or depreciation methods each year. However, methods used for new acquisitions can be selected, and questions about expense vs capitalization arise frequently and can be answered uniquely as they arise.

[6]An example of this would arise where management wished to report a particular amount for earnings per share.

and its operations, and to the extent that accounting information is utilized as part of their decision processes, it will affect these decisions. However, the goals of the decision-makers external to the firm presumably may differ from the objectives of the firm or objectives which concern decision-makers within the firm. This possibility (as well as the obvious diversity of goals in the sets of outsiders) makes analysis of effects of accounting information on decisions of this class of decision-makers very difficult.

Nevertheless, the classification of decision-makers yields an important hypothesis: *if a decision-maker can affect the accounting system as well as the activities of the firm, and if he conceives accounting information as a goal, accounting information will affect decisions about either or both the accounting system and operations.*

NON-ACCOUNTING INFORMATION

The final hypothesis to be introduced in this model concerns the role played by information which is not a product of the accounting system in determining the impact of accounting information on decisions. Above, accounting information was defined as information of the type that might be contained in a conventional financial report. In many respects, the effects of non-accounting information on decisions can be analyzed in the same framework as accounting information. However, the importance of non-accounting information here is that it may determine the effects of accounting information on decisions.

If non-accounting information becomes a goal or is perceived as having special relevance for decisions undergoing evaluation, the impact of accounting information will be reduced. If non-accounting information is not relevant to decisions, the effects of relevant accounting information will be enhanced. Therefore, we hypothesize: *the impact of accounting information on decisions is affected by the perceived relevance of other information also available to the decision-maker.*

A MODEL FOR ANALYZING THE EFFECTS OF
ACCOUNTING INFORMATION ON DECISIONS

The hypotheses developed above are all summarized and their interrelationships are made clear in Figure 1. Rather than restate all hypotheses or describe the model in detail, a summary of hypotheses which lead to the principal outcomes predicted by the model will be used to reveal the interrelationships within it.

I. *Accounting information will either affect decisions or affect decisions about the accounting system if*
   (a) accounting information is relevant to decisions
      (b) the decision-maker conceives accounting as a goal,
and   (c) the decision-maker is a member of the firm who can control the selection and operation of the accounting system.

II. *Accounting information will affect decisions if*
   (a) accounting information is relevant to decisions,
      (b_1) the decision-maker conceives accounting as a goal,
and   (c_1) the decision-maker is a member of the firm who cannot control the selection and operation of the accounting system,

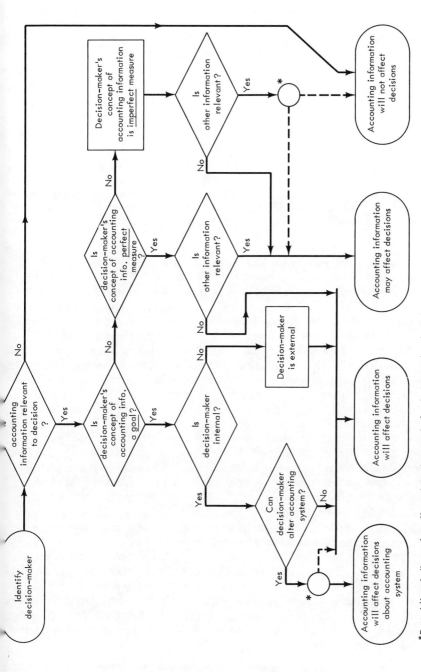

FIGURE 1   Accounting Information and Decisions

*Dotted lines indicate that effects depend on particular decision rule selected

or	(c_2)	the decision-maker is external to the firm;
or	(b_2)	the decision-maker conceives accounting as a perfect measure,
and	(c)	non-accounting information is not relevant to the decision.

III. *Accounting information may affect decisions* if

	(a)	accounting information is relevant to decisions,
	(b_1)	the decision-maker conceives accounting as a perfect measure,
and	(c)	non-accounting information is relevant to the decision;
	(b_2)	the decision-maker conceives accounting as an imperfect measure,
but	(c)	non-accounting information is not relevant to the decision.

IV. *Accounting information will not affect decisions* if

	(a_1)	accounting information is not relevant to decisions;
or	(a_2)	accounting information is relevant to the decision,
but	(b)	the decision-maker conceives accounting information as an imperfect measure[7]
and	(c)	non-accounting information is relevant to the decision.

SOME FURTHER EXPLORATION OF THE MODEL

The flow chart format used in Figure 1 is extremely demanding and, possibly, too restrictive. This format demands that we state precisely what will happen at each branch of the model. Yet there appear to be some situations in which it would be more satisfactory to think in terms of effects along a continuum.

Examine, for example, the lower right-hand portion of Figure 1, where the model predicts the impact of other information when accounting has been perceived as relevant and when the decision-maker perceives accounting information as being either perfect or imperfect. The model predicts that accounting information perceived as perfect may have some effect on decisions. However, when the decision-maker perceives accounting information as being something less than perfect (for example, recognizes that errors or biases may have been introduced into the measurements reported), the impact of other information becomes less certain. The degree of conceived imperfection and the amount and quality of other information are important variables in such cases. Likewise, even in cases where accounting information is perfect, and other information is relevant, the decision might be affected but not altered by accounting information. Similar questions can be raised at other points and simply reinforce conclusions about the need for testing the hypotheses on which this model is based.

While these uncertain conclusions beg for clarification and discriminating research, they are perhaps the least interesting. In cases where decisions may be little affected by accounting information, the choice of a particular accounting system, or particular accounting methods used in that system, may be of little importance. It is at the other extreme, where the model predicts that accounting information will affect decisions that the choice of accounting systems and methods becomes critical.

[7]The degree of conceived imperfection is important for this conclusion. If accounting information is conceived as being so imperfect it is of no use it will not affect decisions in this case. If, however, the degree of imperfection conceived is not great enough to preclude the use of accounting information in the decision process, accounting information may or may not affect decisions.

INTERACTION WITHIN THE MODEL

Further complications in interpreting or using the model stem from possible interaction between the method of accounting used and/or the accounting system developed and the perceived relevance of accounting for decision-making purposes. If the decision-maker feels that a particular method or system of accounting is inappropriate as a basis for measurements relating to a particular problem, he will be led to a position where the effective accounting information will be reduced. Unless we know something about the particular class of decision-makers and their perceptions of accounting methods, it is difficult to predict whether any examination of the conception of accounting held by the decision-maker will be of importance. Likewise, if the method chosen, or the process of selecting a method, affects the conception of accounting held by the decision-maker, then this will affect the relationship between a particular method and decisions.

A DIGRESSION: THE MEANING OF RELEVANCE

The proposal made here to recognize relevance as a primary determinant of the effect of accounting on decision-making is not new. The degree of relevance has frequently been suggested as a basis for choosing between alternative accounting methods and forms of accounting information. This has been particularly true in the literature relating to accounting within the firm, where it is frequently asserted that those methods that result in revelation of cost-volume-profit relationships are most appropriate. Likewise, in the recent *Statement of Basic Accounting Theory,* formulated by a committee of the American Accounting Association, relevance is proposed as a primary standard for selecting among alternative forms of accounting information.[8]

However, the meaning of relevance appropriate for its use as a criterion in the development of accounting methodology and theory is not clear. While users are frequently the point of reference in analyses employing "relevance," the determination of "relevant information" is left to the accountant, who uses some standard, generally accepted model for decision-making as the criterion in determining what should be reported. In the formulation which has been presented above, relevance is determined by the user of the information, and the effect of this choice creates several problems which require careful consideration before this criterion is employed.

If the user determines relevance, we should expect that, in some cases, what the user feels is relevant would not be relevant in those standard, accepted models with which we are familiar, such as those drawn from economics. Suppose the accountant knows the objectives of the firm and those objectives correspond to those in an accepted model of decision-making, but the decision-maker feels the relevant information is different from that called for by the model. The accountant may be placed in a position of second guessing the user, in order to provide the data that will allow him to make a correct decision, because the user's idea of what information is relevant is wrong from the standpoint of the decision models. This is a position in which I believe most accountants would feel somewhat uncomfortable.

---

[8]*A Statement of Basic Accounting Theory* (American Accounting Association, 1966), especially Chapter 2.

We must also be concerned with the possibility that the conception of accounting held by the decision-maker affects the perception of relevance to a significant degree. The more a decision-maker conceives of accounting as being perfect, the more relevant accounting information is likely to be for decision-making purposes, and the more importance can be attached to the part that accounting systems and methods will play in the decision-making process. In so far as this writer is aware, this relationship has seldom been considered, and never carefully explored.

If the hypotheses developed in this paper are valid, then it is clear that relevance alone cannot serve as a primary standard for the development of accounting theory and methods. If accounting is to serve users of accounting information then something besides whether or not the data is relevant must be known. These hypotheses would lead us to believe that critical variables are the conception of accounting held by a decision-maker and the perceived relevance of other kinds of information to the problems under examination at the time the user chooses to employ or not to employ accounting information.

SOME EXAMPLES OF THE USE OF RELEVANCE AND THE CONCEPTION OF ACCOUNTING AS BASES FOR ACCOUNTING SYSTEMS DEVELOPMENT

Suppose that research fails to lead to rejection of the hypotheses presented above, and consider a case in which we are concerned with designing an appropriate accounting system to facilitate effective decision-making. Imagine that the organization in question is a business firm. Among the products of an accounting system are financial statements issued at regular intervals. These intervals may vary in length from very short periods to relatively longer periods, that is, financial statements may be prepared for internal use as frequently as daily or weekly, or they may be issued less often, perhaps annually, to employees of the firm. It is possible to hypothesize that the more frequently financial reports are issued and attention is drawn to the financial condition of the firm, the more relevant accounting information will appear to people within the firm who are making decisions about prices, promotion policies, and production quantities.[9] Yet, for many decisions of this type, we might argue that other information would be more important and relevant. Therefore, we might be led to a situation in which we wish to reduce the perceived relevance of accounting information by reducing the frequency of reports, so that decision-makers within the firm would rely more heavily on other information which would allow their decisions to be more appropriate for the conditions under which the firm was operating.

Consider pricing decisions. In general, economists and other analysts would agree that the financial condition of the firm is not necessarily an appropriate basis for choosing a price strategy and selecting terms of sale. However, if financial statements are issued very frequently, thus enhancing their perceived relevance, and the conception of accounting held by decision-makers is such that we might expect

---

[9] An attempt to test whether decisions might be affected by varying the time periods between accounting reports is reported in William J. Bruns, Jr., "The Accounting Period Concept and Its Effect on Management Decisions," in *Empirical Research in Accounting: Selected Studies, 1966* (The Institute of Professional Accounting, University of Chicago, 1967), pp. 1-14.

accounting information to have some effect, then favorable or adverse profit information and/or other financial information might affect decisions with respect to price. It is possible, then, that by developing an accounting system in which the frequency of reporting reduces the perceived relevance of accounting information we could improve pricing decisions in the firm.

In other cases, we might come to an opposite conclusion. In decision-making related to the acquisition and management of working capital, the availability of frequent information on the status of assets and liabilities of the firm may be very important, and we might choose to issue reports to persons concerned with these matters very frequently in hopes of increasing the efficiency of such decisions.

The point of these examples is that changes in the accounting system may affect perceived relevance of accounting information and may determine the effect of accounting information on decisions, and furthermore, that the interactions between relevance and conceptions of accounting which we have considered above may be important also. In designing an accounting system, relying on cliches like ". . . the more information, the better . . ." may lead to surprising results.

Consider another example, in which we are concerned with a choice between alternative accounting methods for reporting on a particular class of assets or liabilities. For sake of illustration, let us consider a choice between two alternative inventory valuation methods—LIFO and FIFO. Assuming that the reader is familiar with the characteristics of these methods, we can quickly conclude that in cases where prices are changing frequently that LIFO will reveal through the income statement the effects of these changes on the profitability of the firm more rapidly than FIFO. To the extent that this is important for the types of decisions being made, this model might provide us with the basis for preferring one method of accounting for inventories over another.

Let us assume that the prices of raw materials for the production process or the price of goods to be resold is rising. From the standpoint of decision-makers within the firm, this is important information, and information which we would expect to be important for decision-making purposes within the firm. To the extent that the decision-maker felt accounting information was relevant to his decisions, a conception of accounting as perfect information would make the choice of LIFO more important than if the decision-maker's conception of accounting information was that it was an imperfect measure. If accounting information is not perceived as relevant, or if the decision-maker feels accounting measures are imperfect and other information is also relevant for decision-making, the choice of inventory valuation methods is unlikely to affect decisions.

Here also we can consider the possible usefulness of this model for evaluating the selection of a method for reporting to external users. Assume that external users feel accounting information is relevant for their decisions. The more perfect their conception of accounting, the more likely that the choice between methods of accounting will affect their decisions. If the current performance of the firm is important to external users because they wish to use it as a basis for decisions, then LIFO may be more appropriate than FIFO for inventory valuation purposes.

In either of these last two cases, if accounting information were perceived as being irrelevant and/or if accounting information were conceived as being so imperfect a measure that it is not weighted heavily by the decision rule, then a decision on an inventory valuation method might not be very important. Such would be the case in any choice between accounting systems or methods. The implication of this is, I believe, quite clear: until we know more about the conditions that affect perceived relevance of accounting information for decision-making and until we know more about the conceptions of accounting held by users we do not have adequate bases on which to reduce diversity in accounting or to increase it selectively.

IMPLICATIONS FOR FURTHER RESEARCH

It is clear that a great deal more research about behavioral relationships between accounting and decision-making is required. The hypotheses which comprise the model presented here demand that we learn more about the factors that influence a decision-maker's perception of the relevance of accounting information. We need to know more about the conceptions of accounting held by individuals, both within business enterprises and external to them, and it would be useful also to know more about the magnitudes of difference required before perceptions of relevance and conceptions would be affected.

One way of finding data about these variables would be to go into the field and do field research about the perceived relevance of accounting for various decision problems. Some attempts have been made in this direction, and while the results are still inconclusive, they provide a basis for the design of further studies.[10] It is also necessary that something be learned about the conceptions of accounting held by users. Is it true that the majority of users feel accounting is a valid and good source of information? Or do most experienced users of accounting information conceive of accounting as being imperfect in the sense that the term is used here, and hence, the types of decisions made about accounting systems and accounting methods are relatively unimportant?

Another approach to this type of problem is the experimental approach, where in a laboratory or a simulated environment, we place people in alternative conditions in hopes of comparing their behavior under the conditions we have created. This, in my opinion, provides a most promising avenue for testing some of the hypotheses we have created in this study.

Consider, for example, an experiment to determine if the relevance of accounting information is a determinant of the effect of that information on decision-making. We could, for example, take a sample group and partition it to obtain a control section and an experimental section. The experimental section could be instructed as to the types of situations in which, given generally accepted models of decision-making, accounting information is relevant. Having provided this background, this group could then take part in a simulated exercise—a business game—in which accounting information and other information are controlled. The control group would receive no instructions about the role of accounting. The decisions of the groups could be compared, and if there were differences, there might be reasons to believe that when accounting information is perceived as being relevant, it will have an effect and that relevance, then, is something that can be affected through educational experiences.

---

[10]See for example James L. Gibson and W. Warren Haynes, *Accounting in Small Business Decisions* (University of Kentucky Press, 1963). Results of this study were summarized in James L. Gibson, "Accounting in the Decision-Making Process," THE ACCOUNTING REVIEW (July 1963), pp. 492-500. The faculty of the Ohio State University conducted two seminars in early 1966 during which users of accounting information discussed prepared papers on their work and the effects of accounting. See Thomas J. Burns, *The Use of Accounting Data in Decision Making* (College of Commerce and Administration, The Ohio State University, 1967).

In like manner, it should be possible to explore in the laboratory the effect of conception of accounting. After determining through tests or interviews the conception of accounting held by subjects, we could partition the group in such a way that those having one conception of accounting are used for a control group, while those having another conception of accounting serve as an experimental group.

Experiments of the type proposed above would have to be replicated many times before we could employ the findings with confidence. Nevertheless, the "obvious" character of the hypotheses developed here gives hope that they may provide keys to new criteria for use in the design of accounting systems and reports.

SUMMARY

Relationships between accounting methods, accounting information, and business decision-making are largely unexplored. Hypotheses developed here relate the user of accounting information, the relevance of accounting information for decisions, the decision-maker's conception of accounting, and other information available, to the effect of accounting information on decisions. No tests of the hypotheses have been made and additional research is warranted.

16

THE EFFECTS OF ACCOUNTING ALTERNATIVES ON MANAGEMENT DECISIONS

YUJI IJIRI / ROBERT K. JAEDICKE / KENNETH E. KNIGHT

INTRODUCTION

A growing interest has arisen among accountants in understanding accounting in relation to the entire business decision process. They have questioned such factors as the role of accounting in the whole complex process of decision making in business and what effects, if any, different accounting methods have on this decision process. Research has been aimed at finding out if decisions made in an organization can be influenced by changing its accounting system.

*In *Research in Accounting Measurement,* Robert Jaedicke, Yuji Ijiri, and Oswald Nielson, eds. Evanston, Illinois, American Accounting Association, 1966, pp. 186-199.

Until recently, discussions of alternative accounting methods hae been directed primarily toward how outputs from accounting systems differ, depending upon the accounting methods that are used. We know that in many cases LIFO and FIFO can result in different inventory values, and hence will produce different profit figures even though the firm operates in an identical business environment. But a more important question is whether these different profit figures affect managers' decisions and, if so, under what conditions? Unless we can show that the different figures (or more precisely different patterns of figures) lead to different decisions under a given set of conditions, there is no point in arguing the merits or demerits of alternative accounting methods.

Some recent studies have been directed toward understanding how differences in the data affect the behavior of the users. Bonini [1] carried out a simulation of business activity based on some assumptions about how business managers behave, and found that a firm with the LIFO inventory method tends to generate more profit under given conditions than a firm with the average cost method of inventory valuation. The reasoning behind this finding is that the LIFO inventory method increases the variability of profits from period to period more than does the average cost inventory method, and hence it stimulates more attention and pressures by managers toward better profit.

On the other hand, the experimental study by Bruns [2] leads to contradictory conclusions. He found that there is no apparent relationship between inventory valuation methods and managers' decisions on selling price, promotion, production volume, etc. An even more recent experiment by Dyckman [7] also came to the same conclusions.

It is, however, difficult to derive general statements from the results of these three studies concerning the influence of different accounting methods upon managers' decisions. We cannot conclude from Bonini's study that the LIFO method should be preferred to the average cost method of inventory valuation because the former tends to generate higher levels of profits, nor can we conclude from Bruns' study or Dyckman's study that inventory valuation methods have no effect on business decisions. Accounting variations may have significant effects under some conditions, and may have no effect under other conditions. The basic problem in these studies is an inability to generalize from a single case.

Therefore, an even more important question than whether different accounting methods have *any* effects upon decisions is: *under what conditions do variations in accounting methods produce different decisions,* and *why* are (or *are not*) different decisions produced by using different accounting methods?

In order to answer these questions, we need, in addition to empirical studies, a theoretical clarification of the mechanism by which an accounting process and a decision making process are related. The purpose of this paper is to develop a theoretical analysis of the relationship between the accounting and decision making processes of a firm. This analysis is then used to study the effect of alternative accounting methods on managers' decisions. Instead of analyzing one empirical situation and deriving conclusions based on that particular example, we have derived some general conditions under which alternative accounting methods do have an effect upon the decision making process and other conditions under which different accounting methods do not have any effect. For each individual empirical situation we are then able to specify a set of variables which will allow us to predict whether or not alternative accounting methods have an effect upon management decisions. In the following section we concentrate on the role of information in the decision making process. In Parts 3 and 4, respectively, the effects on decisions of

(a) *changes* in accounting method and (b) *alternative* accounting methods are discussed.

THE ROLE OF INFORMATION IN THE DECISION PROCESS

The Decision Process as a Function

A decision process is characterized by three factors: i) decision inputs, ii) decision outputs, and iii) a decision rule. *Decision inputs* are factors which are considered by the decision-maker in making his decision. *Decision outputs* are decisions made by the decision-maker. A *decision rule* is a rule by which a set of decisions is associated with a set of decision inputs. For example, in an investment decision, let us assume that investments are to be based only upon the rate of return of the project (say, invest if the rate of return is greater than or equal to 15 percent per year; otherwise, do not invest). Here the decision input is the project's rate of return and the decision output is either "invest" or "do not invest." The decision rule is to associate all rates of return greater than or equal to 15 percent per year with the decision output "invest," and all other rates of return with the decision output "do not invest."

Of course, an actual investment decision will be much more complicated involving many other decision inputs and outputs. However, suppose if we focus on only one input (e.g., rate of return) and one output (invest or not invest) keeping other decision inputs constant, then it would be reasonable to assume that there is a relationship between the value of the input and the value of the output which is relatively stable for some period of time. This is what is meant by a decision rule.

If we let x represent a variable for the input and z a variable for the output, then the decision rule concerning the input x and the output z can be represented as a function h as follows:

$$z = h(x).$$

In an actual decision process, the value of the output for a given value of the input may not be unique: that is, the function h may not be single-valued. For example, the decision-maker may decide to invest on a project A and decide not to invest on a project B even though the two projects have an identical rate of return. In this case, a single value of the decision input yields two different values of the decision output, i.e., "invest" and "do not invest": that is, the decision function is not single-valued. However, we may assume that by making finer specifications on the environmental conditions (i.e., the values of other decision inputs) under which the decision function is supposed to be applied, it can eventually be converted into a single-valued function. We shall, therefore, deal with only a single-valued function in the following analysis.

Principals versus Surrogates as Decisions Inputs

In order to understand the role of accounting data in a decision process, it is crucial to distinguish between *principal* decision inputs and *surrogated* decision inputs. We will emphasize that accounting data are generally surrogated inputs rather than principal inputs.

By a *principal input* or a *principal* we mean a decision input upon which the decision-maker *wants* to base his decision ultimately. A *surrogated input*[1] or a

---

[1] Webster's *Seventh New Collegiate Dictionary* defines a surrogate as a substitute to be put in place of another. Also see Charnes & Cooper [3, p. 369], for a further elaboration on the relationship between the principal and its surrogates.

surrogate is a decision input upon which the decision-maker bases his decision *only insofar as the surrogate reflects a principal.*

For example, a thermometer reading is a surrogate for a temperature reading. We want to base our decision upon the thermometer reading only insofar as it reflects the real temperature. Similarly, in a pricing decision the decision-maker may want to base his decision upon the cost of the product that is reported in an accounting statement only to the extent that the reported cost reflects what he considers to be the "real" cost of the item.

For a given principal, there may be a hierarchy of surrogates which reflect the principal. For instance, if the reported sales volume of the firm reflects the reported profit of the firm which, in turn, reflects the real profit of the firm, the decision-maker may base his decisions upon this indirect surrogate, the reported sales volume, as a surrogate of the real profit of the firm.

Characteristics Required for a Surrogate

Obviously, in order to effectively use a surrogate instead of a principal in a decision process, the surrogate must have certain characteristics. We now want to investigate these characteristics.

Identifiability. The surrogate must reflect the principal input. Since the decision-maker wants to base his decision upon the principal input, it is necessary for him to be able to estimate the value of the principal input from the value of the surrogated input. More precisely, the decision-maker must be able to use the surrogate to identify the key factors necessary for his decision. In the above example of the investment decision, the decision-maker can use any input as a surrogate for the rate of return if, and only if, he can identify whether the rate of return is greater than or equal to 15 percent per year. Note that in this case it is not necessary that the decision-maker be able to identify the exact value of the rate of return. For decision purposes he only needs to know whether the rate of return is greater than or equal to 15 percent per year. This is what we mean by the decision-maker being able to obtain *the key factors which affect the decision.* A surrogate which reflects the principal in this sense will be called a *satisfactory surrogate.* Obviously, whether or not a surrogate is satisfactory depends not only upon the surrogate-principal relationship but also the decision function which defines the key factors of the principal input.[2]

The notion of *identifiability* (of the key factors for the decision) raises the question of the reliability of the surrogate-principal relationship. The surrogate-principal relationship can be represented by

$$y = f(x),$$

where x is a variable representing the principal input, y a variable representing the surrogated input, and f a function representing the surrogate-principal relationship. This relationship is reliable if it is *stable* enough so that the decision maker can *identify* the key factors of the principal input from the value of the surrogate. We can use again our earlier example of the investment decision. An unstable surrogate

---

[2]Since it is not the purpose of this paper to analyze the functional relationship between a surrogate and a principal, the above statements are not as precise as they otherwise should be. The readers who are interested in pursuing this topic in a more rigorous manner are referred to Ijiri [11], where the notions of a perfect, a satisfactory, and a reasonable measure are defined, based upon the functional relationship involved. Also refer to Ijiri [12], where the relationship between a management goal and an accounting indicator as a surrogate for the goal is analyzed. The analysis is called "goal analysis," which is an extension of breakeven analysis.

is one where, for example, a value of 15 percent means that the real rate of return of the project is 19 percent per year at one time and the same value of 15 percent means that the real rate of return of the project is 12 percent per year at another time. When this *unstable* condition arises, the decision-maker can no longer rely upon the value of the surrogate in making his investment decision. An example of this situation is the use of the payback factor as a surrogate for the rate of return. That is, a payback factor of 3 gives a rate of return of 12 percent (approximately) if the life of the project is 4 years. On the other hand, the same payback factor of 3 gives a rate of return of 19 percent (approximately) if the life of the project is 5 years. In this case, the decision-maker cannot *rely* on this surrogate only, because he cannot *identify* the key factor which affects his decision.[3]

Timing. In addition to the requirement of *identifiability*, a surrogate must be available to the decision-maker at the time of the decision: that is, the surrogate must meet the requirement of *timing*. The significance of this requirement is made clearer in the following discussion on the *need* for a surrogate in a decision process.

Need for a Surrogate in a Decision Process

Why does a decision-maker need a surrogate? That is, why doesn't he always use the principal input in his decision process? The following cases summarize those instances in which the decision-maker needs a surrogated input.

Case 1. Difficulty in Obtaining the Principal. When it is too expensive (either timewise or costwise or both) for the decision-maker to use the principal input in making his decision or when it is practically impossible for him to obtain the principal input, a surrogated input will be preferred to the principal. For example, a bank manager may be willing to base his lending decisions upon financial statements certified by a C.P.A. even if he has the right to perform an independent investigation, and the necessary auditing talent to do so.[4]

Furthermore, when the value of a principal is not available at the time of the decision, it is necessary for the decision-maker to use a surrogate insofar as he does not want to delay the decision (time lag). For example, if the profit figure of a division cannot be made available until the end of the month, the division manager may want to base his decision upon a surrogate such as the sales volume to date (which may be available on the daily basis). Another example is the use of a predetermined overhead rate as a surrogate for the "actual" overhead rate which is not available until the end of the accounting period.

Case 2. Difficulty in Using the Principal. A surrogate may be used to simplify a decision problem where the decision-maker may actually want to base his decision on a large number of inputs. This will occur when the number of inputs to be considered exceeds the capacity of the decision-maker. It is a well-known fact that a human being can use effectively only a limited number of inputs in making his decision.[5] If the decision environment is too complicated, the decision-maker is

[3]Refer to Ijiri and Jaedicke [13] where the reliability of an accounting system is discussed by using statistical concepts. Here, for our subsequent discussions, it is sufficient to define reliability as the possibility of identifying the *key factors* of the principal input *consistently* from the value of the surrogate.

[4]Here again, the reliability of real world data that are used in decision making is often not as satisfactory as that defined above. Occasionally, one may use an unsatisfactory surrogate which sometimes leads to a wrong decision. We often tolerate such a case if the wrong decision does not lead to a fatal outcome and if the cost of obtaining the unsatisfactory surrogate is much cheaper than the cost of obtaining a completely satisfactory surrogate. For a discussion of the use of unsatisfactory surrogates, see Ijiri [11] and [12].

[5]See, for example, Simon [17,pp. 241-60], and Garner [8,pp. 98-187].

likely to simplify the problem by grouping or aggregating a number of factors or by simply neglecting some of them. For example, a president of a firm may be able to obtain detailed data on the activities of the firm without too much cost, but he may want to base his decision upon a summary statement prepared by an accountant. The use of a representative figure such as a mean, median, mode, maximum, minimum, variance of a set of data is an example of the use of a surrogate to reflect many different principal inputs.

Surrogate-Principal Relationship—Cause and Effect

In discussing the surrogate-principal relationship earlier, we avoided any mention of the cause-and-effect problem. In the case of accounting data as surrogates, it is usually the principal which determines the value of the surrogate. That is, the principal is usually the cause and the surrogate (the accounting report or reported amount) is the effect. Therefore the usual functional relationship is

$$x \xrightarrow{\quad f \quad} y,$$

where x represents the principal input, y the surrogated input, f the functional relationship between x and y, and the arrow the fact that x is the cause of y.

However, this cause-and-effect relationship is occasionally reversed. The following two examples illustrate situations where this can occur.

Example 1. A division manager wants to exercise more pressure upon his subordinates if the manager's supervisor feels that the performance of the manager's division is unsatisfactory. In other words, his superivsor's evaluation x of the division is the principal for the manager's decision as to the amount of pressure z that he exerts on his subordinate, namely:

$$x \xrightarrow{\quad h \quad} z.$$

Suppose that the division manager knows, however, that the supervisor's evaluation x is based upon the reported divisional profit y (i.e., $x = \phi(y)$). Then the division manager may want to base his decision z upon the reported profit as a surrogate of the supervisor's evaluation ($z = g(y)$). In this case, the surrogate y is the cause of the principal x:

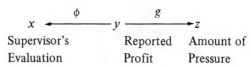

$x \xleftarrow{\quad \phi \quad} y \xrightarrow{\quad g \quad} z$
Supervisor's   Reported   Amount of
Evaluation   Profit   Pressure

whereas in an ordinary case we have

$$x \xrightarrow{\quad f \quad} y \xrightarrow{\quad g \quad} z$$
Principal   Surrogate   Decision

Example 2. As another situation where the principal input is caused by a surrogate (rather than vice versa) consider the role of income taxes in decisions. The income tax is based on the reported profit which is a surrogate for the real profit. Yet the income tax may be a principal input for many decisions. If the decision-maker bases his decision (e.g., the amount of money to be borrowed from banks) upon the reported profit as a surrogate for the actual income tax, the situation may be represented as follows:

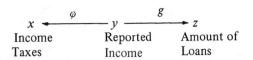

$$x \xleftarrow{\quad \varphi \quad} y \xrightarrow{\quad g \quad} z$$

Income	Reported	Amount of
Taxes	Income	Loans

To summarize, we have identified two different surrogate functional relationships. One relationship is where the surrogate (y) is determined by the principal (x). That is,

$$x \xrightarrow{f} y.$$

The other relationship is where the surrogate (y) causes the principal (x). That is,

$$y \xrightarrow{\phi} x.$$

The value of the surrogate resulting from the former relationship represents the principal which is a *past* state or event. In the latter case, the value of the surrogate is used to *predict* the principal, which is a *future* state or event. Let us distinguish between the two types of surrogates (or more precisely the two types of uses of surrogates) by calling the former a "descriptive" surrogate and the latter a "predictive" surrogate. For example, the reported profit is a descriptive surrogate of the operations of the firm, but it is a predictive surrogate of its future profit.

However, whether a given surrogate is a descriptive surrogate or a predictive surrogate of a given principal may be more complicated than in the cases described above. Consider the situation in which a decision-maker wants to base his price decision on the real *future* cost. Since the real future cost is unknown at the time of his decision, he may use a measure of the real *current* cost. In this case, the real current cost would be a *predictive* surrogate and not a descriptive surrogate. On the other hand, the decision-maker may use the reported (accounting) cost as a *descriptive* surrogate of the real current cost. In this case, the reported cost is a descriptive surrogate of the real current cost, which is a *predictive* surrogate of the real future cost.

In an earlier section we stated the timing requirements for a surrogate: it must be available to the decision-maker at the time of his decision. When a decision-maker needs to base his decision upon factors in the future, the use of a predictive surrogate is obviously necessary and highly important. In fact, where it may be possible to eliminate a descriptive surrogate from the decision process by actually observing the principal it is never possible to eliminate a predictive surrogate if the decision must be based on a factor that will occur in the future.

EFFECTS OF A CHANGE IN ACCOUNTING METHOD
ON MANAGEMENT DECISIONS

Accounting and Decision Processes

In Part 2 we analyzed the role of surrogates in the decision process. Accounting data as well as other types of business information are surrogates which the decision-maker uses to carry out the decision process. Of course, he will want to use surrogates only insofar as they reflect principal inputs (as discussed in the previous section).

To illustrate the interaction between an accounting process and a decision process let us consider the following simplified example. Suppose that a decision-maker wants to quote a price (z) on each job so as to recover 300 percent of the direct cost for the job (x). In the absence of a surrogate, his decision process is represented by

$$\underline{z} = 3\underline{x}.$$

Suppose also that the firm's accounting process provides the full cost (y) for each job by adding to the direct cost a standard overhead which is 100 percent of the direct cost (x). Then this accounting process is represented by

$$\underline{y} = 2\underline{x}.$$

If the decision-maker wants to achieve the same result by basing his decision upon the surrogate (the full cost) instead of the principal (the direct cost), he must adjust his decision so that he quotes a price equal to 150 percent of the full cost of the job, i.e.,

$$\underline{z} = 1.5\underline{y}.$$

Therefore, the accounting process and the decision process collectively constitute the decision process that the manager would use in the absence of a surrogate. Namely, the decision process which was formerly

$$\underline{x} \xrightarrow{3\underline{x}} \underline{z}.$$

is now decomposed as

$$\underline{x} \xrightarrow{2\underline{x}} \underline{y} \xrightarrow{1.5\underline{y}} \underline{z}.$$

If the accounting process is changed and the full cost (y) is calculated as 150 percent of the direct cost (x) instead of 200 percent, the decision-maker must adjust his decision process from $z = 1.5y$ to $z = 2y$ in order to keep the overall process ($z = 3x$) unchanged.

Obviously, this is an extremely oversimplified example, but nonetheless it shows the important interaction between the accounting process and the decision process, i.e., *the decision-maker must, in general, adjust his decision process (g) when the accounting process (f) is changed if he wants to keep the overall process (h) unchanged.*

The Decision-Maker's Adjustment to a Change in an Accounting Method

Using the relationship between the accounting process and the decision process as described above, we can now discuss the central question to be investigated. *"Under what conditions can (or cannot) a decision-maker adjust his decision process (g) to a change in the accounting process (f)?"* We will discuss this question by considering two different factors that would indicate when the manager cannot adjust. One is the lack of feedback on the performance of the accounting process, and the other factor is the possibility of "functional fixation" on the accounting concepts and measurements that are used in the decision process.

Lack of Feedback. A key factor which will determine whether or not the decision-maker can adjust to a change in the accounting process is simply whether or not he receives appropriate feedback on the performance of the accounting process. That is, he must be able to determine whether the process is performing as he expects it to perform. A type of direct feedback is for the decision-maker to observe the value of the principal input and compare it with the value of the surrogate. A cash count or a physical inventory is a good example of direct feedback. In addition to direct feedback, a decision-maker often has a means of obtaining indirect feedback. Instead of checking the process by himself, he may have somebody who checks the process for him. The use of an auditor to check any significant change in the accounting process is one way which might be used to discover when the accounting method is performing differently from what it is supposed to perform. Stockholders who, in their decisions, use profit figures as reported in financial statements are protected by auditors who report any significant changes in the accounting method used in generating profit figures. The decision-maker may have a number of surrogates which will collectively indicate any irregular performance of the accounting process, or an unexpected outcome from a decision may cause him to investigate the accounting process in detail.

It seems almost inconceivable to have a situation in business where a decision-maker has absolutely *no* feedback whatsoever on the performance of the accounting process. Therefore, it is highly unlikely to have a decision change which results solely from a change in an accounting process, where this is *caused only by the lack of feedback to the decision-maker.* This is especially true if we exclude a possible short-run effect due to the time lag between the change in the accounting process and the indication of the change to the decision-maker through feedback.

Therefore, if a modification in the accounting process results in any change in the decisions even though proper feedback exists for the decision-maker, it must be attributable to his inability to *use* the feedback in order to adjust to the alteration. No matter how good the feedback is in indicating the change, if the decision-maker cannot effectively use this feedback, he cannot hope to make the same decisions as before. There do appear to be instances in which decision-makers are unable to adjust. We believe the inability to adjust when it exists can be explained by a psychological factor called "functional fixation."

Functional Fixation. Psychologists have found that there appears to be "functional fixation" in most human behavior in which the person attaches a meaning to a title or object (e.g., manufacturing cost) and is unable to see alternative meanings or uses. People intuitively associate a value with an item through past experience, and often do not recognize that the value of the item depends, in fact, upon the particular moment in time and may be significantly different from what it was in the past. Therefore, when a person is placed in a new situation, he views the object or term as used previously.[6] If the outputs from different accounting methods are called by the same name, such as profit, cost, etc., people who do not understand accounting well tend to neglect the fact that alternative methods may have been used to prepare the outputs. In such cases, a change in the accounting process clearly influences the decisions.

When accounting data are used as predictive surrogates, the accounting process represented by the function f does not come directly into the principal-surrogate-decision relationship, as shown below.

$$\text{Principal} \qquad \text{Surrogate} \xrightarrow{\;g\;} \text{Decision}$$
$$x \longleftarrow y \longrightarrow z$$
$$\Big\uparrow f$$
$$x'$$

Input to the Accounting Process

---

[6]This phenomenon was discussed by Duncker [6].

However, if the functional fixation occurs on the ϕ-function (i.e., if the ϕ-function remains the same even after the f-function has been changed), then a change in the f-function affects the principal x; this, in turn, affects the decision z. For instance, in Example 1 in section 2.5, if the supervisor is unable to adjust to the change in the accounting process which generates the reported profit and continues to evaluate the division in the same manner (specified by the ϕ-function) as before even though the meaning of the reported profit has now been changed significantly, then the change in the accounting process of generating the reported profit will influence the amount of pressure exerted by the division manager. Such an influence occurs even if the division manager himself is perfectly capable of adjusting his decision function g to the change in the accounting process f, since what he is concerned with is not the performance of his division *per se* (which is the input x' to the accounting process) but his supervisor's evaluation x of his divisional performance.

EFFECT OF ACCOUNTING ALTERNATIVES ON MANAGEMENT DECISIONS

In the preceding section we discussed the question of whether or not a *change* in accounting methods affects management decisions. Our conclusion is that an accounting change will not affect decisions if there is feedback on the performance of the accounting system and if there is no functional fixation, i.e., the manager is able to effectively *use* the feedback information. A second question of great importance is whether or not the *choice* of one method from a set of accounting alternatives has any influence on the management decisions.

As a first step we will analyze one set of environmental conditions where existing research shows us that the choice of accounting method definitely affects decisions. This set of conditions can be referred to as an *ill-structured* environment.

Decision Making in Ill-Structured Environment

Authors who write about the management decision environment point out the ill-structured nature of the problems that confront business managers. That is, in today's business world, managers face problems for which there is great uncertainty about which alternatives are available and what constitutes an acceptable solution. Leavitt explains that in most managerial situations the decision-makers do not have a decision criterion that enables them to know exactly when they have made the correct decision.[7] Some of the reasons for the ambiguity is that there is usually a long delay between a positive step (a decision) and the recorded outcome. Then, too, there are many events that occur simultaneously in the organization which makes it almost impossible to determine the results of one particular decision. Therefore, as the manager views his world, he is always faced with the question—would another action have worked better? This difficulty means that the manager cannot unambiguously determine the decision function [in (1) $z = h(x)$] that he *should* use.

Recent research describing how people behave in ill-structured or uncertain situations has shed some light on how people probably use accounting information in the ill-structured situations.[8] The results show that when a person is confronted

[7]Leavitt [15,pp. 352-54].
[8]See, for example, Knight [14], and Cyert and March [4].

by such a situation, it is unlikely that he will remain in it very long. He will use his previous experience, available data, friends, etc. to define and structure his situation.[9] This problem is closely related to the one presented in section (2.4), where we discussed the limits of the human decision making capacity. There we emphasized that the human mind can handle only a limited amount of information. We mentioned that humans simplify their problems by using surrogates which are aggregates of a number of principals or by neglecting some of the principals. These procedures represent two of the methods which the individual uses to define and structure his world.

Studies that have described a manager's actual decision making behavior have found that he tries to avoid uncertainty and arrange the environment so that it has a predictable future. This is usually done in an organization by creating and following "standard operating procedures" in order to perform roles "safely."[10] The "standard operating procedures" are used to operationally define the decision-maker's environment and thus remove him from the previously ill-structured situation. We will now show how accounting information will sometimes be used to determine a decision-maker's "standard operating procedures;" that is, *to define the goals and decision procedures of the manager.*

We find that the surrogates generated by accountants often become used as predictive surrogates to define the decision-maker's environment, his goals and decision procedures. We mentioned (in the initial presentation of the concept of predictive surrogates in section 2.5.) the example in which the reported profit determined the goals of the division manager $(x = \phi(y))$, since the supervisor used the reported profit as a basis for the evaluation of the division manager and not what he considers as the "real" profit.

Another way that an accounting system determines the goals for a manager is by defining an area for him to pay attention to. For example, let us assume the accountants suddenly report scrap cost for the first time. The manager now modifies his goals in that he creates a new goal that specifies his objectives in regard to the control of scrap cost. In this example, the manager's g function changes to incorporate the new piece of accounting data. Furthermore, the accounting procedure, in addition to specifying goals for a manager, may also be used by him to help define his decision function. If the accountant chooses to report a given set of surrogates, this set may provide a basis around which the manager structures his decision process. In these cases, we expect that alternative accounting methods will affect the manager's decisions.

There are examples in the behavioral science literature that describe situations where accounting information has been used in the way we have just described and has been found to influence both the goals of the decision-maker and the alternatives which he considers in making his decisions. Ridgeway, studying the problem of accounting measures and behavior in American industry, found that "even where performance measures are instituted purely for purposes of information, they are probably interpreted as definitions of the important aspects of that job."[11] The results of Ridgeway's study represent direct support for the theoretical framework that we have presented in this section.

Additional support for our analysis comes from studies of the behavior in Russian industrial firms. These studies show that when specific performance

---

[9]Refer to Knight [14] for a further elaboration of this topic.

[10]See Cyert and March [4].

[11]Ridgeway [16,p. 377].

surrogates are provided, they are used by the decision-maker to structure his uncertain world. Smolinski reports how "the project of the Novo Lipetsk steel mill . . . comprises 91 volumes totaling 70,000 pages. (One is not surprised to learn that the designers are paid by sheet . . .) . Literally, everything is anticipated in these blueprints, the emplacement of each nail, lamp or washstand. Only one aspect of the project is not considered at all: its economic effectiveness."[12] What Smolinski shows is, that by measuring and recording the number of pages in a report, this surrogate has become a factor that defines the decision-maker's world. The decision-maker then restricts his goals and alternatives to ones other than those which are most useful for the organization.[13]

In a study of the Russian executive, Granick points out several dramatic shortcomings of a system where pressures result in the decision-maker receiving a limited number of performance surrogates and these are then used to determine his goals and alternatives. Granick discusses the "standard operating practice" of "storming," the phenomenon of getting everything possible out at the end of the month because monthly bonuses are determined by the volume produced.[14] He found that the volume of production was used as a descriptive surrogate of other principals that should have been considered by the decision-maker in determining his overall effectiveness. The result of the limited accounting information available to the Russian managers shows how these accounting systems greatly influence the behavior of the decision-maker in an ill-structured situation. Phenomena similar to that observed in Russia frequently are found in the United States, where surrogates such as direct cost as a percentage of total cost, scrap costs, maintenance costs, return on investment, etc, are used to define the manager's goals and alternatives. In the examples just described, the choice of an accounting method becomes very important in view of the fact that alternative accounting systems will tend to produce different decisions.

Area for Further Research

Our analysis in the last section leaves unanswered the question of whether or not the choice of accounting methods will affect decisions as we consider the infinite number of possible environments between ill-structured and well-structured. We have not been able to specify the general environmental conditions to predict when a choice of accounting methods would (or would not) affect decisions.

To establish a description of these general conditions we need to investigate many issues in addition to the ill-structuredness of the environment such as (1) the extent to which good or poor timing of accounting data affects decision, (2) the degree to which different methods of presentation of accounting data affect decisions, and (3) the extent to which the reliability (or lack thereof) of an accounting process affects decisions. In this paper we have begun to outline the variables that determine the effects of alternative accounting methods on manage-

[12]Smolinski [18 pp. 602-13].

[13]Note that many of the arguments in support of transfer pricing have been based on arguments about their psychological advantages or disadvantages. (See Hirshleifer [10] and Dean [5].) See also Ijiri [12] where the degree of the divergence between the organizational goal and the goals of its sub-system is analyzed by means of a "goal indicator chart" and a "goal indicator divergence coefficient."

[14]Granick [9,pp. 227-47].

ment decisions. There is a need for extensive additional research both to find other important variables and to test empirically hypotheses already proposed.

SUMMARY

We now summarize our above analysis as follows:

1. A decision process may be characterized by three factors: decision inputs, decision outputs, and a decision rule.

2. A surrogate may be used in place of a principal input if a surrogate is available at the time of the decision (timing) and if it is possible for the decision-maker to identify the key factors of the principal input which affect his decision (identifiability). The notion of a satisfactory surrogate is introduced in connection with the requirement of identifiability.

3. A decision-maker may need to use a surrogate (i) if it is difficult for him to obtain the principal input (cost consideration, time lag, etc.), or (ii) if it is difficult for him to use the principal input due to the limit in his capacity to consider it in making his decision.

4. The two types of surrogates are: (i) a descriptive surrogate and (ii) a predictive surrogate. A descriptive surrogate is one which is caused by a principal. A descriptive surrogate succeeds the principal timewise, such as in the case where the reported cost is used as a surrogate for the real cost.

On the other hand, a predictive surrogate is one which causes the principal. A predictive surrogate precedes the principal timewise. An example is the use of the current cost as a predictive surrogate for the future cost.

5. The intimate relationship between the accounting process which produces a surrogate (y) from a principal (x) and the decision process which generates a decision (z) based upon a surrogate (y) is explained by means of a simple example:

$$ x \xrightarrow{\ f\ } y \xrightarrow{\ g\ } z. $$

6. Then, the question "Under what condition can (or cannot) a decision maker adjust his decision process to change in the accounting process?" is considered in terms of (i) lack of feedback and (ii) "functional fixation" upon accounting concepts and measurements.

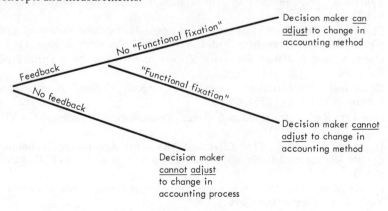

7. Finally, as an important case where the *choice* of accounting method does affect decisions, we considered the role of accounting processes in supplying

operational goals and alternatives for a decision-maker who is confronted with an ill-structured environment.

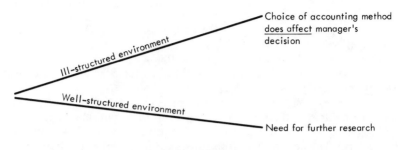

CONCLUSION

We set out to explore the condition under which alternative accounting methods affect decisions. We did this by proposing a theoretical clarification of the mechanics by which the accounting process and the decision process are related. Of course, the relationship between the two processes is a complicated one. We do not claim, by any means, that all variables and their relationships involved in the problem are identified in the above analysis. We believe, however, that at least the *key* factors in the relationship between the accounting process and the decision process are clarified in our theoretical analysis.

Much research still needs to be done before we can make more precise statements concerning the relationship between the accounting process and the decision process and before we can state in precise terms the effects of accounting alternatives on management decisions.

BIBLIOGRAPHY

1. Bonini, Charles P. *Simulation of Information and Decision System in the Firm.* Englewood Cliffs, N.J.: Prentice-Hall, Inc., 1963.
2. Bruns, William. "A Stimulation Study of Alternative Methods of Inventory Valuation." Unpublished Ph.D. Dissertation, University of California, Berkeley, 1962.
3. Charnes, A. and W. W. Cooper. *Management Models and Industrial Applications of Linear Programming.* Vol. I. New York: John Wiley & Sons, 1961.
4. Cyert, R. and J. March. *Behavioral Theory of the Firm.* New York: Prentice-Hall, 1963.
5. Dean, Joel. "Decentralization and Intra-Company Pricing," *Harvard Business Review,* XXXIII, 4 (1955), 65-74.
6. Duncker, Karl. "On Problem Solving," *Psychological Monographs,* LVIII, 5, Whole No. 270 (1945).
7. Dyckman, Thomas R. "The Effects of Alternative Accounting Techniques on Certain Management Decisions," *Journal of Accounting Research,* II, 1 (Spring, 1964).
8. Garner, Wendell R. *Uncertainty and Structure as Psychological Concepts.* New York: John Wiley & Sons, 1962.
9. Granick, David. *The Red Executive.* Garden City, New York: Doubleday & Co., 1961, pp. 227-47.

10. Hirschleifer, J. "On the Economics of Transfer Pricing," *Journal of Business of the University of Chicago*, XXIX (1956), 172-84.
11. Ijiri, Yuji, "Functional Analysis of Aggregation," Working Paper No. 21, Graduate School of Business, Stanford University, August 1964. Presented at the Tenth Annual, First International Meeting of the Western Section of the Operations Research Society of America held on September 14-18, 1964, in Honolulu, Hawaii.
12. Ijiri, Yuji. *Management Goals and Accounting for Control.* Amsterdam: North-Holland Publishing Company, and New York: Rand McNally, 1965.
13. Ijiri, Yuji and Robert K. Jaedicke. "Reliability and Objectivity of Accounting Measurements," Working Paper No. 55, Graduate School of Business, Stanford University, April, 1966.
14. Knight, Kenneth E. *The Organization as an Ill-Structured Problem Solving System. Working Paper No. 56, Graduate School of Business, Stanford University, 1965.*
15. Leavitt, Harold J. *Managerial Psychology.* Rev. ed. Chicago: University of Chicago Press, 1964, pp. 352-54.
16. Ridgeway, V. F. "Dysfunctional Consequences of Performance Measurements." In A. H. Rubenstein and C. J. Haberstroh (eds.). *Some Theories of Organization.* Homewood, Ill.: Irwin Dorsey, 1960, p. 377.
17. Simon, Herbert A. *Models of Man.* New York: John Wiley, 1957.
18. Smolinski, Gern. "What Next in Soviet Planning?" *Foreign Affairs*, XLII, 4, (July, 1964), 602-13.

DISCUSSION QUESTIONS

1. The technology for designing computer-based information systems for managing large organizations has been available for some time. Indeed, there have been many predictions that the manager will make his decisions through having access to the firm's information data base. It is obvious, however, that few if any such information systems have been implemented.

Comment on the difficulties of implementation in terms of administrative man and his capacity for processing information. Assume that technological factors such as hardware and such issues as resistance to change have all been overcome.

2. In a recent set of experiments on risk taking it has been shown that groups will tend to recommend taking greater risks than the mean of the individuals of the same group acting alone. It has been proposed that, if companies wish to increase the risk in some decision, a committee be appointed for that purpose.

Discuss the advisability of using committees for the purpose of increasing the riskiness of a firm's decision. Hint: consider the effect of status differences.

3. Since the revision of the New York City charter in 1961 the power of the mayor has increased through centralization of decision making in the office of the mayor. At a recent session before a committee holding hearings on revisions to the charter, the point was made that the mayor centralizes decision power to such an extent that he is unable to utilize it effectively. The result is that top bureaucrats who are not responsible to the electorate exercise the real power. The testimony was

concluded with a recommendation to decentralize city decision making by transferring power to borough presidents.

Discuss this recommendation in terms of the bounded rationality of humans and in terms of vertical and horizontal organization structures for decision making.

4. Basic inputs to a capital budgeting decision include cost of the investment, projected cash flows over time, and a cost of capital.

a. Contrast the accounting guidelines for relevant inputs regarding projections of cash flow in the decision process with accounting guidelines affecting the reporting of the results of the decision.

b. What would be the impact on capital budgeting decisions if conventional guides for public reporting were to be used as guides for cost inputs in arriving at projections of cash flows for decision making.

5. After extended meetings between the vice president of marketing and the controller of a large corporation engaged in the manufacture and marketing of consumer products, the following directive was issued to product managers who have responsibility for developing and implementing advertising and promotion programs for their products: "Beginning with January 1, 19x1, all advertising and promotion costs specifically identified as relating to the development of new markets or new products will be deferred over the expected benefit period not to exceed three years. Programs to qualify for this treatment must be approved by the vice president of marketing."

The new policy statement represents a clear departure from current practice where in all advertising and promotion costs would be expensed as incurred.

a. What changes in the product managers' decision process would you expect?

b. As vice president of marketing, what criteria for approval and control techniques would you need to implement this program.

c. As president of the company, what response would you make to the directive, assuming you were consulted before implementation?

6. The personnel department of a large service-type corporation (The "A" Company) has for a long time been considered a "cost center" and its costs allocated to the operating divisions that are the consumers of personnel services. Recently, the personnel department was invited to perform some special work for two corporations unrelated to the "A" Company. These projects were completed and some calculations were made, and it was agreed that a profit was made on both jobs.

It is now proposed by the manager of personnel that his department be a profit center and that charges to user divisions of Company "A" be charged for services at a price including profit.

a. What changes in the decision on using services would you expect on the part of the divisions of Company "A" if the manager's recommendation were adopted?

b. Will decision-making processes be altered within the personnel department as a result of the suggested change if adopted?

c. Assume you are opposed to the suggested change. What arguments would you present to the personnel manager, assuming the personnel department will continue to perform external projects at a profit?

PART FOUR

Control

THEORY OF CONTROL IN ORGANIZATIONS

As part of the development of the behavioral model of the firm discussed in Part One, the firm's goals were described as a complex compromise of conflicting demands reflecting a large and varied constituency. In Part Two the process of achieving operational goal congruency was developed through an examination of the budget processes within the firm. A major characteristic of the process is that goal congruency is achieved through a bargaining process, and the budget document can be viewed as a surrogate for an explicit statement of the firm's goals.

Management control has been defined by Anthony as "the process by which managers assure that resources are obtained and used effectively and efficiently in the accomplishment of an organization's objectives."[1] This definition assumes the existence of broad business goals and considers budgeting as part of the control process.

Indeed, the budget is the basis of the control system. If one accepts the concept that managers will behave in a way that will maximize the attainment of

---

[1] Anthony, Robert N., *Management Accounting Principles,* Richard D. Irwin, Inc., 1970, Chapter 14.

their goals subject to achieving the firm's objectives, then their influence is not limited to the setting of objectives but is implicit in the control process as well.

Specifically, management controls are implemented by relating actual performance to the budget, analyzing derivations from the budget, and taking corrective action. It is in the analysis and action phases of the control process that the conflict between individual and organization goals appears.

The two prevalent organizational approaches to control in organizations are centralized and decentralized systems. The type of control system often determines the nature of the intraorganizational conflict that occurs within the organization.

Centralized control systems came about and reflected a direct application of the management by exception principle. The intent was to routinize lower level decision making and centralize discretionary decision making at the top. The result was verticalized organizations.

Decentralized control systems came about partly in response to participative critics of vertical coercive organizations, partly in the hope of improving organizational decision making but mainly in anticipation of tighter control over costs. The main feature of the decentralized control system is the creation of control positions on the division and subdivision level staffed with controllers who formally report directly to the corporate controller.[2]

Whereas decentralized control systems have resulted in lowering decision-making levels within the organization and have partially increased felt participation in decision making, no difference exists between centralized and decentralized control systems in internal resource allocations. Schiff and Lewin report that, to the contrary, in decentralized control systems the divisional controller appears to be intimately involved in managing the division's slack and that overall, the extent to which slack is created within organizations is more deliberate and planned in decentralized organizations than in centralized organizations.[3]

INTRODUCTION TO THE READINGS

The article by Kenneth J. Arrow sets forth the problem and current status of understanding control in large organizations based on the logic of economic theory and the mathematics of maximization. The author addresses himself to the control problem in organizations in the public and private sectors and to economic systems as a whole. The control problem is viewed as one concerned with keeping members of the organization "in step with each other" so as to maximize the organization's objective function.

The problems of centralization and decentralization are considered by examining organizational decision making. The manager is viewed as an information channel of limited capacity operating under overload conditions necessitating decision making at lower levels of the organization.

Thus, Arrow's rationale for decentralized organizations is derived from the limits of information-processing capacity as contrasted to decentralization proposed on the basis of participative management theory.

The control problem resulting from decentralization centers on the fact that

---

[2]D. Solomons, *Divisional Performance: Measurement and Control*, Financial Executives Research Foundation, 1965.

[3]For further detail see Michael Schiff and Arie Lewin, "The Impact of People on Budgets," *The Accounting Review*, April 1970.

the organization's objective is a function of a number of interrelated decision variables concerning individual activities. Different members of the organization have different bodies of knowledge, the latter derived from the notion that transmission and assimilation of information is costly, otherwise each member of the organization would transmit all his knowledge to others.

The price system is suggested as a possible way for choosing operating rules but poses difficulties. The author concludes that systematic analysis of organization control will include price theory and programming methods joined in an "unfamiliar synthesis" with information theory and sampling statistics.

Carmichael's paper can also be considered "a state of the art" evaluation. It is narrower in that it is restricted to internal control systems as part of a total information system and focuses on the behavioral aspects of internal control. The goals of the total information system are viewed as including productivity, reliability, and safeguarding assets. The author then proceeds to examine the literature in related fields and sets forth eight behavioral hypotheses believed to be held by accountants though not previously articulated. These hypotheses focus only on the design, operation, and audit of internal control systems.

A critical evaluation of these hypotheses is then undertaken with due recognition to the fact that the operative organization, the subject of study, emerges from the interaction between the formal and informal organizations. The author concludes, after citing a number of illustrations and utilizing the literature or organization theory, that the hypotheses as stated and currently used cannot be validated and hence, there is a real need for a new set of hypotheses more in agreement with organization reality.

In their analytical and empirical study, Whistler, *et al.* attempt to clarify what they define as the key variables in the theories and models of organization—the centralization of organizational control. Focus is on three concepts of the process of control and the measures associated with them—individual compensation, perceptions of interpersonal influence, and span of control. The authors then turn to concepts and measures of centralization associated with the three concepts of the control process listed above. The transaction from the consideration of control as a dimension of individual behavior to a dimension of organizational behavior is achieved by defining the control structure. This permits the derivation of a concept of centralization related to the control structure and a measurement of centralization in the form of an index. Appropriate indexes for each of the key variables are identified.

The degree of congruence among the indexes of centralization are then examined as they relate to different organizations. Less congruence is revealed by production departments that have broadly defined goals and that frequently encounter the responsibility not only of developing solutions to problems but of defining the problems in the first place.

The second part of the Whistler, *et al.* paper consists of an empirical study addressed to observing the degree of congruence in the three variables using indexes of centralization and to substantiating the broad inferences regarding production type and staff type organizations as noted above.

In the article by Walter, empirical research is the basis for testing two hypotheses. Although observation techniques were used in two municipal government hierarchies, one suspects that a similar research approach in organizations in the private sector would produce similar conclusions. The hypotheses tested have significant relevance in any control system and are: (1) that subordinates were relatively more influential than their superiors in the formulation and execution of non-recurring decisions, and (2) that superiors have greater influence in the formulation and execution of recurrent or programmed decision making.

Walter addresses himself to testing the validity of what has been referred to as "a pair of hypotheses venerated in administrative folklore" that hold that the autonomy of subordinates peaks when making routine choices but declines sharply on novel decisions.

The research supports the first hypothesis that in non-programmed choices the influence of subordinates over superiors exceeds the influence of superiors over subordinates, resulting from the subordinate's greater knowledge or, perhaps, from the shared presumption by superiors that subordinates know more than the superiors do. Perhaps more significant are the conclusions regarding programmed choices. Here the research data are not consistent with the hypotheses. It was found that subordinates are more influential than their superiors in making programmed decisions. The influence of superiors in these decisions consisted of setting priorities among alternative actions suggested by subordinates and external consumers of goods and services supplied by the organization.

17

CONTROL IN LARGE ORGANIZATIONS*

KENNETH J. ARROW

I welcome greatly the opportunity to address a meeting of The Institute of Management Sciences in this land where beauty and efficiency have had such a happy junction. Dr. Geisler's presidential address in Paris two years ago and this one symbolize the internal character of our organization and of the needs which we hope to serve. I rejoice that we are among that small number of scientific organizations who have direct international membership—we stand together as scientific co-workers, with no labels of nationality dividing us.

In considering a topic for a presidential address, I had two motivations. One, of course, was my own interests; one cannot be interesting to others about what one is not interested in. But the second was to use the occasion to bring before you

*Management Science, April 1964, pp. 397-408.

a broad and significant field of inquiry, one transcending the technical papers which are, and should be, the usual objects of our concern. Especially was I interested in speaking on this area, which is implicitly relevant to everything the management scientist does, and at the same time so poorly understood as an object of theoretical and practical study. There are few results to present, but many problems. If I succeed in persuading some of you of the complexity and the challenge of the issues, I will feel well satisfied.

I

The large organization, so prominent on our contemporary social landscape, is of great antiquity. If we had no other evidence, we would know that complex organizations were necessary to the accomplishment of great construction tasks—planned cities like Nara or Kyoto or Ch'ang-An, monuments like the Pyramids and temples of Egypt, irrigation systems such as those in ancient Mesopotamia or northern China. But we also know of organization for less material ends, for the preservation of law and order, the maintenance of peace or the prosecution of war—Persia, the efficiency of whose control mechanism and communication system has been so well described by Herodotus and Xenophon, and the Inca empire of Peru, where a complex and far-flung state was administered in a highly systematic manner with a technology so poor as to include neither writing nor the wheel. Truly, among man's innovations, the use of organization to accomplish his ends is among both his greatest and his earliest.

But it is perhaps only in our era, and even then haltingly, that the rational design of organization has become an object of inquiry. It is characteristic of the present day, as exemplified by the groups meeting here today, that innovation, the solving of problems, is being increasingly systematized. Whereas in the past the improvement in the choice of routes was made by insight and spontaneous inspiration, today we try to arrive at the decision by solving a transportation problem. In the same way, there is an increasing interest in studying how organizations solve their problems so that one can systematically investigate optimal organization.

Let me state the problem at hand a little more precisely; since research in this area is still in its early stages, undue exactness must be avoided. An organization is a group of individuals seeking to achieve some common goals, or, in different language, to maximize an objective function. Each member has objectives of his own, in general not coincident with those of the organization. Each member also has some range of decisions to make within limits set partly by the environment external to the organization and partly by the decisions of the other members. Finally, some but not all observations about the workings of the organization and about the external world are communicated from one member to another. The word "large" in the title is meant to stress the importance of the communications element.

In this address, I wish to set forth some considerations on one aspect of the workings of an organization—how it can best keep its members in step with each other to maximize the organization's objective function. This may be referred to as the problem of organizational *control.* It divides itself naturally into two parts: the choice of *operating rules* instructing the members of the organization how to act, and the choice of *enforcement rules* to persuade or compel them to act in accordance with the operating rules. Various other terms for these two problems have appeared in the literature; a widespread usage is to refer to the operating rules as control-in-the-large and the enforcement rules as control-in-the-small. It should be noted that enforcement, here as elsewhere, includes both the detection and the punishment of deviations from the operating rules.

My point of view is rationalistic and derives, with appropriate changes, from the logic of choice as it has been developed in the pure economic theory of prices and the mathematics of maximization. The rational or economic analysis of organizations has been developing rapidly over the past fifteen years, and the present account is largely derived from the work of such innovators as Jacob Marschak, Herbert Simon, Leonid Hurwicz, Thomas Marschak, and Roy Radner. There is no intention of denying that non-rational factors, sociological and psychological, are of the utmost importance in the study and development of organizations. But a rational point of view is also needed, and indeed much of the value of studies in group dynamics will only be properly realized in the context of rational design of organizations.

I will first discuss in the very broadest outline some typical examples of control problems in modern organizations—the large corporation, government, the economic system as a whole considered as one great organization. From these illustrations, a brief statement of the essentials of the control problem will be derived. Next I will consider the price system as a solution to the problem of control; this is the solution most natural to an economist. While the price system has many values, it also has limitations. Consideration of these will bring out more clearly the basic problems of organizational control, and in particular the crucial role of uncertainty among the causes for the creation of organization. Finally, the need for some additional forms of control will be briefly examined. As can be seen from this summary, this address has as its primary function the delineation of the problem and of the present status of our understanding, not the presentation of any definitive solutions.

II

The issue of centralization or decentralization in the large corporation has received considerable attention in recent years. A large corporation contains many diverse productive activities, which have important connections with each other and yet are separately identifiable. The products of one activity are the inputs of another, and therefore it is costly to the corporation if its activities are not balanced. Some commodities have to be purchased from outside, stored, transported from one place to another among and within plants, and assigned to the activities using them; some activities produce final products which have to be transported, stored, and sold; other activities produce intermediate products, such as component parts of an automobile, which in turn enter other activities, such as assembly, which produce final products or still other intermediate products. Further, the coordination is needed not only at a single point of time but over many time periods; each activity takes time, so its product can only be used in another activity beginning when the first one ends.

What may be called the classic businessman's view is to be so impressed with the complexity of coordination that great stress is placed on the need for central control. Emphasis is placed on vertical, hierarchical relations; control is exercised by orders from above, executed in detail by those below. The coordination between managers of parallel activities is, in this view, achieved by their common obedience to the plans set at higher levels. Accounting systems and other forms of reporting provide higher echelons with all the information needed to detect violations of orders, and dismissal from employment is the punishment.

Of course, the view I have just sketched is a caricature and was probably not held by anyone in all its rigidity. It is immediately obvious that higher management cannot literally know everything about the operations of individual activities and therefore cannot make all decisions. Indeed, management literature recognized this problem under the heading "the span of control." It was held that an official could not exercise effective supervision over more than a relatively small number of subordinates, say six. In the terminology which modern management theory is borrowing from statistical communications theory, a manager is an information channel of decidedly limited capacity. This means, of course, that the junior managers must be receiving information from their juniors which they do not retransmit. Hence, some decisions, if only trivial ones, must be made at lower levels, since the relevant information is discarded in the process of upward transmission to avoid overloading the channels.

The recognition that individual managers will inevitably know more about their own spheres of activity than higher officials has caused decentralization of decision-making to be looked on with much more favor in recent years. It has also been recognized that decentralization can improve the allocation of responsibility; on the one hand, the subordinate has greater possibilities of initiative; on the other, his successes and failures can be more easily recognized by top management.

In the terminology introduced earlier, the operating rules under a centralized system take the form, "do this or that," while under a decentralized system they rather take the form, "do whatever is necessary to maximize a certain objective function."

But the problems of articulating more specifically the operating and enforcement rules of a decentralized organization have not been faced systematically. The objective function for the corporation as a whole may be well defined to be aggregate net worth, but its value depends on the decisions of many managers; the objective function to be maximized by an activity manager must depend in some well defined way on his decisions, to provide an appropriate set of directions to him.

Further, even when the objective function for the manager is defined, there remains the problem of enforcement. When the goal is stated in terms of an objective function, it becomes a matter of more or less, not of yes or no, as it would be if instructions were stated in terms of specific tasks. The top management can never, strictly speaking, know if the activity manager's objective function has been maximized; instead, their enforcement rules should be such as to encourage him to increase the value of the objective function as much as possible. In more usual terms, the problem is to create such incentives to activity managers for performance as will best enhance the corporation's net worth. There are (at least) two problems in devising incentive systems. (1) An effective incentive system creates new demands for information; the reward is a function of performance, so top management must have a way of measuring performance. This may be the objective function itself, or it may be some other, more easily measurable, index. If the index is something other than the objective itself, the manager's incentives may not be directed optimally from the viewpoint of the corporation; for example, if the index of the manager's performance is based primarily on output rather than profits, he will be tempted to be wasteful of inputs. However, an index which supplies better incentives may require more information; in organizational control, as in automobiles, cuisine, and every other commodity, the benefits of improved quality must always be compared with its costs. (2) Even if the index is thoroughly appropriate, the relation between the reward and the index remains to be determined. Suppose there is no difficulty in isolating the contribution of a manager to the net worth of the firm. The fullest incentive to the manager would be achieved by fixing a base salary and a target level of contribution to net worth or profits and then giving the manager as a bonus the difference between his contribution to profits and the target level. If his contribution fell below the target level, the difference would constitute a negative bonus, to be subtracted from his salary. Such an arrangement would clearly not be satisfactory in spite of its desirable effects; the corporation of course intends to share in the profits attributable to the skill of its managers and not to give them all away to him, and the manager may also be reluctant to face the risks, especially if the contribution of his activity depends in part on factors not under his control and about which his knowledge is uncertain.

III

The design of control systems in large corporations is already a formidable task, but it is several orders of magnitude simpler than the control system for a government. To keep the discussion within reasonable bounds, I will confine my remarks to one particular, though very important, phase of governmental activity, the determination of the annual budget. This is the process by which it is determined how much of the resources of society shall be diverted to the different activities carried on by government. The budgetary decisions are a major determinant of the direction of government activities, though, of course, there are many aspects of government decision-making, for example, foreign policy, where budgetary considerations are secondary.

The governmental decision process has all the complexities of the corporate, but there are two major additions: the consumer-like character of the government, and the varied nature of its activities. Economic theory, as well as ordinary experience, tells us that the process of consumer's choice is harder to make rational than the decision-making of the corporation. In theory, the corporation maximizes a well-specified objective function, profits or net worth, with no constraints other than those imposed by its technology. The consumer, on the contrary, maximizes a subjective magnitude, under a budget constraint. This implies that the consumer cannot seriously be expected to write down in any explicit way his maximand. Rather, the process of optimization consists of a series of comparisons among alternative ways of spending marginal dollars; the utility function is revealed to the consumer himself in the process. Further, the common budget constraint means that the marginal comparisons must be made among highly disparate alternatives—travel as compared with clothing, for example.

The government's choices are analogous to those of the consumer, with the additional problem that the single utility function is replaced by the great variety of utility functions of the different groups in the political system, the final choice being the resultant of political pressures in many different directions. The government's budget to be allocated among activities is relatively fixed in any one year, though there is some opportunity for change in the total. Alternatively, and perhaps better, it could be said that society's total resources constitute the budget constraint, with the government deciding both the overall allocation between public and private activities and the allocation among public activities. In any case, the budget constraint is a basic element in the government's financial decisions.

The great scope of the government's activities means that marginal comparisons have to be made among some exceedingly remote alternatives: Is an improvement in a national park to be preferred to increased defense?

These choice problems are all institutionalized in the budget-making process. Budgetary requests are made by individual bureaus and then presented to some central agency—in the United States, the Bureau of the Budget. Symbolically, the bureaus represent the utilities of different activities, the Bureau of the Budget the overall resource constraint. But of course no simple separation is possible. The Budget Bureau has to make decisions in cutting down the total requests to the desired budget total, and these decisions involve two types of judgments: (1) the relative social value of the functions of the different bureaus, and (2) the efficiency with which the bureaus are performing their functions. The first judgment has necessarily to be made in a centralized fashion; the Budget Bureau might be thought of for this purpose as the agent of the legislative authority. It is the second type of judgment, that of the efficiency with which government activities are performed, that is more relevant to the problem of control.

For the Bureau Budget to judge efficiency would in principle require it to know as much or more about individual activities as the bureaus themselves. As the affairs of government have become increasingly complex and differentiated, the impossibility of such a concentration of knowledge has become increasingly patent. Traditional analysis of the budgetary process tended to stress the virtues of centralized budgetmaking, strict lines of control, and avoidance of duplicating activities among bureaus. Some current writers, notably Lindblom, Enthoven, and Rowen, now argue that a good deal of apparent inefficiency and duplication are essential elements of the control process. To replace the impossible demands for knowledge on the part of the Budget Bureau, reliance is placed on the self-interest and mutual rivalry of bureaus. The bureaus act like individuals before a court; they are required to supply the information which will justify their requests, and if two bureaus have overlapping functions, the information supplied by one can be used to check on that of the other.

This theory of the invisible hand in government, though a significant contribution, is as limited a view as the earlier theory of the all-knowing Budget Bureau. The search for a more satisfactory theory of government budget control must still go on.

IV

Up to this point, the boundaries of an organization have been taken as given. The line which separates governmental from non-governmental actions, or which separates a corporation from its customers and suppliers, has been implicitly taken as well defined. But in fact we really have a nesting of organizations inside larger organizations; indeed, the whole economic system can be regarded as one large organization, and in many respects it is fruitful to do so. A socialist system is one in which the organizational unity of the economy is made explicit in its institutions, but it has long been a commonplace of traditional economics, certainly since the time of Pareto, that the apparent anarchy of capitalism conceals a complex organization fundamentally similar to socialism.

Consider the following three examples of commodity transfers: (1) An engine is placed on an assembly line to be installed into an automobile body. (2) An automobile factory receives a shipment of steel from a mill owned by the automobile manufacturing company. (3) An automobile factory receives a shipment of steel from a mill owned by a steel company. The first is certainly a transaction within an organization and is carried out in accordance with operating rules laid down by authority. The third is a commercial transaction, the result of a contract in which goods are exchanged for money, and would usually be regarded as taking place between different organizations. Yet the second, the steel shipment from a mill to an automobile factory of the same ownership, is identical to the third in its economic content and to the first in the form of the transaction.

This continuous sequence of cases shows that drawing any boundary lines for an organization has a somewhat arbitrary element. If the entire economy is thought of as a single organization, one is led naturally to think of the price system as one of the major devices for coordinating different activities, and a great deal of effort by economists has succeeded in clarifying its virtues and limitations.

The very importance of price-mediated transactions suggests that it is worth while distinguishing them from others. The boundary of an organization then will be taken as the line across which only such transactions take place. As the examples just given show, we must be prepared in such a classification to recognize that some intra-organizational transactions will have the same economic content as price-mediated transactions.

It is important and illuminating to note, however, that many transactions have both price and non-price characteristics. Professional services, such as medicine and legal services, are not carried on solely on the basis of an impersonal cash-for-service exchange. There is an expectation of personal responsibility, of fidelity and trust; physician and patient behave in many ways more like coworkers in the same organization than like a large manufacturer and his remote and unseen customers. Similar relations are typical of labor services, agents, and in general of transactions involving goods or services where quality standards are significant and not easily checkable in detail by the purchaser. Speaking broadly, these non-market relations reflect the same sort of problems that arise in control within an organization—the need for services coupled with an incompleteness of knowledge by the receiving party about the activities of the supplier.

V

From these examples of organizations, we can abstract the central problem of organizational control. It arises when two conditions hold: (1) The objective of the organization is a function of a number of interrelated decision variables concerning individual activities; (2) the different members of the organization have different bodies of knowledge. The second condition, of course, implies that the transmission and assimilation of information is costly, for otherwise each member of the organization would transmit all his knowledge to all the others.

Uncertainty is simply the complement of knowledge; when I speak of different bodies of knowledge, I could equally well speak of different uncertainties. For definiteness, let us suppose that uncertainty can be represented by probability distributions over all possible states of the world. Then the following model may serve to illuminate organizational behavior: Each member of the organization is in possession of a signal from Nature, and his probability distribution of states of the world is the conditional distribution given that signal. (The "signal" is understood to be his knowledge based on learning and experience.) Each member can, at a cost, transmit his signal, or a weaker signal compatible with it, to one or more other members of the organization. Each member who has received an additional signal appropriately modifies his conditional distribution. On the basis of the resulting distributions and the operating rules laid down by the organization, each manager makes a decision. The decisions made in turn generate further information which is transmitted in one form or another, and leads to new signals and new decisions. New signals are also coming in from outside the organization and also leading to new decisions. Finally, the messages being transmitted within the system are used to modify the operating rules and to execute the enforcement rules.

VI

It has already been observed that many of the transactions within an organization are similar to those that take place in the market. This has led both theorists and business firms to suggest that prices can be used to regulate transactions within the firm; these are usually referred to as "transfer prices." In the purest form, a price is attached to each commodity or service produced or consumed by any activity in the organization; if the commodity is sold to, or bought from, other firms, the transfer price has to be the same as the market price (with some modifications in the case of imperfect competition). The operating rule for the manager of each activity is then to maximize its profit, as computed by valuing its inputs and outputs at the transfer prices.

This is straightforward, but merely restates the control problem as that of choosing the correct prices. They have to be such that, if each manager does choose his inputs and outputs so as to maximize profits, then for each intermediate good (one not bought or sold on an open market) the total supply and demand by all activities balance.

If the organization calculates its optimum by the Lagrange method for constrained maxima, where the constraints are precisely that the activities producing intermediate products produce enough to meet the requirements of the activities consuming them, then the Lagrange multipliers are the prices. This method of determining the prices is itself centralized and does not satisfy the informational limitations which are the heart of the organizational problem. Of course, radical improvements in the techniques of constrained maximization, such as the modern work in linear and nonlinear programming, decrease the costs of centralized information handling and thereby reduce the problem of organizational control. But, as has been shown in many different forms, an informationally economical decentralization is possible if we solve the constrained maximization problem by a suitable form of successive approximations. If the prices are first set by guesswork, each manager can make a set of tentative decisions. If the resulting inputs and outputs of intermediate goods match, then the prices were indeed the correct ones; if not, the normal procedure would be to raise the prices of those intermediate goods for which demand in the aggregate exceeds supply, and lower those for which the contrary is true. Under certain assumptions as to the technologies of the activities, this process will converge to the optimum for the organization.

The price system, conceived in this way as a process of successive adjustments, is a satisfactory way of choosing operating rules when the appropriate assumptions hold. Each tentative set of rules is defined by the tentative set of transfer prices; the successive adjustments in the prices, and therefore, in the rules, require information only about the supplies and demands of the individual activities, information which would have to be transmitted under almost any sensible control system; and there is a guarantee that the decisions at least tend toward full optimality for the organizations.

Though the price system for operating an organization possesses these merits, and though I believe that it is capable of much greater use than it now receives, it has intrinsic limits. Indeed, the very existence of large organizations in the commercial world is a proof of the existence of these limits. When the price system is fully operative, the large organization is equivalent to a large number of separate activities whose connections are the same as those of unrelated firms. Hence, the large organization would have no differential advantage in economic competition, and we would not expect to find it so dominant.

The difficulties in applying a price system to the control of an organization can be classified into four mutually interacting types: (1) the choice of enforcement rules; (2) the complexity of the operating rules; (3) the limits on the theoretical validity of the price system; and (4) the presence of uncertainty, which we have seen to be inherent in the problem of organizational control.

The first problem, the choice of enforcement rules, has already been discussed in some measure in the case of the large corporation. Since we have supplied each manager with an objective function, the profits of his branch evaluated at transfer prices, the most natural enforcement rule would be an incentive system; the payment to the manager should be a strictly increasing function of the branch profits. If the slope of this relation is close to one, then the branch manager is bearing most of the uncertainties due to successive revisions of the transfer prices for which, as a risk-averter, he may well require a large fixed compensation. If the slope is close to zero, then the incentive effect to the manager is small.

The second problem, the complexity of the operating rules, can be appreciated only after a little reflection on the scope of a really thoroughgoing price system. The need of coordination in time is perhaps the chief source of complications; deliveries of specific commodities have to be made at specific times, and in a pure price system there would have to be a separate price for each commodity for each possible date of delivery. One might, to take an example from the government's sphere of activity, use a price system to settle traffic problems; there would be varying prices to be paid for different priorities at intersections and in passing lanes at different moments of time. It is not hard to see the confusion such a system would cause; a traffic signal may lead to an allocation of traffic which is less than optimal in some theoretical sense but it is a far simpler system to operate.

The third problem, the limits on the theoretical validity of the price system, has received a great deal of attention in the literature of welfare economics. There are two basic conditions under which the price system is invalid, in the sense that the equilibrium prices do not represent an optimum: One is that there are increasing returns (or, more generally, non-convexity) in some of the activities, and the other is the presence of externalities, relations between the productivities of different activities which are not classified as commodity transfers. Smoke emitted by one activity may, for example, interfere with the productivity of another. Externalities are essentially a matter of classification; we can always call any externality a new commodity and attach a price to it. Indeed, the elimination of externalities can proceed much farther within an organization than in the market; there is no technically satisfactory way in the marketplace for making the smoke producer pay for his damage to others, but an organization can fix a price for the privilege of emitting smoke and order it to be paid. Of course, special enforcement rules are needed to make sure that the appropriate payments are made. Further, the elimination of externalities increases the list of commodities and thereby again complicates the operating rules.

Although the matter is too technical to be discussed in a brief space, it can be asserted that increasing returns can be handled by modifications of the price system, but these necessarily introduce some degree of centralization. There is still room for significant research to minimize the informational requirements needed for optimal allocation under these conditions.

VII

The fourth difficulty in applying the price system, the presence of uncertainty, is of major importance and yet has received relatively little theoretical study. The one case that has been studied in some detail is that in which all activity managers have the same information about the world outside the organization. Clearly, the appropriate transfer prices can easily depend on the unknown state of the outside world; the simplest illustration would be the case where production plans have to be made now for sale in the future, and at a price which cannot be known now with certainty. We may regard the organization as being faced with a probability distribution of states of the world, product prices in the example. For each state of the world, there will be a corresponding set of transfer prices, so that each activity manager will be faced with a probability distribution of transfer prices. The instructions to maximize profits is no longer meaningful; it must be replaced by the operating rule of maximizing the expected value of utility of profits, where utility is a strictly increasing function.

If the organization itself is risk-neutral, then it would want each activity manager to maximize expected profits. But now the already-mentioned problem of enforcement rules becomes even more acute. If the reward of the manager depends in some measure on his observed profits and if he is a risk-averter, he will wish to play safe by following a course which leads to more predictable profits, even if the expected value is lower. To avoid this outcome, the organization should provide insurance against unfavorable external contingencies, which the manager may buy at his option. In this way, it can be shown that the manager will be motivated to maximize expected value and at the same time have all the protection against risk that he wishes.

Such a system does really exist in the sense that a manager is not normally held accountable for unfavorable outcomes or credited with favorable ones if they are clearly due to causes not under his control. However, there is a deep problem here which is well known in insurance theory and practice under the name of the "moral hazard"; it is, in general, almost impossible to separate causes outside the organization from the efficiency of the manager himself. If an activity does badly, it may be because of external uncontrollable events, or it may be mismanagement. To distinguish between them may never be completely possible and, to the extent that it is, may require costly information. Thus, the occurrence of a fire may be partly due to failure to take precautions or may be completely independent of them; the fire insurance company will not only charge a premium but also engage in additional information-gathering in the form of inspection of premises.

Still further complications occur when the different managers have access to different amounts of information about the external world; this is the problem treated by Marschak and Radner in their theory of teams. Though operating rules can indeed be devised, the problem of enforcement has not yet been approached except in a very rudimentary case (studied by Good and McCarthy).

VIII

Even without going any further, it is clear that in the control of the typical organization, perfect decentralization is not possible because of the limitations on enforcement rules associated with uncertainty and risk aversion. The top management of the organization will always have to have some information about the internal workings of the individual activity. This is far from saying that they have to have complete information. One of the most promising lines of study is that of sampling inspection—it should be equally applicable to the control of the quality of management as to that of goods. A relatively small amount of information, properly chosen, may have large incentive effects.

The problem of organizational control is just beginning to be analyzed systematically. Already it is clear that price theory and programming methods will have to join in an unfamiliar synthesis with information theory and sampling statistics to achieve the state where the rational design of the organization becomes a reality.

18

BEHAVIORAL HYPOTHESES OF INTERNAL CONTROL

D. R. CARMICHAEL

The principal function of an internal control system is to influence (or control) human behavior. It follows that the nature and form of internal control systems must be materially influenced by the view of human behavior which is held by the accountants who design, operate, and audit these systems. Yet, there has been no significant attempt to make this view of human behavior explicit.[1] This paper clarifies the behavioral hypotheses which underly the design, operation, and audit of internal control systems.

THE INFORMATION PROCESSING SYSTEM

In modern complex business organizations the internal control system is an integral part of the information processing system. Consequently, a discussion of internal control must begin with a consideration of some of the general aspects of information processing systems. The goals normally established by management for the information processing system are described first. Second, the general means of accomplishing these goals are discussed. Finally, the behavioral hypotheses underlying these means are clarified.

Goals for the System

Management establishes the goals for the information processing system by factoring the overall organizational goals. In the chain of organizational goals and means, these information processing *goals* are the *means* by which the goals of higher levels in the organization are achieved. The information system goals are productivity, reliability, and safeguarding assets. The goal of productivity places emphasis on the output of the system. Reports must be prepared in a timely and economical manner. Payroll checks must be prepared and distributed on schedule. Customers must be billed at designated times. The factoring of the productivity goal to individual workers results in task specialization. Individuals are assigned simple repetitive tasks to increase efficiency. Measures of performance are then

The Accounting Review, April 1970, pp. 235-245.

[1] The behavioral hypotheses underlying the content of management accounting data have been explored by Edwin H. Caplan in "Behavioral Assumptions of Management Accounting," THE ACCOUNTING REVIEW, (July 1966), pp. 496-509. This paper accepts the content of the data processed as a given and explores the working relationships involved in the processing activity.

established as productivity goals for individuals, e.g., number of transactions posted per hour.

Timely and economical processing of information is not the only goal. To be useful in meeting other goals of the organization, the information must also be reliable. Management will use the information output of the system as a means to make the decisions necessary for the achievement of other organizational goals. For decision-making purposes, reliability is important.

The goals of safeguarding assets and reliability are related. Abstraction of assets is usually considered to be one source of unreliability of information. Elimination of this source of unreliability is identified as a separate goal because of its importance for selecting means of achieving information processing goals. Little purpose would be served by extending this discussion of information processing system goals much beyond their identification. For purposes of analysis, they will be accepted as given.

The Means of the System

The means of achieving information processing productivity may be generally characterized as a refined application of the methodology of Frederick W. Taylor.[2] No attempt will be made to give a comprehensive summary of the means of increasing office productivity; a brief analysis should suffice.[3] Generally, the methodology involves elimination of unnecessary steps and wasted motion, minimizing idle time, and improving work methods and procedures. Task specialization is a central element in the productivity goal. For example:

Individual work productivity may be considerably increased by rearranging work assignments so as to permit employees to develop special skills. It is axiomatic that the fewer different tasks an employee has to perform, the greater his opportunity for proficiency in each of them.[4]

The criterion of efficiency—maximization of output in relation to input—is then applied in a grouping process; tasks are grouped into jobs and jobs are grouped into departments. Measures of task performance are then developed, as productivity subgoals, and departmental supervisors are charged with the responsibility of effecting achievement of these subgoals.

The means of achieving the goals of reliability and safeguarding assets are normally referred to as internal control. A traditional benchmark in discussions of internal control is a definition contained in a special report published by the Committee on Auditing Procedure of the AICPA.

Internal control comprises the plan of organization and all of the coordinate methods and measures adopted within a business to safeguard its assets, check the accuracy and reliability of its accounting data, promote operational efficiency, and encourage adherence to prescribed managerial policies.

[2]Frederick W. Taylor, *The Principles of Scientific Management,* (Harper & Brothers, 1911).

[3]For representative works on office productivity see: Earl P. Strong, *Increasing Office Productivity*, (McGraw-Hill Book Co., Inc., 1962) and George R. Terry, *Office Management and Control,* (Richard D. Irwin, Inc., 1966).

[4]Strong, *op. cit.,* p. 119.

The characteristics of a satisfactory system include:

A plan of organization which provides appropriate segregation of functional responsibilities,

A system of authorization and record procedures adequate to provide reasonable accounting control over assets, liabilities, revenues and expenses,

Sound practices to be followed in performance of duties and functions of each of the organizational departments, and

A degree of quality of personnel commensurate with responsibilities.[5]

The traditional rationale supporting such a system is that it:

... makes it impossible for a defaulter to abstract funds or other assets for which he is responsible and at the same time cover up his manipulations by entering corresponding amounts in the accounting records. As long as accounting and custody are separated, fraud can be completely concealed only through collusion between employees responsible for each of these functions. Fraud by an employee in either function is virtually certain to be discovered when quantities on hand (as reported by the custodian function) are verified with what the records show should be on hand (a product of the accounting function).[6]

This rationale and other more complete expositions on internal control are supported by a number of basic assumptions or behavioral hypotheses. These behavioral hypotheses are usually implicit in discussions of internal control, and even those which are made explicit are widely scattered in the literature.

Accounting writers have not remained oblivious to the behavioral aspects of internal control. The most concise and penetrating analysis was made by Mautz and Sharaf in their attempt to formulate a concept of due audit care for the independent auditor's review of internal control:

To borrow a phrase, "internal control is people." A system of internal control is made up of people and procedures, procedures in which people are expected to perform and report in a normal fashion. But unknown to the reviewer, the pressures which motivate the people in the "system" may change sufficiently that they cease to act in an expected fashion, whereupon the internal control procedure loses its effectiveness.

There are so many events and relationships which can work to offset the most effective internal control measures and which at the same time would be neither apparent to nor necessarily discoverable by the independent auditor that acceptance of responsibility for the review of internal control is hazardous at best.[7]

Rather than treating these factors as imponderables, the approach taken here is to identify and classify these factors and show that they are related to recognized concepts in other fields and that they, therefore, can be studied and analyzed.

[5]Committee on Auditing Procedure, American Institute of Accountants, *Internal Control,* (American Institute of Certified Public Accountants, 1949), p. 6.

[6]Eric L. Kohler, *A Dictionary for Accountants,* 3rd ed., (Prentice-Hall, Inc., 1963), p. 275.

[7]R. K. Mautz and Hussein A. Sharaf, *The Philosophy of Auditing,* (American Accounting Association, 1961), p. 145.

BEHAVIORAL HYPOTHESES OF INTERNAL CONTROL

A hypothesis is first presented, in a somewhat formal manner, and numbered (H*i*) for later identification. Each formally presented hypothesis is followed by supporting evidence drawn from the literature. The hypotheses presented are those apparently held by accountants who design, operate, and audit internal control systems; the validity of the hypotheses is considered at a later point.

H1: Individuals have inherent mental, moral and physical weaknesses; therefore, internal control methods and measures are necessary to achieve information processing system goals.

The organizational concept of specialization of task is a common adaption to the mental and physical shortcomings of people. The statement is frequently made that the cause of fraud is a constitutional or moral weakness on the part of the embezzler. An early writer hypothesized about these weaknesses as follows:

Such men may be placed in two classes—first, the weaklings who fall under the pressure of fancied necessity; second, the egotists who, being dishonest at heart, feel themselves able to escape detection.[8]

The human weakness emphasized may be a base tendency, e.g., "the human craving for something for nothing,"[9] or "he probably would not be embezzling at all if he weren't greedy."[10] On the other hand, the embezzler's actions may be attributed to a hidden weakness:

... There is usually some defect in background or training which permits the defaulter to justify to himself his departure from generally accepted moral standards.[11]

H2: An effective internal control system, by threat of prompt exposure, will deter an individual from committing fraud.

Most studies of fraud conclude that the solution is a strengthening of internal controls:

If ... an employee is constantly faced with the opportunity to steal, either through inadequate accounting procedures and/or lack of proper internal control, management is at fault. All employers have a definite moral obligation to safeguard their employees' integrity. . . .[12]

[8]L. U. Crawford, "Defalcations," *The Journal of Accountancy,* Vol. 20, (August 1915), p. 112.

[9]Henry Brodish, "Fraud in Business and Its Control," *The Internal Auditor,* Vol. 17, (Fall 1960), p. 25.

[10]Earl Soder, "Trustees—Audits—Defalcations," *The Arthur Andersen Chronicle,* Vol. 18, (April 1958), p. 137.

[11]Bradford Cadmus and Arthur J. E. Child, *Internal Control Against Fraud and Waste,* (Prentice-Hall, Inc., 1953), p. 13.

[12]J. D. Forbes, "Good Internal Control—a Necessity for Effective Fraud Prevention," *The Ohio CPA,* Vol. 26 (Winter 1967), p. 28.

Another writer extolls the merits of good internal control in this manner:

> Accountants generally believe that sound systems of internal control, devised, installed, and operated in accordance with the best business practices, will deter by threat of prompt exposure many such persons from violating their trusts.[13]
>
> *H3: An individual who is independent, i.e., functionally and structurally situated so that he does not perform incompatible actions, will recognize and report irregularities which come to his attention.*

This assumption must necessarily be made before any internal control system could be considered effective. The elaborate procedures creating interdependence of records and independence of people, so that the work of one employee is continuously verified by that of another, would be merely ritualistic if an employee did not report the irregularities in the work of other employees. The importance of this hypothesis is given explicit recognition in an authoritative work on internal control:

> The value of "independence" on the part of persons performing many of the procedures of internal check is based upon the assumption that an independent person will report to knowledgable authority deliberate errors, falsification or improper use of documents, forgeries, or other irregularities coming to his attention. To be "independent" in this sense, the employee must be free to report such matters both from the standpoint of the duties assigned to him and that of his position in the line of organization. When there is such freedom, failure to report to proper authority should occur only if the employee is incompetent, or if there is collusion between employees presumed to be independent.[14]
>
> *H4: The consequences of rejection for suggestions of irregularities will normally be considered prohibitive and, therefore, the probability of collusion is low.*

This assumption is necessary because of the commonly expressed opinion with regard to internal control that the system collapses with collusion. If the custodian and the record keeper collaborate, the abstraction of assets can be concealed and the system fails.

The reluctance of one individual to approach someone in another group with a suggestion to commit fraud is assumed to be high. The reason for the assumed reluctance is usually attributed to fear of exposure, i.e., fear that the person approached will report the suggestion to a supervisor and disciplinary action will be taken. In relation to H3, a party to a collusive fraud scheme would not report irregularities.

H5: The plan of organization is the only determinant of power in the information processing system.

This assumption is not given explicit recognition in accounting literature; rather the evidence for this assumption is implicit in the emphasis of the existing literature. Discussions of the plan of organization stress establishing clear lines of

---

[13]Robert L. Williams, "Two Costs of Poor Internal Control: Fraud and Unreliable Accounting Information," *The Journal of Accountancy,* Vol. 94, (November 1952), p. 583.

[14]Normal J. Lenhart and Philip L. Defliese, *Montgomery's Auditing,* 8th ed., (The Ronald Press Company, 1957), p. 517.

authority and responsibility.[15] This singular emphasis on prescribed duties and responsibilities and the heavy reliance placed on organization charts suggest that the organizational hierarchy is assumed to be the only determinant of power, in the sociological sense. In other words, there is a general acceptance by accounting writers of the proposition that in an organization "all authority comes from the top and is cascaded down by progressive delegations, while responsibility comes from the bottom and is owed to the next superior and to no one else."[16] The extent to which it is implied that clear lines of authority and responsibility contribute to internal control effectiveness suggests that power is assumed to be attainable only through the formal organization.

More direct evidence for this assumption is provided by considering assertions that H3 is modified by superior-subordinate relations as specified by the plan of organization.

> . . . If these persons [people assigned functions that would be incompatible if combined] report to a common chief who has hire-and-fire or disciplinary control over them, their functional independence may be impaired by their job dependence on their chief.[17]

This statement is in reality a corollary assumption that an individual is not independent of his superior. Combining this corollary assumption of H5 with H3 yields another corollary assumption that an individual will not report irregularities of his superior which come to his attention. On the other hand, because the power distributed by the hierarchy rests in the position of the superior, a superior is considered to be independent of his subordinates.[18] This leads to another corollary assumption that an individual will report the irregularities of subordinates which come to his attention.

H6: Actions not specified by the formal organization are dysfunctional for information processing goals.

This assumption is supported by the emphasis given to the necessity of continuous review to ensure that internal control methods are functioning as prescribed and the stress placed on adherence to procedures, e.g., "whenever we permit deviations from prescribed routines, we are creating a potentially dangerous situation, because deviations are the embezzler's meat and drink."[19] Furthermore, the involved processes of specialization of tasks and separation methods are aimed at adherence to procedure. In fact, one of the characteristics of a satisfactory system of internal control listed in the previously cited Institute study, "sound

---

[15]"Responsibilities and the attendant delegation of authority should be clearly defined and wherever possible set forth in either an organizational chart or manual. . . ." "The chain of responsibility does not stop with the departmental heads. Within a particular department it should move downward, but always in a *continuous* line." Committee on Auditing Procedure, *op. cit.*, pp. 9 and 10 respectively.

[16]Victor A. Thompson, *Modern Organization*, (Alfred A. Knopf, Inc., 1963), p. 74.

[17]Lenhart and Defliese, *loc. cit.*

[18]This is evidenced by the importance of supervision duties for effective internal control as discussed by James B. Bower and Robert E. Schlosser, "Internal Control—Its True Nature," THE ACCOUNTING REVIEW, Vol. 40, (April 1965), p. 340.

[19]J. D. Forbes, *op. cit.*, p. 34.

practices," seems to mean, primarily, adherence to the procedures specified in two other characteristics, a plan of organization and a system of authorization and record procedures.[20]

H7: A record system provides adequate evidence of actions, such as acknowledging performance and transferring responsibility, i.e., the existence of documentary evidence implies the prior existence of concomitant actions.

Any review of past action based on documentary evidence must necessarily make this assumption. When a reviewer examines documents to determine that prescribed actions have been taken, he is actually observing the documentary manifestations of company activity. Such a review requires:

... two basic assumptions (1) that there is a universe of events and of actions in response to these events stable enough so that criteria for appropriate action can be set up and (2) that there is a way of recording these actions and events so that the recording process can be verified in order that the correspondence with the relevant events and the actions can be ascertained.[21]

H7 is a composite of these two assumptions. Further support for H7 comes from consideration of the emphasis placed on providing documentary evidence for such actions as transferring responsibility and acknowledging performance and the subsequent review of those documents.[22]

H8: There is no inherent conflict among the information processing goals of productivity, reliability, and safeguarding assets.

There seems to be no reason to question the complementary nature of the goals of reliability and safeguarding assets. A similar claim is often made for internal control and productivity.

Planning of procedures to put to best use the specialized talents of each employee will almost automatically provide the separation of responsibility that is a prime essential of internal control.[23]

In other words, "the optimum degree of specialization is very likely to produce the necessary degree of internal control as a by-product."[24]

The behavioral hypotheses specified above are not offered as *the* assumptions underlying internal control but, rather, are submitted as a partial and tentative attempt to develop such assumptions. If the behavioral hypotheses developed here

[20]"Practices adopted in carrying out the procedures would be largely determinative as to whether satisfactory internal control exists. Thus, punching clock cards becomes effective internal control only through *observance* by timekeepers *to determine* that properly authorized cards are punched by the employees to whom they were issued." (emphasis added) Committee on Auditing Procedure, *op. cit.*, p. 13.

[21]Neil C. Churchill, "Behavioral Effects of an Audit: An Experimental Study," unpublished Ph.D. thesis, (University of Michigan, 1962), p. 34.

[22]Bower and Schlosser, *op. cit.*, pp. 341-342.

[23]Bradford Cadmus and Arthur J. E. Child, *op. cit.*, p. 20.

[24]*Ibid.*, p. 21.

are an accurate indication of the view of human behavior held by the accountants who design, operate, and audit internal control systems, then the accountant's view of the organizational setting of internal control coincides very closely with what organization theorists have referred to as the formal organization.

Formal organization is a term for one set of characteristics of the business organization; it is the "structural expression of rational action."[25] The formal organization presents a blueprint for coordinating the activities of many groups of people. Since this blueprint must be communicated, the formal organization has been defined as:

> ... all written specification of individual relationships in the group, all rights, duties, and privileges that are formally assigned to personal and group roles, and all rituals and regulations that are created as models of personal and group activity.[26]

The formal organization establishes a hierarchy of authority. This hierarchy specifies the division of power or authority among members of the organization. The higher ranks are responsible for planning and controlling the operation of the organization and have an obligation to supervise the performance of the lower ranks. The lower ranks are given little, if any, power and their obligation to the organization is usually specified in the form of detailed tasks.

Organization theorists, however, have long realized that the formal organization does not consider all essential aspects of organizational interaction because:

> ... the human actors who fulfill organizational roles rarely can limit themselves merely to the performance of these activities required by the organizational blueprint.[27]

Those activities that arise among the members of a formal organization which are not called for by the blueprint are referred to as the informal organization. Organization theorists feel that both the formal and informal organization are necessary for the effective functioning of the organization. For example:

> ... No organization can function effectively if it does not contain a parallel spontaneous network of interpersonal relations.[28]

In contrast to the specificity of the formal organization, the informal organization is a complex blend of social relations and modifications of organizational relations.

> It is composed of the animosities and friendships among the people who work together. It contains primary groups, cliques, and congeniality groups that develop in shop or office. It further consists of the folkways, mores, norms,

[25]Philip Selznick, "Foundations of the Theory of Organization," ed. Amitai Etzioni, *Complex Organizations: A Sociological Reader,* (Holt, Rinehart and Winston, Inc., 1961), p. 19.

[26]Delbert C. Miller and William H. Form, *Industrial Sociology,* (Harper & Row, Publishers, 1964), p. 117.

[27]Edgar H. Schein, *Organizational Psychology,* (Prentice-Hall, Inc., 1965), p. 9.

[28]Miller and Form, *op. cit.,* p. 226.

and values which guide the behavior of workers, sometimes in the fulfillment of the goals of formal organization and sometimes in the blockage of those goals.[29]

The concepts of formal and informal organization are ideal typologies. Organizational behavior cannot be neatly compartmentalized into these categories. The actual operative organization is a product of the interaction of the formal and informal organization.

THE OPERATIVE ORGANIZATION AND INTERNAL CONTROL HYPOTHESES

The operative organization which emerges from the interaction of the formal and informal organization is decidedly different from the formal organization considered in isolation. If the operative organization, rather than the formal organization, is taken as the proper setting of the internal control system, some doubt is cast on the validity of the behavioral hypotheses based on the accountant's conception of the organization. The following discussion highlights some of the phenomena observed in operative organizations by organization theorists and considers their mitigating influence on the validity of the behavioral hypotheses of internal control.

Influence Attempts (H3 and H5)

Influence attempts are a general category of action involving the exertion of power by one individual over another individual or group. First, the type of influence attempt which would have a mitigating effect on H3 will be explained. The attitude of the individual subjected to influence is significant for this type of influence attempt. The use of specialization of task for achieving information processing system goals creates a certain image of the organization in the mind of the employee. Frequently, because he does not understand the contribution he makes to organizational goals, task specialization deprives his work of meaning. In such a situation an employee may counter his perception of his job as impersonal with an attitude of indifference. One possible outcome of this situation has important implications for H3.

> Even if the employees have information that would be of value to management, they would be unlikely to share it because of their image of the organization as basically exploitive and indifferent to human needs.[30]

This attitude would certainly contribute to irregularities.

One employee may use power to persuade another employee that a discovered irregularity in the records is an unintentional error, rather than an intentional error made to conceal an irregularity. An employee attempting to persuade another must have some source or base of power which will cause another employee to accept the explanation. An employee in a supervisory position might use the power vested in his position in the formal hierarchy. This situation was

---

[29]*Ibid.*, p. 119.

[30]Schein, *op. cit.*, p. 33

given explicit recognition in the form of a corollary assumption. The formal hierarchy, however, is not the only source of power. In a discussion of the sources of power of lower ranking members of organizations, David Mechanic suggests that power may be obtained from such personal qualities as expertise, physical attractiveness, and length of service in the organization.[31] An employee, then, might be expected to accept the judgment of another over his own if he knew the other employee had more experience on the job or had reason to believe that he was particularly qualified, for instance, by possessing a CPA certificate.

This suggestion of the possession of power by lower ranking members of the organization indicates that influence attempts may also have a mitigating effect on H5. Influence attempts might be used to gain access to records or assets necessary for the perpetration or concealment of fraud. The potentialities of such a situation have not gone unnoticed. For example:

> ... Most embezzlement losses are due to breakdowns in the control systems prescribed, not to inefficiency of the system. Most large defalcations are not the work of master-minds—they are due to the failure of an employee or auditor to carry out a simple assignment, usually because of an inclination to "let George do it." And right here is where the dishonest employee enters the picture with his offer to take over a part of a fellow-worker's duties.[32]

A recently reported case in a company with an apparently effective internal control system illustrates the use of influence to perpetrate irregularities. A supervisor, under the guise of helping his subordinates, would periodically offer to do such jobs as reconciling a bank account and assisting in account distribution.[33] Thus, he performed tasks for which he was not responsible according to the plan or organization. During these short periods of assistance, he manipulated the records to conceal a fraud of in excess of $100,000 over a period of two years. Although this case concerns a supervisor, a similar method could have been used by a subordinate.

Two of Mechanic's hypotheses concerning the manner in which lower ranking organization members obtain power are particularly appropriate for this type of influence attempt. Mechanic hypothesized that:

> Other factors remaining constant, there is a direct relationship between the amount of effort a person is willing to exert in an area and the power he can command.[34]
> Other factors remaining constant, the less effort higher ranking participants are willing to devote to a task, the more likely are lower participants to obtain power relevant to this task.[35]

[31]David Mechanic, "Sources of Power of Lower Participants in Complex Organizations," ed. W. W. Cooper, H. J. Leavitt, and M. W. Shelly II, *New Perspectives in Organization Research*, (John Wiley & Sons, Inc., 1964), p. 138.

[32]Herbert N. Schisler, "Fraud Can Take Place in a Well-Designed System if Working Rules Are Not Followed," *The Journal of Accountancy*, Vol. 95, (February 1953), p. 176.

[33]Milton M. Broeker, "Audit Problems Relating to Review of Internal Control," *The Journal of Accountancy*, Vol. 123, (February 1967), p. 77.

[34]Mechanic, *op. cit.*, p. 144.

[35]*Ibid.*, p. 145.

These hypotheses imply that an employee could use an influence attempt to perform the approval and authorization or review duties assigned to his superior or to perform the tasks assigned to a fellow worker.

Performance Pressure (H6 and H8)

Organizational pressure for high performance can have consequences which mitigate the effectiveness of internal controls. One common phenomenon in organizations is an over-attachment to the measures of performance used to assess achievement of organizational goals.

Frequent measuring can distort the organizational efforts because, as a rule, some aspects of its output are more measurable than the others. Frequent measuring tends to encourage over-production of highly measurable items and neglect of the less measurable ones.[36]

The information processing system goal of reliability can be used to illustrate the mitigating effect of performance pressure on H6. In an effort to achieve reliability, the quality standard set for certain clerical functions is frequently *no mistakes*. Certain procedures, such as balancing accounts daily, are rigidly adhered to. The possible consequences of such rigid adherence to procedure are revealed by the following comments by the probation officer of a convicted embezzler:

... After one day's business he was approximately $1,000 short in his cash account and was told at the time by Mr. X, who was the cashier, to find the $1,000 before he left the teller's cage or he would lose his job. Defendant says that he checked and rechecked his accounts but was unable to locate the missing money. Consequently, the defendant states he withheld deposit tickets for the day to make up the $1,000 shortage. It was necessary then that he continue withholding deposit tickets at various times to cover the first shortage. After he discovered it was so simple he began withholding deposit tickets and pocketing the difference between the deposit tickets and actual cash.[37]

Contrary to H8, there can easily be a conflict between the goals of productivity and safeguarding assets. In explaining the complementary nature of specialization of task, required to meet the goal of productivity, and separation of duties, necessary to meet the goal of safeguarding assets, Cadmus and Child give the following illustration:

Inquiry answering and delinquent analysis are distinct functions which require very different talents from those of the machine operator [cash posting to accounts receivable]. Thus for this we would have an accounts receivable specialist who might handle the ledgers of several machine operators.

This separation between mechanical operation [posting] and analysis has a further advantage of providing good internal control, since the recording function is separated from the responsibility for analysis and adjustment. If

---

[36]Amitai Etzioni, *Modern Organizations,* (Prentice-Hall, Inc., 1964), p. 9.

[37]Donald R. Cressey, *Other People's Money,* (The Free Press, 1953), p. 62.

the accounts receivable specialist wants to manipulate his accounts he will have to pass the entries to the machine operator.[38]

An empirical study of clerical workers by George Homans involved an office situation with a separation of duties strikingly similar to the situation described by Cadmus and Child. Homans' terminology does differ slightly; cash poster is equivalent to machine operator and ledger clerk equivalent to accounts receivable specialist. According to Homans:

> It was . . . standard daily procedure for their supervisor to take some of the ledger clerks . . . off their stations in rotation and send them to fill in on other jobs, usually cash posting.
>
> Since many of the ledger clerks had been "promoted" from cash posting, they were thoroughly familiar with the work. [39]

In this situation described by Homans, the supervisor is choosing to meet the productivity goal at the expense of separation of duties, a means of achieving the goal of safeguarding assets. Productivity goals usually have easily measured standards of performance, e.g., number of transactions posted per day; therefore, such goals may be emphasized over other less measurable goals, such as safeguarding assets.

A small digression should be made at this point to note a serious lack of empirical evidence in this entire area. Sociological studies of organizations have been chiefly industrially-oriented. In an industrial situation, there is an easily identifiable physical output and, consequently, such studies have focused major attention on the goal of productivity and the effect that workers' personal goals and the goals of informal groups have on productivity. Similarly, sociological studies of clerical workers have been oriented toward organizational productivity.[40] There is a need for sociological studies that focus attention on the goal of safeguarding assets in a clerical situation.

Informal Groups (H3, H4, and H5)

H3 and the corollary assumption from H5 that an individual will report the irregularities of his subordinates that come to his attention are modified by the existence of informal groups or cliques in the organization.

An interesting empirical analysis of cliques by Melville Dalton classifies informal groups into three general categories: vertical, horizontal, and random.[41] In a vertical clique the supervisor frequently conceals the errors of certain subordinates. This action may forestall investigation of an apparently unintentional error which is, in reality, an intentional error being used by a subordinate to

---

[38]Cadmus and Child, *loc. cit.*

[39]George C. Homans, "Status Among Clerical Workers," *Human Organization,* Vol. 12, (Spring 1953), p. 7.

[40]For an example of such a study see: Daniel Katz, Nathan Maccoby, and Nancy C. Morse, *Productivity, Supervision, and Morale in an Office Situation,* (Institute for Social Research, University of Michigan, 1950).

[41]The following discussion on cliques is drawn from: Melville Dalton, *Men Who Manage,* (John Wiley & Sons, Inc., 1959), pp. 57-63. Dalton's classifications are based on empirical studies of organizations.

conceal a fraud. A random clique, composed of members from different levels and different departments, might provide the paths for collusive relationships between members of structurally separated departments. Random cliques, at the least, could considerably reduce the barriers to collusion postulated by H4. Membership in a clique may provide a source of power to be used in the previously explained influence attempts. Such influence attempts involving the tacit collaboration of other employees might be referred to as involuntary collusion.

Horizontal cliques might facilitate another interesting modification of H3 and H5. An internal auditing department is normally used to substantiate adherence to internal control procedures. One might expect the internal auditing department to discover and report a situation in which a supervisor was emphasizing the productivity goal over the goal of safeguarding assets. The existence of cliques, however, can foster an attitude that it is "a lot of bunk about Auditing being independent."[42] Internal auditing, a staff function, is subject to the exertion of power by line supervisors. "Toleration of rule-breaking and even cooperation with the line to sidestep some regulations is essential at times to prevent the line from revealing staff errors to the top."[43] Dalton reports a pertinent case in which a surprise audit of the parts inventory was instituted by top management. The employees in charge of the audit, however, were subjected to influence exerted by department heads in a horizontal clique.

> ... Their solution was not to make unannounced counts, but to telephone various heads before a given inspection telling them the starting point, time, and route that would be followed. By varying these conditions on successive tours, [they] made each inspection *appear* to catch the chiefs off guard.[44]

Attitude Toward Employees (H1)

The assumptions made about people in organizations operate as a theory which determines how employees will be treated. Although the true nature of man has never been determined conclusively, much evidence does exist concerning the influence that the assumptions adopted have on employee behavior. The greatest danger of an assumption such as H1, i.e., that employees have inherent mental, moral, and physical weaknesses, is that it tends to be self-fulfilling. If management's attitude forces employees to conclude that they are expected to behave in a certain manner, the employees may retaliate by exhibiting the behavior the system was intended to control.

A "perfect" internal control system with numerous checks and balances may, in fact, stimulate violation of control procedures. Near the close of a professional lifetime study concerning the influence of assumptions about people in organizations, Douglas McGregor concluded that:

> One fundamental reason control systems often fail and sometimes boomerang is that those who design them fail to understand that an important aspect of human behavior in an organizational setting is that noncompliance tends to appear in the presence of perceived threat.[45]

[42]Dalton, *op. cit.*, p. 32.

[43]*Ibid.*, p. 104.

[44]*Ibid.*, p. 47.

[45]Douglas McGregor, "Do Management Control Systems Achieve Their Purpose?," *Management Review,* Vol. 56, (February 1967), p. 8.

Some of the situations which might be perceived as threatening are application of punitive measures when standards are not met, pressure for higher performance, and use of the concept of accountability. McGregor feels that such a situation could easily provide justification for dishonesty.

SUMMARY

This paper develops the behavioral hypotheses which underly the design, operation, and audit of internal control systems. The traditional conception of the organizational setting of the internal control system in accounting literature resembles very closely what organization theorists have referred to as the formal organization. When the traditional behavioral hypotheses are examined in the light of current thinking in organization theory, however, some doubt is cast on the validity of the traditional hypotheses. Although the traditional hypotheses are not conclusively invalidated in this paper, enough doubt should exist to stimulate formulation of hypotheses more in agreement with organizational reality.

19

CENTRALIZATION OF ORGANIZATIONAL CONTROL

AN EMPIRICAL STUDY OF ITS MEANING

AND MEASUREMENT *

THOMAS L. WHISLER / HAROLD MEYER /

BERNARD H. BAUM / PETER F. SORENSEN, JR.

INTRODUCTION

This study is aimed at clarifying the meaning of a key variable in theories and models of organizations—*centralization of organizational control.* To do so, it is necessary to first examine the concept of control. The study is empirical as well as analytical. We compare certain proposed measures of control, the comparison being designed both to test our inferences about the control concept underlying each of

* *The Journal of Business,* The University of Chicago Press, January 1967, pp. 10-27.

the measures and to assess the degree to which the concepts and measures are interrelated.

Study of the growing literature of organizations makes one aware that, until recently, the centralization variable has usually been lamely handled in empircial research. The probable explanation is that both *control* and *centralization* have always been ambiguous concepts. In view of the importance of the concepts of control and centralization in theory and the growing emphasis on empirical research for the purpose of testing and refining theory, empirical exploration of the meaning and measurement of centralization of control appears urgently required.

The study focuses upon three measures of control already suggested in organizational literature: (1) individual compensation,[1] (2) perceptions of inter-personal influence recorded on a questionnaire,[2] and (3) the span of control in the formal organization.[3]

It appears to us not only that these three measures are based upon different concepts of the process of control in organizations but also that the concepts themselves represent different orders of explanation, with the compensation-related concept being broader than the other two.

The *first* concept, upon which the compensation measure is based, is that of individual control over system (organizational) output, either by influencing other members or by direct personal task inputs. The *second* concept, underlying the questionnaire measure of control, defines control as perceived interpersonal influence—the perceived influence of members upon each other. The *third* concept is that of control as the formally planned influence of organization members upon one another in their roles as superiors and subordinates.

These relationships of concept and measure are summarized in Table 1.

TABLE 1   Measures and Concepts of Control

Measure of Control	Related Concept of Control
A. Individual compensation	A. Control over system output (system control)
B. Scaled perceptions of individual influence	B. Perceived interpersonal control
C. Span of control	C. Formally defined (or intended) interpersonal control

Discussion of Concepts and Measures of Control

Individual Compensation. In our view the concept of system control, upon which this measure is based, is the broadest of the three considered in this study.

[1]Thomas L. Whisler, "Measuring Centralization of Control in Business Organizations," in W. W. Cooper, H. J. Leavitt, and M. W. Shelly II (eds.), *New Perspectives in Organization Research* (New York: John Wiley & Sons, 1964).

[2]Arnold S. Tannenbaum and Robert L. Kahn, "Organizational Control Structure: A General Descriptive Technique as Applied to Four Local Unions," *Human Relations,* X, No. 2 (1957), 127-40.

[3]A. Janger, "Analyzing the Span of Control: How Many Subordinates Should Report to a Single Manager?" *Management Records,* XXII (July-August, 1960), 7-10, and Peter M. Blau and Richard D. Scott, *Formal Organizations* (San Francisco: Chandler Publishing Co., 1962), pp. 168-69.

Each member of the organization provides inputs which, in various ways, influence the outcome of the total effort of the organization. These inputs can be applied either through *direct personal task effort* (commonly, "work" or "problem-solving" at various levels of sophistication) or *through other members* (commonly, "direction" or "supervision"), or both. This concept we define as system control, the "system" being the totality of resources and procedures constituting the organization.

One expects, in any hierarchical organization with specialization of tasks, that there will be differences among individuals in the amount of control they exert over system output. Von Bertalanffy, in a discourse on what he calls "general system theory," argues the universal existence of a principle of centralization, meaning that some elements (individuals) in a system (organization) function as "triggers," because a small change in energy input by those elements results in large (disproportionate) changes in system output.[4] This disproportion results from the design characteristics of the system. The present concept closely parallels this idea.

The measure of control based on this concept is the compensation paid the individual by the organization. Compensation is the "inducement"; control is the "contribution" (expressed in terms of effect upon organizational output) in the terminology used by March and Simon.[5] As these writers point out, the organization seeks always to maintain a balance between contributions and inducements.

The way in which an organization's "role" or job structure and performance-evaluation procedures tie together with market prices to make individual compensation a reflection of individual control has been analyzed in detail elsewhere.[6] But the argument may be briefly restated here:

In the bureaucratic organization, roles are formally structured and control explicitly assigned to them by those in top leadership positions (their own roles included). It seems reasonable to assume that control can be assigned in a variety of alternative patterns at the discretion of leadership, with technology, organization size, and other factors undoubtedly influencing their choices as they seek an effective pattern.

The pattern of control that is established determines a homologous pattern of role demands made upon the individuals who fill these roles (or, in traditional managerial language, a grant of authority carries a corresponding measure of responsibility). These role demands can be expressed in terms of individual attributes: innate intelligence, acquired special or general knowledge, energy, sensitivity and insight, daring—any attribute associated with individual contribution and commitment to organization goals based upon *present activity and upon past investment in himself.*

These attributes are unevenly distributed in the general population, with individuals who possess them in high degree, singly or in combination, being relatively scarce. Given that organizations generally prefer those who possess more, rather than fewer, of these attributes, we have the determinants of a structure of labor prices in any society in which individuals sell their services to organizations.

If we assume the existence of broad, reasonably competitive labor markets, then the organization paying monetary compensation to those who participate in

---

[4]L. Von Bertalanffy, "An Outline of General System Theory," *British Journal for the Philosophy of Science, I*, No. 2 (1950), 150-51.

[5]James G. March and Herbert A. Simon, *Organizations* (New York: John Wiley & Sons, 1958), chap. iv.

[6]Whisler, *op. cit.*

its activities will not be able to influence prices significantly but must regard them as constraints on its choice of control structure. In other words, the leadership of the organization will establish what it conceives to be a satisfactory pattern of control in the role structure, given the prices it must then pay to staff these roles adequately. Given the structure of prices in the market, alternative control patterns will produce different compensation patterns.

In practice, rational bureaucratic organizations act just about this way, devising job-analysis and job-evaluation schemes in order to assess role demands, with this job structure then determining the compensation structure. The official structure of compensation in an organization is periodically examined in light of market and other changes, and discrepancies (evidenced through difficulties in finding people to fill jobs or by the existence of maneuvering and bargaining to obtain overvalued jobs) tend to be rectified. Every organization also has some scheme for assessing individuals that is a counterpart to the one used in assessing jobs. Discrepancies between the control structure and the compensation structure can occur not only because of market changes but also because of changes in individuals and because of initial imperfections in analysis of the control or compensation structures. Those discrepancies may be rectified by adjusting *any* of the variables—the role, role occupant, or the compensation. This process tends to be continuous, consisting of marginal adjustments throughout the organization. It thus becomes possible to infer the control structure of the organization from its compensation structure and to compare organizations with one another at the same or different points in time.

Perceived Interpersonal Control. A more restricted concept of control than that just discussed has been used in organization research by investigators at the University of Michigan. In this case, control is defined as a process of interpersonal influence. Control is exerted *by* members, *on* members in accomplishment of the organization task. Further, control is exerted only to the extent that it is perceived by members of the organization. Those individuals who work in relative isolation from most other members of the organization, therefore, will likely be seen as having relatively little influence (control) over others. Research personnel and staff analysts would be examples, as would presidents.[7] For that matter, anyone in the organization lying beyond the perceptual range of respondents would also be likely to have little influence attributed to them.

The measure of control is provided by asking all members of an organizational unit to indicate on a scale the amount of influence that other members of the organization—identified by hierarchical levels—exert upon individuals at each level of the hierarchy. (This questionnaire is described in detail on pp. 16-17.) These attributions are then summed and averaged by hierarchical level.[8]

Span of Control. The literature of classical organization theory has given a prominent place to the span of control. It has been argued occasionally that a large span of control (a high subordinate-to-superior ratio) indicates a high degree of decentralization: "If the manager practices close supervision, if he is constantly checking the work of subordinates, and if he insists upon prior approval of all decisions . . . made by the subordinate, then he is decreasing the number of people

---

[7]A recurring phenomenon in empirical studies using the "control graph" is the perception of the top man in the organization as having less influence than his immediate subordinates.

[8]This aggregation greatly reduces the precision of the measure for purposes of the present study. Later, we deal with the problem it created for us—that of inferring the influence or control of the individual.

he can supervise. He broadens his span by granting them more authority to take action without checking back with him on all details. On a company-wide basis, this is analogous to centralized vs. decentralized operations."[9] The costs of queuing time set limits on the span of control, if nothing else does.

The concept of control is again that of interpersonal influence, or control, in this case between a superior and his subordinates. The span of control becomes a visible map of the formally planned or intended pattern of interpersonal control. The span of control defines a two-level work group, with control shared between the two levels, among the superior and his subordinates. The average individual share is inversely proportional to the number-sharing. Thus, increasing the span of control reduces the relative control of the superior, *ceteris paribus*.

Concepts and Indexes of Centralization of Control

Discussion up to this point has been restricted to different concepts of the process of control and to the measures associated with them. We need to give consideration now to concepts and measures of centralization. Starting with the three concepts of control, we can develop concepts of centralization and viable measures of centralization associated with them.

If, as Von Bertalanffy states, centralization is an attribute of a system or structure, to study centralization we need first to specify the structure to which it applies. Our interest centers on control, considered up to this point as a dimension of individual behavior. To get an analogue that is a dimension of organizational behavior we must define the control structure. Given a definition of control structure, we can then derive a concept of centralization related to it as well as an index of centralization based upon this concept.

These concepts and measures of control structure and centralization are spelled out below for each of the three concepts of individual control.

System Control. The structure of control can be defined as the array of individual valences (relative amounts) or control (as reflected in individual compensation) for the entire membership of the organization. Centralization is a condition of concentration of control in the hands of a few members. The limiting case of centralization is the assignment of all control to one member. The limiting case of decentralization is the peer group, with all members assigned equal control.

Appropriate indexes of centralization are measures of inequality of distribution of individual compensation.

Perceived Interpersonal Control. The structure of control again can be defined as an array—in this case, of perceived individual valences (relative amounts) of influence or control over others (as reflected by questionnaire responses). Centralization is the concentration of interpersonal control in a few members, with the extreme case of centralization (approached as a limit) being that where one member has all the perceived control and the others none. The limiting case of decentralization is that where all members have equal perceived control (a peer group).

Again, appropriate indexes of centralization are measures of inequality of distribution of individual influence.

Span of Control. The structure of control is the network of interconnected spans of control as mapped on a typical organization chart. In this case, following

[9]Janger, *op. cit.*

302

the arguments of Janger and others, we define centralization as a condition where the spans of control are relatively narrow, with the limiting case of centralization being a chain of one-for-one superior-subordinate relationships and the limiting case of decentralization being a single superior for the whole organization.

An appropriate index of centralization is the average span of control for the entire organization, or for such part of it as one chooses for study.

In Table 2 we summarize the concepts and measures just discussed and add them to those presented in Table 1.

TABLE 2   Measures and Concepts of Control, Control Structure,
and Centralization of Control

Control as it Pertains to Individuals		Control as it Pertains to Organization		
Concept of Control	Measure of Control	Structure of Control	Concept of Centralization of Control	Index(es) of Centralization of Control
A. System control	A. Individual compensation	A. Array of individual variances of control (individual compensation)	A. Concentration of individual control	A. Measures of inequality of distribution of individual compensation
B. Perceived interpersonal control	B. Scaled perceptions of individual influence	B. Array of individual variances of control (questionnaire responses)	B. Concentration of individual control	B. Measures of inequality of distribution of control variances from questionnaire
C. Formally defined interpersonal control	C. Span of control	C. Network of interconnected individual spans of control	C. Narrowness of control	C. Average span of control

Congruence of Concepts and Measures

We indicated earlier that it appears to us that the concepts underlying the three measures we have chosen to study represent different orders of explanatory power. System control encompasses both interpersonal control and direct task control and is thus broader than either perceived interpersonal control or formally defined interpersonal control.

However, since the broader concept includes the other two, we expect that overlap or congruence would always exist in indexes of centralization developed from them. Furthermore, we believe that it is possible to specify the organizational conditions under which the congruence would be high and those under which it would be low. Specifying these conditions makes it possible to test our earlier inferences about the differences in the control concepts.

The conditions to which we refer relate to the degree of routineness of organization activities and to the derivative standardization of individual tasks and rationalization of the authority and communication structures. There are, on the one hand, organizations, usually operating under stable conditions, with rather narrowly defined goals and detailed programs for achieving these goals. Many production departments fall under this heading. There are, on the other hand, organizations with more broadly defined goals, organizations that not only must devise solutions to problems but often have the responsibility for defining the problems in the first place. A variety of "staff" departments in a modern corporation would fit this description.

In the first kind of organization (routine) we expect a substantial congruence among indexes of centralization based upon the three concepts of control. System control will be exercised largely *through* other members (an operating hierarchy) with only those at the bottom exerting the direct personal-effort kind of control through their work. We would expect continuous efforts at rationalization of tasks to remove ambiguities in the supervisor-subordinate relationship with a consequent reinforcement of formal influence relationships. Perceived influence should reflect this reinforcement. Real differences in concepts should, in this case, have little empirical significance.

In the second kind of organization (problem-solving), low congruence should be expected. Many members of the organization will be working individually and independently for much of the time. Interpersonal influence, whether formally defined or perceived, will describe only part of the behavior of such an organization. Formally defined influence will also describe a smaller subset of behaviors than in the first case, since influence relationships should shift from problem to problem (on the assumption that authority of knowledge dominates and some specialization of knowledge is present). Perceived influence may well be at odds with the formal map.

Our empirical test will involve correlation of indexes of centralization under the different conditions. In a set of organizational units that perform routine tasks, variance should reflect largely errors of measurement, and correlations should be substantial. In a set of problem-solving organizational units, variance should reflect both errors of measurement and the disparity in concepts. Correlations should be low.

THE EMPIRICAL STUDY

Design

The empirical study was designed to get answers to two questions: (1) What is the degree of congruence or overlap of the three concepts when indexes of centralization derived from them are applied to a set of organizations? (2) Can we substantiate our inferences about the differences among the control concepts?

To answer the first question, we obtained compensation, perceived-influence, and span-of-control data for a set of departments. Using these data in the indexes of centralization we generated three series of index numbers for the departments and computed their intercorrelations.

To answer the second question, we obtained a rank ordering of the departments in terms of the degree of routinization of tasks. We then compared size-matched subsets of the departments, subsets chosen from different parts of the continuum. We expected correlations among the index-numbers series to be higher in the more routinized subset than in the size-matched less-routinized subset. We were able to make this comparison twice, for two pairs of samples.

Research Site and Data

Data were gathered on seventy-three departments within a large insurance firm, each with its own head and formal structure. This group of departments includes thirty in the home office performing a variety of functions (personnel, organization analysis, legal, reinsurance, etc.) and forty-three branch claims offices performing an identical function in different locations throughout the United States. The size range of these departments in terms of number of individuals is shown in Table 3. Four kinds of data were collected on these departments:

TABLE 3   Size of Departments Used in the Study

Size	Thirty Home-Office Departments	Forty-three Branch Claims Offices	All Seventy-three Departments
Smallest	3	2	2
Largest	44	75	75
Median	9	7	8
Mean	10.4	11.1	10.8
Standard deviation	8.1	14.5	12.2

1. **Individual Compensation.** Monthly salaries were obtained for every individual in each department for the pay period during which the influence questionnaire was completed within the particular department. These salaries were used as compensation data, fringe items being ignored. No bonuses or incentive payments were involved.

2. **Influence-Questionnaire Responses.** The questionnaire, a portion of which is shown in Figure 1, was used to gather perceptions of influence. It is quite similar to those used by Tannenbaum and others in studies of organizational control. The data used in this study were the responses to the question shown in Figure 1, in which respondents are asked to indicate by check marks their estimate of the influence exerted by each identified group in the department on every other group in that department. Responses were given values from one to five, left to right. The influence of each level or group is the mean value of responses of all members in the department.

3. **Reporting Relationships.** A review of reporting relationships and a classification of organizational levels were made jointly by corporate staff personnel and individual department heads at the same time that other data were gathered. We could thus pinpoint each superior and his span of control.

4. **Ranking on a Task Continuum.** Three staff members of the company (organization and job analysts) made a joint ranking of the seventy-three depart-

In general, how much influence do the people in <u>one</u>* group have on what the following individuals or groups do in the company?	Little or no influence	Some influence	Quite a bit of influence	A great deal of influence	A very great deal of influence
The individuals in group two					
The individuals in group three					
The individuals in group four					
The individuals in group five					
The individuals in group six					

JOB GROUPS
A & H BRANCH CLAIM PERSONNEL

Group One	Divisional Claim Supervisor
Group Two	District Manager
Group Three	District Supervisors
Group Four	Clerical Supervisors
Group Five	Adjusting Personnel (Adjusters, Examiners, etc.)
Group Six	Clerical

*Question repeated for each group, one through six

FIGURE 1   Sample Question on Influence Questionnaire

ments in order, from that with the least routinized tasks to the most routinized. (These analysts have no connection, formal or otherwise, with those who establish wage and salary structure.) All forty-three branch offices, which performed the same task and thus received the same ranking, fell below eighteen less routinized home-office departments and above twelve more routinized home-office departments.

Index Construction

For each of the three definitions of centralization of control we sought indexes of centralization that could be applied to whole organizations or to parts of them, with a minimum of data transformation necessary to their application. It turned out that the only transformation involved was made necessary by the nature of the questionnaire data available to us. (See Section A, below.)

Indexes of Inequality of Distribution of Compensation. Several indexes were devised, all derived from cumulative frequency distributions expressed in percentages (Lorenz distributions). The items in these distributions were individual compensation figures.

As a global index of centralization we used a modified Gini ratio of concentration (see Appendix I). Portions of the total compensation distribution in each department also were examined in indexes calculated. These indexes were the percentages of total compensation earned by the highest paid 20, 30, 40, and 50 per cent of the members.

A data transformation was necessary. The reason lies in the fact that the influence-questionnaire data, with which we wish to compare compensation data, are averages computed from questionnaire responses focused on groups. Since true individual compensation figures are available, true individual influence ratings would be desirable.

Because it was not possible to get such individual ratings,[10] we reduced compensation data to the same level of imprecision as the influence data *for purposes of comparing perceived influence and compensation indexes, only.*[11] That is, we computed the average compensation for each member of each group in each department (the groups being identical to those used in measuring perceived influence). This figure was used to compute indexes of concentration of *adjusted* (average) compensation in the same fashion as indexes of concentration of *true* compensation were computed.

Indexes based upon true compensation were used for comparison with span of control. Indexes based upon adjusted compensation were used for comparison with perceived influence.

Indexes of Inequality of Distribution of Perceived Influence. Indexes similar to those described in Section A were computed. In this case, items in the distributions were individual influence valences.

A problem of data interpretation arose in connection with these indexes. The reason lay, once again, in the fact that questionnaire responses pertained to *groups* and we wanted *individual* valences. The number representing the influence exerted by a group is a mean of individual responses. A critical question arises as to what the respondent intends when he assigns an influence valence to a group. Does this number represent the combined influence of all those in the group or the influence of an average member of the group? Either response could follow logically from the

---

[10]Questionnaire data had already been gathered by corporate personnel for other purposes. We borrowed the data in the only form in which they were available—expressing the influence of groups.

[11]Had we not done so, we would have incorporated an error of measurement substantially reducing correlation coefficients.

wording of the question; the respondent is given no further guidance by the questionnaire.

As far as we know, those who have used this questionnaire have not attempted to answer the question raised. Tannenbaum and Kahn, in describing scaling problems associated with this technique, do not raise the issue.[12]

We asked a sample of the respondents in the company (after a time lapse of three months) to tell us what they meant when they made their responses. They were unable to answer the question with any certainty, except to say that their rating was *not* influenced by the number of people at each level.

Therefore, we made a preliminary comparison of influence and compensation data to get some clue to aid us in interpreting the responses. This procedure is described in Appendix II. On the basis of the two tests described there, we decided to calculate the index of perceived influence on the assumption that respondents were actually describing the influence exerted by the average member in a given group.

Index of Concentration of Formally Assigned Control. We used the simplest global index we could devise, the average span of control. Its computation is simply $(N - 1)/S$, where S is the number of department members who have at least one subordinate, N is the total membership, and $N - 1$ is the number who are subordinates in the department.

TABLE 4 Simple Correlation Coefficients Among Various Indexes
of Centralization

Correlations between:	Home-Office Departments (N = 30)	Branch Offices (N = 43)	All Departments (N = 73)
Concentration of compensation* (adjusted) and concentration of influence*	.62	.48	.53
Concentration of compensation* (true) and average span of control	−.68	−.52	−.60
Average span of control and concentration of influence*	−.66	−.55	−.56
Proportion of total compensation and proportion of total influence held by *i* per cent of department members, where *i* = top:			
20 per cent	.36	.26	.24
30 per cent	.47	.21	.31
40 per cent	.58	.19	.40
50 per cent	.60	.20	.41

*Modified Gini ratios of concentration.

Correlation

In Table 4 we show correlations among the indexes for the seventy-three departments and for the subsamples of thirty home-office departments and forty-three branch claims offices. Where the average span of control is used as an index

[12]*Op. cit.*

the sign is negative as expected, since greater centralization is associated with a larger ratio of concentration and a smaller span of control.

To get at the effects of the degree of task-programing on correlations among the indexes of centralization, we used the forty-three branch offices as a reference group. Performing an identical departmental task, these units had been placed on the task continuum just behind the eighteenth and ahead of the nineteenth home-office departments by the organization analysts who functioned as judges. (The farther down the ranks a department is placed, the more routine and programed its activities are; see Figure 2.)

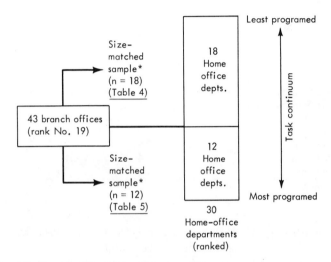

* Ten branch offices appear in both samples

FIGURE 2   Schematic Illustration of Method of Drawing
Size-matched Samples to Show Task Effects

Thus the branch offices came close to being in the middle of the distribution on the task continuum. Taking advantage of the large number of units performing an identical job, we tested the task-effect hypothesis twice.

First of all, we compared the correlations among eighteen home-office departments at the "least programed" end of the task continuum with the correlations among the forty-three branch offices and the latter, in turn, with the correlations among the twelve home-office departments at the "most programed" end. The results are shown in Table 5.

Our second test was performed only because we noticed that the smallest home-office departments were concentrated in the least programed end of the continuum. While we know of no reason a priori to expect departmental size to affect the correlations we are examining, the existence of the branch offices permitted us to control for size by a sample-matching technique.

We matched as closely as possible, on the basis of size (see Table 6), the eighteen departments ranked ahead of the branch offices (toward the least programed end of the continuum) with eighteen of the branch offices. Thus we had two subgroups between which correlations were run as before. The results are shown in Table 7.

TABLE 5   Simple Correlation Coefficients for Control-Structure Measures

Correlations between:	Least Programed Home-Office Departments (N = 18)	Branch Offices (N = 43)	Most Programed Home-Office Departments (N = 12)
Concentration of compensation* (adjusted) and concentration of influence*	.16	.48	.86
Concentration of compensation* (true) and average span of control	−.31	−.52	−.75
Average span of control and concentration of influence*	−.38	−.55	−.64
Proportion of total compensation and proportion of total in influence held by *i* per cent of departments members, where *i* = top:			
20 per cent	.19	.26	.65
30 per cent	.15	.21	.86
40 per cent	.14	.19	.91
50 per cent	.01	.20	.90

*Modified Gini ratios of concentration.

TABLE 6   Pairings of Departments from the Home-Office
and Branch-Office Groups

Department Sizes in the Pairing of Twelve Branch and Twelve Home-Office Departments		Department Sizes in the Pairing of Twelve Branch and Twelve Home-Office Departments	
Branch*	Home Office	Branch*	Home Office
6	5	3	3
11	11	9	9
12	12	9	9
9	9	12	12
9	8	3	3
7	8	2	3
19	18	10	10
7	8	5	5
9	9	6	6
23	24	5	5
14	13	7	7
36	44	14	14
		4	3
		11	12
		6	6
		19	20
		9	9
		7	8

*Ten branch claims offices are common to both samples.

TABLE 7   Simple Correlation Coefficients for Control-Structure Measures

Correlations between:	Least Programed Home-Office Departments (N = 18)	Size-matched Branch Offices (N = 18)
Concentration of compensation* (adjusted) and concentration of influence*	.16	.70
Concentration of compensation* (true) and average span of control	−.31	−.37
Average span of control and concentration of influence*	−.38	−.68
Proportion of total compention and proportion of total influence held by *i* per cent of department members, where *i* = top:		
20 per cent	.19	.23
30 per cent	.15	.32
40 per cent	.14	.41
50 per cent	.01	.42

*Modified Gini ratios of concentration.

Similarly, we compared the twelve departments ranked below the branch offices (more routine) with a size-matched sample of twelve branch offices. Correlations are shown in Table 8. Figure 2 shows, schematically, how these comparisons were made.

ANALYSIS AND DISCUSSION

Over-All Relationships

The three independent indexes of centralization exhibit varying degrees of correlation, in the expected direction, in these seventy-three departments (Table 4). The global indexes (indexes describing centralization in a department as a whole) correlate more highly than do those measuring the relative control exercised by parts of these units (what we have called partial indexes).

The rather low coefficients obtained for fractions of these units could result from discontinuities and errors of measurement in very small groups. A fifth or a third of, say, a nine-person department gives one very little to work with. Our purpose in considering such partial indexes comes from the fact that, especially in large organizations, one often is interested in changes in segments of the control structure. One example would be an assessment of the effectiveness of division-alization as a device for decentralizing corporate top managerial control. Another would be testing the notion that installation of computer systems tends to shift control from middle to upper levels of management.

TABLE 8   Simple Correlation Coefficients for Control-Structure Measures

Correlations between:	Most Programed Home-Office Departments (N = 12)	Size-matched Branch Offices (N = 12)
Concentration of compensation* (adjusted) and concentration of influence*	.86	.49
Concentration of compensation* (true) and average span of control	−.75	−.26
Average span of control and concentration of influence*	−.64	−.28
Proportion of total compensation and proportion of total influence held by i per cent of department members, where i = top		
20 per cent	.65	.52
30 per cent	.86	.59
40 per cent	.91	.55
50 per cent	.90	.36

*Modified Gini ratios of concentration.

Furthermore, a global index may conceal as much as it reveals. Conceivably, shifts in concentration of control from one part of the organization to another could occur without any consequent change in the modified Gini ratio appearing. And a change in the global index simply tells one that a change in concentration of control has occurred without pinpointing its location. Hence our emphasis upon partial indexes.

The low coefficients yielded for the smallest fractions of these small departments would make one cautious about accepting these indexes as effective substitutes for one another under such conditions. In larger organizations, errors of measurement arising out of the discontinuities of small size should be a lesser problem, making partial indexes more reliable and the substitution of one of the three indexes for another more acceptable.

The data in Table 4 provide a tentative answer to the first question the study sought to answer. Were we able to get more precise data we would hope that the correlation among the indexes would be somewhat higher, perhaps by another ten points on the average. But, in any event, the remaining variance is sufficiently large to make tenable our assumptions of differences in basic concepts of control.

Control for Degree of Task-Programing

The second question in the study related our ability to demonstrate empirically the differences imputed analytically to the different concepts of control. Our prediction was that in more highly programed task situations the control concepts would tend toward congruence and that indexes developed from them would show higher correlations.

Tables 6, 7, and 8 show that, on two trials, both the global indexes and the partial indexes behaved as predicted.[13] We believe this behavior to reinforce strongly our assumption that we have identified three basically different ways of defining organizational control and that these indexes give cognizance to them.

General Conclusions

This study must be classified as criteria research. We started with three proposed criteria of an organizational variable—centralization of control—that seemed to us not only to use different organizational data but to have distinctive conceptual underpinnings.

We sought to test empirically the degree to which they yielded comparable results in comparing a group of organizations. In this respect we were motivated by a practical concern. The researcher cannot always get the sort of data in one organization that he can in another. Hence, we hoped that it might turn out that alternative measures would correlate to a degree that would permit free substitution.

We also sought evidence to support our belief that these criteria were based upon different concepts of control and control structure—differences that could be defined formally and operationally. Our interest here was both theoretical and practical. The structure of control has always been a muddy concept and attempts to measure it usually abortive.

We think we have found evidence to support two conclusions: (1) The three measures analyzed do not relate to a common construct or concept but to three different constructs that are closely related under certain specifiable conditions in an organization and that are quite unrelated under others. These "conditions" appear to be summed under the heading of the degree of routinization or programing of the organizational task. Where the organizational task is highly programed, the shape of the formal structure, the distribution of individual control over organizational achievement, and the perception of interpersonal authority and influence relationships will be highly correlated. We found that, with highly programed tasks, correlations varied from [.64] to [.86]. Where the organizational task is relatively unprogramed, they will tend to diverge. In this situation, we found correlation coefficients to range from [.16] to [.38]. (2) Except in studies confined to organizations characterized by loosely structured and unprogramed tasks, the three indexes of centralization may be used empirically as substitutes for one another. For our total group of seventy-three departments, with no control for degree of task-programing, coefficients ranged from [.48] to [.68].

In our judgment, those engaged in empirical research would select one of these measures of centralization of control on the basis of the following considerations:

1. *The control construct most relevant to other variables studied.*—System control is likely to be most relevant where other variables relate to the organization as a whole, for example, cultural or demographic differences in the environment, technological change, changes in size or dispersion. The same is true of span of control, especially when the other variables are "internal" in nature, such as

---

[13]The correlation coefficient between compensation and span of control in the second column of Table 8 takes on a positive sign. In the population of forty-three branch offices, correlation between these two measures is -.52. We found, from examination of the appropriate scatter diagram, that the twelve offices we chose for size-matching purposes unfortunately happened to yield observations producing this small but positive correlation.

technology and task complexity. Perceived control is apt to be most relevant when psychological variables are studied.

2. *The ease of use.*—In this regard, one can see appreciable qualitative differences in these measures. Questionnaire data are costly and difficult to gather. Compensation data, already generated, are often treated as confidential in private business, although they frequently are freely available elsewhere. Formal organization structures are there for the asking, provided one has a reliable and knowledgeable informant or provided that the organization maintains and preserves charts. The availability of various kinds of data is often related to the industry or local research site within which research is carried out.

3. *The research design.*—Two considerations are important here. One concerns specifically the use of a longitudinal (before-and-after) design. If one seeks to compare the present with the past, the influence-questionnaire measure is unfeasible (unless one can find a situation in which the questionnaire had for some reason been administered earlier). It would be necessary to use either the span of control or compensation measures. Second, when one encounters informally organized groups, or organizations that do not use monetary compensation, the influence questionnaire or some variation on it may be the only feasible measure among the three.

APPENDIX I: CONSTRUCTION OF CENTRALIZATION INDEXES FROM CUMULATIVE FREQUENCY DISTRIBUTIONS

Global Index (Modified Gini Ratio of Concentration)

To measure centralization, using compensation data and influence-questionnaire data in the seventy-three departments, we selected the Gini ratio of concentration. This measure has been widely used by others, especially by economists studying income distribution.

The Gini ratio, based upon Lorenz distributions, has some inherent limitations[14] but seemed the best measure available for our purposes where the departments (and distributions) are quite small. However, the very fact of small size made a modification of the Gini ratio necessary.

Consider the Lorenz diagram shown in Figure 3. The side AB represents the cumulative number of members in the department, the side BC the cumulative compensation or influence in the department, and the curve AEC the cumulative frequency distribution of either salaries or influence ratings, ranked from the lowest to the highest.

Normally, the Gini ratio of concentration is computed as the ratio of the area $AECA$ to the area $ABCA$, supposedly the ratio of the observed area of deviation from equality to the largest possible area of deviation. But, strictly speaking, the maximum area of deviation is not $ABCA$ but $AFCA$, where AF is the total membership less one, a situation where all compensation or interpersonal influence is held by one member, while the others hold none. In many applications of the ratio (e.g., large labor markets), it does not matter greatly that $ABCA$ is substituted for $AFCA$. When numbers are large, the area $FCBF$ is very small. But in our case $FCBF$ can be

[14]See Mary Jean Bowman, "A Graphical Analysis of Personal Measure Distribution in the United States," *American Economic Review*, XXV, No. 4 (1945), 607-28, and "The Analysis of Inequality Patterns: A Methodological Contribution," *Metron*, XVIII, Nos. 1-2 (1956), 2 ff.

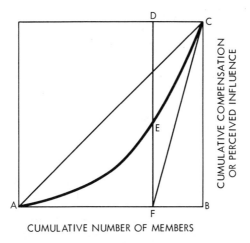

FIGURE 3   Lorenz Diagram, Illustrating the
Modification of the Gini Ratio

quite large (e.g., in a five-member department *FCBF* comprises one fifth and in a two-member department one-half, of *ABCA*). Therefore, in order to adhere to a strict interpretation of the rationale of the Gini index of concentration, it was necessary to use the ratio of area *AECA* to the area *AFCA*.

In addition, to compute indexes of concentration of compensation and perceived influence at various points of the compensation or perceived-influence distributions, we calculated the second, third, fourth, and fifth decile deviation in each of the seventy-three departments. For instance, the second decile deviation indicates the percentage of control (compensation or perceived influence) held by the top 20 per cent of the department's members. In terms of the Lorenz diagram above, this is equal to the ratio of *DE* to *CB,* assuming that *FB* comprises the department's 20 per cent top employees. These decile deviations are relatively easy to understand and compute and have been discussed and used in this context in an earlier study.[15]

APPENDIX II: INTERPRETATION
OF INFLUENCE-QUESTIONNAIRE RATINGS

In order to calculate indexes of centralization of perceived influence for each department, it was necessary to determine whether the influence-questionnaire ratings made by each member for each level of a department represented the perceived influence of the total level or of the average member at that level. To illustrate the point, consider the first four columns in Table 9. These columns contain information obtained from a sample department. If the influence ratings in column (3) are assumed to pertain to the average member at the given level (assumption A), then the total perceived influence exerted in that department is 18.80; if the ratings denote the total control of all members at a level, then the departmental total is 7.34.

[15]Whisler, *op. cit.*

TABLE 9   Salaries and Influence Ratings for a Nine-Member Department

Group (Level)	No. of Members (1)	Salaries Received (Dollars) (2)	Influence Rating (3)	Per Cent of Total Salary Received by Group (4)	Percentage of Total Influence for Group under Assumption	
					A* (5)	B† (6)
1	1	$775	3.52	20.4	18.7	48.0
2	4	467, 550, 500, 425	2.30	51.1	48.9	31.3
3	4	280, 275, 275, 255	1.52	28.5	32.4	20.7
Total	9	3,802	A*: 18.80 B†: 7.34	100.0	100.0	100.0

*Assumption A: The influence rating represents influence of the average member of the group.
†Assumption B: The influence rating represents the influence of the group as a whole.

Several months after administration of the questionnaire, we asked a sample of respondents what they meant when they made their responses. They were unable to answer the question with certainty, except to say that they did not adjust their answer to the number of people at each level.

Since this direct approach proved fruitless, we engaged in two calculations. First, for every department we computed the relative share of total salaries paid to each level and the relative share of total perceived influence for each level under both assumptions (columns (4)-(6). These computations were made for all 273 levels in the seventy-three departments, and correlations between influence and compensation shares were calculated. When assuming the perceived-influence ratings (as in column [3]) to pertain to the average member of the level, then the simple correlation coefficient between the relative share of salaries (column 4) of the 243 levels and the corresponding influence shares (column [5]) was +.93. When assuming the perceived-influence ratings to express the control of the entire level, then the corresponding correlation coefficient is +.27.

We made a second and different kind of test. Choosing the clerical (fourth) level from a random sample of twenty branch claims offices (all performing the same task), we correlated the number of members in each department at this level with the total perceived influence of the level in each department under both assumptions. Under assumption A, the simple correlation coefficient is +.90; assuming the rating reflects the total influence of the level, the correlation coefficient is +.16.

On the basis of the outcome of these two tests, and the rater statements referred to earlier, we assumed the questionnaire ratings to represent ratings of the perceived influence of the average member at a given level.

20

INTERNAL CONTROL RELATIONS IN
ADMINISTRATIVE HIERARCHIES *

BENJAMIN WALTER

In view of the crucial importance of different types of influence relations linking superiors and subordinates for administrative theory, it is astonishing to find that empirical examinations of organizations have given scant attention to the subject.[1] Indeed, the entire problem was barely touched by early administrative theory, which obdurately would acknowledge only hierarchical control relationships, with lines of authority running from boss to employee. Hierarchical position alone conferred the right to issue authoritative directions. At least prescriptively, the ability to exact compliance originated at the very apex of the administrative structure and, by a process of continuous vertical delegation, ramified throughout in an ever-expanding pyramid.[2] Through the chain of command, each superior was supposed to supply his subordinates with the communications needed to coordinate their behavior, a point of view oddly reminiscent of medieval theories of political sovereignty.

So pictured, control relationships in administrative organizations were tidy and asymmetrical; at any level, superiors were able to control subordinates, but at no echelon could subordinates control superiors. This notion of organizational life could not withstand rigorous analysis. Drawing upon a miscellaneous fund of empirical observations, some barely more than anecdote or reminiscence, Chester I. Barnard and Herbert A. Simon noted that many pervasive influence relations diverged sharply from the norm that received theory had certified.[3]

Superiors, Barnard and Simon remarked, often defer to the presumed

*Administrative Science Quarterly, September 1966, pp. 179-206.

[1]For a recent exception, see David Mechanic, Sources of Power of Lower Participants in Complex Organizations, *Administrative Science Quarterly,* 7 (1962), 349-64; and the handful of empirical studies that Mechanic summarizes.

[2]One irritating difficulty in summarizing classical administrative theory springs from the artless way it jumbled descriptive and normative statements together. On one reading it would seem that theorists were asserting that hierarchical control patterns were the rule in operating organizations; on another, that they were desirable to increase the probabilities of maximizing some values. To make bad matters even worse, these desiderata were generally left unspecified. For a sharp criticism of this tendency and an appraisal of the mischief it created, see James G. March and Herbert A. Simon, *Organizations* (New York: John Wiley, 1958), pp. 30-33.

[3]Chester I. Barnard, *Functions of the Executive* (Cambridge, Mass.: Harvard University, 1938), pp. 163-175; Herbert A. Simon, *Administrative Behavior* (New York: Macmillan, 1951), pp. 123-153; and Herbert A. Simon, Donald W. Smithburg, and Victor A. Thompson, *Public Administration* (New York: Alfred A. Knopf, 1950), pp. 189-201.

technical expertise of their subordinates. Though they may be officially announced by superiors, comprehensive policies are often initiated and elaborated by employees six or seven levels beneath them on the organizational chart. Within variable and ill-defined limits, workers are able to band together and haggle over the compensations they are willing to accept in return for their contribution of labor and talent. Employees can exploit a rich ensemble of cunning strategies to redress the severe imbalance of hierarchical sanctions that classical theory granted their superiors. They may obey managerial commands in perversely literal fashion, and "go slow" campaigns are indications that directives to increase output have been subtly but effectively countermanded. They may appeal to some external constituency to impose a veto on an immediate superior. Under extreme conditions, they may mutiny.

The careful distinctions that Barnard and Simon drew were of greater logical than empirical significance. What they showed is that, once an appropriate operational definition has been supplied, it is not at all absurd to speak of subordinates wielding control over superiors. Even the possibility of subordinate control over superiors was conceptually forbidden by earlier administrative theory, which declared that superior position was the sole basis of authority in organizations.

PATHS OF INFLUENCE AND TYPES OF DECISION

The empirical question that arises is: Under what conditions is the influence of subordinates likely to be maximal? William R. Dill has perceptively observed that one pair of hypotheses venerated in administrative folklore holds that the autonomy of subordinates peaks when making routine choices but declines sharply on novel decisions.[4] For decisions that occur repeatedly during the course of everyday organizational routine, the criteria for making correct decisions are so minutely governed by settled precedent, explicit regulation, and standard operating procedure that overt supervision would be either redundant or resented. The complement to this hypothesis states that for the infrequently encountered but momentous choices that irretrievably commit scarce resources and unavoidably entail risk and uncertainty, superiors do not (or should not) allow their subordinates the autonomy they enjoy in making recurrent decisions.

At the outset of this study it was hypothesized (1) that far from being autonomous on nonrecurrent choices, superiors are constrained by their subordinates, and conversely (2) that the autonomy of subordinates declines on routine decisions. The purpose of the study reported here was to subject this pair of hypotheses to empirical test.[5]

It is unfortunate that the concept of autonomy has no settled empirical content, even after long use. A rather straightforward modification of Dill's definition is used here, which equates "autonomy" with "freedom from in-

---

[4]William R. Dill, Environment as an Influence on Managerial Autonomy, *Administrative Science Quarterly*, 2 (March 1958), 409-433.

[5]Robert K. Merton has referred to the "serendipity pattern" in science, the unexpected encounter of data sharply incompatible with accepted theory. Because they are impressionistic, such chance discoveries have only marginal value as evidence, but they do serve to stimulate disciplined inquiry.

As an enlisted man, I noticed that troops could often get their way on what are here called nonprogrammed choices but that it was tough to hoodwink officers on routine matters. These impressions were corroborated by enlisted men in other sections, and suggested the hypotheses here proposed for test.

fluence",[6] the inference "the more a man is influenced, the less autonomous he is" follows directly. The hypotheses may then be rephrased:

1. Subordinates influence superiors on nonrecurring choices more than superiors influence subordinates.
2. Superiors influence subordinates on recurrent choices more than subordinates influence superiors.

RESEARCH DESIGN: RATIONALE AND METHODS

The research design in this analysis was devised to identify and enumerate acts of interpersonal influence as they occurred in making organizational decisions. Although they were continuously supplemented by brief interviews, systematic observations in actual organizations provided most of the data. Few empirical studies of organizational behavior depend principally on "capture-and-record" techniques; most rely on retrospective questionnaires and interviews.[7] The decision to use this rather heterodox procedure was prompted by a report published by Tom Burns over a decade ago.[8] He asked a number of executives in a British engineering firm to keep records of their behavior on precoded forms that Burns had devised. After the journals had been collected, collated, and analyzed, Burns asked each executive to summarize his "typical" behavior in terms of the categories all the executives had used in keeping their diaries. The comparison of the observational data with the summary recollections disclosed many crucial disparities; more to the point, the administrators themselves were astounded by the sharp incongruities between the two. Indeed, analysis of the journals revealed that participants in the same episode of interaction would render accounts at odds with one another. For example, in forty per cent of the cases when a superior announced he had given a subordinate an "instruction," the subordinate would concede only that he had accepted "advice." Burns' article wryly hints that an informant's assessment of his relationships with others may be systematically distorted by his refusal to assault

[6]*Op. cit.,* p. 411. Note that Dill's proposal permits one to speak of varying degrees of autonomy or of relative autonomy. As usually defined, "independence" allows only a dichotomous classification; either a man is independent, or he is not. But, if A influences B more than B influences A, then A is a relatively more autonomous than B. These usages will be followed throughout the paper.

[7]The use of nonparticipant observers to capture some of the more elusive behavioral processes of organizational life was urged some time ago by Herbert A. Simon. See his "Recent Advances in Organization Theory" in Stephen K. Bailey (ed.), *Research Frontiers in Politics and Government* (Washington, D.C.: Brookings Institution, 1955), pp. 23-44.

The inspiration for the particular research strategy used in this study came from the work of Robert Bales in the Harvard Laboratory of Social Relations. See "Some Uniformities of Behavior in Small Social Systems" in Guy B. Swanson, Theodore M. Newcomb, and Eugene L. Hartley (eds.), *Readings in Social Psychology* (New York: Henry Holt, 1952), pp. 146-159.

[8]The Direction of Activity and Communication in a Departmental Executive Group: A Quantitative Study in a British Engineering Factory with a Self-recording Technique, *Human Relations,* 7 (1954), 73-87.

Rensis Likert has also warned "An individual's reaction to any situation is always a function not of the absolute character of the interaction, but of his perception of it. It is how he sees things that counts, not objective reality." See "A Motivation Approach to the Modified Theory of Organization and Management," in Mason Haire (ed.), *Modern Organization Theory* (New York: John Wiley, 1959), p. 191.

the integrity of his own perceived status. To rely *exclusively* on a respondent's appraisal of his own behavior is to introduce perceptual errors of unknown magnitude. Despite the impressive achievements of survey techniques and the prestige they have deservedly enjoyed, they seemed singularly inappropriate for this study. For this reason it was decided to combine interview and observation, rather than depend uncritically upon participant reports alone.[9]

The core of the research design is the categorization of behavior acts as they are observed, one by one, in making a composite organization decision. The design is composed of two separate elements: (*1*) a *communications audit*, a classification of different types of organizational communications and a tracing of the paths they follow, and (*2*) a *categorization* and *tabulation* of the recipient's reaction to the information transmitted by the communicator. This is the phase of the research design where influence transactions are operationally identified for tabulation.

AUDITING COMMUNICATIONS[10]

Within any organization, men transmit information to one another. As organizations increase in size, the number of possible two-person channels and multiperson nets soon becomes very large. However, some linkages are never used at all; others convey information only intermittently; and only a small proportion of all those possible are used intensively. As communications flows are traced from initiation to destination, it is found that they tend to describe two distinct but overlapping networks; one, the hierarchical and lateral paths recognized by the official organization chart; the other, a luxuriant webbing established and maintained by tacit convention. The flow of information within an organization is *patterned*, not random, and whatever is patterned can be mapped.

For this research, organizational communications were separately classified in terms of two distinct dimensions: (*1*) the scope or type of decision to which the communication was relevant, and (*2*) the kind of information that the communication conveyed. Each dimension is treated in turn.

Scope or Type of Decision

The information that communications carry may be associated with either programmed or nonprogrammed decisions, to use a distinction that Herbert A.

[9]I wish to express my gratitude to David L. Mundy and William Smith, at one time graduate students in the department of psychology at the University of North Carolina. They observed and logged communications flows and influence reactions among a half-dozen top administrators in the governments of two North Carolina cities. Thanks are also due Judith Kovenock, Angell G. Beza, and Clyde Z. Nunn, all of whom assisted materially in coding and analyzing the data.

[10]What follows is an abbreviated sketch of the operational procedures. Limitations of space forced omission of the conventions used to transform messages as naturally written or spoken into individual premises or statements, which are the primary units for the quantitative analyses. For a more complete description, see David M. Kovenock, "Communications and Influence in Congressional Decision-Making: Employing the Communications Audit Technique in a U.S. House of Representatives Sub-Committee," unpublished paper delivered before the 1964 annual meeting of the American Political Science Association. As the title indicates, Kovenock adapted the procedures for use in another context.

Simon has repeatedly urged.[11] A programmed decision may be regarded as a largely (but not completely) prefabricated sequence of interrelated choices evoked by demands so frequently made that they can be stereotypes. The "program" is simply a shorthand expression for the battery of rules, directions, and criteria that specify how organizational actors are to respond to signals or other clearly defined stimuli. Portions of some programs are set in print, generally in manuals presenting standard operating procedures; more complicated and subtle decision-making routines are likely to be filed away in the memories of employees and managers. Organizations economize their resources by disaggregating complex tasks into components that can be easily managed by trained personnel. The program reduces each component of the job to a standardized and settled routine. All the routines are serially linked, so that the output of one simplified procedure becomes the input for the next. (In this respect, it resembles ordinary long division.) Programs may be simple or elaborately detailed. An example of a simple routine is the procedure followed by the billing clerk in sending accounts six months overdue to the organization's attorney for legal action. All she has to do is ascertain the date when the order was filled; from then on, her responses are determined by the authorized program. The leader of a bombing squadron uses a more complicated program in selecting targets. It permits him a small number of options, each one contingent on certain critical or limiting variables: his fuel supply, anticipated wind currents, and the casualties his unit has suffered along the way. His program is composed of a number of sub-routines, and he switches from one to another as the limiting factors dictate.[12]

Distinguished from such recurrent choices are the largely unprecedented actions called nonprogrammed decisions. Unlike programmed decisions, they cannot be resolved into a sequence of simple routines. They commonly call on the decision makers to construct models that summarize and define the situation confronting them. The models typically contain enough detail to promote comprehensive calculation of the impact that contemplated alternatives will make on the variables that are postulated and interrelated in an expanded network of means-ends relationships.[13] The model is used to explore and rehearse the consequences of proposed alternatives. For example, in deciding whether to break up large country estates in countries receiving foreign aid, decision makers would use a simplified model of the social structure in the recipient country to trace out the repercussions of land redistribution on the productivity of agricultural labor, the consumption of capital goods, prices in urban centers, and reactions of political elites. The standard operating procedures that govern programmed decision making furnish only slender guidance when comprehensive actions are undertaken. In fact,

---

[11] Simon seems to have first drawn attention to this distinction in "Recent Advances in Organization Theory" in Stephen K. Bailey, *op. cit.,* pp. 38-42. It was further refined and elaborated in his *The New Science of Management Decision* (New York: Harper, 1960), and most persuasively in James G. March and Herbert A. Simon, *op. cit.,* pp. 136-210, *passim.*

[12] See March and Simon, *op. cit.,* pp. 142-150 for an extended discussion of how to differentiate among varying levels of complexity in the structure of performance programs.

[13] It should not be assumed that the elements and relations comprising the model are in any sense "given" or empirically unproblematic data. What to put in the model and what to exclude from it, are crucial in devising strategies and programs. Both social workers and policemen incorporate images of slum dwellers and dope addicts in their simplified representation of reality, but their hypothetical models differ enormously, both cognitively and affectively. The representations that social workers and police have of one another also place limits

one key objective of a nonprogrammed decision may be to overhaul and thoroughly redo an inherited program; reformulating a graduate curriculum is a familiar example.

It should be noted that the degree to which a decision is programmed is no measure of its importance for the organization or for those whom organizational choices affect. A programmed decision is not necessarily synonymous with a trivial decision, and "nonprogrammed" is not just another way of proclaiming importance. These terms describe processes for making decisions; they do not evaluate the significance of the product.

For simplicity, programmed and nonprogrammed decisions are treated as though they formed separate classes. Actually they represent little more than the end points of a continuum. No decision is ever wholly novel or completely repetitive, it is only more or less so. Even the municipal employees who collect garbage each morning have to improvise responses on occasion, and one way of reducing the uncertainties inherent in making nonprogrammed decisions is to compare proposed alternatives with established routines that have worked in the past. (If an organization were perfectly programmed, its rigidities would forbid the learning of new responses. It would not even be incrementally adaptive.) If one could devise criteria for ranking decisions according to their relative saturation by settled routines, it would be possible to transpose the beguiling simplicity of this classification into a more finely calibrated serial order. Since these criteria are not available, it was necessary to force each decision to one extreme or the other of what is known to be a continuum.

To stipulate and clarify conceptual distinctions by example is one thing; to pair these distinctions with observed behavior, quite another. The operational problem was to prepare a program that would permit an observer to classify an impending decision as either programmed or nonprogrammed. One way was for the observers to ask the officials such questions as, "About this matter that the City Manager just mentioned, have you come across anything like it before?" or,

"As far as the planning director's request for that map is concerned, is there any standard way of drafting it that you follow?" Affirmative answers indicated programmed decisions.

The observers did not always have to ask questions; the officials themselves would often provide cues. The following examples are taken from transcripts. A subordinate telephoned his superior to say: "Jack, I've looked through every goddamned manual we have. Nothing covers it, and nobody remembers seeing anything like it before." The superior responded: "Well, do what you can, but let me know what you come up with." The exchange indicated that the processes for arriving at a decision were not programmed. On another occasion, a division head turned to the observer and complained: "Whewee—this park business is a mess. Nobody knows what the hell to do, even the old timers." This remark allowed the observer to infer a nonprogrammed decision. At times, administrative personnel would ransack manuals of procedure and files of old correspondence for hints as to how tasks ought to be handled. "Ah, here it is!" indicated that the searcher had found a program which bore on the present case. "This is no help at all!" suggested that the quest for a settled program was unsuccessful. If nothing in the administrator's

---

on their ability and willingness to collaborate in a joint undertaking. For a lucid discussion of the ways professional identification shape the cognitive maps here called "models," see March and Simon, *op. cit.*, pp. 150-154.

behavior permitted the observer to infer whether the decision was programmed or nonprogrammed, he asked the question designed to discriminate between the two classes.

Typology of Information

For this research, the information conveyed in communicated messages was classified as follows:

Factual Assertion. This is a sentence in any tense of the indicative mode. It may describe states of affairs previously or presently experienced, or it may predict future occurrences. At the outset, it was decided to distinguish two different types of factual assertions on the hunch that each would play a distinct role in making organizational decisions.

The first type is the *sensitizing* or attention-directing assertion, a signal summoning the recipient to attend to a matter requiring his consideration. A simple example (drawn from the observer's transcripts) is: "We have to do something about the machine card installation in the water department. We are not billing quickly enough." The superior who received this message called a meeting of his subordinates and a representative of the firm that had installed the equipment in order to consider the alternative plans.

The second type is the *problem-solving* assertion, a supposition estimating the probably consequences of selecting an alternative in an empirically problematic situation. Two distinct varieties of problem-solving assertions were distinguished: (*1*) estimates of costs and (*2*) estimates of benefits.

An estimate of cost forecasts the penalties or deprivations that will be suffered if a contemplated alternative is chosen. The costs may be expressed as diminutions in the levels of resources: gallons of paint consumed, man-hours expended, inventory depletions, and the like. Or they may be formulated in less generalized terms as specific alternatives forgone; the sacrificed alternative is a measure of the cost. An estimate of cost does not have to be explicitly measurable in quantitative terms; indeed, in many situations, numerical indices of incurred costs are simply not available. When decision makers appraise proposed courses of action, they typically try to predict the deprivations that others—a Congressional committee, the Federal Drug Administration, leaders of important interest groups— might inflict. It is not always possible to quantify these deprivations in comparable values, even when they are considered significant constraints.

An estimate of benefits predicts the rewards of choosing certain alternatives. These may be immediately enjoyed, such as man-hours set free for alternative uses, or they may be dividends harvested and stored away for future valued purposes, such as the good will of an influential public.

Imperative Sentence. This is an imperative or directive. It is a request for the performance of a specific act or a sequence of activities. Proposed alternatives were coded as imperatives; so were value judgments.[14]

[14]Trial observations disclosed that value judgments were actually directives that organizational etiquette had muffled and were so treated by the administrators. Characteristically, the subordinate employed the judgmental locution in addressing a superior: "I think it's a good idea to ...." The pointed imperative was reserved for the superior: "Let's go and ...." Although both superior and subordinates are here proposing alternatives, the niceties of administrative status and protocol evidently decreed that only superiors were entitled to use the more forceful and direct expression.

IDENTIFYING AND MEASURING INFLUENCE

How the analysis of organizational communication may be related to the study of influence has been expressed by Herbert A. Simon with his accustomed economy and lucidity:

> The central notion is that a decision can be regarded as a conclusion drawn (though not in any strict logical sense) from premises; and that influence is exercised by transmitting decisions, which are then taken as premises for subsequent decisions.[15]

To study influence, one must first study communication, for influence without communication is as wildly implausible as action at a distance. Influence is always accompanied by some form of communication, blunt or subtle, overt or tacit: advertising, lobbying, arguing a case before a jury or on a suitor's knee.

For this study, the relevant "premises" are the imperative sentences and factual assertions that have just been described. "Influence" and "failure to influence" are operationally defined by a recipient's observed reactions to a communicated premise, provided the premise was not redundant. Assume that an observer has just seen administrator A receive a premise from administrator B. If A carries out B's order, or if he concurs in B's factual statement, then B has been successful in exerting influence over A. If, however, A rejects the factual statement, or if he refuses to obey the order, then B has failed in his efforts to influence A.

It is one thing to claim that A has "accepted" B's communicated premise, and another to show that he has done so in fact. The observer did not record an act of influence unless the recipient of a message subsequently performed some action that could reasonably be taken to indicate he had accepted the premise in deed as well as in word; for example, undertaking the actions specified in a command, incorporating another person's suggestions in his own reports, and orally defending another's estimates in conference. (Like everybody else, administrators sometimes nod "yes" just to shoo pests away.) When events made it impossible to discover the response to a particular message, the observer dropped the entire episode from his tabulations.

To ascertain whether the communicated premise was redundant for the recipient, the observer simply asked him if he had been previously aware of what the communicator had said. A negative answer indicated that the premise was not redundant. Alternatively, if a recipient disputed a premise before going along with it, the observer concluded that the premise was not redundant. It appeared unlikely that any person would quarrel with a premise he had already accepted.[16]

An actual vignette and some hypothetical variations may help clarify the recording and coding procedures used in this study. A pessimistic forecast had given the Parks and Recreation Department a small surplus in its "New Projects" budget. The director proposed to one of his crew chiefs that the funds be used to prepare and plant a new flower bed in one of the older city parks. The decision was

---

[15]Comments on the Theory of Organization, *American Political Science Review,* 41 (1952), p. 1134.

[16]These procedures introduce opposing types of measurement error. The observer may mistakenly conclude that no premise was transmitted, which is an error of omission; or he may incorrectly record a redundant premise as influential, which is an error of commission. The frequency of these errors is unknown, and there is no way to arrive at estimates of their magnitude. It is hoped that the errors will cancel one another in the aggregate.

nonprogrammed, for nothing (the observer was told) in any city ordinance or organizational manual told him what to do if a surplus appeared before the end of the fiscal year. Had the crew chief concurred, the department head would have been credited with the successful transmission of a nonprogrammed imperative. But the crew chief said: "If we plant roses, we'll eat up part of the budget we need for a new truck. There isn't enough left over to put the new bed in anyway, and we'll have to dip into the new equipment budget."[17] The department head responded: "Say, you're right. I hadn't thought of that before. I promised you a new truck a while ago." The observer scored the transaction by giving the crew chief credit for the transmission of two factual assertions: one sensitizing the department head to the fact that the surplus was not enough for a new flower bed, and another, an estimate of cost, pointing out that planting flower beds now would consume resources that could later be used in buying a new truck.

Suppose the director had said: "Yes, I know all about that, but go ahead and plant the bed anyway." The observer would then have concluded that the crew chief had communicated redundant information, and no record would have been kept of the transaction. If the crew chief then ordered his men to plant the bed, the department head would have been given credit for the successful transmission of one nonprogrammed imperative. (Since the planting of flower beds is a routine activity for the Parks and Recreation Department, any subsequent interaction between the crew chief and subordinates would have been classified as programmed. There is no contradiction involved in asserting that a nonprogrammed decision may initiate programmed activity.)

Now suppose that the department head had remarked: "Say, I haven't thought of that. We'll certainly be strapped." Then, after mulling the matter over, he concluded: "I'll tell you what we'll do. You go ahead and get the bed planted. I'll enlarge next year's budget to cover what we spend planting the bed." The crew chief still would have been given credit for the two factual assertions, but the department head would also have been given credit for the successful transmission of an imperative.

One way to measure the amount of influence possessed by A over B is to divide arithmetically the number of premises that A has successfully transmitted to B by all the premises he has sent. The resulting quotient is simply a concise and convenient way of expressing observed frequencies, calculated in much the same way as a batting average. A value of zero is another way of saying that A has never influenced B; a figure of 1.00, that he has never failed. If one wishes to compare the influence of two actors over one another or over a third, the actor with the higher measure is the more influential of the two.

Although this simple procedure provides at least a tolerably accurate way of ranking the members of an organization according to their degree of influence, it falls short of an ideal measure for the following reasons:

1. It is a simple measure of unweighted proportions, and therefore obscures the total frequency of cases entering into its computation. It may correlate postively, or inversely, or not at all, with a measure that simply sums the successful attempts and ignores the failures.

2. It measures interpersonal influence in an organizational context, not organizational influence. A may relay a premise through B to many other actors in

[17]The crew chief was not taking liberties in shifting around budgetary categories. Planting a new flower bed would have required the replacement of some specialized equipment. That expenditure would have had to be absorbed by the new equipment budget.

an organization, but the attention given to communications channels linking successive *pairs* of actors compels the neglect of relationships where one man acts as proxy for another.

3. It speciously makes it appear as though all influence episodes are unilateral. Yet the influence relationships encountered in business firms or in governmental organizations are frequently bilateral or even multilateral in structure and composition. In the process of dickering for advantage, each party permits itself to be bound in the future by alternatives the other has selected; a wage contract reached through collective bargaining is an obvious example. Like all aggregative measures, those used in this study wrench episodes from sequence and context. Thus, they cannot be used to portray relationships of reciprocal control.

4. The units of computation refer to discrete transactions temporally bounded by the transmission of a premise at one end and its acceptance or rejection at the other. It spuriously treats influence outcomes as perfectly determinable within the immediate organizational field. But human behavior in any sort of social organization is hemmed in by a myriad of rules, constraints, and codes, which make a large number of responses predictable.[18] Through social indoctrination, individuals absorb certain generalized commitments defining the content of required, permitted, and prohibited behavior. The presence and importance of these commitments are detectable only when they are flouted—they are seldom overtly communicated; thus, crucial as they are, they will not succumb to identification and measurement by the techniques described here.

5. Perhaps the most crucial inadequacy of all is that no method was devised which would enable the weighting of premises by their importance or significance for the organization. The discrete premise was the unit of tabulation; no distinction could be drawn between important and relatively insignificant premises.

RESEARCH SITES AND OPERATIONS

The research sites were Alpha and Beta, pseudonyms for two neighboring Southern cities. Both cities had populations of approximately 100,000, city managers, and nonpartisan boards of aldermen. A small number of top administrators in Alpha were observed one summer; in Beta, the summer following. In each city, the observer had the city manager's permission to read all correspondence received and dispatched, to attend all conferences, and to listen to all calls on an extension telephone. If private citizens and representatives of civic associations came in personally to discuss some problem, the administrator explained that the anonymity of the visitor would be safeguarded and that the substantive content of his business would be concealed by the coding procedures.[19]

After a preliminary run of two weeks' duration, used to develop proficiency

[18]See Simon's statement: "Individual choice takes place in an environment of 'givens'—premises that are accepted by the individual as bases for his choice; and behavior is adaptive only within the limits set by these 'givens.'" *Administrative Behavior, op. cit.,* p. 79.

[19]It turned out that all the fretting about anonymity was largely unnecessary. Most visitors assumed that the observer was a minor functionary who had been told to remain silent while learning his job. To the few outsiders interested enough to ask who the observer was, the administrator remarked that the observer was a college student, allowing the visitor to conclude he was some sort of management intern or summer employee.

in recording observations and to improve rapport with the administrators,[20] the samples for observation were drawn: The city planner and the head of the Department of Public Works were originally included in the Beta sample, but at the last minute the former withdrew and the latter unexpectedly decided to retire in a few weeks. In each city, the city manager was the direct superior of all the other officials in the sample, and, of course, all the officials communicated daily with men situated on lower organizational echelons.

Each observer rotated his observations among the administrators comprising his sample, staying with each administrator a morning or an afternoon at a time. Since the number of administrators in each sample was odd, a man observed in the morning during the first cycle would be seen during the afternoon on the second, and so on. The order of observation *within* each cycle was randomized, so that no administrator would be able to forecast when his turn was due. On precoded log

Alpha	Beta
City manager	City manager
Head, Department of Public Works	Traffic engineer
Head, Department of Recreation	Head, Department of Recreation
City engineer	City engineer
Head, Department of Finance	Building inspector
Head, Department of Parks	
City Planner	

forms, the observer classified the premises contained in incoming messages and recorded the reactions of the administrator (acceptance or rejection) to each one he received.

The premises were assembled into sampling blocks, each one consisting of all the premises that were recorded during an encounter involving two or more participants. Each telephone call was usually regarded as a sampling block, as was each memo or letter. It was also decided to terminate a sampling block when a conversation switched from one topic to another, making it possible for ten or fifteen sampling blocks to nest in one conversation or conference. The number of premises contained in each sampling block varied widely. A single curt order could comprise a sampling block. Although many sampling blocks consisted of only a handful of premises, a protracted administrative conference on a particularly ticklish issue could yield many hundreds of premises in a single sampling block. For the analysis, a ten per cent simple random sample of blocks was selected for Alpha and Beta separately. After eliminating premises for which no conclusive determination of influence could be made, 2,011 remained for analysis in Alpha and 1,228 in Beta.

Because of the data collection methods used in this study, only a fragmentary check on the observers' accuracy was possible. Though hardly conclusive, the results are encouraging. Tape recordings were made of administrative conferences in

[20]We found out that there can be too much rapport. With time, the observers became more familiar and less threatening. In fact, some of the administrators began to ask the observers what they thought of proposed plans and how they felt other administrators were reacting to suggested lines of action. One great danger in monitoring a communications network is that if the observer is not careful, he may become part of it.

Alpha. (Permission was not granted for the use of recording equipment in Beta.) After the observer had logged, classified, and recorded the premises, another coder repeated the operation independently. Only in about fifteen per cent of the sampling blocks did the count vary by more than four premises per block; in about fifty-five per cent of the blocks, the count of premises differed only by one. The average number of premises in each Alpha sampling block was thirty-four. There was perfect agreement in the classification of premises.

OBSERVATIONS

Table 1 presents a synoptic quantitative overview of communications patterns in Alpha and Beta. Well over half (66%) of all the premises transmitted in Alpha and Beta during the observations dealt with programmed decisions. The disparity between the proportions recorded for each city reflects differences in organizational situation. Observations in Alpha were begun during a period of great turmoil and innovation. The city administration was in the throes of installing high-speed data-recording and data-manipulating equipment for preparing water bills, and for automating internal audit procedures and inventory controls. The planning director was negotiating plans for an urban renewal project, the first in the state. Beta, by contrast, had just hired a new city manager who wanted to familiarize himself thoroughly with all the intricacies of organizational routine—filling in potholes, repairing traffic lights, installing parking meters—before attempting any major innovations.

TABLE 1   Distribution of Programmed and Nonprogrammed Decision Premises

Premise	Alpha $N = 2011$	Beta $N = 1228$	Combined $N = 3239$
Programmed			
Assertion	44%	75%	56%
Imperative	8	14	10
Nonprogrammed			
Assertion	42	10	30
Imperative	6	1	4

Nonprogrammed Premises: A Hypothesis Confirmed

Confirmation. Subordinates originated slightly more than half of all the nonprogrammed decision premises, as Table 2 shows. Of the assertions dispatched by superiors to subordinates, approximately three of every four (278 of 375) were sensitizing in function. Relatively few explored the likely costs and benefits of proposed alternatives. By contrast, only about two premises of every three (286 of 427) transmitted by subordinates to superiors were sensitizing. In terms both relative and absolute, subordinates sent more assertive premises anticipating the likely costs and benefits of contemplated actions than they received from their superiors. Only in transmitting of imperative premises did superiors retain an edge over their subordinates.

Table 2 clearly sustains the summary hypothesis. Subordinates were more influential than superiors in transmitting decisional premises relating to non-programmed decisions. The results, tabulated in the row labelled Total Premises, show that superiors set aside fewer than two per cent of all the premises their subordinates originated, although many were accepted only after protracted and spirited argument. This finding does not mean that superiors were entirely impotent in shaping nonprogrammed choices. The data indicate that they were able to win the consent of their subordinates on more than eighty per cent of all the premises they communicated. For assertions and imperatives taken separately, the subordinates' influence index is higher than the corresponding figure calculated for their superiors. Thus, the summary pattern presented in the last row is not disturbed by treating factual and imperative premises individually.

When the totals for assertive premises are divided into sub-classifications, a more sharply detailed picture emerges. The largest difference between superior and subordinate indices occurs when dealing with estimates of costs. Superiors in Alpha and Beta accepted every cost forecast which their subordinates communicated. Their subordinates modified or nullified outright approximately thirty per cent of the estimates presented by their superiors. The other differences, though less striking in their magnitude, all lie in the same direction.

Influence Relations. These findings are informative, for they point to discernible and systematic differences in influence patterns among the administrators in the two cities. Acts of influence were operationally identified, abstracted

TABLE 2   Distribution and Influence Indexes* of Nonprogrammed Decision
Premises Transmitted by Superiors and Subordinates in
Alpha and Beta (Combined)†

Type of Premise	Subordinate to Superior		Superior to Subordinate		
	Influence Index	N	Influence Index	N	Difference‡
Sensitizing assertion	.986	(286)	.838	(278)	.148
Estimate of cost	1.000	(75)	.707	(58)	.293
Estimate of benefit	1.000	(66)	.872	(39)	.128
Total assertions	.991	(427)	.821	(375)	.170
Total imperatives	.951	(41)	.773	(75)	.178
Total premises	.987	(468)	.813	(450)	.174

*Influence index = no. of premises accepted/no. of premises transmitted.
†The figures separately recorded for the two cities have been combined in order to conserve space. Separate tabulations for each city do not reverse any of the relationships presented in the summary tables.
The totals are smaller than those in Table 1, because communications going from peer to peer or crossing orgnizational lines have been dropped.

‡A positive difference indicates confirmation of the hypothesis; a negative difference, that the observations ran counter to the prediction.

The data in each row can alternatively be presented as proportions rather than as differences by rearranging the frequencies in the customary fourfold table. A Chi-square test can then be calculated to decide whether the differences between the proportions can be ascribed to sampling variability when the true difference is actually zero. For total assertions and total premises, the difference between the proportions would occur fewer than one time in a thousand under a population difference of zero; for total imperatives, about twice in a hundred random samples of identical size. The Chi-squares have been adjusted for continuity, even when the large size of the smallest expected cell frequency makes the adjustment, strictly speaking, unnecessary. Thus, if anything, the tests are biased in a conservative direction.

from temporal sequence, and summed over the periods of observation. It is important not to read surplus meaning into the data. To be influenced is *not necessarily* to be cornered into adopting a position one would not freely choose. The influenced administrator was not being subtly coerced; he was simply concurring in a communicated premise. Superiors in the two organizations had many opportunities to sample the operational consequences of heeding their subordinates; acceptance was justified by previous experience. As one administrator remarked: "If I had anything like his experience on the job, I would know enough to be able to argue the point. As it is, I have to take his word for it."

Supplementing the aggregate statistics with the observers' running notes helps to define more sharply the texture of the relationships between communicator and recipient.[21] In many cases, a subordinate would parry and finally annul a superior's estimate before successfully proposing one of his own, a path of behavior necessarily submerged from view in the summary table. The comments also provide tangible grounds for delineating the bases of authority, the reasons why a communicated premise elicited compliance. A superior would often openly acknowledge his inability to match or master his subordinates' knowledge of crucial decisional factors or constraints: the anticipated reactions of an influential public that "might cause trouble if rubbed the wrong way," the actual capabilities of a new piece of equipment, or "what would go over" in Washington or the state capitol. Already confronted by clogged agenda and lacking contextual information or technical competence (and sometimes both), he was likely to accept the inferences that his subordinates extracted from the data they had assembled and analyzed. Very seldom did the superior examine the facts and documentation himself; instead he relied on the technical virtuosity and expertise of his subordinates.[22] In Alpha and Beta, superiors in effect delegated to their subordinates the responsibility for procuring and evaluating information as to the costs and benefits of proposed alternatives.

Nor is it altogether clear that superiors tossed rationality to the winds in permitting subordinates to limit their discretion. From the comments that the observers recorded, it seems reasonably clear that superiors hoped to take advantage of their subordinates' greater technical competence, previous specialized training, and detailed information about the immediate decisional environment. Moreover, superiors apparently did not resent granting authority to their subordinates. The bureaucratic organization embodies specialization of knowledge as well as a differentiation of labor and skill. The superior who accepted his subordinates' advice was able to purchase expert opinion at relatively low cost compared to the expenditures of time and effort he would have had to incur to gather and appraise the same data. To know as much as the director of planning about the proposed urban renewal project, for example, Alpha's city manager would have needed the

---

[21]The observers sometimes recorded the comments that passed between the administrators and sometimes simply asked the influenced administrator why he "went along" with the newly communicated premise. These procedures could not be followed in every case. Interrupting conferences and staff meetings is often resented, and to put the same question to an administrator twenty or thirty times in a single morning would likely encourage hasty and stereotyped responses. Thus it would be senseless to attempt to analyze statistically what fragments of data were obtained by these procedures.

[22]March and Simon, *op. cit.,* p. 165, term this relationship "uncertainty absorption." The recipient is bound by error and uncertainty in a communicator's appraisal when he "takes his word for it."

equivalent of a Master's degree in city planning. In order to draft the basic plan, he would have had to supervise the collection of data relating to the physical and topographic characteristics of the blighted area and conduct lengthy negotiations with private developers, title insurance firms, banks and other lending agencies. Moreover, he would have had to divert time and energy, resources seldom in plentiful supply, to master the intricate maze of federal procedures and regulations controlling urban renewal projects. The immediate costs the city manager bore in obtaining all this information from the city planner were relatively slight, for most of it was carried around in the planner's head. Possible future costs were discounted, primarily because administrators at different organizational echelons were linked in fiduciary relationships. There never was the whisper of a suggestion that the planning director was trimming the data to maximize preferences at variance with the city manager's.

Students of organizational behavior correctly stress the strains that may emerge from the clash of authority legitimated by professional expertise with the authority validated by the incumbency of a superior organizational status. It is undeniable that organizations from time to time are transformed into quasi-Hobbesian universes. Administrators do wrangle, sometimes decorously and at other times bitterly. They occasionally contrive and scheme to overcome their organizational opponents with all the strategic advantages that position, chance and skill place at their disposal: presumed technical competence, control over information, and the stimulation or maintenance of alliances with politicians or other superiors entrusted with doling out grants of legal authority and other scarce resources to one or another of the battling claimants. Disagreements sometimes result in anarchy; how often is another matter. But to explain how differences are avoided and composed is as important a topic for organizational theory as it is to explain what happens on the relatively infrequent but more dramatic occasions when irreconcilable disagreement flares into open struggle.

Evidence from Other Studies. Nonprogrammed decision making has not been intensively explored in actual organizations, although imaginative work has been carried out in simulations of various kinds.[23] Thus there is little corroborating data available. Since most analyses of organizations do not distinguish between programmed and nonprogrammed decisions, what fragmentary evidence there is comes from organizations that have never been able to factor their tasks into a set of interrelated routines. One example is presented in Dill's study of control patterns in a Norwegian firm that designed, installed, and maintained highly specialized electrical equipment for a wide variety of commercial users.[24] The decisions the firm had to make could not be programmed, because each installation had to be custom designed. Using entirely different measures from those employed in this study, Dill underscores the point that the home-office superiors were tightly constrained by their nominal subordinates, the engineers and representatives who procured business for the firm and negotiated terms with its customers. In planning

[23]For some representative examples, see Alex Bavelas, Communication Patterns in Task-oriented Groups, *Journal of the Acoustical Society of America*, 22 (1950), 725-730; Harold J. Leavitt, Some Effects of Certain Communication Patterns on Group Performance, *Journal of Abnormal and Social Psychology*, 46 (1951), 38-50; Harold Guetzkow and Herbert A. Simon, "The Impact of Certain Communication Nets upon Organization and Performance in Task-oriented Groups" in Albert H. Rubenstein and Chadwick J. Haberstroh (eds.), *Some Theories of Organization* (Homewood, Ill.: Dorsey, 1960), pp. 259-277.

[24]*Op. cit.*

an installation, cost schedules were not initially known, even by the field personnel. They were dependent upon the quotations made by the firm's suppliers, who were themselves producing nonstandardized components. In addition, product requirements and hence aggregate costs fluctuated drastically as inadequacies in early working sketches and blueprints were spotted and corrected. By the time information could be compressed and relayed to the firm's central headquarters, the situation in the field had once again changed. Superiors could do little more than endorse the decisions of their field representatives, for they alone had the most current information.

Ely Devons provides an informative account of the pattern of controls that developed within the Ministry of Aircraft Production.[25] In time of war, hierarchical controls largely displace the cues and incentives mediated through a decentralized price system as techniques for allocating goods and services. Decisions as to the direction of production and the distribution of economic resources are made by a large number of hierarchical organizations especially created for the purpose. Almost by definition, the procedures they evolve and the decisions they make are nonprogrammed; in fact, such agencies are the most perfect real-world analogues to the mock organizations of the small-group laboratory.

The Ministry was supposed to devise comprehensive plans for organizing the production of finished aircraft, spare parts, and aircraft components. At the onset of the war, participating plants drew up monthly schedules informing central planners of their resource requirements and projected output. The planners were supposed to coordinate the member firms by telling them what they were to produce and by shifting resources among the plants in such a way as to fulfill the comprehensive plan. Early in the war, each participating firm planned its requests and gauged its productive capacity on the supposition that all the necessary factors of production—labor, space, raw materials, finished components—were free goods. They never were. From one month to the next, different bottlenecks and scarcities occurred, and the Ministry's coordinators could simply not keep up with the rapidly oscillating realities of production. The Ministry personnel could not reduce the decisions to a small number of simple routines. Only when differences between supply and demand happened to be fairly small were central planners able to make incremental adjustments to reflect the scarcities. When they were large, the coordinators were helpless to continue central control and direction. As the firms became increasingly cynical of the Ministry's ability to develop and implement comprehensive directives, there occurred an odd inversion of the prescriptive operational plan. Production and distribution were supposed to be guided by central planners. But, as Devons writes:

> The central allocating authorities could not consider the use of all resources, interrelated though they were. Separate committees dealt with manpower, raw materials, factory building, etc. *No committee even considered whether the allocation of resources in total to each use was correct, but took the existing plans of the individual departments . . . as given.*[26]

The central planners accepted the estimates of cost and output given them by their subordinate committees, and the committees were, in turn, given these estimates by the participating firms. Production did not follow the central plan; the central plan

[25]Ely Devons, *Planning in Practice* (Cambridge, Engl.: Cambridge University, 1950).
[26]*Ibid.*, pp. 19-20.

merely recorded the actual figures of production. Subordinate control supplanted central direction.

In Germany too, when the war began, planning authorities had to allocate labor and commodities to a multiplicity of competing users. The leather control authority, for example, had to apportion existing and expected future stocks of leather among shoe manufacturers, harness makers, manufacturers of rifle slings, fabricators of drive belts, and so on. Requests for tanned hides, plant space, labor, and rolling stock were sent to the leather control office by subordinate government divisions, which had previously received them from individual manufacturers. The overall hierarchical arrangement resembled that employed by the British Ministry of Air Production, and the effects were the same. The German planners soon found that the most advanced mathematical and statistical techniques of the time could not cope with the problems of allocation springing from a variegated array of shoe styles, each demanding a different combination of resources. The German planners, unlike the British Ministry of Aircraft Production which in effect granted subordinate groups control of nonprogrammed decision making, ordered the standardization of shoe styles to a handful of basic patterns. Simplification permitted calculation, and the feasibility of making calculations allowed the leather control authority to exert control over subordinate firms. Superiors, in effect, converted from nonprogrammed to programmed decision making in order to permit centralized control.[27]

Programmed Premises: A Hypothesis Confounded

The data derived from observations support the hypothesis that on nonprogrammed choices the influence of subordinates over superiors exceeds the influence of superiors over subordinates. It was also proposed that superiors are more influential than their subordinates on programmed choices. This hypothesis fared very poorly. As Table 3 shows, subordinates actually had a somewhat greater measure of success than their superiors in getting programmed premises accepted. Only in the transmission and acceptance of imperatives did the observations sustain the hypothesis. Not only did superiors issue more commands than their subordinates, but theirs' were also more likely to elicit compliance. The hypothesis is therefore confirmed by imperatives, but denied by assertions. The observers' running notes again provide insights into the structure of the relationships. In many cases, subordinates on routine surveillance would report a situation requiring action, and the superior would authorize the repair. This sequence of behavior is reflected in the large number of sensitizing assertions from subordinate to superior. Often, however, private citizens would call in complaints directly to the superior, who would simultaneously inform a subordinate of the condition and direct him to fix it. The major impact of top executives was registered in the way they paced organizational action, rather than the number of orders they issued for the repair of broken traffic lights and similar directives. They were strategically located where

[27]Walter Eucken, On the Theory of the Centrally Administered Economy, *Economica*, 15 (1948), 79-100. The development of electronic automata may have nullified some of the lessons Eucken and Devons drew. The basic difficulty confronting the central planners was the large number of simultaneous equations that needed to be solved in order to minimize wasted resources and maximize output. High-speed computers and linear programming might have made their problems more tractable. See Benjamin Walter, Organizations, Computers, Logic, *Public Administration Review*, 21 (1961), 226-233.

TABLE 3   Distribution and Influence Indexes* of Programmed Decision
Premises Transmitted by Superiors and Subordinates in
Alpha and Beta (Combined)

Type of Premise	Superior to Subordinate		Subordinate to Superior		Difference†
	Influence Index	N	Influence Index	N	
Sensitizing assertion	.972	(503)	.996	(540)	−.024
Estimate of cost	.972	(36)	.982	(56)	−.010
Estimate of benefit	1.000	(41)	1.000	(26)	.000
Total assertions	.963	(580)	.991	(622)	−.028
Total imperatives	.961	(207)	.783	(46)	.178
Total premises	.971	(787)	.981	(668)	−.010

*Influence index = no. of premises accepted/no. of premises transmitted.
†A positive difference indicates confirmation of the hypothesis; a negative difference, that
the observations ran counter to the prediction.

they could either initiate programmed decisions immediately or postpone them; in
effect, to establish and enforce priorities among the activities competing for
organizational action. Superiors countermanded ten imperatives in all. In every case
the refusal to acquiesce to the suggestion of the subordinate represented a change
of priority rather than an outright veto.

The observations suggest an alternate hypothesis: that the influence of
superiors in programmed decision making lies chiefly in their ability to specify
priorities among the alternative actions suggested by their subordinates and clients.
Although this hypothesis is consonant with the data here reported, they cannot be
used to test it. The analytic operations are diagnostic, no more. The aggregate totals
were subdivided to discover which proportions affirmed the hypothesis and which
negated it. Nothing the analysis turned up has any probative value until it is tested
on other samples. It is obviously methodological naivete to treat chance discoveries
as though one had suspected that they were there all the time.

CONCLUSIONS AND IMPLICATIONS

The evidence presented sustains one hypothesis and refutes the other. The
influence of subordinates over superiors on nonprogrammed choices is greater than
the influence of superiors over subordinates. This outcome is apparently a function
of the subordinates' greater knowledge, or, perhaps, the shared presumption by
superiors that subordinates know more than they do. Lest too much confirmation
be read from too little data, it would be valuable to know whether the relationships
reported here also hold in other organizational settings; for example, between
junior and senior faculty in devising curricula and designing research, between
engineers and top management in developing new products, or between administrative agencies and Congressional committees.[28]

[28]A perennial justification for Congressional seniority is that it leads to competence in
evaluating administrative requests. As Daniel S. Greenberg notes, "Scientists may seek to
persuade the government to pursue this or that line of research, but after twenty years of
dealing with scientist-supplicants, both the Congress and the Executive have developed an ear
for sound argument." See The Myth of the Scientific Elite, *The Public Interest,* 1 (1965), 57.

The data reported in this paper were inconsistent with the other hypothesis. On making programmed choices, subordinates were more influential than their superiors. The influence of superiors over programmed decisions consisted of their ability to set priorities among alternative routine tasks.

DISCUSSION QUESTIONS

1. Cite five situations wherein the operative organization resulting from the interaction of the formal and informal organization raises doubts as to the validity of the hypotheses stated by Carmichael. (Do not use illustrations involving fraud or embezzlement.)

2. Arrow points out that a good deal of the inefficiencies and duplications in organizations in the public sector are essential elements of the control system. Recognizing the difficulties in the impossible demand for knowledge on the part of the budget office, he cites current writers' suggestions that greater reliance be placed on the self-interest and mutual rivalry of bureaus. It is proposed that bureaus act as do individuals before a court in justifying their requests; and where overlapping functions exist, the information supplied by one can be used to check on that of the other.

Evaluate the usefulness of this approach to control in a large private organization where independent divisions can be viewed as bureaus and the corporate executive committee as the budget office.

3. In developing or evaluating control systems in the private sector, reference is made to investment centers, cost centers, and profit centers. Refer to the Whistler et al. article and indicate how their conclusions regarding congruence might help in better defining control systems for the following functional areas in a large corporation:

   a. Manufacturing
   b. Marketing
   c. Research and Development
   d. Finance and Administrative Services

4. Arrow observes that ". . . a manager is an information channel of decidedly limited capacity." This means, that managers receive information from their subordinates that they do not retransmit. Hence, some decisions, if only trivial ones, must be made at lower levels, because the relevant information is discarded in the process of upward transmission to avoid overloading the channel.

"The recognition that individual managers will inevitably know more about their own sphere of activity than higher officials has caused decentralization of decision making to be looked on with much more favor in recent years. It has also been recognized that decentralization can improve the allocation of responsibility; on the one hand, the subordinate has greater possibilities of initiative; on the other, his successes and failures can be more easily recognized by top management." Compare this observation with the conclusions reached by Walter in his empirical study regarding both programmed and non-programmed decisions.

5. In his delightful book, "Parkinson's Law," C. Northcote Parkinson's view of the

process of decision making in large corporations is illustrated in the following proceedings before the finance committee.

The first proposal for a $10 million dollar atomic reactor is made by the treasurer in a few sentences as the formal documents are put before the committee. The treasurer's presentation includes the approval of the project by the firm's consulting engineer accompanied by some technical gibberish supplied by a consulting geophysicist. After two and one-half minutes of discussion involving only one member apart from the chairman the project is approved.

The next item on the agenda is a proposal for a $2,350 aluminum-roofed bicycle shed for the use of the clerical staff. The discussion on this issue is extended and runs for forty-five minutes with all members of the committee totally involved. It is finally resolved with a possible cost saving of $300.

Refer to the readings in Part Four and indicate wherein Parkinson's notion of the decision process is confirmed or denied.

6. A very large commercial bank has recently reviewed its control system for branch offices. The bank has a centralized computer service organization that services all the bank's many branch offices and the central office. It has been suggested that computer service be treated as a "profit center," charging all the users of its service a price that will include a profit. This is justified on the grounds that the computer service operation entails a large investment in capital equipment as well as significant costs and in "selling" its service to its customers (branch offices, and so on), it should yield a profit on the investment. This reflects the view of the director of computer service.

An alternate suggestion offered by the controller is that computer service should be considered a "cost center" because it provides a service necessary for the completion of the end product, in this case a banking service to the customers. As such, computer service is not unlike maintenance service in a manufacturing plant.

Discuss the behavioral implications implicit in each of the proposals.

7. An exposure draft of the American Institute of Certified Public Accountants entitled "Proposed Statement on Auditing Procedure: The Auditor's Study and Evaluation of Internal Control" (August 10, 1972) states: "As defined in this Statement, accounting control is within the scope of the study and evaluation of internal control contemplated by generally accepted auditing standards, while administrative control is not" (emphasis added) (Paragraph 49).

The draft defines administrative control as including "but not limited to, the plan of organization and the procedures and records that are concerned with the decision process leading to management's authorization of transactions." Accounting control, the draft continues, "comprises the plan of organization and the procedures and records that are concerned with the safeguarding of assets and reliability of financial records and consequently are designed to provide reasonable assurance . . . ." This section continues with a listing of assurances relating to (1) execution of transactions in accordance with management authorization, (2) the recording necessary to prepare financial statements and maintain accountability for assets, (3) access to assets permitted in accordance with management's authorization, (4) accountability for asset as compared with existing assets at reasonable intervals.

How does this explicit separation of accounting control relate to Carmichael's "Behavioral Hypotheses of Internal Control"?

PART FIVE

Financial Reporting

REPORTING OPERATING RESULTS

In a recent paper, Dyckman notes the need for stressing behavioral complexities in trying to link decision models and accounting. In his words:

I intend to show that present accounting measurement practice may lead to serious diseconomies for internal organizational decisions. Further, I believe that the way decision makers respond to accounting information is a key factor in conditioning the decision making system. The importance of these relationships extends beyond the direct decision consequences which will occupy our initial attention, to other decisions and policies affected indirectly by the decision and decision-evaluation process.

Moreover the internal decision making process is inexorably tied to decisions made by, and hence to information given to, those outside the organization. It is necessary then that the initial discussion be extended to embrace external uses of accounting data and related measurement issues. The internal and external decisions are not independent because the external reactions to accounting reports may not only have immediate decision effects but also often rebound to affect the future of the organization.[1]

"Generally accepted accounting principles" permit choices between alternatives in accounting reporting. The choice among available alternatives reflects aspirations of managers, yet as was noted earlier, affects decision making, both within and without the firm. Relatively little research has been done in studying this linkage. What is available is some initial work on the behavioral implications in the choice of accounting alternatives for external reporting.

Some work has been done in exploring income smoothing or income management. It is assumed that stockholders and prospective investors favor smooth gradual growth in earnings over widely fluctuating earnings. The results are not totally conclusive with regard to the selective choice among accounting alternatives that may achieve smoothed income growth. What has not been adequately researched is the ability of management to smooth income without resorting to accounting alternatives, focusing instead on the timing of transactions such as disposal or acquisition of assets or specific businesses, building or reducing inventories, timing shipments or purchases among others.

Returning to the matter of choice among accounting alternatives, there is one so-called principle in accounting that appears to result in smoothing yet is rarely associated with it. Conservatism as a guiding principle has long been used by accountants; in fact, conservatism is associated with the public image of an accountant. There is a close linkage between conservatism and income smoothing, the latter being an objective sought in earnings behavior over time. The immediate write-off of intangibles, for example, can result in income smoothing. These expenditures increase in periods of high economic activity and high profits, and they are the first to be curtailed during periods of economic stress. Yet there is a significant lag between the period of expenditure and the periods of benefit. Accordingly, in periods of high economic activity such expenditures reduce profits with minor impact on profit whereas the subsequent periods of depressed economic activity have the benefits with no related expenditures. The effect is a reduction in profits in very profitable periods and an increase in profits in not so profitable periods.

One can observe, then, that the accountant's conservatism meshes well with management's desire for smoothed income. Yet there is still another party to this conservatism bias—specifically, the external user, as suggested by Backer:

> Research findings suggest that accounting conservatism is something more than a bias based on tradition and that there is a rationale behind the widespread support of this doctrine. Bankers are concerned with loan safety and their experience indicates that conservatism furnishes an additional margin of protection. Security analysts prefer to rely on a conservatively constructed income base as a guide to future income projections. They regard risk of a possible overstatement of income to be greater than that of an understatement. Analysts generally comment adversely on the quality of earnings of companies that employ unconservative practices.

It would appear that conservatism with its implicit effects on income smoothing serve not only the aspirations of management with its responsibility for

[1]T. R. Dyckman, "Decision Models and Accounting Measurement: A Challenge for Accountants," Stanford Lecture Series in Accounting, 1971.

reporting to external users but actually is encouraged by key users of financial reports—the credit extenders and financial analysts who advise the investing public.

The papers presented in this section are samples of the research in external reporting and its behavioral linkage.

INTRODUCTION TO THE READINGS

In his paper, Hawkins examines the induced behavior generated by generally accepted accounting principles and the related alternative accounting treatments permitted by them and questions if this behavior is in the best interest of the stockholders and society. The author reviews several opinions of the A.P.B., examining their behavioral implication, and then goes on to point out areas where modifications in principles are necessary so as to achieve better goal congruence between corporate management's objectives and stockholders' objectives.

Several variations between accounting practices for internal reporting and external reporting are examined, contrasting the desired behavior of managers and the behavior induced by the accounting practices used in external reporting. Reference is made to the possibility of utilizing some of the research results of studies on the behavioral implications of internal control systems and their relationship to accounting practices to fill the void, albeit temporarily, in the limited research that has been done on the behavioral implication of accounting for public reporting.

Gynther takes a more theoretical approach in attempting to relate behavioral hypotheses to accounting. His frame of reference, unlike Hawkins,' are two basic concepts underlying accounting reporting theory rather than specific existing generally accepted accounting principles. For these principles to be developed, an underlying concept is necessary, and Gynther examines two possibilities—the proprietary and the entity concept. Delineation between these concepts is necessary because of the effect on the accounting principles associated with profit determination, definition of balance sheet elements, and historical cost versus current values, among others.

It is Gynther's position that the general acceptance of the proprietary view has its basis in the value systems of individuals that in turn have their roots in the family and cultures of individuals, and he feels that what can be reasoned on a logical basis to be a superior approach will not be adopted until the frames of reference of individuals change. In short, he sees the change as a gradual one with the expectation that the entity theory will evolve as the dominant theory. Indeed, it is the entity theory that comes closest to providing a theoretical basis for a logical accounting approach consistent with the modern theory of the firm. (See Monsen and Downs, "A Theory of Large Managerial Firms" in Part One.)

The paper by Gordon, Horowitz, and Meyers and the one by Schiff both address themselves to the subject of income smoothing in external financial reports. Recognizing the existence of alternatives in the accounting treatment of specific transactions, the authors address themselves to choices made by management in the selection of a specific alternative and the impact on trends in earnings over time. Gordon *et al.* refer to a prior paper wherein a series of propositions is stated leading to a theorem regarding income smoothing. This theorem is consistent with the behavioral theory of the firm.

An effort to test the theorem is made in reviewing choices with regard to the alternative methods for accounting for the investment credit—deferral versus flow-through. In this connection, the behavior of several large chemical firms over a series of years was reviewed. In addition, the choice among a series of accounting alternatives was studied for a single steel firm.

The article by Schiff examines a single firm and its implied smoothing occasioned by deferral or expensing of marketing costs associated with entry into new markets. Here the accounting theory regarding the treatment of marketing costs is examined, and the shift in the application of the theory suggests an explicit effort on the part of management to smooth income. The findings confirm the reality of the behavioral theory of the firm.

In their paper, Sorter *et al.* illustrate an innovative research approach in exploring the relationship between what is referred to as a corporate personality and the choice in accounting methods for external reporting. Indeed, they go even further and observe that one can predict decision on alternatives in equity management and liquid asset management as well, once the personality characteristics have been identified.

It is noted in this paper that a corporation facing a choice between consistency or inconsistency in reporting depreciation for tax purposes and public reporting purposes reflects its tolerance or intolerance toward ambiguity. Consistent treatment of depreciation for different reports indicates an intolerance of ambiguity, hence a need for one set of records and one identifiable net income figure for all reports. It reflects, according to the authors, an ability to cope with what are orderly and predictable stimuli. Even if unpredictable, messy stimuli cannot be avoided, they are treated as if they were orderly and predictable. This in contrast to the corporation that can deal with the unpredictable and in psychological terms, possesses an ability to respond to vague undefined stimuli. The authors associate characteristics of risk averting and conservatism with corporations that cannot tolerate ambiguity and the reverse for the others.

21

BEHAVIORAL IMPLICATIONS
OF GENERALLY ACCEPTED ACCOUNTING PRINCIPLES *

DAVID HAWKINS

Generally accepted accounting principles can condition the decisions of managers as well as measure their performance. Unfortunately, this does not always lead to desirable results. A number of these principles have a built-in bias which motivates managers under certain circumstances to adopt them in preference to alternative principles that may better reflect the operating results and financial condition of their company. In addition, other generally accepted accounting principles may induce managers to adopt specific operating policies, even though these policies may not necessarily be the most appropriate.

NEED TO CONSIDER BEHAVIORAL IMPLICATIONS

The Accounting Principles Board and its predecessor, the Committee on Accounting, have reduced the number of behaviorally undesirable accounting principles, but some still persist. The goal of the accounting and management professions should be to eliminate these remaining objectionable practices and to create a set of generally accepted principles that will motivate managers to make sound economic and reporting decisions. If this is not possible, our corporate reporting system should at least not encourage managers to act against what appear to be the best interests of their stockholders and society.

The Accounting Principles Board and others who influence the definition of what constitutes acceptable corporate accounting principles must ask themselves in each case:

What might this accounting principle or practice motivate managers to do in their own selfish interest?

Could this possible action obscure actual managerial performance, give the illusion of performance where none exists, or lead to unsound economic actions?

If the answer to any part of the second question is "Yes" and the probability that it will occur is reasonably high in even a few cases, then the use of the accounting practice should not be encouraged, unless it is obviously justified by clearly defined business circumstances. Such accounting practices should not be encouraged even though sound from the technical viewpoint of accounting theory.

Another important determinant of the strength, character, and prevalence of

*California Management Review, Winter 1969, pp. 13-21.

managerial response to any improvements in the behavioral aspect of financial accounting is the attitude of the "managers" of the system toward corporate reporting. The "managers" include the Securities and Exchange Commission, the major stock exchanges, the ethics and professional practice committees of the American Institute of Certified Public Accountants, the courts, and Congress. If these manager groups follow a vigilant, tough, aggressive program to root out and expose undesirable accounting practices, corporate managers and the accounting profession will be more inclined to respond to the desirable biases in our accounting system rather than the undesirable. Fortunately, this seems to be increasingly the case today.

The continuing controversy over the appropriate handling of deferred taxes illustrates the need to consider the behavioral aspects of an accounting principles decision. Deferred tax accounting problems arise when a company uses different accounting methods for book and tax purposes, i.e., capitalizes research and development expenses on its books and expenses them for tax purposes. The timing differences between the book and tax recognition of revenues and costs can lead to a deferral of tax payments. There are three different proposals for handling these tax deferrals in financial statements. The flow-through method would report the taxes due to the taxing authorities as the tax expense for book purposes. The comprehensive allocation approach bases the book tax expense upon the book profits before taxes. The difference between this tax expense and the taxes shown on the tax return is carried as a deferred tax liability on the balance sheet; irrespective of when it is anticipated, the deferred taxes will fall due. The partial allocation approach is a variation of the flow-through method. It would include in the deferred tax liability calculation only those taxes which are thought by management to be actually payable in the near future plus the taxes due on the current tax return.

In my opinion the Accounting Principles Board came to the correct decision on this issue when it decided on the comprehensive allocation method, but it did so on bookkeeping grounds. Neither the Board nor those who opposed its decision appear to recognize the behavioral aspects of the contending approaches proposed.

There are some undesirable motivation implications associated with the partial allocation and flow-through methods—the two approaches the Accounting Principles Board rejected. These stem from two facts: (1) the first-year profit boost inherent in the method per se from the deferral of tax payments; (2) the accounting decision necessary to create the circumstances which give rise to tax deferral, such as the bookkeeping decision to use straight-line depreciation for public reporting purposes and some accelerated method for tax purposes. Thus, by simply adopting a bookkeeping change, profits can be improved by the cost difference between the two accounting treatments of depreciation plus the differential cost times the tax rate. This is potentially undesirable since it can encourage a manager to substitute the illusion of performance for the realities of performance. (See my article, "Controversial Accounting Changes," *Harvard Business Review,* March-April 1968.) In my opinion, this is enough reason to reject flow-through methods as acceptable accounting principles.

In contrast, the comprehensive allocation approach to tax allocation has the desirable behavioral quality of encouraging and permitting management to make their tax and book accounting decisions independently of each other. Also, it reduces the strength of the incentive to make bookkeeping switches to create a timing difference between book and tax recognition of items. The comprehensive allocation method still permits a company to get the profit differential between, say, straight-line and accelerated depreciation, but it eliminates the additional incentive of the profit differential times the tax rate gained under the flow-through methods.

Side Effects

The potentially undesirable motivational implications of the flow-through approaches to tax accounting extend to many accounting and tax decisions which can create timing differences between the recognition of revenues and costs for tax and book purposes. For example, the extra profit bonus flowing from applying flow-through methods biases managers toward the following:

Selling in an expanding sales situation on the installment basis rather than for cash. (An expanding company which accounts for installment sales on the accrual method for book purposes and the installment method for taxes could show greater current profits than a company either using the accrual method for both book and tax purposes or selling for cash.)

Capitalizing dubious research and development and similar expenditures for book purposes and expensing them for tax reports.

Recognizing profits on questionable long-term contracts on a percentage-of-completion basis in stockholder reports and in tax returns on a completed contract basis.

Including the earnings of marginal foreign subsidiaries in the accounts currently, but in tax returns when later remitted.

In the case of the marginal firm these accounting inducements to improve profits may well work toward management's accepting some methods simply because they improve profits, regardless of tax deferral and underlying business considerations. The added profit bonus resulting from applying flow-through accounting to tax deferrals would make it harder to resist adopting these methods. Under these circumstances the potentially undesirable behavioral aspects can interfere with the application of managerial judgment necessary to make financial reporting more meaningful, more responsible, and more responsive to the peculiar aspects of each business enterprise.

A Strong Profession

It is conceivable that in particular instance the accounting methods cited above may most fairly reflect the actual circumstances. For instance, some expenditures for research activities may be just as good as an investment in bricks and mortar. In this case the research expenditures should be capitalized and written off over future accounting periods. However, the circumstances which might justify capitalization are not always clearly stated or clearly determinable in operational terms.

Herein lies the problem: Can those accounting methods with potentially undesirable motivational characteristics be eliminated from the list of generally accepted accounting principles without reducing the responsiveness of corporate reporting to the unique characteristics of each company?

In my opinion, the answer to this question is "Yes." Certainly, the accounting profession must continue its work in reducing the inducements to adopt the obvious flagrant misuse of accounting options. Also, the profession must, as it is, work to eliminate those practices not justifiable by different circumstances. Beyond these actions, the dilemma posed above points up:

1. The need for an independent and knowledgeable public audit function with a strong commitment to "fairness" in corporate reporting and protecting third parties from accounting misrepresentations.
2. A clearer definition of the circumstances under which alternative accounting practices are justifiable.

Management Control Analogy

With one exception our corporate financial reporting systems perform operationally in a behavioral sense in our total economy in a way somewhat analogous to the management control systems used internally by top corporate management to communicate with, understand, measure, and influence the actions of their operating unit managers. Because of this similarity, I believe that we can move toward a desirable behavioral set of accounting principles for public reporting practices by applying to our financial accounting recommendations and practices the same type of thinking which is applied to management control to influence behavior through the use of measurement devices.

The financial reports to stockholders represent the information output of the public system to control managerial actions. In this case the control system is designed by the accounting profession to the extent it defines "generally accepted accounting principles," and by the managers themselves insofar as they make accounting policy decisions for individual companies within this framework.

The principal operational difference between the motivational aspects of internal managerial control systems and our corporate reporting system lies in who sets the objectives the system is to achieve. Operationally, however, the desired results are the same: optimum use of resources with the system.

In the case of managerial controls every manager within the system is an employee who is working toward specific goals that his superior has established with or without his participation. Also, resources within the company are allocated by a few managers at the top level of the company.

In contrast, the reporting units in the corporate reporting system are independent of each other and act in their own self-interest. The resources of society are allocated between these units through a competitive free market capital allocation mechanism, the effectiveness of which rests in large measure on the reliability and relevance of the information in corporate financial reports. To the extent that accounting principles are used to construct corporate financial statements, our society's resource allocation decisions rely in part on these principles. If these principles bias management toward unsound economic decisions or lead to financial reports which are misleading, then the effectiveness of society's resource allocations will be unnecessarily reduced.

Even though those who establish accounting principles are not responsible for planning our economic development, they must seek to reflect society's best interests and desires in their actions related to accounting principles. This is a heavy responsibility, but it will do this more effectively if it is recognized that accounting principles can influence corporate and investor behavior.

Like the typical management control system, our financial reporting system serves as a two-day communication device between management and society. Everyone recognizes that financial reports are a communication between management and their stockholders. The communication from society to management is less obvious and less clearly defined. This aspect of communication is achieved through the accounting principles that society sanctions in the form of generally accepted accounting practices. Consequently, if some of these principles encourage management to do things that are contrary to the current modes of thought in society, then society must share part of the blame.

It is very difficult to define the current mode of thoughts as to what is acceptable corporate behavior. It is equally difficult to adjust accounting principles to changes in this standard. Thus, all too often our corporate financial reporting system is not as responsive to new attitudes as is, say, the typical management control system, where the communication from top management to operating managers is under the control of a few people who can readily determine what is acceptable behavior in their company. Nevertheless, as difficult as it is to make our system more responsive, the messages carried by accounting principles from society to management can be clearer and closer to today's modes of thought if the groups charged with responsibility for maintaining our corporate reporting system recognize the two-way communication potential in our system and use it to the best of their ability to communicate society's goals to management.

A key element of any management control system is the standard against which actual performance is measured. This relationship gives meaning to the control system. Experts in the field have long recognized that the measure of a manager's performance index can influence in a crude way the behavior of the managers subjected to the system.

For example, if a manager of a foreign subsidiary in a country such as Brazil, with a continuously devaluating currency, is measured in terms of his net profit in local currency, he is not necessarily encouraged, by this measure to protect the parent company's investment from devaluation. Devaluation has no direct effect on this particular measure of performance.

On the other hand, if the manager's profit performance is measured in the dollar equivalent of his local profits after adjustments for devaluation gains or losses, he may be stimulated toward taking actions to reduce the devaluation erosion of the parent's investment.

However, what specific actions the manager takes to reduce the effects of devaluation may in part be influenced by the particular technique used to translate the local currency statements into dollars. Some translation techniques encourage managers to shift their assets from monetary items to nonmonetary items. Other methods induce the manager to switch his assets from the current to the long-term category.

Thus, the measure of performance may be the same for two managers, but the way it is determined may lead them toward making different decisions on how to protect their operations from devaluation losses.

The performance standards of our corporate reporting system are established in a variety of ways: Managers can set these standards themselves by publicly predicting their company's future earnings-per-share results. Similarly, standards can be set by the public predictions of security analysts and others who advise investors. The actual or predicted results of competitors are often used as a standard against which actual performance is measured. Another standard used widely is the common expectation that a corporation should improve upon its last year's results. From these standards stockholders and potential investors pick the financial measures of performance they consider most relevant, which, despite its limitations, in most cases seems to be principally earnings-per-share.

Despite the fact that the earnings-per-share performance measurement is a crude measure of performance it influences managerial behavior in two ways:

In the way corporations are capitalized.

In the way accounting and economic decisions made along the way in the creation and calculation of profit.

The strength of the direction of a control systems motivational bias depends in large measure on the relationship of the manager's compensation to his performance measurement. The closer this relationship the more likely is the system to influence the behavior of the manager.

The economic and psychic rewards received by managers for successfully meeting the earnings-per-share measures of performance in our corporate reporting system are attractive. Modern managers understand this fact of life. Unfortunately, the pressures to meet these standards are sometimes so strong that some chief executive officers acting under the weight of an adverse business situation have stretched the credibility of their accounting reports to meet their stockholders' insatiable appetite for continually improved performance.

It is these incentives—plus the pressures for producing successful performance together with the fact that managers are human beings—that give meaning to the behavioral aspects of generally accepted accounting principles. It is reasonable to expect that managers acting in their self-interest will seek to meet their performance standards by whatever reasonable legitimate accounting methods are available to them. Hopefully, the accounting means they use will be in the best interests of society. This will be more likely to occur if corporate accounting policy decisions and corporate action are not complicated by the fact that available techniques used to measure and report performance have built-in biases toward the reporting of misleading results and the structuring of corporate decisions to justify the use of these methods.

RECENT PROGRESS

During the last five years the Accounting Principles Board has made a number of significant decisions which have influenced the motivational bias of generally accepted accounting principles.

Unconsolidated Subsidiaries

Opinion No. 10's amendment to Accounting Research Bulletin No. 51 reduced the motivational bias inherent in the old principles governing consolidation. These principles presented a strong inducement for companies to establish unconsolidated subsidiaries whose principal business activity was leasing property or facilities to their parents. This often led to an inadequate and unfair presentation of the consolidated financial position of the total enterprise. Significant assets and liabilities were excluded from the consolidated statements. Subsequent to Opinion

No. 10 such subsidiaries must be consolidated. Thus, the strength of accounting inducement to establish this particular type of subsidiary was reduced.

Extraordinary Income and Losses

Prior to Opinion No. 9 the accounting principles related to writing off extraordinary losses provided strong incentives for corporations to defer facing up to potential write-offs of costs, such as goodwill, bad debts, etc., and then write them off against retained earnings, rather than income.

Opinion No. 9 reversed this situation. Henceforth, the general presumption is that net income will reflect all items of profit and loss recognized during the period, except for those rare items which were actually adjustments to prior period income calculations. Now the accounting motivation tends to bias corporations away from capitalizing costs which may some day have to be written off against revenues, but do not have any offsetting related income. However, should a corporation build up large potential write-offs on its balance sheet, the effect of Opinion No. 9 may be to make the company more reluctant than ever before to write these costs off the balance sheet. In most cases these costs now would have to be charged against income. The option of a "painless" write-off against retained earnings is no longer available.

Common Stock Equivalents

Opinions No. 9 and 15 reduced the incentive for managers to issue convertible securities, particularly those which at the time of their issuance are the equivalent of common stock. Previously, the potential dilution from such securities was not included in the earnings-per-share calculation. This encouraged corporations to issue convertible securities to acquire other companies and for new financing. Beginning in late 1968, however, the Securities and Exchange Commission stated that the actual earnings-per-share calculation of corporations in its jurisdiction had to include all classes of common stock outstanding, all outstanding securities with participating dividend rights with common stock, and all securities deriving a major portion of their value from the conversion rights or common stock characteristics. This accounting change reduced one advantage of convertible securities as a financial device to the extent that they might now dilute primary and fully diluted earnings per share.

Retroactive Poolings

Prior to Opinion No. 10 the business combinations consummated during or shortly after the close of the accounting period but before the financial statements of the continuing business were issued to stockholders, were includable on a pooling-of-interest basis in the results at the close of the accounting period. There was no requirement for disclosing the results of operations and the fiscal condition of the acquiring company before effecting the combination. The stockholder could not distinguish that part of reported earnings which related to operations and that part which related to acquisitions. This accounting practice was a strong inducement to some managers to acquire companies in order to reach previously announced projected earnings levels.

347

Opinion No. 10 did not remove the accounting incentive for such acquisitions, but it did reduce the strength of the inducement. Opinion No. 10 recommended: "In order to show the effect of poolings upon their earnings trends, companies may wish to provide reconciliations of amounts of revenues previously reported with those currently presented." The effectiveness of such disclosure admonitions upon corporate behavior has yet to be fully tested. The assumption is however, that this disclosure requirement will contribute to more responsible managerial behavior in merger decisions.

Each of these changes sponsored by the Accounting Principles Board reduced the opportunity for managers to improve or hide profits through accounting manipulations. While the Board was not able to remove the conditions which led to managers adopting these practices for nonoperating reasons, it did eliminate or reduce the strength of the potentially undesirable accounting inducements inherent in these reporting practices.

CURRENT AREAS OF CONCERN

There are still a number of accounting practices which have undesirable behavioral characteristics since they can condition managerial decisions in such a way that the resulting measurement of performance is misleading. The major areas of current concern are the treatment of poolings-of-interest, leases, unconsolidated financial subsidiaries, and investment tax credits. In each of these cases there is a need to tighten current accounting practices so as to reduce the temptation for managers to gear their operating or reporting decisions to take advantage of the profit or balance sheet improvements inherent in the relevant accounting options.

Pooling of Interests

An important feature of the prolonged trend of corporate mergers and acquisitions is the "pooling-of-interest" accounting practice. Originally, this treatment was reserved for the merger through an exchange of equity stocks of two companies of comparable size. The sales and profits of the two companies were added together and presented as though they had always been one company. Similarly, the assets, liabilities, and retained earnings were combined and the remaining capital accounts adjusted to bring the totals of the left- and right-hand sides of the new balance sheet into equilibrium and to reflect the new stock issued.

Before the mid-1950's the relative size of the acquired company tended to be an important criteria in determining how to account for the acquisition. As often as not this meant acquisitions of smaller companies by larger ones for either cash or stock were usually treated as a purchase. In these cases the sales, expenses, and profits of the acquired company were added to the income statement of the acquiring company only as earned from the date of acquisition. Usually the assets of the acquired company were added to those of the acquiring company at their book or fair market value. Any excess of purchase price over the net asset value of the acquisition was listed as goodwill among the acquirer's assets.

The purchase treatment was unpopular with a number of managers, and, in general, it did not encourage them to actively seek acquisitions of smaller companies. Managers were reluctant to show large amounts of goodwill on their balance sheet, even though there was no requirement to write this intangible asset off against earnings or retained earnings, except if there was a permanent decline in the profitability of the acquired business. Also, they were reluctant to attribute some of this goodwill to the assets they had acquired. This would have raised their annual depreciation costs and lowered profits.

Beginning about ten years ago the pooling treatment was slowly expanded to cover more and more mergers until today nearly every acquisition involving a taxfree exchange of stock is treated as a pooling-of-interest. Now bigger companies can acquire smaller ones without being burdened with the troublesome goodwill item.

Thus, an accounting consideration changed from a disincentive to an incentive to merge. In fact, much of the merger movement can be attributed to this development. It made it possible for some companies with high price/earnings ratios to grow faster and easier through acquisitions than through operations.

The power of the pooling incentive is increased significantly when one considers the disincentive inherent in the accounting presumption that the costs of such programs as research and development and new product development and marketing are written off as incurred. If these costs are heavy this could have a depressing effect on profits since the revenues from such activities are usually relatively small in the early years of the program. Thanks to the pooling treatment a company can avoid this situation by acquiring new products and research know-how through a merger. The development costs can be avoided and the risks can be less.

Off-the-Balance-Sheet Financing

A significant factor in the growth of leasing companies is the current accounting practice which does not require lessees to capitalize future rental payments and list them as a liability on the balance sheet. This fact has encouraged corporations to enter into leasing arrangements rather than acquire assets through debt. The result is a more attractive debt-equity ratio, even though in most leasing situations it is hard to see how the substance of the lease contract and the intentions of the parties differ from those associated with a normal debt agreement. Consequently, the accounting treatment of leases has a built-in bias toward leasing. The debt equivalent of the lease is kept off the balance sheet.

Another so-called "off-the-balance-sheet" financing device encouraged by accounting is the creation of financial subsidiaries to handle the debt financing of credit sales. These subsidiaries do not necessarily have to be consolidated with their parent company in reports to the public. Consequently if the financial subsidiary is not consolidated, the debt held by the finance company is not included in the debt-equity ratio of the parent, even though in some cases it is the general credit of the parent that guarantees the debt. In my opinion, the exclusion of many of these financial subsidiaries from the parent company statement can lead to misleading parent company statements.

Investment Tax Credit

The flow-through accounting treatment of the investment tax credit which permits a company to recognize the full income benefit of the credit in the year it is granted leads to a misleading statement of current profits. This profit-enhancing potential of the credit biases management toward purchasing assets, although like the examples cited above it is not the only factor in the decision.

The strength of the influence of the accounting treatment on the investment decision would be reduced if investment tax credits had to be accounted for by the deferral method which spreads the credit's profit improvement influence over the economic life of the asset. This handling of the credit relates profit recognition more closely to the use of assets in operations which adds to the company and society's capital and makes profits less of a derivative of accounting treatment and capital outlays.

Protection Through Disclosure

It is possible that the potentially undesirable behavioral implications of the foregoing cases may be diminished by the disclosure requirements relating to them. This would be true if security analysts and stockholders fully understood the accounting practices involved and explicitly made adjustments for the influence of accounting on corporate profits and actions in their evaluations. The enthusiasm of the public and the investment community for conglomerate company stocks whose managements have molded their actions in large part to take advantage of accounting profit enhancers would seem to indicate that this is not the case. If this is so, disclosure is not necessarily an adequate safeguard for investors or an adequate motivator for improved reporting.

The existence of an accounting principle with potential behavioral implications is seldom enough alone to encourage management to adopt a principle for reporting purposes. Certain nonaccounting facts, when combined with the reporting opportunities inherent in the accounting practice, activate the motivational biases of the accounting principle.

One basic condition is the existence of a general operating need. For example, managers are not likely to lease a new building simply because of the accounting treatment of leases. The need for a building has to be there first. However, the "off-the-balance-sheet" financing aspect of the lease treatment may well induce a manager to lease the needed building, rather than purchasing it through regular mortgage financing. Of course, other factors beside the accounting consideration may lead the managers to decide to lease or not lease.

There are a variety of other circumstances which may give added strength to the undesirable behavioral bias of some accounting principles. These include the case where a corporation fails to reach its "earnings-per-share" standard through operations. The opportunity to increase profits through accounting devices is present. It takes a strong-minded management to resist the temptation inherent in these methods, especially when the competition is adopting these practices to boost profits.

Another common circumstance is a company seeking, for one reason or another, to project a particular financial image. A common example of this phenomena is the company that seeks a growth image. The "pooling-of-interest" accounting encourages this to be done through acquisition for the reasons outlined above. A second illustration is the company which seeks to project a high return on capital image. The accounting treatment of unconsolidated subsidiaries encourages companies with this goal to establish unconsolidated financial subsidiaries. The equity method allows management to include the profits of financial subsidiaries in the consolidated statement, but not the assets or liabilities.

In summary, within the accounting practice the direction of any bias is clear. However, the strength of this bias depends on the attendant circumstances.

A number of companies have recognized the motivational implications of specific generally accepted accounting practices and have explicitly made decisions for behavioral reasons to use or not use these principles to calculate the internal measures of performance through which the actions of managers are controlled in part. Some of these companies use these principles for internal statement purposes, but oppose their use for reports to stockholders. The reverse is true of others. Here are four illustrations:

1. Very few corporations show capitalized leases on their public statements, yet a great number of them require divisional managers to capitalize leases on their divisional statements. Why? Top management recognizes that managers can improve their return on total assets by leasing rather than buying new plant equipment. The leased assets never enter into the investment base whereas the purchased assets do. As noted earlier, this can encourage excessive leasing in some situations. Also, comparing divisional performance can be more difficult when some divisions lease and others buy assets. To facilitate comparison, some companies require all divisions leasing assets to capitalize the leases and then depreciate the offsetting asset like any ordinary purchased assets. This puts all divisions on the same basis.

2. Few companies permit divisional managers to capitalize research and development, principally because this "tends to let them off the hook." If they were permitted to capitalize research and development the managers might be less inclined not to terminate projects with poor prospects of success because their costs could be kept out of the income statement. Yet, in the case of external reporting it is often those companies who are in trouble and whose research projects are the most dubious that try to capitalize these costs.

3. For somewhat similar motivational reasons a number of companies use accelerated depreciation for internal purposes. The early heavy depreciation charges tend to make managers more careful about making investments with marginal prospects. On the other hand, some of these same companies use straight-line depreciation in public reports.

4. Apparently, few companies give divisions credit for investment tax credits flowing from their investments. Their reason is that it might encourage divisions to make investments primarily to get the credit. Yet, a number of these same corporations report the credit for public purposes by the flow-through methods, which gives them the full credit in the year they acquired the asset.

Examples such as the above raise the disturbing question: If an accounting method is not a useful measure of performance for internal purposes because: (1) it motivates managers to follow operating policies not desired by the company; (2) it provides top management with a misleading measure of performance; or (3) it fails to reflect the company's prospects, then why would the same considerations not govern the selection of the method for reporting these same facts to stockholders? The presumption is that the internal and external application of generally accepted accounting principles should be the same. In both cases the underlying purpose is the same—to measure performance and to motivate managers to operate in such a way as to achieve the company's goals.

The challenge to those who create generally accepted accounting principles is to develop a set of principles that are both behaviorally and technically sound. They should be behaviorally sound in that they

Inhibit managers from taking undesirable operating actions to justify the adoption of an accounting alternative.

Inhibit the adoption of accounting practices by corporations which create the illusion of performance.

The traditional approach to defining generally accepted accounting principles has focused principally on technical considerations. Typically, this has been done well. The time has come, however, to pay greater attention to the possible impact of accounting practice on people's actions. If this is also done well, financial accounting will do a better job of communicating the financial facts of a business situation, rather than the illusion of performance.

Some accountants and regulatory agencies would go further than I suggest. These people argue that financial reports should be reports on management, not reports by management. They seem to believe it is both desirable and feasible that some all-wise body construct a set of accounting principles for business that will make the financial statements of corporations more accurate and more comparable as well as motivate managers to make sound economic decisions. These are desirable goals. However, the degree to which this can be achieved by some super-accounting body is limited. Our management control experience in the smaller environment of a single firm indicates that the use of financial controls can be a useful—but somewhat imperfect—crude tool for motivating managers. Also, within the confines of the single firm it is very difficult to design a uniform system of reporting for all of the economic subunits which produce meaningful results.

Despite my reservations about how far we can go in using our financial reporting system to encourage managers to report fairly and make sound economic decisions, I nevertheless believe we should seek to improve the behavioral aspects of the system.

In order to do this we must know more about the behavioral aspects of generally accepted accounting principles in a business climate. More research is needed in this area, particularly as it relates to the motivational relationship between external reporting and the internal management control system.

Until such research is available we will have to rely on the many studies in management control for our direction. One important conclusion of these studies that we could well work with now is that control systems with behavioral attributes which allow and encourage responsible management by self-control, rather than command through inflexible rules, are the most appropriate in times of change within complex business environments. Such an approach is needed today for our financial accounting system if we are to encourage positive managerial operating and reporting responses.

22

ACCOUNTING CONCEPTS AND BEHAVIORAL HYPOTHESES*

REGINALD S. GYNTHER

The discipline of accounting suffers in many ways from our inability to devise, deduce, or build a general theory on which to base the many necessary lesser theories for specific events, operations, organizations, etc. Until this general theory is produced we will continue to operate with the variety (and often duplicity) of theories which cannot be interrelated or fitted to any one framework of accounting in a logical fashion. Unbeknown to the participants, many debates on accounting "theories," practices, and procedures stem from differences in their basic concepts of accounting. As Oliver Wendell Holmes once said:

> I will tell you what I have found spoil more good talks than anything else; long arguments on special points between people who differ on the fundamental principles upon which these points depend. No men can have satisfactory relations with each other until they have agreed on certain ultimata of belief, not to be disturbed in ordinary conversation, and unless they have sense enough to trace the secondary questions depending upon these ultimate beliefs to their source.[1]

This paper is a humble attempt to open the door far enough to permit a little light to be thrown on these matters in the hope that we might proceed a step further towards a general theory of accounting. After examining what appear to be looked upon as the main concepts of accounting and the different attitudes and consequences involved, we shall analyze some of the underlying behavioral factors causing the existence of these different perceptions. It will then be suggested that these underlying behavioral factors nullify two notable attempts to provide a solution to this dilemma; and reasons for the apparent irreconcilability of the various basic concepts will be given. A discussion of the implications for the future and the author's suggestions will then follow.

DIFFERENT PERCEPTIONS OF THE FIRM

The subject of "basic concepts of accounting" is one that has often been discarded, only to be stumbled upon by another academician and to be dragged out of the corner for another "chewing over" before being discarded once again. With

---

* *The Accounting Review*, April 1967, pp. 274-290

[1]Baxter, W. T. (ed.), *Studies in Accounting*. (Sydney: Law Book Co. of Australasia Pty. Ltd., 1950), p. 243.

few exceptions, basic textbooks have ignored the matter, and it is seldom, if ever, discussed outside academic circles.

Over the years two main concepts, [2] the proprietary concept and the entity concept, have been discussed at odd times in the literature, and there have been occasional appearances of refinements, modifications, and alternatives reflecting slight variations in viewpoint, [3] as well as attempts at reconciliation. [4]

The Proprietary Concept

Those who hold the proprietary concept perceive the firm as being owned by a sole proprietor, a set of partners, or a number of shareholders. The firm's assets are looked upon as being the property of these people and the liabilities of the firm are their liabilities. "The business is merely a segregated portion of their financial interests, accounted for separately because it is convenient or necessary for various reasons to do so." [5] The proprietors are the center of interest at all times, and their viewpoints are the ones reflected in the accounting records. Total assets minus total liabilities equals that portion of their net worth that is vested in the firm. Revenue and expense items immediately increase or decrease this net worth, which is another way of saying that profits are perceived to be the proprietors (and not the firm) at the time they are earned, whether they are distributed or not.

When corporations do distribute dividends, they are seen to be actually placing in the hands of the proprietors something which has been part of their private individual property for some time. Payments of interest and taxation by the firm are expenses to the proprietors and reduce their net worth in the same way as the firm's other operating expenses do. Where the firm does pay taxation, there is "double taxation."

However, there are different shades of the proprietary concept, depending chiefly in who is perceived as belonging to the proprietorship group. Husband sees the proprietorship function belonging to those who really are entrepreneurs, and "on the theory that the common stockholders occupy the entrepreneurship position in the corporation, preferred stock, like bonds, represents hiring of capital service. Consistent therewith, preferred stock dividends are best treated as a cost." [6] This is the narrowest version of the proprietary concept and it appears to be identical to the "residual equity" concept which has been put forward by Staubus. He also sees the proprietors of the firm as being the ordinary shareholders only:

[2] Sometimes referred to as "theories."

[3] For example, Suojanen, W. O., "Accounting Theory and the Large Corporation," THE ACCOUNTING REVIEW, July 1954, pp. 391-398; Husband, G. R., "The Entity Concept in Accounting," THE ACCOUNTING REVIEW, October 1954, pp. 552-563; Sprouse, R. T., "The Significance of the Concept of the Corporation in Accounting Analyses," THE ACCOUNTING REVIEW, July 1957, pp. 369-378; Staubus, G. J., "The Residual Equity Point of View in Accounting," THE ACCOUNTING REVIEW, January 1959, pp. 3-13; Li, D. H., "The Nature of the Corporate Residual Equity Under the Entity Concept," THE ACCOUNTING REVIEW, April 1960, pp. 258-263; Li, D. H., "The Nature and Treatment of Dividends Under the Entity Concept," THE ACCOUNTING REVIEW, October 1960, pp. 675-679; Lorig, A. N., "Some Basic Concepts of Accounting and Their Implications," THE ACCOUNTING REVIEW, July 1964, pp. 563-573.

[4] For example, Vatter, W. J., *The Fund Theory of Accounting and Its Implications for Financial Reports.* (The University of Chicago Press, 1947); Goldberg. L., *An Inquiry into the Nature of Accounting,* (American Accounting Association; 1965), pp. 162-174. These are discussed later in this paper.

[5] Lorig, A. N., op. cit., pp. 564-565.

[6] Husband, op. cit., p. 561.

Those who have been friendly to the proprietary theory should see some merit in narrowing the focal area to a single point by excluding preferred stock (unless it is participating preferred). . . . In the residual equity theory, all investors in a corporation except common stockholders are thought of as outsiders.[7]

However, Lorig's perception of the firm is such that he widens the proprietorship group to admit the preferred shareholders:

Just who constitute the proprietors in a business corporation is not entirely clear. Certainly the common stockholders are included. The preferred stockholders also are generally considered in that category, though normally they have no voice in operating the business. In practice, the financial return to them is always considered a distribution and is chargeable only to net profits, current or accumulated, and payable only when declared in the form of a dividend. Both classes of stockholders, therefore, are distinctly different from the creditor group, and this distinction is basic in the proprietary concept.[8]

Then there is the minority who see *all* long-term investors as being proprietors of the firm—i.e., bond and debenture holders as well as shareholders. For example, Chow considers that "a concept of proprietor broadly defined as the totality of private interests or the long-term investors as a class would be more logical and workable from the standpoint of theory and practice."[9]

The Entity Concept

The entity concept, like the proprietary concept, is a viewpoint, an attitude of mind; and it, too, is not confined to accountants. For example, Eells and Walton say:

The perception of managers is often such, that the shareholders as well as the creditors are outside the organization which they are concerned in operating.[10]

This is the essence of the entity concept of accounting. The holders of this concept see the entity as something separate and distinct from those who contributed capital to it. They see the assets and liabilities as being those of the entity itself and not those of the shareholders or proprietors. As profits are earned by the entity, they become the property of the entity; they accrue to the shareholders *only* if and when a dividend is declared. It follows that any undistributed profits remain the property of the entity and constitute part of the entity's "equity in itself"[11] in the eyes of those who hold an entity concept, and this is not affected

---

[7]Staubus, op. cit., p. 12.

[8]Lorig, op. cit., p. 565.

[9]Chow, Y. C., "The Doctrine of Proprietorship," THE ACCOUNTING REVIEW, April 1942, p. 162.

[10]Eells, R., and Walton, C., *Conceptual Foundations of Business.* (Richard D. Irwin, Inc.; 1961), p. 149. W. A. Paton, in his remarkable book published 44 years ago (*Accounting Theory,* The Ronald Press Company; 1922), was probably the first to recognize *and* describe this entity viewpoint.

[11]Husband, op. cit., p. 554.

by the inclusion of undistributed profits in the stockholders' section of the printed balance sheet. The entity concept person sees this as mere conforming to conventional and regulatory reporting procedures.

It should be emphasized at this stage that those who have the entity viewpoint actually see the net assets as being the property of the entity itself, and not that of the shareholders. A few writers have indicated that the mere creation of a separate accounting system for the entity's activities provides evidence of the existence of the entity concept, but it is suggested here that these few writers do not perceive the firm in the way a holder of the "pure" entity viewpoint does.[12] The "independence" or "separateness" of the entity's accounting records is commonly referred to as the "entity convention" and not the "entity concept." If the hot dog vendor maintains separate accounting records for his business as he should (the entity convention), it does not follow that he has an entity viewpoint regarding the business—although this is possible.

> It is to be noted that in the proprietary theory, as well as in the entity theory, the business is the center or the area of attention. No extended argument is necessary to establish that the area of attention for a given set of records and reports must be limited.... Hence, both proprietary and entity theory recognize the independence of certain activities from each other for accounting purposes; and the unit of accounting under either theory is the business venture or enterprise.[13]

It was seen that different shades of the proprietary concept exist, and so it is with the entity concept. Here, too, all those with an entity concept do not perceive the firm in exactly the same way.

Those people who see the entity from a holistic viewpoint look upon all dividend, interest, and taxation payments as being expenses of the entity, and this is the picture of the entity concept that Husband paints so well.[14] All of these are outgoings which reduce the undistributed profits that form part of the entity's equity in itself. This way of looking at the firm is not unlike that in Vatter's fund theory; he has said that "the fund theory viewpoint is something of an extension of the entity theory."[15] Li, who might be "accused" of holding an extreme entity viewpoint, looks upon dividends not as a financing cost, as most entity people do, but as being "akin to institutional advertising ... a cost incurred with a view to the

---

[12]For example, Louis Goldberg says, "The entity theory—or, as it is frequently referred to, the entity convention—has been the subject of varying degrees of exposition," op. cit., pp. 109-110; and "if we take the entity theory to its ultimate end, we reach the stage where a person may become an (accounting) entity distinct from himself," *An Outline of Accounting* (Sydney: Law Book Co., 1957). p. 29.

Gilman S., in *Accounting Concepts of Profit* (The Ronald Press Company; 1939), tends to blur the "entity convention" and the "entity theory" together. (See Chapters 4 and 5.) At page 47 Gilman says, "Accounting records are still written from the *viewpoint* of an entity until it has now become an accounting convention" (emphasis added). Incidentally, although Gilman seems to profess to hold the entity viewpoint (p. 64), he says at p. 52, "The entity is as soulless and automatic as a slot machine.... In and of itself the entity makes no profits, suffers no losses"; and "increases in entity property automatically become additional liabilities to the proprietor." See further "proprietary-type" statements of his on pp. 61, 87, 88, 123, 246, and 604.

[13]Vatter, op. cit., p. 3.

[14]Husband, op. cit.

[15]Vatter, W. J., in *Handbook of Modern Accounting Theory* (M. Baker, ed., Prentice-Hall, Inc.; 1955), p. 367.

future"; he also says that they may be "viewed as an insurance cost."[16] He sees dividends as being necessary to create both a favorable investment atmosphere and a favorable corporate image, both with the idea of protecting the corporation's objective of survival.

Even though dividends are seen by some entity theorists as being an expense of running the business, the taxation authorities will not allow them to be treated as a deduction for tax purposes. Taxes are calculated on profits before deducting dividends. To this extent, those with this entity outlook also see a form of double taxation.

However, Vatter says that "under entity theory interest charges are distributions of income, not expense. Similarly, dividends would be regarded as income distributions rather than proprietary withdrawals of capital. Taxes on net income also would seem to fall in the category of distributions of income rather than determinants of 'profit'."[17] This writer considers that this is not the contradiction that might appear at first sight, but merely the description of the viewpoint of a person who is in charge of production and/or distribution activities for an entity and who is not looking at the entity as a whole. After such a person makes "profits" for the entity, he "hands them over" to top management (which is also responsible for arranging finance for the entity) for the paying of interest, dividends, and taxation. This contention seems to be supported by Vatter:

> Under entity theory, expense is the cost assigned to the production of revenue. The business unit (entity) is one part of the vast machinery of production and distribution of goods and services. As a part of the business system, the firm is a device for converting goods and services into new and different forms. Expense is simply the financial measure (cost) of the product of the firm. . . . Entity theory tends to recognize financing transactions and income distributions as distinct from either proprietary or income-determining transactions.[18]

At one end of the entity viewpoint of the firm continuum, the capital supplied by the stockholders (including undistributed profits) is also viewed as being part of the entity's equity in itself and *not* as a debt of an indefinite nature. For example, Li sees such capital remaining with the entity as long as it remains a going concern and he argues that the lack of a due date "denies a claim" by the stockholder to capital contributed. "From the present-value concept, the present value of a claim due at infinity is zero, the same as if there were no claim at all."[19]

The Social Responsibilities Concept

Some people perceive the firm as a social institution that is operated for the benefit of all members and groups in the society. They see the firm as being responsible to stockholders, management, employees, suppliers, customers, the government, and other members of the public. Ladd, for example, says:

> Virtually all segments of the community, including corporation managers, have come to have important interests in the status and progress of the large

---

[16]Li, op. cit., October 1960, p. 675.

[17]Batter in Backer op. cit., p. 367.

[18]Vatter, ibid., p. 366.

[19]Li, op. cit., April 1960, p. 261.

corporation, which is by way of saying that the corporation has important responsibilities to all of them. These responsibilities are a function of the corporation's role as our principal instrument for the utilization of human, material, and monetary resources in the production and distribution of goods and services, and for rewarding those who provide these goods and services.[20]

Instead of providing a third concept (in addition to the proprietary and entity concepts discussed above), it seems to this writer that the social responsibility ideas concern the way the entity *acts* and the way it goes about carrying out its activities. It seems to be related to ethics, goals, objectives, and the ways of obtaining them, and in no way alters the perception of a firm as an entity owning net assets. In fact, the social responsibility notions seem to fit completely within the entity viewpoint of the firm when the writings of the two main accounting exponents of these ideas are examined.

Suojanen's "enterprise theory"[21] is based on the concept of the large corporation as an "enterprise or institution with wide social responsibilities," and his main (or sole) requirement is in the reporting process where he wants the financial statements to show "value added" as in national income accounting.

.If the enterprise is considered to be an institution, its operations should be assessed in terms of its contribution to the *flow* of output of the community. If the income generated in the enterprise is to be analyzed on the basis of social considerations, then the traditional type of income statement is insufficient.[22]

But Suojanen definitely perceives the firm as a separate and distinct entity; the following statements by him are completely consistent with the way the firm is seen by those with an entity outlook:

The enterprise theory of the area of accounting application accepts the concept of the large corporation as "an institution in its own right."[23]

The enterprise exists apart from any of the participants.[24]

The stockholders in an enterprise and their rights are subsidiary to the organization and its survival.[25]

The other main exponent of the social responsibility ideas in the accounting area, Ladd, is also mainly concerned with the reporting function and this is reflected in his strong advocacy of "the uniformity and the degree of disclosure modern conditions require."[26] At the same time, he, too, seems to remain completely within the entity outlook described in the previous section. He thinks that "corporate survival and growth are the principal objectives of contemporary

[20]Ladd, D. R., *Contemporary Corporate Accounting and the Public* (Richard D. Irwin, Inc.; 1963), p. 13.
[21]Op. cit.
[22]Ibid., p. 395.
[23]Ibid., p. 393.
[24]Ibid., p. 394.
[25]Ibid.
[26]Ladd, op. cit., p. 165.

corporations and that these objectives are implicitly accepted by most of those to whom corporations are responsible."[27]

To summarize, it is thought that the social responsibilities idea is an adjunct to the entity concept, and that it concerns the way the entity carries out its activities in society and then reports back to the members of that society.

Economic Theories of the Firm

It is clear that the entity and proprietary concepts of the firm are also present in the discipline of economics, but they do not appear to have been delineated and labeled as clearly there as they have been in the discipline of accounting. McGuire says that this area has been "clouded by the economists who discuss the enterprise and the entrepreneur as one and the same, and who sometimes term profits the returns to the firm, and at other times talk about profits as the return to the firm's owners"; and that "there appears to be little unanimity among economists on the proper answer to the question: are profits a return to individuals or to business units."[28]

McGuire considers, and this writer agrees, that most economists have the proprietary outlook and perceive "the net income stream flowing to the owners of the firm";[29] and he finds it difficult to "accept the convenient fiction of the impersonal institution—the firm—as an ultimate income recipient separated completely by convention from the people who inhabit it."[30] The viewpoints of the economists Due and Bober are identical to those of Husband, because they see the stockholders, even in the modern large corporation, making the decision to hire, fire, or retain the management; and they therefore are really the entrepreneurs.[31]

Stauss and Davis, however, are representative of those economists who adopt the entity concept and who look on the firm itself as the entrepreneur and on profit as the net income of the enterprise.[32] This, of course, eliminates the inconvenient "undistributed profits" from the economic models.

The proprietary concept seems to personify the traditional, classical ideology of capitalism. This is reflected in a statement by the economist, Milton Friedman, a prominent advocate of that ideology, when he decries the concept of social responsibility that many corporate officials "profess" to have adopted:

> Few trends could so thoroughly undermine the very foundations of our free society as the acceptance by corporate officials of a social responsibility other than to make as much money for the stockholders as possible.[33]

---

[27] Ibid., p. 18.

[28] McGuire, J. W., *Theories of Business Behavior* (Prentice-Hall, Inc.; 1964), pp. 52-53.

[29] Ibid., p. 54.

[30] Ibid., p. 53.

[31] Due, J. F., *Intermediate Economic Analysis* (Richard D. Irwin, Inc.; 1951), p. 415; and Bober, M. M. *Intermediate Price and Income Theory* (W. W. Norton & Company, Inc., 1955), pp. 425 ff.

[32] Stauss, J. H., "The Entrepreneur: The Firm," *Journal of Political Economy,* June 1944, pp. 112-117, and Davis, R. M., "The Current State of Profit Theory," *American Economic Review,* June 1952, pp. 252-252.

[33] Friedman, M., *Capitalism and Freedom* (The University of Chicago Press, 1962), p. 133.

Also, "The corporation is a instrument of the stockholders who own it."[34]

The entity concept, on the other hand, seems to be the essence of Monsen's "managerial ideology of capitalism,"[35] which sees the businessman and the large corporation as having replaced the entrepreneur. This ideology is also tinged with the idea of social responsibility, which we saw previously is consistent with the entity concept.

Consequences of the Different Viewpoints

In the sections above on the proprietary and entity concepts, it was seen that the different ways of perceiving the firm resulted in different ways of viewing profits. Several different ways of looking at the treatment of interest, dividends, and income taxes in the profit determination process were discussed.

Lorig lists differences in accounting and reporting that he sees as being caused by the existence of two main viewpoints.[36] However, it has been shown above that there are several gradations or shadings within both the proprietary and entity concepts, and for this reason it might be difficult to find many that would agree with all of the specific differences that he lists using his perception of these viewpoints. For example, he says that a person with an entity concept would probably create a charge (and accrue the resultant liability) for arrears of dividends on preferred stock, while a person with a proprietary outlook would not.[37] It is suggested here that Husband and Staubus, whose viewpoints place them at the extreme end of the proprietary concept continuum, would be just as likely as the entity theorist to accrue this item because they see preferred stockholders as being outside the proprietary group and in a category similar to bondholders. On the other hand, we saw that Lorig views preferred stockholders as being in the entrepreneur category. The main point here is that it is difficult to prepare any one comprehensive listing of differences to depict all the various viewpoints within the two main categories.

Much of the Lorig list relates to ways in which items are treated in financial statements prepared for the purpose of reporting to stockholders, and this writer does not believe that these financial statements necessarily reflect the attitudes or concepts of the firm or of those responsible for preparing them. When statements are being prepared, every consideration must be given to agency regulations, convention, and the style and methods used on previous occasions. Further, it is thought that a person with an entity viewpoint might deliberately prepare these statements in the way he thought they would please the shareholders. For example, Li can be imagined to be expanding his "institutional advertising" in this fashion.

Lorig suggests that all those with an entity concept are not interested in revaluing assets in times of changing price levels, while those with a proprietary viewpoint are.[38] People with an entity viewpoint are usually most concerned with the survival and growth of the entity, and besides other things this entails ensuring that all assets are being used profitably within the various divisions of the organiza-

[34]Ibid., p. 135.

[35]Monsen, R. J., Jr., *Modern American Capitalism—Idealogies and Issues* (Houghton Mifflin Company; 1963). pp. 25-29.

[36]Lorig, op. cit.

[37]Ibid., p. 571.

[38]Ibid., p. 572.

tion. To control this and the performance of managers effectively, it is necessary to look at the current values of the assets employed and the divisional profit percentages on those current values. Revaluations of assets are often necessary to enable this to be done. To the entity person such revaluations of assets would result in increases (assuming rising prices) to the entity's equity within itself (and not to stockholders' funds), and while this is not "meaningless" it is certain that entity people concentrate their attention mainly on the asset side of the balance sheet.

However, there are some significant differences between the entity and proprietary concepts in the *way* that assets are revalued. These will be dealt with later in this paper.

SOME BEHAVIORAL HYPOTHESES FOR THE DIFFERENT CONCEPTS

The same firm, i.e., the same set of "facts," can be seen in several different manners, which merely illustrates a matter that psychologists have been concerned with for many years. What is an "objective fact" is often only that which is perceived as being such by an individual. Each of us sees the world in a manner slightly different from the next one; many variations in perception are possible.

The world-as-we-see-it is not necessarily the same as the world-as-it-"really"-is. Our answer depends on what we heard, not on what was really said. The housewife buys what she likes best, not what is best. Whether we feel hot or cold depends on us, not on the thermometer. The same job may look like a good job to one of us and a sloppy job to another.[39]

The realization that different perceptions are often possible brings tolerance and permits the acceptance of other viewpoints as "legitimate"; but as Stagner has pointed out, people often become so strongly involved in a situation that they fail to distinguish between their own personal involvement and the specific facts.[40] This is particularly so in situations involving conflict.

Reasons for Different Perceptions

The matters of perceptions, attitudes, frames of reference, values, reference groups, group norms, environment, culture, and personality systems overlap and are inextricably interrelated in interacting patterns. As many volumes have been written concerning these matters, the discussion here can do no more than give a scant outline necessary to an understanding of the issues at hand.

To understand the manner in which man responds to and copes with his social environment, we must know what that environment is to him. Although it is certain that those things that seem to be aids to the satisfaction of one's needs tend to be perceived more quickly than other things,[41] perception depends to a large extent on the assumptions that an individual brings to any particular occasion. The meanings and significances that we assign to things, people, and events depend on the meanings and significances we have built up into a frame of reference through

[39]Leavitt, H. J., *Managerial Psychology* (The University of Chicago Press; 1958), p. 27.

[40]Stagner, R. *The Psychology of Industrial Conflict* (John Wiley & Sons, Inc.; 1956), Chapter 3.

[41]Leavitt, op. cit., p. 36.

our past experiences.[42] This frame of reference, which may be called our value system, is something that is molded over the years as we form attitudes to a variety of situations, persons, groups, etc. Katz says, "When specific attitudes are organized into a hierarchical structure, they comprise value systems."[43]

These attitudes are psychological formations learned in the course of our development,[44] and once learned they tend to demand that we react in a characteristic way.

In our daily life, many of our major attitudes are formed on the basis of short-cut value dictums from other people, *before* we make up our minds ourselves through actual contact with the situations, persons and things. In other words, the relationships are structured, crystallized for us through these value dictums before we form our own attitudes in relation to them on the basis of sufficient facts.[45]

This indicates the impact of "family" on the development of each individual's attitudes; and many consider that this is the major direct influence because it is the "usual filter through which the cultural, class, religious, and other sources flow to the individual" in his early years.[46] Evidence of this is provided by Lipset who, from empirical findings, reported that there was a relatively high congruency between "father's vote and the vote of first-voters."[47]

But there are other important influences on the development of attitudes besides the family. Culture (meaning the customs, habits, traditions, and beliefs that characterize a people or a social group) is a most important influence that varies greatly from one society to another. Anthropologists have shown how different cultures are responsible for vastly different attitudes to many things; but for our purpose in this paper, total culture will not be an important factor because we are examining differences in perception within one culture.

Each individual in this complex society is influenced by the many groups of which he is a member. Geographic, religious, educational, peer, and socio-economic group memberships all provide a person with group norms and standards as to what attitudes he "should" learn; and many of these attitudes relate to both work situations and industrial society.[48] It is not suggested that each individual will take over and internalize all the values of the social groups in which he moves, but they will have some lasting effect on him if he becomes psychologically involved. In some cases, too, the attitudes of people have been developed, not by membership within a reference group, but because they aspire to membership within the group and so adopt its viewpoints.

It follows that it is difficult to validate an argument that a person "should" or "should not" have certain perceptions or concepts of the firm. Why? Because these perceptions and concepts are derivatives of attitudes (via a reference frame of

[42]Cantril, H., "Perception and Interpersonal Relations," *American Journal of Psychiatry,* February 1957, p. 120.

[43]Katz, D., "The Functional Approach to the Study of Attitudes," in Costello, T. W., and Zalkind, S. S., *Psychology in Administration.* (Prentice-Hall, Inc.; 1963), p. 253.

[44]Sherif, M., *An Outline of Social Psychology* (Harper & Brothers, 1948), p. 208.

[45]Ibid., p. 228.

[46]Costello and Zalkind, p. 261.

[47]Lipset, S. M., *Political Man* (Doubleday & Company, Inc.; 1963).

[48]Costello and Zalkind, p. 261.

values), and these attitudes, in turn, are a function of many things—including the person's environmental and social history.

Further, it should be mentioned that people are not consciously aware of all facets of their value structure or of the various attitudes that have gone into its construction. Therefore, they are not consciously aware of what their perceptions are or might be in certain circumstances. Much lies dormant in the subconscous awaiting possible motivation.

The hypotheses that follow are based on informal observations made over several years of accountants in public practice, accountants in commerce and industry, businessmen shareholders with holdings of all sizes, graduate students, and others. Most were not aware in the first instance of the terms "proprietary concept" and "entity concept" because discussions under these headings have appeared almost exclusively in the academic writings. It was by discussing matters such as the "property" in net assets and profits, and the treatment of interest, dividends, and income taxes that it was possible to classify their perception of the firm in most cases. Further, it was found that most of these people were not even aware that two different main concepts exist, and that they felt there was or should be only one way of viewing the firm. Their viewpoint, whether strong or not, had remained in their subconscious until the matter was discussed.

Some Hypotheses Concerning the Proprietary Concept

The intention is not to list hypotheses in a formal fashion, but to include them in the general discussion. Some are fairly "obvious" and might not cause debate, but it will be interesting to attempt to prove (or disprove) others by empirical research some time in the future.

It is hypothesised that most stockholders with substantial holdings of shares in corporations have the proprietary outlook, and that this is particularly so with holders of substantial quantities of common stock. Further, it is claimed here that most accountants in public practice have a proprietary outlook, and those with whom this has been discussed seem to agree that this is a result of their adopting the viewpoint of the shareholder when carrying out the many audits of corporations. To most public accountants the prime function of the accounting system is to reflect the interests of the shareholders. In Australia, auditors are actually appointed by shareholders at each company's annual meeting, and their short audit report at the foot of the balance sheet is addressed to the shareholders who appointed them. The examinations conducted by professional bodies of accountancy tend to be oriented in style and flavor towards the proprietary concept, and this results in slanting the preparatory education of public accountants in the same direction. The result is that they tend to see the net assets as really being the property of the shareholders, and they look upon profits as "belonging" to the shareholders as soon as they are earned.

The influence of family in these discussions should not be forgotten. Many wives and children of large shareholders become shareholders, and the proprietary concept is absorbed in the home atmosphere. Many public accountants have followed in the footsteps of their fathers; and even where sons go into different occupations, they often take many parental values with them.

It is certain that most sole proprietors, members of partnerships, and shareholder-directors of small companies look upon the firm with a proprietary viewpoint. It is difficult for many to separate, in their subconscious, their business from their private interests. All is "owned" and tends to be blurred into the one "net worth." In this regard Bernstein, after looking at profit concepts of large and small firms from his "external" position, said:

> The profits [of the large firm] has an "impersonality" about it, whereas in the case of the small business, the relationship between the entrepreneur and his company's earnings is very intimate indeed . . . . In brief, while conceptually small business profit seems to accrue to *people* big business profit belongs to "the corporation."[49]

However, as claimed in a previous section, most economists have a proprietary concept, and this seems to apply particularly to those who are solid members of the classical school. All economists have been exposed to the classical models of the entrepreneur, expecially in their formative years, and it could be that this leaves its imprint. Further, although economists are objectively concerned with the firm, most do their viewing from an external position, which is not the best place to acquire by psychological processes the values of one who is imbued with the welfare and survival of the entity itself. It is those on the "inside looking out," and those associated with such people, who are most likely to acquire, consciously or subconsciously, an entity concept.

It has been suggested by some with whom this matter has been discussed that the proprietary concept is a "carry-over" from the Protestant ethic and the focus on the entrepreneur that preceded the large corporation, and that this concept will gradually fade out of our culture as we get further away from that era, and as we come to accept more and more the separation of management from "ownership" in an advanced corporate society. It could be that the influence of such a culture change would result in all small sole proprietors' looking upon their businesses as something entirely distinct and separate from their private lives and possessions. With regard to culture change Sherif has said:

> In spite of all the forces in society that work toward social change, as a general rule the change in attitudes of individuals and groups tends to lag behind the change in actual conditions. Because of this "cultural lag" many prevalent attitudes are highly at variance with existing facts, social and otherwise . . . . Unless acceptable new anchoring frames are presented, a person will tend to cling tenaciously to the old. The reason for this psychological fact is wrapped up in ego-involvement."[50]

Some might argue that Sherif's observations have much significance with respect to the proprietary concept.

Then again, others might argue that more people will see the firm from the proprietary viewpoint as (and if) the ownership of stocks and shares becomes more diffused under "People's Capitalism."[51] Over 16 million Americans owned stocks in 1962, but it seems certain that most of the large number of small investors in that number did not look upon themselves as being anything more than "small investors."

When ownership is diffused among thousands of stockholders, the owners are

[49]Bernstein, P. L., "Profit Theory—Where Do We Go From Here?" *Quarterly Journal of Economics,* August 1953, p. 411.

[50]Sherif, op. cit. pp. 241-242.

[51]See Monsen, op. cit., pp. 36-42.

almost indistinguishable from the general public[;] ... hence the public image of the firm is very likely to be the owners' image too.[52]

None of the many small stockholders with whom this matter has been discussed looked upon themselves as being "owners" of the corporations whose stocks they held; their varying viewpoints seemed to have been conditioned by other factors.

Some Hypotheses Concerning the Entity Concept

It is hypothesized that most corporation employees to whom responsibilities have been delegated (including controllers and accountants) hold the entity concept, and that the higher up the hierarchical scale these people are situated, the more strongly they tend to hold this concept. The majority of these employees, consciously or subconsciously, see the entity as being the owner of both the profits as they are earned and the net assets, and they tend to look upon shareholders as being important to the corporation, but not as owners of it.

It is an almost automatic response for management to assume that all internally generated funds over and above the customary dividend will be used for investment requirements before any other source is given serious consideration.[53]

Those who see payments of dividends, interest, and income taxes as "expenses" of the entity tend to be top executives, while those who see these payments as being "distributions of profit" tend to be members of middle management responsible for the production of such profits. To most controllers and accountants employed by corporations, the prime function of the accounting records is to provide management with data to assist with its planning, decision-making, and control functions.

The influence of the environment within the organization is such that the norms of executive groups include the basics of the entity concept, and these are soon internalized by the group member who becomes psychologically involved in his position. Even the fact that they might be small to medium-sized stockholders in a corporation seems to make little or no difference to the entity viewpoint held by such executives. It is also hypothesized, therefore, that the issue of stock options to executives will not alter the view that their welfare is dependent on and secondary to the survival and success of the entity. They will not see themselves as "owners."

The writer's informal discussions with people have revealed many with an entity outlook even though they have no direct affiliations with corporations. The values of some of these may have been influenced by close relatives who had been corporation executives, but the majority seemed to have been conditioned by the way corporations are structured and by their significant role in our soceity. Since most have mentioned the legal restrictions on the withdrawal of profits or capital by stockholders, the fact that stockholders must buy and sell their shares at the stock exchange (and not at the company's offices), and that the average stockholder has no voice in the management of the corporation, it would seem that the

---

[52]Monsen, R. J., Jr., and Downs, A., "A Theory of Large Managerial Firms," *Journal of Political Economy,* June 1965, p. 231.

[53]Donaldson, G., "Financial Goals: Management vs. Stockholder," *Harvard Business Review.,* May-June 1963, p. 125.

fictional legal entity has become real in the perceptions of many. This could be further evidence of the cultural change mentioned in the previous section.

There have been others, of course, who have no significant concept of the firm. Their environmental history had been such that they had not yet been exposed to factors which motivated attitudes of consequence in this area.

ATTEMPTS TO RECONCILE THE BASIC CONCEPTS WITHIN ACCOUNTING

Two attempts to reconcile the proprietary and entity concepts within accounting theory will be discussed here. Almost twenty years ago Vatter showed tremendous insight into the need for such a reconciliation when he produced his work on the fund theory of accounting.[54] Then in 1965 Goldberg produced his commander theory.[55] This, he says, "does not destroy either the entity notion or the proprietary theory, but it can be used to reconcile the two."[56]

The Fund Theory of Accounting

Vatter's fund theory of accounting was not designed to be an expression of the way people perceive the firm, even though "the fund theory viewpoint is something of an extension of entity theory," designed "to embrace a less personalistic set of ideas, and to emphasize even more the 'statistical' viewpoint in dealing with accounting problems."[57] He says:

> Under the fund theory, the basis of accounting is neither proprietor nor a corporation. The area of interest covered by a set of accounts is independent of legal patterns or organization. The accounting-unit-area is defined in terms of a group of assets and a set of activities or functions for which these assets are employed. *Such a group of assets is called a fund.*[58]

Such funds can exist in private-enterprise, government, social and other types of institutions. This way of looking at assets, together with the way Vatter looks on equities and debts as merely being restrictions on the use of these assets (and not as being legal liabilities)[59] and the way he sees the fund itself (the group of assets) as being increased by inflows (revenues) and decreased by outflows (expenses), is consistent with the manner in which those with an entity concept perceive the firm.

However, Vatter intended his fund theory to be an impersonal, neutral notion; and to achieve this end he would include much detail in his financial statements so that the reader might compute the profit figure that meets his own personal needs or desires.

It might be said that it would be desirable to force the reader of the state-

[54]Vatter, op. cit.
[55]Goldberg, op. cit.
[56]Ibid., p. 173.
[57]Vatter, in Backer, op. cit., p. 367.
[58]Ibid.
[59]Ibid., p. 368. "Legally, debts only 'accrue' on their due date."

ment to make his own calculations of income from the data thus presented.[60]

For example, the reader could take as the profit figure the one before or after deducting items for interest, income taxes, dividends, etc., depending on his perceptions of the firm and the set of values that prompt them. The fund theory is "directed primarily at the problem of *reporting*,"[61] but the notions underlying it go much closer to satisfying those with an entity concept than they do those who have a proprietary viewpoint. However, it is believed that the personal values that underlie the proprietary and entity concepts nullify (unfortunately) this attempt at a reconciliation.

Nullifying Factors

The fund theory idea is based on the assumption that both entity and proprietary theorists would agree on the inclusion of all the various items in the financial statements (which they interpret to suit themselves), and that both would agree on the way each item is calculated or valued. It is claimed by this writer that such agreement is not possible on certain items and for this reason the preparation of "neutral" financial statements is not a practicable one. Some of the problem items are mentioned in this section.

The entity concept has its emphasis on the firm itself, on its assets and its operating capacity. The proprietary concept emphasizes the interests of the proprietary group in the firm and in its assets. To an entity theorist, a firm's profit for a period could be defined as "the maximum amount expressed in dollars, which, if there were no capital transaction during the period, could be distributed by the firm to its beneficiaries without impairing its operating capacity." To a proprietary theorist, a firm's profit could be defined as "the maximum amount which if there were no capital transactions during the period could be distributed by the firm to its beneficiaries without the contraction of the amount of shareholder equity."

These are two different concepts of profit, and they arise out of two different concepts of capital. When prices and values change, different accounting results can be obtained as a result of these different concepts held by entity and proprietary theorists.

As Hendriksen says, assets to the person with an entity viewpoint "represent the rights of the *firm* to receive specific goods and services or other benefits," and "the valuation of assets, therefore, should reflect the value of the benefits to be received by the enterprise."[62] It follows that the entity theorist, when revaluing inventories and non-current assets, will use current market values (or specific indexes in their absence) in order to reflect the new value of the benefits to be received by the firm. Further, the person with the entity viewpoint will see the *total* movement in the current market values of operating assets as being one of a capital nature. That is, it does not result in any increase or decrease in the physical assets (or in operating capacity) which comprises its capital.

[60]Vatter, W. J., *The Fund Theory of Accounting and Its Implications for Financial Reports*, p. 36.

[61]Goldberg, op. cit., p. 108.

[62]Hendriksen, E. S., *Accounting Theory* (Richard D. Irwin, Inc., 1965), p. 396.

On the other hand, although many of those with a proprietary viewpoint would also revalue inventories and non-current assets with the aid of current market values, they would recognize a holding gain (or loss) to the extent that increases in the current market values of these assets are greater (or less) than the movement in the general price index which reflects the change in the purchasing power (to the shareholders) of the shareholder equity.

It is claimed here that those who really hold an entity viewpoint do not see these holding "gains" and "losses" as gains and losses to the firm itself. They would point to the statement by the American Accounting Association's Committee on Concepts and Standards—Long-Lived Assets that holding gains, although forming a part of "total net income," are "not distributable without contraction of operating capacity and therefore do not enter into the measurement of income from ordinary operations."[63] Real entity theorists would then claim that if something cannot be distributed because it would impair the operating capacity of the firm, it cannot really be "profit" to the firm and therefore should not be recorded in the firm's books at all.

There are other proprietary theorists who would actually revalue inventories and non-current assets (as well as shareholder equity) in accordance with the movements in the general price index which reflect the change in the shareholders' purchasing power. Such methods produce different depreciation and costs of goods sold, and hence different profit figures from those calculated from the current market values of the specific assets which make up the entity theorist's "operating capacity."

It is considered that reporting under the fund theory idea could not handle these different perceptions of profit and capital, nor could it deal with holding gains and losses, which are recognized by some but not by others. Further, when prices change if some of the firm's capital has been contributed by long-term bondholders and/or by preferred stockholders, more difficulties are encountered. (Price rises will be assumed in the discussion, but price declines present identical problems.)

To those who see the firm from the proprietary viewpoint, gains are made on capital contributed by bondholders when prices rise because the debt is a fixed one and will be repaid in dollars of a lower value. "Proprietary theory is an expression of events from the point of view of the proprietor."[64] To those who have the extreme proprietary view, similar gains are seen on capital contributed by preferred stockholders. For example, L. A. Wilk says:

> There is no reason to maintain the original purchasing power of preference capital since it is only entitled to a portion of the company's assets equivalent to the nominal value of such preference shares. Capital maintenance reserve will therefore be restricted to maintaining the purchasing power of ordinary capital.[65]

However, to those who hold the entity concept, *all* "obligations are considered the obligations of the corporation itself; there is no significant distinction to be made between common shareholders, preferred shareholders, bondholders, and

[63]"Accounting for Land, Buildings and Equipment," The Accounting Review, July 1964, p. 607.

[64]Goldberg, p. 117.

[65]Wilk, L. A., Accounting for Inflation (London: Sweet & Maxwell Ltd., 1960), p. 80.

other long-term obligees."[66] This writer now contends that the viewpoint of a real entity theorist is as follows:

> As far as the firm itself is concerned there is no "profit" on these items of long-term debt when prices are rising. . . . All of these long-term debt items form part of the permanent capital of the firm in the same way as do amounts contributed by shareholders. Therefore, to calculate "profit" on items of long-term debt would be just as illogical as calculating "profit" on funds received from shareholders, i.e., in times of rising prices. It cannot make "profits" out of one sort of capital and not out of another.[67]

Once again, if such profits were calculated on long-term debt, their distribution would result in a contraction of operating capacity—and therefore could not really be profits to the firm as perceived by the entity theorist.

So, reporting under the fund theory idea could not handle the calculation of profits and losses on monetary items when prices rise or fall. Not only do entity and proprietary people have different perceptions of what constitutes profits and losses, but there are also different perceptions within the proprietary ranks.

A matter of smaller importance is that of imputed interest. Those who would actually impute "the interest due to the entrepreneurs" within the accounting records have a strong proprietary outlook. (It is not being suggested that *all* those with a proprietary concept would impute interest.) Those with an entity viewpoint are unable to see any interest accruing to the firm itself as time elapses. Here, too, the one set of statements cannot be prepared in a neutral fashion to depict the financial position and results in the ways perceived by both entity and proprietary theorists.

The author has noticed other problem items (e.g., in the areas of goodwill and selecting interest rates for discounting purposes), but the above should be sufficient for the purposes of this paper.

The Commander Theory

In introducing the commander theory, Goldberg says:

> Neither the entity nor the proprietary theory . . . is wholly satisfactory in explaining the point of view from which accounting procedures . . . are carried out. Each is based, fundamentally, on the notion of ownership; ownership, however, is a nebulous concept and is extremely difficult to define and analyse in any way suitable for use as a basic accounting notion.[68]

But even if the notion of ownership is difficult to define or analyze, it is true that it is difficult to avoid having perceptions on "ownership" because our culture is permeated with notions of the ownership of property. Most people do see the net assets and profits of the firm as being the property of either the shareholders or proprietors on the one hand, or of the firm itself (entity) on the other.

---

[66]Sprouse, p. 370.

[67]Gynther, R. S., *Accounting for Price-Level Changes: Theory and Procedures* (Oxford: Pergamon Press Ltd., 1966), p. 140.

See also Hendriksen, E. S., *Price-Level Adjustments of Financial Statements* (Pullman: Washington State University Press, 1961), pp. 86-88.

[68]Ibid., p. 162.

Goldberg's commander theory, which he believes should be adopted, is not one that is meant to reflect the viewpoints of most people. He seems to confirm this when he says that "instead of focusing attention upon 'the corporation as a distinct but abstract entity . . . we *should* direct our attention to the function of control which can only be exercised by human beings."[69] He goes on to say:

> Once the position of the commander is recognised, it becomes clear that accounting functions are carried out for and on behalf of commanders. Accounting reports are reports by commanders to commanders, that is, by commanders at one level of command to commanders at a higher level . . . along a whole chain of command; accounting records are set up and maintained to enable effective reports to be made and to provide documentary evidence for decisions to be made by commanders.[70]

And most importantly he adds:

> Accounting procedures are carried out from the point of view of the commander rather than from the point of view of the owner or from a hypothetical point of view of an artificial entity.[71]

And now we must ask, "What is the point of view of the commander? Is it the proprietary point of view or the entity point of view?"

It is suggested here that the answer to this question depends upon the behavioral matters discussed in this paper, i.e., on his value system, which in turn depends on his environmental and social history. Unfortunately, the commander theory does not seem to provide the reconciliation of the proprietary and entity concepts of the firm within accounting theory.

IMPLICATIONS AND CONCLUSION

At the outset it was claimed that the discipline of accounting suffers from the lack of a general theory of accounting and that this lack is due to the lack of agreement on the basic concepts of accounting. In the previous section under the heading of "The Nullifying Factors," some examples were given of the ways in which the two concepts can (and do) lead to different accounting results because of the varying perceptions people have of the firm. The fact that different accounting results occur makes a reconciliation between the proprietary and entity concepts of accounting impossible. What then is the answer?

Both of these concepts emerge from value frames of reference of people in our society, and it is seldom possible to alter these by sophisticated or theoretical arguments. Therefore, if we want a general theory of accounting, together with the higher degree of uniformity and comparability in accounting and reporting that it will provide (from the small firm through to national income accounting), we shall have to make an arbitrary decision as to whether to base it on the proprietary concept or the entity concept.

[69] Ibid., p. 163.

[70] Ibid., p. 167.

[71] Ibid., p. 168. Incidentally, it is thought that very few suggest that accounting be carried out from the "point of view of an artificial entity." What is suggested by most entity theorists is that the accounting be carried out from the way they and many others perceive the entity.

This author votes for the entity theory, and in so doing he admits that his twelve years in industry as an accountant-controller before entering academic life have shaped his frame of reference in such a way that he has an entity viewpoint. However, he hopes that the following points, given to support his vote, are devoid of bias and prejudice.

1. The interests of the members of the various subcoalitions interested in the firm depend on the results of the firm (entity) and its survival, and therefore the focus of attention is (should be) on the entity itself, and not on any particular member or subcoalition.

2. "In accounting we should be concerned with expressing the truth (a word of high degree of abstraction) about *the social unit* to which accounts or reports are related, so far as is ascertainable and expressible in the units elected as appropriate for this purpose."[72]

3. It follows that we should not attempt to express the entity's activities within the entity's accounting records from the point of view of the shareholders (proprietary concept). We should be expressing the entity's activities from the point of view of those primarily interested in the survival of the entity (entity concept). As we have seen these two expressions can be very different.

4. The place for the recording of the interests of the shareholder is in his own private accounting records. He is a separate entity, and his records should include his various business investments along with his other assets and liabilities. When his investments are listed on the stock exchange, he does not have the valuation problems that he might otherwise have, and he has no difficulty in forming an opinion as to the way the entities are being managed.

5. In private enterprise economies, capital investments are channelled into the various corporations and different industries by decisions based largely on accounting data. Therefore, the optimum allocation of resources depends to a marked degree on the soundness of the results shown by this accounting data. It is thought that they will be sound only if expressed in the values and costs of the entity itself, and not those of the shareholders.

6. In other words, it is considered that shareholders will be in a far better position to make decisions regarding the buying, selling, or holding of securities if the reports reflect the entity viewpoint, and if they do not contain misleading "gains" and "losses" which are not gains and losses to the corporation itself. If shareholders assume that these items affect the profits that can be distributed now or later, they might make incorrect investment decisions. Further, if they insist, for example, on the distribution of gains on holding long-term debt in times of rising prices, this could have adverse effects on the operating capacity and the survival of the corporation—hence on their own long-term interests as shareholders.

7. The entity concept can form the base for a general theory of accounting that applies to *all* forms of organizations in all kinds of economic and political systems. It can form the base for non-profit, fiduciary, and government organizations as well as the private enterprises. Some have suggested to the author that the proprietary concept can be applied to government organizations, but it is doubtful whether many taxpayers look upon themselves as the proprietors of such organizations.

8. Finally, it seems to this author that the proprietary concept of the firm is a carry-over from the era of entrepreneurial ideology when there was a blurring of the business and private interests of the entrepreneur. He sees a gradual change of

[72]Goldberg, p. 5; emphasis added.

beliefs and viewpoints within our culture as enterprise becomes more and more institutionalized, and thinks that this, in time, will result in even the small sole proprietor's seeing a clear distinction between his private and business interests.

23

ACCOUNTING MEASUREMENTS AND NORMAL GROWTH

OF THE FIRM *

MYRON J. GORDON / BERTRAND N. HORWITZ / PHILIP T. MEYERS

Throughout its history the field of accounting has been concerned with correct rules for the measurement of income and wealth. Attempts at standardization, emphasizing comparability and disclosure, have the objective of delineation of accounting principles which lead to measurement rules such that two companies having identical economic histories issue identical accounting reports. If income and wealth are, in part, a function of their measurement rules, it would then seem that at least the measurement rules should be constant. In fact, however, conflicting accounting rules exist, and two economically identical companies may report substantially differing incomes. Thus, income and wealth are dependent upon the choice of measurement rules.

A number of people regard this situation as a sad state of affairs. Leonard Spacek [22, p. 116] has aggressively argued for standardization of accounting rules:

> The opinion paragraph of the standard form of certificate uniformly reads that the financial position and operating results are fairly presented "in accordance with generally accepted accounting principles." While practically every accounting firm uses this standard wording to express its opinion on corporate financial statements, there is no general agreement as to the exact meaning of the phrase or its applicability to the variety of situations in which it is used.

Robert Anthony [4, p. 100] is even more explicit: "Currently, a comprehensive, consistent, and generally accepted body of accounting principles does not exist in the United States. This is a flat statement . . ." Though they may differ somewhat

*In *Research in Accounting Measurement,* Robert Jaedicke, Yuji Ijiri, and Oswald Niel sen, eds. Evanston, Illinois, American Accounting Association, 1966, pp. 221-231.

as to order of attack, both Spacek and Anthony believe the accounting profession should define measurement rules such that the range of alternatives be narrowed and that the remaining alternatives be characterized by the economic reasoning supporting them. Comparability among firms is their goal. In the words of the latter author: "Comparing the financial status or performance of several companies is an extremely difficult task under the best of circumstances. But when the figures for the several companies are prepared under different ground rules, the task is made even more frustrating." [4, p. 100].

Others believe that differences in accounting rules should be allowed to continue. Their position is that conflicting rules develop in response to differing circumstances faced by the business firm. Maurice Peloubet [17, p. 38], in discussing accounting for natural resource enterprises, states, "These differences, while expressed in accounting terms, are not differences in accounting. They are differences in facts and situations, expressed in differing accounting terms." Since no one can know the "correct" measurement rule, the professional accountant must exercise his judgment in approving or disapproving a particular rule applied to particular circumstances. Protection of the public comes from the integrity of the accountant in his demands for consistency of application, for disclosure and for conservatism in the presentation of financial statements. Peloubet [17, p. 39] explains that complete comparability cannot be attained:

> The impossibility of presenting the accounts of different companies in the same industry on a completely comparable basis arises from the fact that physical and financial conditions and management policies are different, and this must be reflected differently in the accounts. The accountant, public or private, cannot influence management decisions in any other way or to any greater extent than is warranted by his role as adviser.

Leonard Savoie [18, p. 160] argues that those who advocate uniformity in accounting measurement rules are "searching for a number" that doesn't exist.

That little progress towards standardization of accounting measurement rules has been made is apparent. That the subject can provoke vigorous, sometimes violent, debate is also apparent. Why this is true is not so apparent. Three major attempts have been made during the past thirty years by the accounting profession to resolve the problem of conflicting accounting measurement rules.[1] Each has failed. In each case the individuals involved have been unable to develop an operational basis for choice between conflicting measurement rules, and between uniformity and diversity as objectives. They have not arrived at a statement of the purpose of accounting and a method of inquiry such that it can be shown that one set of measurement rules is a more effective instrument for realizing the objectives of accounting than any alternative set.

If alternative measurement rules may be applied to a given set of production and exchange activities, what criteria are utilized in the actual process of selection for a firm—how is the choice made? Who makes the choice? Conventionally, corporate financial statements are regarded as the result of a two-stage process. Management submits the statements and the public accountant attests to their

---

[1] A special committee of the American Institute of (Certified Public) Accountants, with George O. May as Chairman, in cooperation with a committee of the New York Stock Exchange, laid the foundation for standardization of accounting principles. The Committee on Accounting Procedure of the AICPA existed for approximately twenty years. The Accounting Principles Board of the AICPA is currently at work. See Storey [23] for a historical analysis of efforts to obtain agreement on accounting principles.

conformity to accepted accounting rules of measurement.[2] Management, therefore, within limits, selects the accounting rule. The purpose of this paper is to present and test a theorem on management behavior when it is faced with a choice among alternative accounting measurement rules, namely, that management will select the rule which will tend to smooth income and smooth the rate of growth in income. This theorem is elaborated below.

In 1953 Hepworth surveyed "... some of the accounting techniques which may be applied to affect the assignment of net income to successive accounting periods ... for smoothing or leveling the amplitude of periodic net income fluctuations." [11, p. 32]. In informal discussions on the choices corporations make among accounting principles, accountants frequently point to income smoothing as the choice criterion. However, apart from a recent paper by Gordon [9], the literature for and against agreement on a set of principles and the efforts at developing a set of principles makes little or no reference to income smoothing as a relevant consideration. That is, the possibility that corporations might use their freedom of choice among accounting principles to smooth income has received scant consideration.[3]

Gordon has theorized on income smoothing as follows:

Proposition 1. The criterion a corporate management uses in selecting among accounting principles is the maximization of its utility or welfare. Whether or not a management should be so motivated is a value judgment that need not concern us here. That managements are in fact so motivated is taken as axiomatic.

Proposition 2. The utility of a management increases with (1) its job security, with (2) the level and rate of growth in the management's income, and with (3) the level and rate of growth in the corporation's size...

Proposition 3. The achievement of the management goals stated in Proposition 2 is dependent in part on the satisfaction of stockholders with the corporation's performance. That is, other things the same, the happier the stockholders the greater the job security, income, etc. of the management. Further, these variables increase by diminishing marginal amounts with stockholder satisfaction. In other words, when stockholders are highly dissatisfied with a management, an increase in their satisfaction greatly increases the management's jobs security, etc., and hence its utility. On the other hand, when stockholders are highly pleased with a management, a further increase in their satisfaction by the same amount will not materially increase job security, income and corporate size...

Proposition 4. Stockholder satisfaction with a corporation increases with the average rate of growth in the corporation's income (or the average rate of

---

[2]Criticism of the lack of standardization in accounting measurement rules has focused upon problems of interpretation by readers of financial statements rather than upon specific cases of "erroneous" choice of accounting rules by management. A typical illustration is that utilized by Spacek [21] to show differing income results to two otherwise identical firms. Of course, management's choice of specific measurement rules is reviewed by the public accountant prior to publication of the financial statements; therefore, the only "erroneous" choices receiving public attention are those in which an opinion is qualified or withheld. [24]. Public criticism tends to concentrate upon the treatment of extraordinary charges and credits. [3].

[3]See the literature cited previously. Of course, the advocates of the all-inclusive income statement in the debate on direct charges to surplus argued that direct charges could be used to manipulate income. The argument on whether equalization reserves should be used during World War II turned on whether they resulted in a more true statement of income during and after the war. See [15].

return on its capital) and the stability of its income. This proposition is as readily verified as Proposition 2.

Theorem: Given that the above four propositions are accepted or found to be true, it follows that a management should within the limits of its power, i.e., the latitude allowed by accounting rules, (1) smooth reported income, and (2) smooth the rate of growth in income. By smooth the rate of growth in income we mean the following: If the rate of growth is high, accounting practices which reduce it should be adopted and vice versa. [9, pp. 261-62].

Neither Gordon nor anyone else to our knowledge has investigated whether corporations do in fact behave this way. Neither has it been shown that under some criterion with respect to the purposes served by financial statements, smoothing is good or bad.[4] We also will not consider the latter question. What we will do is attempt to test the empirical truth of the theorem. Do corporations in fact tend to smooth income?

We have examined the behavior of a single firm (United States Steel Corporation) over a number of years and the behavior of a sample of companies from the chemical industry with respect to a single accounting-rule decision (the investment credit). The empirical results we obtained are not conclusive. As will be seen, a far more ambitious investigation is needed to establish the extent to which income smoothing guides corporations in choosing among the accounting principles they are free to adopt. Our purpose in presenting the results obtained is to reveal and stimulate discussion of the methodological problems we encountered and the approaches to these problems we adopted.

Testing the theorem raises two distinct problems. Management's choice of accounting rules increases, decreases, or does not affect the level of income reported for a particular year. To conclude that such choice smooths reported income requires knowledge of whether income for the year is above or below normal. Definition of normal income is essentially subjective, but we believe it involves the consideration of income in prior years and possibly also a comparison with the average rate of growth in income for the industry. For the purposes of this study, the smoothing theorem was tested by considering whether an accounting measurement rule was selected which tended to: (1) adjust the firm's percentage change in earnings per share to the average percentage change in the industry, or (2) smooth the firm's earnings per share toward a normal value, or (3) smooth the firm's rate of return on common stockholders' equity.

The other and more difficult problem is the identification of the choice decisions made by management. Disclosure of the particular accounting measurement rules which have been used by a corporation management in its financial statements is not at all complete, and the financial statement resources available to us for this study have not been extensive.[5]

Once one embarks on the study a third problem is encountered. Assume that a corporation has adopted some practice, e.g., to charge accelerated depreciation for book and tax purposes or to use an all-inclusive income statement. Clearly, a decision in a subsequent year to adopt an alternative practice is a discretionary action on the part of management. However, is the continued use of principles

---

[4]Even if we postulate that financial statements should be of maximum utility to the users, it has not been proved that income smoothing will not achieve this maximum utility.

[5]We have relied on the companies' annual reports and such secondary sources as Moody's. More information might be obtained from the corporations' 10-K reports to the Securities and Exchange Commission and direct communication with the corporations.

adopted in prior years a discretionary decision? Since consistency is a principle corporations do not like to violate, this question is not easily answered.

THE INVESTMENT CREDIT

The Revenue Act of 1962, Code Section 38, provided for an investment credit which is generally 7 percent of the qualified investment in depreciable property which is acquired after December 31, 1961.[6] The investment credit reduces the amount of federal income tax otherwise payable for the year in which the qualified asset is acquired.[7] According to the Act of 1962, the basis of the asset is reduced by the allowed investment credit for determining tax depreciation over the life of the asset.

The crucial problem for financial reporting is the method of reporting the permanent tax-saving portion of the investment credit. Two alternatives exist: (1) to allow the savings to be realized entirely in the year of acquisition, i.e., to "flow through" to the current year's income, or (2) to allow the savings to affect income over the life of the qualified asset, i.e., to allocate the savings over a number of periods.

Subsequently, the AICPA's Accounting Principles Board issued a draft of a position, which it had tentatively adopted, advocating the allocation approach. Reaction to the Board's position was immediate; of approximately 600 opinions it solicited from corporation officials, accounting practitioners and accounting educators, almost one-half opposed the position of the Board. [1].

Although the Board later formally adopted its original position, the vote was very close. Moreover, the force of its position was further reduced when the Securities and Exchange Commission issued a release shortly afterwards which stated that either of the two positions could be used in reports filed with it providing that there was disclosure of all material facts. [12].

Since there were likely to be a large number of annual reports filed in 1963 which would account for the investment credit both ways, it appears that the treatment of the investment credit in 1962 and 1963 by a sample of corporations in one industry would be a useful basis for testing the hypothesis that the choice of accounting alternatives leads to results which tend to smooth earnings per share or to adjust it toward an external norm.[8]

To carry out this test of the hypothesis it is necessary to establish for each corporation: (1) how it treats the investment credit, and (2) whether its income for the year is above or below the figure it considers normal or satisfactory.

Measurement

On the investment credit, let q be the percentage effect of the investment credit savings on earnings per share. If the investment credit savings is carried to

[6]If the useful life of the property is eight or more years, the entire cost qualifies; if the life is six or seven years, only two-thirds of the cost qualifies; if four or five years, only one-third qualifies; property with a useful life of less than four years does not qualify.

[7]The maximum credit allowed is $25,000 plus one-fourth of the tax liability over $25,000.

[8]The 1963 edition of AICPA, *Accounting Trends and Techniques,* indicates that of 256 companies which revealed the method of treatment in their annual reports 38 percent "flowed through." [2, p. 123].

income, q is equal to the investment credit savings divided by net income after taxes and is positive. If, on the other hand, the investment credit savings is allocated then q is equal to the investment credit savings divided by net income after taxes and is negative.

Three alternative definitions have been developed to establish whether a corporation's earnings per share is above or below normal. First, R, the rate of growth in a corporation's earnings per share is established as follows. Let Y_t = actual earnings per share in time period t. Then

$$(1) \qquad \overline{Y}_t = \alpha Y_t + (1 - \alpha)\, \overline{Y}_{t-1}$$

where $\overline{Y}_t$ is smoothed earnings per share in time period t.

To get an initial value of $\overline{Y}_t$, we define

$$(2) \qquad \overline{Y}_{52} = \frac{\alpha Y_{52} + \alpha(1 - \alpha)Y_{51} + \alpha(1 - \alpha)^2 Y_{50}}{\alpha[1 + (1 - \alpha) + (1 - \alpha)^2]}$$

with a arbitrarily assigned a value of .3.

Thus, the smoothed values for 1962 and 1963 have been obtained by successive application of Equation (1). $\overline{Y}_t$, however, understates (overstates) the smoothed earnings per share for a year if there has been an upward (downward) trend in income.

Accordingly, the change in smoothed earnings per share is defined as

$$(3) \qquad G_t = \overline{Y}_t - \overline{Y}_{t-1}$$

The smoothed change in earnings per share is

$$(4) \qquad \overline{G}_t = \alpha G_t + (1 - \alpha)G_{t-1} \text{ and } \alpha = .3$$

An initial value is

$$\overline{G}_{55} = \frac{\alpha G_{55} + \alpha(1 - \alpha)G_{54} + \alpha(1 - \alpha)^2 G_{53}}{\alpha[1 + (1 - \alpha) + (1 - \alpha)^2]} \text{ for } \alpha = .3$$

and the smoothed changes in earnings per share for 1962 and 1963 have been determined by successive application of Equation (4).

One measure of the growth in earnings per share we have used is the rate of growth, $R_t = \overline{G}_t/Y_t$ for t = 1962 or 1963. A corporation's earnings per share for 1962 or 1963 is considered above or below normal if R for that corporation is above or below the average industry R. Thus for each corporation in our sample for 1962 and 1963 our variable is

$(5) \quad \lambda_t = R_t - \overline{R}_t$ for t = 1962 or 1963 and $\overline{R}_t$ is a simple average of the industry.

Another measure used to determine whether a corporation's earnings per share is above or below normal for 1962 or 1963 depends upon the trend adjusted normal earnings per share [5, pp. 26-80]. Let

$$(6) \qquad Y_t = Y_t + \frac{1 - \alpha}{\alpha}\ \overline{G}_t \text{ where } \alpha = .3$$

9
$$\frac{\text{Investment Credit Savings}}{\text{Net Income}} = \frac{\text{investment credit savings/number of outstanding common shares}}{\text{net income / number of outstanding common shares}}$$

Also, the negative q is partly overstated since a portion of the investment credit savings would be allocated to current year's income. Where that portion could be determined it is included in the computation and thus reduces slightly the negativity of q.

$\hat{Y}$ is taken as the earnings per share a corporation considers normal, and Z, the second measure of growth, is the percentage amount by which actual earnings per share are above or below normal.

(7) $$Z = \frac{Y_t - \hat{Y}_t}{\hat{Y}_t} \text{ for } t = 1962 \text{ or } 1963.$$

A third measure of growth is to apply a smoothed ratio of actual earnings per share to the book value per share.

Let Y_t = actual earnings per common share
B_t = actual book value pre common share
$P_t = Y_t/B_t$

Thus $\overline{P}_t = \alpha P_t + (1 - \alpha)\overline{P}_{t-1}$ where $\alpha = .3$
An initial value is

$$\overline{P}_{52} = \frac{\alpha P_{52} + \alpha(1 - \alpha)P_{51} + \alpha(1 - \alpha)^2 P_{50}}{\alpha[1 + (1 - \alpha) + (1 - \alpha)^2]} \text{ and } \alpha = .3$$

The smoothed ratio for 1962 and 1963 is then applied to actual book value per common share for 1962 and 1963. We find

$$\widetilde{Y}_t = \overline{P}_t B_t \text{ for } t = 1962 \text{ or } 1963.$$

And so, our third measure of growth, C_t, is defined as

(8) $$C_t = Y_t - \overline{Y}_t \text{ for } t = 1962 \text{ or } 1963.$$

Sources

The sample data consist of 21 firms selected from the chemical industry. For each of these firms the annual report provides information about the accounting treatment of the investment credit and the amount of the savings. In a few cases the accounting treatment and the amounts are given only for 1962; estimates made for 1963 assume that the ratios of investment credit savings to fixed asset acquisition may have been the same for both years.

Data for the adjusted earnings per share, net profit after taxes and book value of net assets for the 21 chemical companies from 1950 through 1963 have been derived from Moody's Industrials, Value Line and the annual reports.

Statistical Analysis

The 21 corporations have been classified in each year according to whether their treatment of the investment credit raised (flow through) or lowered (allocated) income and whether their income was above or below normal under each criterion discussed above. The results appear in Table I in the form of six 2 X 2 contingency tables. Flow through treatment of the investment credit is indicated by $+ q$ and allocation by $-q$. A company has been classified as plus or minus under the λ, Z, and C criteria according to whether its income was above or below normal under each criterion.

The chi-square test was used to test the null hypothesis that the method of

TABLE I   Classification of 21 Chemical Firms According to
Treatment of Investment Credit and Whether Income
was Above or Below Normal

	1962			1963	
	$+\lambda$	$-\lambda$		$+\lambda$	$-\lambda$
+q	4	4	+q	4	6
−q	9	4	−q	8	3
	$+Z$	$-Z$		$+Z$	$-Z$
+q	3	5	+q	6	4
−q	10	3	−q	9	2
	$+C$	$-C$		$+C$	$-C$
+q	1	7	+q	1	9
−q	5	8	−q	8	3

Explanatory note:
+q is an increase in income from the investment credit ("flow through").
−q is a relative decrease in income from the investment credit (allocation).

accounting for the investment credit is independent of the rate of growth of earnings per share. Because the sample was small, expected frequencies in some cells were less than five. Chi-square tests are restricted to large samples and most writers warn against the use of the test when any of the expected values are less than five. When small samples are used, such as the number in this study, the difficulty can be overcome in the case of 2 X 2 tables in a number of ways. One way is to apply a correction for continuity known as the Yates correction [14, pp. 21-26].

Using the Yates correction factor the chi-square values are

Smoothing Criterion	1962	1963
λ	.175	1.15
Z	1.81	.026
C	.6	6.05

The chi-square statistic is not significant at the 5 percent level for λ and Z in 1962 and 1963 and for C in 1962. The observed association could well have been due to chance. Criterion C in 1963 is significant at the 2½ percent level. However, even where the results support the null hypothesis, the fact that the cross multiples of the observations in $(+q+c)$ X $(-q-c)$ are less than the cross multiples of the observations in $(-q+c)$ X $(+q-c)$, where c denotes the smoothing criterion, suggests that the two variables act in a direction which lends support to the smoothing hypothesis.

It should be noted that the C criterion is probably superior to the Z criterion as a basis for establishing whether a corporation's income is above or below normal.[10] The Z criterion superimposes the smoothed growth rate on the smoothed earnings to adjust for the trend in earnings. When the research was substantially completed, Roger Glassey pointed out to us that this operation, double exponential smoothing, introduces more error than it eliminates when the growth rate fluctuates. [See 16.] Accordingly, the accuracy of the λ criterion is also open to question.

Observations

Although a larger sample size would have been more appropriate, the results indicate that there is a positive association between "flow through" and below normal income and vice versa.

It seems to us that a better test of our hypothesis would use the methodology of this study, but would include larger samples from several industries and would encompass all of the discretionary accounting practices. Ideally, our study should have examined each corporation for 1962 and 1963, noted the adoptions or changes in all accounting policies and analyzed the effects on earnings per share. A format for analysis might be:

Item	1962 (1963) Effect on Earnings per Share	Accounting Policy	
	Increase or Decrease (percentage)	Established This Year	Continued This Year
1) Investment credit			
2) Amortization of intangibles			
3) Tax allocation			
4) Mergers			
5) Pension past-service costs			
6) Extraordinary gains or losses			
Etc.			

Thus, a better test of our hypothesis using our methodology would examine the net percentage effect on earnings per share of year t for all accounting policies established in year t. A chi-square test would then be used to determine if there is any association between the percentage change of earnings per share and any of our three definitions of growth, λ, Z and C.

UNITED STATES STEEL CORPORATION

United States Steel Corporation has experienced widely fluctuating profits in recent years. Therefore, it would seem to be a desirable company on which to test the income smoothing theorem. The test would be to identify discretionary accounting rule choices and see if they tended to increase or decrease the rate of growth in income.

[10]For the C criterion the rate of return on book value was smoothed and then multiplied by current book value to get a smoothed trend adjusted earnings. Since there is no a priori basis for believing that rate of return on book value has a trend and because book value has a trend similar to smoothed income, the C criterion provides a smoothed trend adjusted earnings figure without relying on double exponential smoothing.

The reported income for U.S. Steel for the period 1952-63 and the normal income for each of these years appear below.

Year	Reported Income (Millions of $)	Normal Income* (Millions of $)
1952	143.6	177.6
1953	222.1	198.9
1954	195.4	204.8
1955	370.1	271.1
1956	348.1	310.1
1957	419.4	390.4
1958	301.5	374.5
1959	254.5	344.5
1960	304.2	344.2
1961	190.2	297.5
1962	163.7	259.5
1963	203.5	244.5

*Normal income was derived by multiplying $\bar{P}$ for each year by the actual total book value.

Discretionary accounting measurement rules, as disclosed by examination of the corporation annual reports and Moody's Industrials, and their income effect include the following items:

(1) Sometime after January 1, 1954, the corporation began the use of accelerated depreciation at two times the straight line rate. U.S. Steel had been accelerating depreciation since 1947; they also reported substantial "certificate of necessity" depreciation during the 1950's. The dollar effect on income for 1954 and following years of this accounting decision was not discovered; however, it would have tended to decrease reported income.

(2) In 1958, funding of past service pension costs was discontinued and a portion of the previously funded past service costs was applied to the current service cost funding. The effect was to increase reported income for 1958 by $46.6 million; this was 15.5 percent of 1958 income. Funding of past service pension costs has not been resumed.

(3) In 1962, the corporation revised its procedures for estimating its pension needs, i.e., it recognized appreciation and estimated a higher income rate on pension fund assets, thereby reducing the current contribution to the pension fund. The effect was to increase reported income for 1962 by $20.6 million, an increase of 12.6 percent of 1962 income.

(4) In 1962, guideline lives were adopted for general reporting as well as for income tax reporting. This decision resulted in $44.0 million additional depreciation and decreased reported income by $21.1 million. Reported income was decreased by 12.9 percent.

(5) In 1962 and 1963, the investment credit was allocated over the lives of the assets to which it applied. By not utilizing the "flow through" method, the corporation "reduced" 1962 reported income by $3.9 million, or 2.4 percent, and 1963 reported income by $5.8 million, or 2.8 percent.

These five decisions involving alternative accounting measurement rules are not all of the rule-choice situations which the management of U.S. Steel faced in the years 1952-63. They are the situations which can be easily identified from reading the published financial statements. The results can be summarized as

TABLE II   Discretionary Accounting Measurement Decisions,
U. S. Steel Corporation, 1954-63

| Accounting Measurement Rule Choice Situation | Decision by U. S. Steel Corporation | |
	Smoothing Theorem Prediction	Actual
(1) Accelerated Depreciation	Adopt	Adopt
(2) Stop funding past service pension costs	Stop funding	Stop funding
(3) Revise estimate of pension needs	Revise	Revise
(4) Guidelines lives	Do not adopt	Adopt
(5) Investment credit	Flow through	Allocate

follows: the actions taken in situations (1), (2) and (3) support the smoothing theorem; the actions taken in (4) and (5) do not support the smoothing theorem. However, since actions taken in (3), (4) and (5) involved the reported income for 1962, it may be noted that the effect of (3) is opposite in direction to that of (4) and (5), resulting in a net decrease to reported income for 1962 of 2.0 percent. (See Table II.)

BIBLIOGRAPHY

1. Accounting Principles Board. "Accounting for the Investment Credit," Opinion 2, *The Journal of Accountancy,* CXV, 2 (February, 1963), 70-72.
2. American Institute of Certified Public Accountants. *Accounting Trends and Techniques,* XVII, New York, 1963.
3. Anreder, S. S. "Pitfalls for the Unwary," *Barron's,* LV, 25 (December 24, 1962), 3, 8, 10, 13.
4. Anthony, R. N. "Showdown on Accounting Principles," *Harvard Business Review,* XLI, 3 (May-June 1963), 99-106.
5. Brown, R. G., *Statistical Forecasting for Inventory Control,* New York: McGraw-Hill, 1949.
6. Cary, W. L. "The SEC and Accounting." *The Journal of Accountancy,* CXVI, 6 (December, 1963), 47-50.
7. Dyckman, P. R. "The Effects of Alternative Accounting Techniques on Certain Management Decisions," *Journal of Accounting Research,* II, 1 (Spring, 1964), 91-107.
8. Fox, J. L., " 'Useful Comparability' in Financial Reporting," *The Journal of Accountancy,* CXVIII, 6 (December, 1964), 44-52.
9. Gordon, M. J. "Postulates, Principles and Research in Accounting," *The Accounting Review,* XXXIX, 2 (April, 1964), 251-63.
10. Hawkins, D. F. "Management's Stake in Accounting Reform," *California Management Review,* VI, 2 (Fall, 1963), 27-34.
11. Hepworth, S. R. "Smoothing Periodic Income," *The Accounting Review,* XXVIII, 1 (January, 1953), 32-39.
12. Kaye, G. "Accounting for the 7% Investment Credit," *The New York Certified Public Accountant,* XXXIV, 2 (February, 1964), 108-14.
13. Lindhe, R. "Accelerated Depreciation for Income Tax Purposes—A Study of the Decision and Some Firms Who Made It," *Journal of Accounting Research,* I, 2 (Autumn, 1963), 139-48.
14. Maxwell, A. E. *Analyzing Qualitative Data.* London: Methuen & Co., 1961.
15. Miller, H. E. "Reserve for War Contingencies and Post-War Adjustments," *The Accounting Review,* XIX, 3 (July, 1944), 248-53.

16. Morris, R. H. and C. R. Glassey. "The Dynamics and Statistics of Exponential Smoothing Operators," *Operations Research,* XI, 4 (July-August, 1963), 561-69.

17. Peloubet, M. E. "Is Further Uniformity Desirable or Possible?" *The Journal of Accountancy,* CXI, 4 (April, 1961), 35-41.

18. Savoie, L. M. "Accounting Improvement: How Fast, How Far?" *Harvard Business Review,* XLI, 4 (July-August, 1963), 144-60.

19. Spacek, L. "Are Accounting Principles Generally Accepted?" *The Journal of Accountancy,* CXI, 4 (April, 1961), 41-46.

20. ———. "Are Double Standards Good Enough for Investors But Unacceptable to the Securities Industry?" *The Journal of Accountancy,* CXVIII, 5 (November, 1964), 67-72.

21. ———. "Business Success Requires an Understanding of Unsolved Problems of Accounting and Financial Reporting." New York: Arthur Andersen & Co., 1959.

22. ———. "Challenge to Public Accounting," *Harvard Business Review,* XXXVI, 3 (May-June, 1958), 115-24.

23. Storey, R. K. *The Search for Accounting Principles.* New York: American Institute of Certified Public Accountants, 1964.

24. "Those 'Special Items,' " *Fortune,* LXX 2 (August, 1964), pp. 77-84.

24

ACCOUNTING TACTICS AND THE THEORY

OF THE FIRM*

MICHAEL SCHIFF

Much criticism of the traditional theory of the firm has appeared in recent years.[1] Under particular scrutiny is the relevance of the notion of profit maximization; that is, if managers are motivated by their own self-interest will their policies and decisions give results compatible with the notion of profit maximization for owners. Since owners are not informed of alternative policies available to the firm, they have no way of determining whether profits are maximized. As a result,

Journal of Accounting Research, Spring 1966, pp. 62-67.

[1] R. J. Monsen, Jr. and A. Downs, "A Theory of Large Managerial Firms," *Journal of Political Economy,* June, 1965, p. 221. See their fn. 2.

owners tend to act as "satisficers" instead of "maximizers"; that is, they would like maximum profits, but, because of limited information, they adopt a behavior which is different from the theoretical maximizer.[2]

Even if knowledge of alternative decisions were made available, owners are confronted with different accounting methods employed in the corporate annual report. If there is a conflict between the managers' and owners' interests in corporations with diffuse ownership, the opportunity to choose the accounting method gives an important advantage to the manager.

This paper reviews a case which seems to validate contemporary theory of the firm; the case illustrates the choice of accounting method as a device available to managers attempting to make stockholders happy. Specifically, the illustration concerns the expensing or deferring of advertising and the resultant impact on per share earnings.

Marketing executives refer to a marketing mix as an array of strategies involving personal selling, pricing, packaging, promotion, advertising, credit, etc. aimed at achieving marketing goals. With consumer goods, advertising is perhaps the most important ingredient in the marketing mix. While the bulk of advertising cost is directed toward maintaining current markets, a significant part of this cost is incurred to secure incremental sales—expanding into new markets, more intensive penetration of current markets, and, frequently, to introduce new products. For advertising aimed at securing incremental sales, there may be a significant time lag between the appearance of the advertising and the achievement of the sales program.

Prevailing accounting practices generally do not look to the specific purpose of advertising to determine appropriate reporting. Conservatism is the justification employed for expensing advertising costs as incurred. The absence of an objective measure of the future impact of advertising on sales is the rationale to justify the traditional accounting approach.

It is fair to say that planning in advertising has improved in recent years. Advertising expenditures related to incremental sales programs are evaluated by using analytical tools commonly associated with capital budgeting, including weighting for probability of achievement in stated time periods.

The accounting practice of deferring costs of fixed assets over their economic lives can be applied to advertising expenditures related to new markets and new products. Fixed assets have the qualities of tangibility and long life and these attributes justify the spreading of their cost over their useful lives. But there is a difference in the likelihood of the "long life" occurring when one contrasts general-purpose equipment with special-purpose equipment. The economic life of the latter is more difficult to predict because of the uncertainty of the continuance of the market for the equipment's output and the related absence of a market for the asset itself. This uncertainty in the market for goods is equivalent to the uncertainty in the success of the advertising program aimed at marketing the future output of the equipment. The fact that one expenditure results in a tangible asset and the other yields an intangible asset is hardly an adequate justification for capitalization and deferral in one case and immediate expensing in the other. It is urged, then, that advertising for incremental sales be deferred and amortized over

[2]*Ibid.*, p. 225.

the periods of the expected sales. Any change in market conditions or information that the program is to be halted would result in a write-off of any balance in deferred advertising in the period of such determination, as is the case with tangible long-life assets.

Such a practice was adopted by the management of Chock Full O'Nuts, a publicly held company engaged in consumer goods and services and listed on the New York Stock Exchange. Sales of the company exceed $40 million a year. In annual reports for fiscal years ending prior to 1960, this company indicated that it followed the practice of deferring advertising and promotion costs relating to the development of new markets for established products and similar expenditures for the introduction of new products in established markets. Because of the importance of advertising and promotion costs, particularly in recent years, this policy had a significant effect on earnings, as indicated in Table 1.

TABLE 1   Net Income and Deferred Advertising

Fiscal Year Ended July 31	After Tax Net Income		Deferred Advertising	
	Total	Per Share	Total	Per Share
1960	$1,815,557	$ .54	$334,000	$ .10
1961	2,153,025	.63	699,607	.20
1962	2,420,037	.69	768,123	.22
1963	2,414,669	.69	482,055	.13

The increase in net income per share between 1960 and 1961 was directly associated with the increase in the amount of advertising deferred and was a significant factor in 1962 as well.[3] It is difficult to discern what prompted the special, though logical, treatment of advertising. But the increase in per share earnings and the related publicity on new products and markets indicated that this was a growth company.

Fiscal 1964 was a critical year for two reasons. First, it was unprofitable for the company; second, and more significant to the theme here, it emphasized how the manager's choice of accounting methods can be used to satisfy stockholders.

Stockholders reading the report were faced with two versions of the results of operations for 1964 and prior years. The portion of the 1964 report covered by the accountant's certificate restated per share earnings for prior years calculated by charging back some advertising previously capitalized. The reason given was that the products for which advertising was deferred were no longer distributed and no future benefit existed. Adding to this, the chief executive's letter to the stockholders indicated earnings per share for the past few years calculated on the assumption that advertising and promotion costs had been expensed as incurred, a complete departure from the stated policy in the notes accompanying the financial statement.[4] Accordingly, the stockholder could refer to three series of per share

---

[3]The financial statements were certified without qualification and Forms 10K filed with the Securities and Exchange Commission did not reveal any information beyond that shown in the annual report.

[4]See Editorial on CPA opinion on text of chief executive's letter, *Journal of Accountancy*, January, 1965, p. 21.

earnings as shown in Table 2. (Actually the 1964 report showed the information in columns 2 and 3; the information in column 1 appeared in the 1963 report.)

The notes to the financial statements indicated a continuance of the policy of deferring advertising.[5] Judging by the amount deferred it appears that advertising expenditures in 1964 were far less than in prior years.

TABLE 2   Earnings Per Share

Fiscal Year Ended July 31	Annual Report 1963 (1)	Annual Report 1964 (2)	Chief Executive's Letter Accompanying 1964 Annual Report (3)
1959	$ .47	$ .47	*
1960	.54	.53	*
1961	.63	.60	$ .42
1962	.69	.61	.50
1963	.68	.62	.67
1964			.74

*Not given.

What is of some importance, however, is the adjustment of a significant amount of deferred advertising by shifting the charge back to prior years, thus reducing per share earnings in 1960 by $ .01; 1961, $ .03; 1962, $ .08; and 1963, $ .08.

This company adopted the logical practice of deferring advertising in accordance with the matching concept; it developed a practical procedure and produced income figures which were presumably acceptable. From this it can be inferred that the advertising expenditures for new markets and new products were conceptually equated with expenditures for equipment and amortized over their expected economic life.

When obsolete equipment is discarded prior to its complete amortization, the remaining balance appears as a special charge to income or retained earnings in the year of disposal, with a preference for a charge to income.[6] If the company under discussion had written-off the deferred advertising to income in 1964, the effect would have been to reduce earnings per share from $ .62 to $ .45, close to 30 per cent (the total effect of write-offs to prior years was $ .20 while the impact in 1964 was $ .17, resulting basically from changes in number of shares outstanding). The backward shifting of the write-off had the effect of showing an increase in earnings per share for 1964 on a revised basis.

Even more disturbing is the company's chief executive abandoning a policy of deferring advertising which he implicitly accepted and approved in past years, and which resulted in an image of growth. He now urges an evaluation of his company on the basis of a reversal of this policy and states that on the basis of his revision the company has shown real growth in recent years (Table 2, column 3)–in the same annual report describing the policy of deferring advertising!

With the reports of several years before us it can be inferred that:

1. The initial decision to defer advertising may have been prompted by a

[5]A note accompanying the 1964 report indicated that advertising and promotion relative to new products and markets were not material in that year and were accordingly charged to income. In the absence of any other information, it is assumed that there was no change in accounting policy regarding deferred advertising.

[6]H. E. Arnett, "Application of the Capital Gains and Losses Concept in Practice," Accounting Review, January, 1965, pp. 56-57.

desire to convey a notion of growth, an attribute highly regarded by stockholders.

2. The financial report for 1964 reflecting a carry-back of a write-off of deferred advertising, an undesirable but acceptable treatment, permitted the management to smooth the trend of per share earnings in recent years.

3. Perhaps as a means for impressing the stockholders, the method of smoothing the trend in annual profits was conservative; the chief executive ignored his established policy of deferring advertising and again produced an image of growth by restating earnings with a traditional approach to the write-off of advertising.

It is difficult to avoid the conclusion that a concerted effort on the part of the management was made to examine various accounting methods and select that one which makes for happy, though confused, stockholders.

Some years ago, Boulding referred to the "homeostasis of the balance sheet—that there is some desired quantity of all the various items in the balance sheet, and that any disturbance of this structure immediately sets in motion forces which will restore the status quo."[7] It can be suggested that we now have a "homeostasis of earnings per share" and that the application of generally accepted accounting principles facilitates the reporting of earnings per share in a constant or rising pattern to give the effect of "pseudo" profit maximization. This is true whether the item be advertising, research and development, extraordinary gain or losses, etc.

The illustration presented here was possible only because of full disclosure by the accountant. But is full disclosure adequate? No reference to the chief executive's analysis appears in the accountant's report. Beyond this, it is questioned if full disclosure of all pertinent information can serve as a substitute for fair presentation. Criteria for fairness must rest with those responsible for the attest function and cannot be left to those preparing the financial report.

This does not suggest a series of narrow and restrictive guides to be used in certifying financial reports. Yet one cannot escape the conclusion that annual reports reflect the results of business decisions as well as the results of choice of accounting methods, acknowledging the reader's limited abilities to separate the two. Perhaps reporting should be restricted to the approach and criteria used in the decision-making process. Accordingly, if advertising or a similar expenditure is planned as a program to secure incremental sales over the future and the decision reached on the basis of relating the expenditure to future incremental revenue, it should be amortized over such a period and the balance written-off in the year in which it is decided to delete the new product or to halt the program. As a result, the action and the results would be reported in a consistent way, denying management a second opportunity to report operations in a more desirable way.

This generalization could extend further. Methods employed in the decision process would be employed in reporting results in the annual report. This would apply to such things as depreciation, inventories, research and development, etc. Consistency here would permit the reader to evaluate decisions and operating results without having to cope with alternative accounting treatments. In the absence of the availability of accounting method as a defense against stockholder complaints, perhaps management would have a greater incentive to maximize profits.

---

[7]K. E. Boulding, *A Reconstruction of Economics* (New York: John Wiley & Son, Inc., 1950), p. 27.

25

CORPORATE PERSONALITY AS REFLECTED

IN ACCOUNTING DECISIONS:

SOME PRELIMINARY FINDINGS *

GEORGE H. SORTER / SELWYN W. BECKER / T. R. ARCHIBALD / W. BEAVER

This paper is a report on the first stage of an intended long-run investigation of the influence of an hypothesized "corporate personality" upon accounting, financial, and other business decisions. Our thesis is that a "corporate personality" does exist,[1] that it influences corporate decisions, that it can be determined by an analysis of accounting and financial reports, and that it can be explained and verified by psychological models and tests. If correct, the thesis would permit additional insights into a firm's behavior and should allow better predictions about a firm's future course of action within various areas.

As our initial approach we tried to explain the decisions about depreciation methods employed by firms for both financial reports and income tax purposes on the basis of corporate personality. Here we describe the depreciation decision and present the test results which seem to show that firms categorized by different depreciation methods differ also in the area of equity management, liquid asset management, accounting attitudes, and psychological behavior. While not all the differences are statistically significant, almost all are in the predicted direction. These findings have encouraged us to prepare this paper and to continue our research.

THE DEPRECIATION DECISION

Since 1954, firms have been allowed certain accelerated depreciation methods for tax purposes. If adopted, these accelerated methods need not be used for financial reporting. If we assume that firms choose between one of the accelerated (i.e., diminishing charge) methods or the straight-line method, and if we consider all accelerated methods as substantially identical, then a firm must choose between the alternatives listed in Table 1.

The adoption of accelerated depreciation for tax purposes results in a lower present value of the stream of tax payments for most firms. Similarly, straight-line

*Journal of Accounting Research, Autumn 1964, pp. 183-196.

[1]For an earlier affirmation of the existence of "corporate personality," see William H. Newman, "Basic Objectives Which Shape the Character of a Company," *The Journal of Business,* October, 1953, pp. 211-223.

TABLE 1 Possible Depreciation Combinations

Method for Tax Reports	Method for Financial Reports	Symbol Used to Describe Combination
Accelerated	Straight line	A/S
Accelerated	Accelerated	A/A
Straight line	Straight line	S/S
Straight line	Accelerated	S/A

depreciation in financial reports results in higher reported income for most firms. If firms attempt to achieve both of these goals, we would expect the A/S combination to predominate. Other studies[2] have shown, however, that this is not the case; accordingly we decided to examine the depreciation decision on the basis of corporate personality.

OUR HYPOTHESIS

Lindhe[3] investigated the reasons firms gave for not adopting accelerated depreciation for tax purposes. In our study of the responses he received, it appeared to us that firms seemed *anxious* about using two sets of "books," i.e., one set for tax purposes and another for financial reports. We postulated that this anxiety was due to a corporate "intolerance of ambiguity." Psychologically, intolerance of ambiguity is an implied need to avoid, or an abhorrence of, vague, undefined stimuli. Orderly, predictable, "real worlds" can be dealt with, while messy, unpredictable ones are to be avoided; if unavoidable, they are treated as orderly, predictable sets of stimuli. Social intolerance of ambiguity takes the form of stereotyping behavior—the assigning of real or imagined group characteristics to each member of the group. We hypothesize that accounting intolerance of ambiguity consists of assigning the same number to each financial event regardless of to whom, or for what purpose, the event is communicated.

We further hypothesized that firms intolerant of ambiguity are also risk-averting or conservative firms. Since S/S firms pay a real price for keeping one set of books (more taxes) while A/A firms only pay the price of reduced reported income for this privilege, and since A/A firms were willing to change their depreciation methods after 1954, we assumed that A/A firms would be less conservative and less intolerant of ambiguity than the S/S firms. These considerations led us to the following hypotheses which we attempted to test:

1. The Debt/Asset ratios of S/S firms are smaller than the Debt/Asset ratios of A/A firms which, in turn, are smaller than the Debt/Asset ratios of A/S firms.

2. The defensive or liquid asset position of S/S firms is larger than the defensive asset position of A/A firms which is larger than the defensive position of A/S firms.

3. S/S firms have less tolerant attitudes about controversial accounting issues than A/A firms which, in turn, are less tolerant in this respect than A/S firms.

---

[2]Richard Lindhe, *Accelerated Depreciation for Income Tax Purposes—A Study of the Decision and Some Firms Who Made It*, Unpublished Ph.D. dissertation, University of Chicago, 1962; also, Joseph Littlefield, "Depreciation Allowance Not Fully Utilized," *The Controller*, July, 1960.

[3]Lindhe, *op. cit.*

4. S/S firms have more authoritarian psychological attitudes than A/A firms which, in turn, have more authoritarian attitudes than A/S firms.

Our universe consisted of 698 unduplicated firms listed in *Fortune's* 500[4] and *Accounting Trends and Techniques.*[5] To each of these we sent a simple questionnaire asking which tax depreciation method and which book depreciation method was used for new eligible assets. The questionnaire results appear in Table 2.

TABLE 2   Results of Depreciation Methods Questionnaire

	Number	%
A/A	302	47
A/S	229	36
S/S	92	14
Combination of 2	18	3
S/A	1	—
	642	100
No reply	56	
Total Original Mailing	698	

As indicated, 92 firms responded that they used straight-line depreciation for both tax and financial reporting (S/S firms). We wanted to eliminate those firms which might have a rational (economic) motive for following this policy from the group to be studied. Since other studies[6] have indicated that firms with loss-carry-forwards and those using percentage-depletion might have greater economic justification for using straight-line depreciation, all firms in these categories were eliminated from our group of S/S firms. After this adjustment, 50 firms remained in the S/S group.

THE SAMPLE

For our sample of firms, we used the 50 "pure" S/S firms mentioned above and randomly selected 50 firms each from the A/A and A/S groups which gave a sample of 150. For each of these, we calculated (1) various debt/asset ratios to measure conservatism in equity management and (2) the defensive intervals[7] and current ratios to measure conservatism in liquid asset management. To each firm we sent a two part questionnaire. The first part ascertained attitudes about certain accounting questions with each answer coded as tolerant or intolerant of ambiguity (see Appendix III). The second part consisted of a modified, shortened version of

[4] "The Fortune Directory," *Fortune*, July, 1961.

[5] *Accounting Trends and Techniques in Published Corporate Annual Reports,* Fifteenth Edition (New York: American Institute of Certified Public Accountants, 1961).

[6] Lindhe, *op. cit.,* and Littlefield, *op. cit.*

[7] For a detailed description of the measures and their uses see: George H. Sorter and George Benston, "Appraising the Defensive Position of a Firm: The Interval Measure," *Accounting Review,* October, 1960, pp. 633-640; and Sidney Davidson, George H. Sorter, and Hemu Kalle, "Appraising the Defensive Position of a Firm: Some Empirical Data," *Financial Analysts Journal,* January, 1964, pp. 23-29.

the California F-scale.[8] According to its originators, the scale measured the degree to which an individual exhibited a constellation of behaviors shown to have a high correlation with intolerance for ambiguity. Although there has been recent criticism of this measuring device, no alternative has been proposed; thus, we considered it appropriate to use a modified version of the F-scale as a psychological measure of intolerance of ambiguity.

ANALYSIS OF RESULTS

Equity Management

The debt/asset ratios were calculated for each firm in the sample. For the first ratio we used the book-value of long-term debt to the book-value of total assets. Deferred taxes and preferred stock were not considered part of long-term debt. The mean and standard deviation of the debt/asset ratios were computed for each depreciation group, and the differences between the means of each group were compared in the manner indicated in Table 3.[9]

TABLE 3   Debt/Asset Ratios (Computed with Book Values)

Depreciation Groups Compared	Direction Predicted	Level of Significance
A/S and S/S	Yes	.001
A/S and A/A	Yes	.088
A/A and S/S	Yes	.043
A/S and (A/A & S/S)	Yes	.004

The directions predicted for the debt/asset ratios, as well as for the other ratios to follow, may be determined by reference to the hypotheses listed above. A "yes" in the Direction-Predicted-Column indicates that the observed difference of the means was in the direction predicted by the hypothesis, while a "no" would imply the opposite. The level of significance, as a test of differences of two means, is the probability of obtaining the observed difference if, in fact, there is no "true" difference in the means (i.e., the "true" difference is zero). Since the standard deviation of the population is unknown and must be estimated by the standard deviation of the sample, a *Student's* distribution was used in calculating all of the significance levels shown in this paper. For example, referring to Appendix I, Table 3, the means of the A/S and S/S depreciation groups were .159 and .093, respectively. The observed difference is .066, and the problem is to determine whether this difference is statistically significant or just due to chance. If the assumption is made that there is no real difference between the two groups, the probability is .001 (or one chance in a thousand) of obtaining a difference between means of .066. The remaining levels of significance may be interpreted in the same way.

It will be observed that all of the levels of significance in Table 3 are below the 10% significance level, and thus it seems reasonable to assume that there is a relationship between depreciation policy and the magnitude of the debt/asset

[8]Theodore W. Adorno, *et al.,The Authoritarian Personality: Studies in Prejudice* (New York: Harper & Row, 1950).

[9]The means and standard deviations for all of the observations presented in Tables 3 through 10 are detailed in Appendix I.

ratios. In order to insure, however, that these differences were not due merely to industry patterns of depreciation and/or debt/asset ratios, we made several adjustments in our sample data. Each firm was assigned to an industry, and the mean debt/asset ratio was computed for each industry represented in the sample.[10] The difference between the individual firm's debt/asset ratio and the related mean industry ratio was calculated; then these differences were assigned to their respective depreciation groups. The means and standard deviations of the differences of each depreciation group were computed, and these were compared in the manner indicated in Table 4. The levels of significance of the differences between

TABLE 4   Debt/Asset Ratios (Adjusted for Industry Differences)

Depreciation Groups Compared	Direction Predicted	Level of Significance
A/S and S/S	Yes	.004
A/S and A/A	Yes	.062
A/A and S/S	Yes	.043
A/S and (A/A & S/S)	Yes	.006

means are also illustrated in Table 4. A comparison of Table 4 and Table 3 suggests that industry characteristics do not explain the differences found in Table 3. In one case, the level of significance improved; in another, it stayed the same; and in the other two, it deteriorated. In no case, however, was the change great. Since it is arguable whether a book or a market debt/asset ratio is the best measure of conservative equity management, we calculated the debt/asset ratios on the basis of market values as reported in Table 5. The introduction of market values did not

TABLE 5   Debt/Asset Ratios (Computed with Market Values)

Depreication Groups Compares	Direction Predicted	Level of Significance
A/S and S/S	Yes	.005
A/S and A/A	Yes	.290
A/A and S/S	Yes	.050
A/S and (A/A & S/S)	Yes	.095

materially affect the results although the levels of significance deteriorated in all cases. This was especially true in the comparison of A/S and A/A firms. The important point, however, is that the direction of the differences in the means remained consistent with our hypotheses.

Liquid Asset Management

For each firm in the sample we calculated three measures representing liquid or defensive asset management: the defensive interval, the no-credit interval, and the current ratio. The defensive interval measures the stock of defensive assets in relation to the daily operating outflow of liquid assets, the no-credit interval measures the stock of defensive assets less current liabilities in relation to the daily operating outflow of liquid assets, and the current ratio measures the proportion of current assets to current liabilities.

[10]The industry mean ratios were computed from industry data published by the Federal Trade Commission and the Securities and Exchange Commission in *Quarterly Financial Report for Manufacturing Corporations,* fourth quarter, 1962.

We analyzed the differences in means between the depreciation groups for each of the three measures as shown in Table 6. All the results were in the predicted direction. The levels of significance, however, were not strong. The least significant

TABLE 6   Liquid Asset Ratios

Depreciation Groups Compared	Direction Predicted	Level of Significance
Defensive interval		
A/S and S/S	Yes	.071
A/S and A/A	Yes	.216
A/A and S/S	Yes	.150
A/S and (A/A & S/S)	Yes	.116
No credit interval		
A/S and S/S	Yes	.065
A/S and A/A	Yes	.242
A/A and S/S	Yes	.141
A/S and (A/A & S/S)	Yes	.116
Current ratio		
A/S and S/S	Yes	.098
A/S and A/A	Yes	.386
A/A and S/S	Yes	.149
A/S and (A/A & S/S)	Yes	.177

levels were obtained when we compared the current ratios. We were not too concerned with this since we consider the current ratio an unsatisfactory measure,[11] and we included it only because of its prevalence. The difference in the defensive intervals between A/S and S/S firms was satisfactory.

We again adjusted the data by calculating the difference from industry means for each firm and analyzed the means of the depreciation groups. The results (which appear in Table 7) changed little except for the differences in current ratios

TABLE 7   Liquid Asset Ratios (Adjusted for Industry Differences)

Depreciation Groups Compared	Direction Predicted	Level of Significance
Defensive interval		
A/S and S/S	Yes	.075
A/S and A/A	Yes	.225
A/A and S/S	Yes	.130
A/S and (A/S & S/S)	Yes	.140
No credit interval		
A/S and S/S	Yes	.050
A/S and A/A	Yes	.275
A/A and S/S	Yes	.110
A/S and (A/A & S/S)	Yes	.130
Current ratio		
A/S and S/S	Yes	.084
A/S and A/A	No	.400
A/A and S/S	Yes	.032
A/S and (A/A & S/S)	Yes	.300

[11] Sorter and Benston, op. cit.

between the A/A and A/S firms where, for the first time, the result is not in the predicted direction. However, it can be demonstrated that the current ratio is an artificial measure of liquidity.[12] It may be that firms attempt to maintain an industry average; if so, the industry effect is important. The interval measures, which we feel are more meaningful indications of defensive strength, remained virtually unchanged.

Accounting Attitudes

We sent a questionnaire to the chief financial officer of each firm in the sample asking his opinion on certain accounting questions. Each response was graded as tolerant or intolerant (see Appendix II and III for tabulation of returns and scoring of questions). We calculated the means and variances for tolerance and intolerance for each depreciation group. The results are presented in Table 8. In

TABLE 8   Tolerance and Intolerance Responses

Depreciation Groups Compared	Direction Predicted	Level of Significance
Tolerance scores		
A/S and S/S	Yes	.225
A/S and A/A	Yes	.100
A/A and S/S	No	.296
A/S and (A/A & S/S)	Yes	.105
Intolerance scores		
A/S and S/S	No	.362
A/S and A/A	Yes	.179
A/A and S/S	No	.116
A/S and (A/A & S/S)	Yes	.355

relation to our original hypotheses, they are disappointing. We have only two consolations: the questions and scoring were arbitrary, and the results may prove interesting in regard to accounting attitudes currently held. The tabulation of answers to various questions are found in Appendix III.

Psychological Attitudes

We asked the chief financial officer of each sample firm to answer a modified F-scale questionnaire. The analysis of the results is in Table 9. As can be seen for all respondents, in each case the differences are in the predicted direction, but the levels of significance are weak. Two responses, one in the S/S group and one in the

TABLE 9   F-Scale Responses

Depreciation Groups Compared	Direction Predicted	Level of Significance
All observations		
A/S and S/S	Yes	.402
A/S and A/A	Yes	.435
A/A and S/S	Yes	.443
A/S and (A/A & S/S)	Yes	.419

[12]*Ibid.*

A/S group, seemed extremely suspicious to us. That is, the S/S respondent had a minus 60 score where the next largest minus score was 25; the A/S respondent had a plus 40 score where the next highest plus score was 15. We were curious to see what results would obtain if we excluded the two respondents whom we felt had not answered seriously. These results are shown in Table 10. We are aware that the

TABLE 10   F-Scale Responses

Depreciation Groups Compared	Direction Predicted	Level of Significance
Omitting two deviant observations		
A/S and S/S	Yes	.075
A/S and A/A	Yes	.303
A/A and S/S	Yes	.215
A/S and (A/A & S/S)	Yes	.155

exclusion of extreme observations which bias against our hypothesis is improper. Nevertheless, we thought the improvements in the levels of significance were interesting, especially in the comparison of A/S with S/S firms.

CONCLUSION

In the main, we feel that the evidence supports our original hypotheses, especially for the A/S vs. S/S firms. All of the important differences were in the predicted direction, and many of the levels of significance were encouraging. We think it is clear that A/S, S/S, and A/A firms are different in more respects than merely depreciation policy, although much remains to be done. For one, we would like to analyze A/A firms in the same manner that we did S/S firms. Are there certain conditions under which firms would not wish to maximize reported profits? How does income differ for these groups of firms? More important, we would like to extend the concept of corporate personality beyond depreciation practices. We are presently testing the relationship of debt management and defensive asset management. We are also interested in testing a firm's investments in research and attitudes of risk-taking in relation to "personality." Finally, we will attempt to determine the consequences of conflicts between individual personality traits of major executives and the firm's personality.

This study is at best a first step; further research may prove that this first step was also the last and perhaps not a tenable step at all. The results reported in this paper, however, convince us that the concept of a "corporate personality" deserves further research and exploration.

TABLE 3

Depreciation Group	Mean	Standard Deviation
A/A	.129	.116
A/S	.159	.102
S/S	.093	.089
(A/A & S/S)	.111	.102

TABLE 4

Depreciation Group	Mean	Standard Deviation
A/A	−.013	.112
A/S	.014	.104
S/S	−.040	.087
(A/A & S/S)	−.026	.110

TABLE 5

Depreciation Group	Mean	Standard Deviation
A/A	.118	.119
A/S	.130	.090
S/S	.083	.091
(A/A & S/S)	.101	.107

TABLE 6

Depreciation Group	Mean	Standard Deviation
Defensive Interval		
A/A	.274	.381
A/S	.230	.098
S/S	.407	.832
(A/A & S&S)	.341	.648
No Credit Interval		
A/A	.104	.253
A/S	.077	.087
S/S	.191	.517
(A/A & S/S)	.148	.408
Current Ratio		
A/A	3.21	1.21
A/S	3.15	1.10
S/S	3.53	1.75
(A/A & S/S	3.37	1.51

APPENDIX I   Continued

TABLE 7

Depreciation Group	Mean	Standard Deviation
Defensive Interval		
A/A	.015	.365
A/S	−.025	.073
S/S	.164	.837
(A/A & S/S)	.115	.461
No Credit Interval		
A/A	.027	.239
A/S	.004	.079
S/S	.131	.518
(A/A & S/S)	.075	.297
Current Ratio		
A/A	.551	1.20
A/S	.673	1.19
S/S	1.077	1.59
(A/A & S/S)	.141	1.32

TABLE 8

	Mean	Standard Deviation	Replies
Tolerance Scores			
A/S	3.62	1.35	45
A/A	3.26	1.22	43
S/S	3.41	1.19	32
(A/A & S/S)	3.32	1.20	75
Intolerance Scores			
A/S	4.62	1.05	45
A/A	4.81	.91	43
S/S	4.53	1.11	32
(A/A & S/S)	4.69	1.00	75

TABLE 9

F-Scale—All Replies			
A/S	−6.78	13.95	41
A/A	−6.28	13.72	40
S/S	−5.93	14.48	28
(A/A & S/S)	−6.22	14.02	68

TABLE 10

F-Scale—Omit Deviants			
A/S	−7.95	11.92	40
A/A	−6.28	13.72	40
S/S	−3.93	10.06	27
(A/A & S/S)	−5.41	1.20	67

	A/A	%	A/S	%	S/S	%
Reply to Accounting Attitudes, F-Scale	40	80	41	82	28	56
Reply to Accounting Attitudes only	3	6	4	8	4	8
Total returns	43	86	45	90	32	64
Non replies	7	14	5	10	18	36
	50	100	50	100	50	100

APPENDIX III

Accounting Attitude Questionnaire with Summary Responses*
Institute of Professional Accounting.
Survey: Chief Financial Officer

	Yes	No
	61%	39%
1. A. Do you approve of direct costing for internal reporting?	T	A†
B. (If you checked No) Would you be more apt to approve direct costing for internal reporting if it were acceptable for financial reporting?	32% I†	68% A
2. A. (If you presently use LIFO) Would you continue to use it for book purposes if it were not required by the Internal Revenue Service?	53% A	47% T
B. (If you presently do not use LIFO) Would you be willing to use if for tax purposes if tax laws would not require you to use it for book purposes?	46% T	54% A
3. Do you believe that all manufacturing overhead should be allocated to specific departments or cost centers?	65% I	35% T
4. Do you approve of capitalizing a portion of the cost of research programs?	21% T	79% I
training programs?	0% T	100% I
market research?	5% T	95% I
advertising campaigns?	2% T	98% I
5. Do you approve of rounding data in financial reports to the nearest dollar?	98% T	2% I
to the nearest $1,000 dollars?	77% T	23% I

*T indicates tolerance of ambiguity; I indicates tolerance of ambiguity; A indicates ambiguous.
†A "NO" response to Question 1.A. coupled with a "YES" response to Question 1.B. is considered an indication of intolerance.

DISCUSSION QUESTIONS

1. The *Wall Street Journal* in a lead article (August 9, 1972) observed that "The do-good funds aren't doing well, nor are they doing much good."
The funds referred to are mutual funds that invest exclusively in companies they regard as socially responsible. The poor performance of these funds was associated with a declining interest on the part of investors in these funds and the relatively lower profit of the companies whose stocks were selected for the portfolios of these funds.
The above reflects some element of reality on the part of individual behavior—what one says and what one does relative to the corporate social responsibility.
Refer to Gynther's article and indicate whether:
a. The *Wall Street Journal* observation relates to the proprietary or entity concept of the firm
b. What behavioral hypotheses are implicit in the concept selected in answer to (a).
2. Indicate the difference in accounting treatment and/or definition of the following under the entity and proprietary concepts of the firm:
    a. Profit
    b. Dividends - common stock
    c. Dividends - preferred stock
    d. Increase in value in assets associated with changes in price level.
3. It has been argued that income smoothing may be achieved to a degree by choice of alternative accounting reporting criteria.
a. Illustrate several operational non-accounting alternatives which may be used to achieve smoothing.
b. Does accounting "conservatism" encourage or disencourage income smoothing? Explain and illustrate by reference to (1) inventory costing, (2) expensing or capitalizing research and development costs and advertising and promotion costs, (3) depreciation policy.
4. Refer to Part Two, Budgeting and Planning, and comment on the possibilities of income smoothing by division managers in reporting their results. Note similarities and differences in potential for smoothing and the means available to achieve smoothing.
5. Hawkins cites areas in which work had to be done (as of 1969 when his article was published) to influence motivation bias in external reporting. Indicate four A.P.B. Opinions published since January 1, 1970 that have achieved or failed to achieve these objectives. Explain.
6. Hawkins makes the point that the APB should be concerned that their pronouncements should not ". . . lead to unsound economic decisions." He goes on to observe that the rejection of the APB of partial allocation and flow-through methods, although not initially based on behavioral implication, did in effect prevent "some undesirable motivation implications."

Review Hawkins' analysis of comprehensive allocation and the deferral method and comment on whether or not the decisions of the APB in these two matters did indeed minimize unsound economic decisions regarding the acquisition of fixed assets.
7. In a paper presented by Horngren, a member of the APB, at the Dr. Scott Memorial Lectures in Accountancy, University of Missouri, Columbia, Missouri,

1972 he reflects on criticism of the APB for its vacillating "Caspar Milquetoast" image in setting accounting standards. He says:

In my view, as a minimum such criticism should be leveled at *both* the SEC and the APB together. Furthermore, the restriction on the freedom of these bodies should not be overlooked. From time to time, I have heard grumbling by various APB members that we do not have to consider the SEC—that we will decide what is right and what is not. But this is wishful thinking, a clinging to the false ideas that a private body is determining accounting principles. Until late 1971, Congress had delegated the bulk of the power to the SEC. In turn the APB has formulated principles subject to whatever constraints the SEC exerts. This point may be obvious to individuals who are acquainted with APB activities, but it is not at all clear to many others. As a result the APB has endured some undeserved flak.

Horngren infers that the organizational structure for developing accounting principles (likened to a product) has the SEC as top management, the APB at the next level as the operating division producing the product (principles), which are in turn used by customers (reporting company). What behavioral characteristics would you ascribe to the APB, assuming you accept the description of the structure?

Do you agree that it is "wishful thinking" as cited by Horngren that the APB should decide what is right in accounting principles and issue opinions accordingly? Explain.

PART SIX

Selected Bibliography

PART ONE—The Theory of the Firm and Managerial Behavior

Alexis, Marcus, and Charles Z. Wilson. *Organizational Decision Making.* Englewood Cliffs, N.J.: Prentice-Hall, 1967.

Anton, Hector R. "Activity Analysis of the Firm: A Theoretical Approach to Accounting (Systems) Development." *The Journal of Business Economics,* 4 (1961): 290-305.

Barnard, C.I., *The Functions of the Executive.* Cambridge, Mass.: Harvard University Press, 1938.

Benston, George J. "The Role of the Firm's Accounting System for Motivation." *Accounting Review,* 38, no. 2 (April 1963): 347-54.

Birnberg, Jacob C., and Raghu Nath. "Implications of Behavioral Science for Managerial Accounting." *Accounting Review,* 42, no. 3 (July 1967): 468-79.

Bonini, Charles P. *Simulation of Information and Decision Systems in the Firm.* Englewood Cliffs, N.J.: Prentice-Hall, 1963.

Caplan, Edwin H. *A Comparison of Behavioral Assumptions of Management Accounting and Some Behavioral Concepts of Organizational Theory.* Unpublished doctoral dissertation. University of California, Berkeley, 1965.

———. "Behavioral Assumptions of Management Accounting." *Accounting Review,* 41, no. 3 (July 1966): 496-509.

———. "Behavioral Assumptions of Management Accounting—Report of a Field Study." *Accounting Review,* 43, No. 2, (April 1968): 342-52.

———. "Management Accounting and the Behavioral Sciences." *Management Accounting,* 50, No. 10 (June 1969): 41-45.

Chambers, R.J. *Accounting, Evaluation and Economic Behavior.* Englewood Cliffs, N.J.: Prentice-Hall, 1966.

Costello, Timothy W., and Sheldon S. Zalkind. *Psychology in Administration, A Research Orientation.* Englewood Cliffs, N.J.: Prentice-Hall, 1963.

Cyert, Richard M., and James G. March. *A Behavioral Theory of the Firm.* Englewood Cliffs, N.J.: Prentice-Hall, 1963.

Gibson, J.L. "Accounting in the Decision Making Process: Some Empirical Evidence." *Accounting Review*, 38, No. 3 (July 1963): 492-500.

Golembiewski, Robert T. "Accountancy as a Function of Organization Theory." *Accounting Review*, 39, No. 2 (April 1964): 333-41.

Herzberg, F. *Work and the Nature of Man.* Cleveland, Ohio: World, 1966.

———. B. Mausner, and B. Snyderman. *The Motivation to Work,* 2nd ed. New York: Wiley, 1959.

Hill, Walter A., and Douglas M. Egan, *Readings in Organization Theory: A Behavioral Approach.* Boston: Allyn & Bacon, 1966.

Hofstedt, T.R., and J.C. Kinard. "A Strategy for Behavioral Accounting Research." *Accounting Review* (January 1970): 38-54.

Jensen, R.E. "Empirical Evidence from the Behavioral Sciences: Fish Out of Water." *Accounting Review* (July 1970): 502-508.

Katz, D., and R.L. Kahn. *The Social Psychology of Organizations.* New York: Wiley, 1966.

Leavitt, Harold J. *Managerial Psychology,* 3rd ed. Chicago: University of Chicago Press, 1972.

Lee, Lucy C., and Norton M. Bedford. "An Information Theory Analysis of the Accounting Process." *Accounting Review*, 44, no. 2 (April 1969): 256-76.

Likert, Rensis. *The Human Organization: Its Management and Value.* New York: McGraw-Hill, 1967.

March, James G., and Herbert A. Simon. *Organizations.* New York: Wiley, 1958.

Maslow, A.H. *Motivation and Personality.* New York: Harper and Row, 1954.

Mautz, R.K. "Accounting as a Social Science." *Accounting Review,* 38, no. 2 (April 1963): 317-25.

Monson, R. Joseph and Anthony Downs. "A Theory of Large Managerial Firms." *Journal of Political Economy* (June 1965): 211-36.

———. "Challenges to the Accounting Profession." *Accounting Review*, 40, no. 2 (April 1965): 299-311.

McGregor, Douglas. *The Human Side of Enterprise.* New York: McGraw-Hill, 1960.

Prince, Thomas R. "The Motivational Assumption for Accounting Theory." *Accounting Review,* 39, no. 3 (July 1964: 553-62

Raia, A.P. "A Second Look at Management Goals and Controls." *California Management Review,* 8, no. 4 (Summer 1966): 49-58.

Rubenstein, A.H., and C.J. Haberstroh, (eds.). *Some Theories of Organization.* Homewood, Ill.: Dorsey & Irwin, 1960.

Schein, Edgar H. *Organizational Psychology.* Englewood Cliffs, N.J.: Prentice-Hall, 1965.

Simon, Herbert A. *Administrative Behavior,* 2nd ed. New York: Macmillan, 1957.

Williamson, O.E. *The Economics of Discretionary Behavior: Managerial Objectives in a Theory of the Firm.* Chicago: Markham, 1967.

Willingham, John J. "The Accounting Entity: A Conceptual Model." *Accounting Review*, 36, no. 3 (July 1964): 543-52.

PART TWO—Budgeting and Planning

Anderson, C.M. "Motivation—The Essential in Budgeting." *Management Accounting,* 44, no. 10 (June 1963): 46.

Anthony, Robert N. *Planning and Control Systems: A Framework for Analysis.* Boston: Harvard Business School, Division of Research, 1965.

Argyris, Chris. "Human Problems with Budgets." *Harvard Business Review,* 31, no. 1 (January-February 1953): 97-110.

——. *The Impact of Budgets on People.* Prepared for the Controllership Foundation, Inc., Cornell University, Ithaca, N.Y., 1952.

——. "Personal Tensions Frequently Sabotage Industrial Budgets, Controller's Research Reveals." *Journal of Accountancy,* 93, no. 5 (May 1952): 603-604.

——. and Frank B. Miller, Jr. "The Impact of Budgets on People." Prepared for the Controllership Foundation, Inc., under the direction of Schuyler Dean Hoslett, Cornell University, Ithaca, N.Y., 1952.

Axelson, Charles F. "What Makes Budgeting So Obnoxious?" *Business Budgeting,* 3, no. 5 (May 1963): 22-27.

Bass, B.M., and H.J. Leavitt. "Some Experiments in Planning and Operating." *Management Science,* 9 (1963): 574-85.

Becker, S. "Discussion of the Effect of Frequency of Feedback on Attitudes and Performance." *Empirical Research in Accounting: Selected Studies, 1967,* supplement to Vol. 5 of *Journal of Accounting Research:* 225-228. Chicago: Institute for Professional Accounting, Graduate School of Business, University of Chicago, 1968.

——. and D. Green, Jr. "Budgeting and Employee Behavior." *Journal of Business,* 35, no. 4 (October 1962): 392-402.

——. "Budgeting and Employee Behavior: A Rejoinder to a 'Reply'." *Journal of Business,* 37, no. 2 (April 1964): 203-205.

Beddingfield, Ronald. "Human Behavior: The Key to Success in Budgeting." *Management Accounting,* 51, no. 3 (September 1969): 54-56.

Boyle, T. P. "Budget Organization and Administration: A Look at the Philosophy of Budget Administration Rather Than its Techniques and Procedures." *Controller,* 27, no. 7 (July 1959): 316-19, 348.

Charnes, A., W.W. Cooper and M.H. Miller. "Application of L-P to Financial Budgeting and the Costing of Funds." *Journal of Business,* 32, no. 1 (January 1959): 20-46.

Crecine, John P. "A Computer Simulation Model of Municipal Budgeting. *Management Science* (July 1967): 786-815.

——. and Andrew Stedry. "Exploratory Models in the Theory of Budget Control." *New Perspectives in Organization Research,* W.W. Cooper, H.J. Leavitt, and M.W. Sheely, eds. New York: Wiley, 1964.

Davis, O.A., A.J. Dempster and A. Wildavsky. "A Theory of the Budgetary Process." *American Political Science Review,* 40 (1966), 529-47.

Decoster, Don T., and John P. Fertakis. "Budget-Induced Pressure and its Relationship to Supervisory Behavior." *Journal of Accounting Research,* 6, no. 2 (Autumn 1968): 237-46.

Dunbar, Roger L.M. "Budgeting for Control." *Management Science* (March 1971): 88-96.

Dunlop, Robert G. "Humanism in Budgeting." *Budgeting,* 12, no. 6 (July 1962): 29-34.

Earley, J.S., and W.T. Carleton. "Budgeting and the Theory of the Firm: New Findings." *Journal of Industrial Economics,* 10, no. 3 (July 1962): 165-73.

——. assisted by M.F. Severance, and F.N. Firestone. "Business Budgeting and the Theory of the Firm." *Journal of Industrial Economics,* 9, no. 1 (November 1960): 23-42.

Gerould, Walter B. "Impact of Budgets on People." *Controller,* 20, no. 3 (March 1952): 116-18, 126-28).

Hofstede, G.H. *The Game of Budget Control.* New York: Van Nostrand, 1967.

Revsine, L. "Change in Budget Pressure and Its Impact on Supervisor Behavior." *Journal of Accounting Research* (Autumn 1970): 290-92.

Schiff, Michael, and Arie Y. Lewin. "The Impact of People on Budgets." *Accounting Review*, 45 no. 2 (April 1970): 259-68.

————. "Where Traditional Budgeting Fails." *Financial Executive,* 36, no. 5 (May 1968): 50-52, 55-56, 61-62.

Stedry, A.C. *Budget Control and Cost Behavior.* Englewood Cliffs, N.J.: Prentice-Hall, 1960.

————. "Budgetary Control: A Behavioral Approach." In *Organizational Decision Making,* M. Alexis and C. Z. Wilson, eds.. Englewood Cliffs, N.J.: Prentice-Hall, 1967.

————. "Budgeting and Employee Behavior: A Reply." *Journal of Business,* 37, no. 2 (April 1964): 195-202.

Wallace M.E. "Behavioral Considerations in Budgeting." *Management Accounting,* 47, no. 12 (August 1966): 3-8.

PART THREE—Decision Making

American Accounting Association. "Report of Committee on Managerial Decision Models." *Accounting Review,* Supplement 1969, 42-76.

Beckett, John A "A Study of the Principles of Allocating Costs." *Accounting Review,* 26, no. 3 (July 1951): 327-33.

Blankenship, L. Vaughn and Raymond Miles. "Organizational Structure and Managerial Decision Behavior." *Administrative Science Quarterly* (September 1969): 192-201.

Bruns, William J., Jr. "Inventory Valuation and Management Decisions." *Accounting Review,* 40, no. 2 (April 1965): 345-57.

————. "Accounting Information and Decision Making: Some Behavioral Hypotheses." *Accounting Review,* 43, no. 3 (July 1968): 469-80.

————. "The Accounting Period and Its Effect Upon Management Decisions." *Empirical Research in Accounting: Selected Studies 1966.* Supplement to Vol. 4 of *Journal of Accounting Research,* Institute for Professional Accounting, Graduate School of Business, University of Chicago (1967): 1-20.

Cartwright, D., and Z. Zander, eds. *Group Dynamics Research and Theory,* 3rd ed. New York: Harper & Row, 1968.

Carzo, Rocco and John N. Vanouzas. "Effect of Flat and Tall Organization Structure." *Administrative Science Quarterly* (September 1969): 192-201.

Chambers, R.J. "The Role of Information Systems in Decision Making." *Management Technology,* 4, no. 1 (June 1964): 15-25.

Coch, L., and J.R.P. French. "Overcoming Resistance to Change." *Human Relations,* 1 (1948): 512-32.

Cyert, Richard M., James G. March and William Starbuck. "Two Experiments on Bias and Conflict in Organizational Estimation." *Management Science* (April 1961): 254-64.

Davidson, H. Justin, and Robert M. Trueblood. "Accounting for Decision Making." *Accounting Review,* 36, no. 4 (October 1961): 577-82.

Dearborn, D.C., and H.A. Simon. "Selective Perception: A Note on the Departmental Identification of Executives." *Sociometry,* 21, no. 2 (June 1958): 140-44.

Demski, J.S. "The Decision Implementation Interface: Effects of Alternative Performance Measurement Models." *Accounting Review* (January 1970): 76-87.

Dickhaut, J.W. "Accounting Information in Decision Making." *Management Services,* 6, no. 1 (January-February 1969): 49-55.

Dickson, G.W. "Information-Decision Systems." *Business Horizons,* 11, no. 6 (December 1968): 17-26.

Dopuch, Nicholas and Jacob G. Birnberg. *Cost Accounting: Accounting Data for Management's Decisions.* New York: Harcourt, Brace & World, 1969.

Dyckman, Thomas R. "Observations on Jensen's Experimental Design for Study of Effects of Accounting Variation in Decision Making." *Journal of Accounting Research.* 5, no. 2 (Autumn 1967): 221-29.

———. "On the Investment Decision," *The Accounting Review.* 39, no. 2 (April 1964): 285-95.

———. "The Effects of Alternate Accounting Techniques on Certain Management Decisions." *Journal of Accounting Research,* 2, no. 1 (Spring 1964): 91-107.

———. *Investment Analysis and General Price-Level Adjustments.* Studies in Accounting Research, no. 1. Evanston, Ill.: American Accounting Association, 1969.

———. "On the Effects of Earning-Trend, Size, and Inventory Valuation." In *Research in Accounting Measurement,* Robert Jaedicke, Yuji Ijiri, and Oswald Nielson, eds. Evanston, Ill.: American Accounting Association, 1966.

Edelstein, R.M. *Risk Taking and Group Decision Making Among Business Professionals.* Unpublished doctoral dissertation. New York: Columbia University, 1971.

Feltham, Gerald A. "The Value of Information." *The Accounting Review,* 43, no. 4, (October 1968): 684-96.

Firmin, Peter A., and James J. Linn. "Information Systems and Managerial Accounting." *Accounting Review,* 43, no. 1 (January 1968): 75-82.

Gibson, James L. "Accounting in the Decision Making Process: Some Empirical Evidence." *Accounting Review,* 38, no. 3 (July 1963): 492-500.

Horngren, Charles T. "Motivation and Coordination in Management Control Systems." *Management Accounting,* 48, no. 9 (May 1967): 3-7.

Ijiri, Yuji. *The Foundation of Accounting Measurement: A Mathematical Economic and Behavior Inquiry.* Englewood Cliffs, N.J.: Prentice-Hall, 1967.

———. "Functional Analysis of Aggregation." Working paper No. 21, Graduate School of Business, Stanford University, August 1964. Presented at the 10th Annual, First International Meeting of the Western Section of the Operations Research Society of America, September 14-18, 1964, Honolulu, Hawaii.

———. Robert K. Jaedicke and Kenneth E. Knight. "The Effects of Accounting Alternatives on Management Decisions." *Research in Accounting Measurement,* Chicago, American Accounting Association, 1966, pp. 186-199.

———. and John L. Livingstone. "The Effect of Inventory Costing Methods on Full and Direct Costing." *Journal of Accounting Research* (Autumn 1966): 224-38.

Jensen, R.E. "An Experimental Design for Study of Effects of Accounting Variations in Decision Making." *Journal of Accounting Research* (Autumn 1966): 224-38.

Johnson, D.M. "A Systematic Treatment of Judgment." *Psychological Bulletin,* 142, no. 4 (April 1945): 193-224.

Khemakhem, A. "A Simulation of Management Decision Behavior: 'Funds' and 'Income'." *Accounting Review* (July 1968): 522-34.

Lawrence, P.R., and J.W. Lorsch. "Differentiation in Complex Organizations." *Administrative Science Quarterly,* 12, no. 1 (June 1967): 1-47.

Leavitt, H.J., ed. *The Social Science of Organizations: Four Perspectives.* Englewood Cliffs, N.J.: Prentice-Hall, 1963.

Livingstone, John Leslie. "A Behavioral Study of Tax Allocation in Electric Utility Regulation." *Accounting Review,* 42, no. 3 (July 1967): 544-52.

Pondy, L.R., and J.G. Birnberg. "An Experimental Study of the Allocation of Financial Resources within Small, Hierarchical Task Groups." *Administrative Science Quarterly,* 14, no. 2 (June 1969): 192-201.

Rappaport, Alfred. "Sensitivity Analysis in Decision Making." *Accounting Review,* 42, no. 3 (July 1967): 441-56.

Simon, H.A. "Theories of Decision-Making in Economics and Behavioral Science." *American Economic Review,* 49, no. 3 (June 1959): 253-83.

Sorter, George H., R. Ross Archibald, and W.H. Beaver. "Accounting and Financial Measures as Indicators of Corporate Personality—Some Empirical Findings." *Research in Accounting Measurement,* Robert K. Jaedicke, Y. Ijiri, O. Nelson, eds. Evanston, Ill. American Accounting Association, 1966, pp. 200-210. (See also "Discussion Comments" by N.M. Bedford and N.C. Churchill, pp. 211-218.)

PART FOUR—Control

Anthony, Robert N. "Cost Concepts for Control." *Accounting Review,* 32, no. 2 (April 1957): 229-34.

Arrow, Kenneth J. "Control in Large Organizations." *Management Science* (April 1964): 397-406.

Beckett, John A. "A Study of the Principles of Allocating Costs." *Accounting Review,* 26, no. 3 (July 1951): 327-33.

Benston, George J. "The Role of the Firm's Accounting System for Motivation." *Accounting Review,* 38, no. 2 (April 1963): 347-54.

Carmichael, D.R. "Behavioral Hypotheses of Internal Control." *Accounting Review,* 45, no. 2 (April 1970): 235-45.

Charnes, A., and W.W. Cooper. "Some Network Characterizations for Mathematical Programming and Accounting Approaches to Planning and Control." *Accounting Review,* 42, no. 1 (January 1967): 24-52.

———. and A.C. Stedry. "Exploratory Models in the Theory of Budget Control." *New Perspectives in Organization Research,* W.W. Cooper, H.J. Leavitt, and M.W. Shelly, eds. New York: Wiley, 1964.

Churchill, N.C., W.W. Cooper, and R. Sainsbury. "Laboratory and Field Studies of the Behavioral Effects of Audits." In *Management Controls,* Bonini, Jaedicke and Wagner, eds. New York: McGraw-Hill, 1964.

Cook D.M. "The Effect of Frequency of Feedback on Attitudes and Performance." *Empirical Research in Accounting, Selected Studies 1967,* Supplement to Vol. 5 of *Journal of Accounting Research.* Chicago, Illinois, Institute of Professional Accounting, Graduate School of Business, University of Chicago, 1968, pp. 213-24.

———. "The Psychological Impact of Certain Aspects of Performance Reports." *Management Accounting,* 49, no. 10 (July 1968): 26-34.

Culpeper, R.C. "A Study of Some Relationships Between Accounting and Decision Making Processes." *Accounting Review* (April 1970): 322-32.

Dean, Joel. "Decentralization and Intracompany Pricing." *Harvard Business Review,* 33, no. 4 (July-August 1955): 65-74.

Dearden, John. "Appraising Profit Center Managers." *Harvard Business Review,* 46, no. 3 (May-June 1968): 80-87.

———. "Limits on Decentralized Profit Responsibility." *Harvard Business Review,* 40, no. 4 (July-August 1962): 81-89.

———. "Problems in Decentralized Profit Responsibility." *Harvard Business Review,* 38, no. 3 (May-June 1960): 79-86.

Dubin, R. "Control Evasion at the Managerial Level." *Human Relations in Administration,* R. Dubin ed. Englewood Cliffs, N.J.: Prentice-Hall, 1968.

Field, John E. "Toward a Multi-level, Multi-goal Information System." *Accounting Review,* 44, no. 3 (July 1969): 593-99.

Horngren, Charles R. *Accounting for Management Control,* 2nd ed. (See especially

Chapter 11, "Responsibility Accounting and the Contribution Process to Cost Allocation"). Englewood Cliffs, N. J., Prentice-Hall, 1970.

———. "Choosing Accounting Practices for Reporting to Management." *National Association of Accountants Bulletin (Management Accounting)*, 44, no. 1 (September 1962): 3-16.

———. "Motivation and Coordination in Management Control Systems." *Management Accounting*, 48, no. 9 (May 1967): 3-7.

Ijiri, Yuji. *Management Goals and Accounting for Control* (See especially Chapter 4, "Accounting for Control: Aggregation and Feedbacks on Goal Attainment"). Amsterdam: North Holland Publishing Co., 1965; and Chicago: Rand McNally & Co., 1965.

Jasinski, Frank J. "Use and Misuse of Efficiency Controls." *Harvard Business Review*, 34, no. 4 (July-August 1956): 105-112.

Jensen, Robert E. "An Experimental Design for Study of Effects of Accounting Variations in Decision Making." *Journal of Accounting Research*, 4, no. 2 (Autumn 1966): 224-37

Likert, R., and S.A. Seashore. "Making Cost Control Work." *Harvard Business Review*, 46, no. 6 (1963): 96-108.

Luneski, Chris. "Some Aspects of the Meaning of Control." *Accounting Review*, 39, no. 3 (July 1964): 591-97.

Miles, Raymond E., and Roger C. Vergin. "Behavioral Properties of Variance Controls." *California Management Review*, 8, no. 3 (Summer 1966): 57-65.

Rappaport, Alfred. "A Capital Budgeting Approach to Divisional Planning and Control. *Financial Executive*, 36, no. 10 (October 1968): 47-48, 55-57, 60-63.

Renner, Robert R. "Introducing an Organization to Budgetary Control." *Controller*, 25, no. 11 (November 1957): 527-30, 549-51.

Ridgway, V.F. "Dysfunctional Consequences of Performance Measurements." *Administrative Science Quarterly*, 1, no. 2, (September 1956): 240-47.

Rosen, L.S., and R.E. Schenck. "Some Behavioral Consequences of Accounting Measurement Systems." *Cost and Management*, 41, no. 9 (October 1967): 6-16.

Schiff, Michael. "Credit and Inventory Management—Separate or Together?" *Financial Executive* (November 1972): 29-33.

Schillinglaw, Gordon. "Divisional Performance Review: An Extension of Budgeting Control." In *Management Controls: New Directions in Basic Research*, C. P. Bonini, R. K. Jaedicke, and H. M. Wagner, eds. New York: McGraw-Hill, 1964.

Shubick, Martin. "Incentives, Decentralized Control, the Assignment of Joint Costs and Internal Planning." In *Management Controls: New Directions in Basic Research*, C. P. Bonini, R. K. Jaedicke, and H. M. Wagner, eds. New York: McGraw-Hill, 1964.

Simon, H.A., H. Guetzkow, G. Kosmetsky, and G. Tyndall. *Centralization vs. Decentralization in Organizing the Controller's Department*. New York: The Controllership Foundation, Inc., 1945.

Solomons, David. *Divisional Performances: Measurement and Control*. New York: Financial Executives Research Foundation, 1965.

Tannenbaum, A.S. *Control in Organizations*. New York: McGraw-Hill, 1968.

Walter, Benjamin. "Internal Control Relations in Administrative Hierarchies." *Administrative Science Quarterly* (September 1966): 179-206.

Whistler, Thomas·L., Harold Meyer, Bernard H. Baum, and Peter F. Sorensen. "Centralization of Organizational Control, An Empirical Study of its Meaning and Measurement." *Journal of Business* (January 1967): 10-27.

Williamson, O.E. *Corporate Control and Business Behavior: An Inquiry Into the Effects of Organization Form on Enterprise Behavior*. Englewood Cliffs, N.J.: Prentice-Hall, 1970.

Willingham, John J. "Internal Control Evaluation—A Behavioral Approach." *Internal Auditor* (Summer 1966): 20-26.

PART FIVE—Financial Reporting

Archibald, T.R. "The Return to Straight Line Depreciation: An Analysis of Change in Accounting Methods." *Empirical Research in Accounting: Selected Studies, 1967*, pp. 164-80.

Baruch, Lev. "The Aggregation Problem in Financial Statements: An Informational Approach." *Journal of Accounting Research*, 6, no. 2 (Autumn 1968): 247-61.

Beaver, W.H., J.W. Kennelly, and W.M. Von. "Predictive Ability as a Criterion for the Evaluation of Accounting Data." *Accounting Review* (October 1968): 675-83.

Comiskey, E.E. "Marked Responses to Changes in Depreciation Accounting." *Accounting Review* (April 1971): 279-85.

Copeland, R.M. "Income Smoothing." *Empirical Research in Accounting: Selected Studies, 1968*, pp. 101-16.

Coughlin, John W. "Industrial Accounting." *Accounting Review*, 39, no. 3 (July 1959): 415-28.

Cramer, Joe J., Jr. and Thomas Iwand. "Financial Reporting for Conglomerates: An Economic Analysis." *California Management Review*, 11, no. 3 (Spring 1969): 25-33.

Dascher, P.E., and R.E. Malcolm. "A Note on Income Smoothing in the Chemical Industry." *Journal of Accounting Research* (Autumn 1970): 253-59.

Goenedes, N.J. "Some Evidence on Investor Actions and Accounting Messages—Part I." *Accounting Review* (April 1971): 320-28.

Gordon, Myron, Bertrand Horowitz, and Philip Meyers. "Accounting Measurement and Normal Growth of the Firm." In *Research in Accounting Measurement*, R. K. Jaedicke, Y. Ijiri, and O. Nielsen (Madison, Wisc., American Accounting Association, 1966), pp. 221-31.

Gynther, Reginald G. "Accounting Concepts and Behavioral Hypotheses." *Accounting Review* (April 1967): 274-97.

Hawkins, David. "Behavioral Implications of Generally Accepted Accounting Principles." *California Management Review* (Winter 1969): 13-21.

Lev, B. "Industry Averages as Targets for Financial Ratios." *Journal of Accounting Research* (Autumn 1969): 290-99.

Lindhe, R. "Accelerated Depreciations for Income Tax Purposes—A Study of the Decision and Some Firms That Made It." *Journal of Accounting Research* (Autumn 1963): 139-48.

Livingston, J.L. "A Behavioral Study of Tax Allocation in Electric Utility Regulation." *Accounting Review* (July 1967): 544-52.

Puzey, Russell V. "Accounting in Communication." *Journal of Accountancy* 112, no. 3 (September 1961): 55-60.

Schiff, Michael "Accounting Tactics and the Theory of the Firm." *Journal of Accounting Research* (Spring 1966): 62-67.

Simpson, R.H. "An Empirical Study of Possible Income Manipulation." *Accounting Review* (October 1969): 806-17.

Soper, F.J., and R. Dolphin, Jr. "Readability and Corporate Annual Reports." *Accounting Review*, 39, no. 2 (April 1964): 358-62.

Sorter, George, Selwyn Becker, T. Ross Archibald, and William Beaver. "Corporate Personality as Reflected in Accounting Decisions—Some Preliminary Findings." *Journal of Accounting Research* (Autumn 1964): 183-96.

Summers, Edward L. "Observations of Effects of Using Alternative Reporting Practices." *Accounting Review*, 43, no. 2, (April 1968): 257-65.